WHAT PEOPLE ARE SAYING

*"**Healing Practices To Help Kids Grow Up Easier** is unlike any resource I've encountered in the past. It's a wonderful, unique and mind-opening find!"*

Cheyenne Jones, mother and middle school teacher, Portland, Oregon

. . . .

"I will give this book to the parents of my students. Finally I can help my students with their challenges by giving their parents the support of this book."

Sarah, Teacher, Sebastopol, California

. . . .

*"**Healing Practices To Help Kids Grow Up Easier** is an easy-to-read, well organized and valuable resource for parents. This material has helped my children and my grandchildren."*

Lilith Rogers, Grandparent, Monte Rio, California

. . . .

*"**Healing Practices To Help Kids Grow Up Easier** is the resource that all of us working with youth should have at our fingertips! Thank you!"*

Dr. Maura McIntyre, Adjunct Professor,
Ontario Institute for Studies in Education of the University of Toronto, Toronto, Canada

. . . .

*"The authors of **Healing Practices To Help Kids Grow Up Easier** are leaders in their fields. Marie Mulligan, MD, a family physician with extensive experience with children, is also well versed in evidence-based therapeutics. Richard Geggie, M. Ed, is an expert in working with troubled children and youth from inner-city schools and communities, and is simply the most gifted educator that I know."*

Joanne Sulman, Social Worker, Halifax, Nova Scotia, Canada

. . . .

"As a medical practitioner and psychotherapist, I have seen numerous parents in distress about their children's difficulties. I've learned that there is not one single answer for any particular condition. Parents are the best judges of what may or may not work for their child and the more well-qualified approaches on which they are informed the better."

Dan Perlitz, Psychotherapist, Toronto, Ontario, Canada

. . . .

"In this time, when medical care has become less of a personal thing, I will recommend this book as a valuable tool to parents in my practice."

Joel Alter, DO, F.A.C.O.S, Santa Rosa, California

. . . .

*"**Healing Practices To Help Kids Grow Up Easier** is an incredible resource for parents looking to address mental, emotional, and physical problems that our children may be facing. As parents of three boys, we find this book refreshing. It presents a wide-range of practices that vary from medical to spiritual approaches addressing important behavioral concerns in children. This is the first time we have come across such a comprehensive resource presenting the type of problems many parents face along with the type of practices that can help us and our children heal in a wholesome manner. We look forward to using this as a resource in raising our children."*

Kirah and Alejandro Caminos, Parents, Oakland, CA

PARTNERS

Ayni Projects: Ayni Projects is a not-for-profit organization, dedicated to participating in the development of healthy communities by working with local leaders [in the Americas] to co-create and implement initiatives that include all members of the community in a reciprocal way whereby people give what they have to offer, and receive what they need in return.

HEALING PRACTICES
To Help Kids

GROW UP EASIER

A resource for families

Over 35 Healing Practices Helping With Over 100 Problems

Marie Mulligan, MD
Rick Geggie, MEd
Et Al

Thoughts On Parenting by Rick Corrigan
Aikido by Isaiah Wisdom
Aromatherapy by Julia Fischer
Attitudinal Healing by Kathy Harris, Carolyn Smith, Marilyn Robinson
Ayurveda by Marc Halpern, DC, CAS
Biofeedback by Bill Barton, PhD
Child Psychiatry by Kristi Panik, MD
Chiropractic by Lana Surgenor, DC
Craniosacral Therapy by Hugh Milne, DO
Developmental Optometry by Tanya Mahaphon, OD, FCOVD, FAAO
Drumming by Christine Stevens, MT-BC, MSW, MA; Heather MacTavish
EMDR by Sandra Wilson, PhD; Robert Tinker, PhD
Environmentally Healthy Home Consultants by Susan Bahl
Expressive Arts by Lore Caldwell LCXMHC, ATR-BC
Feldenkrais Method by Linda Evans-Delman; Russell Delman
Flower Essences by Katharina Johnson, MD (Austria)
Herbology by Karyn Sanders

Homeopathy by Dian Wagner; Randy Jane Reitzes, LVN, CMT, CCHH; Lisette Narragon CCH, BRCP
Hypnotherapy by Randi Farkas, MA, MFT
Independent Study by June Nason, MsEd
Light Therapy by John Downing, OD, PhD
Massage by Alan Jordan, BA, LMT, NCTMB; Peggy Farlow, MsEd, LMT, CIMI
Meditation by Heather Sundberg
Music Lessons by Nick Simmons, BA
Nonviolent Communication by Inbal Kashtan
Nutrition Consulting by Paula Bartholomy, MS, CNC
Osteopathy by Carlisle Holland, DO
Precision Teaching by Elizabeth Haughton, MA
Psychotherapy by Peter Carnochan, PhD
Safe School Ambassadors by Rick Phillips, MsEd
Support for Parents by Theresa Beldon, MA, MFTI, Bodynamic Analyst
Traditional Chinese Medicine by Bob Flaws, L.Ac., FNAAOM (USA), FRCHM (UK)
Western Medicine by Marie Mulligan, MD
Wilderness Therapy by Robert Cooley, PhD
Yoga by Brenda Bakke, MsEd, PT, CYT

Growing Up Easier Publishing
PO Box 94, Sebastopol, CA 95473
www.GrowingUpEasier.org
(707) 874-1789

Copyright © 2008 by Marie Mulligan & Rick Geggie

All chapters on healing practices © 2008 by individual authors, except where noted in the text.

Cover and book design by Mary Smith of Mary Smith Design.

Mulligan, Marie; Geggie, Rick

Healing Practices To Help Kids Grow Up Easier – a resource for parents

p.cm.

Includes bibliographical references and index.

1.Parenting. 2. Childhood Issues. 3. Teen Issues. 4 Healing Practices.

Library of Congress Control Number: 2008927839

ISBN 978-0-9816702-1-8 (pbk)

Printed in USA

We dedicate this book to all beings.

I especially dedicate this book to my sons,
Billy and Michael,
and to my parents, Denis and Kathleen Mulligan.

Marie Mulligan

I especially dedicate this book to my granddaughters,
Tanya, Cleo and Simone.

Rick Geggie

Contents

DISCLAIMER

This book, based upon our experiences and investigations, is about what we have tried or would try if our children had any of the problems we discuss in this book.

The practices described within have been useful for the patients, clients and students of the contributors. The suggestions in the chapters on the healing practices are based upon the contributors' experiences. The information in this volume should not be construed as personal medical/psychological advice or instruction.

If your child or youth has a serious condition, get two Western Medicine or Western Psychological evaluations before you start. If the child has already been diagnosed, please get a second opinion—even if the cost seems high. Compare the two reports before deciding what to do next.

Learn about the practice(s) you are choosing. Pick practitioners carefully. Watch the child or youth's reactions. Stop the practice if there is even a hint of a problem. Talk with the practitioner and with the heads of their professional associations. (You will find information about associations when you read about the practices). If a problem continues, see your pediatrician, family physician, psychologist, or therapist.

This book is meant for information only. Any information obtained from this volume is not intended to diagnose, treat or cure a psychological/medical condition. The editors and contributors shall have no liability for claims by, or damages of any kind whatsoever to, a purchaser of this book or any other person for a decision or action taken in reliance on the information contained in this volume. Such damages include, without limitation, direct, indirect, special, incidental or consequential damages.

We are not responsible or liable in any way for any problems that develop as a result of using any of these practices or any advice given by their contributors. We do hope this information is helpful to you and the child or youth you are concerned about.

PREFACE

Evidence of the need for healing the earth and all the life upon it, surrounds us. Many children & youth, in particular, are suffering a great deal. With all the other struggles our world, our society and our families face, the needs of our children & youth are too often ignored or inadequately addressed. It is time to choose change and to learn new ways of supporting the young, who are – after all – our future.

At any given moment, far too many children & youth and their families are coping with difficulties of some kind. Some challenges are minor. Many are not. Most challenges can have long-term results if they are not adequately addressed - and the sooner the better.

Too often, children & youth who have suffered and do not receive the help they need, grow to be adults who struggle and are insensitive to the suffering they unconsciously create and tolerate. A cycle of suffering goes on and on.

It is time to stop this cycle. It is time to choose change and to investigate healing practices that have helped other children & youth and which we hope will help yours, too.

Throughout this book, we have used the word "parent(s)" to describe the role of the person(s) responsible for the upbringing of a child or youth, with or without legal custody.

Being a parent can be one of the most wonderful and most difficult life-long tasks anyone can undertake. Everyone starts out wanting to be a great parent. However, little training is given. Unhealed parental wounds can also cause problems. Reliable guidance is often difficult to obtain.

And so, many parents treat their children & youth more or less as they were treated themselves as kids. They do the best they can with the information they have at hand, and sometimes that information is not so good.

When parents are stressed, they may be unaware of the needs of their child or youth and they may unknowingly do wounding things they later regret. The effects of these unhealed and regretted actions can get passed on to future generations. We hope this book helps support parents in breaking family cycles of suffering.

Unfortunately, sometimes things happen to children & youth that parents cannot prevent. The task of parenting then becomes even more challenging when children & youth have problems. Accidents, illnesses, school and social difficulties, and other problems sometimes occur.

Happily for parents, there are now many healing practices that have helped other children & youth. We have presented some of these in *Healing Practices To Help Kids Grow Up Easier*. We hope this book helps parents take healing and protective actions.

The world is changing very rapidly. New information, healing practices, and social structures are developing to strengthen children & youth and the family unit itself. We hope this book helps parents support their children & youth in new ways for them, by investigating and choosing helpful practices.

Some of the material in this book may be difficult to absorb. Many forms of suffering are addressed. Old, unhealed memories of what happened in the past to either the children or youth or to the parents might be reawakened. Parents themselves may need support so they can keep getting and giving assistance for the challenged child or youth.

A happier childhood lasts a lifetime. We hope this book will help you help children & youth grow up easier.

Marie Mulligan/Rick Geggie

MISSION

The world cannot afford to waste a single human being. Each child and youth has a unique set of gifts that can make life better for her/him and everyone else – if they get help in developing these gifts.

The mission of this book is to assist the greatest possible number of children, youth and families by connecting these individuals with healing practices that will help them grow up easier and reach their full potential.

Let us take care of the children, for they have a long way to go.
Let us take care of the elders, for they have come a long way.
Let us take care of those in between, for they are doing the work.

Ancient African Proverb
used by Nelson Mandala

CHAPTER 1

INTRODUCTION

Introduction
- We hope this book is useful to you in helping the child or youth who is important to you.
- We believe that children and youth can be more relaxed, learn how to learn and live fuller lives into adulthood when they get assistance with their challenges as early as possible.
- The goal of this book is to provide vital information about healing practices that we have found helpful for children & youth during our careers in medicine and education.
- We want to help parents skillfully examine which healing practices show the most promise in helping their children & youth.

About This Book
- Chapters on healing practices that have helped children & youth have been written by practitioners who are dedicated to helping kids grow up easier.
- This book provides a straightforward process leading parents and caregivers to the most effective treatments for their child or youth's challenges, hopefully helping to avoid years of trial and error.
- Because no single book could provide all the information about all these healing practices, contributors have included the names of associations, books, articles, research papers and internet addresses so that you may compile as much information as you need to help you make decisions about what can help your child or youth.
- Almost all chapters follow the same organization to make learning easier.
- Problems that can hurt children and youth throughout their lives, if they do not receive assistance, are listed and linked to healing practices.
- A long list of problems is given in the *Problems and Healing Practices* chapter. Beneath each problem we have listed the practices which may heal, help, protect, or ease the suffering of children and youth. The problems are listed in alphabetical order.
- The information beneath each problem comes from the experience of the authors of the chapters on Healing Practices. You will see the information of what the practice helps at the beginning of each chapter.
- We have listed these practices in alphabetical order and not in any order of importance or priority. You will have to decide how to use the information.
- To make this an easy-to-read book, we have written and organized it as simply as possible.

- This book is a work in progress. To save time and get the first edition out to you, we have left out many other healing practices that will be included in the second edition.

How To Use This Book

- Carefully go over the lists of PROBLEMS AND HEALING PRACTICES. With each of the problems there is a list of practices that may heal, help, protect or ease your child or youth. Study the practices linked to your child or youth's problems. Learn about the ones that interest you. This information comes from the practitioner/authors who wrote the chapters on the various healing practices. The information they give is from their experience.

Remember

- Children & youth grow and learn more fully when they get assistance so that they can feel safe, loved, appreciated, understood, relaxed, supported, and happy.
- It is important for you to remember that you are an expert when it comes to your children or youth's well being.
- As an expert, you need to continually assemble as much information as possible in order to quickly act in the child's best interests.
- It is important to address problems early because children & youth can develop learning and living habits that can limit their futures when such problems go unattended.
- Ideally, childhood should be harmonious, productive, satisfying, and happy.
- Children and youth need positive growth-enhancing experiences, not recurring patterns of pain and dissatisfaction.
- Effectiveness as adults is determined in large part by what happens to people during their formative years.
- There are many things to keep in mind when choosing a practitioner and some or many of the practices may be beyond your financial reach. Use your imagination. Find help. Go to family, friends, and networks of all sorts to find the financial support you need. Many practitioners will work with you on this difficulty.
- You may have a hunch that one problem is more important than others. You may find yourself drawn to some method for no reason that you understand. We encourage you to follow your intuition as well as your logic.
- If something sparks your curiosity, investigate it. In many cases, intuition or a gut reaction can be as important as your logical thoughts.
- Be careful and be open. Allow for your and your child or youth's life to be better as soon as possible.

Expensive Yet Economical

- Parents are often disturbed by what seems to be the high cost of many healing practices.
- What is often overlooked are the extremely high costs, both in money and anguish, of children & youth continuing to have unsolved problems throughout their lives – including adulthood.
- Keep in mind that the money, time and *heart* that you invest today could save you and your child or youth much more money, time and *heartache* in the future.

Choosing A Practitioner

- Find practitioners from professional associations, recommendations from friends, and any trusted professionals you know.
- Begin by contacting the practitioner and gathering information.
- Ask what training or other qualifications the practitioners have. Ask about their education, additional training, licenses, and certifications. If you have contacted a professional organization, see if the practitioner's qualifications meet the standards for training and licensing for that profession.

- Ask about their experiences treating other children or youth similar to your child or youth in terms of age, gender, and problem.
- Ask if it is possible to have a brief consultation in person or by phone with the practitioners. This will give you a chance to speak with the practitioner directly. The consultation may or may not involve a charge.
- Ask if the practitioners believe their healing practice can effectively address your child or youth's challenge and if there is any scientific research supporting its use.
- Ask about charges and payment options. Ask how much treatments cost.
- Ask about the hours appointments are offered. How long is the wait for an appointment? Consider whether this will be convenient for your schedule.
- Ask about office location. If you need a building with an elevator or a wheelchair ramp, ask about it.
- Ask what will be involved in the first visit or assessment.
- Observe how comfortable you and your child or youth feel during these first interactions.
- Once you have gathered the information, assess the answers and determine which practitioner was best able to respond to your questions and best suits your needs.
- To begin your search for a practitioner, check out the following website which contributed much of the information in this section: www.nccam.nih.gov/health/practioner/index.htm.

Cautions

- No single practice is effective for everyone all of the time.
- In choosing a method or practitioner you have to be discerning and careful without allowing your fears to rule your life or that of your child.
- You and your child or youth will probably have to experiment and investigate to find what works to solve a challenge and make growing up easier.
- In some cases using one method may lead to another until the problem is diminished or resolved.
- Choosing the right combination of healing practices can be helpful. There can be synergy between different healing practices—for example, osteopathy or another manual therapy in conjunction with Traditional Chinese Medicine or Aryuveda.
- Remember that some methods work better than others and that what works for one child or youth might not work for another. Each child or youth is unique, has different parents, different conceptions, different womb experiences, birth experiences, bodies, combinations of experiences, accidents, childhood illnesses, diet, and so on.

Disclaimer

You and your child or youth deserve support in reducing suffering. The intention of this book is to assist you in learning about healing practices. If you or your child or youth are experiencing severe challenges, we strongly recommend that you seek out appropriate help from medical, psychological, psychotherapy or educational professionals. Please share the healing practices in this book with those professionals. Contact appropriate professionals immediately if you or your child or youth have any adverse reactions to any of the practices presented in this book.

CHAPTER 2

THOUGHTS ON PARENTING

By Rick Corrigan,   © Copyright 2008.

- Parenting is our most important responsibility.

- Parenting is a full-time, super-human job that no one can handle without considerable help. These practices may help when things get tough. (And if you use them even when times are easy, they'll come to mind much more easily in the tight spots.)

- Parenting is a sacred responsibility.

- Raising our children & youth to the best of our ability is simply the right thing to do. If we can keep this in mind, we and our children & youth will learn that there are commitments more important than our challenges.

- Our children & youth have important jobs to do as they grow up: namely, to discover the world, to learn who they are and how they can happily manage in the world.

- Our job is to make their journey as enjoyable, easy, exciting, profound and safe as possible.

- When we accept our job, the process of parenting becomes a lifelong exploration.

- We have to keep an experimental attitude. We and our children & youth can teach each other and learn from each other.

- Our relationship with our children & youth works best when it is based on respect. When we respect our children & youth, they will learn to respect us, themselves and others.

- Remember, parent/child & youth relationships are about reciprocity, not equality. It is about giving and receiving. But it is also about parents accepting the responsibility that comes with parenting.

- We can and must establish boundaries and safety so that our children & youth can feel safe and flourish. If we do this with respect, we make it possible for our children & youth to respect those boundaries and to make their own.

- Parenting is not about our power over our children & youth; it's about our service to a process larger than us.

- Like it or not, we model what it means to be a human being for our children & youth.

- We don't have to be heroes, or larger than life. Although it can be difficult, we have to be real and honest.

- It's important that we show up for our children & youth, and stand up for what we believe with honesty.

- Our children & youth learn what real strength and humanity means when they see us handling the "tough stuff" that scares us, with honesty, compassion and all the strength and skill we have.

- "What do you need?" is the most important question we can continually ask of our children & youth (out loud or not!).

- If we are truly willing to show up and provide what's needed (distinguished from what our children & youth might want in any given moment), our children & youth will learn to trust what we provide, and to relax into the process of living.

- The relationship between us and our children & youth is what makes our family.

- Children & youth's family is their first model of community.

- Children & youth learn what love is when we make commitment and service to our family the center and heart of our relationship.

- When love is practiced every day, parenting becomes easier and easier. Our children & youth learn that love is a natural and every day occurrence, not something fleeting and unobtainable. This is a priceless gift that brings endless bounty.

- Parenting is a "practice, not perfection," for everyone.

- Do your best and keep learning.

Rick Corrigan is a dad of a grown up child. He lives in Monte Rio, California. He can be contacted through email: rickcorrigan@growingupeasier.org.

PROBLEMS AND HEALING PRACTICES

CHAPTER 3

PROBLEMS AND HEALING PRACTICES

How To Use This Chapter

In this we have listed events, illnesses and conditions that can cause challenges with living and learning for children & youth unless something is done. Some items will not apply due to the child or youth's age and challenges.

Under each challenge we have tried to explain why it is important to help the child or youth with this challenge. With several challenges we have listed some possible causes, or combination of causes, of that challenge. Whole books could be written about each one of these challenges, and more study is being done all the time. We have provided as much, and as current information as we feel you will need to get started with your child or youth.

Under each challenge, we have also listed practices that we have found to be helpful to many children & youth. One or both of us has had direct experience with each of the practices that we mention. Some practices are better for young children. Others work best for teenagers & youth.

Since each child & youth is so unique, it is very difficult to predict what will work most effectively with each one. Differences in practitioners can affect results as well. Some children & youth don't like or respond to one practice, while others do. We have tried to offer many choices to investigate. You need to pay attention to how the child or youth reacts, and remember that some help takes quite a bit of time to have a good effect.

It is important to remember that many of the stressful events that we have listed may not be what is causing your child or youth's condition, but might be making the underlying condition worse.

The lists of challenges and things to investigate can sometimes be painful, overpowering and confusing. The lists may cause panic and big emotional reactions. Take your time. Read a bit at a time. Keep breathing. Drink water. Study the lists with a friend. Read the material out loud if it helps. Remember why you got this material. Keep focusing on the child or youth you want to help.

We are not pretending to be the Harvard Medical School Health Line. We are relating information that we have experienced, seen, and that we have heard about from practitioners and parents. We want to share what we know with you. Practitioners of the different practices can discuss the details.

When we put all this together, we thought about our children and our grandchildren. Some practitioners and some professionals may disagree with us, and we do not always agree amongst ourselves. However, until we find otherwise, we have listed what we would investigate for our children and grandchildren if they had a specific challenge.

We have listed the practices we would first investigate, followed by our second choices for investigation. We then have listed practices for you to investigate which have helped many children maintain the gains they have made. Finally, we have listed some suggestions you can try on your own with your child or youth. In each section we have listed practices in order of importance.

There are many things to keep in mind while making choices. Age is one of them. The age of the child or youth is very important in choosing practices. Some of the practices are not appropriate for all ages.

Later on in this book, in the chapters devoted to specific practices, we have usually included the ages most appropriate for that practice.

Consulting with local practitioners can help decision-making as well. Ultimately however, you have to decide which practices are most suitable for your child or youth.

Because children & youth are so different, very few practices will work completely every time. You have to find the right practices that will help your child or youth to grow and learn more easily. Hopefully these lists will make your investigations a little quicker and more efficient.

ABANDONMENT

By Parent; Parents; Family Members

Without help, abandonment can cause challenges with intelligence, learning, living, relationships, judgment and/or self-esteem throughout life. Abandonment can destroy faith, trust, ability to love, and willingness to communicate. It can lead to anxiety, depression or other mental illness, physical illnesses, severe antisocial behavior and violence. Adult relationships can become challenging. It can make being a parent very difficult.

First, We Would Investigate	Second, We Would Investigate	For Long Term Support We Would Investigate
• Psychotherapy • Psychiatry • Independent Study • Massage • EMDR • Hypnotherapy • Attitudinal Healing • Music Lessons • Expressive Arts • Drumming • Support For Parents • Wilderness Therapy • Flower Essences • Nonviolent Communication	• Aromatherapy • Herbolology • Yoga • Meditation	• Aikido • Drumming • Music Lessons • Aromatherapy • Ayurveda • Traditional Chinese Medicine • Homeopathy • Flower Essences • Independent Study • Massage • Support For Parents • Meditation • Independent Study • Nonviolent Communication

On Our Own We Would Try: • Pets • Long Walks/Hikes • Nature • Bedtime Stories and Chats • Wholesome Pleasures • Back Rubs and Foot Massages • Replace sodas, juices, sugars, fats, fast foods with water, veggies, whole grains, protein, fruit, slow food • Less or No TV

. . . .

For Parents: • Get help to deal with the memories of when you as a child were abandoned. Doing this will help you be there for your child or youth. • Get some help also to forgive yourself for abandoning your child or youth. • Kids like structure. Mean what you say, say what you mean, do what you say you are going to do. Get help so the child or youth has routines. • Acknowledge and express your regret that the abandonment happened. • Home schooling can help for a year or two when everything calms down.

Check out: www.Childtrauma.org (Parents of Traumatized Children); www.traumasoma.com/index.shtml (very technical); www.acestudy.org.

ACCIDENT

Being Involved In An Accident Or Crash

There are many kinds of accidents, many levels of intensity and risk and many causes of accidents. It is essential to seek medical care as soon as possible. Seek out doctors who are familiar with the practices listed below and follow their advice. There are some children & youth who may get some relief from the practices below when they are used in conjunction with western medical care. Try any of these practices only with the cooperation of your child or youth's primary physician. Without help, accidents can cause a number of challenges that can slow optimal progress. Children & youth can appear to recover quickly, but the effects of any accident can grow. Emotional as well as physical discomfort can develop from tensions resulting from accidents. Effects can take some time to cause challenges such as headaches, pain, perception challenges, memory, learning, emotional calm and physical movement. Initially appearing to be OK after accidents should not be trusted.

First, We Would Investigate	Second, We Would Investigate	For Long Term Support We Would Investigate
• Western Medicine • Osteopathy • Craniosacral Therapy • Chiropractic • Aromatherapy • Homeopathy • Herbolology • Flower Essences • Massage • Feldenkrais • Psychotherapy • Psychiatry • Support For Parents	• EMDR • Hypnotherapy • Massage • Expressive Arts • Meditation • Developmental Optometry • Light Therapy • Nonviolent Communication	• Craniosacral • Osteopathy • Chiropractic • Aromatherapy • Flower Essences • Aruveda • Traditional Chinese Medicine • Homeopathy • Psychotherapy • Developmental Optometry • Light Therapy • Flower Essences • Nonviolent Communication

On Our Own We Would Try: • Back Rubs and Foot Massages • Bedtime Stories and Chats • Wholesome Pleasures • Replace sodas, juices, sugars, fats, fast foods with water, veggies, whole grains, nuts, protein, fruit, slow food • Long Walks/Hikes • Nature • Pets • Less or No TV, Movies, Video/Computer Games, Movies, Video/Computer Games

. . . .

For Parents: • Get a medical evaluation as soon as possible. • Tell the child or youth you know things are going to be OK. • Do whatever you can to make things as OK as you can. • Watch for long term consequences of what happened.

Check out: www.traumasoma.com/index.shtml (very technical); www.acestudy.org.

ACCIDENT PRONE

Hurt Often

Without help, the effects of being accident prone can slow emotional and physical growth and learning. Being accident-prone can be due to, and complicated by a combination of: pre-existing medical conditions; perceptual difficulties; physical disorganization; impulsivity; stress; emotional preoccupation; emotional and/or physical discomfort from other unhealed accidents, traumas or abuses of all kinds; nutritional imbalances; exposure to environmental pollutants; inability to focus. Children & youth can be so preoccupied with thoughts and feelings that they are not in touch with their bodies and surroundings.

First, We Would Investigate	Second, We Would Investigate	For Long Term Support We Would Investigate
• Psychotherapy • Psychiatry • Western Medicine • Osteopathy • EMDR • Hypnotherapy • Craniosacral • Feldenkrais • Chiropractic • Developmental Optometry • Aromatherapy • Homeopathy • Herbolology • Light Therapy • Massage • Nutrition Consulting • Biofeedback • Environmentally Healthy Homes	• Aikido • Drumming • Expressive Arts • Flower Essences • Meditation • Independent Study • Traditional Chinese Medicine • Ayurveda • Yoga	• Psychotherapy • Chiropractic • Craniosacral • Osteopathy • Aikido • Aromatherapy • Feldenkrais • Environmentally Healthy Homes

On Our Own We Would Try: • Long Walks/Hikes • Back Rubs and Foot Massages • Replace sodas, juices, sugars, fats, fast foods with water, veggies, whole grains, nuts, protein, fruit, slow food • Bedtime Stories and Chats • Wholesome Pleasures • Nature • Pets • Less or No TV, Movies, Video/Computer Games

• •

For Parents: • Get your child or youth's doctor to evaluate and diagnose any underlying conditions that might be causing being accident prone. • Crawling around on the floor together can help as well. • Engage the child or youth in regular, fun, physical activity. Reassure the child or youth that you know things are going to be OK.

Check out: www.MedLinePlus.gov; www.KidsHealth.org; www.traumasoma.com/index.shtml (very technical); www.acestudy.org.

ACNE

There are many kinds of Acne, many levels of intensity and risk, and many causes. It is essential to seek medical care as soon as possible. There are some children & youth who may get some relief from the practices below when they are used in conjunction with western medical care. Try any of these practices only with the cooperation of your child or youth's primary physician. Without help, Acne is painful and can leave permanent scars on the body, self-confidence and emotions. Acne can be caused by a combination of: stress; genetic factors; nutritional imbalances; environmental pollutants; and molds. It can be difficult to treat. Each therapy should be tried for at least two months because the skin healing needs that long.

First, We Would Investigate	Second, We Would Investigate	For Long Term Support We Would Investigate
• Western Medicine • Osteopathy • Psychotherapy • Aromatherapy • Ayurveda • Herbolology • Traditional Chinese Medicine • Homeopathy • Attitudinal Healing • Hypnotherapy • Support For Parents • Nutrition Consulting	• Drumming • Biofeedback • EMDR • Light Therapy	• Western Medicine • Nutrition Consulting • Aromatherapy • Traditional Chinese Medicine • Ayurveda • Herbolology

On Our Own We Would Try: • Long Walks/Hikes • Nature • Bedtime Stories and Chats • Wholesome Pleasure •Massage • Replace sodas, juices, sugars, fats, fast foods with water, veggies, whole grains, nuts, protein, fruit, slow food • Pets • Less or No TV, Movies, Video/Computer Games • Back Rubs and Foot Massages

. . . .

For Parents: • Sometimes the over the counter acne remedies are effective (like Benzylperoxide). • Make sure the child or youth knows they are loved and have gifts. • Reduce stress as much as possible.

Check out: www.MedLinePlus.gov; www.KidsHealth.org.

ADDICTIONS

To: Alcohol, Drugs, Tobacco, Sex, Sugar, Fats, Carbohydrates, Fast Food, TV, Video, Computer Games And The Internet, Consumerism, Collecting Stuff, Looking Good, Looking Like A Particular Social Group

There are many kinds of addictions, many levels of intensity and risk, and many causes. It is essential to seek medical care as soon as possible. There are some children & youth who may get some relief from the practices below when they are used in conjunction with western medical care. Try any of these practices only with the cooperation of your child or youth's primary physician. Addictions are often children's & youth's easiest choice to make themselves feel better in the face of their pain and suffering. Addiction can be a short-term solution to emotional or physical pain, loneliness, confusion, anger, unhappiness, frustrations, and chaos in their lives, having powerful emotions they are trying to forget or stay away from. Things that become an addiction are often first tried as ways to have social connection with other children & youth who often have the same types of challenges. Addictions are a substitute for being able to grow up easier and cope with unhappiness, depression, boredom, pain, confusion, anxiety and powerlessness. Children & youth are the ones who suffer the most from ineffective and dysfunctional ancestral and family patterns. Addictions can be viewed as a strong sign of the child or youth losing connection with their nature or soul. Addictions can also be a sign that they feel unimportant to life. Addictions can also give children & youth temporary relief from the effects of nutritional imbalances which can cause painful emotional, psychological, or physical challenges. Addictions can cover emotional and/or physical discomfort caused by unhealed accidents, traumas and abuses of all kinds. Addictions are often associated with covering up a lack of communication skills. All addictions can be a major waste of time/life and a loss of learning valuable skills needed for adult success.

Alcohol, Drugs, Tobacco, Sex: Alone or together addiction to any of these can damage the body, mind, emotions in childhood and into adulthood. They can lead to life-threatening diseases. Tobacco and alcohol are legally promoted and made socially attractive. Tobacco and alcohol kill more people annually than all other drugs combined. Alcohol is one of the leading causes of teen death. Tobacco is one of the most addictive and harmful of all drugs. Tobacco use can be an entry into addictive patterns. Smoking, drinking, drug taking and compulsive sexual activity are often social experiences that children & youth use to make up for unmet family needs. These addictions can be protection against the feeling of helplessness to make life better. They can also be due to a combination of: coping with painful life experiences; abuses of all kinds; family patterns; social isolation; lack of communication skills; genetic factors; exposure to environmental pollutants; nutritional imbalances and physical discomforts.

Sugar, Fats, Carbohydrates, Fast Food: This can be a major challenge for emotional balance, memory, ability to concentrate, and meeting the nutritional needs of growing. These foods can lead to hyperactivity, irritability, laziness, impulsivity and other serious behavior challenges. They can lead to a number of serious conditions including: obesity, diabetes, heart disease. They can be a sign of a number of physical and emotional difficulties. These addictions can be due to a combination of: prolonged stress; environmental pollutants; family patterns; nutritional imbalances.

TV, Internet, Video and Computer Games: This addiction is slightly less destructive than other forms of addictions. It can also cover up and help children & youth avoid feelings of depression, boredom, pain, confusion and anxiety. These addictions are also major losses of time that could be spent learning, accomplishing skills, playing, which help children & youth build confidence and learn valuable social and thinking skills needed for adult life. These addictions can be due to a combination of: low self-confidence; hopelessness; depression or other mental illnesses; boredom; feeling powerless; feeling disconnected socially; exposure to environmental pollutants; nutrition imbalances; hyperactivity.

Consumerism, Collecting Stuff, Looking Good, Looking Like a Particular Social Group: Attachment to things, appearances, looking good, are often cover ups and substitutes for challenges with confidence, self-esteem and friendships. They are substitutes for ability, skill and accomplishment. These addictions can be complicated by media advertising, which tries to create dissatisfaction and shame about appearance, social class and not having stuff. Often this addiction can also be due to parental and/or societal examples. It is necessary for children and teens to love themselves for who they are without all the stuff and particular appearances.

First, We Would Investigate	Second, We Would Investigate	For Long Term Support We Would Investigate
• Psychotherapy • Nonviolent Communication • Attitudinal Healing • Wilderness Therapy • Expressive Arts • Yoga • Aikido • Aromatherapy • Ayurveda • Traditional Chinese Medicine • Herbology • Flower Essences • Biofeedback • EMDR • Hypnotherapy • Flower Essences • Nutrition Consulting • Support For Parents • Independent Study	• Light Therapy • Massage • Drumming • Music Lessons • Craniosacral	• Nonviolent Communication • Psychotherapy • Support For Parents • Aromatherapy • Ayurveda • Traditional Chinese Medicine • Herbology • Flower Essences • Yoga • Aikido • Massage • EMDR • Hypnotherapy • Wilderness Therapy • Independent Study

On Our Own We Would Try: • Replace sodas, juices, sugars, fats, fast foods with water, veggies, whole grains, nuts, protein, fruit, slow food • Long Walks/Hikes • Bedtime Stories and Chats • Wholesome Pleasures • Back Rubs and Foot Massages • Nature • Pets • Less or No TV, Movies, Video/Computer Games

• •

For Parents: • First begin by taking good care of yourself as a caregiver. Get help for your own addictive patterns. 12 step programs for yourself and your child or youth can help. Your example can create a safe container for your child or youth. • Engage the child or youth in regular, fun, physical activity. Go on hikes or backpacking trips in the wildest countryside you can manage. • Learn and eat what is nutritious, avoiding processed food. • Empathize with your own suffering and also the suffering of your child or youth. • Compassion and empathy are powerful healing tools. • Say what you mean and mean what you say and do what you say you are going to do. • Tolerate only what you say you are going to tolerate.

Check out: www.MedLinePlus.gov; www.KidsHealth.org; www.traumasoma.com/index.shtml (very technical); www.acestudy.org.

ADOPTION

Learning About Being Adopted Late In Childhood, Meeting Birth Parents (With Their Current Families), Mixed Race And International Adoptions

Without ongoing support, adoption can be a very complex situation. Adopting parents can try too hard and worry too much. Adopting parents often get worried and clumsy when the children or youth show their special needs. Professional help is frequently necessary to help the parents to cope with their own feelings—which indirectly affect the child or youth. Adopted children & youth can feel unwanted, rejected at the same time they feel loved and wanted. Children & youth can often construct unreal ideas about themselves. These strange ideas, combined with feeling unwanted and rejected by their family of origin, can effect self-esteem, confidence and emotional calm. There is major debate amongst professionals about the nature and depth of the emotional wounds caused by being abandoned by the birth mother. (see Abandonment above)

Learning about being adopted late in childhood: Without great care this can be a shock to self-esteem, confidence, and can cause children & youth to feel insecure and untrusting for many years or even their whole life. We believe children & youth need to be gently and appropriately told what is true as soon as possible. Adopted children & youth, adoptive parents and birth parents all need support with establishing trust and healthy bonding.

Meeting birth parents (with their current families): Even when this is strongly desired, this can be a shocking experience for everyone. Without great support this can cause confusion and insecurity effecting self-esteem and feeling secure. It can also give children & youth strange ideas about what they will be like when they grow up. Handled with love, care and sensitivity, however, this can sometimes be a wonderful healing experience.

Mixed race and international adoptions: Without support, this can be a very complex situation affecting self-esteem, confidence and social relations. Parents of the dominant culture's ethnicity often overlook the possibly difficult effects of looking different.

First, We Would Investigate	Second, We Would Investigate	For Long Term Support We Would Investigate
• Psychotherapy • Psychiatry • Support For Parents • Nonviolent Communication • Attitudinal Healing • EMDR • Hypnotherapy • Massage • Independent Study • Flower Essences	• Aikido • Drumming • Expressive Arts • Feldenkrais • Music Lessons • Independent Study	• Aikido • Homeopathy • Traditional Chinese Medicine • Ayurveda • Aromatherapy • Herbology • Nutrition Consulting • Support For Parents • Flower Essences • Nonviolent Communication

On Our Own We Would Try: • Wholesome Pleasures • Bedtime Stories and Chats • Long Walks/Hikes • Nature • Back Rubs and Foot Massages • Replace sodas, juices, sugars, fats, fast foods with water, veggies, whole grains, nuts, protein, fruit, slow food • Pets • Less or No TV, Movies, Video/Computer Games

. . . .

For Parents: • Make connection with other parents with similar experiences. There are now online support groups available for most ethnicities and races.

Check out: www.MedLinePlus.gov; www.KidsHealth.org; www.traumasoma.com/index.shtml (very technical); www.acestudy.org.

ANTI-SOCIAL BEHAVIOR

Without some help, this can become habitual and can affect the way the child or youth is treated by family, friends and authority. Reputations can be destroyed. Anti-social behavior can be caused by a combination of: body discomfort; body chemistry and nutritional imbalances; exposure to environmental pollutants; emotional blockages; anti-social family patterns; low self-esteem; and the need to learn social and communication skills.

First, We Would Investigate	Second, We Would Investigate	For Long Term Support We Would Investigate
• Nutrition Education • Aikido • Attitudinal Healing • EMDR • Hypnotherapy • Craniosacral • Psychotherapy • Psychiatry • Support For Parents • Expressive Arts • Environmentally Healthy Homes • Nonviolent Communication • Flower Essences	• Aromatherapy • Massage • Homeopathy • Herbology • Ayurveda • Traditional Chinese Medicine • Music Lessons • Independent Study	• Vitamin Therapy • Nutrition Consulting • Aikido • Aromatherapy • Ayurveda • Traditional Chinese Medicine • Independent Study • Support For Parents • Nonviolent Communication • Flower Essences

On Our Own We Would Try: • Routines • Pets • Less or No TV, Movies, Video/Computer Games • Replace sodas, juices, sugars, fats, fast foods with water, veggies, whole grains, nuts, protein, fruit, slow food • Bedtime Stories and Chats • Wholesome Pleasures • Back Rubs and Foot Massages • Long Walks/Hikes • Nature

· ·

For Parents: • Kids like structure. Mean what you say, say what you mean, do what you say you are going to do.

Check out: www.MedinePlus.gov; www.KidsHealth.org; www.traumasoma.com/index.shtml (very technical); www.acestudy.org.

ANXIETY

Frequent

There are many kinds of anxiety, many levels of intensity and risk, and many causes. It is essential to seek medical care for anxiety as soon as possible. There are some children & youth who may get some relief from the practices below when they are used in conjunction with western medical care. Try any of these practices only with the cooperation of your child or youth's primary physician. Without treatment, anxiety can be painful and may slow or stop learning, lower self-esteem, lead to social isolation, depression, physical illness. It can cause havoc with the child or youth's reputation and how others treat the child or youth. Frequent anxiety can be due to a combination of: genetics, prolonged stress; unresolved abuses and traumas of all kinds; family patterns; nutrition imbalances; exposure to environmental pollutants.

First, We Would Investigate	Second, We Would Investigate	For Long Term Support We Would Investigate
• Homeopathy • Osteopathy • Western Medicine • Psychiatry • Flower Essences • Ayurveda • Herbology • Nutrition Consulting • Traditional Chinese Medicine • Massage • Biofeedback • EMDR • Hypnotherapy • Chiropractic • Craniosacral • Light Therapy • Aromatherapy • Nonviolent Communication • Independent Study	• Feldenkrais • Aikido • Expressive Arts • Drumming • Music Lessons • Wilderness Therapy • Attitudinal Healing	• Aikido • Nutrition Consulting • Aromatherapy • Homeopathy • Ayurveda • Herbology • Traditional Chinese Medicine • Flower Essences • Independent Study • Nonviolent Communication

On Our Own We Would Try: • Less or No TV, Movies, Video/Computer Games • Replace sodas, juices, sugars, fats, fast foods with water, veggies, whole grains, nuts, protein, fruit, slow food • Long Walks/ Hikes • Nature • Bedtime Stories and Chats • Wholesome Pleasures • Back Rubs and Foot Massages • Pets

• •

For Parents: • Get a medical evaluation. • Give your family the best food you can afford. • Explore bio-feedback devices such as E-wave from HeartMath. • Remember that the child or youth's fears and anxieties are forms of communication that tell you that you need to give the child or youth assistance. • Try to see the world through the child or youth's young eyes. Think of what might be upsetting or confusing to your vulnerable child or youth. • Never belittle or cater to the fears but do acknowledge them. • Consider if expectations are too high. • Look up local resources on the Internet, at school and in the community for parenting skills and support. • Beware of drug ads on the Internet. • Kids like calm, relaxed structure, predictability, novelty, encouragement and parental support/faith. Get help and learn how to give the child or youth effective, consistent routines and opportunities for success. • Engage the child or youth in regular, fun, physical activity. • Find and express faith that everything will work out well.

Check out: www.MedLinePlus.gov; www.KidsHealth.org; www.traumasoma.com/index.shtml (very technical); www.acestudy.org.

ARITHMETIC/MATHEMATICS CHALLENGES

Calculates Slowly; Difficulty Organizing Information On Paper; Difficulty Understanding Abstract Concepts; Lack Of Challenge Solving Strategies; Reverses Numbers/Mixes Up Numbers; Difficulty Learning Basic Operations; Difficulty Remembering Number Facts; Gets Very Frustrated/Lacks Confidence

It appears that proficiency in math has some connection to being successful. Higher salaries appear to be paid to people who are comfortable with mathematics. It is therefore very important to solve these challenges with learning mathematics as quickly as possible. These challenges create increasing anxiety, habits of quitting, and ineffective attitudes towards learning. This difficulty can be due to a combination of: learning style/instruction style mismatch; family patterns and expectations; lack of effective family support and acknowledgement; vision challenges; perceptual challenges; anxiety; nutritional imbalances; chaotic environment; damage to the head; allergies; exposure to pollutants; inability to focus; ineffective teaching and insufficient practice; insufficient study habit instruction; inability to relax and think; a lack of hearing storybooks read every night.

First, We Would Investigate	Second, We Would Investigate	For Long Term Support We Would Investigate
• Precision Teaching • Developmental Optometry • Light Therapy • Craniosacral • Biofeedback • Flower Essences	• Ayurveda • Traditional Chinese Medicine • Herbology • Homeopathy • Hypnotherapy • EMDR • Feldenkrais • Music Lessons • Independent Study	• Nutrition Consulting • Aikido • Aromatherapy • Ayurveda • Expressive Arts • Flower Essences

On Our Own We Would Try: • Less or No TV, Movies, Video/Computer Games • Replace sodas, juices, sugars, fats, fast foods with water, veggies, whole grains, nuts, protein, fruit, slow food • Bedtime Stories and Chats • Back Rubs and Foot Massages • Wholesome Pleasures • Long Walks/Hikes • Nature • Pets

For Parents: • Give the best low sugar, low additive diet you can afford. High protein, low sugar breakfasts can help a great deal. • Carefully explore tutors, systems, companies and books that successfully help children or youth be successful and comfortable with math. • Until High School graduation, read your child or youth stories, biographies, or anything that interests them. The art of focusing, listening and organizing information helps abstract thinking and math skills.

Check out: www.MedLinePlus.gov; www.KidsHealth.org; www.traumasoma.com/index.shtml (very technical); www.acestudy.org.

ASHAMED, BLAMED, SUFFERING DEBILITATING GUILT

About What Has Been Done; About Feeling Worthless; About Shame For Being Alive

Feeling guilty or ashamed a little is pretty natural–like regret. Feeling ashamed a great deal can be both physically and psychologically painful and disabling. It can slow learning. Unchecked, shame can destroy confidence and success in later life. It make children & youth very fearful of attempting anything. Shame is learned. It can be due to a combination of: clumsy attempts at control; exposure to a lack of compassion and forgiveness; being blamed or teased; unskilled guidance by ashamed parents, family, friends, teachers and other professionals; unresolved traumas or disfigurements; having apparent difficulties; poverty; racism; uncertain gender identification; sexual orientation; learning challenges; communication difficulties; emotions--expressed and unexpressed; abuse of all kinds including spiritual abuse. Shame can be made more confusing by nutritional imbalances and exposure to environmental pollutants.

First, We Would Investigate	Second, We Would Investigate	For Long Term Support We Would Investigate
• Attitudinal Healing • EMDR • Hypnotherapy • Biofeedback • Psychotherapy • Psychiatry • Expressive Arts • Meditation • Support For Parents • Nonviolent Communication • Flower Essences	• Homeopathy • Ayurveda • Traditional Chinese Medicine • Wilderness Therapy • Aikido • Yoga • Massage • Drumming • Music Lessons • Independent Study	• Aikido • Aromatherapy • Nutrition Consulting • Massage • Nonviolent Communication • Flower Essences

On Our Own We Would Try: • Bedtime Stories and Chats • Wholesome Pleasures • Replace sodas, juices, sugars, fats, fast foods with water veggies, whole grains, protein, fruit, slow food • Back Rubs and Foot Massage • Long Walks/Hikes • Nature • Faith and Hope • Pets • No or Less TV

• •

For Parents: • It is very important for the family to learn how to effectively give support, acknowledge each other, forgive self and others and to have compassion. • Investigate over the counter at health food stores: Bach Flower Essence remedies including: Crabapple for shame and self hatred; Larch for lack of self-confidence; Pine for self reproach/guilt; and Rescue Remedy for general well-being.

Check out: www.MedLinePlus.gov; www.KidsHealth.org; www.traumasoma.com/index.shtml (very technical); www.acestudy.org.

ASTHMA

Asthma attacks can be really terrifying for everyone. Asthma can affect vitality, achievement, and self-fulfillment and self-confidence. It can produce a lot of fear. It can prevent full participation in life. Asthma creates distrust of one's body. Asthma can be due to a combination of: fear, stress and anxiety; genetics; family patterns; exposure to pollutants; parental income levels; unexpressed emotions; nutritional imbalances; body shock; allergies to dust, certain foods, some pets; physical and neurological disorganization.

First, We Would Investigate	Second, We Would Investigate	For Long Term Support We Would Investigate
• Western Medicine • Osteopathy • Aromatherapy • Herbology • Traditional Chinese Medicine • Ayurveda • Biofeedback • Homeopathy • Craniosacral • Meditation • Environmentally Healthy Homes • Hypnotherapy • Nutrition Consulting • Chiropractic • Support For Parents • Nonviolent Communication • Flower Essences	• Aikido • Expressive Arts • Yoga • Psychotherapy • Feldenkrais	• Aikido • Aromatherapy • Ayurveda • Environmentally Healthy Homes • Music Lessons • Expressive Arts • Wilderness Therapy • Nonviolent Communication • Flower Essences

On Our Own We Would Try: • Replace sodas, juices, sugars, fats, fast foods with water, veggies, whole grains, nuts, protein, fruit, slow food • Long Walks/Hikes • Bedtime Stories and Chats • Wholesome Pleasures • Back Rubs and Foot Massages • Nature • Less or No TV, Movies, Video/Computer Games

• •

For Parents: • Get a medical evaluation. • Do what is necessary to help the child or youth have a good time. Reducing stress and anxiety can make a great difference. • Make sure you protect your child or youth from second hand smoke and other air pollutants. Explore air purifiers. • You may have to move to a neighborhood with cleaner air. • Help the child or youth maintain a healthy body weight by engaging the family in exercise and good diet. • Investigate Buteyko Breathing Method. • Contact Dorisse Neal in Ashland, TN.

Check out: www.MedLinePlus.gov; www.KidsHealth.org; www.traumasoma.com/index.shtml (very technical); www.acestudy.org.

ATTACHMENT DISORDERS

Has Difficulty With Social Relationships; Family Relationships; Does Not Relate And Interact Easily; Very Withdrawn And/Or Very Argumentative And/Or Very Aggressive And/Or Very Manipulative

These disorders can cause havoc in adult relationships, accomplishment, and conscience. They can be signs of challenges with relationships, feeling connected to home, school and community. These disorders can be due to perceptual challenges or not being able to pay attention to social cues. They can be a sign of difficulties being empathetic, having a conscience, and being able to have successful relationships. They can also be due to a combination of: exposure to physical, emotional, or spiritual abuse; being traumatized; not being loved; abandonment; or exposure to crazy adult behavior. They may also be due to or made worse by nutritional imbalances and exposure to pollutants.

First, We Would Investigate	Second, We Would Investigate	For Long Term Support We Would Investigate
• Psychotherapy • Psychiatry • Support For Parents • Expressive Arts Therapy • EMDR • Hypnotherapy • Independent Study • Biofeedback • Massage • Music Lessons • Flower Essences • Nonviolent Communication	• Vitamin Therapy • Nutrition Consulting • Aikido • Ayurveda • Homeopathy • Herbology • Traditional Chinese Medicine • Yoga	• Support For Parents • Aikido • Ayurveda • Homeopathy • Aromatherapy • Herbology • Traditional Chinese Medicine • Nonviolent Communication • Flower Essences • Independent Study

On Our Own We Would Try: • Pets • Bedtime Stories and Chats • Wholesome Pleasures • Back Rubs and Foot Massages • Replace sodas, juices, sugars, fats, fast foods with water, veggies, whole grains, nuts, protein, fruit, slow food • Less or No TV, Movies, Video/Computer Games • Long Walks/Hikes • Nature

• •

For Parents: • Remember that the child or youth's behavior is a form of communication that you need to give assistance. • Try to see the world through the child or youth's young eyes. Think of what might be upsetting or confusing to the vulnerable child or youth. • Look up local resources for parenting skills and support. • Kids like structure and predictability. Mean what you say, say what you mean, do what you say you are going to do. • Get help and learn how to give the child or youth effective, consistent routines.

Check out: www.MedLinePlus.gov; www.KidsHealth.org; www.traumasoma.com/index.shtml (very technical); www.acestudy.org.

ATTENDS SCHOOLS THAT HAVE DRUG AND ALCOHOL USE CHALLENGES

Children & youth who attend schools where many students use, and can easily access, drugs/alcohol are at greater risk of using drugs/alcohol and being unsafe. Sadly, few schools are free from some drug/alcohol use among students. Children & youth often use drugs to feel better, for excitement, acceptance and companionship. Children & youth could be using drugs to self-medicate pain, frustration, low self-esteem and social disconnection. Drug use often has "rite of passage" qualities that some children & youth seem to need to grow up. Drug use can be a plea for help. Drug/alcohol challenges in schools reflect a society that uses drugs/alcohol to self-medicate suffering, loneliness and boredom. Media messages contribute distorted ideas for children & youth. Children & youth need support and communication skill to resist peer pressure and find alternatives to self-medication. Often society and school programs do not engage the child/youth in making meaningful contributions/expressions. "Just Say No" programs have not solved this challenge. Schools have to provide a safe haven from effects of other students using drugs. This is an extremely difficult task and school budgets often do not allow for effectively dealing with this challenge. Children & youth from families with communication and problem-solving skills appear less interested in drug use. Nevertheless, they too are at risk from coercion and violence from drug/alcohol using school-mates.

Drug/alcohol experimentation/use/abuse: This can be related to and complicated by a combination of: peer pressure; curiosity; family patterns and modeling; low self-esteem; the need to escape emotional pain from unresolved traumas and abuses; feeling disconnected from family; feeling anger, fear, hopelessness and depression. Prolonged stress, nutritional imbalances and exposure to environmental pollutants may also be involved.

First, We Would Investigate	Second, We Would Investigate	For Long Term Support We Would Investigate
• Safe School Ambassadors • Independent Study • Nonviolent Communication • Attitudinal Healing • Aikido • Meditation • Wilderness Therapy • Expressive Arts • Psychotherapy • Psychiatry • Support For Parents • Nutrition Consulting • Precision Teaching • Flower Essences • Homeopathy	• Aromatherapy • EMDR • Hypnotherapy • Biofeedback • Music Lessons • Massage	• Aikido • Independent Study • Nonviolent Communication • Safe School Ambassadors • Nutrition Consulting • Aromatherapy • Meditation • Herbology • Homeopathy • Traditional Chinese Medicine • Ayurveda • Flower Essences

On Our Own We Would Try: • Less or No TV, Movies, Video/Computer Games • Replace sodas, juices, sugars, fats, fast foods with water, veggies, whole grains, nuts, protein, fruit, slow food • Bedtime Stories and Chats • Wholesome Pleasures • Back Rubs and Foot Massages • Long Walks/Hikes • Nature • Pets

• •

For Parents: • Keep family communication open and positive. • Be involved with your child or youth's friends and their parents. • Join with other concerned parents to assist school staff in dealing with this problem. • Praise sobriety. • Have an alcohol and drug free home. • Explore and teach alternative methods of having a good time.

ATTENDS SCHOOL WITH GANGS AND VIOLENCE

Attending schools and living in communities with gang activity puts children & youth at great risk of being badly hurt in many ways. It also increases the risk that children & youth will become violent or join gangs in self-defense. Attending schools with gangs and violence can lead to death, permanent disability, imprisonment, addictions of all kinds, and being abused in many ways. Gangs and violence can be signs of families, schools and communities not meeting the children's or youth's needs for: meaningful skills; realistic, effective self-esteem; communication skills; effective alternatives; security/safety; success; social connection; and hope. Children & youth also join gangs for reasons of friendship in the face of loneliness and feeling useless/worthless. The existence of gangs and violence can also reflect alienation from the community, a lack of communication skills and poor nutrition. Too often the unresolved, unsupported pain and suffering of youth abnormalize the normal and normalize the abnormal. Children and youth become so desperate and alienated from society that gang life looks attractive. Society, so far, is not forgiving and compassionate when anyone makes a mistake or breaks the law. This lack of compassion condemns children & youth, who can come to think of themselves as "bad" forever. Gangs help kids feel normal and welcomed. Nutritional imbalances and exposure to environmental pollutants can also be involved in making children & youth anxious, angry and violent.

Without help, gang violence can be life threatening and can lead to dangerous and crippling lifetime habits. Changing to a safer school is not always possible, but still a good idea to explore. Being in such dangerous schools makes learning very difficult, due to the stress of fearing for personal safety. Violence and willingness to participate in gang life is often caused by survival needs (safer to be violent or in a gang because there are no alternative safe options). The violent behavior is often due to and complicated by a combination of: mental illness; unacknowledged fear; anger; low self-esteem; boredom; hopelessness; family modeling; loneliness. Drugs and alcohol can be involved in both violence and gang membership, as can alienation from society, insufficient communication and negotiation skills, a history of a lack of school funding and inappropriate school staffing. Nutritional imbalances and exposure to pollutants may also be factors.

First, We Would Investigate	Second, We Would Investigate	For Long Term Support We Would Investigate
• Safe School Ambassadors • Independent Study • Nonviolent Communication • Aikido • Attitudinal Healing • Meditation • Expressive Arts • Psychotherapy • Psychiatry • EMDR • Hypnotherapy • Biofeedback • Wilderness Therapy • Support For Parents	• Precision Teaching • Light Therapy • Developmental Optometry • Drumming • Environmentally Healthy Homes • Flower Essences • Herbology	• Aikido • Safe School Ambassadors • Independent Study • Nutrition Consulting • Meditation • Aromatherapy • Herbology • Homeopathy • Nonviolent Communication • Psychotherapy • Meditation

On Our Own We Would Try: • Pets • Less or No TV, Movies, Video/Computer Games • Wholesome Pleasures • Replace sodas, juices, sugars, fats, fast foods with water, veggies, whole grains, nuts, protein, fruit, slow food • Bedtime Stories and Chats • Back Rubs and Foot Massages • Long Walks/Hikes • Nature

. . . .

For Parents: • Talk with other parents. Form or find a parent support group so you have support. Help your child or youth feel reassured by joining with other parents and school staff interested in changing this situation. • Learn nonviolent communication and negotiation skills and teach them to your child or youth. • Move into a safer neighborhood if possible. • Take your child or youth out of the environment whenever possible for as long as possible. • Go camping together as often as possible. • Encourage education and getting employable skills. • Enroll in educational programs yourself. • Enroll in Aikido yourself. • Tell the truth about what you think and feel. • Get in touch with having faith that the child or youth will be OK. Communicate this often.

ATTENDS SCHOOLS WITH LOW PERFORMANCE

Without help, attending such schools can be very dangerous for children & youth and their future. Besides not being able to gain necessary skills or to catch up on missing skills, children & youth can lose their curiosity and may not develop necessary life-long learning skills. Without success, they can develop low self-esteem as learners. Moving to another school may be a good option, but may not be possible. Low school performance is often due to and complicated by: society and governments not spending enough money on hiring and effectively supervising enough good teachers, programs and equipment. The lack of community political will and finances for safe school environments, catch-up, remedial, or extra support programs is also a factor. Low school performance can also be affected by and contribute to student violence, drug and alcohol use. Too often, low school performance is blamed on parents and families for not effectively preparing and supporting their children & youth. Research is showing that nutritional imbalances and exposure to environmental pollutants also have importance in school performance.

First, We Would Investigate	Second, We Would Investigate	For Long Term Support We Would Investigate
• Precision Teaching • Independent Study • Nonviolent Communication • Safe School Ambassadors • Meditation • Yoga • Nutrition Consulting • Expressive Arts • Attitudinal Healing • Music Lessons • Environmentally Healthy Homes • Support For Parents	• Homeopathy • Flower Essences • EMDR • Hypnotherapy • Massage • Craniosacral • Developmental Optometry • Light Therapy	• Precision Teaching • Independent Study • Nonviolent Communication • Meditation • Yoga • Expressive Arts

On Our Own We Would Try: • Bedtime Stories and Chats • Less or No TV, Movies, Video/Computer Games • Wholesome Pleasures • Replace sodas, juices, sugars, fats, fast foods with water, veggies, whole grains, nuts, protein, fruit, slow food • Back Rubs and Foot Massages • Long Walks/Hikes • Nature • Pets

. . . .

For Parents: • Helping teachers and elected officials can improve schools. Your involvement will give your child or youth hope. • Giving curiosity-based learning programs at home can also be important. • Become a learner yourself. Enroll in a class learning something new. • Consider Independent Study or an apprenticeship program.

ATTENTION DEFICIT DISORDER (ADD), ATTENTION DEFICIT HYPERACTIVE DISORDER (ADHD)

Inattentive, Hyperactive And Combined Impulsive Behavior

These are very overused diagnostic labels that can limit children & youth, parents and teachers. The label often gets treatment. The child or youth may not. A variety of conditions get lumped together. This often hides the needs of each individual child or youth. Special classes, special drugs can sometimes be very helpful. Sometimes they may only deal with symptoms and may not help the child or youth feel good about themselves and give them good skills for the future. The conditions that can add up and combine to make learning and living extremely difficult include: perceptual challenges; body chemistry imbalances; impulse control difficulties; auditory processing; focusing difficulties; prolonged unresolved stress; unresolved traumas—especially to the body; depression or other mental illnesses; anxiety; lack of effective communication skills; difficulty relaxing.

Without support, the condition can lead to a lifetime of misery, confusion, poor performance, unfulfilling relationships and suffering for everyone. Children & youth often develop antisocial behavior patterns in clumsy attempts to feel good when they feel so unsuccessful. This condition may be related to a combination of a vast number of factors including: genetics; exposure to environmental pollutants; stress; nutritional imbalances; anxiety; learned behavior; low self-esteem; unreleased body tension resulting from traumatic birth; falls and other childhood accidents. With proper help, children can learn to use their ADD/ADHD condition to their and society's advantage.

First, We Would Investigate	Second, We Would Investigate	For Long Term Support We Would Investigate
• Nutrition Consulting • Environmentally Healthy Homes • Ayurveda • Traditional Chinese Medicine • Hypnotherapy • Craniosacral • Light Therapy • Developmental Optometry • Chiropractic • Osteopathy • Herbology • Independent Study • Support For Parents • EMDR • Biofeedback • Western Medicine • Flower Essences • Nonviolent Communication	• Aikido • Aromatherapy • Wilderness Therapy • Feldenkrais • Drumming • Music Lessons • Expressive Arts	• Aikido • Aromatherapy • Herbology • Nutrition Consulting • Nonviolent Communication • Flower Essences • Independent Study

On Our Own We Would Try: • Less or No TV, Movies, Video/Computer Games • Replace sodas, juices, sugars, fats, fast foods with water, veggies, whole grains, nuts, protein, fruit, slow food • Long Walks/Hikes • Nature • Wholesome Pleasures • Bedtime Stories and Chats • Back Rubs and Foot Massages • Pets

• •

For Parents: • Restrict sugars, provide high protein, low sugar breakfasts, encourage drinking lots of water.   • Address anxiety, depression, desperation and ADHD patterns in the whole family.   • Explore support for being a parent.   • Find family structures and methods that fit the child or youth and you.   • Support the children or youth in finding positive things they enjoy and in which their high energy helps them succeed.

•Watch out for websites and information sponsored by drug companies. They want your business and may not give you all the information you need.   • Be patient and kind with the child or youth and yourself.   • Explore references to short term memory; working memory; auditory processing; visual processing; temporal and special sequencing.

Check out: www MedLinePlus.gov; www.KidsHealth.org; and wwwSchwabLearning.org (very technical); www.acestudy.org.

ATTITUDE CHALLENGES

Attitude challenges can lead to difficulties in living, learning, and having successful relationships. They can be caused by or lead to addiction challenges. Attitude challenges may be due to a combination of: poor role models; family patterns; depression, anxiety or other mental illnesses; frustration; nutritional imbalances; exposure to pollutants and unresolved body tension resulting from traumatic birth; accidents; abuses of all kinds; and other traumatic events. Unexpressed emotion, low self-esteem, and a lack of communication skills may also be involved.

First, We Would Investigate	Second, We Would Investigate	For Long Term Support We Would Investigate
• Support For Parents • Nutrition Consulting • Attitudinal Healing • EMDR • Hypnotherapy • Psychotherapy • Psychiatry • Aikido • Craniosacral • Chiropractic • Expressive Arts • Independent Study • Environmentally Healthy Homes • Nonviolent Communication • Flower Essences	• Aromatherapy • Massage • Homeopathy • Herbology • Ayurveda • Developmental Optometry • Light Therapy • Music Lessons • Drumming	• Vitamin Therapy • Nutrition Consulting • Aikido • Aromatherapy • Ayurveda • Traditional Chinese Medicine • Herbology • Homeopathy • Nonviolent Communication • Flower Essences • Independent Study • Support For Parents

On Our Own We Would Try: • Replace sodas, juices, sugars, fats, fast foods with water, veggies, whole grains, nuts, protein, fruit, slow food • Long Walks and Hikes • Bedtime Stories and Chats • Wholesome Pleasures • Back Rubs and Foot Massages • Nature • Pets • Less or No TV, Movies, Video/Computer Games

• •

For Parents: • Remember that behavior is language that children or youth use to indicate their needs for assistance. Get help learning how to have ongoing non-judgmental dialogue with your child or youth. • Check out local parent/child/youth communication resources. • Learn about the art of acknowledgement. • Learn how to provide meaningful self-expression and self-esteem boosting accomplishments. Get support for being a parent. Remember that the child or youth's behavior is a way of communicating that you need to give assistance.

•Try to see the world through the child's or youth's young eyes. Think of what might be upsetting or confusing to the vulnerable child or youth. • Look up local resources for parenting skills and support. • Kids and teens like structure and predictability. Mean what you say, say what you mean, do what you say you are going to do. • Get help and learn how to give the child or youth effective, consistent routines. • Be patient and kind with the child or youth and yourself.

Check out: www.MedLinePlus.gov; www.KidsHealth.org; www.traumasoma.com/index.shtml (very technical); www.acestudy.org.

ATTRACTED TO STRANGERS

An attraction to strangers can put children & youth at great risk of being badly hurt and abused. It can be caused by family denial about the impact of the child or youth being exposed to activities that can be frightening and confusing. It may also be due to unconscious family patterns; lack of emotional connection; not being able to recognize what love feels like; needing attention; and traumas and abuses of all kinds. An attraction to strangers is often associated with perceptual challenges: ineffective memory skills; low self-esteem; lack of social skills; confusion and impulsivity. Nutritional imbalances and exposure to environmental pollutants may also be involved.

First, We Would Investigate	Second, We Would Investigate	For Long Term Support We Would Investigate
• Support For Parents • Expressive Arts Therapy • Psychotherapy • Psychiatry • EMDR • Hypnotherapy • Massage • Music Lessons • Flower Essences • Independent Study • Nonviolent Communication	• Vitamin Therapy • Nutrition Consulting • Aikido • Ayurveda • Homeopathy • Herbology • Traditional Chinese Medicine • Yoga	• Support For Parents • Aikido • Ayurveda • Homeopathy • Aromatherapy • Herbology • Traditional Chinese Medicine • Nonviolent Communication • Independent Study

On Our Own We Would Try: • Replace sodas, juices, sugars, fats, fast foods with water, veggies, whole grains, nuts, protein, fruit, slow food • Long Walks/Hikes • Bedtime Stories and Chats • Wholesome Pleasures • Back Rubs and Foot Massages • Nature • Pets • Less or No TV, Movies, Video/Computer Games

. . . .

For Parents: • Remember that the child's or youth's behavior is a way of communicating that he/she needs assistance. If you see the child or youth being too friendly with strangers you need to take action. • Try to see the world through the child or youth's young eyes. Think of what might be upsetting or confusing to the vulnerable child or youth. • Look up local resources for parenting skills and support. • Kids like structure and predictability. Mean what you say, say what you mean, do what you say you are going to do. • Get help and learn how to give the child or youth effective, consistent routines. • Be patient and kind with the child or youth and yourself.

Check out: www.traumasoma.com/index.shtml (very technical); www.acestudy.org.

AUTISM

Autistic Tendencies; Autism Spectrum Disorders; Pervasive Developmental Disorders; Asperger's Syndrome; Rett's Disorder; Non-verbal Learning Disabilities; Non-Verbal Disorders

Having even mild autism can be extremely difficult on everyone–especially the child or youth. Without support, families can burn out and disintegrate, causing many more burdens on the child or youth dealing with autism. Without support, children & youth with autistic tendencies or a full diagnosis of autism, suffer isolation and deepening confusion, which can make the symptoms even more severe. Some unaware children and youth and adults treat children & youth dealing with autism as weird, crazy, and sources of fear. This further affects the child or youth's self-esteem, emotional control, social connection and communication skills. Autism may be due to a combination of: genetic factors; exposure to environmental pollutants; nutritional imbalances; viral or bacterial infection. The causal links between vaccinations, food and air containing mercury and autism remains controversial. One thing that is known is that the number of children & youth with autism and with associated challenges is increasing globally as is environmental pollution.

First, We Would Investigate	Second, We Would Investigate	For Long Term Support We Would Investigate
• Support For Parents • Attitudinal Healing • Psychiatry • Nutrition Education • Precision Teaching • Environmentally Healthy Homes • Drumming • Expressive Arts • Light Therapy • Massage • Yoga • Nonviolent Communication • Flower Essences	• Ayurveda • Traditional Chinese Medicine • Herbology • Homeopathy • Feldenkrais • Aikido	• Nutrition Consulting • Massage • Attitudinal Healing • Support For Parents • Aikido • Yoga • Nonviolent Communication • Flower Essences

On Our Own We Would Try: • Replace sodas, juices, sugars, fats, fast foods with water, veggies, whole grains, nuts, protein, fruit, slow food • Long Walks/Hikes • Pets • Bedtime Stories and Chats • Wholesome Pleasures • Back Rubs and Foot Massages • Nature

. . . .

For Parents: • Make sure to get a medical assessment. • Organize involvment with healing practices as early as you can. • Have compassion for your child or youth and yourself. • Having a child or youth with autism to any degree is extremely difficult and energy consuming. You must get real support for yourself and other family members from people and groups. • Avoid isolation. • Hang out with people who make you feel good about yourself and who can help you relax. • Be your own expert for your child or youth.

•Remember, each child or youth is different. Keep looking for educational and behavior practices that help.   • You have to be careful.   • You may have to move to an environmentally safer neighborhood.   • Providing as much organic food as possible may help.

•Get help in connecting with the child or youth's soul. Learn to connect with the genius within the child or youth that is hidden by all the symptoms called autism, etc. Figure out ways to communicate under or around or through the disconnections. Watch for the ways the child or youth is trying to communicate.   • Be patient and kind with the child or youth and yourself.

Check out: Samahria Lyte Kaufman and Barry Neil Kaufman's website; www.autismtreatmentcenter.org: www.MedLinePlus.gov; and www.KidsHealth.org.

BEREAVEMENT/DEATH OF FAMILY MEMBER

Death of a family member is extremely difficult and painful for children & youth, even if they appear calm about it. Their whole world has changed. A great deal of confusion and fear are created. This can slow or even stop physical, intellectual and social development. Trust and hope and being able to truly relax can become extremely difficult. Left unsupported, bereavement can lead to physical, emotional, social, and success challenges in adult life. Even though there may be no logical explanation for it, the child or youth may feel responsible for the loved one's death. Expression of grief is essential for effective mental health.

First, We Would Investigate	Second, We Would Investigate	For Long Term Support We Would Investigate
• Attitudinal Healing • Parental Support • Massage • Expressive Arts Therapy • Psychotherapy • Nonviolent Communication • Flower Essences	• Aromatherapy • Ayurveda • Homeopathy • Herbology • Traditional Chinese Medicine • Wilderness Therapy • Independent Study	• Aikido • Aromatherapy • Homeopathy • Nonviolent Communication • Flower Essences

On Our Own We Would Try: • Wholesome Pleasures • Long Walks/Hikes • Nature • Pets • Bedtime Stories and Chats • Back Rubs and Foot Massages • Replace sodas, juices, sugars, fats, fast foods with water, veggies, whole grains, nuts, protein, fruit, slow food • Less or No TV, Movies, Video/Computer Games

. . . .

For Parents: • Get help grieving and suffering the loss so that you can give the child or youth the support they need. Avoid seeking support from your child or youth. • Don't rush grieving. • Seek out local organizations which can help with grieving and loss, such as hospice organizations.

Check out: www.MedLinePlus.gov; www.KidsHealth.org; www.traumasoma.com/index.shtml (very technical); www.acestudy.org; www.bbc.co.uk/relationships/coping_with_grief/bereavement_effectschildren.shtml.

BIRTH TRAUMA

Dry Birth; Long Hard Labor; Premature Birth; Challenging Pregnancy; Caesarean

Without support and sensitive treatment, the effects of traumatic birth can be powerful and long lasting. Problematic behaviors, impulsivity, irritability, restlessness, sleeplessness, often disappear when the emotions and physical effects of birth trauma are given support through various therapies. Birth trauma can be due to a complicated pregnancy, long, hard labor, etc. Without assistance, the child or youth's mind and body can remain in shock with post-traumatic syndrome throughout adult life. Children & youth born through caesarean processes may dislike being hurried and may lack much will power in later life. Research is ongoing.

First, We Would Investigate	Second, We Would Investigate	For Long Term Support We Would Investigate
• Craniosacral • Aromatherapy • Massage • Yoga • Nutrition Consulting • Ayurveda • Traditional Chinese Medicine • Massage • Osteopathy • Chiropractic • Psychotherapy • Psychiatry • Herbology • Homeopathy • Nonviolent Communication • Flower Essences	• EMDR • Hypnotherapy • Feldenkrais • Precision Teaching • Light Therapy • Developmental Optometry • Meditation • Independent Study	• Aikido • Aromatherapy • Massage • Music Lessons • Expressive Arts • Flower Essences

On Our Own We Would Try: • Bedtime Stories and Chats • Wholesome Pleasures • Back Rubs and Foot Massages • Long Walks/Hikes • Nature • Replace sodas, juices, sugars, fats, fast foods with water, veggies, whole grains, nuts, protein, fruit, slow food • Pets • Less or No TV, Movies, Video/Computer Games

. . . .

For Parents: • Empathy, soothing music and comforting touch are very helpful with children or youth who have experienced birth trauma. • Massage and lots of exercise can be helpful, too.

Check out: www.MedLinePlus.gov; www.KidsHealth.org; www.traumasoma.com/index.shtml (very technical); www.acestudy.org.

BORED A LOT OF THE TIME; BORED AT SCHOOL

Boredom can lead to habits not conducive to learning and success. Although it may be a normal part of growing up, it can be used by the child or youth to express unhappiness. Boredom is an important part of deciding what is interesting. It can be due to a combination of: lack of engaging activities; over-stimulation and being overwhelmed by the number of choices of activities; fear/anxiety; depression/sadness; mental illness; unresolved body tension left from shock and trauma; lack of success and acknowledgement for accomplishments and having curiosity; lack of confidence; fear of making mistakes; perceptual difficulties; lack of suitable stimulation; over-expectations; under-expectations; family patterns of boredom and inactivity; lack of effective communication skills; patterns of avoiding new situations; nervous system challenges; perception challenges; nutritional imbalances; exposure to environmental pollutants. Having things to do that are important to the life of the family and thus feeling connected is important for any child or youth and is helpful in counteracting boredom.

First, We Would Investigate	Second, We Would Investigate	For Long Term Support We Would Investigate
• Nutrition Consulting • Flower Essences • Traditional Chinese Medicine • Ayurveda • Precision Teaching • Herbology • Homeopathy • Music Lessons • Expressive Arts Therapy • Drumming • Environmentally Healthy Homes • Wilderness Therapy • Independent Study	• Aikido • Aromatherapy • Light Therapy • Developmental Optometry	• Aikido • Aromatherapy • Nutrition Consulting • Precision Teaching • Independent Study • Flower Essences

On Our Own We Would Try: • Bedtime Stories and Chats • Wholesome Pleasures • Back Rubs and Foot Massages • Pets • Replace sodas, juices, sugars, fats, fast foods with water, veggies, whole grains, nuts, protein, fruit, slow food • Long Walks/Hikes • Nature • Less or No TV, Movies, Video/Computer Games

. . . .

For Parents: • Get interested in doing what you like to do. Set an example of having fun learning and doing things. • Engage the child or youth in meaningful family activities. • Encourage drinking lots of water, having high protein meals with lots of vegetables and fruits. Avoid supplying sugars, sodas, fruit juices and processed foods. • Have shared wholesome pleasures: regular, predictable shared family meals, rituals, celebrations, religious observances–with extended family if possible. • Engage the child or youth in regular, fun, physical activity. • Find and express faith that everything will work out well.

Check out: www.MedLinePlus.gov; www.KidsHealth.org; www.traumasoma.com/index.shtml (very technical); www.acestudy.org.

BRAIN DAMAGE

Accidents; Birth Trauma; Fetal Alcohol Or Fetal Drug Syndrome; High Fevers

Take action as soon as possible. Other parts of the brain and nervous system can be trained to compensate for the damage. Brain damage can affect emotional, physical, intellectual growth and success. It can be due to a combination of: birth traumas, stresses during pregnancy, genetic considerations, exposure to environmental pollutants, nutritional imbalances, infections and accidents.

First, We Would Investigate	Second, We Would Investigate	For Long Term Support We Would Investigate
• Western Medicine • Osteopathy • Psychiatry • Support For Parents • Feldenkrais • Craniosacral • Chiropractic • Massage • Nutrition Consulting • Ayurveda • Traditional Chinese Medicine • Light Therapy • Developmental Optometry • Yoga • Precision Teaching • Independent Study	• Herbology • Homeopathy • Aikido • Drumming • Expressive Arts	• Aromatherapy • Nutrition Consulting • Feldenkrais • Precision Teaching • Independent Study • Massage

On Our Own We Would Try: • Replace sodas, juices, sugars, fats, fast foods with water, veggies, whole grains, nuts, protein, fruit, slow food • Long Walks and Hikes • Bedtime Stories and Chats • Wholesome Pleasures • Back Rubs and Foot Massages • Nature • Predictable Routines • Pets • Less or No TV, Movies, Video/Computer Games

• •

For Parents: • Get medical assessment. • Get support from other parents and from organizations focusing on helping parents and children or youth with this challenge. • It may take a lot of energy and effort to assist your child or youth. Encourage high protein diets, eating lots of vegetables and fruit, drinking lots of water, avoiding sugars, sodas, fruit juices. • Learn skillful methods of nonjudgmental encouragement. • Avoid expressing pity or worry about the child or youth. These destroy self-confidence. • Protect the child or youth from bullies. • Hyperbaric chambers may help.

Check out: www.MedLinePlus.gov; www.KidsHealth.org; www.traumasoma.com/index.shtml (very technical); www.acestudy.org.

BULLYING – AGGRESSIVE

Rages, Fights, Argues

Without careful support, this can become a habitual lifelong difficulty–making relationships of any kind extremely difficult. This can be a sign of challenges in the child or youth's life which they cannot overcome or do anything about. Aggressive behaviors can be due to and complicated by a combination of: lack of training how to manage anger and fear; prolonged stress; family patterns; ineffective role models; copying violent family behaviors; copying violent media; anxiety; depression or other mental illnesses; low self-esteem; much body tension; physical and emotional traumas; abuse of any kind; a lack of effective communication skills; nutritional imbalances; exposure to pollutants; brain damage; hormone imbalances; or acting out aggression in the home.

First, We Would Investigate	Second, We Would Investigate	For Long Term Support We Would Investigate
• Western Medicine • Osteopathy • Psychotherapy • Psychiatry • Nonviolent Communication • Nutrition Consulting • Aikido • Aromatherapy • Attitudinal Healing • Traditional Chinese Medicine • Ayurveda • Independent Study • Biofeedback • Homeopathy	• Safe School Ambassadors • Expressive Arts Therapy • Osteopathy • Chiropractic • Environmentally Healthy Homes • Herbology • Wilderness Therapy	• Aikido • Aromatherapy • Traditional Chinese Medicine • Ayurveda • Herbology • Homeopathy • Massage • Independent Study

On Our Own We Would Try: • Pets • Less or No TV, Movies, Video/Computer Games • Bedtime Stories and Chats • Wholesome Pleasures • Back Rubs and Foot Massages • Replace sodas, juices, sugars, fats, fast foods with water, veggies, whole grains, nuts, protein, fruit, slow food • Long Walks/Hikes • Nature
. . . .
For Parents: • Avoid sugar, greasy food, fast food, sodas, caffeine and aspartame. Eat more fruit, vegetables, whole grains. • Engage the child or youth in regular, fun, physical activity to release energy. • When a child or youth becomes very aggressive, getting them to simply lie down can be a good, calming experience. • Teaching exhaling can help as well. • Remember that most aggressive children & youth are covering up being very frightened, so don't frighten them more. • Loving touch can also help at the right moment.

Check out: www.MedLinePlus.gov; www.KidsHealth.org; www.traumasoma.com/index.shtml (very technical); www.acestudy.org.

CAN'T ACCEPT LOVE, KINDNESS, COMPASSION

Not being able to love and receive love and compassion can affect how a child or youth treats the world and how the child or youth is treated by others. It can cause havoc in adult relationships, accomplishment and compassion for themselves and others. Lack of acceptance of love can lead to habits of insensitivity, loneliness, isolation, breaking home, school and community rules. This can affect the child or youth's whole future. Often, stressed-out, worried parents are not able to give children or youth the attention and love they need to develop the capacity to receive love.

This challenge can also be due to a combination of: abandonment; abuses of all kinds; not being loved and taught to love, trust and relax; living in a chaotic, unpredictable environment; being hurt emotionally and/or physically; challenges with self-esteem; lack of acknowledgment and praise; being blamed and shamed; perceptual challenges; neurological difficulties; being exposed to crazy adult behavior. It can also be due to: family patterns of relationship; exposure to environmental pollutants; nutrition difficulties. Workaholism can also contribute to this difficulty.

First, We Would Investigate	Second, We Would Investigate	For Long Term Support We Would Investigate
• Support For Parents • Attitudinal Healing • Massage • Biofeedback • Aikido • Psychotherapy • Psychiatry • Nutrition Consulting • Flower Essences • Nonviolent Communication	• Expressive Arts • Music Lessons • Wilderness Therapy • Traditional Chinese Medicine • Ayurveda • Herbology • Homeopathy • Drumming • Meditation • Independent Study	• Massage • Vitamin Therapy • Nutrition Consulting • Expressive Arts Therapy • Support For Parents • Nonviolent Communication • Flower Essences

On Our Own We Would Try: • Replace sodas, juices, sugars, fats, fast foods with water, veggies, whole grains, nuts, protein, fruit, slow food • Long Walks/Hikes • Bedtime Stories and Chats • Wholesome Pleasures • Back Rubs and Foot Massages • Nature • Pets • Less or No TV, Movies, Video/Computer Games

. . . .

For Parents: • Get support from other parents and from local self-help groups on how to release guilt and how to love the child or youth who has trouble trusting and receiving love and compassion. • Find people who can help you not share your frustrations, guilt, fears and worries with your child or youth. They need continued faith and consistency.

Check out: www.MedLinePlus.gov; www.KidsHealth.org; www.traumasoma.com/index.shtml (very technical); www.acestudy.org.

CANCER: TUMORS; LEUKEMIA

There are many kinds of cancer. There are many levels of severity. Without treatment, cancer is often fatal. Often the causes of cancer remain unknown. A combination of the following factors are suspected: genetics; exposure to environmental pollutants; infections; nutritional imbalances; prolonged stress. Children & youth often deal with these situations better than adults. A child or youth with cancer is very frightening and affects the whole family. It can drain energy from all family members and can cause great family tension making it even more difficult for the child or youth with cancer who can sense the burden she/he is creating. Support for all family members is vital. Getting second medical opinions is very important.

First, We Would Investigate	Second, We Would Investigate	For Long Term Support We Would Investigate
• Western Medicine • Osteopathy • Attitudinal Healing • Psychotherapy • Nutrition Consulting • EMDR • Hypnotherapy • Meditation • Support For Parents • Nonviolent Communication • Flower Essences • Independent Study	• Aromatherapy • Biofeedback • Ayurveda • Traditional Chinese Medicine • Herbology • Homeopathy • Massage • Drumming • Expressive Art Therapy	• Aromatherapy • Psychotherapy • Nutrition Consulting • Attitudinal Healing • Support For Parents • Nonviolent Communication • Flower Essences • Independent Study

On Our Own We Would Try: • Replace sodas, juices, sugars, fats, fast foods with water, veggies, whole grains, nuts, protein, fruit, slow food   • Long Walks/Hikes   • Bedtime Stories and Chats   • Wholesome Pleasures   • Back Rubs and Foot Massages   • Nature   • Pets   • Less or No TV, Movies, Video/Computer Games

. . . .

For Parents: • Get support from wherever you can: psychotherapy, group support, prayer.   • Investigate visualization practices to teach to the child or youth.   • Let your fears, worries, doubts, sadness, frustrations out with friends and professionals and not with the child or youth.   • Be honest with the child or youth who is dealing with cancer but don't dwell on the worst symptoms or possibilities.   • Look after your own and other family members' health and well being.

Check out: www.MedLinePlus.gov; www.KidsHealth.org; www.traumasoma.com/index.shtml (very technical); www.acestudy.org.

COLDS AND FLU: FREQUENT AND LONG

Occasional colds and flus are a necessary part of growing up, giving the body a chance to cleanse and readjust. Without help, frequent colds and flus can become a bigger challenge debilitating the body and leading to ear infections, stomach and/or intestinal illnesses. All this illness takes up time better used learning/playing, further affecting vitality and success in living and learning. Colds and flus can be due to a combination of: genetic factors; nutrition, vitamin and mineral imbalances; family patterns, exposure to environmental pollutants; lack of exercise; prolonged stress; breathing challenges; weakened immune system; disorganization of the body and mind as a result of trauma. If the child or youth is having frequent, long-lasting flus and colds it is important to see a health practitioner. It is normal for babies, toddlers and preschoolers to get up to eight colds a year. School age children can average up to six colds a year. Teens and adults can get up to four a year. Strong, healthy children & youth get over their colds quickly. All this is part of the body adjusting to new germs and viruses. Very frequent runny noses can be a sign of allergic reactions to something.

First, We Would Investigate	Second, We Would Investigate	For Long Term Support We Would Investigate
• Western Medicine • Osteopathy • Nutritional Education • Massage • Aromatherapy • Ayurveda • Traditional Chinese Medicine • Ayurveda • Herbology • Homeopathy • Chiropractic • Environmentally Healthy Homes • Yoga	• Aikido • Light Therapy • Craniosacral • Biofeedback • Hypnotherapy	• Aikido • Aromatherapy • Nutrition Consulting • Music Lessons • Drumming • Expressive Arts.

On Our Own We Would Try: • Replace sodas, juices, sugars, fats, fast foods with water, veggies, whole grains, nuts, protein, fruit, slow food • Long Walks/Hikes • Bedtime Stories and Chats • Wholesome Pleasures • Back Rubs and Foot Massages • Nature • Pets • Less or No TV, Movies, Video/Computer Games

. . . .

For Parents: • Hand washing habits help prevent the spread of colds, flu, etc, even within families. • Sneezing and coughing manners and face masks can also help. • Careful dish washing helps as well.

•The healing professions of the world agree that massage, exercise, movement, happiness, fresh air and good food build healthy bodies that can resist illness and recover faster.   • All the time and especially during cold/flu times, encourage drinking lots of water; avoid juices and sodas; limit sugar intake. Offer your child or youth more vegetables than fruit.   • Differences of opinion exist on whether to provide a high or low protein, high bulk/low bulk diet during colds.   • You have to find what works to help your child or youth recover quickly.   • Return the child to regular activities as soon as possible.   • Make sure your child is not exposed to second hand smoke and other air pollutants.   • Going to small daycare centers and schools can help reduce the number of exposures and infections.

•Avoid anti-bacterial soaps and wipes. These keep children, youth and adults from being exposed to the minimal amounts of bacteria they need to develop natural immunities.

Check out: www.MedLinePlus.gov; www.KidsHealth.org.

COMMUNICATION CHALLENGES: INTERPERSONAL, EMOTIONAL, SOCIAL

Argues And/Or Withholds; Does Not Know How To Settle Arguments With Words; Cannot Communicate Easily Or Effectively; Withdrawn; Over-Stimulated; Not Aware Of Impact Of Communication Given; Over-Reactive To Communication Received

Without help, these challenges can establish patterns making all social relations very difficult throughout life. They can erode self-esteem. These types of learned unhelpful listening and speaking habits are different from communication challenges due to neurological conditions (see below). Communication challenges can be due to a combination of: a build up of habits the child or youth has developed to cope; nutritional imbalances; exposure to environmental pollutants; lack of training in how to manage anger and fear; prolonged stress; family communication patterns; ineffective role models; perceptual challenges; emotional challenges; low emotional and social intelligence levels; copying media and poor role models; anxiety; depression or other mental illnesses; low self-esteem; much body tension; physical and emotional traumas; abuses of any kind; genetics; stress; impatient adults; body tension; painful physical or psychological disorganization due to accidents, abuses of all kinds and trauma; or difficult birth. Poor communication habits can affect auditory processing (the brain becomes unable to figure out what the sounds mean) and can contribute to challenges with language and/or speech and/or listening. Further challenges can develop through having to use a second language without help.

First, We Would Investigate	Second, We Would Investigate	For Long Term Support We Would Investigate
• Western Medicine • Osteopathy • Psychiatry • Nutrition Consulting • Aikido • Attitudinal Healing • Expressive Arts Therapy • Support For Parents • Psychotherapy • Environmentally Healthy Homes • Nonviolent Communication	• Craniosacral • Chiropractic • Wilderness Therapy • Aromatherapy • Traditional Chinese Medicine • Biofeedback • Ayurveda • Flower Essences • Homeopathy • Herbology	• Aikido • Aromatherapy • Traditional Chinese Medicine • Ayurveda • Herbology • Homeopathy • Massage • Environmentally Healthy Homes • Flower Essences

On Our Own We Would Try: • Replace sodas, juices, sugars, fats, fast foods with water, veggies, whole grains, nuts, protein, fruit, slow food • Long Walks/Hikes • Bedtime Stories and Chats • Wholesome Pleasures • Back Rubs and Foot Massages • Nature • Pets • Less or No TV, Movies, Video/Computer Games

. . . .

For Parents: • Get support from other parents. • Encourage your child or youth to replace sodas and juices with lots of water. Replace sugars and processed food with fresh vegetables and fruits. Eat them yourself. • Learn Nonviolent Communication at local classes and teach it to your child or youth. • Be the role model for what you want your child or youth to become. • Listen to your child or youth more than you talk. • Avoid judgments and expressions of frustration. Children & youth can achieve good communication when they feel safe and heard. • Find and express faith that everything will work out well.

Check out: www.MedLinePlus.gov; www.KidsHealth.org; www.traumasoma.com/index.shtml(very technical); www.acestudy.org.

COMMUNICATION CHALLENGES: PHYSICAL/NEUROLOGICAL

Cannot Communicate Easily Or Effectively; Has Developmental Delays; Has Physical Conditions Making Communication Difficult; Does Not Appear To Comprehend Communication Received; Cannot Express Self In Ways Understood By Others; Communication Disorders Of Many Labels Including Dysarthria, Aparaxia Of Speech, Asperger's Syndrome, Autism, ADHD

Without help these communication challenges can establish patterns making learning and social relations very difficult in later life. Children & youth with these challenges can be considered to be unintelligent, which further destroys self-esteem and can produce antisocial behavior. A combination of therapies is often needed.

Communication challenges can be due to a combination of: genetics; exposure to environmental pollutants; birth trauma; complications during pregnancy; nutritional imbalances; neurological disorganization; hearing difficulties; perceptual challenges; emotional challenges; much body tension; physical and emotional traumas; abuses of any kind.

First, We Would Investigate	Second, We Would Investigate	For Long Term Support We Would Investigate
• Western Medicine • Osteopathy • Psychiatry • Nutrition Consulting • Feldenkrais • Craniosacral • Chiropractic • Expressive Arts Therapy • Precision Teaching • Yoga • Support For Parents • Massage • Biofeedback • Nonviolent Communication • Flower Essences	• Environmentally Healthy Homes • Music Lessons • Herbology • Homeopathy • Attitudinal Healing	• Aikido • Aromatherapy • Traditional Chinese Medicine • Ayurveda • Herbology • Massage • Support For Parents • Aromatherapy • Traditional Chinese Medicine • Ayurveda • Nonviolent Communication • Flower Essences

On Our Own We Would Try: • Replace sodas, juices, sugars, fats, fast foods with water, veggies, whole grains, nuts, protein, fruit, slow food • Long Walks/Hikes • Bedtime Stories and Chats • Wholesome Pleasures • Back Rubs and Foot Massages • Nature • Pets • Less or No TV, Movies, Video/Computer Games

. . . .

For Parents: • Get a medical assessment. • Get into a support group with parents of children & youth with the same challenges. You can help each other help your children & youth. • Read lots of bedtime stories, sing lots of songs, even if you can't see them being understood. • Remember that your child or youth is very normal and brilliant somewhere inside. • Remember that she/he has gifts for the world. • Keep believing that your communication will be understood by your child or youth someday, and that he/she is going to be able to communicate effectively with the world.

•The pathways into your child's or youth's essence need to be opened. The pathways from your child's or youth's essence need to be opened. • Remember that behavior is another language, for children and for adults. Watch for amazingly subtle ways of communicating.

CONCENTRATION PROBLEMS

Paying Attention Is Difficult; Attention And Focus Wanders Or Bounces; Loses Or Forgets Things; Disorganized

Lacking concentration skills can make effective learning very challenging. It can lead to overlooking social cues, and thus getting into trouble a great deal. It can make social relations difficult, and can reduce joy and self-confidence. Children & youths with these conditions are often considered as unintelligent or emotionally disturbed. Difficulty concentrating may be a sign of other learning difficulties. It may be due to a combination of: age; over or under-expectation; nutritional imbalances; lack of exercise; lack of deep rest and relaxation; over or under-stimulating environments; exposure to environmental pollutants; allergies; poor health; physical disorganization due to stress, abuses of all kinds; accidents; emotional challenges; genetics; family patterns; isolation; problematic physical organization; family patterns and role models; lack of purpose for concentrating; inconsistent and unappreciative home/school environment.

First, We Would Investigate	Second, We Would Investigate	For Long Term Support We Would Investigate
• Western Medicine • Osteopathy • Psychiatry • Nutrition Consulting • Craniosacral • Chiropractic • Light Therapy • Developmental Optometry • Environmentally Healthy Homes • Biofeedback • Aikido • Nonviolent Communication • Flower Essences • Drumming • Music Lessons	• Traditional Chinese Medicine • Ayurveda • Herbology • Homeopathy • Aromatherapy • Wilderness Therapy • Yoga • Expressive Arts • Independent Study	• Aikido • Aromatheraphy • Traditional Chinese Medicine • Ayurveda • Herbology • Homeopathy • Flower Essences • Nonviolent Communication

On Our Own We Would Try: • Replace sodas, juices, sugars, fats, fast foods with water, veggies, whole grains, nuts, protein, fruit, slow food • Long Walks/Hikes • Bedtime Stories and Chats • Wholesome Pleasures • Back Rubs and Foot Massages • Nature • Pets • Less or No TV, Movies, Video/Computer Games

. . . .

For Parents: • Get support from other parents. Become a learner or do things where your child or youth can see you concentrating. • Play lots of games the child or youth enjoys even if you think they are too childish. • Playing card games can be helpful. • Ask teachers to recommend useful games.

Check out: www.MedLinePlus.gov; www.KidsHealth.org; www.partnershipforlearning.org; www.schwablearning.org; www.kidshealth.org; www.traumasoma.com/index.shtml (very technical); www.acestudy.org.

CONCUSSION: HEAD TRAUMA; HEAD INJURIES

After your child or youth has had a head injury, seek prompt medical care if you notice changes—even if there was no obvious swelling or lumps. If you do notice changes, use the lists below. Without quick help, even minor head injuries, concussions, can lead to challenges with coordination, frequent headaches, visual and auditory challenges, difficulties with perception, attention, behavior, memory and learning. These can eventually create challenges with social relations and success in learning and living. More severe head injuries can lead to seizures. They can create a weakness such that challenging symptoms return with repeated falls and blows to the head. Concussions can disorganize the brain, skull and spine. All these challenges can add up to be painful and can reduce self-esteem and make success and good health difficult to attain.

First, We Would Investigate	Second, We Would Investigate	For Long Term Support We Would Investigate
• Western Medicine • Osteopathy • Craniosacral • Chiropractic • Feldenkrais • Developmental Optometry • Light Therapy • Biofeedback • Massage • Flower Essences	• EMDR • Hypnotherapy • Aromatherapy • Homeopathy • Herbology • Traditional Chinese Medicine • Ayurveda	• Aromatherapy • Homeopathy • Herbology • Craniosacral • Osteopathy • Chiropractic • Nutrition Consulting • Flower Essences

On Our Own We Would Try: • Wholesome Pleasures • Back Rubs and Foot Massages • Replace sodas, juices, sugars, fats, fast foods with water, veggies, whole grains, nuts, protein, fruit, slow food • Long Walks/Hikes • Nature • Less or No TV, Movies, Video/Computer Games • Bedtime Stories and Chats • Pets

. . . .

For Parents: • Get medical attention as soon as possible. Seek medical advice before you try anything else. • The practices above may help prevent aftereffects. • For shock, immediately use Bach Flower Remedies from your Health Food Store—especially Rescue Remedy.

•Give the child or youth plenty of time to rest and heal. Cuddle your child or youth after injuries. • Give them lots of water to drink. Give them lots of protein and vegetables. • Pay attention to changes in living and learning. • When children & youth are involved in activities that can lead to concussion, make sure they have proper supervision and protective equipment—particularly helmets. • Engage the child or youth in regular, fun, physical activity to build physical confidence. • Find and express faith that everything will work out well.

Check out: www.kidshealth.org; www.medlineplus.gov; www.traumasoma.com/index.shtml (very technical); www.acestudy.org.

COORDINATION CHALLENGES

Inability To Connect The Mind And Body; Having The Body Do What The Mind Wants; Difficulty Planning And Making Small Movements Such As Handwriting, Catching, Throwing, Playing Music, Singing, Dancing; Difficulty Planning And Making Big Movements Such As Walking, Running, Throwing, Kicking, Riding Bikes, Swimming

Coordination challenges can be large or small. Without help, a lack of coordination can lead to inactivity, a lack of confidence, challenges with learning and social relations. It can cause ineffective movement patterns throughout life, which may produce other physical and emotional complications. These challenges may be due to a combination of: genetics; birth trauma; uncoordinated role models; nervous system challenges; nutritional imbalances; and exposure to environmental pollutants. Not enough play, relaxation, practice and lack of encouragement may also be factors.

First, We Would Investigate	Second, We Would Investigate	For Long Term Support We Would Investigate
• Western Medicine (occupational and physical therapy) • Osteopathy • Craniosacral • Nutrition Consulting • Chiropractic • Feldenkrais • Aikido • Precision Teaching • Developmental Optometry • Light Therapy • Music Lessons • Drumming	• Massage • Traditional Chinese Medicine • Ayurveda • Yoga	• Aikido • Nutrition Consulting • Craniosacral • Chiropractic • Feldenkrais • Music Lessons • Drumming.

On Our Own We Would Try: • Long Walks/Hikes • Replace sodas, juices, sugars, fats, fast foods with water, veggies, whole grains, nuts, protein, fruit, slow food • Bedtime Stories and Chats • Wholesome Pleasures • Back Rubs and Foot Massages • Nature • Less or No TV, Movies, Video/Computer Games • Pets

• •

For Parents: • Play with your child or youth as much as possible. Focus on specific tasks and practice them if necessary; however, have fun doing it. • Have fun moving, singing and dancing together. • Lots of walking is a huge help. • Encourage getting enough rest, getting enough movement, drinking lots of water, staying away from sugar, sodas, fruit juices. • Give lots of enjoyable practice when learning a new coordination skill.

Check out: www.MedLinePlus.gov; www.KidsHealth.org; www.pbs.org/wgbh/misunderstoodminds.

DAYDREAMS: FREQUENT

Daydreams, although they may look like a waste of time, can be a source of creativity, emotional calm, and intellectual clarity. Daydreams can frighten parents who want their child or youth to be successful in the world. They can also be a sign of conditions that can lead to serious learning difficulties. Daydreams can also become a habit of avoidance of engagement with living and learning. As a negative factor, daydreaming can be due to a combination of: neurological conditions; attention and focusing difficulties; emotional trauma; avoidance of suffering; not appearing alert; unstimulating environment; over-stimulating environment; boredom; role models of avoidance; nutritional imbalances; exposure to environmental pollutants; over-expectations; under-expectations; inappropriate and unstimulating curricula; teaching styles not matching the child's or youth's learning styles; perceptual challenges; difficulty with attention; physical disorganization; abuses of all kinds. Daydreaming as a positive factor may be due to: creativity; preparing for creativity; resting.

First, We Would Investigate	Second, We Would Investigate	For Long Term Support We Would Investigate
• Nutrition Consulting • Environmentally Healthy Homes • Craniosacral • Chiropractic • Developmental Optometry • Expressive Arts • Music Lessons • Aikido • Feldenkrais • Flower Essences • Nonviolent Communication	• Aikido • Aromatherapy • Ayurveda • Homeopathy • Herbology • Psychotherapy • Psychiatry • Independent Study	• Aromatherapy • Nutrition Education • Flower Essences • Nonviolent Communication

On Our Own We Would Try: • Replace sodas, juices, sugars, fats, fast foods with water, veggies, whole grains, nuts, protein, fruit, slow food • Long Walks/Hikes • Bedtime Stories and Chats • Wholesome Pleasures • Back Rubs and Foot Massages • Nature • Pets • Less or No TV, Movies, Video/Computer Games

. . . .

For Parents: • Avoid teasing or blaming children or youth about daydreaming. Treating the child or youth as normally as possible is essential. • Give calm, loving, gentle engagement and acknowledgement. • Trust the child or youth's nature while investigating practices and giving support.

Check out: www./MedLinePlus.gov; www.KidsHealth.org; www.pbs.org/wgbh/misunderstoodminds; www.traumasoma.com/index.shtml (very technical); www.acestudy.org.

DEPRESSED: FREQUENTLY

Without help, childhood or youth depression can affect learning and growth throughout life. Depression can become habitual and chronic. Long term depression can affect body chemistry, making treatment more difficult. Depression can lead to unrealistic ideas about living. It can lead to suicide. Depression can be due to a combination of: genetics; traumas and prolonged stresses of all kinds, unexpressed anxiety; feeling powerless; fear; anger; poor role models; allergies; exposure to environmental pollutants; nutritional imbalances; poverty and resulting low self-esteem; lack of choice; lack of effective stimulation; uncontrollable chaos. Depression is often due to the child or youth being very intelligent and sensitive to what is going on in the family/world, yet feeling powerless to change anything. See the depression as a language that things in the child or youth's life are not right and that the child or youth needs support, compassion and love. Depression is not a word to use to describe sadness or loneliness. Illness and medical conditions can cause or contribute to depression. Sadness and loneliness are necessary parts of growing up and being human.

First, We Would Investigate	Second, We Would Investigate	For Long Term Support We Would Investigate
• Psychotherapy • Psychiatry • Western Medicine • Osteopathy • Ayurveda • Traditional Chinese Medicine • Herbology • Homeopathy • Chiropractic • Craniolsacral • Biofeedback • Nutrition Consulting • EMDR • Hypnotherapy • Light Therapy • Aikido • Environmentally Healthy Homes • Support For Parents • Flower Essences	• Nonviolent Communication • Aromatherapy • Expressive Arts Therapy • Wilderness Therapy • Yoga • Drumming • Music Lessons • Massage • Feldenkrais	• Aikido • Aromatherapy • Nutrition Consulting • Expressive Art • Massage • Flower Essences

On Our Own We Would Try: • Replace sodas, juices, sugars, fats, fast foods with water, veggies, whole grains, nuts, protein, fruit, slow food • Long Walks/Hikes • Nature • Bedtime Stories and Chats • Wholesome Pleasures • Back Rubs and Foot Massages • Pets • Less or No TV, Movies, Video/Computer Games

• •

For Parents: • Get a medical assessment. • Treat your child or youth's depression seriously. Do not tease or make fun of this condition. • Listen as much as you can if your child or youth is willing to talk. • Get support from other parents whose children & youth are afflicted with these symptoms.

Check out: www.KidsHealth.org; www.Medlineplus.gov; a book, *The Mood Cure* by Julie Ross. www.traumasoma.com/index.shtml (very technical); www.acestudy.org

DEPRESSED PARENT(S)/CAREGIVER(S)

Without help, this is very hard on children or youth and on their development. Parental and caregiver mood swings prevent the child or youth from learning how to trust. Children & youth need to have a predictable foundation of emotional support to feel secure. Parental/caregiver depression can produce fear and confused emotions in children & youth. It can produce lack of confidence and unrealistic ideas about life. It can confuse children & youth and make them afraid to try new things. Children & youth can learn to be depressed and to fear their own emotions. Severe parental/caregiver depression can be life-threatening. The loss of a parent/caregiver through suicide may be life-crippling for the children or youths involved. Postpartum depressions have to be identified early and supported rapidly. The family of a mother in postpartum depression needs immediate and ongoing support.

First, We Would Investigate	Second, We Would Investigate	For Long Term Support We Would Investigate
For Parents: • Psychiatry • Psychotherapy • Western Medicine • Nutrition Consulting • Biofeedback • Hypnotherapy • Aromatherapy • Ayurveda • Traditional Chinese Medicine • Homeopathy • Herbology • Light Therapy **For Children & Youth:** • Attitudinal Healing • EMDR • Hypnotherapy • Biofeedback • Meditation • Western Medicine • Psychotherapy • Psychiatry	**For Parents:** • Music Lessons • Expressive Arts Therapy • Drumming • Environmentally Healthy Homes **For Children & Youth:** • Aikido • Attitudinal Healing • Drumming • Music Lessons • Expressive Arts • Wilderness Therapy	**For Parents, Children & Youth:** • Nonviolent Communication • Aikido • Aromatherapy • Nutrition Consulting • Meditation • Attitudinal Healing • Ayurveda • Traditional Chinese Medicine

On Our Own We Would Try: • Less or No TV, Movies, Video/Computer Games • Replace sodas, juices, sugars, fats, fast foods with water, veggies, whole grains, nuts, protein, fruit, slow food • Long Walks/Hikes • Bedtime Stories and Chats • Wholesome Pleasures • Back Rubs and Foot Massages • Nature • Pets

• •

For Parents: • Depressed parents need evaluation by and support from trained professionals. • Children or youth have to be helped to realize that they are not responsible for the condition of their parent/caregivers.

• Depressed parents and caregivers can explore Flower Essences sold over the counter at health food stores—such as Rescue Remedy. They can also explore cutting out sodas, coffee, sugars, processed fast foods. Drinking water, eating vegetables, proteins and fruits can help improve mood.   • Getting friends and relatives to give support to the child or youth is essential. Extended family members and friends can assist the child or youth a great deal by providing non-depressed experiences.   • Pets can provide loving companionship to both parents and children or youth.

Check out: www.mentalhelp.net; www.traumasoma.com/index.shtml (very technical); www.acestudy.org.

DISORGANIZED: SCATTERED

Without support, disorganization can slow learning and success. It can challenge relationships and reduce self-confidence. Disorganization may be related to and complicated by a combination of: genetic factors; learning disabilities; short-term memory challenges; focusing challenges; chaotic environment; allergies; exposure to environmental pollutants; nutritional imbalances; emotional disorganization due to physical/emotional trauma; ineffective instruction; lack of practice; disorganized role models; abuses of all kinds; troubled parents and caregivers.

First, We Would Investigate	Second, We Would Investigate	For Long Term Support We Would Investigate
• Western Medicine • Osteopathy • Nutrition Consulting • Precision Teaching • Environmentally Healthy Homes • Ayurveda • Traditional Chinese Medicine • Hypnotherapy • EMDR • Craniosacral • Light Therapy • Developmental Optometry • Chiropractic • Feldenkrais • Herbology • Support For Parents • Biofeedback	• Nonviolent Communication • Aikido • Aromatherapy • Wilderness Therapy • Drumming • Music Lessons • Expressive Arts • Meditation • Flower Essences	• Aikido • Aromatherapy • Herbology • Nutrition Consulting • Support For Parents • Meditation • Flower Essences • Nonviolent Communication

On Our Own We Would Try: • Replace sodas, juices, sugars, fats, fast foods with water, veggies, whole grains, nuts, protein, fruit, slow food • Long Walks/Hikes • Bedtime Stories and Chats • Wholesome Pleasures • Back Rubs and Foot Massages • Nature • Pets • Less or No TV, Movies, Video/Computer Games

. . . .

For Parents: • Restrict sugars, provide high protein, low sugar breakfasts, encourage drinking lots of water. • Address anxiety, depression, desperation and ADHD patterns in the whole family. • Watch out for websites and information sponsored by drug companies. They want your business and may not give you all the information you need. • Explore support for being a parent. • Find family structures and methods that fit your child or youth and you. • Seek out classes in Nonviolent Communication, learn it and teach it to your children or youth. • Explore references to short term memory; working memory; auditory processing; visual processing; temporal and spacial sequencing.

Check out: wwwSchwabLearning.org.; www.MedLinePlus.gov; www.KidsHealth.org; www.traumasoma.com/index.shtml (very technical); www.acestudy.org.

DYING: CHILD HAS TERMINAL ILLNESS

This is often emotionally easier on children or youth than their families. Without support (emotional, physical, spiritual), families can disintegrate, making the child or youth's passing even more traumatic on everyone.

First, We Would Investigate	Second, We Would Investigate	For Long Term Support We Would Investigate
For the child or youth and for the family: • Support For Parents • Attitudinal Healing • Western Medicine • Osteopathy • Psychotherapy • Expressive Arts • Meditation • Music Lessons • Drumming • Aromatherapy • Herbology • Homeopathy • Nonviolent Communication	**For the child or youth and for the family:** • Ayurveda • Chiropractic • Traditional Chinese Medicine • EMDR • Hypnotherapy • Flower Essences	**For the child or youth and for the family:** • Aromatherapy • Homeopathy • Herbology • Support For Parents • Attitudinal Healing • Psychotherapy • EMDR • Hypnotherapy • Nonviolent Communication • Flower Essences

On Our Own We Would Try: • Pets • Bedtime Stories and Chats • Wholesome Pleasures • Back Rubs and Foot Massages • Replace sodas, juices, sugars, fats, fast foods with water, veggies, whole grains, nuts, protein, fruit, slow food • Nature • Less or No TV, Movies, Video/Computer Games

. . . .

For Parents: • Try to arrange for at-home care. Parents need rest and support. When possible, seek and use local children or youth hospices which can give specialist and respite care for caregivers. • Marriages get stressed and parental depression is common, so get support from other people, family members and parents in the same situation. • Be choosy with whom you spend time. Pick people who can help you feel relaxed. • Find family structures and methods that fit the child or youth and you. • Let the child or youth know you will be okay when they are gone. Talk about what is happening. • Be patient and kind with the child or youth and yourself.

Check out: www.chionline.org, for children's hospice and end of life care information; www.traumasomaom/index.shtml (very technical); www.acestudy.org.

DYSLEXIA

Without being managed well, dyslexia can prevent children & youth from achieving their full potential in later life. Without support, it can produce lifetime challenges with self-esteem, learning, confidence and success. Dyslexia can make adult relationships very difficult. It may be linked to a number of perceptual difficulties and may be caused and complicated by a combination of factors including: genetics; exposure to environmental pollutants; nutritional imbalances; challenges during pregnancy; physical disorganization due to trauma; and prolonged physical stress.

First, We Would Investigate	Second, We Would Investigate	For Long Term Support We Would Investigate
• Western Medicine • Osteopathy • Support For Parents • Nutrition Consulting • Precision Teaching • Craniosacral • Chiropractic • Light Therapy • Developmental Optometry • Feldenkrais • Yoga • Expressive Arts • Music Lessons • Nonviolent Communication • Independent Study	• Aikido • Traditional Chinese Medicine • Ayurveda • Aromatherapy • Herbology • Homeopathy • Wilderness Therapy • Hypnotherapy	• Aikido • Nutrition Consulting • Support For Parents • Expressive Arts • Music Lessons • Flower Essences • Nonviolent Communication • Independent Study • Yoga

On Our Own We Would Try: • Less or No TV, Movies, Video/Computer Games • Long Walks/Hikes • Nature • Replace sodas, juices, sugars, fats, fast foods with water, veggies, whole grains, nuts, protein, fruit, slow food • Bedtime Stories and Chats • Wholesome Pleasures • Back Rubs and Foot Massages • Pets

. . . .

For Parents: • Get support from other parents. Deal with your fear and frustrations with other adults outside your home. • Mean what you say, say what you mean, do what you say you are going to do. • Sing lots of songs together. Dancing can help.

Check out: www.MedLinePlus.gov; www.KidsHealth.org; www.SchwabLearning.org; and www.traumasoma.com/index.shtml (very technical); www.acestudy.org.

EAR CHALLENGES

Chronic/Frequent; Frequent Ear Aches; Many Infections; Has Drainage Tubes Inserted; Build Up Of Wax

Ear health is vitally important to children & youth. Seeing, hearing and balance needed for organizing the body for action are intimately connected. Challenges with vision and hearing are linked in the brain. Functioning ears are essential for easy learning. Without prompt help, chronic ear challenges can seriously slow learning, lower self-confidence, cause behavior challenges, and establish poor learning, listening, speaking and reading habits. They can be extremely painful and confusing. Ear challenges may be associated with creating perceptual and speech challenges. Some ear challenges can be easily addressed. They can be related to a combination of: genetics; accidents and physical trauma; physical disorganization; allergies; prolonged stress; nutritional imbalances; exposure to environmental pollutants. Some osteopaths and naturopaths consider frequent exposure to antibiotics as possibly creating hearing challenges.

First, We Would Investigate	Second, We Would Investigate	For Long Term Support We Would Investigate
• Western Medicine • Osteopathy • Craniosacral • Chiropractic • Ayurveda • Traditional Chinese Medicine • Herbology • Homeopathy • Nutrition Consulting • Light Therapy • Developmental Optometry • Environmentally Healthy Homes	• Attitudinal Healing • Aromatherapy • Music Lessons • Drumming • Massage	• Aromatherapy • Nutrition Consulting • Attitudinal Healing • Craniosacral

On Our Own We Would Try: • Replace sodas, juices, sugars, fats, fast foods with water, veggies, whole grains, nuts, protein, fruit, slow food • Long Walks/Hikes • Bedtime Stories and Chats • Wholesome Pleasures • Back Rubs and Foot Massages • Nature • Pets • Less or No TV, Movies, Video/Computer Games

. . . .

For Parents: • Get a medical evaluation. • Make sure teachers are aware of these challenges so they can help position the child or youth for better hearing.

Check out: www.MedLinePlus.gov and www.KidsHealth.org.

EATING DISORDERS

Anorexia/Bulimia; Eating/Not Eating Problems; Compulsive Overeating

As soon as challenges like overeating, (with or without purging), or not eating are noticed get as thorough a medical evaluation as possible. Try to find practitioners who know a lot about the practices listed below. Without help, eating disorders can cause death, organ damage, relationship challenges in adult life, emotional confusion, reduction in learning ability and decrease already low self-esteem. They can be signs of great emotional upset and confusion; the need for communication opportunities and skills; social isolation; media created self loathing. These disorders are often linked to a combination of: depression or other mental illnesses; anxiety; unhealed abuses of all kinds; traumas of all kinds; lack of opportunity to heal. They may be affected by nutritional imbalances or exposure to environmental pollutants. Low self- esteem combined with ideas from advertisers can complicate self-destructive patterns.

First, We Would Investigate	Second, We Would Investigate	For Long Term Support We Would Investigate
• Support For Parents • Western Medicine • Osteopathy • Psychotherapy • Psychiatry • Attitudinal Healing • Hypnotherapy • EMDR • Ayurveda • Traditional Chinese Medicine • Expressive Arts • Nutrition Consulting • Nonviolent Communication • Wilderness Therapy • Flower Essences • Homeopathy	• Flower Essences • Herbology • Aromatherapy • Meditation • Aikido • Music Lessons • Drumming • Massage • Yoga	• Support For Parents • Nonviolent Communication • Attitudinal Healing • Expressive Arts • Nutrition Consulting • Psychotherapy • Flower Essences • Herbology • Homeopathy

On Our Own We Would Try: • Replace sodas, juices, sugars, fats, fast foods with water, veggies, whole grains, nuts, protein, fruit, slow food • Long Walks/Hikes • Bedtime Stories and Chats • Wholesome Pleasures • Back Rubs and Foot Massages • Nature • Pets • Less or No TV, Movies, Video/Computer Games

. . . .

For Parents: • Keep focusing on love. • Monitor computer access to websites that support eating disorders. • Seek out parents of other children or youth with the same kind of challenges. Support each other. • Find and express faith that everything will work out well.

Check out: www.MedLinePlus.gov; www.KidsHealth.org; www.edap.org, Elizabeth Scott; www.traumasoma.com/index.shtml (very technical); www.acestudy.org.

EDUCATIONAL ABUSE/EDUCATIONAL WOUNDING

Lack Of Help For Child Or Youth's Uncorrected Learning Challenges; Lack Of Support For Child Or Youth's Unique Ways Of Learning; Inappropriate Curriculum For Child Or Youth's Age, Ability And Learning Style; Not Enough Success To Build Confidence; Punitive Teachers Who Shame And Who Do Not Acknowledge Feelings, Thoughts And Actions; Teachers Lacking Knowledge Of The Child's Or Youth's Birth Cultures

Uncorrected, educational abuse can profoundly slow learning, damage self-esteem and can create an unwillingness to try to be successful. This is incredibly frustrating for children & youth. Educational abuse often causes behavior challenges and poor attitudes towards learning. It creates damaged learners. Children & youth can become very anxious, frightened learners. They can begin to think they are the problem. Educational abuse is often caused by and complicated by a combination of: learning disabilities; ADHD, OCD; budget cutbacks resulting in insufficient time with the teacher; outmoded educational practices; outmoded educational material; inappropriate curriculums; excessive work load for teachers; lack of political will to address these challenges.

A Lack Of Help For Child Or Youth's Uncorrected Learning Challenges: Can cause children & youth to fall further and further behind when a missing skill is not learned or taught. Missing school for even a few days can have a powerful effect because essential skill learning is missed. The same is true if the child or youth is preoccupied with worries or confusing emotions. Nutritional imbalances can distort the child or youth's ability to focus and pay attention—thus creating a learning gap that gets wider and wider. Remedial help is needed to catch up—sometimes on a daily basis.

Lack Of Support For Child Or Youth's Unique Ways Of Learning; Inappropriate Curriculum For Child Or Youth's Age, Ability And Learning Style: Programs that revolve around text books do not usually take into account the uniqueness of each child's or youth's learning styles. Much talent and confidence is lost when the child is expected to fit the program and not having the program fit the child. Old-fashioned education based on obedience creates low or phony self-esteem—both of which create future challenges.

Not Enough Opportunities To Succeed To Build Confidence: Children & youth soon get bored learning and succeeding at tasks that appear to have no use to them or to society. It takes skill to learn things that are boring. These skills are often not taught. When the curriculum and the instruction methods do not fit the child or youth, little success will happen, thus eroding self-confidence even further.

Punitive Teachers Who Shame And Who Do Not Acknowledge Feelings, Thoughts And Actions: These tactics are signs of insecure teachers who themselves have had this treatment. These bullying tactics are used by ineffective teachers who blame the children or youth for the learning challenges, rather than learning new methods to be more effective. Everyone ends up being more and more frustrated, with lower and lower self-confidence.

Teachers Lacking Knowledge Of The Child's Or Youth's Birth Cultures, Community Cultures And Cultural Developmental Milestones: Without this knowledge, the teacher cannot fit the curriculum and teaching styles to the child or youth.

Low Expectations Based On Race, Gender And Economic Status: Negative stereotypes reduce success because the real child or youth is not seen. The teacher's eye is not truly present. The teacher is treating the pupil not as a real person, but as the teacher's idea of who the pupil should be.

Inability To See The Child Or Youth's Strengths And To Use Them For Learning: Stressed, insecure, overworked adults often are too burned out to see the child or youth through positive eyes. The lack of acknowledgement of skill and strength is hard on children or youth, creating worry, hesitation, lack of confidence and negative focus on what is not right.

Teachers Lacking Knowledge And Appreciation Of The Child Or Youth's Birth Cultures: Such teachers cannot use what the child or youth already knows as a source of meaningful learning. Ignorance is often seen as disapproving of the culture and thus the child or youth.

First, We Would Investigate	Second, We Would Investigate	For Long Term Support We Would Investigate
• Precision Teaching • Light Therapy • Developmental Optometry • Expressive Arts • Independent Study • Music Lessons • Drumming • Support For Parents • Psychotherapy • Attitudinal Healing • Nutrition Consulting • Meditation • Nonviolent Communication • Safe School Ambassadors • Hypnotherapy • EMDR • Aikido	• Homeopathy • Herbology • Flower Essences • Feldenkrais • Massage • Wilderness Therapy	• Aikido • Expressive Arts • Independent Study • Psychotherapy • EMDR • Hypnotherapy • Nutrition Consulting • Meditation • Independent Study

On Our Own We Would Try: • Less or No TV • Long Walks/Hikes • Bedtime Stories and Chats • Replace sodas, juices, sugars, fats, fast foods with water, veggies, whole grains, nuts, protein, fruit, slow food • Wholesome Pleasures • Back Rubs and Foot Massages • Nature • Pets

. . . .

For Parents: • Listen and acknowledge your child's or youth's frustration. • Get involved in your child's or youth's school or daycare center. • To model how to be a learner become one yourself, take a course in something that interests you. • Get support from other parents of children or youth with the same challenge. • Stay calm. • Engage the child or youth in regular, fun, physical activity. • Investigate responsible Independent Study. • Find and express faith that everything will work out well.

Check out: www.drsimonelli.com; www.traumasoma.com/index.shtml (very technical); www.acestudy.org; www.oprah.com/tows/pastshows/tows_2002/tows_past_20020327_b.jhtml.

EMOTIONAL ABUSE–PSYCHOLOGICAL ABUSE

Being Called Stupid, An Idiot, Bad, Ugly; Frequently Belittled And Unacknowledged; Child Or Youth Often Threatened And Frightened By Adults And Teachers; No Guidance/No Limits, Allowed To Do Anything; Stifled By Over-Control And Worry, Lack Of Faith And Trust; Yelled At Frequently; Verbal Abuse; Prolonged Exposure To Chaos

Emotions are a person's radar. The rest of the human body has as many nerve cells as the brain. The whole body is a gigantic sense organ; that includes all the other sense organs like the skin, nose, mouth, eyes, ears. The mind, body and all the sense organs are involved in the creation of emotions. Emotions tell us what is happening around us, whether we are safe or not safe, whether to relax or be ready for trouble. Babies are born with some basic emotions--fear, displeasure, pleasure. They learn other emotions as they get older. Children & youth gain intelligence about what their emotions mean when they are living in peaceful, loving environments, with adults who are pretty relaxed and who have had enough security to become emotionally intelligent. Such parents teach their children & youth what to do with emotions.

Emotions cause physiological effects that can be stored in the body when the emotions are unexpressed. The body is good at sensing emotions, but is not good at releasing the effects of emotions that prepare the body for action, defense or trouble. When children & youth are emotionally overloaded, other emotions cannot be felt. Children & youth lose information that can help them control their behavior, think clearly, learn easily and be relaxed enough for their bodies to grow easily.

Children & youth become emotionally abused when they are bombarded with too much negative emotion (like anger, fear, hate, apathy); too much activity; too much shocking information; too many frightening actions done to and around them; too much lack of success; when they receive too little love, caring attention, acceptance and encouragement. The child's or youth's nervous system can also be further damaged by nutritional imbalances and exposure to pollutants of all kinds. (Exposure to pollutants and nutritional imbalances can cause symptoms similar to ones associated with emotional abuse.) Being abused physically, sexually, intellectually, or spiritually all involve emotional abuse.

To recover from emotional abuse and to develop emotional intelligence, children & youth need stability, caring attention from relaxed adults, interesting activities, good food, exercise, safe environments, some novelty.

Children & youth who are abused often resort to doing many things which can temporarily make them feel safer and help them forget the pain of being abused. These include: vandalism; violence; bullying; sexually acting out; smoking; drug abuse; substance abuse; eating disorders; cutting themselves; suicide attempts; theft; isolation; abusing other children and youth; breaking home, school and community rules.

Being Called Stupid, An Idiot, Bad, Ugly; Frequently Belittled And Unacknowledged: Without help, a child or youth's self-confidence disappears. Later success in learning, living, relationships, and being an effective parent is extremely difficult. These actions are often related to parents and teachers who need education, support and therapy so they can be more patient and attentive to the child or youth. Some adults discharge their stress onto children & youth by acting abusively .

Child Or Youth Often Threatened And Frightened By Adults And Teachers: This fear often immobilizes the child or youth's learning and willingness to participate, destroys self-confidence and can cause emotional, social and intellectual challenges later in life. The child or youth does not learn effective communication skills, but rather learns to intimidate. Frightened children & youth often try to frighten other children & youth. This fear can be due to and complicated by a combination of: adults being stressed out from their own family patterns as children or youth; economic worries and stresses; nutritional imbalances; exposure to environmental pollutants; and a lack of practice at being calm. Adults discharge their own stress onto the children or youth they abuse.

No Guidance/No Limits, Allowed To Do Anything: Unchecked, this can effect concentration, impulse control , and can lead to disorganized learning and inability to cooperate with others. This can make children & youth very self-centered and can place them in very dangerous situations. Often it deteriorates a child or youth's ability to trust, learn, perceive and discriminate. It can make impulse control, cooperation, following directions very difficult throughout life. This can be due to a combination of: stressed adults who are in need of support themselves; encouragement; help for adults being effective caregivers.

Stifled By Over-Control And Worry, Lack Of Faith And Trust: This lowers a child or youth's self-confidence and can create fear, timidity, or a lack of self-worth. It can stifle perseverance. The child or youth can also become a bully in order to compensate. This kind of abuse often leads the child or youth to making poor choices later in life. It can often be due to stressed out, frightened adults who need help in being effective caregivers.

Unloved: Unchecked, this can be fatal. A child or youth can become disconnected from society and can become angry, depressed, frightened, having no confidence and being unable to love or have compassion. Being unloved is often due to caregivers who need support, love, attention, therapy, good nutrition, and success themselves.

Yelled At Frequently: Unchecked, this can create a lack of self-confidence and an inability to work through intense situations. This type of emotional abuse can create anxiety, depression, hopelessness, anger, and muddled thinking. Being yelled at is often due to the child or youth being exposed to stressed out adults who need support in: being effective with children & youth; fear management; anger management; impulse control. Adult nutrition imbalances and their exposure to environmental pollutants might also be involved.

Verbal Abuse: Frequently being yelled and screamed at, humiliated, shamed. Everything that happens to children & youth effects their bodies. Without help, children & youths' bodies can be twisted into postures of defeat which can become habitual. Emotions caused by being yelled at, ridiculed and criticized can become locked in body posture. Slouching, holding stiffly upright, frozen facial expression, inner tension can all cause distorted growth, discomfort, pain, and other challenges in adult life. As well as the causes listed above, people saying cruel things to a child or youth can be caused by a combination of: the perpetrator feeling insecure and/or angry; perpetrator guilt and shame; having low self-esteem; family and community patterns; silence of people rejecting these ideas.

Prolonged Exposure To Chaos: Without assistance, exposure to chaos can cause the child or youth to be tense and unable to relax. A lack of relaxation can eventually hurt the body, mind and spirit. The child or youth abused this way can habitually create chaos in adult life. Without help, such children & youth can harbor powerful and confusing emotions about not being cared for properly. These emotions can effect self-confidence and decrease success as adults.

First, We Would Investigate	Second, We Would Investigate	For Long Term Support We Would Investigate
• EMDR • Hypnotherapy • Light Therapy • Psychotherapy • Attitudinal Healing • Expressive Arts • Drumming • Homeopathy • Aromatherapy • Flower Essences • Herbology • Nutrition Consulting • Wilderness Therapy • Family Therapy • Music Lessons • Environmentally Healthy Homes • Psychiatry • Western Medicine • Osteopathy • Independent Study	• Aikido • Ayurveda • Traditional Chinese Medicine • Craniosacral • Chiropractic • Precision Teaching • Feldenkrais	• Aikido • Aromatherapy • Flower Essences • Attitudinal Healing • Nutrition Consulting • Meditation • Support For Parents • Independent Study

On Our Own We Would Try: • Less or No TV, Movies, Video/Computer Games • Wholesome Pleasures • Back Rubs and Foot Massages • Nature • Replace sodas, juices, sugars, fats, fast foods with water, veggies, whole grains, nuts, protein, fruit, slow food • Long Walks/Hikes • Bedtime Stories and Chats • Pets

• •

For Parents: • Get help for yourself. • Listen and acknowledge your child's or youth's frustration. • Stay calm. • Your child's or youth's challenges may make you feel upset about your own challenges. Acknowledge this and do what you can to work on your own challenges.

•Keep sodas, diet sodas, juices, sugars, processed foods out of your home. • Mean what you say, say what you mean, do what you say you are going to do.

Check out: www.medlineplus.gov; www.acestudy.org; www.traumasoma.com/index.shtml (very technical); www.acestudy.org.

EMOTIONAL CHALLENGES

After Accidents, Beatings, Fevers, Shocks, Traumas, Family Trouble

Emotional challenges are often expressed through misbehavior. Children & youths' problematic behavior is a language often based upon emotional confusion. Without sensitive help and guidance, children's & youths' emotions can cause behavior that upsets adults, can hurt the child or youth, can hurt others, can hurt property, can develop hard-to-change reputations. Children & youth who have had bad things happen to them are often confused, frightened, or angry (or all of these). Their behavior can often be seen as discharging the stress and confusion they have accumulated. Without help these shocks can create changes in attitude and ability to learn and stay calm. They can create difficulties that can make relaxing, living and learning difficult into adult life. Emotional challenges are often due to and complicated by: physical tensions and resulting chemical imbalances; confusion; isolation.

First, We Would Investigate	Second, We Would Investigate	For Long Term Support We Would Investigate
• Western Medicine • Osteopathy • Psychiatry • Craniosacral • Chiropractic • Attitudinal Healing • EMDR • Hypnotherapy • Homeopathy • Aromatherapy • Herbology • Nutrition Consulting • Family Therapy • Flower Essences • Support For Parents • Independent Study	• Expressive Arts • Drumming • Music Lessons • Aikido • Feldenkrais • Meditation • Nonviolent Communication • Wilderness Therapy	• Aromatherapy • Nonviolent Communication • Craniosacral • Family Therapy • Psychotherapy • Expressive Arts • Drumming • Music Lessons • Aikido • Flower Essences • Support For Parents • Independent Study

On Our Own We Would Try: • Replace sodas, juices, sugars, fats, fast foods with water, veggies, whole grains, nuts, protein, fruit, slow food • Long Walks/Hikes • Bedtime Stories and Chats • Wholesome Pleasures • Back Rubs and Foot Massages • Nature • Pets • Less or No TV, Movies, Video/Computer Games

. . . .

For Parents: • Get support from other parents whose child or youth has the same challenge. • Get family and community support in supporting the child or youth, who is often frightened by her/his own erratic behavior. • Do whatever you can to reduce stress on the child or youth. You will reduce stress on the child or youth by taking action and by having faith that everything is going to work out.

Check out: www.traumasoma.com/index.shtml (very technical); www.acestudy.org.

EYE CHALLENGES

Blurry Vision; Straining; Double Vision; Squints; Eyes Itchy Or Red After Reading Or Looking At Small Things; Many Infections; Ineffective Vision/Needs Glasses; Eyes Do Not Work Together--Crossed Or Wandering

When you learn of any of these challenges, make sure you quickly get the child or youth to a medical doctor. There could be many complications related to these symptoms. Then get an optometric examination. Follow the advice given about which of the practices below might be of some assistance. You may have to hunt around to get doctors and optometrists who know about these practices. Unchecked, challenges with the eyes can severely effect learning, living, and success in later life. Since eyes are connected directly or indirectly to most parts of the brain, almost all of the child's or youth's activities are affected negatively. Without help these challenges can make learning and living very difficult. Reading and remembering what is read can also be affected. Many eye challenges are closely related to disorganization in the brain. Eye challenges can be due to and complicated by: genetics; illnesses and fevers; physical, social or emotional trauma; falls and injuries to the spine, face and head; exposure to environmental pollutants; stress; allergies; nutritional imbalances.

First, We Would Investigate	Second, We Would Investigate	For Long Term Support We Would Investigate
• Western Medicine • Osteopathy • Developmental Optometry • Light Therapy • Craniosacral • Chiropractic • Traditional Chinese Medicine • Ayurveda • Nutrition Consulting • Support For Parents	• Herbology • Homeopathy • Massage • Feldenkrais • Biofeedback • Meditation	• Developmental Optometry • Light Therapy • Osteopathy • Chiropractic • Nutrition Consulting • Support For Parents

On Our Own We Would Try: • Replace sodas, juices, sugars, fats, fast foods with water, veggies, whole grains, nuts, protein, fruit, slow food • Bedtime Stories and Chats • Wholesome Pleasures • Back Rubs and Foot Massages • Long Walks/Hikes • Nature • Less or No TV, Movies, Video/Computer Games

. . . .

For Parents: • Take action. These challenges can slow a child's or youth's learning and cause them to miss important lessons. • Get medical and optometric attention quickly. • Have your children play outdoors when possible. • Avoid sugars, caffeine in sodas, candies and chocolates. • Provide adequate lighting in the home, but avoid over lighting. • Check hygiene practices.

Check out: www.MedLinePlus.gov.

EXPOSURE TO DRUG/ALCOHOL INTOXICATED FAMILY MEMBERS

Without help, this exposure can make growing up very difficult and confusing. It can make living, learning and relationships very challenging throughout adult life. It is very hard on children & youth's trust, faith, safety, confidence, self-worth and ability to succeed. Too often, this can lead to the children & youth's growing into adults with the same challenges themselves. This exposure can lead to the child or youth's being abused in many ways by unconscious, confused family members and friends. Adults who have not been helped with challenges in childhood often abuse drugs and alcohol.

First, We Would Investigate	Second, We Would Investigate	For Long Term Support We Would Investigate
• Nonviolent Communication • Aikido • Attitudinal Healing • Psychiatry • Psychotherapy • EMDR • Hypnotherapy • Biofeedback • Nutrition Consulting • Expressive Arts • Drumming • Music Lessons • Wilderness Therapy	• Aromatherapy • Flower Essences • Herbology • Homeopathy • Traditional Chinese Medicine • Ayurveda • Precision Teaching • Meditation	• Nonviolent Communication • Aikido • Aromatherapy • Attitudinal Healing • EMDR • Hypnotherapy • Psychotherapy • Wilderness Therapy • Nutrition Education

On Our Own We Would Try: • Less or No TV, Movies, Video/Computer Games • Replace sodas, juices, sugars, fats, fast foods with water, veggies, whole grains, nuts, protein, fruit, slow • Bedtime Stories and Chats • Wholesome Pleasures • Back Rubs and Foot Massages • Long Walks and Hikes • Nature • Pets

• •

For Parents: • Get the child or youth away from intoxicated family members as fast as possible. • People who are intoxicated are unconscious and abuse children & youth in all kinds of ways without knowing it. • Tell the child or youth that the challenge is not their fault. • Attend 12 step meetings whenever possible. • Get the consciousness of sobriety and bring it into the home. • Attend 12 step family social events. • Make family life as safe and predictable as possible. • Have regular meals. • Make sure you get help yourself. • Look at what you need to do to support the child or youth. • Get help with the painful memories of your own childhood from good therapists.

Check out: www.traumasoma.com/index.shtml (very technical); www.acestudy.org/.

EXPOSURE TO VIOLENCE

Emotional Abuse; Physical Abuse; Sexual Abuse; Family Violence;
Seeing Or Hearing Family Members Beaten

Being around violence of any kind is extremely hard on children & youth—even if they are only witnesses. Without help, most children & youth exposed to violence and abuse can react as if they were abused directly themselves. Or, they can become abusers themselves as children or youth or in later life. Exposure to violence generates feelings of helplessness, diminishes trust and faith, creates low self-esteem and low achievement in later life. Children & youth can develop behavior patterns based upon fear and anger. This exposure can be due to and complicated by: family patterns; adult depression or other mental illnesses; adult mental illness; addictions; adults exposed to violence as children; abuses of all kinds; media messages condoning violence; addiction; substance abuse; nutritional imbalances; family exposure to environmental pollutants.

Seeing or hearing family members beaten: Without support, this can create lifelong patterns that make living very difficult. The immediate effect of this stress can deteriorate self-esteem and create ongoing patterns of anxiety and depression, along with increasing the likelihood of becoming a bully or a victim of violence. In addition, family violence can create intellectual or social perceptual challenges.

First, We Would Investigate	Second, We Would Investigate	For Long Term Support We Would Investigate
• Nonviolent Communication • EMDR • Hypnotherapy • Psychotherapy • Psychiatry • Attitudinal Healing • Expressive Arts • Drumming • Aikido • Wilderness Therapy • Craniosacral • Light Therapy • Nutrition Consulting • Flower Essences • Aromatherapy • Herbology • Homeopathy • Support For Parents	• Music Lessons • Massage • Precision Teaching • Meditation Yoga	• Nutrition Education • Aikido • Aromatherapy • Traditional Chinese Medicine • Ayurveda • Flower Essences • EMDR • Hypnotherapy • Psychotherapy • Precision Teaching • Meditation • Yoga

On Our Own We Would Try: • Bedtime Stories and Chats • Wholesome Pleasures • Back Rubs and Foot Massages • Replace sodas, juices, sugars, fats, fast foods with water, veggies, whole grains, nuts, protein, fruit, slow food • Long Walks/Hikes • Nature • Pets • Less or No TV, Movies, Video/Computer Games

. . . .

For Parents: • Get the child or youth away from the violence and abuse as quickly as possible. • Make life as predictable and as pleasant as possible.

•Explain that they are not to blame. To validate the child or youth's own sanity, explain that the behavior witnessed is crazy. Tell the child or youth that what happened is not his/her fault and he/she could do nothing to stop these things from happening.

Check out: www.traumasoma.com/index.shtml (very technical); www.acestudy.org.

EXPOSURE TO SUFFERING, DEPRESSION, ECONOMIC DESPAIR, ADDICTIONS, ILLNESS, HOMELESSNESS

Without help, children & youth can feel overwhelmed and powerless. They can learn helplessness. They can come to believe that life is too hard and that they can do nothing to help themselves. Children & youth can often think that the suffering they are witnessing is their suffering. This slows their emotional, intellectual and physical development. Children/teens often feel isolated, alone, depressed and abandoned in the face of such suffering. This affects later relationships and the ability to give and receive help for the rest of their lives.

First, We Would Investigate	Second, We Would Investigate	For Long Term Support We Would Investigate
• Psychotherapy • Nonviolent Communication • Attitudinal Healing • EMDR • Hypnotherapy • Biofeedback • Expressive Arts • Flower Essences • Aromatherapy • Homeopathy • Herbology • Massage • Meditation • Independent Study • Support For Parents	• Drumming • Music Lessons • Aikido • Wilderness Therapy • Safe School Ambassadors	• Psychotherapy • Nonviolent Communication • Nutrition Consulting • Ayurveda • Traditional Chinese Medicine • Aikido • Aromatherapy • Attitudinal Healing • Independent Study • Expressive Arts • Chiropractic • Osteopathy

On Our Own We Would Try: • Less or No TV, Movies, Video/Computer Games • Long Walks/ Hikes •Nature •Bedtime Stories and Chats •Wholesome Pleasures •Back Rubs and Foot Massages •Replace sodas, juices, sugars, fats, fast foods with water, veggies, whole grains, nuts, protein, fruit, slow food • Pets

. . . .

For Parents: • Get support for yourself and for the child or youth as soon as possible. Find people for you and the child or youth to talk to. • Pick people who are compassionate listeners who do not blame you or the child or youth.

•Do things together that will remind the child or youth that she/he is loved and valued. Talk together. • Keep trying even if the child or youth refuses to stop being silent or angry. Her/his silence or anger is helping her/him feel protected and strong in a situation where she/he has lost power and faith.

Check out: www.traumasoma.com/index.shtml (very technical); www.acestudy.org.

FAILURE

Frequent

Learning is extremely difficult without some failure. Learning involves experimenting. But without help and encouragement, frequent failure eats self-confidence. It negatively affects most children & youth physically, emotionally and socially. It can stop them from trying to succeed. It can start children trying to fail. (At least they are in control of something.) Failure is a poor motivator, success is a much better one. Continued failure can lead to very distorted ideas about self and life. Failure is often due to and complicated by a combination of: exposure to caregivers who have unresolved fears due to their failures; learning disabilities; over-expectations; inappropriate curriculum and learning tasks; nutrition imbalances; exposure to environmental pollutants.

First, We Would Investigate	Second, We Would Investigate	For Long Term Support We Would Investigate
• Nonviolent Communication • Precision Teaching • EMDR • Hypnotherapy • Nutrition Consulting • Western Medicine • Attitudinal Healing • Psychiatry • Psychotherapy • Wilderness Therapy • Support For Parents • Environmentally Healthy Homes	• Flower Essences • Homeopathy • Herbology • Aromatherapy • Aikido • Expressive Arts • Music Lessons • Drumming • Yoga • Massage • Independent Study	• Aikido • Aromatherapy • Nutrition Consulting • Precision Teaching • Flower Essences • Traditional Chinese Medicine • Ayurveda • Independent Study

On Our Own We Would Try: • Pets • Bedtime Stories and Chats • Wholesome Pleasures • Back Rubs and Foot Massages • Less or No TV, Movies, Video/Computer Games • Replace sodas, juices, sugars, fats, fast foods with water, veggies, whole grains, nuts, protein, fruit, slow food • Long Walks/Hikes • Nature

• •

For Parents: • Do things together that are enjoyable. • Limit learning experiences to ones where success is assured until confidence has grown back up. • Teach perseverance by example. • Get lots of exercise.

Check out: www.traumasoma.com/index.shtml (very technical); www.acestudy.org.

FALLING

Hard Many Times On Head, Face, Neck Or Back Followed By Changes In Attitude, Learning Ability, Balance, Behavior

Get medical evaluation as soon as possible. Find doctors who are familiar with the practices below and follow their advice on which ones to investigate. Falling can have immediate or long-term effects on impulse control, emotions, learning ability and perception. It can affect hearing, vision, speech, reading and handwriting ability long after the event. Unchecked it can be the cause of much physical pain later in life. All of these can make learning, living and behaving harmoniously very difficult.

First, We Would Investigate	Second, We Would Investigate	For Long Term Support We Would Investigate
• Western Medicine • Psychiatry • Osteopathy • Chiropractic • Craniosacral • Light Therapy • Developmental Optometry • Feldenkrais • Massage • Nutrition Consulting • Support For Parents	• Aromatherapy • Herbology • Traditional Chinese Medicine • Ayurveda • Flower Essences • Aikido • EMDR • Hypnotherapy	• Nonviolent Communication • Aikido • Support For Parents • Craniosacral • Chiropractic • Nutrition Consulting • Massage

On Our Own We Would Try: • Long Walks/Hikes • Nature • Replace sodas, juices, sugars, fats, fast foods with water, veggies, whole grains, nuts, protein, fruit, slow food • Bedtime Stories and Chats • Wholesome Pleasures • Back Rubs and Foot Massages • Pets • Less or No TV, Movies, Video/Computer Games

. . . .

For Parents: • Take action as quickly as possible. • Without transmitting worry, keep alert to even small changes after falling. • Keep taking action until attitudes, learning ability, balance and behavior are better. • Stay optimistic. • Discourage processed food, sugars, caffeine in sodas, candy and chocolates. • Spend extra time getting easy exercise like walking, hiking, cycling.

Check out: www.traumasoma.com/index.shtml (very technical); www.acestudy.org.

FIDGETS AND SQUIRMS

A Great Deal

If this goes on for more than a few months, get a medical consultation. Try to find doctors who are familiar with the practices below and follow their advice about which ones to investigate. Without help, fidgeting can slow success intellectually, physically, emotionally and socially. It can lead other people to treat the child or youth inappropriately and often negatively, which decreases self-esteem. Fidgeting and squirming is often a sign of the need for relieving physical and/or emotional pressure. It is often considered to be a major symptom of a number of other conditions such as ADHD/PTSD and others. It can be due to and complicated by a number of factors including: shock; birth trauma (regardless of the age of the child or youth); prolonged stress; lack of exercise, fun and movement; unresolved physical/emotional trauma and accidents; abuses of all kinds; exposure to environmental pollutants; out of balance nutrition and body chemistry; emotional insecurity/anxiety; and a lack of sleep. Sometimes fidgeting, squirming can help children & youth learn easier.

First, We Would Investigate	Second, We Would Investigate	For Long Term Support We Would Investigate
• Western Medicine • Psychiatry • Osteopathy • Chiropractic • Craniosacral • Developmental Optometry • Light Therapy • Traditional Chinese Medicine • Ayurveda • Nutrition Consulting • Support For Parents	• Nonviolent Communication • Massage • Expressive Arts • Drumming • Music Lessons • Aromatherapy • Herbology • Flower Essences • Homeopathy	• Aromatherapy • Nonviolent Communication • Massage • Herbology • Homeopathy

On Our Own We Would Try: • Replace sodas, juices, sugars, fats, fast foods with water, veggies, whole grains, nuts, protein, fruit, slow food • Long Walks/Hikes • Bedtime Stories and Chats • Wholesome Pleasures • Back Rubs and Foot Massages • Nature • Pets • Less or No TV, Movies, Video/Computer Games

. . . .

For Parents: • Release unresolved shock by playing with the child/teen through encouraging squirming and fidgeting on purpose. • This can help the child or youth become aware of what they are doing. • Getting enough exercise and cutting down on sugars and caffeine by cutting out candies, sodas and chocolate can also help. • Asking the child or youth to pretend that the jiggling part of their body can talk and allowing that part to say what needs to be said is fun and useful, too.

Check out: www.nlm.nih.gov/medlineplus.html; www.traumasoma.com/index.shtml (very technical); www.acestudy.org.

FIGHTS

Very Often; Quick Tempered

Children & youth who fight a lot should be given a medical evaluation. Pick doctors who are familiar with the practices listed below and follow their advice. The child or youth who throws the first punch is often the child or youth in the most pain and frustration. Fighting and starting fights is often related to needing to feel safe, be in control of something and release pent-up emotions which cannot be expressed appropriately. Unchecked and not replaced by alternative problem solving methods, fighting can become a life-long pattern with very negative consequences to adult success. Fighting can be related to and complicated by: family patterns; modeling; exposure to family violence; media messages; learning disabilities; listening challenges—including auditory processing, hearing; communication challenges; prolonged stress; depression or other mental illnesses; anxiety; low self-esteem; physical or emotional trauma; abuses of any kind; exposure to environmental pollutants; out of balance nutrition.

First, We Would Investigate	Second, We Would Investigate	For Long Term Support We Would Investigate
• Western Medicine • Osteopathy • Psychiatry • Traditional Chinese Medicine • Ayurveda • Nonviolent Communication • Chiropractic • Craniosacral • Nutrition Consulting • Support For Parents • Environmentally Healthy Homes • Flower Essences • Drumming • Safe School Ambassadors	• Expressive Arts • Aikido • Wilderness Therapy • Massage • Aromatherapy • Homeopathy • Herbology • Music Lessons	• Support For Parents • Nonviolent Communication • Aikido • Aromatherapy • Homeopathy • Herbology • Flower Essences • Safe School Ambassadors

On Our Own We Would Try: • Long Walks/Hikes • Nature • Back Rubs and Foot Massages • Replace sodas, juices, sugars, fats, fast foods with water, veggies, whole grains, nuts, protein, fruit, slow food • Bedtime Stories and Chats • Wholesome Pleasures • Pets • Less or No TV, Movies, Video/Computer Games

. . . .

For Parents: • Too many TV programs, video games, movies and music stimulate, frighten and support fighting. • Channel the child or youth's fighting energy by getting involved as a family in community activities that help other people and/or the environment.

Check out: www.raisingkids.co.uk/abt/abt.asp; www.acestudy.org; www.traumasoma.com/index.shtml (very technical).

FOCUSING PROBLEMS

Difficulty Paying Attention; Difficulty Finishing An Activity; Easily Distracted

If this lasts more than a few weeks, get a medical evaluation by the child's or youth's primary physician. Pick doctors who know about the practices below and follow their advice about which ones to investigate. Focusing challenges can destroy self-confidence, limit success and be very difficult in relationships. These challenges may lead the child or youth to be stereotyped as slow or difficult. They can lower the ability to learn and remember. Focusing challenges can be very frustrating for children & youth and anyone around them. These challenges may be linked to and complicated by a combination of: genetics; family patterns; lack of training; hearing and vision challenges; depression; anxiety; over stimulation; other psychiatric conditions; developmental conditions; ADD/ADHD; abuses of all kinds; unresolved physical trauma (especially to the head and spine); exposure to environmental pollutants; nutrition additives and food processing; nutritional imbalances.

First, We Would Investigate	Second, We Would Investigate	For Long Term Support We Would Investigate
• Western Medicine • Psychiatry • Osteopathy • Craniosacral • Chiropractic • Traditional Chinese Medicine • Ayurveda • Nutrition Consulting • Developmental Optometry • Light Therapy • Precision Teaching • Environmentally Healthy Homes • Support For Parents • Nonviolent Communication	• Aromatherapy • Homeopathy • Herbology • Flower Essences • Wilderness Therapy • Hypnotherapy • EMDR • Drumming • Music Lessons • Expressive Arts • Meditation • Yoga • Aikido	• Aikido • Aromatherapy • Flower Essences • Homeopathy • Nutrition Consulting • Herbology • Meditation

On Our Own We Would Try: • Replace sodas, juices, sugars, fats, fast foods with water, veggies, whole grains, nuts, protein, fruit, slow food • Long Walks/Hikes • Bedtime Stories and Chats • Wholesome Pleasures • Back Rubs and Foot Massages • Nature • Pets • Less or No TV, Movies, Video/Computer Games

. . . .

For Parents: • Keep home calm, tidy and simple. Play lots of music. • Get lots of gentle exercise. • Avoid TV. • Family games and puzzles can replace TV and teach focusing.

Check out: www.Medlineplus.gov; www.SchwabbLearning.org; www.acestudy.org.

FOOD AND BEVERAGE DANGERS

Insecticide And Fungicide Residues On Fruits And Vegetables; Plant And Animal Growth Promoters In Food Possibly Linked To Children & Youth's Development, Hormone Balances And Premature Puberty; Antibiotics In Meats; Chemicals Dangerous To Growing Children & Youth In Veggies, Grains, Fruits, Fish, Poultry, Livestock; Foods With Poor Nutrition Due To Manufacturer Ignorance; Foods With Poor Nutrition Due To Soil Depletion; Consuming "Diet" Foods & Colas With Chemical Sweeteners; Cravings/Addictions Especially Fats, Sugars, Salt, Chocolate; Diet Not Balanced; Drinks Sodas And Juices Frequently - Causing Blood Sugar Challenges, Mood Swings, Concentration Challenges; Malnutrition/Not Enough Nourishing Food; Not Drinking Enough Pure Water; Bacterial Infection Of Crops And Animals Due To Industrialized Agriculture Practices–Animal Overcrowding, Poor Sanitation/Hygiene While Handling Crops And Food Products.

Foods that have poor nutritional value are dangerous when consumed more than occasionally. Foods that are high in salt, fats, sugars, and often lacking in protein and fiber are not nutritious. Food companies produce foods and beverages without nutrition because they are inexpensive to make and produces big profits. In addition, such food lasts a long time on the shelf. When children & youth consume these foods that have cleverly crafted, exciting tastes, they do not get the benefits needed from full nutrition foods and beverages. They cannot grow physically, intellectually and socially to their best without enough nutritious foods and water. Children & youth can become addicted to fats, salt and sugars and flavor enhancers, which are unfortunately placed in the foods by manufacturers to create addiction and sell more products. It is very important to read the chapters on Nutrition Education and Vitamin Mineral Supplements. Some children & youth are particularly vulnerable to the harmful effects of consuming too much fat, salt, sugars and chemicals found in highly processed foods and beverages.

Another eating danger involves fungicides, insecticides and growth promoters used in producing vegetables, grains, fruits, fish, poultry and livestock. Food activists consider that residues of these chemicals may be dangerous to some children & youth, perhaps most. Experts argue about the research. Parents have to make food choice decisions without that complete certainty. Many parents avoid these food dangers by reducing the amount of chemical exposure their children & youth experience, in case the food activists are correct.

Eating dangers can be due to and complicated by a number of factors, including: genetics; lack of parental information about nutrition; family patterns and habits; lack of meals eaten by the whole family together; food industries and advertising agencies' managers and stockholders believing they need to make big profits at the expense of children & youth's health (count the number of nutrition-empty food and beverage commercials); eating habits and addictions; children & youth learning to prefer foods that are not healthy; poverty and the cost and lack of availability of good food; power struggles with parents and family; tensions due to accidents and/or abuses of all kinds, resulting in self-medication by consuming tasty, nutrition-empty foods; bodily nutritional imbalances; exposure to environmental pollutants.

Some children & youth act out their frustration about other things with their parents by being picky eaters.

Insecticide And Fungicide Residues On Fruits And Vegetables: There is much ongoing debate about this. Organic food proponents feel that any chemical designed to kill insects or molds cannot be good for growing bodies in any quantity. The food industry position is that the chemicals do no harm at the levels that children & youth consume them. The food activists disagree and bring up the cumulative effects of these chemicals. Research is still mixed. Parents have to decide the risks but caution is called for.

Plant And Animal Growth Promoters In Food Possibly Linked To Children & Youth's Development, Hormone Balances and Premature Puberty: There is much debate about this subject as well. Synthetic growth promoters are applied to grains, farm fish and meat animals to increase production and profit. The bodies of growing children and teens are not designed to consume these growth promoters in quantity. Many adverse conditions are now being suspected as being linked to growth promoters in foods. Research is mixed. Parents have to decide the risks but caution is called for.

Antibiotics In Meats: There is much debate and even lawsuits about whether antibiotics in foods cause challenges. More and more research is indicating that germs are developing that are resistant to antibiotics because people have so many antibiotics in their systems from eating commercial meat products. (See food challenges above.)

Insecticide And Fungicide Residues On Fruits And Vegetables: There is much ongoing debate about this. Organic food proponents feel that any chemical designed to kill insects or molds cannot be good for growing bodies in any quantity.

Chemicals Dangerous To Growing Children & Youth In Veggies, Grains, Fruits, Fish, Poultry, Livestock: There is again ongoing research on how chemicals dangerous to growing children & youth get into the food and into the children & youth when they eat the food. The United States government has lists of foods that have become dangerous and gives recommendations on how much of such food is considered safe. This can be very frightening information for parents and even more so for children & youth. Parents have to decide the risk of not knowing this information.

Foods With Poor Nutrition Due To Manufacturer Ignorance: Some children & youth get so addicted to sugars, fats, and nutrition-empty fast foods that they throw tantrums when they are presented with alternatives, and if they are allowed to have their way, they end up not eating the protein they need for healthy growth, calm behavior and clear thinking.

Foods With Poor Nutrition Due To Soil Depletion: The United States Congress has determined that modern agricultural practices have depleted soils in America of minerals that are necessary for children's & youth's growth. This important information is largely ignored. Fertilizers appear not to contain a wide enough range of mineral supplements for healthy soil. Ideally, these minerals should pass from the soil into plants which are then consumed by children & youth.

Consuming "Diet" Foods & Colas With Chemical Sweeteners: Again there is much debate about the quality of the research about the long term effects of chemical sweeteners. Some research maintains that sweeteners are harmless. Some people think they are dangerous. Again, parents should exercise caution.

Cravings/Addictions Especially Fats, Sugars, Salt, Chocolate: Children & youth get addicted early by the interesting taste and mood enhancing results of eating fats, sugars, salt, chocolate. These addictions can often be due to nutritional imbalances.

Diet Not Balanced: Sadly, so far, corporations and media advertisers are more interested in selling products than in being concerned about children & youths getting the habit of eating balanced diets. Many parents do not know what constitutes a balanced diet.

Drinks Sodas And Juices Frequently - Causing Blood Sugar Challenges, Mood Swings, Concentration Challenges: Corporations and advertisers have not yet awakened to the challenges caused by sugars and chemicals in drinks. Few people have the research skills to find out. The flavors are designed to taste better than water so that children & youth will crave them.

Malnutrition/Not Enough Nourishing Food: There are levels of malnutrition. There are levels of under–nutrition. Many children & youth get enough food to keep going and to do okay. However, research is showing that children & youth's learning capacity goes up, emotional calm increases, emotional outbreaks and anger go down when children & youth get good nutrition. This is why so much of this book relates to nutrition. Vitamin supplements of a good quality can make a huge difference.

Not Drinking Enough Pure Water: This is another one of those areas of great concern. More and more research is coming in suggesting that pure water may be one of the most important things humans can consume. While challenges can happen from drinking too much water, far more challenges happen from not drinking enough, including dental cavities. Children & youth can get so addicted to commercial tastes that they do not know what thirst for water feels like.

Bacterial Infection Of Crops And Animals Due To Industrialized Agriculture Practices—Animal Overcrowding, Poor Sanitation/Hygiene While Handling Crops And Food Products: Since federal budget cuts have reduced the number and effectiveness of food health inspectors/inspections, extra care must be made to ensure hygienic food. Food workers getting low wages and no health care means workers who are sick often bring their illness to the food they handle. Make sure all foods are checked thoroughly, washed carefully and are well cooked. Cooking can help reduce bacterial content.

First, We Would Investigate	Second, We Would Investigate	For Long Term Support We Would Investigate
• Western Medicine • Osteopathy • Nutrition Consulting • Ayurveda • Traditional Chinese Medicine • Environmentally Healthy Homes • EMDR • Hypnotherapy • Support For Parents • Nonviolent Communication • Attitudinal Healing	• Herbology • Homeopathy • Flower Essences • Aikido • Expressive Arts • Aromatherapy • Massage • Precision Teaching • Expressive Arts • Drumming • Music Lessons	• Nutrition Consulting • Support For Parents • Nonviolent Communication • Herbology • Homeopathy • Flower Essences

On Our Own We Would Try: • Replace sodas, juices, sugars, fats, fast foods with water, veggies, whole grains, nuts, protein, fruit, slow food • Family Dinners • Long Walks/Hikes • Bedtime Stories and Chats • Wholesome Pleasures • Back Rubs and Foot Massages • Nature • Pets • Less or No TV, Movies, Video/Computer Games • Grow as much organic food as you can with your children & youth • Shop at your local farmer's market or join a community supported agricultural co-op.

· ·

For Parents: • Get support from other parents who have the same concerns. • Expect resistance when you begin to change the family eating habits. • Expect withdrawal symptoms of crankiness, mood swings, headaches from caffeine withdrawal and power struggles. • Plan carefully. • Learn how to make good-tasting alternatives. • Reduce or get rid of TV and exposure to advertisements selling refined foods.

• Purchase foods as fresh and pure as you can. Local seasonally grown organic food is less expensive. • Fresh, organic food usually costs extra money; however, it saves money in the long run since it is a good protection for growing children & youth as they develop. • If you cannot afford or find organic foods, follow the US Food and Drug Administration's advice to thoroughly wash all vegetables, fruits and berries. This does not help in all cases. • This will remove residues, but not chemicals embedded in the cells of the food. • If you can, grow and cook you own food as a family. • Make meals from scratch using basic ingredients. • Keep in mind that going up against mainstream culture's food addictions is not easy. • Your local health food store will give you one set of information. Supermarkets will give you another. Your local health department can help. • Parents must decide.

Check out: www.Medlineplus.gov/childnutrition.

FRUSTRATION: FREQUENT

Since frequent frustration can be a sign of medical challenges, get a medical evaluation from a doctor. Try to pick a doctor who's open to appropriate alternative practices and follow her/his advice about which practices to investigate for your child or youth. Without help, feeling frustrated frequently can become a lifetime pattern which prevents learning and success. Frustration is the language the child or youth uses to express difficulty. It can easily lead to rage or anxiety. It stops activity. Frustration can be a sign that the child or youth is having learning difficulties or challenges with too-simple learning activities. It can be caused by and complicated by a combination of factors including: family patterns; attention seeking; perceptual difficulties; learning challenges; teaching methods not appropriate to child/teen's learning style; inability to focus; inappropriate or overly complicated activities; over expectations; fear of making mistakes; anxiety; lack of self-confidence; emotional/physical/intellectual overload; lack of training; memory challenges; nutritional imbalances; exposure to environmental pollutants. Some frustration is a normal and necessary part of learning and accomplishment. Persevering and learning to stay calm while frustrated is very important.

First, We Would Investigate	Second, We Would Investigate	For Long Term Support We Would Investigate
• Western Medicine • Osteopathy • Psychiatry • Ayurveda • Traditional Chinese Medicine • Psychotherapy • Biofeedback • EMDR • Hypnotherapy • Precision Teaching • Homeopathy • Herbology • Aromatherapy • Flower Essences • Nutrition Consulting • Support For Parents • Nonviolent Communication	• Meditation • Aikido • Drumming • Expressive Arts Therapy • Music Lessons • Massage • Environmentally Healthy Homes	• Nutrition Consulting • Meditation • Environmentally Healthy Homes • Aromatherapy • Homeopathy • Herbology • Flower Essences

On Our Own We Would Try: • Replace sodas, juices, sugars, fats, fast foods with water, veggies, whole grains, nuts, protein, fruit, slow food • Long Walks/Hikes • Bedtime Stories and Chats • Wholesome Pleasures • Back Rubs and Foot Massages • Nature • Pets • Less or No TV, Movies, Video/Computer Games

. . . .

For Parents: • It sometimes helps to get the child or youth to simply lie down if possible during frustration attacks. • A drink of cold water can help as well. Exhaling many times through the nose is worth trying. • Set good examples for the child or youth by showing how you can keep learning while frustrated.

Check out: www.Medlineplus.gov; www/casabalt/prs/trauma.htm; www.acestudy.org.

GENDER IDENTITY CONCERNS

Gender Dysphoria

Gender Dysphoria is a condition characterized by intense feelings of being the wrong gender. It is extremely confusing having the body of one gender and the experience, thoughts and feelings are of the opposite gender. No one knows for sure what causes it. Children & youth can be aware of this very early in their lives–feeling different, wrong, and often bad because of it. Without support this can be very crippling physically, emotionally, intellectually and socially. Without assistance, a child or youth's self-confidence can be severely damaged–possibly lasting throughout life. Self-loathing, isolation and withdrawal can result. Children & youth often know quite early in their lives that their gender identity is not the one expected by their parents, family and schoolmates. Anxiety results when the child or youth does not feel support for who he/she is. Gender identity anxiety can create confusion and alienation. Gender identity anxiety can be due to and complicated by: a lack of celebration and appreciation for differences; community and family patterns of judgment; parental fear and misunderstanding; a lack of sensitive support from the extended family and friends; adult ignorance; prejudice; fear; fear of differences; complicity in allowing suffering; simplistic thinking; social pressure.

First, We Would Investigate	Second, We Would Investigate	For Long Term Support We Would Investigate
• Parental Support • Western Medicine • EMDR • Attitudinal Healing • Hypnotherapy • Psychotherapy • Expressive Arts • Nonviolent Communication	• Aikido • Aromatherapy • Flower Essences • Homeopathy • Herbology • Drumming • Music Lessons • Massage • Nutrition Education	• Nonviolent Communication • Attitudinal Healing • Aikido • Aromatherapy • Flower Essences

On Our Own We Would Try: • Long Walks/Hikes • Bedtime Stories and Chats • Wholesome Pleasures • Back Rubs and Foot Massages • Nature • Less or No TV, Movies, Video/Computer Games

. . . .

For Parents: • Support your child or youth in his/her exploration of what is true for her/him and protect him/her from prejudice. • Get therapeutic help in releasing emotional and intellectual blocks which prevent you from giving support and protection. • Get therapy/counseling to help deal with your anxiety and mixed emotions about issues of gender identity. Locate therapists who are knowledgeable and comfortable with issues of gender. • Get support from other parents wanting to support their children & youth facing these concerns. • Learn about the gender identity your child or youth chooses. • Your love and support is needed by your child or youth. Your child or youth needs your love, acceptance and support not your fears and embarrassments. • Avoid teasing or pressure. Protect your child or youth from it. • Enjoy and celebrate whatever gender identity your child or youth expresses. • Overcome the mainstream medical, psychological and religious communities' ideas of what is sane, healthy, normal about gender. • Some families choose to find doctors who use medicines to delay puberty until the youth is sure about her/his gender identity, thus allowing time to avoid the challenges of transitioning.

Check out: www.critpath.org/pflag-talk/gid.htm; www.Medlineplus.gov.

GRIEF

Grief is natural. The expression of grief is valuable to children & youths' minds, bodies and spirits. Grieving may involve periods of wailing, weeping, crying, sobbing, anger, quietness, shyness, withdrawal, avoidance, depression, mood swings, memory loss. Changes in behavior, interests, and school performance are to be expected. Children & youth need to grieve and to feel safe to express these emotions. Adults may mistakenly want to protect the child or youth from grief. It can be difficult for adults to be around children or youth who are grieving. Children & youth are often stopped from grieving by adults who are unable to grieve themselves and who can't stand seeing their children or youth suffer. It is essential that children & youth grieve fully, which may take some time. Without help, unexpressed grief can negatively effect mental, emotional, and physical health. Withdrawal from life can result from incomplete grieving. Grieving deeply helps children & youth get over the pain of loss and get back to living fully more quickly. Some physical effects of unexpressed grief may stay in the child's or youth's body all of their lives. Unexpressed grief can contribute to becoming an unemotional, cold, and often insensitive/cruel adult.

First, We Would Investigate	Second, We Would Investigate	For Long Term Support We Would Investigate
• Expressive Arts • Attitudinal Healing • Aromatherapy • Flower Essences • Herbology • Homeopathy • Nonviolent Communication • Support For Parents • Nutrition Consulting **If grief is blocked/held in:** • EMDR • Hypnotherapy • Psychotherapy • Psychiatry • Biofeedback • Expressive Arts • Drumming • Massage • Wilderness Therapy • Flower Essences	• Ayurveda • Traditional Chinese Medicine • Massage • Drumming • Music Lessons • Wilderness Therapy • Chiropractic • Osteopathy • Craniosacral	• Aikido • Expressive Arts • Aromatherapy • Flower Essences • Herbology • Homeopathy • Attitudinal Healing • Nutrition Consulting

On Our Own We Would Try: • Replace sodas, juices, sugars, fats, fast foods with water, veggies, whole grains, nuts, protein, fruit, slow food • Long Walks/Hikes • Nature • Bedtime Stories and Chats • Wholesome Pleasures • Back Rubs and Foot Massages • Pets • Less or No TV, Movies, Video/Computer Games

. . . .

For Parents: • Be honest. Get help if you are not comfortable with the loss yourself. • Get support for your own grief. • Be patient. Grief often takes quite a while. Each child or youth grieves differently. • Try not to force anything. • Try not to deny anything. What is, is. This will help you support your child or youth.

• Allow the child or youth to keep crying until he/she is done.   • Make lots of eye contact.   • Have lots of physical contact.   • Favorite comfort foods are good, however make sure that lots of water is consumed   • Check out grief camps and local hospice programs.   • If you are grieving as well, avoid alcohol and medications that take you away from your child or youth. You need each other.

Check out: www./medlineplus/bereavement; www.acestudy.org.

HANDWRITING/PRINTING IS INEFFECTIVE

Lacks Size & Shape Consistency; Letters Unreadable; Dysgraphia; Dyslexic Dysgraphia; Motor Dysgraphia; Spatial Dysgraphia

Unreadable printing or writing can slow educational progress and can also be a great nuisance in later life. It can be due to and complicated by a combination of: co-ordination difficulties; lack of instruction based on learning styles; lack of practice; lack of encouragement; genetic factors; vision challenges; family coordination patterns; nervous tension due to accidents, prolonged emotional stress, and all types of abuses; lack of sleep; learning difficulties; focusing/perceptual challenges; memory challenges. It can also be a sign of depression, anger, frustration, and a lack of confidence. Being worried about and reminded of poor handwriting tends to make the challenge worse. Alert relaxation improves it. Using computers can help children & youth whose handwriting is not clear; however, using computers for communicating can deteriorate handwriting and printing because good handwriting needs practice.

First, We Would Investigate	Second, We Would Investigate	For Long Term Support We Would Investigate
• Western Medicine • Osteopathy • Chiropractic • Precision Teaching • Feldenkrais • Craniosacral • Developmental Optometry • Light Therapy • Attitudinal Healing • Nutrition Consulting • Expressive Arts • Music Lessons • Homeopathy • Flower Essences • Aromatherapy • Herbology • Ayurveda • Traditional Chinese Medicine	• EMDR • Hypnotherapy • Biofeedback • Psychotherapy • Aikido • Yoga • Meditation • Drumming • Support For Parents • Nonviolent Communication • Environmentally Healthy Homes	• Nutrition Consulting • Feldenkrais • Expressive Arts • Flower Essences • Homeopathy • Herbology • Ayurveda • Traditional Chinese Medicine

On Our Own We Would Try: • Replace sodas, juices, sugars, fats, fast foods with water, veggies, whole grains, nuts, protein, fruit, slow food • Long Walks/Hikes • Bedtime Stories and Chats • Wholesome Pleasures • Back Rubs and Foot Massages • Nature • Pets • Less or No TV, Movies, Video/Computer Games

. . . .

For Parents: • Get a medical evaluation from a practitioner who is familiar with these practices. Follow their advice when it makes sense to you. • Praise effort. • Acknowledge success. • Practice printing and handwriting as an art/craft form in enjoyable ways.   • Eye-hand coordination games such as Pick-Up-Sticks can help   • Calligraphy classes can help. Include the child or youth in the functioning of family life that involves handwriting. • Express confidence that the child or youth will solve this challenge.

Check out: www.MedlinePlus.com.

HAS REPEATED A GRADE AT SCHOOL

This is a very complicated and controversial issue. Repeating a grade can be devastating to self-confidence and success in later life. The majority of children & youth who repeat a grade do not finish high school. Repeating a grade should most often be avoided at all costs. A child or youth who has repeated a grade should be promoted as soon as possible to catch up with her/his age group to undo the negative effects of grade repetition on self-confidence. Special help has to be given so the child or youth experiences a great deal of academic success. Getting a thorough medical checkup is highly recommended the minute grade repeating is considered. Undetected medical conditions can cause poor school performance.

There are many types of intelligence and styles of learning. With support, intelligence can be improved. With support, learning styles can be enhanced. When educators and parents blame children or youth for being lazy, they are avoiding responsibility for finding what will help them be successful. Having young children begin school when they are older is a good formula for success. The oldest children in a class often are the most successful and learn the easiest throughout their lives.

Occasionally, children & youth are relieved when they are required to repeat a grade because the pressure to be successful has been so uncomfortable. This can be a short term gain, since they will carry the stigma into the rest of their lives. Better to repeat the grade, get lots of extra help to catch up and rejoin the social group. Sometimes, however, when the children or youth are the youngest in a class, repeating a grade actually connects them with their social group, carries less stigma, and turns out to be beneficial for them.

Most often making a child or youth repeat a grade indicates a failure of the school, not the child or youth. Usually falling behind the other children or youth and being forced to repeat a grade is due to the child being amongst the youngest in the class and thus being immature intellectually and socially. These factors can cause stress and slow learning.

Insufficient progress in academic programs is also often due to and complicated by: learning disabilities; perceptual challenges; learning styles not compatible with teaching style; difficulties following instructions; challenges remembering; genetics; family patterns; lack of sleep; lack of regular nutritious meals; family turmoil and change including illness, separation, divorce, incarceration; parental addictions; poverty; prolonged stress; challenges with physical organization/coordination; challenges with concentration and focusing; unsafe schools; moving schools and homes often. All of these can be complicated by frequent illnesses; high stress; peer pressure at school, gang involvement; child, youth and parental substance abuse challenges; child or youth or parent depressions/anxiety; physical, emotional and neurological imbalance due to traumas and abuses of all kinds. Exposure to environmental pollutants may also be involved.

First, We Would Investigate	Second, We Would Investigate	For Long Term Support We Would Investigate
• Western Medicine • Osteopathy • Precision Teaching • Light Therapy • Developmental Optometry • Nutrition Consulting • Craniosacral • EMDR • Hypnotherapy • Attitudinal Healing • Psychiatry • Chiropractic • Traditional Chinese Medicine • Ayurveda • Herbology • Homeopathy • Nonviolent Communication • Independent Study • Expressive Arts • Music Lessons • Drumming • Safe School Ambassadors • Support For Parents	• Environmentally Healthy Homes • Aromatherapy • Flower Essences • Wilderness Therapy • Psychotherapy • Aikido • Wilderness Therapy • Massage	• Nutrition Consulting • Ayurveda • Traditional Chinese Medicine • Herbology • Homeopathy • Flower Essences • Aromatherapy • Aikido • Expressive Arts • Attitudinal Healing • Nonviolent Communication • Independent Study • Support For Parents

On Our Own We Would Try: • Less or No TV, Movies, Video/Computer Games • Bedtime Stories and Chats • Replace sodas, juices, sugars, fats, fast foods with water, veggies, whole grains, nuts, protein, fruit, slow food • Long Walks/Hikes • Nature • Wholesome Pleasures • Back Rubs and Foot Massages • Pets

. . . .

For Parents: • Get the school district psychologist to test for learning difficulties. • If you can, also get a private psychologist to do the same for a second opinion. • Get the school district to support your child or youth more effectively. • Keep advocating for your child or youth. • Avoid blaming the child or youth. • Acknowledge skills, gifts, talents of everyone in the family often. • Rebild confidence by singing, dancing, cooking and making things together as a family. • Learn new things as a family–like dancing or singing or a new language. • Help your child or youth fall in love with learning. • Restricting TV gives the child or youth more time for activity. • Find parents of children or youth with the same challenge and support each other.

• Avoid homework wars. • Learn study skills yourself and teach them to your child or youth. • Develop study and homework routines by setting aside regular, predictable times for learning. Do homework in as quiet and safe a place as possible. • Make homework a game/chore and pleasantly accompany the child or youth while doing it. • Find someone who is cheerful and who the child or youth likes to act as a learning coach. Have that person teach learning strategies as well as assist with the task of catching up.

• Keep your worry to yourself.

Check out: www. MedlinePlus.org; www.kidshealth.org.

HEAD INJURIES

Traumatic Brain Injury, Bangs To The Head, Falls, Accidents, Beatings, Slapped On The Head/Face

There are a wide range of head injuries–from extreme to mild brain damage to no apparent ill effects (except a bump on the head). Even seemingly mild bangs on the head, however, can later effect living, learning and behavior–possibly profoundly. After any head injuries, get medical attention as soon as possible. Later, get regular checkups to watch out for any long term consequences. If possible, use doctors who support the practices listed below and follow their advice about which ones to investigate for your child or youth. Without help, head injuries of all kinds have the potential of contributing to physical, neurological and chemical imbalances that can contribute to future learning perceptual challenges, concentration challenges, behavior challenges, and social challenges. The effects of head injuries can lie dormant for many years and can emerge as learning difficulties, physical challenges throughout the whole body or emotional challenges. It is essential to keep track of the details of any head injuries. Childhood & youth challenges with being able to use and remember what they hear, see and feel may be related to head injuries. Frequent head injuries, falls, bangs to the head, accidents can be caused by or complicated by a number of factors including: perceptual challenges, vision and hearing challenges; attention/focusing/coordination challenges; depression or other mental illnesses: anger; low self-confidence and low self-esteem and peer pressure leading to reckless, dangerous behavior. Substance use and abuse, nutrition challenges and exposure to environmental pollutants may also be involved.

First, We Would Investigate	Second, We Would Investigate	For Long Term Support We Would Investigate
• Western Medicine • Osteopathy • Craniosacral • Chiropractic • Traditional Chinese Medicine • Ayurveda • Nutrition Consulting • Light Therapy • Developmental Optometry • Feldenkrais • Precision Teaching • EMDR • Hypnotherapy • Biofeedback • Nonviolent Communication • Support For Parents • Aikido • Yoga	• Herbology • Homeopathy • Massage • Expressive Arts • Drumming • Environmentally Healthy Homes • Aromatherapy • Flower Essences • Safe School Ambassadors • Meditation • Music Lessons	• Western Medicine • Osteopathy • Chiropractic • Craniosacral • Aromatherapy • Herbology • Homeopathy • Flower Essences • Nutrition Consulting • Nonviolent Communication • Support For Parents

On Our Own We Would Try: • Long Walks/Hikes • Nature • Back Rubs and Foot Massages • Replace sodas, juices, sugars, fats, fast foods with water, veggies, whole grains, nuts, protein, fruit, slow food • Bedtime Stories and Chats • Wholesome Pleasures • Pets • Less or No TV, Movies, Video/Computer Games

· ·

For Parents: • Get a medical evaluation. • After a head injury of any severity be very alert for a few months to any changes in appearance, posture, behavior, vision, hearing, memory, learning ability. • Get additional medical attention as soon as you notice any changes. • Avoid frightening the child or youth. • Avoid letting yourself or her/him use the head injury as an excuse to misbehave or slack off with learning and behaving properly. • Acknowledge successes and efforts, as well as giving instructions using Nonviolent Communication processes.

Check out: www.MedLinePlus.gov.

INACTIVITY: HABITUAL PHYSICAL INACTIVITY

Without help, this can become a very dangerous habit resulting in obesity, stress related conditions, loss of sleep, poor self-esteem, depression, reduced learning ability, low school performance, confused emotions, distorted ideas, chronic medical challenges, lack of survival skills, social isolation.

Habitual inactivity has become epidemic (especially in the US) for children, youth and adults. There are many reasons for this including; societal, technological, industrial, financial, and commercial factors. Children & youth are being driven to school for safety concerns and lack of good schools in local neighborhoods. Budget cuts have resulted in inadequate physical education in schools. For safety reasons, children & youth are often not able to play outside after school at home. Too many children & youth are spending hours and hours each day watching TV or playing computer games, instead of being physically active.

Low energy, inactivity, listlessness and disinterest may also be caused by and complicated by medical and psychiatric conditions, which need to be evaluated. Nutritional imbalances involving diets high in sugars and fats and incomplete proteins also add to the challenge of inactivity. Exposure to environmental pollutants—air pollution in particular—can also limit activity.

However, whole families are losing the habit of being physically active. Children & youth are not learning the enjoyments of movement and physical accomplishment from their families.

Children & youth learn and grow through activity. Increased physical activity is good for: heart health; preventing diabetes; controlling weight; improving psychological and emotional well being; improving self image; raising energy levels.

First, We Would Investigate	Second, We Would Investigate	For Long Term Support We Would Investigate
• Western Medicine • Osteopathy • Support For Parents • Nonviolent Communication • Nutrition Consulting • Music Lessons • Expressive Arts • Drumming • Yoga • Wilderness Therapy • Herbology • Homeopathy • Flower Essences • Traditional Chinese Medicine • Ayurveda • Psychiatry • Psychotherapy • Attitudinal Healing	• Environmentally Healthy Homes • Safe School Ambassadors • EMDR • Hypnotherapy • Biofeedback • Light Therapy • Developmental Optometry • Precision Teaching • Massage	• Nutrition Consulting • Nonviolent Communication • Expressive Arts • Flower Essences • Music Lessons • Drumming • Wilderness Therapy

On Our Own We Would Try: • Less or No TV, Movies, Video/Computer Games • Replace sodas, juices, sugars, fats, fast foods with water, veggies, whole grains, nuts, protein, fruit, slow food • Long Walks/Hikes • Nature • Bedtime Stories and Chats • Wholesome Pleasures • Back Rubs and Foot Massages • Pets

. . . .

For Parents: • Increase moderate and extreme physical, enjoyable activity as a family to replace TV, computer, and stay-at-home times. • Become as active as you want your child or youth to be. • Find physically active things the whole family likes to do together and do them regularly. • Instead of using a car or bus, rediscover walking or cycling as a form of transportation. • Join with other parents interested in this topic. • Pressure your local political leaders to provide daily physical education in schools, safe streets, bicycle and walking paths, team sports, more parks, playgrounds and swimming pools, and effective public transportation. • Ask your doctor, local business people and school staff to help you get your child or youth motivated.

Check out: www.gov/Medlineplus/exerciseforchildren; www.kidshealth.org; www.actionforhealthykids.org.

INJURY

Falls/Injury To The Face, Head, Limb, Neck, Pelvis, Spinal Chord; Falling Or Dropping On Head Or Tail Bone; Being In Many Accidents; Experiencing Intense Pain After Injuries

Falls/Injury To The Face, Head, Limb, Neck, Pelvis, Spinal Chord: Get a medical evaluation as soon as possible. Try to pick medical practitioners who know about the practices listed below and follow their advice on which ones to investigate. Often children & youth may seem to be okay, however challenges can occur later if the trauma is not released. Unreleased trauma like this can make living, learning and growing very difficult. Without help human bodies can store the results of injuries which can cause a lot of challenges later in life, sometimes years later. Unreleased injuries can cause behavior and learning challenges. They can also result later in learning challenges, memory challenges, perceptual challenges, movement challenges, digestive challenges, and sleep difficulties. Very often, children & youth's bodies, minds and emotions tighten up in fear. This tightening up process can spread to other parts of the body and mind. Injuries can create fear.

Too often, parents and professionals overlook subtle signs and symptoms and do not provide experiences that can help children & youth release the negative effects of injury. Occasionally, children, youth and families can use old injuries as excuses and ways of avoiding the struggles of growing up and succeeding. Children & youth can also get in the habit of using repeated injury to the same body part as ways of getting attention.

Falling Or Dropping On Head Or Tail Bone: The height of the fall is often less critical than the angle that the child or youth lands on in creating severe difficulties immediately of later in life. Too often, parents assume that the child or youth is okay if the child or youth gets up and moves around without reporting much pain. Parents are advised to watch out for new behavior difficulties or new learning challenges after such a fall--even years later.

Being In Many Accidents: Having too many injuries and accidents can be an indicator of perceptual, coordination or emotional difficulties. It may indicate that the child or youth is preoccupied and not present or is subconsciously self-abusive and reckless. Without help, having injuries can become an habitual way of avoiding problems, avoiding success, and getting attention.

Experiencing Intense Pain After Injuries: Without help in learning how to relax, intense pain can create more fear of future pain and can diminish the child's full participation in life. Feeling pain intensely can be due to a combination of severe trauma, genetic factors, problematic breathing patterns, prolonged stress, excessive fear and an overall inability to relax.

Resulting In Becoming Unconscious: Loss of consciousness is one of the body's responses for protecting against further injury. Getting medical help as soon as possible is extremely critical. Maintaining soft and gentle physical, emotional and verbal contact with a child or youth in a coma is vitally important for the child or youth and the adults.

First, We Would Investigate	Second, We Would Investigate	For Long Term Support We Would Investigate
• Western Medicine • Osteopathy • Chiropractic • Craniosacral • Feldenkrais • Developmental Optometry • Light Therapy • Traditional Chinese Medicine • Ayurveda • Herbology • Flower Essences • Homeopathy • Aromatherapy • Psychiatry • Support For Parents • Nonviolent Communication	• Expressive Arts • Drumming • Music Lessons • Yoga • Massage • EMDR • Biofeedback • Hypnotherapy	• Osteopathy • Chiropractic • Craniosacral • Feldenkrais • Aromatherapy • Herbology • Flower Essences • Nutrition Consulting • Nonviolent Communication

On Our Own We Would Try: • Replace sodas, juices, sugars, fats, fast foods with water, veggies, whole grains, nuts, protein, fruit, slow food • Long Walks/Hikes • Nature • Bedtime Stories and Chats • Wholesome Pleasures • Back Rubs and Foot Massages • Pets • Less or No TV, Movies, Video/Computer Games

• •

For Parents: • Seek medical attention immediately. Stay calm but take action. • Watch for long term effects so you can support full recovery of your child or youth. • Avoid frightening the child or youth or giving them excuses for acting or avoiding effort because of injuries. • Practice patience, compassion and encouragement for effort. • Ask your physician, public health department and local school about ways to prevent further injuries.

Check out: www.medlineplus.gov.

INTELLECTUAL/EDUCATIONAL ABUSE

Being Called Stupid, Idiotic, Bad, Ugly; Exposure To Racism; Exposure To Sexism; Teaching, Instruction Methods Not Matching Learning Styles; Over-Stimulation, Too Much Going On; Exposure To Chaos; Too Little Stimulation/Uninteresting Environments; Intellectual Abuse By Neglect

Without help, a child or youth's ability to learn can be temporarily or permanently damaged by improper education and wrong ideas. Children & youth tend to become what they are taught to believe about themselves. Learning can be decreased by learning environments that are not calm enough and structured enough, or by learning environments that are too controlled and too structured. This abuse can come from insensitive family members, neighbors, educators and anyone having contact with children & youth. Media can also deliver abusive ideas. Without help, intellectual abuse can result in a lifetime of having a lack of confidence in one's learning ability. This can lead to a lack of success, frustration, self-condemnation and depression. Parents, schools, community and society too often conspire to ignore intellectual abuse by overvaluing academic achievement and success, and by under-funding education. The child or youth's learning ability is abused when the teaching styles do not fit the nature of the child or youth. Intellectual abuse can also be complicated by a combination of: genetic factors; nutrition challenges; exposure to environmental pollutants; unhealed abuses of other types, and as a result of accidents.

Being Called Stupid, Idiotic, Bad, Ugly: It is not true that "sticks and stones can break your bones but words can't ever hurt you". Children & youth are very hurt by names and insensitive labeling by parents, family, teachers, or their peers. This can lower self-esteem so severely that learning and living can almost stop.

Exposure To Racism: Racism can come in many forms – economic, social, emotional and personal. Racism can shape expectations, limit access to learning resources, limit achievement and can create distorted self-concepts. Often, educational programs are not culturally sensitive, which can cause failure. Racism challenges logic: it can prevent success, yet the student and their family are blamed. It hurts children & youths' self-esteem. Without help, racism can limit children & youths' achievement in life. The causes of racism are many and complex and beyond the scope of this book. The good news is that racism is being openly acknowledged and actively addressed in many areas of American life.

Exposure To Sexism: Sexism can come in many forms – economic, social, emotional and personal. It can effect both boys and girls. Like racism, sexism can shape expectation, limit access to learning resources, limit achievement, and can create distorted self-concept. Without help, exposure to sexism gives children & youth distorted ideas about themselves and others. These distorted ideas can be damaging to self-esteem and self-confidence, as well as relationships. Sexism based patterns can become habitual and can deteriorate adult relationships. Without help, sexism can limit children & youth's achievement in life. The causes of sexism are many and complex and beyond the scope of this book. The good news is that girls & young women are catching up to boys & young men in some sport and academic fields and out-performing them in others.

Teaching, Instruction Methods Not Matching Learning Styles: Without help, children & youth can develop habits of severe underachievement throughout their lives. Children & youth can become convinced they are stupid and that they are to blame for underachievement because they did not try hard enough. These self-concepts can be acted out throughout adult life. Each child or youth learns in a particular set of ways. Too often, children & youth are forced to learn in one or two ways. This can be due to society not being willing to invest money in teacher education and in small enough classes to allow for individual instruction. Traditional education tends to stress obedience and compliance rather than teaching how to be successful learners.

Over-Stimulation, Too Much Going On; Exposure To Chaos: Too much stimulation can cause children & youth to short-circuit. Over stimulation can lead to habitual challenges with focus and being present. It can also lead to memory and school performance challenges. Children & youth can become addicted to intensity. This makes necessary practice of skills difficult and boring. Being negatively affected by over stimulation can be due to a combination of: genetic factors; family patterns; nutritional imbalances; exposure to environmental pollutants; prolonged stress; unreleased body tension due to accidents and unhealed abuses of all kinds. Prolonged exposure to over stimulation may have the same physiological and emotional effects as prolonged stress.

Too Little Stimulation/Uninteresting Environments; Intellectual Abuse By Neglect: This is very hard on bright, talented children & youth. They begin to dislike themselves for not being interested and for being bored/frustrated. This happens for a number of complicated reasons, including community unwillingness to pay for quality education, parental depression or addiction, family blindness to the child's or youth's gifts and talents.

First, We Would Investigate	Second, We Would Investigate	For Long Term Support We Would Investigate
• Attitudinal Healing • Psychotherapy • Psychiatry • Precision Teaching • Expressive Arts • Western Medicine • Osteopathy • Hypnotherapy • EMDR • Biofeedback • Flower Essences • Herbology • Homeopathy • Aikido • Yoga • Meditation • Craniosacral • Feldenkrais • Nutrition Consulting • Support For Parents • Nonviolent Communication • Music Lessons	• Traditional Chinese Medicine • Ayurveda • Drumming • Wilderness Therapy • Massage • Light Therapy • Developmental Optometry • Safe School Ambassadors	• Aikido • Yoga • Meditation • Support For Parents • Nonviolent Communication • Nutrition Consulting • EMDR • Hypnotherapy • Biofeedback • Chiropractic • Osteopathy

On Our Own We Would Try: • Bedtime Stories and Chats • Less or No TV, Movies, Video/Computer Games • Wholesome Pleasures • Replace sodas, juices, sugars, fats, fast foods with water, veggies, whole grains, nuts, protein, fruit, slow food • Long Walks/Hikes • Nature • Back Rubs and Foot Massages • Pets

. . . .

For Parents: • Make sure that you protect your child or youth from the above abuses. • This may bring up painful memories of your own upbringing and childhood & youth. • Get help from other supportive parents, religious leaders, your family practitioner, and school officials. • Listen carefully to what your child or youth is telling you about her/his experiences. • Be compassionate about his/her struggles and suffering, but let her/him know you have faith that he/she will be okay. • Instead of blaming your child or youth for misbehavior, depression, etc., determine how the learning program is not suiting his/her needs and talents and work to change the situation.

ISOLATION

This is a very complicated issue. Isolation is dangerous for children & youth. Children & youth learn how to learn and love and get along with others through interaction and conversation with other children, youth and adults. Children & youth learn self control, language and communication skills through interaction with others, particularly with other children & youth. Isolation can prevent them from learning what is real and what is not.

Without help, isolation can damage a child or youth intellectually, emotionally, spiritually and physically. Lifelong inappropriate habits can develop. If the child or youth voluntarily isolates, it can be a sign of trouble; depression, mental illness, abuse, social difficulties, drug or alcohol involvement, exposure to confusing information, and cruising the Internet without supervision. Isolation can also be due to parental anxiety, often focused on unsafe neighborhoods and inappropriate playmates. It can also be due to the child or youth having a prolonged illness. When children or youth isolate themselves it can be due to and complicated by a combination of: family patterns; lack of communication skills; genetics; prolonged stress; unresolved abuse; nutritional imbalances; exposure to environmental pollutants; depression or other mental illnesses; low self-esteem; gender confusion.

First, We Would Investigate	Second, We Would Investigate	For Long Term Support We Would Investigate
• Western Medicine • Osteopathy • Psychotherapy • Psychiatry • Nutrition Consulting • Ayurveda • Traditional Chinese Medicine • Homeopathy • Herbology • Flower Essences • EMDR • Hypnotherapy • Biofeedback • Support For Parents • Nonviolent Communication • Akido • Attudinal Healing • Expressive Arts • Safe School Ambassador	• Yoga • Music Lessons • Drumming • Massage • Aromatherapy • Craniosacral • Feldenkrais • Light Therapy • Developmental Optometry • Wilderness Therapy	• Expressive Arts • Aikido • Flower Essences • Attudinal Healing • Nonviolent Communication

On Our Own We Would Try: • Less or No TV, Movies, Video/Computer Games • Pets • Bedtime Stories and Chats • Wholesome Pleasures • Nature • Replace sodas, juices, sugars, fats, fast foods with water, veggies, whole grains, nuts, protein, fruit, slow food • Long Walks/Hikes • Back Rubs and Foot Massages

. . . .

For Parents: • Pressuring the child or youth to just "get friends" or "do something" is not advised. This tends to create more anxiety and pressure. If they could, they would.   • Find in yourself the faith that the child or youth will be okay.   • Follow the child or youth's quirks and interests.   • To start, you may have to bring the world into your home rather than taking your child or youth into the world. Having tutors, teachers, come to the home may cost more; however, the child or youth may, with their help, develop enough confidence, interests and social connection to venture into the world.

LANGUAGE/SPEAKING DIFFICULTIES

Afraid To Make A Mistake; Can't Speak Clearly; Difficulty Sequencing Thoughts; Does Not Use Rich Speech With Adverbs And Adjectives; Lacks Confidence

Language is an essential part of being human. Success in living, learning, succeeding, and social connection is very difficult without language skills. There are many aspects of language (See below).

Challenges with language development can be due to and complicated by a combination of: hearing difficulties; difficulty processing/figuring out what has been heard; voice/speaking challenges; lack of language experience; family patterns; genetic factors; physical or emotional trauma; perceptual challenges; exposure to environmental pollutants; nutrition imbalances.

Language/speaking difficulties may be due to and complicated by a combination of factors including: learning/developmental conditions; medical conditions; genetics; memory challenges; family speech patterns; over correction; lack of exposure to people talking clearly; over or under stimulating environment; family patterns of tension and anxiety; unresolved traumas and abuses of all kinds; nutrition imbalances; exposure to environmental pollutants.

Afraid To Make A Mistake: Children & youth who have been overcorrected are at risk. Learning requires making and correcting mistakes. Over-correction can eat a child or youth's confidence to risk making necessary mistakes. Relaxed speaking leads to success. For students learning English as a second language, this challenge may be due to inadequate and under-funded education.

Can't Speak Clearly: Spoken language is critical to living in the world. Being able to speak clearly makes learning to read easy.

Difficulty Sequencing Thoughts: It is important to solve this challenge as quickly as possible. Language difficulties can create ineffective attitudes toward learning, lower self-esteem, great frustration, isolation and habits of quitting. Sequencing difficulties affect the ability to write language clearly.

Does Not Use Rich Speech With Adverbs And Adjectives: Without help, this can make learning to read and write very difficult. People often mistake children or youth with this challenge as being not very intelligent. Without help, children & youth will have difficulties communicating their thoughts and feelings clearly.

Lacks Confidence: Children & youth who have been criticized, teased or ignored learn not to trust and communicate their own ideas and thoughts. Untreated, this can make learning very difficult and can establish life-long patterns of poor communication, isolation, and lack of success. A lack of language confidence is often due to exposure to well-meaning adults who lack knowledge of how children & youth learn.

First, We Would Investigate	Second, We Would Investigate	For Long Term Support We Would Investigate
• Western Medicine • Osteopathy • Precision Teaching • Nonviolent Communication • Expressive Arts • Chiropractic • Craniosacral • Developmental Optometry • Light Therapy • Biofeedback • Attitudinal Healing • Ayurveda • Traditional Chinese Medicine • Flower Essences • Homeopathy • Support For Parents • Nutrition Consulting • Environmentally Healthy Homes	• Aikido • Drumming • Music Lessons • Feldenrais	• Nutrition Consulting • Expressive Arts • Nonviolent Communication • Aikido • Traditional Chinese Medicine • Ayurveda • Herbology • Homeopathy

On Our Own We Would Try: • Bedtime Stories and Chats • Wholesome Pleasures • Replace sodas, juices, sugars, fats, fast foods with water, veggies, whole grains, nuts, protein, fruit, slow food • Long Walks/ Hikes • Back Rubs and Foot Massages • Nature • Pets • Less or No TV, Movies, Video/Computer Games

• •

For Parents: • Get a medical/developmental evaluation as soon as you notice any of these conditions. • Check out hearing, vision, coordination of the eyes. • Pay a compliment before every correction. • Play a game of making mistakes on purpose.• In relaxed ways tell family stories, read stories, play "I spy" games, read signs, and use open ended invitations to communicate like: "Tell me about that …." • Try to avoid questions that elicit a "yes" or "no" response. • Ask librarians and teachers to help you learn these skills. • Learning Nonviolent Communication and teaching it to your child or youth can help them and you.

LANGUAGE/WRITTEN PROBLEMS

Difficulty Communicating Easily And Clearly; Dyslexia; Dysgraphia; Afraid To Make A Mistake So Does Not Try; Difficulty Sequencing Thoughts So Writing Does Not Make Sense; Does Not Know About Sentences And Paragraphs; Does Not Know Writing Strategies; Does Not Know How To Put Ideas Into Words Or Written Words; Does Not Use Rich Speech Or Written Language With Descriptive Words And Complex Sentences

Speaking is a very complicated skill that we take for granted. Writing language is even more complicated. Writing well is a remarkable achievement for children & youth. Learning to write well and effortlessly is easier when a child or youth can speak clearly, has a large vocabulary and uses descriptive words and phrases. Having a large vocabulary depends on hearing a great deal of rich, descriptive language and then having opportunities to use the words. Descriptive language is more easily learned through example by hearing and talking.

Written language challenges can be due to or complicated by: learning/developmental challenges; dyslexia; dysgraphia; genetics; family patterns; vision/hearing challenges; coordination difficulties; medical conditions; insufficient teaching and practice; adult over/under expectation; challenges from unresolved shock, abuses and other traumas; inability to relax and think; coordination challenges; emotional turmoil; memory challenges; body chemistry imbalances; nutrition imbalances; allergies and exposure to environmental pollutants.

Dysgraphia and Dyslexia: are neurological conditions that can cause various levels of difficulties in reading, spelling and writing language. They can be complicated by other factors and learning challenges.

Dysgraphia: is the term describing difficulty in the ability to write due to difficulties with eye-hand co-ordination.

Dyslexia: is the term describing difficulty reading and spelling.

Afraid To Make A Mistake So Does Not Try To Communicate: Without help, this can seriously slow school performance. It can create ineffective attitudes towards learning and habits of quitting and lower self-esteem.

Difficulty Sequencing Thoughts So Writing Does Not Make Sense: Without relaxed help, this can create failure at school and adulthood.

Does Not Know About Sentences And Paragraphs: Learning about sentences and paragraphs is a natural step in written language development. Not knowing this can be due to and complicated by a combination of a lack of effective instruction, premature expectations and/or a lack of sufficient practice.

Does Not Know Writing Strategies/Does Not Know How To Put Ideas Into Words or Written Words: It is important to solve these challenges quickly. Not knowing these skills can create habits of quitting and ineffective attitudes towards learning and can lower self-esteem.

Does Not Use Rich Speech Or Written Language With Descriptive Words (adverbs and adjectives) And Two Part Sentences: Without help, learning to communicate effectively using written language is extremely difficult. A lack of this skill can often contribute to a lack of success in school and adulthood—especially with society's use of computer communication.

First, We Would Investigate	Second, We Would Investigate	For Long Term Support We Would Investigate
• Western Medicine • Osteopathy • Feldenkrais • Nonviolent Communication • Precision Teaching • Craniosacral • Biofeedback • Expressive Arts • Chiropractic • Developmental Optometry • Light Therapy • Biofeedback • Aikido • Ayurveda • Traditional Chinese Medicine • Flower Essences • Homeopathy • Support For Parents • Nutrition Consulting • Environmentally Healthy Homes • Support For Parents	• EMDR • Hypnotherapy • Attitudinal Healing • Music Lessons • Drumming • Herbology	• Precision Teaching • Developmental Optometry • Light Therapy • Flower Essences • Traditional Chinese Medicine • Homeopathy • Ayurveda

On Our Own We Would Try: • Bedtime Stories and Chats • Wholesome Pleasures • Back Rubs and Foot Massages • Replace sodas, juices, sugars, fats, fast foods with water, veggies, whole grains, nuts, protein, fruit, slow food • Long Walks/Hikes • Nature • Pets • Less or No TV, Movies, Video/Computer Games

• •

For Parents: • Check out hearing, vision, eye coordination. Get a medical/psychological evaluation as soon as you notice any difficulties with these. • The best way to give a child or youth a large vocabulary is to read stories rich in language to them every night (from infancy to graduating High School) and then to have talks later about the stories you read. • Frequent, easy, relaxed, interesting conversations are essential. • Make time each day when everyone in the family reads to themselves or out loud. • Play a game of making mistakes on purpose. • In relaxed ways, tell family stories, read stories, play "I spy" games, read signs, and use open-ended invitations to communicate like: "Tell me about that …." • Try to avoid questions that elicit a "yes" or "no" response. • Ask librarians and teachers to help you learn these skills. Learning Nonviolent Communication and teaching it to your child or youth can help them and you. • Pay a compliment before every correction.

LEARNING DIFFICULTIES/DISABILITIES

Children & youth with learning difficulties have difficulty learning, regardless of their intelligence. There are many different kinds of learning difficulties. Learning difficulties can affect listening, speaking, thinking, organizing, remembering, reading, spelling, writing. Without help, learning difficulties can limit a child or youth's future. Social relations and self-esteem can also be very difficult because social cues are not noticed/learned. May be caused by and complicated by a combination of: genetic factors; physical or neurological challenges with hearing/vision; discomfort from emotional and physical traumas (falls, accidents and abuses of all kinds); exposure to environmental pollutants; nutritional imbalances; fevers; prolonged stress of any kind. Occasionally a lack of training can be mistaken for a learning difficulty. Children & youth have an even harder time when they are stigmatized and stereotyped as being damaged, not intelligent, lazy.

First, We Would Investigate	Second, We Would Investigate	For Long Term Support We Would Investigate
• Western Medicine • Osteopathy • Psychiatry • Craniosacral • Feldenkrais • Biofeedback • Hypnotherapy • Precision Teaching • Developmental Optometry • Light Therapy • Environmentally Healthy Homes • Nonviolent Communication • Support For Parents • Expressive Arts • Music Lessons • Traditional Chinese Medicine • Ayurveda • Homeopathy	• Aikido • Yoga • Chiropractic • Massage • Aromatherapy • Meditation • Herbology • Flower Essences • Aromatherapy • Wilderness Therapy • EMDR	• Expressive Arts • Aikido • Yoga • Meditation • Aromatherapy • Herbology • Flower Essences

On Our Own We Would Try: • Less or No TV, Movies, Video/Computer Games • Bedtime Stories and Chats • Back Rubs and Foot Massages • Replace sodas, juices, sugars, fats, fast foods with water, veggies, whole grains, nuts, protein, fruit, slow food • Long Walks/Hikes • Wholesome Pleasures • Nature • Pets

. . . .

For Parents: • Get a medical/psychological evaluation as soon as you notice difficulties. • Try to find practitioners who are supportive of the above practices. • Check out gluten allergies. • Have enjoyable activities based on what the child or youth likes to do and is good at. • Keep life interesting but simple. • Calm homes are easier for kids with these challenges. • Get help and support from the many resources you can find on the Internet, at your local school, through your medical team.

LIFE THREATENING ILLNESS

Of The Child Or Youth; Of A Family Member

Of The Child Or Youth: Family energy gets directed to helping the child or youth who is ill. This can create social havoc within the rest of the family. It can leave the child or youth who is ill with fear and tension. Time, energy and money spent dealing with the life threatening illness can create gaps in ordinary living and learning for the whole family. It can drain the parents so they cannot provide support for each other and the child or youth's needs. The illness can create negative patterns of behavior in sisters and brothers, which can cause further stress and can slow healing.

Of A Family Member: Children & youth can develop serious challenges in self-confidence and in asking for what they want. They can become fearful, jealous, confused, guilty, moody and or uncooperative during and after the illness. It is important to give the child or youth lots of attention after the illness has passed.

First, We Would Investigate	Second, We Would Investigate	For Long Term Support We Would Investigate
• Western Medicine • Osteopathy • Psychotherapy • Psychiatry • Attitudinal Healing • Nonviolent Communication • Nutrition Consulting • Hypnotherapy • EMDR • Expressive Arts • Flower Essences • Homeopathy • Aryuveda • Traditional Chinese Medicine • Herbology • Aromatherapy	• Support For Parents • Massage • Biofeedback • Aikido	• Aromatherapy • Flower Essences • Nonviolent Communication • Support For Parents • Attitudinal Healing • Ayurveda • Traditional Chinese Medicine

On Our Own We Would Try: • Bedtime Stories and Chats • Back Rubs and Foot Massages • Long Walks/ Hikes • Wholesome Pleasures • Nature • Pets • Replace sodas, juices, sugars, fats, fast foods with water, veggies, whole grains, nuts, protein, fruit, slow food • Less or No TV, Movies, Video/Computer Games

For Parents: • Get support for the person who is ill, yourself, other caregivers, the children or youth. • Focus on as much normal living as possible. • Make sure to take rests from caregiving. • Communicate your need for support with your family, your medical team, local health departments, religious groups. • Join with other parents having this situation. • Make sure to take time for yourself.

LISTENING PROBLEMS

Can't Remember Or Easily Understand What Has Been Heard, Despite No Major Challenges Reported Through Medical Examination And Audiometer Tests; Can't Follow Directions; Does Not Pay Attention Does Not Remember; Hears Some Things And Not Others, Lack Of Focus; Needs Constant Reminding

Listening is taken for granted until challenges arise. Listening is a very complicated learned skill. Listening challenges can dramatically slow a child or youth's learning and reduce their ability for getting along in the world. Listening challenges can confuse everyone. They can be due to and complicated by: complex genetic factors; family patterns; depression or other mental illnesses; anxiety; blocked emotions – especially anger and isolation; perceptual challenges; memory habits; focusing and concentrating challenges; lack of listening training; prolonged stress; mental patterns resulting from accidents and abuses of all kinds; post traumatic syndrome; exposure to environmental pollutants; nutritional imbalances; poor hygiene; and unresolved physical difficulties.

Can't Remember Much, Despite No Major Challenges Reported Through Medical Examination And Audiometer Tests: Get a medical and psychological evaluation. Pick practitioners who are familiar with the practices listed below. Without help, difficulty listening can cause difficulties living and learning. Can make speaking and reading very challenging. It can create frustrating social challenges through the resulting inability to respond to directions, commands, directions, and social cues.

Can't Follow Directions: Without help, listening challenges can negatively affect success in living and learning, even into adulthood. They can also produce academic challenges. Directions, instructions and warnings can be missed.

Does Not Pay Attention: Without help, this can become habitual. Children can learn how to not listen. They miss much learning by doing this. This challenge can also be due to, and complicated by, a combination of factors including: being preoccupied with painful thoughts and memories, resisting authority, choosing to be isolated, seeking negative attention, family patterns of not paying attention, a lack of training.

Does Not Remember: Without help, this can make much learning extremely difficult and can reduce self-esteem. This can lead other people to treat the child as not intelligent. This can also be due to a combination of factors including: blockages in the middle ear created by traumas and accidents to the head, neck, spine and pelvis.

Hears Some Things And Not Others, Blocked Ears, Lack of Focus: Put your hands over your ears when someone is talking and then every so often take you hands off and then put them back on. This on-again-off-again hearing is what some children experience. It makes living and learning impossibly frustrating. Following directions becomes extremely difficult. Everything becomes confused. This challenge is often associated with frequent ear and eye infections. It can also be caused by and complicated by a combination of factors including: injuries to the head, spine and pelvis, and vision difficulties.

Needs Constant Reminding: This nuisance can drive adults crazy which can create tension for the child. It can become habitual. It can also create an idea within the child of a lack of intelligence. Having this habit can lower self-confidence. Can also be due to and complicated by a number of factors including: attention seeking, controlling adults, needing some control in the world, family patterns, physiological challenges, unresolved emotional difficulties.

First, We Would Investigate	Second, We Would Investigate	For Long Term Support We Would Investigate
• Western Medicine • Osteopathy • Precision Teaching • Craniosacral • Chiropractic • Biofeedback • Ayurveda • Traditional Chinese Medicine • Environmentally Healthy Homes • Precision Teaching • Nutrition Consulting • Nonviolent Communication	• Drumming • Music Lessons • Expressive Arts • Aikido • Feldenkrais • Light Therapy • Developmental Optometry • Massage • Herbology • Homeopathy • Flower Essences	• Nonviolent Communication • Nutrition Consulting • Precision Teaching • Osteopathy • Craniosacral • Chiropractic • Herbology • Flower Essences • Aromatherapy • Music Lessons • Drumming • Aikido

On Our Own We Would Try: • Bedtime Stories and Chats • Less or No TV, Movies, Video/Computer Games • Replace sodas, juices, sugars, fats, fast foods with water, veggies, whole grains, nuts, protein, fruit, slow food • Long Walks/Hikes • Wholesome Pleasures • Back Rubs and Foot Massages • Nature • Pets

. . . .

For Parents: • Encourage drinking water, eating veggies, grains, protein and fruit. • Sing together. • Talk less and mean more. • Say what you mean, mean what you say, do what you say you are going to do. • Put away the TV and talk together as a family. • Learn about and practice active listening. Teach it to your child/teen. • Nonviolent Communication classes can help as well.

LOW GRADES

Without support this can escalate to even lower grades, less self-esteem, defeatism and depression. Low grades can create enormous and dangerous physical/emotional stress. They can be a sign that school programs are not appropriate. Low grades and low self-esteem may put children & youth at risk for gang participation, substance abuse, and other risky behaviors. Low grades can be caused by and complicated by a combination of: medical conditions; perceptual/learning/developmental challenges; nutritional imbalances; prolonged stress; family patterns; emotional and/or physical discomfort from physical trauma (especially head, neck, spine, pelvis) and/or abuses of all kinds; environmental pollutants; unresolved emotional difficulties; depression and other mental illness; loneliness; grief; over expectations or under expectations; substance abuse.

First, We Would Investigate	Second, We Would Investigate	For Long Term Support We Would Investigate
• Western Medicine • Osteopathy • Psychotherapy • Psychiatry • Nutrition Consulting • Environmentally Healthy Homes • Precision Teaching • Developmental Optometry • Light Therapy • Flower Essences • Hypnotherapy • EMDR • Biofeedback • Craniosacral • Chiropractic • Support For Parents • Expressive Arts • Nonviolent Communication • Attitudinal Healing	• Wilderness Therapy • Aikido • Yoga • Massage • Meditation • Aromatherapy • Music Lessons • Drumming • Homeopathy • Traditional Chinese Medicine • Ayurveda • Herbology	• Precision Teaching • Expressive Arts • Ayurveda • Traditional Chinese Medicine • Nutrition Consulting • Aikido • Yoga • Meditation • Aromatherapy • Flower Essences • Homeopathy

On Our Own We Would Try: • Much Less or No TV, Movies, Video/Computer Games • Bedtime Stories and Chats • Wholesome Pleasures • Back Rubs and Foot Massages • Replace sodas, juices, sugars, fats, fast foods with water, veggies, whole grains, nuts, protein, fruit, slow food • Long Walks/Hikes • Nature • Pets

. . . .

For Parents: • Get a medical evaluation. • Get assistance on catching up from the school and by using Internet resources. • Get family, friends, community and religious organizations to help the child or youth learn study skills and get caught up academically in enjoyable ways. • Become a learner yourself. • Find and use humor and hope.

"LOW INTELLIGENCE"

Given This Label

What is intelligence? How is it measured? Many times children & youth given this label are hurt by how people react to them as a result of the label "low intelligence". There are many different kinds of intelligence. Often children & youth are considered to have "low intelligence" because the method of evaluating intelligence and/or their curriculum does not recognize their learning strengths. And, the child or youth's true challenges are often not identified by parents or teachers. Getting this label can be caused by and complicated by a combination of: medical conditions; learning/developmental challenges; genetic factors; unmet educational needs; nutritional imbalances; family patterns; too much or too little stimulation; exposure to environmental pollutants; prolonged stress; frequent illness; abuses of all kinds.

First, We Would Investigate	Second, We Would Investigate	For Long Term Support We Would Investigate
• Western Medicine • Osteopathy • Psychiatry • Nutrition Consulting • Craniosacral • Precision Teaching • Light Therapy • Developmental Optometry • Yoga • Feldenkrais • Biofeedback • Meditation • Hypnotherapy • EMDR • Ayurveda • Traditional Chinese Medicine • Homeopathy • Expressive Arts • Support For Parents • Meditation	• Aikido • Aromatherapy • Flower Essences • Herbology • Masssage • Music Lessons • Drumming • Environmentally Healthy Homes • Chiropractic	• Precision Teaching • Meditation • Yoga • Aikido • Expressive Arts • Flower Essences • Feldenkrais • Massage • Aromatherapy

On Our Own We Would Try: • Bedtime Stories and Chats • Less or No TV, Movies, Video/Computer Games • Replace sodas, juices, sugars, fats, fast foods with water, veggies, whole grains, nuts, protein, fruit, slow food • Long Walks/Hikes • Wholesome Pleasures • Back Rubs and Foot Massages • Nature • Pets

. . . .

For Parents: • Discover all the ways the child or youth is intelligent and skillful. • Find activities they enjoy and can be good at. • Remember that each child or youth has gifts which when involved help them learn more easily and quickly. • Get family, friends, community and religious organizations to help the child or youth learn study skills and get caught up academically in enjoyable ways.

LOW SELF–ESTEEM, LACKS CONFIDENCE

Low self-esteem can make living and learning very painful. It can create behavior challenges. Low self-esteem can prevent future success in adult life. It can lead to a very painful and costly life. Low self-esteem can be due to and complicated by a combination of: medical conditions; learning and developmental challenges; a lack of consistent, meaningful success; family communication patterns; over/under expectations; unrealistic expectations; family members competing for attention; lack of acknowledgement; exposure to environmental pollutants; nutritional imbalances; exhaustion; prolonged stress; emotional and/or physical discomfort from accidents, traumas and abuses of all kinds; insufficient educational programs.

First, We Would Investigate	Second, We Would Investigate	For Long Term Support We Would Investigate
• Western Medicine • Osteopathy • Psychotherapy • Psychiatry • Support For Parents • Nonviolent Communication • Nutrition Consulting • Precision Teaching • Craniosacral • Chiropractic • Feldenkrais • Attitudinal Healing • Aikido • Yoga • Meditation • EMDR • Hypnotherapy • Expressive Arts • Homeopathy • Flower Essences • Wilderness Therapy • Light Therapy • Developmental Optometry • Environmentally Healthy Homes	• Independent Study • Ayurveda • Traditional Chinese Medicine • Aromatherapy • Herbology • Music Lessons • Drumming	• Nonviolent Communication • Support For Parents • Yoga • Feldenkrais • Aikido • Expressive Arts • Aromatherapy

On Our Own We Would Try: • Less or No TV, Movies, Video/Computer Games • Wholesome Pleasures • Replace sodas, juices, sugars, fats, fast foods with water, veggies, whole grains, nuts, protein, fruit, slow food • Long Walks/Hikes • Bedtime Stories and Chats • Back Rubs and Foot Massages • Nature • Pets

• •

For Parents: • Get a medical evaluation from a practitioner who is familiar and supportive of the above practices. • Discovering how the low self-esteem got started is the first step. Learning about this may be painful for the family. • Facing the child or youth's low self-esteem may be difficult. • Taking action will boost everyone's self-esteem. • Choose to change how you are bringing up your child or youth. • Find courses in parenting from your medical team, public health department, local schools or religious organizations. • Have daily family time spent reading and also having enjoyable physical activity (for at least an hour).

LYING

Habitual

Lying is normal at young ages when children are trying out things and do not know the difference between truth and fiction. However as the child grows older, lying becomes a challenge. Habitual lying harms relationships. It erodes trust. Without help, frequent lying/avoiding telling the truth can become a lifetime habit. Habitual lying can prevent children & youth from facing reality, accepting consequences and getting on with living and learning. Lying feeds patterns of fear, avoidance. Lying tries to control situations and other people. Often children & youth lie when they have been criticized for their thoughts and when they have been frightened by punishment or seeing other children or youth punished. Children & youth's thinking and feelings can be distorted. The causes of lying can be due to and complicated by combinations of: low self-esteem; family patterns; family stress; family communication patterns; fear of and avoidance of punishment and rejection; anxiety about the unknown; confusing, prolonged stress; nutritional imbalances; exposure to environmental pollutants. Children & youth will also lie to get their own way and to avoid having someone else know and perhaps control their thoughts and actions. Children & youth who are over-controlled often lie the most.

First, We Would Investigate	Second, We Would Investigate	For Long Term Support We Would Investigate
• Psychotherapy • Attitudinal Healing • Nonviolent Communication • Support For Parents • Nutrition Consulting • Flower Essences • Homeopathy • Hypnotherapy • EMDR • Wilderness Therapy • Biofeedback • Precision Teaching • Psychiatry • Western Medicine • Osteopathy • Chiropractic • Craniosacral	• Feldenkrais • Massage • Environmentally Healthy Homes • Aromatherapy • Aikido • Yoga • Meditation • Ayurveda • Herbology • Traditional Chinese Medicine	• Nutrition Consulting • Nonviolent Communication • Aikido • Yoga • Precision Teaching • Flower Essences • Aromatherapy • Homeopathy • Herbology • Ayurveda • Traditional Chinese Medicine

On Our Own We Would Try: • Bedtime Stories and Chats • Wholesome Pleasures • Replace sodas, juices, sugars, fats, fast foods with water, veggies, whole grains, nuts, protein, fruit, slow food • Long Walks/Hikes • Back Rubs and Foot Massages • Nature • Pets • Less or No TV, Movies, Video/Computer Games

• •

For Parents: • Tell the truth yourself. • Praise truth telling. • Remember that lying is a normal part of growing up. • Acknowledging lies when you catch them takes great skill. Harsh acknowledgment can train children & youth to become better liars. • Getting support from parents with the same challenge, religious leaders, local schools can also help. • Health departments and your medical team can help you find parenting classes which will help you avoid power struggles that can cause lying. • Family meetings where children & youth are listened to by adults can also help. • Explain/discuss why telling the truth is important. • Have consistent, not harsh, consequences for lying. • Avoid rewarding or shaming lying. • Figure out why the child or youth is lying and deal with it.

MEMORY CHALLENGES

Can't Remember Details; Names Of Things; Has Small Vocabulary;
Can't Remember What Has Been Seen; Can't Remember What Has Been Heard

Without help, memory challenges can make living and learning very difficult and frustrating. They can erode self-confidence. Memory challenges can prevent learning easily and are often a major factor involved in difficulties in learning mathematics, reading, language, and following instructions. Memory challenges can be due to and complicated by a combination of: medical conditions; learning/developmental challenges; genetic factors; discomfort from unhealed physical trauma (especially to the head, neck, spine, and pelvis); abuses of all kinds; repressed emotions; chaotic family patterns; environmental pollutants; nutritional imbalances; prolonged illness; medications; a lack of instruction and practice with memory strategies.

Can't Remember Details, Names Of Things; Has Small Vocabulary; Can't Remember What Has Been Seen; Can't Remember What Has Been Heard: Often given the label "short term memory problem." Or "working memory problem." This can make learning difficult - especially in reading, writing and arithmetic. Children & youth begin to doubt their own intelligence and begin to become tense when they have to learn something. This doubt can reduce self-esteem which can further slow learning.

First, We Would Investigate	Second, We Would Investigate	For Long Term Support We Would Investigate
• Western Medicine • Osteopathy • Psychiatry • Nutrition Consulting • Environmentally Healthy Homes • Precision Teaching • Craniosacral • Light Therapy • Developmental Optometry • Biofeedback • Feldenkrais • Hypnotherapy • EMDR • Chiropractic • Ayurveda • Traditional Chinese Medicine • Herbology • Psychotherapy • Attitudinal Healing • Flower Essences • Homeopathy • Support For Parents • Music Lessons	• Expressive Arts • Drumming • Yoga • Aikido • Meditation • Nonviolent Communication • Aromatherapy • Independent Study	• Biofeedback • Aikido • Homeopathy • Ayurveda • Traditonal Chinese Medicine • Aromatherapy • Craniosacral • Developmental Optometry • Light Therapy • Precision Teaching • Environmentally Healthy Homes

On Our Own We Would Try: • Less or No TV, Movies, Video/Computer Games   • Bedtime Stories and Chats   • Replace sodas, juices, sugars, fats, fast foods with water, veggies, whole grains, nuts, protein, fruit, slow food   • Long Walks/Hikes   • Wholesome Pleasures   • Back Rubs and Foot Massages   • Nature   • Pets

• •

For Parents: • Get a medical and psychological assessment if these challenges persist.   • Identify which type of memory challenge your child or youth experiences with the help of school district psychologists and teachers.   • Get family, friends, community and religious organizations to help the child or youth learn memory skills.   • They can help the child or youth get caught up academically in enjoyable ways.

MOOD SWINGS

Without help, mood swings can be very upsetting to the child or youth, family, teachers and friends. They can be very confusing. They isolate the child or youth. Mood swings can lead to habits of lying and pretending. They affect success in living, learning and social situations into adult life. They can result in low self-confidence and being stereotyped as untrustworthy. Mood swings can be due to and complicated by a combination of factors including: medical conditions; learning and developmental challenges; family patterns; mental illness such as bipolar disorder; nutritional imbalances; exposure to environmental pollutants; discomfort from unhealed emotional and physical traumas (falls, accidents) and abuses of all kinds (physical, emotional, sexual, intellectual); prolonged stress; stress due to family turmoil; lack of success; ineffective educational programs; exhaustion.

First, We Would Investigate	Second, We Would Investigate	For Long Term Support We Would Investigate
• Western Medicine • Osteopathy • Psychotherapy • Psychiatry • Nutrition Consulting • Environmentally Healthy Homes • Attitudinal Healing • Aromatherapy • Craniosacral • Light Therapy • Ayurveda • Traditional Chinese Medicine • Homeopathy • Herbology • Flower Essences • EMDR • Hypnotherapy • Biofeedback • Support For Parents • Nonviolent Communication	• Aikido • Yoga • Massage • Meditation • Precision Teaching • Expressive Arts • Music Lessons • Drumming • Chiropractic • Osteopathy	• Aikido • Yoga • Meditation • Aromatherapy • Flower Essences • Nonviolent Communication • Support For Parents • Homeopathy • Herbology • Ayurveda • Traditional Chinese Medicine

On Our Own We Would Try: • Replace sodas, juices, sugars, fats, fast foods with water, veggies, whole grains, nuts, protein, fruit, slow food • Long Walks/Hikes • Bedtime Stories and Chats • Wholesome Pleasures • Back Rubs and Foot Massages • Nature • Pets • Less or No TV, Movies, Video/Computer Games

• •

For Parents: • Get early medical evaluation. • Daily, enjoyable family physical activity works wonders. • Avoid making the child or youth feel guilty or ashamed. • Parenting classes can help with power struggles which often result from mood swings.

MOVING OFTEN

Changing Addresses Often

Moving often can be extremely difficult for children & youth. Moving any time is stressful. Home and neighborhood stability are important parts of learning and knowing how to relax. Living in familiar surroundings helps confidence and feeling safe enough. Children & youth who move often have to get used to a new home, new neighborhood, new groups of other children & youth. Older children & youth will have a more difficult time with many moves because their friends are very important to them. Without support, relationships in later life can be shallow and having long time friends can be difficult. Progress in school can be slowed. However, if handled well, even frequent moving can be a positive experience leading to increased self-confidence and inter-personal skills. Strong family ties, good communication skills, and attending to the child or youth's developmental needs really help.

First, We Would Investigate	Second, We Would Investigate	For Long Term Support We Would Investigate
• Psychotherapy • Nonviolent Communication • Nutrition Consulting • Attitudinal Healing • Support For Parents • Aikido • Yoga • Meditation • Music Lessons • Expressive Arts • Drumming • Biofeedback • Wilderness Therapy • Flower Essences • EMDR • Hypnotherapy	• Homeopathy • Aromatherapy • Herbology • Ayurveda • Traditional Chinese Medicine	• Flower Essences • Aikido • Yoga • Meditation • Music Lessons • Expressive Arts • Drumming • Attitudinal Healing • EMDR • Hypnotherapy • Nonviolent Communication

On Our Own We Would Try: • Nature • Wholesome Pleasures • Replace sodas, juices, sugars, fats, fast foods with water, veggies, whole grains, nuts, protein, fruit, slow food • Long Walks/Hikes • Bedtime Stories and Chats • Back Rubs and Foot Massages • Less or No TV, Movies, Video/Computer Games • Pets

. . . .

For Parents: • Make sure to apologize to your child or youth for uprooting their lives often. • Spend time with family and friends who live in the same place for long periods of time. • If possible, revisit favorite places often. These visits can give a needed sense of stability. • If you have to move, involve your children or youth in the process. They may have to talk repeatedly about their feelings. Ask questions and listen.

Check out: www.parents.com.

MUSIC DIFFICULTIES

Can't Remember Words, Tunes; Can't Sing Or Play In Tune; Sounds Hurt Ears; Not Interested In Practicing

The importance of creating music is very underrated–whether singing or playing instruments. Without support, children & youth can lose or not develop an important tool for increasing physical, intellectual, emotional, and spiritual well being. Creating music can stimulate and can calm. It can help children & youth with learning mathematics, language acquisition, increasing memory capacity, and refining physical coordination. It also promotes listening skills. Music can build self-confidence and give a tool for self-expression and connecting with others. A lack of musical ability can be due to and complicated by a combination of: hearing challenges; a lack of positive musical experience; ineffective, not-enjoyable instruction and practice; lack of encouragement/acknowledgement; criticism and teasing; mismatch of instrument and child or youth; unrealistic expectations; learning and developmental factors; focusing challenges; physical and/or emotional discomfort caused by unhealed accidents, traumas and abuses of all kinds; prolonged stress; lack of relaxation training; lack of good, enjoyable, comfortable instruction, experimentation and practice; nutritional imbalances; exposure to environmental pollutants. Challenges with music can be indicators of confusing emotions. Children & youth are also often intimidated by not being able to sound like professional musicians immediately with no practice.

Can't remember words, tunes: This can make music an uncomfortable experience. With good instruction this can be overcome.

Can't sing or play in tune: This can make music a not-pleasant experience. It can lead to being ridiculed and teased which can discourage. It can create a loss of an enjoyable, relaxing experience. With good instruction, this can be overcome.

Not interested in practicing: It is extremely difficult to get better at making enjoyable music without practice. Not practicing can often be a way to get a reaction from the parents, or can be about feeling lonely. With good instruction and parental non-nagging support, this can be overcome.

First, We Would Investigate	Second, We Would Investigate	For Long Term Support We Would Investigate
• Nonviolent Communication • Support For Parents • Music Lessons • Expressive Arts • Drumming • Nutrition Consulting • Aromatherapy • Flower Essences • Craniosacral • Meditation • Yoga • Aikido • Hypnotherapy • Biofeedback • Precision Teaching • Feldenkrais • Attitudinal Healing	• Ayurveda • Traditional Chinese Medicine • Herbology • Homeopathy • Massage • Light Therapy • Environmentally Healthy Homes • EMDR • Osteopathy • Chiropractic	• Music Lessons • Support For Parents • Nonviolent Communication • Expressive Arts • Yoga • Aikido • Meditation

On Our Own We Would Try: • Less or No TV, Movies, Video/Computer Games   • Wholesome Pleasures   • Back Rubs and Foot Massages   • Replace sodas, juices, sugars, fats, fast foods with water, veggies, whole grains, nuts, protein, fruit, slow food   • Long Walks/Hikes   • Bedtime Stories and Chats   • Nature

• •

For Parents: • Have family fun with music and song.   • Make sure to pick a music teacher who the child or youth really likes.   • Have a lesson with the teacher yourself.   • Become involved with music yourself, however you are comfortable. Enjoyment is contagious.• Work with local schools and community centers to become involved in music education.   • Protect your child or youth from having musical experiences that reduce their self-esteem and joy of playing. Being rejected from trying out for something too soon can be painful.

NERVOUS

Tense - Stressed

Without help this can seriously affect learning and success in living. Staying calm enough to learn and practice is extremely difficult. Tension can be very hard on the child or youth's body and self-esteem. Being nervous, jumpy and stressed out can become habitual. It can become a focus of teasing and taunting. Tension and stress can be due to and complicated by a combination of: genetic factors; chaotic family patterns; learning and developmental challenges; depression, anxiety and other mental illnesses; Attention Deficit Hyperactivity Disorder; too much stimulation; over expectations; lack of success; living with fearful circumstances; too much stress; prolonged stress; nutritional imbalances; exposure to environmental pollutants; digestive disorders; serious illnesses; exhaustion; lack of skill relaxing; emotional and/or physical discomfort from unhealed physical trauma (accidents, falls) and abuses of all kinds (physical, emotional, sexual, intellectual).

First, We Would Investigate	Second, We Would Investigate	For Long Term Support We Would Investigate
• Western Medicine • Osteopathy • Psychotherapy • Psychiatry • Craniosacral • Chiropractic • Homeopathy • Ayurveda • Traditional Chinese Medicine • Flower Essences • Herbology • Aromatherapy • Biofeedback • Hypnotherapy • EMDR • Yoga • Aikido • Massage • Meditation • Nonviolent Communication • Expressive Arts • Nutrition Consulting	• Support For Parents • Environmentally Healthy Homes • Feldenkrais • Light Therapy • Developmental Optometry • Precision Teaching • Wilderness Therapy • Safe School Ambassadors • Independent Study	• Environmentally Healthy Homes • Flower Essences • Herbology • Aromatherapy • Homeopathy • Ayurveda • Traditional Chinese Medicine • Aikido

On Our Own We Would Try: • Less or No TV, Movies, Video/Computer Games • Back Rubs and Foot Massages • Replace sodas, juices, sugars, fats, fast foods with with water, veggies, whole grains, nuts, protein, fruit, slow food • Long Walks/Hikes • Bedtime Stories and Chats • Wholesome Pleasures • Nature • Pets

• •

For Parents: • Daily physical family activity that is enjoyable can help reduce stress. • Find family relaxations that involve being active–such as; reading to one another, doing art, community service projects, learning to make music together. • This can help the child or youth discharge tensions by having fun.

NOT LOVING OR AFFECTIONATE TO FAMILY, FRIENDS

Most Of The Time

Different cultures have different ways of being loving, kind and affectionate. When a child or youth in any culture becomes not loving, kind and affectionate it is seen as a danger signal. Without help, this can become a habit leading to isolation. Being not loving/affectionate can also lead to being stereotyped as unfriendly and "cold." Once stereotyped, it can lead to being treated in ways that can cause even further alienation. It can prevent success in living, learning and social relations. All this can build into anger, being a bully, being a victim, and being crippled by anxiety and/or depression and/or other mental illness. A lack of affection can often be due to and complicated by a child or youth's need to protect themselves emotionally from confusing events in their lives. It can be due to and complicated by a combination of: family patterns; a lack of receiving love and acknowledgement; chaotic and/or unhappy family life; lacking effective communication skills; perceptual difficulties; learning and developmental challenges; exposure to environmental pollutants; nutritional imbalances; physical/emotional discomfort due to unhealed accidents, trauma and birth traumas and abuses of all kinds; exposure to environmental pollutants.

First, We Would Investigate	Second, We Would Investigate	For Long Term Support We Would Investigate
• Psychiatry • Psychotherapy • Western Medicine • Attitudinal Healing • Nonviolent Communication • Support For Parents • EMDR • Hypnotherapy • Biofeedback • Flower Essences • Homeopathy • Herbology • Nutrition Consulting • Environmentally Healthy Homes	• Aromatherapy • Ayurveda • Traditional Chinese Medicine • Meditation • Light Therapy • Developmental Optometry • Wilderness Therapy • Independent Study • Safe School Ambassadors	• Nonviolent Communication • Attitudinal Healing • Psychotherapy • Psychiatry • Aikido • Aromatherapy • Ayurveda • Flower Essences • Homeopathy • Traditional Chinese Medicine • Herbology • Meditation • Yoga

On Our Own We Would Try: • Long Walks/Hikes • Bedtime Stories and Chats • Replace sodas, juices, sugars, fats, fast foods with water, veggies, whole grains, nuts, protein, fruit, slow food • Wholesome Pleasures • Back Rubs and Foot Massages • Nature • Pets • Less or No TV, Movies, Video/Computer Games

. . . .

For Parents: • Get medical evaluation as soon as possible. • Learn how to set limits if the child or youth becomes disrespectful or abusive. • Try to avoid having this behavior create emotional barriers to your expressing your affection for your child or youth. • Try to find and repair the causes of this behavior. • Get support from other parents whose children or youth have this challenge.

OBESITY–UNHEALTHY OVERWEIGHT

Obesity can often be physically and emotionally harmful. Without help, being overweight or obese can be very hard on a child or youth's self-esteem/confidence and can lead to chronic illness–including diabetes and sleep apnea. Obesity can make learning and living activities challenging. Criticism, worry and teasing can be very painful and can lead to lower self-esteem. Obesity can be due to and complicated by a combination of: family and community patterns of overeating and under exercising; medical conditions; chronic depression, anxiety and other mental illnesses; physical and/or emotional discomfort from unhealed accidents, traumas, and abuses of all kinds; eating high calorie, high fat, high sugar foods and sweetened drinks as entertainment; eating as a distraction and/or defense against uncomfortable emotions; genetic factors; allergies; economic poverty; prolonged stress and anxiety; exposure to environmental pollutants; nutritional imbalances.

First, We Would Investigate	Second, We Would Investigate	For Long Term Support We Would Investigate
• Western Medicine • Osteopathy • Psychiatry • Psychotherapy • Attitudinal Healing • Nonviolent Communication • Traditional Chinese Medicine • Ayurveda • Nutrition Consulting • Aromatherapy • Flower Essences • Homeopathy • Herbology • Hypnotherapy • EMDR • Biofeedback • Support For Parents	• Environmentally Healthy Homes • Aikido • Craniosacral • Yoga • Meditation • Massage • Feldenkrais • Chiropractic	• Vitamin Supplements • Nutrition Consulting • Aikido • Yoga • Meditation • Massage • Aromatherapy • Nonviolent Communication • Traditional Chinese Medicine • Ayurveda • Herbology • Hypnotherapy • EMDR • Biofeedback

On Our Own We Would Try: • Replace sodas, juices, sugars, fats, fast foods with water, veggies, whole grains, nuts, protein, fruit, slow food • Less or No TV, Movies, Video/Computer Games • Long Walks/Hikes • Bedtime Stories and Chats • Wholesome Pleasures • Back Rubs and Foot Massages • Nature • Pets

For Parents: • Be a role model for healthy eating and activity. • Enjoyable family exercise for an hour a day can also help. • Slow down the preparation and eating of food. • Eat out less. • Limit sweetened drinks and juices. • As a family, practice being hungry and get help with the troublesome feelings that can emerge. • Seek help from community support groups. If you can't find a group, start one. • Avoid extreme diets, diet pills, unless medically supervised. • Avoid teasing and nagging. • Have realistic expectations about weight loss.

PAINFUL MEMORIES

Recurring; Disabling

Without appropriate help, recurring painful memories can cause all sorts of challenges to easy living and learning. They can cause so much stress that physical, intellectual and social growth are difficult. Self-esteem/confidence can be eroded. Children & youth with painful memories often distract themselves, sooth themselves, get rid of the memories with unhealthy, risky behaviors like substance experimentation and/or abuse, unsafe sexual practices, self-mutilation, violence, as well as gang membership. Painful memories can be embedded in the body and can be evoked without warning. Can be due to and complicated by; the severity of the originating trauma; the number of times traumas occurred; the delay or lack of appropriate, family, community acknowledgement of, and help with, the emotions caused by the events originating the painful memories. Painful memories can be due to and complicated by a combination of: emotional and/or physical discomfort caused by accidents, traumas, painful events and abuses of all kinds; mental illness; lack of training and support in the skills of releasing painful memories of physical, emotional, intellectual, or spiritual accidents, trauma or abuses. Help that happens as soon as possible after traumas can prevent recurring painful memories.

First, We Would Investigate	Second, We Would Investigate	For Long Term Support We Would Investigate
• Psychotherapy • Psychiatry • Western Medicine • Osteopathy • Craniosacral • Hypnotherapy • EMDR • Biofeedback • Expressive Arts • Flower Essences • Homeopathy • Aromatherapy • Herbology • Support For Parents • Nonviolent Communication • Nutrition Consulting	• Ayurveda • Traditional Chinese Medicine • Light Therapy • Aikido • Yoga • Meditation • Music Lessons • Drumming • Wilderness Therapy • Chiropractic	• Psychotherapy • Expressive Arts • EMDR • Hypnotherapy • Biofeedback • Flower Essences • Aromatherapy • Nonviolent Communication • Wilderness Therapy • Aikido • Yoga • Meditation • Music Lessons • Drumming

On Our Own We Would Try: • Less or No TV, Movies, Video/Computer Games • Bedtime Stories and Chats • Back Rubs and Foot Massages • Wholesome Pleasures • Replace sodas, juices, sugars, fats, fast foods with water, veggies, whole grains, nuts, protein, fruit, slow food • Long Walks/Hikes • Nature • Pets

• •

For Parents: • Get help for yourself so you can help your child or youth. • Learn the skills of dealing with painful memories. • Learn and teach your children or youth healthy self soothing practices so they won't use unhealthy ways to sooth their emotional pains. • Daily enjoyable family physical exercise can help.

PARENT HOSPITALIZED

Serious Illness; Long Term Illness

Having a seriously ill parent can be very hard on children or youth who feel their own and the family's anxiety and worry. They want to help but can't. This can lead to distrust of feelings, love and relationships. Without help, it can lead to children or youth being self-centered, withdrawn, fearful, angry, anxious, depressed and suspicious. These qualities can be harmful to self-confidence and successful engagement in learning. Early help can make growing up a lot easier for children & youth. They can have more full and successful adult lives.

First, We Would Investigate	Second, We Would Investigate	For Long Term Support We Would Investigate
• Psychotherapy • Psychiatry • Western Medicine • Oseopathy • Attitudinal Healing • Nutrition Consulting • Meditation • Flower Essences • Homeopathy • Herbology • EMDR • Hypnotherapy • Nonviolent Communication • Support For Parents	• Aromatherapy • Aikido • Yoga • Music Lessons • Drumming • Expressive Arts • Music Therapy • Ayurveda • Traditional Chinese Medicine	• Nutrition Consulting • Meditation • Expressive Arts • Attitudinal Healing • Flower Essences • Aromatherapy

On Our Own We Would Try: • Pets • Bedtime Stories and Chats • Wholesome Pleasures • Back Rubs and Foot Massages • Replace sodas, juices, sugars, fats, fast foods with water, veggies, whole grains, nuts, protein, fruit, slow food • Long Walks/Hikes • Nature • Less or No TV, Movies, Video/Computer Games.

. . . .

For Parents: • Many hospitals have social workers and therapists who can be very helpful to children & youth with hospitalized parents. • Involving friends and families can also help the child or youth get energy. • The adults in the family need to get emotional support so they can support the children or youth. • Caretakers need to take very good care of themselves to avoid burnout. • Getting respite care is very important for everyone.

PARENT/FAMILY MEMBER DYING/DEAD

Without very sensitive support, this can be devastating for surviving children & youth for the rest of their lives. They want to help but don't know what to do. They can become afraid about the health and stability of the surviving parent. They can fear being left alone for a long time. Life and love seem to become dangerous. Guilt from not being able to help prevent the death can erode self-esteem. The child or youth can become isolated, withdrawn, anxious, tense, hyper-vigilant and even ill. Children & youth often get confused, thinking they caused the death and/or that they could have prevented it, etc. Children & youth may seek attention and energy in inappropriate ways because all the family energy is going toward the dying/dead person. Family shock, misunderstanding children & youth's normal needs during grieving, insufficient communication skills, discomfort with intense feelings may prevent other family members from seeing the needs of the child or youth, especially for grieving. Unexpressed grief can effect physical, intellectual and emotional growth. School performance can drop considerably. Negative effects can surface years later in many forms of suffering. Surviving children or youth often have difficulty making good decisions for themselves. Children & youth's behavior communicates their emotions, particularly, grief, loneliness, pain and confusion. Fortunately, there are many resources available to make children & youth's lives easier with the death of a parent or family member.

First, We Would Investigate	Second, We Would Investigate	For Long Term Support We Would Investigate
• Psychotherapy • Psychiatry • Attitudinal Healing • Expressive Arts • Nutrition Consulting • EMDR • Flower Essences • Homeopathy • Herbology • Aromatherapy • Massage • Support For Parents • Nonviolent Communication • Meditation	• Traditional Chinese Medicine • Ayurveda • Music Lessons • Drumming • Yoga • Wilderness Therapy • Biofeedback • Hypnotherapy	• Psychotherapy • Attitudinal Healing • Expressive Arts • Nutrition Consulting • EMDR • Hypnotherapy • Flower Essences • Herbology • Aromatherapy • Support For Parents • Nonviolent Communication

On Our Own We Would Try: • Pets • Less or No TV, Movies, Video/Computer Games • Bedtime Stories and Chats • Wholesome Pleasures • Back Rubs and Foot Massages • Replace sodas, juices, sugars, fats, fast foods with water, veggies, whole grains, nuts, protein, fruit, slow food • Long Walks/Hikes • Nature

• •

For Parents: • Seek support from community grief groups available through public health departments, hospice, religious organizations. • Daily physical enjoyable family activity can be helpful. • Allow yourself and your children or youth to grieve fully. Grief takes time.

PARENTAL ADDICTION

Alcoholism; Drugs; Food; Gambling; Shopping; Pornography; Sex; Violence; Workaholism

Children & youth need a great deal of extra support when one or both parents have addictions of any kind. Addictions rob children & youth of their parents' time, attention, connection. Addicted parents often model harmful behaviors and communication styles. Parental addictions make for a chaotic, unpredictable life for children & youth. Family energy is centered mainly on the parent's needs and not the needs of the child or youth. Having an addicted parent can make living, learning and achieving very difficult. All addictions are hard on children and youth. Children & youth of addicted parents may engage in unsafe behaviors such as: risk taking, unsafe sex, violence, substance abuse, gang membership. The impact of parental addictions on children & youth are often complicated by a combination of: genetic factors; emotional and/or physical discomfort caused by unhealed accidents, traumas, shocks, and abuses of all kinds (physical, emotional, sexual, intellectual); poverty; physical and/or mental illness; nutritional imbalances; exposure to environmental pollutants; family communication patterns; the child or youth's own addictions.

First, We Would Investigate	Second, We Would Investigate	For Long Term Support We Would Investigate
• Support For Parents • Nonviolent Communication • Psychotherapy • EMDR • Hypnotherapy • Biofeedback • Psychiatry • Western Medicine • Osteopathy • Attitudinal Healing • Wilderness Therapy • Flower Essences • Homeopathy • Herbology • Aromatherapy	• Nutrition Consulting • Ayurveda • Traditional Chinese Medicine • Massage • Drumming • Music Lessons • Expressive Arts • Meditation • Yoga • Aikido	• Attitudinal Healing • Support For Parents • Meditation • Yoga • Aikido • Aromatherapy • Flower Essences

On Our Own We Would Try: • Less or No TV, Movies, Video/Computer Games • Bedtime Stories and Chats • Wholesome Pleasures • Back Rubs and Foot Massages • Replace sodas, juices, sugars, fats, fast foods with water, veggies, whole grains, nuts, protein, fruit, slow food • Long Walks/Hikes • Nature • Pets

• •

For Parents: • If you are the addicted parent – get help – for the love of your child or youth. • If you are the non-addicted parent, get help as well. • Fortunately, Twelve Step Programs for every addiction and for family members can be effective. The programs exist all over the world. • Local health departments, medical teams, religious organizations and phone book directories can help you locate a program. Most cities have Twelve Step programs for families of people with addictions. • Let your love of your child or youth give you the strength to work the program. • Break the habit so your child or youth will not have to suffer. • Have daily family enjoyable physical exercise. • When possible, make amends to your child or youth for the chaos they have had to live through.

PARENTAL FIGHTING, ARGUING, FAMILY UNHAPPINESS

Frequent; Ongoing

Without assistance for both children & youth and their parents, this sort of thing can slow learning and teach patterns that can last into adulthood. Without assistance, children & youth tend to copy their family patterns when they grow up. Children & youth learn to be both bullies, victims and unsuccessful communicators. They are stopped from learning how to effectively get what they need. Children & youth are hurt emotionally, socially, physically and spiritually when their parents are continually arguing, fighting or are unhappy. When parents argue/fight and show unhappiness, the children or youth get frightened because they can't help their parents. This fear takes energy away from living, growing and learning. Children & youth exposed to frequent parental fighting can become anxious and/or depressed. Parents who often argue or physically fight show their unhappiness these ways for a number of reasons including: being exhausted, frightened, lonely and needing energy; trying to get their own way; copying patterns learned in childhood during the parents' own childhoods; poor role models for being parents; lack of self awareness; lack of communication training; prolonged depression/anxiety or other mental illness; addictions; financial stresses; low self-esteem; nutritional imbalances; exposure to environmental pollutants. Such parents often have been bullied and victimized themselves, so that they cannot even imagine seeking professional or spiritual help to learn new ways of handling stress and communicating needs. Such parents are often unaware of the pain they cause their children or youth.

First, We Would Investigate	Second, We Would Investigate	For Long Term Support We Would Investigate
For Parents: • Support For Parents • Psychotherapy • Nutrition Consulting • Nonviolent Communication • EMDR • Hypnotherapy • Biofeedback • Psychiatry • Flower Essences • Aromatherapy • Craniosacral • Massage • Attitudinal Healing • Wilderness Therapy • Environmentally Healthy Homes **For Children & Youth:** • Attitudinal Healing • Psychotherapy • Nutrition Consulting • Expressive Arts • EMDR • Hypnotherapy • Aromatherapy • Flower Essences • Biofeedback	**For the Whole Family:** • Aikido • Yoga • Meditation • Drumming • Music Lessons • Ayurveda • Traditional Chinese Medicine • Homeopathy • Herbology	**For the Whole Family:** • Expressive Arts • Aikido • Aromatherapy • Flower Essences • Attitudinal Healing • Psychotherapy • Meditation • Aikido • Yoga

On Our Own We Would Try: • Wholesome Pleasures • Bedtime Stories and Chats • Back Rubs and Foot Massages • Replace sodas, juices, sugars, fats, fast foods with water, veggies, whole grains, nuts, protein, fruit, slow food • Long Walks/Hikes • Nature • Pets • Less or No TV, Movies, Video/Computer Games

· ·

For Parents: • This is an important family pattern for you to change. If you can't change this pattern, your children or youth will have to or they will pass it on to your grandchildren. • Find other parents who have the same challenge and support each other in protecting your children or youth by freeing yourselves from fighting habits. • Learn some alternative methods of expression and problem solving. • Focus on the love you have for your children or youth to give you courage to get over your fears of changing these patterns. • Healing this pattern of fighting/arguing can often involve remembering painful events from your own childhood. Don't try to do this change alone. • Get some assistance or at least some company of people who also want to change.

PARENTAL WORRY ABOUT THE CHILD OR YOUTH

Habitual; Ongoing

There is healthy parental concern and then there is the ongoing habit of worrying. Habitual parental worry diminishes a child or youth's self-confidence and self-esteem. Worrying parents expect difficulty for the child or youth or expect that the child or youth will not be able to handle whatever challenges arise. Children & youth are very sensitive to parental emotions and attitudes. Parental worry teaches children & youth not to trust themselves and to expect difficulty. All this often can make success difficult in later life. Parental worry teaches children & youth to have fear and anxiety and to believe that getting help is very difficult. Parental worries may be due to and complicated by a combination of: parents having had little real help themselves as children & youths; having had many frightening experiences as children, youth and adults; having not experienced hope and success. Such parents often don't know how to support their children or youth effectively because they were not successfully parented themselves. Having a lack of support and guidance in being a parent can cause misunderstandings and can create anxiety, fear and worry. Parental exposure to stresses, addictions, financial challenges, exhaustion, nutritional imbalances and environmental pollutants may also be a factor. The effects of parental worry upon children & youth can be complicated by a combination of: parental, child or youth medical or mental illness; learning and developmental delays; physical and/or emotional discomfort from unhealed accidents, traumas and abuses of all kinds; exposure to environmental pollutants.

First, We Would Investigate	Second, We Would Investigate	For Long Term Support We Would Investigate
For Parents: • Support For Parents • Nonviolent Communication • Attitudinal Healing • Psychotherapy • Psychiatry • Biofeedback • EMDR • Hypnotherapy • Nutrition Consulting • Environmentally Healthy Homes • Flower Essences • Homeopathy • Aromatherapy • Herbology • Meditation • Aikido • Yoga **For Children or Youth:** • Expressive Arts • Aikido • Yoga • Meditation • Flower Essences • Herbology • Homeopathy • Aromatherapy • Wilderness Therapy • Attitudinal Healing • Nonviolent Communication • EMDR • Hypnotherapy • Biofeedback • Psychotherapy • Psychiatry	**For Whole Family:** • Aryuveda • Traditional Chinese Medicine • Drumming • Music Lessons	**For Whole Family:** • Attitudinal Healing • Flower Essences • Herbology • Aromatherapy • Aikido • Yoga • Meditation • Expressive Arts • Music Lessons • Wilderness Therapy • Psychotherapy • Psychiatry

On Our Own We Would Try: • Wholesome Pleasures   • Back Rubs and Foot Massages   • Bedtime Stories and Chats   • Replace sodas, juices, sugars, fats, fast foods with water, veggies, whole grains, nuts, protein, fruit, slow food   • Long Walks/Hikes   • Nature   • Pets   • Less or No TV, Movies, Video/Computer Games

· ·

For Parents: • Practice expressing genuine confidence in your child or youth's ability to problem solve and succeed even if you don't know how they will do it.   • Keep your habitual worry away from your child or youth.   • Be careful what you say to your child or youth with your voice and with your facial expressions.   • Find a support group or at least trusted friends or religious leaders and talk out your fears.

PARENTS NOT HAVING ENOUGH MONEY TO PAY
FOR HEALING PRACTICES & TREATMENTS TO HELP THEIR CHILDREN OR YOUTH

Not having enough money to help their child or youth can be very upsetting for parents and family. Such parents can feel defeated and can slide into depression, mental illness or addictions. Not having enough money to help can make the whole family feel isolated. This can play into parental hopelessness and shame, which blocks problem solving creativity. The depression, isolation, shame and despair often makes it harder to solve challenges and to ask others for assistance. All of this can create fear in the child or youth. Lack of money is often caused by and complicated by a number of parental factors including: misfortune; illness; learning difficulties as children, youth or adults; inappropriate money management instruction as children or youth; lack of retraining programs; family patterns; nutritional imbalances; exposure to environmental pollutants; addictions of any and all types; physical, emotional and/or intellectual discomfort from unhealed accidents, traumas and abuses of all kinds.

First, We Would Investigate	Second, We Would Investigate	For Long Term Support We Would Investigate
For Parents: • Nonviolent Communication • Support For Parents • Flower Essences • Homeopathy • Nutrition Consulting • Aromatherapy • Psychiatry • Psychotherapy **For Children or Youth:** • Attitudinal Healing • Flower Essences • Homeopathy	**For Whole Family:** • Aikido • Yoga • Drumming • Herbology • Aromatherapy • Expressive Arts • Meditation	**For Whole Family:** • Support For Parents • Flower Essences • Homeopathy • Nonviolent Communication • Herbology • Meditation

On Our Own We Would Try: • Less or No TV, Movies, Video/Computer Games • Replace sodas, juices, sugars, fats, fast foods with water, veggies, whole grains, nuts, protein, fruit, slow food • Long Walks/Hikes • Nature • Bedtime Stories and Chats • Wholesome Pleasures • Back Rubs and Foot Massages • Pets

. . . .

For Parents: • Read the *Healing Practices To Help Kids Grow Up Easier* appendix on Money. • Call practitioners of practices you are interested in and ask them to help you find no cost or low cost clinics where your child or youth might get help. • Some practitioner schools offer very effective, supervised, free or low cost clinics, classes, etc. • Some practices lend themselves well to less costly groups or classes.

PEER PRESSURE

Children & youth pay more attention to each other than they do to adults. Children & youth who have good open, supportive, communication with their parents and family are less likely to be led into risky behavior by their friends and social group. Children & youth who are insecure and not sure of who they are can more likely "follow the crowd" to get approval, attention, and to feel safe–even if they "know" better. Without help and good models, peer pressure can lead children & youth into risky behavior that could cause or lead to dangerous challenges for the rest of their lives. Risky behaviors include: low school performance, tobacco, alcohol and drug use/abuse, gang participation, violence, crime, unsafe sex, unsafe driving, etc. Being unable to resist peer pressure can be due to and complicated by: lack of engagement and connection with family and extended family; lack of effective models; immigrant cultural differences; lack of communication and problem solving skills; parental anxiety and worry; parental inability to teach alternatives to peer pressure; learning or developmental delays; physical or emotional discomfort resulting from unhealed accidents, traumas, or abuses of all kinds; prolonged stress; lack of success at school; family financial challenges; nutritional imbalances; exposure to environmental pollution. With support, children & youth can be strong and can resist dangerous peer pressure. Peer pressure happens throughout life. Learning how to deal with it early is good for the whole family.

First, We Would Investigate	Second, We Would Investigate	For Long Term Support We Would Investigate
• Aikido • Attitudinal Healing • Nonviolent Communication • Support For Parents • Flower Essences • Aromatherapy • Expressive Arts • Safe School Ambassadors • Independent Study • Nutrition Consulting • Wilderness Therapy • Psychotherapy • Hypnotherapy • EMDR • Precision Teaching • Massage • Meditation	• Drumming • Music Lessons • Light Therapy • Herbology • Homeopathy • Ayurveda • Traditional Chinese Medicine • Environmentally Healthy Homes	• Nonviolent Communication • Safe School Ambassadors • Independent Study • Meditation • Aikido • Yoga • Attitudinal Healing • Support For Parents • Flower Essences • Homeopathy • Expressive Arts • Nutrition Consulting

On Our Own We Would Try: • Wholesome Pleasures • Back Rubs and Foot Massages • Bedtime Stories and Chats • Replace sodas, juices, sugars, fats, fast foods with water, veggies, whole grains, nuts, protein, fruit, slow food • Long Walks/Hikes • Nature • Pets • Less or No TV, Movies, Video/Computer Games • Nonviolent Communication

For Parents: • Make sure that your child or youth knows that you have faith in them and in their ability to make the right choices. • Practice responses to possible peer pressures. • Do not cave in to your child or youth's claiming "everyone else does it". Check out these claims with other parents. • Get involved with your child's life. Ask questions. Meet with other parents. • Take parenting classes as soon as you can. • Don't abandon your child or youth. Take their complaints seriously.

Check out: http://www.kidshealth.org/kid/kh_misc/about.html;
www.kidshealth.org/teen/your_mind/relationships/peer_pressure.html.

PHYSICAL ABUSE

Has Been Allowed To Be In Dangerous Situations; Beaten, Burned, Hair Pulled, Punched, Thrown, Whipped; Withholding Enough Food; Slapped, Shaken, Spanked As Punishment

Physical abuse is very complicated–it can involve the child or youth's body, sensations, mind, thoughts, emotions, social relations. Without healing assistance, being physically abused can create great difficulties learning, living, and getting along with others. Physical abuse diminishes self-esteem and confidence. It can make success in life sporadic. Physical abuse can create physical, emotional, perceptual, communication and learning difficulties. It can create distrust, fear, anxiety, anger, withdrawal and isolation. Physically abused children & youth can learn to be bullies and victims. They can become insensitive to themselves and others. Being physically abused can make growing up to be a non-abusive parent difficult. People who are physically abusive often have been physically abused themselves. Perpetrators often suffer from a combination of: mental illness; learning and developmental delays; addictions; emotional and physical discomfort from unhealed accidents, traumas and abuses of all kinds; prolonged stress; nutritional imbalances; exposure to environmental pollutants.

Has been allowed to be in dangerous situations: Without help, children & youth can have difficulty learning how to be careful because they have not been taught to discriminate between safety and danger. Such children & youth can also have difficulty trusting love. They're also being taught that they are not worthy of protection. Parents and caretakers who allow children to be in dangerous situations are often self absorbed, unaware and not present.

Beaten, burned, hair pulled, punched, thrown, whipped: Without sensitive assistance, children & youth often have difficulty recovering their sanity as adults. Often teens and adults who have been abused this way become very good at pretending that they are O.K. Even the repressed memory of such abuses can sabotage adult success in careers, relationships and being a parent. This can lead to powerful, confusing thoughts and behaviors.

Withholding enough food: Without help, children & youth who have not been given enough food can experience all kinds of emotional and physical difficulties relating to not being loved or cared for. Eating disorders often result. Such children & youth can become bullies and/or victims and can be very resentful. They can also be so hungry for attention or affection that they cannot perceive dangerous situations or people. This is one of the ways that poverty can be physically abusive.

Slapped, shaken, spanked as punishment: This is a very controversial topic. How often, how forceful, how emotionally aroused the perpetrator is, and whether other parenting techniques are being used are also very important topics for families to discuss. Such treatment teaches children & youth that violence is acceptable. Too often, parents who were treated this way do the same to their children or youth when frustration erupts. Often this sort of abuse is considered acceptable discipline. Being slapped, shaken or being spanked can be dangerous on all levels. Without assistance in releasing the psychological, physical and spiritual effects of suffering this abuse, children & youth can develop learning disabilities, inability to control themselves, inability to trust themselves, and an inability to enjoy their own bodies. Learning challenges can develop or be made worse by the long term effects of this abuse. Such children & youth stand a good chance of growing to be parents who do the same thing. This behavior is legally banned for use in the home by many countries.

First, We Would Investigate	Second, We Would Investigate	For Long Term Support We Would Investigate
For Parents: • Support For Parents • Nonviolent Communication • Psychotherapy • Psychiatry • Western Medicine • Osteopathy • Flower Essences • EMDR • Hypnotherapy • Biofeedback • Nutrition Consulting • Environmentally Healthy Homes **For Children or Youth:** • Nonviolent Communication • Craniosacral • Chiropractic • Psychiatry • Psychotherapy • EMDR • Hypnotherapy • Biofeedback • Developmental Optometry • Attitudinal Healing • Expressive Arts • Wilderness Therapy • Nutrition Consulting	**For the Whole Family:** • Herbology • Drumming • Music Lessons • Feldenkrais • Massage • Meditation • Traditional Chinese Medicine • Ayurveda	**For the Whole Family:** • Support For Parents • Nutrition Consulting • Craniosacral • Feldenkrais • EMDR • Hypnotherapy • Nonviolent Communications • Expressive Arts • Aikido • Yoga • Meditation

On Our Own We Would Try: • Back Rubs and Foot Massages • Wholesome Pleasures • Bedtime Stories and Chats • Long Walks And Hikes • Nature • Pets • Less or No TV, Movies, Video/Computer Games • Replace sodas, juices, sugars, fats, fast foods with water, veggies, whole grains, nuts, protein, fruit, slow food

. . . .

For Parents: • Get medical and mental health evaluations for the whole family. • Get assistance and support for yourself. • Protect the child or youth from future abuses. • Remember to focus on the child or youth's strengths. Acknowledge these frequently. • Get support for healing the causes of your being physically abusive so that the abuse stops. • Learn how to make amends and make them to children or youth who have been physically abused.

POST TRAUMATIC STRESS DISORDER (PTSD)

The Consequences Of Shock And Trauma

PTSD is the name given to what happens to the mind, body, emotions and spirit of people and animals who have been under prolonged stress or who have experienced horrific experiences—even once. Without sensitive support, children & youth can suffer challenges in living, learning and growing up. Children & youth's bodies, minds, emotions and spirits protect the life of the child or youth by shutting down emotionally/intellectually, or becoming hyper-vigilant. Too often adults do not want to consider that the child or youth is suffering. This results in not noticing that the child or youth is changed—either by becoming shy and withdrawn or very aggressively moody. Memory can also be effected. With sensitive help and patience, children & youth who are well loved, supported and accepted can recover more rapidly from a traumatic experience. In addition, such recovered children & youth gain new strengths and skills.

First, We Would Investigate	Second, We Would Investigate	For Long Term Support We Would Investigate
• Western Medicine • Osteopathy • Psychotherapy • Psychiatry • EMDR • Hypnotherapy • Biofeedback • Feldenkrais • Craniosacral • Chiropractic • Massage • Nonviolent Communication • Support For Parents • Attitudinal Healing • Expressive Arts • Nutrition Consulting • Herbology • Aromatherapy • Flower Essences • Homeopathy • Traditional Chinese Medicine • Ayurveda	• Drumming • Music Lessons • Developmental Optometry • Light Therapy • Independent Study • Wilderness Therapy	• Expressive Arts • Nutrition Consulting • Flower Essences • Massage • Herbology • Homeopathy • Aromatherapy • Traditional Chinese Medicine • Ayurveda

On Our Own We Would Try: • Pets • Less or No TV, Movies, Video/Computer Games • Long Walks/Hikes • Nature • Wholesome Pleasures • Bedtime Stories and Chats • Back Rubs and Foot Massages • Replace sodas, juices, sugars, fats, fast foods with water, veggies, whole grains, nuts, protein, fruit, slow food

· ·

For Parents: • Early, sensitive care can really help the child or youth for the rest of their lives.   • They need your faith, hope and willingness to stand by them.   • Protect your child or youth from your worry. They have enough on their minds.   • Develop and express compassion.   • Get help yourself so you can give the child or youth emotional, social, spiritual support.   • Acknowledge the child or youth's strengths, especially to yourself.

Check out: www.nlm.nih.gov/medlineplus; www.acestudy.org/; www.traumasoma.com/index.shtml (very technical).

READING PROBLEMS

Can't Read At All When Other Same-Age Children Or Youth Can; Can't Read Easily At Grade Level: Can't Read Out Loud; Can't Remember What Has Just Been Read Out Loud And/Or Silently; Can't Remember What Words Look Like; Can't Understand What They Have Read; Skips Words

In modern life, reading is one of the most important skills a child or youth has to learn. It is important to solve reading challenges as quickly as possible. Reading challenges can create poor attitudes toward learning. Reading challenges can lower self-esteem and can begin habits of quitting. Reading challenges make going to school frustrating and unpleasant for children & youth. Children & youth who are frustrated with school may make themselves feel better with isolation or acting in ways dangerous to themselves or others. Reading challenges can be due to and complicated by a combination of factors, including: medical conditions; communication challenges; lack of practice using descriptive language; hearing and vision challenges; prolonged stress; physical or emotional discomfort caused by accidents, traumas and abuses of all kinds; nutritional imbalances; exposure to environmental pollutants; ineffective instruction; insufficient practice; inability to relax and think due to family patterns. Reading challenges can also be created when the parents are anxious for the child or youth to read well. Reading challenges are often signals that healing deeper issues is needed.

First, We Would Investigate	Second, We Would Investigate	For Long Term Support We Would Investigate
• Western Medicine • Osteopathy • Psychiatry • Developmental Optometry • Precision Teaching • Light Therapy • Craniosacral • Chiropractic • Nutrition Consulting • Environmentally Healthy Homes • Hypnotherapy • EMDR • Biofeedback • Meditation • Flower Essences • Nonviolent Communication • Support For Parents • Expressive Arts	• Psychotherapy • Aikido • Yoga • Music Lessons • Drumming • Homeopathy • Herbology • Attitudinal Healing • Ayurveda • Traditional Chinese Medicine • Independent Study • Safe School Ambassadors	• Precision Teaching • Developmental Optometry • Craniosacral • Light Therapy • Meditation • Yoga • Aikido • Nonviolent Communication

On Our Own We Would Try: • Less or No TV, Movies, Video/Computer Games • Bedtime Stories and Chats • Wholesome Pleasures • Back Rubs and Foot Massages • Replace sodas, juices, sugars, fats, fast foods with water, veggies, whole grains, nuts, protein, fruit, slow food • Long Walks/Hikes • Nature • Pets

· ·

For Parents: • Uncorrected reading challenges severely limit a child or youth's future. Reading is a survival skill that children & youth need to thrive.   • Take action! Invest in your child or youth's future.   • It's important not to panic or make a big deal out of the child or youth having this challenge. Reading happens best when the reader is relaxed.   • Read out loud to your child or youth as much as possible—as early as possible and up to secondary graduation. Have lots of long talks about what has been read.   • Get someone to help you if this is difficult. Let the child or youth choose the reading matter and discussion talks.   • Good diet, enough deep sleep, calm home and daily exercise are also vitally important.

RELAXATION CHALLENGES

Can't Relax; Jumpy; Restless

Relaxation allows for better concentration, learning performance, health and successful relationships. Human bodies are designed to need more relaxation than stress. Without help, not being able to relax can lead to headaches, poor coordination, learning difficulties and physical pain. These challenges can be due to and complicated by a combination of: genetics; family patterns and family models; fear-producing and over-stimulating environments; nutritional imbalances; exposure to pollutants; and unresolved traumas, accidents and abuses of all kinds.

First, We Would Investigate	Second, We Would Investigate	For Long Term Support We Would Investigate
• Western Medicine • Osteopathy • Traditional Chinese Medicine • Ayurveda • Psychotherapy • Psychiatry • Homeopathy • Herbology • Massage • Biofeedback • Meditation • EMDR • Light Therapy • Nutrition Consulting • Craniosacral • Developmental Optometry • Nonviolent Communication • Flower Essences • Aromatherapy • Support For Parents • Expressive Arts	• Environmentally Healthy Homes • Chiropractic • Aikido • Drumming • Music Lessons • Feldenkrais • Attitudinal Healing	• Nutrition Consulting • Massage • Aikido • Aromatherapy • Flower Essences • Homeopathy • Nonviolent Communication

On Our Own We Would Try: • Pets • Less or No TV, Movies, Video/Computer Games • Replace sodas, juices, sugars, fats, fast foods with water, veggies, whole grains, nuts, protein, fruit, slow food • Long Walks/Hikes • Nature • Bedtime Stories and Chats • Wholesome Pleasures • Back Rubs and Foot Massages

. . . .

For Parents: • Learning how to relax is a family affair. Relaxation takes time, so make time each day and each week. • Make a priority to take a non-structured day off each week to experience the joys of relaxation. • Avoid TV and get creative. • Deep sleep, good water, good food and daily exercise are also essential to being able to relax. • Be wary of websites offering products. Some are great, many are not. • Walking, human contact, compassion, communication, loving kindness are free and work well.

Check out: websearch Relaxation Techniques; wso.williams.edu/orgs/peerh/stress/relax.html; http://search.nlm.nih.gov/medlineplus.

RUDE BEHAVIOR

Frequent; Habitual

Without help and guidance being rude can become habitual and can lead to a lifetime of loneliness and difficulties in living and learning. It can lower already low self-esteem and can lead to social difficulties in the family, school and community. Rudeness can be due to and complicated by a combination of: prolonged stress; trying out new behavior; power struggles; peer pressure; being unacknowledged and unseen; insufficient instruction about effective social behavior; family patterns and modeling; exhaustion; hunger; physical and emotional discomfort due to unhealed accidents, traumas and abuses of all kinds; nutritional imbalances; exposure to environmental pollutants.

First, We Would Investigate	Second, We Would Investigate	For Long Term Support We Would Investigate
• Psychotherapy • Nonviolent Communication • Attitudinal Healing • Nutrition Consulting • Craniosacral • Osteopathy • Chiropractic • Psychiatry • Western Medicine • Osteopathy • Flower Essences • Aromatherapy • Herbology • Homeopathy • Environmentally Healthy Homes • Support For Parents	• Aikido • Yoga • Meditation • Expressive Arts • Music Lessons • Drumming • Wilderness Therapy • Traditional Chinese Medicine • Ayurveda • Biofeedback • EMDR • Hypnotherapy	• Nonviolent Communication • Aikido • Yoga • Meditation • Aromatherapy • Homeopathy • Flower Essences • Attitudinal Healing • Traditional Chinese Medicine • Ayurveda

On Our Own We Would Try: • Replace sodas, juices, sugars, fats, fast foods with water, veggies, whole grains, nuts, protein, fruit, slow food • Pets • Less or No TV, Movies, Video/Computer Games • Bedtime Stories and Chats • Wholesome Pleasures • Back Rubs and Foot Massages • Long Walks/Hikes • Nature

• •

For Parents: • Watch your reactions to the child or youth's rude behavior habit. • Let your child or youth know that the rude, sassy behavior is not effective communication. • Model effective communication. • Take parenting classes through schools and health departments. • Learn and use Nonviolent Communication. It will have a good result.

Check out: http://search.nlm.nih.gov/medlineplus; http://california.startingouthealthy.com/index.html; www.becomingtheparent.com/subsections1/question28.html.

SARCASTIC; CRITICAL

Frequent

Without help, sarcasm and being critical can lead to isolation, loneliness and being unable to interact and learn from others successfully. Consider this behavior as communication, telling you that something is bothering the child or youth. When children or youth use criticism and sarcasm frequently, they are often letting you know that they do not feel understood, appreciated, listened to, or important. Child & youth sarcasm and criticism can be considered as ineffective ways of asking for help and assistance. Adults can see the signals that something the child or youth cannot talk about is bothering them. Sarcasm can be due to and complicated by a combination of: depression, anxiety or other mental illness; low self-esteem; being anxious; lack of effective communication skills; lacking confidence; lacking acknowledgement for talents and successes; over expectations or under expectations; isolation; family patterns and modeling; addicted parents; lack of meaningful activities; nutritional imbalances; exposure to environmental pollutants.

First, We Would Investigate	Second, We Would Investigate	For Long Term Support We Would Investigate
• Nonviolent Communication • Attitudinal Healing • Hypnotherapy • EMDR • Biofeedback • Craniosacral • Traditional Chinese Medicine • Ayurveda • Western Medicine • Osteopathy • Psychotherapy • Expressive Arts • Psychiatry • Flower Essences • Environmentally Healthy Homes • Support For Parents	• Nutrition Consulting • Aikido • Aromatherapy • Homeopathy • Herbology • Light Therapy • Developmental Optometry • Precision Teaching • Music Lessons • Drumming • Wilderness Therapy • Chiropractic	• Nonviolent Communication • Attitudinal Healing • Aikido • Aromatherapy • Flower Essences • Herbology • Homeopathy • Nutrition Consulting • Traditional Chinese Medicine • Ayurveda

On Our Own We Would Try: • Less or No TV, Movies, Video/Computer Games • Bedtime Stories and Chats • Wholesome Pleasures • Back Rubs and Foot Massages • Replace sodas, juices, sugars, fats, fast foods with water, veggies, whole grains, nuts, protein, fruit, slow food • Long Walks/Hikes • Nature • Pets

. . . .

For Parents: • Learn and use Nonviolent Communication to respond to child or youth sarcasm and criticism. • Make sure there is enough unstructured family time without distractions, so that conversations can happen easily. • Regular enjoyable family physical activity can relieve some of the tension and promote friendly communication. • Parenting classes can help establish new communication patterns.

SEEING KILLING

Of Parent, Family Member, Friend

Without careful help and emotional support this can create emotional, intellectual, and spiritual blockages that can lead to severe challenges as adults – in relationships, being able to trust, relax and learn easily. This event is a major shock for children & youth. Seeing the killing of strangers, friends and loved ones can be very upsetting and confusing for children & youth. It can stunt their emotional growth. It can create fear, anger, depression, nightmares, sleep loss, isolation and great loneliness. Can diminish school performance. Without help, can cause recurring nightmares and disabling fears. Without help, seeing anyone killed can lead the children or youth to become adult victims or perpetrators of violence. Children & youth can overcome this trauma and often become dedicated to creating safer communities.

First, We Would Investigate	Second, We Would Investigate	For Long Term Support We Would Investigate
• Psychotherapy • Expressive Arts • EMDR • Craniosacral • Hypnotherapy • Aromatherapy • Massage • Attitudinal Healing • Psychiatry • Homeopathy • Flower Essences • Support For Parents • Nonviolent Communication	• Aikido • Yoga • Biofeedback • Ayurveda • Traditional Chinese Medicine • Herbology • Nutrition Consulting • Drumming • Music Lessons • Chiropractic • Osteopathy	• Psychotherapy • Attitudinal Healing • Expressive Arts • Support For Parents • Aikido • Aromatherapy • Meditation • Nutrition Consulting • Herbology • Ayurveda • Traditional Chinese Medicine

On Our Own We Would Try: • Wholesome Pleasures • Less or No TV, Movies, Video/Computer Games • Replace sodas, juices, sugars, fats, fast foods with water, veggies, whole grains, nuts, protein, fruit, slow food • Bedtime Stories and Chats • Back Rubs And Foot Massages • Long Walks/Hikes • Nature • Pets

. . . .

For Parents: • Get help with your own and your child or youth's grieving process. • Investigate grief groups for the family. • Avoid isolation. Reach out to family, friends and community for help. • Get lots of exercise in nature. • Treat your family to flowers. • Ask neighbors and friends to help keep the child or youth in non-intrusive company. Don't hurry healing this wound. Grief takes a long time to heal or it can turn into bitterness..

SEEING STRANGER KILLED

Seeing anyone killed is very confusing and upsetting for children & youth – so much so that they often can hardly talk about it. The reactions of adults to the event are a very important model. Adults' ability and willingness to talk about the event with compassion is of utmost importance in helping the child or youth recover trust and calm. Depending upon their age, children & youth can go into shock very easily and can become withdrawn emotionally – occasionally for long periods of time. Without help, children & youth can also behave erratically, be confused, fearful or very angry. The event can create unexplained fears and nightmares and interfere with learning and success. Children & youth can become very angry, depressed and fearful if there are many killings in their neighborhoods.

First, We Would Investigate	Second, We Would Investigate	For Long Term Support We Would Investigate
• Psychotherapy • Nonviolent Communication • Attitudinal Healing • Expressive Arts • Hypnotherapy • EMDR • Craniosacral • Biofeedback • Flower Essences • Aromatherapy • Homeopathy • Support For Parents	• Osteopathy • Chiropractic • Aikido • Music Lessons • Drumming • Massage • Herbology • Traditional Chinese Medicine • Ayurveda	• Psychotherapy • Nutrition Consulting • Flower Essences • Homeopathy • Aromatherapy • Yoga • Aikido • Meditation • Biofeedback • EMDR • Hypnotherapy • Attitudinal Healing • Expressive Arts

On Our Own We Would Try: • Wholesome Pleasures • Pets • Less or No TV • Replace sodas, juices, sugars, fats, fast foods with water, veggies, whole grains, nuts, protein, fruit, slow food • Bedtime Stories and Chats • Back Rubs and Foot Massages • Long Walks/Hikes • Nature

. . . .

For Parents: • Get help from religious leaders, therapists, public health staff. • Staff at funeral homes can sometimes be helpful as well. • Make sure to have unstructured, relaxed family time where discussions and questions can arise when the child or youth is ready. • Do what you can to support the release of the shock of seeing a killing. • Get help yourself.

SELF-ABUSE

Cutting; Slashing; Self-Tattooing

Without sensitive support, cutting, slashing, and self-tattooing can be dangerous and life threatening to children & youth. This is a sign that sensitive support is needed quickly. Youth often report that these behaviors are attempts to cope with overwhelmingly painful feelings. This behavior also can be influenced by peer pressure and the desire to belong to a particular group. Self-abuse can be caused by and further complicated by a number of factors including: medical illness; depression, anxiety or other mental illness; family patterns of miscommunication; lack of family understanding; lack of being listened to and acknowledged realistically; unhealed abuses of all kinds (physical, sexual, emotional, intellectual); abandonment; isolation; loneliness; nutritional imbalances; sleep deprivation; unexpressed fear, anger, self-loathing, confusion; emotional and/or physical discomfort caused by unhealed accidents; exposure to environmental pollutants.

First, We Would Investigate	Second, We Would Investigate	For Long Term Support We Would Investigate
• Psychotherapy • Psychiatry • Nonviolent Communication • Support For Parents • EMDR • Hypnotherapy • Expressive Arts • Flower Essences • Homeopathy • Herbology • Ayurveda • Traditional Chinese Medicine • Western Medicine • Osteopathy • Biofeedback • Nutrition Consulting • Massage	• Environmentally Healthy Homes • Drumming • Music Lessons • Yoga • Attitudinal Healing • Light Therapy • Developmental Optometry	• Attitudinal Healing • Support For Parents • Nonviolent Communication • Flower Essences • Expressive Arts • Light Therapy • EMDR • Biofeedback • Precision Teaching • Nutrition Consulting

On Our Own We Would Try: • Replace sodas, juices, sugars, fats, fast foods with water, veggies, whole grains, nuts, protein, fruit, slow food • Less or No TV, Movies, Video/Computer Games • Bedtime Stories and Chats • Wholesome Pleasures • Back Rubs and Foot Massages • Long Walks/Hikes • Pets • Nature

• •

For Parents: • Get a medical evaluation as soon as possible. This is very frightening for families. • Stay calm and acknowledge what is happening. "I'm sorry and I love you" are powerful things to feel and say when you can't think of anything else. • Learn and use Nonviolent Communication to respond. • Make sure there is enough unstructured family time, without distractions, that conversations can happen easily. • Through local health departments, therapists, you can learn how to hold effective, enjoyable weekly family meetings to keep the child or youth connected to the family. • Good food, safe sleep and exercise are important and likely difficult to get to happen.

SELF-CRITICAL/PERFECTIONISTIC

Without support this habit can diminish taking chances necessary for successful and satisfying life and learning. Learning is often about making mistakes and trying again. Children & youth who are self-critical can defeat themselves before they start. This attitude often stops children & youth from enjoying their successes. This can often be covered by unrealistic confidence and bravado. Children & youth become self-critical to reduce expectations placed upon them. Being self-critical/perfectionistic can be due to and complicated by a combination of factors: low self-esteem; ineffective family communication skills; family patterns of criticism and belittlement; physical and/or emotional discomfort caused by unhealed accidents (especially even slight damage to the spine or head); traumas, abuses of all kinds; nutritional imbalances; exposure to environmental pollutants. Children & youth enjoy learning and living much more when they get over this habit.

First, We Would Investigate	Second, We Would Investigate	For Long Term Support We Would Investigate
• Psychotherapy • Attitudinal Healing • Nonviolent Communication • Expressive Arts • Homeopathy • Flower Essences • Herbology • Aromatherapy • EMDR • Hypnotherapy • Craniosacral • Aikido • Yoga • Precision Teaching • Nutrition Consulting • Environmentally Healthy Homes • Support For Parents	• Psychiatry • Light Therapy • Developmental Optometry • Wilderness Therapy • Yoga • Drumming • Music Lessons • Massage • Traditional Chinese Medicine • Ayurveda	• EMDR • Hypnotherapy • Aikido • Yoga • Flower Essences • Nutrition Consulting • Traditional Chinese Medicine • Ayurveda • Herbology • Homeopathy • Aromatherapy

On Our Own We Would Try: • Wholesome Pleasures • Replace sodas, juices, sugars, fats, fast foods with water, veggies, whole grains, nuts, protein, fruit, slow food • Long Walks/Hikes • Bedtime Stories and Chats • Back Rubs and Foot Massages • Nature • Pets • Less or No TV, Movies, Video/Computer Games

. . . .

For Parents: • Model unconditional love. • Avoid trying to convince your child or youth not to be self-critical. • Let them know you don't feel that way about their accomplishments, character, talents, appearance, etc. • Play games of making mistakes and laughing about it. • Get support from other parents whose children or youth do this.

SEPARATION/DIVORCE

Bitter, Contested Divorce/Separation; In Infancy; In Childhood; In Teen Years

Without sensitive help, most children & youth take years to recover from their parents' separation(s)/divorce–even peaceful ones. Negative reactions can be expected from the children or youth when parents draw them into the adult relationship challenges. Negative reactions can also occur even when the child or youth know that separation/divorce is a good idea due to troublesome parental addiction, abandonment, violence, or mental illnesses. Without help, life-long emotional blockages and fears of love and relationship can develop. Children & youth need calm, protection, security, predictability and relaxation to grow and learn easily. Separation/divorce should be seen by adults only as a very last resort. Sometimes separation and/or divorce is a good idea. However parents set dangerous examples when they terminate relationships with hostility rather than using problem solving skills, conversation, negotiation, and honesty. The impact of separation and divorce on the children or youth can be complicated by a combination of factors, including: the child or youth's past family traumas; depression and other mental illnesses; parents' unresolved childhood traumas, family patterns and perceptual difficulties. Other factors can include: communication skill levels; emotional intelligence levels; prolonged anxiety, physical and/or emotional discomfort from unhealed accidents, traumas and abuses of all kinds; addictions; exhaustion; nutritional imbalances; exposure to environmental pollutants.

Bitter, contested divorce/separation: Without help, this can be very difficult and frightening for children & youth and can set very bad examples for the child or youth's future relationships. Unless parents are very careful, children & youth can get "caught in the middle" and are forced to "take sides" for their own emotional safety. During any separation/divorce, children & youth are suffering loss through no fault of their own and need as much reassurance as possible. Children & youth can get very stressed during these situations–often because they are helpless to stop something that affects them. Their learning can be reduced–perhaps for years. Children & youth can become very tense, confused, angry and withdrawn. Or, they can begin breaking rules at home, school and in the community. Children & youth often believe that they are the only ones in their schools to suffer from parental conflict/separation/divorce.

In infancy: Infants do not have a verbal language to express their sense of loss; however, they can become depressed during separation/divorce. Without help, this depression can last a lifetime. Infants involved in separation/divorces need extra love, attention and touch to recover and grow. Keeping contact with both parents is important, if possible. Parents making peace is also very helpful to the child or youth's wellbeing. Infants may stop making eye contact unless coaxed into it.

In childhood: Children & youth can become so confused and tense during separation/divorce that their school performance can suffer for up to two years or more. It's important for both parents to be involved with the child or youth if possible, so the the child or youth feels loved and supported. Children & youth need to be reassured that they are not to blame for the separation/divorce. Without help, they often blame themselves and this guilt can reduce their confidence and make them feel like they are bad children or youth. They then can begin to act like bad children or youth. Children & youth often lose respect for one or both of the parents during separation/divorce. Children & youth may become overwhelmed because they want to "look after" their unhappy parents. This takes energy from the child or youth living and learning fully.

In teen years: Without help, teenagers of divorcing/separating parents can act disinterested and uncaring. They can withdraw even more than usual from the parents, becoming sullen, uncommunicative, or sarcastic and cuttingly critical. Teens can "get back" at the parents for disrupting their lives and for scaring them by becoming involved with unsavory friends and activities. Without help, teenagers can also take out their mixed emotions by hurting themselves in various ways that upset the parents.

First, We Would Investigate	Second, We Would Investigate	For Long Term Support We Would Investigate
• Psychotherapy • Expressive Arts • Nonviolent Communication • Support For Parents • Attitudinal Healing • Aikido • Psychiatry • EMDR • Hypnotherapy • Biofeedback • Craniosacral • Meditation • Nutrition Consulting • Flower Essences • Aromatherapy • Herbology • Homeopathy • Wilderness Therapy	• Ayurveda • Traditional Chinese Medicine • Drumming • Music Lessons • Developmental Optometry • Precision Teaching • Light Therapy • Feldenkrais • Osteopathy • Chiropractic • Environmentally Healthy Homes	• Attitudinal Healing • Expressive Arts • Flower Essences • Precision Teaching • Nonviolent Communication • Ayurveda • Traditional Chinese Medicine • Herbology • Homeopathy • Aromatherapy

On Our Own We Would Try: • Bedtime Stories and Chats • Wholesome Pleasures • Back Rubs And Foot Massages • Pets • Replace sodas, juices, sugars, fats, fast foods with water, veggies, whole grains, nuts, protein, fruit, slow food • Long Walks/Hikes • Nature • Less or No TV, Movies, Video/Computer Games

. . . .

For Parents: • When difficulties begin to arise in relationships try to find help from wise friends, elders, religious leaders, marriage therapists. Get and try ideas from books. Parents can profit by learning to negotiate, communicate honestly and effectively as soon as possible. • Making extra eye contact is important to the child during infancy to help the child or youth have successful future relationships • If separation/divorce cannot be avoided, get into a separation/divorce support group as soon as possible. • Communicate with ex-partners as calmly as you can, as soon as possible, using Nonviolent Communication. This can help, even if only one partner does it. Eventually two way communication will be safer and less painful. Remember you have a relationship with your "ex" through your child or youth. • Parents are advised to make peace as soon as possible–for the sake of the children or youth. • Celebrate family times with your "ex" as soon as possible. Focus on whatever love and compassion there is between you. • Suffering parents are advised to get professional counseling and support, or at least to talk with some friendly adult, rather than share their misery with their child or youth.

SEXUAL ABUSE

Definition: "Harmful touching of the child or youth's genitals, (vagina, breasts, anus, penis, testicles); Penetration of mouth, vagina or anus with body parts or objects for any unnecessary reason; Non touching abuse is exposing the child or youth to pornography or to another persons genitals; Watching/Hearing Sexual Acts–in person or media images."
www.stopitnow.com

Incest; Knowledge Of Incest Of Other Family Members; Rape/Date Rape/Gang Rape/Sexual Behavior Initiated By Someone More Powerful–By Stranger(s) Or Friends–Oral, Anal, Vaginal Penetration; Sexual Coercion; Inappropriate Touching Of The Child Or Youth's Genitals/Improper Touch Of Any Body Part–Especially Breasts And Genitals; Exposure To Suggestive Talk About Sexual Matters; Exposure To Pornography/Sexually Charged Images In Film, Magazine, Internet, Exposure To Sexual Prejudice, Exposure To Sexism/Gender PreJudice/Gender Stereotypes

Without help and even with help, sexual abuse has many difficult and harmful consequences including: physical pain; emotional pain; confusing fears; intellectual confusion; isolation; shame; loss of body feelings; loss of trust; possible guilt about feeling some pleasure; possible confusing excitement and enjoying "special" attention–to name a few. Children & youth who have suffered from sexual abuse can often grow up with: low self-esteem; confusing angers and fears, unhappiness; depression; addiction; challenges with their sexuality/sensuality; relationship challenges; inability to happily care for themselves - physically, emotionally, intellectually and spiritually. Often sexual abuse of any kind is so confusing and awful that the child or youth goes into shock and cannot remember what happened, even for decades. Abused children & youth can often live in their own world completely, "forgetting" the abuse, even as its happening. This "forgetting" process can spread to affect all aspects of learning and living. Without help many victims of sexual abuse may constantly need confirmation about who they really are throughout their lives. Without effective assistance, successful adult relationships can be extremely difficult. Continued help is often needed throughout life to reduce the stressful effects of the abuse(s). The effects on the child or youth of being sexual abused can be complicated by any number of factors including: having a previous or ongoing history of neglect; abandonment; abuses of all kinds (emotional abuse, physical abuse, verbal abuse, intellectual abuse).

Being sexually active at a young age or having sexual behavior between children of the same age can be extremely dangerous in many ways: fatal sexually transmitted disease; guilt; addiction; relationship challenges; distorted self - concept; childhood pregnancy; organ damage. Sexually active children and youth can become so sexually preoccupied that education suffers. This can often be due to and complicated by: childhood sexual abuse; low self-esteem; powerful needs for attention and affection; acceptance; premature sexual knowledge; exposure to pornography; hormone imbalances; exposure to environmental pollutants; nutritional imbalances. Some childhood sexual play/touching/exploration are normal behavior up to adolescence. Performing sexual acts usually reflects some previous exploitation by older children or self-centered abusive adults with poor boundaries.

Without help children & youth's bodies can retain the memory of the great pain involved in having oral, vaginal or anal penaration. Joints can be dislocated, muscles ripped and stretched, physical and emotional sensations lost. Without sensitive help, normal body functioning can be challenging or extremely difficult. If the abuse is remembered, the great fears and confusions that can be caused by the abuse can last for the child or youth's whole lifetime unless given effective help. Without help, unexpressed fear, rage and confusion can build up over many years and can erupt suddenly during adulthood (often during seemingly unconnected events–like staying in a motel). The shock of such sexual abuse can be locked in muscles and nerves making easy moving, feeling, thinking and learning very difficult. All of this emotional and physical discomfort can cause illnesses later in life. Thankfully, with skilled help, healing is possible.

The causes of children or youth being abused can be due to and complicated by a combination of factors including: perpetrator mental illness; repressed and unresolved childhood abuse of perpetrators; perpetrator alcohol and drug use/abuse; perpetrator low self-esteem; perpetrator having very distorted ideas about sex; lack of perpetrator consciousness and conscience; perpetrator self-centeredness; perpetrator nutrition imbalances; exposure to pollutants causing perpetrator to have bizarre thinking patterns.

Incest: Without help, incest can be one of the most damaging sexual abuses because it combines coercion, pain, pleasure and a violation of love and trust by a formerly safe family member. It can create guilt, betrayal, loss of love and confusion. These can cause great havoc in adult life unless considerable help and support are given. Children & youth are often not believed when they report incest often due to fear of family breakdown. Not being believed when reporting incest can create even more confusion, mistrust, guilt, rejection and isolation. "Telling" risks the loss of whatever appropriate love and attention is available to the child or youth. The physical sensations and pain of incest are very harmful; however, the psychological pain is even greater. Recovery from incest is very complex and difficult. The causes of children or youth being incested can be due to and complicated by a combination of factors including perpetrators having: mental illness; repressed and unresolved childhood abuse; alcohol and drug use/abuse; low self-esteem; distorted ideas about sex; lack of conscience; immature and self-centered personality structure; prolonged anxiety, depression or other mental illness; nutritional imbalances; exposure to pollutants causing bizarre thinking patterns.

Knowledge of incest of other family members: Without sensitive help, not being able to help brothers or sisters who are being incested leaves children & youth with crippling guilt, fear, shame, pain and confusion. Without sensitive help, hearing family stories of parents themselves being sexually abused as children or youth can be also very disorienting, confusing and painful for the children or youth. As with all sexual abuse, without help, this experience creates great fear and tension around intimacy, pleasure, trust, and sexuality throughout adult life.

Rape/date rape/gang rape/sexual behavior initiated by someone more powerful–by stranger(s) or friends–oral, anal, vaginal penetration: Without sensitive help, such abuse has painful lifetime consequences, notably: physical, emotional, spiritual, intellectual shock and pain. Healing can take a great deal of time. Distrust, doubt, confusion, memory loss, shame, guilt, depression, hopelessness are common and recurring emotions.

Often rage about having suffered this abuse does not come to the surface until much later in the healing process. Rape is often caused by and complicated by a combination of factors, including; perpetrator(s') mental illness; perpetrators having bizarre ideas about sexuality fed by media misuse of images of sexuality for purposes of financial profit. Shame, ignorance and discomfort about sex has also contributed to perpetrator ideas about sex/rape/gang rape. Countries with the most society-wide open discussions about sexuality have the least rape. The causes of children or youth being raped can be due to and complicated by a combination of factors including perpetrators': mental illness; lack of impulse and rage control; repressed and unresolved childhood abuse of perpetrators; alcohol and drug use; low self-esteem; exposure to pollutants causing bizarre thinking patterns. Happily, preventative and protective programs are coming into existence in some communities through the public health department, schools and child protective agencies.

Sexual coercion: Sexual coercion involves using pressure, lies, threats, tricking, blackmail, alcohol, drugs or force to have sexual contact with someone against his or her will. Sexual coercion also includes persistent attempts to have sexual contact with someone who has already refused advances. Perpetrators do this for a wide variety of reasons, including factors involving: family and community patterns; peer pressure; mental illness; prejudice; stereotyping; media images. Happily, preventative and protective programs are coming into existence in some communities through the public health department, schools and child protective agencies.

Inappropriate touching of the child or youth's genitals/improper touch of any body part–especially breasts and genitals: Children & youth need to be taught what constitutes "safe touch" and "unsafe touch". They need to learn where touch is okay and where it is not. They need to be taught who is safe to touch them and who is not. The popular "good touch/bad touch" ideas have many benefits and some drawbacks. It is a complicated issue that needs calm, comfortable, mature adult explanation. Children & youth can profit from learning verbal and physical self-defense techniques. Open communication patterns between families and children or youth are important so that children & youth can get help in releasing the emotions they feel if they were inappropriately touched. Some exploratory play is normal with young children & youth. Adults who touch inappropriately or abusively often have distorted ideas through being touched inappropriately themselves as children or youth. Happily, preventative and protective programs are coming into existence in some communities through the public health department, schools and child protective agencies.

Exposure to suggestive talk about sexual matters: Without effective help, teaching, reinterpretation and emotional release, such abuse can be confusing, frightening, depressing and can make the child or youth feel lonely and often sexually preoccupied. This type of abuse is often a precursor to more severe abuse. Insecure children & youth simultaneously often enjoy the attention. Such behavior gives children & youth damaging ideas about sex and pleasure.

Exposure to pornography/sexually charged images in film, magazine, Internet, exposure to sexual prejudice, exposure to sexism/gender prejudice/gender stereotypes: Without effective assistance in reframing and reinterpreting, exposure to pornography can give children & youth confusing ideas about sex that can prevent having happy sexual, sensual relationships as adults. Pornography gives children & youth too much information which confuses them. Many adults are uncomfortable talking with children or youth about sex, either healthy sex, or pornographic sex. In mainstream media, powerful sexual images are cleverly used to sell products to teens and adults. Children & youth need to know that pornography/media are huge industries which exploit sexuality.

First, We Would Investigate:	Second, We Would Investigate	For Long Term Support We Would Investigate
• Psychotherapy • Psychiatry • Nonviolent Communication • Support For Parents • Craniosacral • EMDR • Hypnotherapy • Aikido • Yoga • Attitudinal Healing • Expressive Arts • Nutrition Consulting • Western Medicine • Osteopathy • Flower Essences • Homeopathy • Aromatherapy • Ayurveda • Traditional Chinese Medicine • Herbology • Light Therapy	• Chiropractic • Feldenkrais • Wilderness Therapy • Drumming • Music Lessons • Developmental Optometry • Massage • Precision Teaching	• Psychotherapy • Psychiatry • Flower Essences • Attitudinal Healing • Expressive Arts • Aikido • Yoga • Aromatherapy • Craniosacral • Ayurveda • Support For Parents • Nonviolent Communication • EMDR • Hypnotherapy • Flower Essences • Homeopathy • Aromatherapy • Ayurveda • Traditional Chinese Medicine • Herbology

On Our Own We Would Try: • Long Walks/Hikes • Nature • Pets • Wholesome Pleasures • Bedtime Stories and Chats • Back Rubs And Foot Massages • Replace sodas, juices, sugars, fats, fast foods with water, veggies, whole grains, nuts, protein, fruit, slow food • Less or No TV, Movies, Video/Computer Games

• •

For Parents: • Become familiar with age-appropriate sexual behavior.   • Learn the signs of sexual abuse.   • Learn how to talk about these issues with your child or youth before anything happens.   • Ask your health provider for assistance.   • If your child or youth has been abused, get professional support for yourself so that you can be very soothing, loving, compassionate, considerate and effective in supporting your abused child or youth.• Do not try to deal with this issue alone. You may have to hunt carefully to get the right kind of support for yourself and your child or youth.   • Remember that, unless you take effective action, the confusing and painful consequences of sexual abuse will keep emerging, possibly for the abused child or youth's lifetime.   • Do not try to rush healing and recovery. It takes time.   • Give the child or youth lots of loving support, acceptance and patience.   • Know that effective recovery is possible.   • Good nutrition, safe sleep, enjoyable exercise are essential.   • There are effective preventative programs available which can help children & youth develop healthy boundaries and self-protective skills.

Check out: National Child Traumatic Stress Network: www.nctsn.org;
Med Line Plus: www.nlm.nih.gov/medlineplus; Stop It Now: www.stopitnow.com; W. Polack, author of *Real Boys* and *Real Boys' Voices*: www.williampollack.com; Reviving Ophelia: Saving the Selves of Adolescent Girls by Mary Pipher, www.marypipher.net.

SHOCK

Emotional And Psychical Effects Of Accidents, War, Natural Disasters, Abuses Of All Kinds, Beatings

When bad things happen to children & youth, their minds, bodies, emotions and spirits can go into shock, which protects them from dying or going totally crazy. Their muscles tighten up or go limp. Their memory may stop. They may shake and quiver or they may appear as though nothing happened. They may not make eye contact. They may stare off into space blankly. Without sensitive, effective help, patterns of muscular organization caused by shock can cause physical challenges later in life. Unreleased shock can also produce confusing psychological challenges, learning challenges, irrational anger and/or fear, withdrawal, isolation and nightmares. Long forgotten or repressed strong, frightening thoughts and emotions can erupt suddenly from shock–sometimes years or decades later. This can be very frightening and confusing. Children & youth can develop strong fears and angers that are confusing because the memory of the original causes of the shock have been submerged. This is especially true after accidents, abandonments, being beaten, attacked, bitten, sexually abused, raped, incested, abandoned, or being very badly frightened–such as being held down or being unprotected in dangerous situations.

First, We Would Investigate	Second, We Would Investigate	For Long Term Support We Would Investigate
• Craniosacral • Flower Essences • Aromatherapy • Homeopathy • Herbology • Western Medicine • Psychotherapy • Psychiatry • Attitudinal Healing • Ayurveda • Traditional Chinese Medicine • Osteopathy • Chiropractic • EMDR • Hypnotherapy • Biofeedback • EMDR • Massage • Nutrition Consulting • Expressive Arts • Support For Parents • Nonviolent Communication	• Light Therapy • Developmental Optometry • Aikido • Yoga • Drumming • Music Lessons • Independent Study • Precision Teaching	• Flower Essences • Craniosacral • Attitudinal Healing • Meditation • Aikido • Yoga • Aromatherapy • Herbology • Nonviolent Communication • Osteopathy • Chiropractic

On Our Own We Would Try: • Replace sodas, juices, sugars, fats, fast foods with water, veggies, whole grains, nuts, protein, fruit, slow foods • Pets • Long Walks/Hikes • Bedtime Stories and Chats • Wholesome Pleasures • Back Rubs And Foot Massages • Nature • Less or No TV, Movies, Video/Computer Games

. . . .

For Parents: • Get medical evaluation as soon as possible, preferably with practitioners who are familiar with the practices listed above.   • Release the shock as soon as possible.   • Ordinary living, good food, safe sleep, enjoyable exercise are very important.   • Patience with the child or youth is important.

Check out: www.Childtrauma.org, Parents of Traumatized Children: www.traumasoma.com/index.shtml (very technical); www.acestudy.org.

SHY/TIMID

Children & youth who are shy and timid are often more intelligent than people know. They are often empathetic and are deeply caring. Too often they don't want to bother anyone by speaking out or taking action. Being shy and timid and being treated as being shy and timid can lead to avoidance of trying, getting involved, accomplishing things which in turn can lead to a loss of self-confidence or nothing to build self-confidence upon. Shy/timid children & youth often have been punished or criticized for their thoughts, insights, wisdom and actions. They often feel trapped with lots of awareness and have fear of taking action. Often they have no one to listen to their thoughts, awarenesses and fears. Such children & youth need much support and encouragement as well as experiences that give them self-confidence. Being shy/timid can also be caused by and complicated by: a combination of family patterns; perceptual difficulties; nutritional imbalances; exposure to environmental pollutants as well as unresolved shock, trauma, or abuses of all kinds.

First, We Would Investigate	Second, We Would Investigate	For Long Term Support We Would Investigate
• Flower Essences • Aromatherapy • Homeopathy • Herbology • Ayurveda • Expressive Arts • Aikido • Traditional Chinese Medicine • Western Medicine • Psychotherapy • Psychiatry • Attitudinal Healing • Biofeedback • Independent Study • Hypnotherapy • EMDR • Support For Parents • Nonviolent Communication • Environmentally Healthy Homes • Light Therapy • Developmental Optometry • Precision Teaching • Nutrition Education	• Chiropractic • Osteopathy • Massage • Wilderness Therapy • Yoga • Meditation • Drumming • Music Lessons • Feldenkrais • Independent Study	• Flower Essences • Aittitudinal Healing • Expressive Arts • Yoga • Aikido • Meditation • Aromatherapy

On Our Own We Would Try: • Replace sodas, juices, sugars, fats, fast foods with water, veggies, whole grains, nuts, protein, fruit, slow food   • Long Walks/Hikes   • Bedtime Stories and Chats   • Wholesome Pleasures   • Back Rubs And Foot Massages   • Nature   • Pets   • Less or No TV, Movies, Video/Computer Games

. . . .

For Parents: • Remember that shy/timid children & youth are often very bright, sensitive and are more aware of things than others. Make sure to appreciate and acknowledge their natures, gifts and talents.   • Encourage self-expression.   • Forcing children & youth to be different often only compounds the shyness.   • Nonviolent Communication skills are very useful.

Check out: http://www.shakeyourshyness.com/parentingshychildren.htm; Dr. Bruce Perry's Attunement: Reading the Rhythms of the Child.

SOCIALIZING CHALLENGES

Continual Difficulty Making Friends, Playing With Others, Being Withdrawn, Shy, Fighting, Controlling, Arguing

Without help, this difficulty can lead to isolation, loneliness and continuing challenges with identity and self-esteem. Without help, this can become habitual and can lead to challenging or extremely difficult adult relationships in later life. Socializing challenges can be due to and complicated by a combination of : family patterns; perceptual challenges; physical tension from unhealed accidents; anxiety; lack of acknowledgement of talents, skills, appearance; lack of social practice; lack of social contact; lack of direction and good models; lack of communication skills and communication practice; depression or other mental illnesses; low self-esteem; lack of success; confusion; anger; abuses of all kinds; substance abuse; nutrition imbalances; exposure to environmental pollutants; racial/religious prejudice; gender prejudice; living in hostile and/or frightening environments. Can also be caused/complicated by locked cranial and spine bones which causes ongoing tension.

First, We Would Investigate	Second, We Would Investigate	For Long Term Support We Would Investigate
• Psychotherapy • Attitudinal Healing • Nonviolent Communication • Aikido • Yoga • Flower Essences • Aromatherapy • Homeopathy • Expressive Arts • Wilderness Therapy • Psychiatry • Western Medicine • Osteopathy • Nutrition Consulting • Support For Parents • Hypnotherapy • EMDR • Biofeedback • Craniosacral	• Chiropractic • Drumming • Music Lessons • Meditation • Traditional Chinese Medicine • Ayurveda • Herbology • Developmental Optometry • Light Therapy • Massage • Environmentally Healthy Homes	• Flower Essences • Homeopathy • Aikido • Yoga • Meditation • Aromatherapy • Attitudinal Healing • Music Lessons • Expressive Arts • Traditional Chinese Medicine • Ayurveda • Herbology • Homeopathy

On Our Own We Would Try: • Replace sodas, juices, sugars, fats, fast foods with water, veggies, whole grains, nuts, protein, fruit, slow food • Long Walks/Hikes • Bedtime Stories and Chats • Wholesome Pleasures • Back Rubs and Foot Massages • Nature • Pets • Less or No TV, Movies, Video/Computer Games

. . . .

For Parents: • Parental worry about this challenge can erode the child or youth's confidence.   • Get into a parent support group so you can discharge your worry about this.   • You can learn ways to effectively support your child or youth in making healthy relationships.   • The strongest tool you have to help your child or youth is your relationship with them.   • Your child or youth needs you to have faith that things will work out for them.   • Enjoy and have pleasure in your relationships–especially with your child or youth. Get professional help if this is difficult for you.   • Nonviolent Communication skills can be a big help.

SPELLING CHALLENGES

Does Not Hear The Sounds Of Words; Does Not Remember Letter Names, Letter Combinations And Letter Sounds; Does Not Transfer Knowing Combinations And Patterns From One Word To Another; Lacks Correct Pronunciation

Without help, spelling challenges can profoundly slow learning and reduce performance in school and adult life. They can be very embarrassing. Spelling challenges can severely reduce confidence, and can create much emotional stress and tension around learning and communicating. Can be caused by and/or complicated by a combination of: perceptual problems; vision and/or hearing difficulties; speech difficulties; memory challenges; low self-confidence; fear of making a mistake; prolonged stress; unresolved physical and emotional issues relating to accidents and injuries to the head and spine: genetic factors; neurological difficulties; traumas and abuses of all kinds; nutritional imbalances; exposure to environmental pollutants.

Does not hear the sounds of words: Not being able to tell the difference between sounds makes reading and spelling difficult. Standard learning tests do not measure enough sound ranges. Spelling is a complicated process that includes accurate hearing, curiosity, paying attention and remembering what has been heard. It also underlies coordination of eyes, memory and muscle movement. Children & youth can often hear some sounds and not others. Spelling challenges can be caused by a combination of genetic factors; jammed cranial bones due to accidents to the head, ears and face; eye challenges; prolonged stress; trauma and shock; memory challenges; nutritional imbalances; environmental pollutants.

Does not remember letter names, letter combinations and letter sounds; does not transfer knowing combinations and patterns from one word to another; lacks correct pronunciation: These challenges make good spelling feel extremely difficult—which leads to much frustration and loss of confidence. The tension and stress of trying to spell better often makes performance worse. Not remembering may be caused by hearing and/or eye challenges and a combination of other neurological disorganizations in the brain which can reduce memory efficiency. All of this may be caused by and/or complicated by a combination of: perceptual challenges; genetic factors; accidents or falls or blows to the head, face, neck, ears or eyes; prolonged stress; chaotic environment; infections in eyes, ears, mouth; nutritional imbalances; exposure to environmental pollutants; a lack of interesting intellectual stimulation; a lack of exposure to strategies for perceiving accurately—noticing patterns and remembering. Not being read to nightly can also contribute.

First, We Would Investigate	Second, We Would Investigate	For Long Term Support We Would Investigate
• Western Medicine • Osteopathy • Craniosacral • Precision Teaching • Nutrition Consulting • Light Therapy • Developmental Optometry • Biofeedback • Hypnotherapy • Music Lessons • Traditional Chinese Medicine • Ayurveda • Environmentally Healthy Homes • Support For Parents • Attitudinal Healing	• Aikido • Yoga • Expressive Arts • Drumming • Meditation • Massage • Flower Essences • Aromatherapy • Chiropractic	• Precision Teaching • Light Therapy • Developmental Optometry • Craniotherapy • Aikido • Yoga • Meditation • Traditional Chinese Medicine • Ayurveda • Herbology • Homeopathy • Flower Essences • Meditation

On Our Own We Would Try: • Bedtime Stories and Chats • Back Rubs and Foot Massages • Long Walks/ Hikes • Replace sodas, juices, sugars, fats, fast foods with water, veggies, whole grains, nuts, protein, fruit, slow food • Wholesome Pleasures • Nature • Pets • Less or No TV, Movies, Video/Computer Games

. . . .

For Parents: • Daily rigorous physical exercise will help.• Playing games involving noticing and memory of patterns as well as listening to stories and music can help. • Staying relaxed about poor spelling performance, and yet communicating the need to spell well are also important. • Many poor spellers have very speedy minds which benefit from learning how to slow down. • Spelling difficulties can create shame. Counteract anything that shames your child or youth. Help overcome this by giving your child or youth positive encouragement about their skills and accomplishments. • Performance anxiety needs to be addressed by helping children & youth not fear making mistakes.

Check out: www.SchwabbLearning.org; www.acestudy.org.

STEALING

Practically all children "steal" while they are learning about the moral concepts of "mine," "yours," "ours" and paying for things. Children & youth often form habits of stealing when their first attempts are not caught, and met with skillful responses that diminish the excitement and promote self-esteem and self-control. Without redirection, effective punishments & consequences, the excitement of stealing can become addictive, offering short-term satisfaction, stimulation and relief from suffering. It can be a way of connecting with friends. Association with similar children & youth encourages stealing. Habitual stealing can harm relationships, and create pain and suffering. Stealing lowers realistic self-esteem. It can lead to jail terms and loss of opportunity. Habitual stealing can lead to more harmful habits and activities. Stealing can be caused by and complicated by a number of factors including: family relationship patterns; family focus on material possessions and status; lack of family attention, enjoyment, trust and faith; feeling isolated and powerless; low self esteem; depression; boredom; perceptual problems; memory problems; poor impulse control; communication problems and blockages; unexpressed and misdirected anger; poor role models; and peer pressures. Other related factors can include: sleep deprivation; nutrition imbalances; emotional confusion; mental illness; brain injury; poverty and exposure to environmental pollution.

First, We Would Investigate	Second, We Would Investigate	For Long Term Support We Would Investigate
• Support For Parents • Nutrition Consulting • Nonviolent Communication • Precision Teaching • Hypnosis • EMDR • Flower Essences • Aikido • Psychiatry • Psychotherapy • Expressive Arts • Attitudinal Healing • Music Lessons • Wilderness Therapy	• Craniosacral • Chiropractic • Light Therapy • Biofeedback • Developmental Optometry • Meditation • Herbology • Ayurveda • Traditional Chinese Medicine • Western Medicine • Osteopathy • Massage • Yoga	• Support For Parents • Nutrition Consulting • Nonviolent Communication • Flower Essences • Herbology

On your own you can try: • Wholesome Pleasures • Long Walks And Hikes • Back Rubs And Foot Massages • Nature • Pets • Less or No TV • Replace sodas, juices, sugars, fats, fast foods with water, veggies, whole grains, nuts, protein, fruit, slow food • Bedtime Stories and Chats

• •

For Parents: • Know where you child or youth is and who they are with. • Get calming support for yourself from friends, schools, religious leaders, and therapists. • Stay connected with other parents who share your concern about this problem. • Stay connected with your child or youth's friends and their families. • Continually set good examples about theft and being part of society. • Be observant but not suspicious. • Calmly check out stories about new things. • Ensure that stolen things are returned in person with apologies and repayment consequences. • Explain the effect of any theft on others. • Avoid causing fear (which can lead to excitement). • Learn and practice Nonviolent Communication. • Express faith, forgive and ensure temptations are as secure as possible.

Check out: www.//medlineplus.gov.

STUDY SKILL CHALLENGES - CHALLENGES KNOWING HOW TO LEARN

Without help, many very intelligent children & youth have trouble learning. Learning how to learn and how to study something can stop the spiral into more and more school challenges which affect future learning, living, social relationships. When children & youth do not do well in school their behavior patterns eventually get self-destructive or overly aggressive. Self-concept and self-esteem can be eroded when learning and succeeding is difficult. Children & youth can come to believe that they are stupid and that trying to learn is a waste of time. Study skill challenges can be due to and complicated by a combination of factors including: lack of instruction on how to learn; being ill and missing important lessons; being frightened of making a mistake; living in a chaotic and frightening environment; family patterns; being teased or called stupid; not being carefully taught; intellectual abuse as well as abuses of all kinds; genetics; vision/hearing challenges; memory challenges; perceptual challenges; nutritional imbalances; exposure to environmental pollutants.

First, We Would Investigate	Second, We Would Investigate	For Long Term Support We Would Investigate
• Western Medicine • Osteopathy • Precision Teaching • Developmental Optometry • Aikido • Light Therapy • Craniosacral • Nutrition Consulting • Feldenkrais • Yoga • Support For Parents • Nonviolent Communication • Meditation • Biofeedback • Hypnotherapy • Expressive Arts • Homeopathy • Flower Essences • Music Lessons	• Environmentally Healthy Homes • Psychotherapy • Psychiatry • Herbology • Traditional Chinese Medicine • Ayurveda • Chiropractic	• Precision Teaching • Light Therapy • Developmental Optometry • Craniosacral • Meditation • Nutrition Consulting • Aikido • Yoga

On Our Own We Would Try: • Replace sodas, juices, sugars, fats, fast foods with water, veggies, whole grains, nuts, protein, fruit, slow food • Long Walks/Hikes • Bedtime Stories and Chats • Wholesome Pleasures • Back Rubs and Foot Massages • Nature • Pets • Less or No TV, Movies, Video/Computer Games

. . . .

For Parents: • There are many quick-to-read books on the subject. • Visit a bookstore and find a book that you can learn from. • Read the book over, learn the techniques and teach them to your child or youth through example. • Learn something new together that interests both of you.

SUBSTANCE EXPERIMENTATION - SUBSTANCE ABUSE

Substance abuse and substance experimentation are very dangerous. Aside from dangers to life, substance abuse can rob a child or youth of valuable learning and living skills. Substance experimentation is also very dangerous due to the exposure to a group of other children or youth who can be reckless, ignorant of risks and competing for attention. Substance use can become a barrier between the child or youth and reality. The child or youth does not learn survival and growth skills that are real. Children & youth who use substances are often medicating themselves against powerful and difficult feelings about frustrating situations they think they cannot do anything about. Substance abuse/experimentation can be due to and complicated by: low self-esteem; physical and emotional pain and discomfort caused by unhealed accidents, traumas and abuses of all kinds; isolation; poverty; little intellectual success; little social success; peer pressure; media messages; family patterns; dysfunctional family communication skills; lack of social skills; lack of communication skills; fascination with excitement, novelty, bizarre stimulation; nutrition imbalances; exposure to environmental pollutants; media models supporting substance abuse. Children & youth are often seeking relief from a lack of meaning and connection in their lives.

First, We Would Investigate	Second, We Would Investigate	For Long Term Support We Would Investigate
• Western Medicine • Osteopathy • Psychotherapy • Psychiatry • Nonviolent Communication • Ayurveda • Traditional Chinese Medicine • Chiropractic • Attitudinal Healing • Nutrition Consulting • EMDR • Hypnotherapy • Biofeedback • Support For Parents • Expressive Arts • Meditation	• Safe School Ambassadors • Craniosacral • Flower Essences • Homeopathy • Aromatherapy • Herbology • Drumming • Wilderness Therapy • Precision Teaching • Independent Study • Music Lessons • Environmentally Healthy Homes	• Expressive Arts • Nonviolent Communication • Psychotherapy • Psychiatry • Attitudinal Healing

On Our Own We Would Try: • Replace sodas, juices, sugars, fats, fast foods with water, veggies, whole grains, nuts, protein, fruit, slow food • Long Walks/Hikes • Bedtime Stories and Chats • Wholesome Pleasures • Back Rubs and Foot Massages • Nature • Pets • Less or No TV, Movies, Video/Computer Games

• •

For Parents: • It is essential to stay calm, keep communication open, avoid blame and panic, and to focus on your child or youth's skills and strengths. • Get support from other parents and groups who know about this challenge. • Your local health department, law enforcement agencies, schools and religious organizations can help you find support. • Learn how to communicate more effectively and how to set realistic protections for yourself, your family and child or youth. • It is essential to heal the sources of isolation from the family, community and peer groups not needing substance abuse/experimentation. • Twelve step programs for families of substance abusing children or youth can be very helpful.

TEMPER TANTRUMS

Temper tantrums are a normal part of growing up for infants. Without assistance, however, children & youth can develop temper tantrum habits which prevent them from learning to be more effective in getting what they want while getting along with family, friends and community. Having temper tantrums is a natural part of learning to communicate as a human being. It is necessary to know how to be heard and taken seriously. Eventually children & youth learn how to curb temper tantrums. Temper tantrums involve knowing what you want and emotional release. Some children & youth learn to use temper tantrums as ways to power struggle and be in control. Often children & youth learn that sometimes temper tantrums get them what they want by being aware of parental frustration and embarrassment around emotional release. Children & youth can get so self-absorbed and feeling impoverished that they become unaware of the needs of the rest of the family. After early childhood, having temper tantrums can be a sign that consistent assistance is needed in the form of teaching effective communication tools that work better than temper tantrums in getting attention or what they want. Having temper tantrums later in life can be due to and complicated by a number of factors including: family communication patterns; lack of training in parenthood skills; parental insecurity and embarrassment; inconsistent parenting techniques; children feeling they are not listened to; children learning how to get their own way in a family context through emotional release; children trying to get their own way through force; children trying to get attention; children learning how to be in relationship; depression or other mental illnesses; frustration; physical discomfort from unresolved accidents, shocks, traumas and abuses of all kinds; nutritional imbalances; exposure to environmental pollutants.

First, We Would Investigate	Second, We Would Investigate	For Long Term Support We Would Investigate
• Nonviolent Communication • Support For Parents • Flower Essences • Aromatherapy • Expressive Arts • Attitudinal Healing • Psychotherapy • Psychiatry • Nutrition Consulting • Environmentally Healthy Homes • Ayurveda • Traditional Chinese Medicine • Western Medicine • Osteopathy • Craniosacral • Chiropractic • Herbology • Homeopathy • Biofeedback • EMDR • Hypnotherapy	• Drumming • Music Lessons • Yoga	• Nonviolent Communication • Support For Parents • Expressive Arts • Homeopathy • Herbology • Flower Essences • Support For Parents

On Our Own We Would Try: • Replace sodas, juices, sugars, fats, fast foods with water, veggies, whole grains, nuts, protein, fruit, slow food • Long Walks/Hikes • Bedtime Stories and Chats • Wholesome Pleasures • Back Rubs and Foot Massages • Nature • Pets • Less or No TV, Movies, Video/Computer Games

. . . .

For Parents: • Ignoring temper tantrums is often a good idea. However this can be hard to do—especially if your child or youth has learned to have tantrums in inconvient places for the maximum embarrassment/harassment effect—in the middle of busy traffic, social events, etc. • Learning and teaching Nonviolent Communication skills is essential. • Avoiding a strong emotional reaction is also important. Use role play games. Play games of pretending to have temper tantrums. Put on little performances where all family members display their temper tantrum skills. This helps everyone realize how much control children, youth and adults have and how temper tantrums are attempts at controlling situations, while releasing emotional frustration in ineffective ways. • Use role playing games to teach effective ways of communication when frustrated. • Family role playing of having temper tantrums can reduce the emotional charges and show the child or youth that they are rather silly when tantruming. • Get support from friends and from professionals who know about temper tantrums. • Find Parenting classes through your local school, public health office or religious organizations. • The Internet also contains lots of information on what to do about temper tantrums. • Seek out books in libraries and bookstores that fit for your family.

TRAUMA

Emotional And Physical Effects Of Accidents, War, Natural Disasters, Abuses Of All Kinds

One of the hardest things in the world is being with children or youth who are suffering after they live through traumatic events– accidents, deaths, war, natural disasters, emotional abuse, sexual abuse, verbal abuse, physical abuse, intellectual abuse. Witnessing any these can be very traumatic as well. The effects can be physical or emotional or social or all of the above. Having unexplained physical pain, being withdrawn, depressed, moody, anxious, tense, easily startled, explosive, highly emotional, or seemingly disconnected are all very common. Some children & youth recover quickly. Others do not.

Without careful help, the effects of trauma on children & youth can last all their lives and can hold them back from being all they could have been. Giving support to traumatized children & youth is a very delicate task. The effects of trauma are very complicated, physically, emotionally, socially, intellectually and spiritually, regardless of what kind of trauma the child/teen has suffered. Trust that children/teens are very resilient if treated with skill. (See Shock above.)

First, We Would Investigate	Second, We Would Investigate	For Long Term Support We Would Investigate
• Psychotherapy • Psychiatry • Western Medicine • Osteopathy • EMDR • Hypnotherapy • Biofeedback • Flower Essences • Aromatherapy • Homeopathy • Herbology • Ayurveda • Traditional Chinese Medicine • Craniosacral • Chiropractic • Feldenkrais • Attitudinal Healing • Expressive Arts • EMDR • Support For Parents • Nonviolent Communication	• Light Therapy • Wilderness Therapy • Yoga • Drumming • Music Lessons • Developmental Optometry • Independent Study • Precision Teaching • Massage	• Biofeedback • Hypnotherapy • Aikido • Yoga • Flower Essences • Aromatherapy • Craniosacral • Chiropractic • Osteopathy • Feldenkrais • Psychotherapy • Psychiatry • Nutrition Consulting • Support For Parents • Nonviolent Communication

On Our Own We Would Try: • Pets • Long Walks/Hikes • Bedtime Stories and Chats • Wholesome Pleasures • Back Rubs and Foot Massages • Nature • Replace sodas, juices, sugars, fats, fast foods with water, veggies, whole grains, nuts, protein, fruit, slow food • Less or No TV, Movies, Video/Computer Games

For Parents: • Get skilled help as soon as possible. It is important to offer opportunities to participate in regular routines of life. • Give the child or youth the space and time to feel whatever they are feeling. • It is also helpful to let them know they are loved and that you have faith they will get through the panic. Get into a local support group for yourself. • Calm, regular, predicable routines, safe sleep, good food, enjoyable exercise, and companionship are helpful as well.

Check out: www.nctsn.org, National Child Traumatic Stress Network; www.medlineplus.gov.

UNCOOPERATIVE

Most Of The Time; Frequently

Being uncooperative can be a message about the child or youth feeling powerless, frightened, confused or angry. Being uncooperative can be an attempt to gain power and control, and it can be an attempt to avoid pain and fear. Without assistance, being uncooperative can become an ineffective habit that can last into adult life. When this happens, learning and living and having successful relationships and careers can be challenging or extremely difficult. Being uncooperative can be caused by a combination of factors including: family patterns; unpredictable environments; over or under stimulating environments; weak communication skills; physical and or emotional discomfort and pain from unresolved shocks, traumas, accidents, difficult births and abuses of all kinds; failures; low self-esteem, depression or other mental illnesses; vision/hearing difficulties; memory challenges; perception challenges; nutritional imbalances; exposure to environmental pollutants.

First, We Would Investigate	Second, We Would Investigate	For Long Term Support We Would Investigate
• Western Medicine • Osteopathy • Traditional Chinese Medicine • Ayurveda • Craniosacral • Chiropractic • Light Therapy • Flower Essences • Homeopathy • Aromatherapy • Environmentally Healthy Homes • Nutrition Consulting • Aikido • Biofeedback • EMDR • Hypnotherapy • Nonviolent Communication • Support For Parents • Psychotherapy • Psychiatry • Expressive Arts	• Developmental Optometry • Precision Teaching • Herbology • Yoga • Meditation • Music Lessons • Wilderness Therapy	• Nonviolent Communication • Support For Parents • Flower Essences • Craniosacral • Chiropractic • Osteopathy • Aromatherapy • Attitudinal Healing • EMDR • Hypnotherapy • Biofeedback • Aikido • Yoga

On Our Own We Would Try: • Replace sodas, juices, sugars, fats, fast foods with water, veggies, whole grains, nuts, protein, fruit, slow food • Long Walks/Hikes • Bedtime Stories and Chats • Wholesome Pleasures • Back Rubs and Foot Massages • Nature • Pets • Less or No TV, Movies, Video/Computer Games

• •

For Parents: • Get a medical evaluation as soon as you notice this challenge. Avoid blaming the child or youth or becoming emotionally reactive to the uncooperative behavior. • Remember that the behavior can be a communication that something is not right in the child or youth's world. • Learn and practice Nonviolent Communication to open communication lines. • Make sure that the family learns how to relax and have a good time together. • Get support from other parents of children or youth having the same challenge. Seek out the assistance of professional guides and therapists you trust.

UNDERACHIEVING

There are many kinds of underachieving. Not being able to meet a set of standards can be the result of expectations that are too high or unrealistic. Another type of underacheiving involves not being interested in achieving what adults want. Some children or youth like to learn only what they are interested in. It can appear to be rebellion. Children & youth are often expected to learn, behave, conform regardless of their type of intelligence or learning style. Without help, adults with underachieving children or youth have a difficult task. Rebellion or defeat can occur with too much pressure and expectations. Other challenges can happen with too little expectation. Yet others can happen when what is to be learned or done simply does not fit with the child or youth's uniqueness. Without help, underacheiving can lead to low self-esteem, refusal to attempt success, loss of skills needed for adult life. It can be due to or complicated by a combination of factors: genetic considerations; family patterns; family communication patterns; prolonged stress; physical or emotional discomfort caused by unhealed accidents, traumas and abuses of all kinds; unique learning styles; lack of appropriate instruction and practice; nutritional imbalances; exposure to environmental pollutants. Often children & youth can become so frightened of failure that they avoid trying anything new.

First, We Would Investigate	Second, We Would Investigate	For Long Term Support We Would Investigate
• Precision Teaching • Nonviolent Communication • Support For Parents • Craniosacral • Chiropractic • Osteopathy • Developmental Optometry • Light Therapy • Expressive Arts • Music Lessons • Aikido • Yoga • Feldenkrais • Meditation • Western Medicine • Ayurveda • Traditional Chinese Medicine • Nutrition Consulting • Environmentally Healthy Homes • Wilderness Therapy	• Aromatherapy • Flower Essences • Independent Study	• Nonviolent Communication • Precision Teaching • Aikido • Yoga • Meditation • Feldenkrais • Aromatherapy • Homeopathy • Hypnosis • Nutrition Education

On Our Own We Would Try: • Replace sodas, juices, sugars, fats, fast foods with water, veggies, whole grains, nuts, protein, fruit, slow food • Long Walks/Hikes • Bedtime Stories and Chats • Wholesome Pleasures • Back Rubs and Foot Massages • Nature • Pets • Less or No TV, Movies, Video/Computer Games

• •

For Parents: • Do whatever you can to involve your child or youth in activities they can be successful with. • Positive, enjoyable tutoring can help. • Get other people to teach your child or youth how to learn, how to study, how to keep focused and how to keep trying. • Identify and acknowledge what the child or youth is good at and interested in.

UNSOCIAL

Prefers To Avoid Social Contact; Likes To Create Social Challenges

Without help, both of these types of unsocial behavior can become habitual and can ruin living and learning well into adulthood. Some children & youth are shy and retiring because they are intelligent, sensitive and deeply care about what is happening. However, they often feel unable to stop the suffering or chaos they perceive. Others feel angry, scared, fearful, hurt, insufficient, unsuccessful and lonely. They get social contact through bullying, bothering and harassing others. These patterns can be caused by, and complicated by a wide range of factors which can include: lack of communication and challenge-solving skills; family patterns; perceptual challenges; genetics; anxiety; low self-esteem; physical and emotional discomfort caused by unhealed accidents, traumas and abuses of all kinds; depression or other mental illnesses; inability to relax; nutritional imbalances; exposure to environmental pollutants.

First, We Would Investigate	Second, We Would Investigate	For Long Term Support We Would Investigate
• Nonviolent Communication • Support For Parents • Western Medicine • Osteopathy • Ayurveda • Traditional Chinese Medicine • Craniosacral • Chiropractic • Nutrition Consulting • Precision Teaching • Light Therapy • Developmental Optometry • Attitudinal Healing • Meditation • Psychotherapy • Psychiatry • Expressive Arts • Aikido • Yoga • Music Lessons • Drumming • Flower Essences • EMDR • Hypnotherapy • Biofeedback	• Independent Study • Feldenkrais • Homeopathy • Aromatherapy • Herbology	• Nonviolent Communication • Support For Parents • Aikido • Aromatherapy • Flower Essences

On Our Own We Would Try: • Replace sodas, juices, sugars, fats, fast foods with water, veggies, whole grains, nuts, protein, fruit, slow food   • Long Walks/Hikes   • Bedtime Stories and Chats   • Wholesome Pleasures   • Back Rubs and Foot Massages   • Nature   • Pets   • Less or No TV, Movies, Video/Computer Games

• •

For Parents: • Get medical and psychological evaluations. • Get professional help. • Learning and teaching Nonviolent Communication skills is essential. • Avoiding strong emotional reaction is also important. Use role play games. Playing games of pretending to be unsocial. Have fun with this without mimicking or making fun of the child or youth. Put on little performances where all family members display their unsocial skills. This helps everyone realize how much control children, youth and adults have and how unsocial behaviors are attempts at controlling situations while releasing emotional frustration in ineffective ways. • Use role playing games to teach effective ways of communication when frustrated, angry, worried, frightened, or lonely. • Family role playing of being unsocial can reduce the emotional charges and show the children or youth that they are rather silly being unsocial. • Get support from friends and from professionals who know about unsocial behavior. • Find Parenting classes through your local school, public health office or religious organizations. • The Internet also contains lots of information on what to do about unsocial behavior. • Seek out books in libraries and bookstores that fit for your family. • Often children & youth can learn social skills by being involved with younger children. • Nonviolent Communication skills can make a big difference.

Check out: www.KidsHealth.org; National Mental Health Information Center, www.mentalhealth.samhsa.gov/15plus/aboutbullying.asp.

VICTIM

Is Picked On By Playmates, Brothers, Sisters

Without help, being a victim can ruin self-concept, self-esteem, social relations, and succeeding at living and learning into adult life. Thinking of oneself as a victim results in behaving in ways that promote more harassment, bullying, suffering and pain. Other children often pick on victims because they are frightened of the victim's helplessness and because the tormentors believe they can get away with being cruel and mean. Most perpetrators are very insecure themselves. With sensitive help, children can learn to stop this cycle. Being a victim can be caused by a combination of factors including: having low energy; unhappiness; depression or other mental illnesses; anxiety; low self-esteem; shyness; family patterns; looking insecure; lacking social training; lacking confidence; nutritional imbalances.

First, We Would Investigate	Second, We Would Investigate	For Long Term Support We Would Investigate
• Nonviolent Communication • Attitudinal Healing • Psychotherapy • Aikido • Yoga • Meditation • Expressive Arts • Feldenkrais • Drumming • Music Lessons • Flower Essences • Homeopathy • Hypnotherapy • EMDR • Biofeedback • Herbology • Support For Parents	• Aromatherapy • Independent Study • Craniosacral • Chiropractic • Osteopathy	• Nonviolent Communication • Aikido • Yoga • Feldenkrais • Expressive Arts • Music Lessons • Flower Essences • Aromatherapy

On Our Own We Would Try: • Replace sodas, juices, sugars, fats, fast foods with water, veggies, whole grains, nuts, protein, fruit, slow food • Long Walks/Hikes • Bedtime Stories and Chats • Wholesome Pleasures • Back Rubs and Foot Massages • Nature • Pets • Less or No TV, Movies, Video/Computer Games

. . . .

For Parents: • Take Aikido and Nonviolent Communication training with your child or youth. • Being a victim is a state of mind that can change. • Remember that some children & youth are never bullied. • Help your child or youth understand how frightened bullies are and how to avoid them.

VIOLENCE IN THE HOME, SCHOOL AND COMMUNITY

Without help, the fear, intensity, and emotional stress caused by violence in homes, schools and communities can lower intelligence, self-esteem, self-confidence, and can make academic achievement extremely difficult. Violence can create long lasting psychical and emotional pain, which if left unhealed can make success in adult life extremely difficult. Exposure to violence in home, school and/or community can force children & youth to become violent themselves. Joining gangs often happens as a self-defensive act.

Children & youth can become violent as a defense against feeling hopeless, powerless and/or inferior. Violence can often be a release for pent-up depression, anger and frustration. Alcohol and drugs only make the situation worse by diminishing thinking and communication skills, increasing blood pressure and impulsivity, decreasing compassion and decreasing intelligence. Without help, violence can become a habit that can last into adulthood.

Violence can have its roots in, and be complicated by a combination of factors including: lack of communication skills; parental communication skill levels; despair; frustration; hopelessness; poverty; parental addiction; overcrowding; lack of opportunity/successful future; comparison with more fortunate children & youth; exposure to ugliness; exposure to violence at a young age; physical and emotional discomfort from unhealed accidents, traumas, beatings and abuses of all kinds; exhaustion; nutrition imbalances; exposure to environmental pollutants.

First, We Would Investigate	Second, We Would Investigate	For Long Term Support We Would Investigate
• Nonviolent Communication • Support For Parents • Safe School Ambassadors • Attitudinal Healing • Meditation • Aikido • Nutrition Consulting • Yoga • EMDR • Hypnotherapy • Biofeedback • Ayurveda • Traditional Chinese Medicine • Wilderness Therapy • Psychotherapy • Psychiatry • Expressive Arts • Drumming • Homeopathy • Herbology	• Music Lessons • Feldenkrais • Flower Essences • Aromatherapy	• Nonviolent Communication • Meditation • Aikido • Expressive Arts • Attitudinal Healing • Flower Essences • Herbology • Ayurveda • Traditional Chinese Medicine • Support For Parents

On Our Own We Would Try: • Replace sodas, juices, sugars, fats, fast foods with water, veggies, whole grains, nuts, protein, fruit, slow food • Long Walks/Hikes • Bedtime Stories and Chats • Wholesome Pleasures • Back Rubs and Foot Massages • Nature • Pets • Less or No TV, Movies, Video/Computer Games

· ·

For Parents: • Become a nonviolent parent/adult as fast as you can.   • Get help for yourself and any victim patterns you have.   • Learn and teach Nonviolent Communication.   • Get involved with any organization working to stop violence.   • Become a nonviolent activist. Your example will give your child or youth security, good examples and hope.   • Keep setting good examples of being honest and safely communicative.

HEALING PRACTICES

CHAPTER 4

AIKIDO FOR CHILDREN & YOUTH

By Isaiah Wisdom,   © Copyright 2008.

Aikido Has Helped Kids With
- Confidence issues
- Dealing with bullies
- Helps children/teens avoid the traps of drugs, violence, negativity, crime and suicide
- Improves grades
- Improves overall performance in all things

Aikido Can Help In The Following Areas
Spirit: Aikido develops win/win philosophy… everyone wins.

Body: Aikido is physically challenging but not impossible, and it is good for strength training and weight loss.

Mind: Children & youth can understand their minds. They learn that the mind is a tool; therefore, they learn problem solving skills and mental discipline.

Emotions: Aikido is self-empowering no matter how the child or youth may feel. Children learn that emotions are tools.

Social: Aikido builds social skills using "no loser" games, teaching consensus, teamwork, cooperation and community activities.

Brief Description Of Aikido
- Aikido is a non-violent, non-resistant martial art from Japan.
- Aikido means unifying energy, the way of harmony.

Success With Aikido
- Kids in group homes grow up with fear because there is no order or center in their lives. When they practice Aikido they learn about their own power. They learn to speak and act for themselves but in harmonious ways.

- Children & youth with physical, psychological, and/or developmental challenges learn about their center and how to have real internal self-control.
- Good athletes and high achievers become even more skilled.

Aikido Is Appropriate For Ages
- 4 to 104

Children & Youth's Reactions To Aikido
- Joy
- More confidence
- If the child or youth is timid or frightened, they will like Aikido because it will teach them self-defense.
- Usually children are surprised that they have so much physical power.
- Children with developmental challenges may not know the names of the techniques, however they learn the moves and enjoy their power.

Extra Care Is Needed
- Make sure you tell the teacher or the head instructor about old injuries and conditions.
- Classes may have to be modified when people come with old injuries.
- Children with developmental challenges may need Aikido sessions to be modified. For instance, a child with Down Syndrome cannot understand the esoteric practice, however they can learn basic moves and how to be non-violent.

Contraindications: When Aikido Should Be Avoided
- Sometime parents and children misunderstand what Aikido is and think that aggressive moves are part of the practice.
- When children, teens and parents think that Aikido is for attacking
- If the child has certain disabilities (physical, mental or emotional) that severely impair ability to participate
- When it is used by a child to hurt others
- Anger/violence levels are out of control.

History
- Aikido is a relatively modern martial art.
- Historically, Aikido is derived from aggressive, Samurai, and war practices like Aikijitsu (or Aikijujitsu).
- After World War Two, the founder, O'sensei Morihei Ueshiba, was advised by one of his teachers, Onisaburo Deguchi, to call the practice "Aikido" (O'sensei means Honored Teacher).
- Aikido means "the way" or a way of life. The practice became one of non-resistance.
- By the end of his life, O'sensei Morihei Ueshiba believed that Aikido should be practiced in non-violence.
- Some people still teach a rigid form of aggressive pre-war practice.
- It was illegal to practice martial arts in Japan after the war. Aikido was practiced in secret. It spread rapidly in the Japanese military.
- Aikido is now practiced all over the world.
- In Japan there are Aikido clubs in elementary and secondary schools.

Basic Concepts And Components Of Aikido
- Attack energy or tense energy can be redirected.
- Integrates body, mind and spirit
- Joins with and uses the energy (attack) in order to redirect
- Uses circular, spiraling movements instead of direct movements (kicks, punches) and blocks, reduces anger, which takes people out of the present moment and causes a loss of focus, power and judgement
- Finding peace in chaotic situations is possible.
- Relies on being relaxed, focused, balanced and grounded
- Cultivates gentle power
- Practices the loving protection of all beings

Description Of A Typical Session
- Information about new students is taken.
- Information is given to new students about terms and Dojo rules.
- Sessions start with a bowing ceremony which shows respect and is a representation of the way Aikido is practiced.
- Next is a meditation.
- Physical warm-ups get the students ready for new teaching or review of a particular Aikido technique.
- Practice with a Partner.
- The lesson ends with a Misogi (purification meditation).
- Bowing out
- Sweep the mat/clean up.

Major Differences Of Opinion Between Practitioners
- Some practitioners feel that Aikido is a spiritual practice, while others see it as a martial art. Some feel that Aikido is both.

Fees/Costs In 2007
Prices vary:
- For children - $40 to $60 a month
- For teens/adults - $40 to $60 a month

Average Time Per Session
- One hour
- All day seminars and camps are also available.

Recommended Length Of Time Between Sessions
- Recommended two sessions per week

Estimated Length Of Time Before Improvements Can Be Expected
- Four to six sessions
- Once the child or youth is engaged with full participation, changes can be noticed.

Suggestions To Make Aikido More Effective With Children
- Parents should not practice the moves with their children.
- Artistic freedom
- Positive discipline.

Other Methods That Complement Aikido
- Tai chi and other Martial Arts
- Music
- Dance
- Yoga
- Calligraphy
- Any activity that involves focus
- Meditation
- Leadership development courses
- Any activity that involves focus

Nature And Length Of Training To Be A Practitioner
- Practitioners are certified by their teachers going back to the founder.
- It takes a minimum of four to six years of regular rigorous training for an adult to become a black belt. It takes longer for children.
- Black belt is considered beginning level and is an indication of competence, but not expertise.
- The holder of a black belt may teach classes if invited to do so by their instructor.

Special Training Needed To Work With Children & Youth
- Knowledge of children and teaching styles
- Behavior management skills
- Conflict resolution skills
- Communication skills
- Mostly, people learn how to teach kids' classes "on the job".
- Look for someone who enjoys working with children.

Professional Associations To Contact For Names Of Local Practitioners
- AikiWeb; Website: www.aikiweb.com
- Ki Society of the U.S.; P.O. Box 75433; Seattle, WA 98125-0433; 206-527-2151; Fax: 206-522-8702; Website: www.ki-aikido.net; Email: info@ki-aikido.net

Number Of Certified Practitioners In U.S., Canada, And Mexico
- Unknown
- In Sonoma Country, California, there are seven dojos (training halls).

What To Look For When Choosing The Best Practitioner
- Showing kindness
- Moving gracefully
- Exhibiting a sense of joy and play in their practice
- Teaching Aikido as the opposite of aggressiveness

Resources, Research Papers, Books, DVDs, Websites

- AikiWeb - The Source for Aikido Information: Its principal purpose is to serve the Internet community as a repository and dissemination point for aikido information. Website: www.aikiweb.com
- Downloadable video (mpeg) clips of aikido in action: www.stenudd.com/aikido/video.htm

Bibliography

- Stevens, John. *Abundant Peace*. Boston: Shambhala Publications, 1987.
- Deguchi, Kyotaro. *The Great Onisaburo Deguchi*. Japan: Oomoto Foundation, 1973.
- Dobson, Terry and Jan Watson. *It's a Lot Like Dancing: An Aikido Journey*. Berkeley, CA; Frog, Ltd., 1993.

Helpful Tips For Parents

- Remind children to focus and take time each day to sit for a second to get focused or to meditate.

Biography Of Isaiah Wisdom, Author

- Years Experience: 17
- Approximate total number of clients who are children, or teens (in a school year): 200 children a week

Isaiah Wisdom's Personal Statement

Aikido's unifying principal is love.

To Contact Isaiah Wisdom, Who Contributed This Chapter

Isaiah Wisdom; 880 Piner Road, #55; Santa Rosa, CA 95403; Ph: 707-571-2013; Web page: www.newschoolaikido.org; Email: info@newschoolaikido.org

· ·

Marie Mulligan's Comment About Aikido: The choice of teacher is often more important than the martial art form. Aikido and martial arts can improve physical confidence. It can complement Nonviolent Communication skills. My younger son and godchildren have benefited from their involvement with martial arts.

Rick Geggie's Comment About Aikido: I have been very impressed with the effects of most of the martial arts upon children & youth. I have noticed that Aikido has the biggest effect in helping children be balanced, harmonious, and able to respond. With any martial art, children's confidence grows, as does their coordination. One of the biggest benefits is learning to control fear and aggression. Children & youth feel safer when they feel they can defend themselves. As always, having the right teacher is very important, so make sure you feel good about who you and your child choose.

CHAPTER 5

AROMATHERAPY FOR CHILDREN & YOUTH

By Julia Fischer,   © Copyright 2008.

Aromatherapy Has Helped Kids With

- Acne & rosacea
- Allergic skin reactions
- Baby care (colic, colds, cradle cap, diaper rash, diarrhea, etc.)
- Burns & sunburns (1st, 2nd & 3rd degree)
- Deodorant (replaces harmful chemical deodorants)
- Dental problems (toothache, teething pain, gum infections, abscesses, etc.)
- Diarrhea
- Ear infections (earache, otitis, swimmer's ear, etc.)
- Eczema
- Eye infections (conjunctivitis, sties) using Aromatic hydrosols ONLY!!!
- Fever

- Food poisoning
- Hair problems (lice, itchy scalp, dandruff, etc.)
- Immune system
- Indigestion
- Infections, bacterial (colds, intestinal, skin, strep throat, tonsillitis, urinary tract, etc.)
- Infections, fungal (athlete's foot, candida, ringworm, etc.)
- Infections - parasitic (dysentery, worms, etc.)
- Infections - viral (flu, herpes, pneumonia, swollen glands, etc.)
- Inflammations (skin, muscles, etc.)

- Insomnia
- Itching
- Menstrual disorders (PMS, hormonal imbalances, painful or irregular menses, etc.)
- Mental alertness, clarity & focus
- Nausea
- Pain (arthritis, bruises, joints, muscles, sports injuries, etc.)
- Psoriasis
- Relaxation
- Respiratory infections, upper & lower (sinusitis, rhinitis, bronchitis, etc.)
- Scars
- Spasms
- Wounds

Aromatherapy Can Help In The Following Areas

Spirit: Influences imagination & inspiration
Body: Alleviates physical ailments & injuries
Mind: Enhances mental clarity & focus
Emotions: Uplifting & calming effects on moods
Social: Healthy, authentic aromas support healthy relationships

Brief Description Of Aromatherapy

- Aromatherapy is a form of herbal medicine that relies on the healing properties of essential oils from plants.
- These essential oils interface with the body directly through inhalations, topical applications and in some cases internally.
- When properly chosen they are safe and suitable for use by everyone for treatment of a wide range of complaints.

Success With Aromatherapy

- CASE #1: Alice was less than a year old when she developed thrush (candida) inside her mouth. I instructed her mother, Lisette, who was breastfeeding Alice, to massage 10 drops of a potent anti-infectious Aromatic solution on her chest and back every 3 hours. The essential oils were carefully chosen with full consideration of safety concerns, while being potent enough to address the flare-up. Essential oils pass rapidly through the skin into the bloodstream and will also appear in breast milk. Sure enough, within 48 hours the thrush had vanished. Lisette, who had a slight vaginal discharge at the same time, reported that it too had disappeared!
- CASE #2: Marielle, age 30, called in desperation. Both she and her 9-year old son, Sylvain, had terrible toothaches caused by an abscess and accompanied by fever. Marielle was fearful that if she waited too long before seeing a doctor both she and Sylvain would end up with serious consequences. Her resistance to taking antibiotics unless absolutely necessary was in question.

  However Marielle was a firm believer in Aromatherapy and had confidence in my practice. I quickly prepared a strong, antibacterial mouth wash and an even more potent topical blend for direct application to the gum area near the abscess.

  When Marielle arrived at my doorstep I could see that fully half of her face was swollen to double its normal size. There was no time to waste and she began using the preparations right away. Within 1½ hours the swelling was down considerably as was the fever and the pain. After another hour she decided to return home to begin treating Sylvain. She knew she was on the right track.

  Later that evening Marielle called to say that both she and Sylvain were "out-of the-woods" and well on the way to recovery. Most importantly, both individuals had a real life experience that built a powerful case for relying on Aromatherapy, their treatment of choice.

Aromatherapy Is Appropriate For Ages

- Prenatal Aromatherapy care for mothers may assist with common complaints of pregnancy.
- Newborns benefit from a non-pharmaceutical approach to home care.
- Young children and adolescents can easily learn to treat themselves, building self-esteem, self-reliance & confidence in their new ability to address their own health care issues.

Children & Youths' Reactions To Aromatherapy

- Aromatherapy is perhaps the most enjoyable and empowering modality available to children of all ages. Infants benefit as much from the fragrance of an Aromatic bath or massage as from the healing properties inherent in the oils.

- Young children newly enraptured with the love of Nature seem to delight in using and identifying smells which are so familiar to them from their foods (i.e. cinnamon, orange) and the outdoors (i.e. eucalyptus, pine).

Extra Care Is Needed
- There are a number of essential oils that should be avoided by infants, the elderly, during pregnancy or by those with certain health conditions.
- Consulting with a qualified Aromatherapy practitioner and using high-quality, medicinal grade essential oils as directed will ensure safe and effective treatment. Essential oils should NEVER be put into eyes or ears, and unless carefully supervised by an experienced Aromatherapy practitioner, should not be taken orally.

Contraindications: When Aromatherapy Should Be Avoided
- It is specific essential oils, rather than Aromatherapy as a whole, which should be avoided by certain individuals at certain times.
- That said, persons who should use most caution when using essential oils are newborns, pregnant women, fragile elderly and epileptics.
- It is wise to consult with a qualified Aromatherapy practitioner to determine which oils are best avoided under which conditions.

History
- Although essential oils have been used by many cultures for thousands of years, modern Aromatherapy as we know it today has only gradually become part of the mainstream.
- The term "Aromatherapy" is most popularly associated with French chemist Dr. Rene Maurice Gattefosse. His groundbreaking text, *Aromatherapy: Essential Oils – Vegetal Hormones*, published in Paris in 1928, is still a respected reference for Aromatherapy practitioners around the world.
- Since that time, more subtle and sophisticated uses of essential oils for healing have developed and flourished, especially with the wider demand for and acceptance of complementary and alternative health care options.

Basic Concepts & Components Of Aromatherapy
- The cornerstone of Aromatherapy is the selection of high quality, medicinal grade essential oils obtained from a reputable supplier.
- It must be stressed that the use of synthetic fragrances or perfumes does not constitute either a safe or therapeutic practice of Aromatherapy.
- The beauty of this therapy is that with the understanding of some basic principles and techniques Aromatherapy can be practiced safely at home to manage more commonly encountered health problems as well as acute flare-ups and chronic conditions.

What Essential Oils Are & A Guide To Determining Their Quality For Use In Aromatherapy
- What distinguishes Aromatherapy from other types of Herbal Medicine is the way in which the medicinal properties (in the form of essential oils) are extracted from aromatic plants.
- Most essential oils are steam-distilled, which concentrates the most volatile (evaporative) components and which results in by-products known as Aromatic Hydrosols. Aromatic Hydrosols may be used for treatments where essential oils cannot or should not be used.
- Essential oils are highly concentrated, and therefore are used in the smallest quantities for therapeutic purposes.

- High quality essential oils will appear in brown or blue glass bottles as they are sensitive to light and will dissolve soft plastic.
- The label (or accompanying literature) should include: botanical (Latin) name; part of the plant used (root, seed, leaf, etc.); cultivation method (organic, biodynamic, wild, etc.); extraction method and country of origin.
- Prices will vary widely depending on factors such as availability and country of origin, and especially on how much essential oil the plant itself will yield.

Description Of A Typical Session
- Because most qualified Aromatherapy practitioners combine different modalities there is no "typical" Aromatherapy treatment session.
- However, given a particular complaint, an Aromatherapist may request a medical history or ask questions to determine a possible origin of the problem and may prepare a custom blend.
- Some practitioners like to involve the child by offering oils for him/her to smell. As much as possible, individual likes and dislikes are factored into the preparation of the blend.
- A parent or child would be instructed specifically how, when and for how long the blend should be used. Depending upon the condition, Aromatic baths, inhalations or massages may be recommended in conjunction with the use of the blend.
- Once a treatment plan is in place, self-care at home is invited and encouraged.

Major Differences Of Opinion Between Aromatherapy Practitioners
- It has been observed that some differences of opinion regarding Aromatherapy lie across international lines.
- In France where modern Aromatherapy was born, an intensive or "hard-core" approach is common (i.e. higher dosages, internal uses).
- England is known for its excellent Aromatherapy schools but the usage continues to be more superficial or "soft-core", usually relegated to Aromatic skin care, baths and massage.
- North American Aromatherapy appears to have embraced both of these approaches and perhaps is the most integrative of all.

Fees/Costs In 2007 (Average - Northern California)
- Fees vary widely depending on length of session, services offered, education and experience of the practitioner.
- Costs for custom blends are most likely additional and will also depend on the specific oils used.
- Anywhere from $50-$100 per session seems to be the going rate with follow-ups, if necessary, significantly lower.

Average Time Per Session
- Depending on the adjunct therapy (or therapies), the Aromatherapy practitioner combines a 1 to 1 ½ hour session including an intake interview. As stated earlier, once a treatment plan is in place, self-care at home is invited and encouraged.
- Follow-up visits may be necessary in order to fine-tune the treatment, but telephone consultations are sometimes sufficient.

Estimated Length Of Time Before Improvements Can Be Expected
- Relief of symptoms of minor health problems may be experienced almost immediately or within several hours.

MARIE MULLIGAN • RICK GEGGIE

- Chronic or more deep-seated illnesses may require days or weeks of repeated applications. It must be noted that, depending on the specific application, effects of an Aromatherapy treatment may be felt for between a few hours to a few days.
- Important factors for a successful Aromatherapy treatment include: correct assessment or diagnosis of the problem, quality of essential oils, proper selection and dosage of essential oils, method and frequency of application.

Suggestions To Make Aromatherapy More Effective

- Parents can best provide all the relevant medical (and/or emotional) history necessary for a practitioner to make a proper assessment of the child's current health issues. Some practitioners use a customized intake form that provides important data for determining which oils should or should not be used.
- Most importantly the parent can observe their child's ailment and should be able to accurately report onset, symptoms, factors which influence changes in those symptoms, monitor temperature, stool, etc. if applicable.
- Other recommendations (i.e. diet, herbal and vitamin supplements, avoidance of offending chemical agents in lotions, soaps, etc.) should be followed and monitored by the parent to ensure best possible outcome.
- Right advice: Get guidance from a qualified Aromatherapy practitioner you can trust.
- Right oils: Use high quality, medicinal grade essential oils from a reputable supplier.
- Right assessment: Correctly evaluate health concern.
- Right selection: Choose essential oils and/or Aromatic hydrosols appropriate to ailment.
- Right dosage: Use proper dosage appropriate to condition and to the individual.
- Right application method: Choose between inhalations, topical treatments, etc.
- Right timing: Act swiftly and decisively once treatment decisions are made.
- Right attitude: Be diligent and optimistic about treatment.

Other Methods That Are Similar To Aromatherapy

- Ayurveda
- Balneotherapy (therapeutic baths)
- Massage
- Phytotherapy (herbal medicine)
- Thalassotherapy (sea water & seaweed therapies)
- Traditional Chinese Medicine

Nature And Length Of Training To Be A Practitioner

- A competent practitioner should be well schooled in all aspects of Aromatherapy – from the fragrance effects, to a working knowledge of Aromatic Chemistry.
- An ability to combine modalities certainly makes a practitioner better-rounded, as well as increasing the odds of successful treatment.
- Experience, education, sensitivity and enthusiasm all make for a better Aromatherapist.
- Dowsing for essences may be an intuitive way to create a perfume blend but is hardly adequate for dealing with illness.
- Most importantly, you should insist on high quality, medicinal grade essential oils for the care of yourself and your child.

Special Training Needed To Work With Children & Youth

- No special training in Aromatherapy is needed for working with children as the treatment principles remain the same.

- The differences lie in dosage, application method and the careful selection of oils appropriate to the size and sensitivity of the child.

Certification/Licenses Held By Practitioners
- Some certification programs take place over a weekend, whereas others last for over a year and require practical experience.
- Certification in Aromatherapy does not assure competency.

Professional Associations To Contact For Names Of Local Practitioners
- NAHA (National Association for Holistic Aromatherapy)

What To Look For When Choosing The Best Practitioner
- A competent practitioner should be well schooled in all aspects of Aromatherapy – from the fragrance effects, to a working knowledge of Aromatic Chemistry.
- An ability to combine modalities certainly makes a practitioner better-rounded, as well as increasing the odds of successful treatment.
- Experience, education, sensitivity and enthusiasm all make for a better Aromatherapist.
- Dowsing for essences may be an intuitive way to create a perfume blend, but is hardly adequate for dealing with illness.
- Most importantly, you should insist on high quality, medicinal grade essential oils for the care of yourself and your child.

Aromatherapy Classes, Correspondence Courses, Certifications, Conferences & Consultations
- Atlantic Institute of Aromatherapy; Sylla Sheppard-Hangar; 16018 Saddlestring Dr.; Tampa, FL 33612; 813-265-2222; Website: http://atlanticinstitute.com; Email: sylla@tampabay.rr.com
- Jeanne Rose Aromatherapy; 219 Carl Street; San Francisco, CA 94117; 415-564-6785; Fax: 415-564-6799; Website: http://www.jeannerose.net; Email: info@JeanneRose.net
- NAHA (National Association for Holistic Aromatherapy); 3327 W. Indian Trail Road, PMB 144; Spokane, WA 99208; 509-325-3419; Fax: 509-325-3479: Website: www.naha.org; Email: info@naha.org
- Pacific Institute of Aromatherapy; Dr. Kurt Schnaubelt; P.O. Box 6723; San Rafael, CA 94903; 415-479-9120; Fax: 415-479-0614; Website: www.pacificinstituteofaromatherapy.com; Email: osa_pia@yahoo.com

Resources, Research Papers, Books, DVD's, Websites
Books
- Schnaubelt, Kurt. *Medical Aromatherapy.* Berkeley: North Atlantic Books, 1999
- Schnaubelt, Kurt. *Advanced Aromatherapy: The Science of Essential Oil Therapy.* Rochester, VT: Healing Arts Press, 1995
- Sheppard-Hangar, Sylla. "Aromatherapy Practitioner Reference Manual." Available from the Atlantic Institute of Aromatherapy; Website: http://atlanticinstitute.com/index.html
- Balazs, Tony and Robert Tisserand. *Essential Oil Safety: A Guide for Health Care Professionals.* London: Churchill Livingstone, 1995
- Gattefosse, Rene-Maurice and Robert Tisserand. *Gattefosse's Aromatherapy: The First Book on Aromatherapy.* United Kingdom: Random House, 2004 (2nd Rev. Ed.)
- L'Aromatherapie Exactement/Pierre Franchomme & Dr. Daniel Penoel (in French)

Periodicals
- *Aromatherapy Journal.* Available from the National Association for Holistic Aromatherapy; Website: http://www.naha.org/journal.htm

Where To Get Good Quality Essential Oils
- Amrita Aromatherapy; 1900 West Stone Ave., Suite C; Fairfield, IA 52556; 641-472-9136; Fax: 641-472-8672; Website: www.amrita.net; Email: info@amrita-essentials.com
- Essential Aura Aromatherapy; 1935 Doran Road; Cobble Hill, BC, Canada VOR 1L0; 250-733-2035; Fax 250-733-2036; Website: http://www.essentialaura.com; Email: info@essentialaura.com
- Floracopeia; 206 Sacramento Street, Suite 304; Nevada City, CA 95959; 530-470-9269; Website: http://www.floracopeia.com
- Original Swiss Aromatics; P.O. Box 6842; San Rafael, CA 94903; 415-459-3998; Fax 415-479-0614; Website: www.originalswissaromatics.com; Email: osa_pia@yahoo.com
- Oshadhi USA; 1340-G Industrial Avenue; Petaluma, CA 94952; 888-674-2344; Fax 707-769-7342; Website: www.oshadhiusa.com; Email: info@oshadhiusa.com
- Naprodis Inc.; 13000 Danielson St., Suite K; Poway, CA 92064; 888-367-2529; Fax 858-486-7768; Website: www.naprodis.com
- Simplers Botanical Company; P.O. Box 2534; Sebastopol, CA 95473; 800-652-7646; Website: www.simplers.com; Email: contact@simplers.com
- White Lotus Aromatics; 602 S. Alder Street; Port Angeles, WA 98362; Fax: 360-457-9235; Website: www.whitelotusaromatics.com; Email: somanath@aol.com

Bibliography
- Rose, Jeanne. *Aromatherapy Book: Inhalations and Applications.* Berkeley: North Atlantic Books, 1992.
- Rose, Jeanne. *375 Essential Oils and Hydrosols.* Berkeley: Frog, Ltd/North Atlantic Books, 1999.
- Lavery, Sheila. *Aromatherapy: A Step-By-Step Guide.* London: Element Books, 1997.
- England, Allison and Lola Borg. *Aromatherapy for Mother and Baby: Natural Healing With Essential Oils During Pregnancy and Early Motherhood.* Rochester, VT: Healing Arts Press, 1994.
- Tisserand, Maggie. *Aromatherapy for Women: A Practical Guide to Essential Oils for Health and Beauty.* Rochester, VT: Healing Arts Press, 1985.
- Tisserand, Robert. *The Art of Aromatherapy.* C.W.Daniel, 2004 (Rev. 2nd Ed.)
- Tisserand, Robert. *Aromatherapy: To Heal and Tend the Body.* Wilmot, WI: Lotus Press, 1988.
- Fischer-Rizzi, Susanne. *Complete Aromatherapy Handbook: Essential Oils for Radiant Health.* Sterling Publishers, 1991.
- Worwood, Valerie Ann. *The Complete Book of Essential Oils & Aromatherapy: Over 600 Natural, Non-Toxic and Fragrant Recipes to Create Health - Beauty - a Safe Home Environment.* Novato, CA: New World Library, 1991.
- Catty, Suzanne. *Hydrosols: The Next Aromatherapy.* Rochester, VT: Healing Arts Press, 1991.
- Lawless, Julia. *The Illustrated Encyclopedia of Essential Oils: The Complete Guide to the Use of Oils in Aromatherapy and Herbalism.* London: Element Books, 1995.
- Penoel, M.D. Daniel. *Natural Home Health Care Using Essential Oils.* Essential Science Publishing, 1998.
- Valnet, Jean and Robert Tisserand. *The Practice of Aromatherapy: A Classic Compendium of Plant Medicines and Their Healing Properties.* Rochester, VT: Healing Arts Press, 1982.

Biography of Julia Fischer, Author
- Julia Fischer is a lover and enthusiastic voice of aromatic plants with 20 years of experience studying and practicing Aromatherapy. A seasoned instructor, her emphasis in Aromatic Chemistry is key to understanding the pharmacology of essential oils. Her classes cover all aspects of Aromatherapy, from the chemical to the alchemical, and are hugely empowering for anyone interested in Aromatherapeutics and health independence. Through

her company, Kinarome, she prepares custom blends and is available for private consultations, staff trainings and Aromatherapy intensives.

Julia Fischer's Personal Statement

People often ask me, "Does Aromatherapy work?". I remind them that long before we had pharmaceuticals, we had plants. In fact, many over-the-counter as well as prescription drugs available today are still derived from medicinal plants. This point seems to win over those for whom a scientific seal-of-approval is necessary to separate the "real" medicine from the snake oil. That effective healing has been achieved by the use of medicinal plants (and foods) by the world's peoples for thousands of years should be sufficient, but alas, it is not. Among those who are "believers" in Aromatherapy are individuals who, through direct experience, saw their health issues resolved without turning to the more conventional, western medical doctors and pharmaceutical drugs.

It is my conviction that the less we use chemical drugs the less toxic load we inflict on our bodies and on the earth. Effective and safe natural medicine also lessens the unnecessary burdens on hospitals and health care professionals.

As I see it, the aim of Aromatherapy is to be an effective alternative to basic care normally administered by an expensive and overburdened health care system.

When I discovered Aromatherapy 20 years ago I immediately understood that bringing sensory pleasure and potent healing together in one therapy was a unique and special treasure. I have witnessed, experienced and facilitated hundreds of successful Aromatherapy treatments and yet I never cease to be amazed by the power and efficacy of essential oils.

Friends, family, students and clients are all delighted to find in Aromatherapy very simple solutions to basic health concerns. Children in particular are intuitively drawn to smells and are often far more descriptive of them than adults. To realize that these wonderful aromas are also their medicine is perhaps the main reason Aromatherapy is the perfect modality to use with children.

My greatest influences along the way have been the enthusiastic, the scientific, the innovative and tireless teachers who seemed to share an innate commitment to the advancement and proliferation of Aromatherapy. My deepest gratitude is reserved for all the Aromatic plants, without whom our sense of smell would be greatly deprived.

To Contact Julia Fischer, Who Contributed This Chapter

Julia Fischer; c/o KINAROME; 3 Ray Court; San Anselmo, CA 94960; Ph: 415-457-3673; Email: kinarome@yahoo.com

. . . .

Marie Mulligan's Comment About Aromatherapy: I use essential oils in a diffuser during study times for myself and for my children. Consult a medical practitioner before using Aromatherapy on children two years and under. Do the same for children & youth with Asthma, Eczema, and other chronic conditions. Be on the alert for allergic reactions (skin and lungs) as well as sun sensitivity reactions. When in doubt consult a practitioner. Aromatherapy can be quite useful in easing tension, and improving mood and focus.

Rick Geggie's Comment About Aromatherapy: Compared to many other things that can help children, essential oils are very inexpensive. They dramatically shift children's moods and physical conditions. I use them myself. I have known many families who make constant use of them to make growing up easier. Getting the best quality oils you can afford is important. They all work. Some have a faster effect than others.

CHAPTER 6

ATTITUDINAL HEALING FOR CHILDREN & YOUTH

By Kathy Harris, Carolyn Smith, Marilyn Robinson, © *Copyright 2008.*

Attitudinal Healing Has Helped Kids With
- Any kind of challenge
- The Center for Attitudinal Healing holds specific groups for children with life threatening illnesses, bereavement groups and teen groups to help with anger management.
- Groups are held in various children's centers and schools to help children learn to express their feelings and cope with their problems.
- Depending on the children's ages, artwork is used and various games are played to help the children express themselves.
- When fear is seen for what it is, only love remains.
- Through group dialogue, or sometimes one-on-one, trained facilitators help children with long-term illnesses, disabilities, behavior problems, or the loss of a loved one.
- Healing is not seen as the absence of illness, but the attainment of peace.

Attitudinal Healing Can Help In The Following Areas
Spirit: Attitudinal Healing (AH) gets children in touch with the knowledge that they are not just their bodies; that no matter how ill their bodies are on the outside, they are always whole inside.

Body: AH helps children shift their thinking that contributes to suffering. Pain may still be there, but the child is relieved of the anxiety they felt about it.

Mind: AH helps the child make a mental shift to focus on the whole of life, not just the fragments of the body or parts of their life that are falling apart.

Emotions: AH emphasizes that there are no right or wrong emotions. Children can stop holding their emotions in, out of fear of expressing them. Instead they have a safe place in which to express and discuss their emotions and realize they're not they only ones to have such feelings.

Social: Because AH usually happens in groups, children learn about taking turns, listening, asking questions, and about compassion.

Brief Description Of Attitudinal Healing

- AH is based on the belief that it is possible to choose peace rather than conflict and love rather than fear. This belief is expressed in the "Twelve Principles", a non-sectarian set of spiritual guidelines.

Success With Attitudinal Healing

- Jane, a six year old in a bereavement group, really exercised her right to remain quiet. She passed in every session for four months. During the "weather report" (the term given to the process when every child and adult facilitator tells how they are feeling in terms of the weather) she would draw expressively but not discuss her drawings. One night a candle was lit in the group's ritual for a new group member whose parent had just died, and Jane burrowed into the facilitator's arms and started crying and talking. She shared her feelings in every session after that.
- Ivan, an eight year old in Russia who had a life threatening cancer, had been told his diagnosis. (In Russia, doctors and parents rarely discuss a diagnosis with the child.) He was quiet, withdrawn, isolated from the other children in the hospital. He loved to draw, though, and began to draw pictures of his feelings. One day, during a bean bag toss, he began to laugh and express himself. He went back to his room a happy child.
- Carlos, a 13 year old with a brain tumor, loved to tell jokes and tell how sharing his feelings was helping him. When his cancer went into remission, he often participated in group training sessions. Three years later, Carlos's cancer returned and he died. Within a month, his mother came to group sessions and shared how AH had pulled her family together and how grateful she was for that.
- Janet, an 8 year old at the Children's Center, was withdrawn and depressed when she started attending AH sessions there. When another young girl shared that she was being molested by her father, Janet was able to open up and talk about her own molestation. Knowing that she was not alone released her from her shame and silence.

Attitudinal Healing Is Appropriate For Ages

- 5 years old in one-on-one situations
- 6-18 years old in group settings
- There are teen and young adult groups in some schools.

Children & Youths' Reactions To Attitudinal Healing

- Most children really like it and look forward to the sessions.
- AH helps children learn to listen and participate in groups.
- AH can help children learn to sit still for an hour and that's not always easy.
- Children learn to extend love to others and experience how that feels.

Extra Care Is Needed

- If a child is acting out too much and disrupting the group, it may be necessary for one of the facilitators to take that child to another room and have a one-on-one session with them.

Contraindications: When Attitudinal Healing Should Be Avoided

- There is no time when AH should be avoided. However, children under five may be too young to benefit fully.

History

- AH is based upon the teachings of *A Course in Miracles*, which can be described as a form of spiritual psychotherapy that is self-taught.

- The Center for AH began in 1975 under the guidance of Dr. Gerald Jampolsky and four volunteers. Its purpose was to create a safe environment of support and trust where children could express their deepest feelings, to begin a process of letting go of the many fears associated with their illness and experience peace of mind.
- Within a short while, attention was also given to the needs of the parents and siblings of these children.
- The program at the Center was designed to supplement traditional health care which places a heavy emphasis on the physical/physiological side of the illness. More specifically, the purpose of the Center's programs is to enable individuals to let go of the emotional pain and fear that usually accompany an illness and then to begin to lead a more fulfilling and peaceful life.
- Since the beginning, the Center has provided its services free of charge to all who wish to participate.
- The Center operates under the premise that true healing has a spiritual and emotional component that must be addressed. The principles of AH include universal, nonsectarian spiritual truths.

Basic Concepts And Components Of Attitudinal Healing
- True healing has a spiritual and emotional component that must be addressed.
- Through using the tools of AH, children can let go of the emotional pain and fear that usually accompany an illness and begin to lead a more fulfilling and peaceful life.
- In the groups, children recognize that love is listening and they agree to listen with an open heart, to give mutual support and to practice non-judgmental listening and sharing.
- Children support each other's inner guidance and assist one another in finding their own best answers.
- The roles of student and teacher are interchangeable. They shift from one to the other, regardless of age or experience.
- Children practice being present with others, seeing only the light and not the lampshade.
- Children learn to keep in mind that they always have a choice between peace and conflict; between love and fear.

Description Of A Typical Session
- The children arrive and break into small groups of no more than twelve. There are always at least two trained adult facilitators per group.
- The children gather by holding hands in a circle. At this time the children's energy is focused on one another and the group.
- Introductions and check-ins occur.
- A short game is played to break the ice and help any newcomers feel more comfortable.
- The children are given a project – drawing, painting, clay work, etc. to do for about twenty minutes. The project focuses on a theme (such as remembering the deceased parent in a bereavement group or a visit to the doctor or hospital in a Living with Illness group), an emotion like anger, sadness, worry, hope, pride, etc.
- After the project, the children are encouraged to share their drawings, etc. and to talk about what they mean to them. But no child is made to talk if they are not comfortable doing so.
- The facilitator helps the children speak about their feelings by asking questions that cannot be answered with a "yes" or "no." For example "What was the hardest part about being in the hospital?"
- After the group discussion, there is a closing circle. During this time, the facilitator touches on the themes that were brought up during the session and relates them to the AH Principles.
- Sometimes the closing circle also becomes a healing circle with members putting someone in the center they want to send love to.
- The circle closes with the passing of an energy squeeze.

Major Differences Of Opinion Between Practitioners
- There really aren't any. A major principle of AH is not to give the children advice. If someone doesn't follow that or any of the other principles of AH, then they don't participate in AH at all.

Fees/Costs In 2007
- All groups in the Sausalito Center are free and are run by trained volunteers. The center trains others who hold groups all over the country and they may charge fees but are encouraged not to do so.
- The Center charges a reasonable fee for volunteer trainings.

Average Time Per Session
- Sessios run an hour to an hour and a half. There's usually a free meal first – the food being donated by local merchants.

Recommended Length Of Time Between Sessions
- One week is best, but also bi-monthly is okay.

Estimated Length Of Time Before Improvements Can Be Expected
- After 3-4 sessions usually, but sometimes on that first night driving home, the children begin sharing feelings.

Suggestions To Make Attitudinal Healing More Effective
- Parents need to ensure their child gets to their group on time.
- Parents need to demonstrate the importance of talking about feelings by doing it themselves.
- When parent and child are having an AH session one-on-one, it is a time for parents to listen and understand, not a time to correct or scold the child.
- Parents can practice reflective listening, asking leading questions and not trying to give answers to help their child come up with their own strategy for changing problematic behaviors.
- Parents can spend time with the principles of AH themselves by going to adult support groups.
- Underscore that giving is receiving.
- Play games with their children that come from the AH Handbook.

Other Methods That Are Similar To Attitudinal Healing
- The Work, founded by Byron Katie, is similar.

Other Methods That Complement Attitudinal Healing
- Any other healing method complements AH. AH complements any other modality the parent chooses.

Nature And Length Of Training To Be A Practitioner
- The trainee joins a support group themselves and attends at least ten sessions.
- The trainee attends an intensive three-day training workshop.
- The trainee then attends a support group made up completely of volunteers for at least eight sessions.
- The trainee is then invited to become an apprentice facilitator.

Special Training Needed To Work With Children & Youth
- The Center has special three-day trainings that the facilitators attend after completing the initial training sessions.

Certification/Licenses Held By Practitioners
- There are none. The trainees leave all their degrees at the door. Sometimes the people with licenses or degrees are the toughest to train because it is harder for them to learn how to express their own feelings.
- The best facilitators are people who can express their own feelings, have a spiritual focus, and love kids.

Professional Associations To Contact For Names Of Local Practitioners
- To obtain the names and addresses of centers all over the world, contact: The Center for Attitudinal Healing; 33 Buchanan Drive; Sausalito, CA 94965; 415-331-6161; Fax 415-331-4545; Website: www.attitudinalhealing.org; Email: info@attitudinalhealing.org.
- The Center has trained hundreds of volunteers as facilitators and many of these facilitators have opened their own centers throughout the world. However, these centers are not affiliated with the International Center for AH in Sausalito, and therefore, the Center can make no endorsements or recommendations involving them.

Number Of Certified Practitioners In U.S., Canada, And Mexico
- There is no official certification but thousands of facilitators have been trained.

What To Look For When Choosing The Best Practitioner
- Because each group is unique, parents will have to attend a few sessions at the center nearest them to decide whether or not it's right for their child.
- Parent and child should feel uplifted, not further depressed by the experience.

Famous Practitioners/Famous Centers
- The leading practitioner is still Gerald Jampolsky, the founder of both the practice and the Center.

Leading Clinics, Centers, Practitioners
- The leading center is the original one in Sausalito (see above).

Resources, Research Papers, Books, DVD's, Websites
- Center for Attitudinal Healing; 33 Buchanan Drive; Sausalito, CA 94965; 415-331-6161; Fax 415-331-4545; Website: www.attitudinalhealing.org; Email: info@attitudinalhealing.org.

Bibliography
- Bearison, David. *They Never Want to Tell You, Children Talking About Cancer.* Boston: Harvard University Press, 1991.
- Huber, Cheri and June Shiver. *How You Do Anything Is How You Do Everything: A Workbook.* Keep It Simple Books, 1988.
- Jampolsky, Gerald G. *There is a Rainbow Behind Every Dark Cloud.* Berkeley: Celestial Arts, 1979.
- Jampolsky, Gerald G. *Love Is Letting Go of Fear.* Berkeley: Celestial Arts, 1979.
- Foundation for Inner Peace. *A Course In Miracles.* Mill Valley: Foundation for Inner Peace, 1975.

Helpful Tips For Parents
- Share what was hard that day and what was easy.

- Parent and child each choose one of the Principles of AH each day and share why they picked it.

Biographies of Kathy Harris, Carolyn Smith and Marilyn Robinson, Co-Authors
- Kathy Harris no longer works with children and youth. She presently facilitates adult groups. She also facilitates in a large prison.
- Carolyn Smith has 18 years experience working with Attitudinal Healing with children & youth.
- Marilyn Robinson has 20 years of experience with Attitudinal Healing.

To Contact Carolyn Smith or Marilyn Robinson, Who Contributed This Chapter
Carolyn Smith; 195 Aylor Rd.; Madison, VA 22727; Ph: 540-923-4170; or CA 415-388-9172; Email: catheal@mac.com

Marilyn Robinson; 1287 Mysty Woods; Victoria, BC V8Y 3G6 Canada; Ph: 250-881-1109; Email: home123@aol.com

. . . .

Marie Mulligan's Comment About Attitudinal Healing: I personally have people in my life who have benefited greatly from being involved in this program. Children and their families benefit from this non-denominational spiritual experience.

Rick Geggie's Comment About Attitudinal Healing: Children and parents of children in the program have all spoken highly of it. Children feel safe to open up and relax.

CHAPTER 7

AYURVEDA FOR CHILDREN & YOUTH

By Dr. Marc Halpern, DC, CAS,   © Copyright 2008.

Ayurveda Has Helped Kids With

• Allergies	• Cancer	• Influenza
• Anemia	• Cerebral Palsy	• Learning difficulties
• Anorexia/Bulimia	• Chronic Fatigue Syndrome	• Measles
• Arthritis	• Colds	• Migraine Headaches
• Asthma	• Dental problems	• Mumps
• Attention Deficit Disorder	• Depression	• Nausea
• ADHD	• Developmental delays	• Nutrition problems
• Middle ear dysfunction	• Diabetes	• Personality disorder
• Balance problems	• Digestion problems	• Psychotic episodes
• Bipolar disorder	• Ear Infections	• Short term memory problems
• Blindness(certain types)	• Epilepsy	• Spasticity
• Brain damage	• Hyperactivity	• Stress
	• Hypoglycemia	

Ayurveda Can Help In The Following Areas
Spirit: Clarity deepens ones personal connection.
Body: Ayurveda supports all body functions.
Mind: Ayurveda brings peace and calm to the mind.
Emotions: Ayurveda brings emotional balance.
Social: Ayurveda supports social skills.

Brief Description Of Ayurveda

- The traditional medicine of India--which literally translated means "the science or knowledge of life," can support the healing process from almost any condition or illness.
- It is often referred to as "the Mother of all healing" and focuses on health, rather than illness.
- Ayurveda truly treats the whole person.
- It is based on the idea that each person is unique, each imbalance is unique, and each person's path toward healing is unique.
- Therapies utilized include dietary, herbal, aroma, color, sound, massage, meditation, yoga, and lifestyle.

Success With Ayurveda

- Tom, an eight year old, suffered from frequent urination. With Ayurveda, the frequent urination was resolved in three months.
- Jackie, a three year old, had recurrent episodes of pneumonia. After six months of Ayurvedic treatment, the frequency of lung infections decreased dramatically.
- Alice, a four year old, was plagued with eczema on her legs and elbow. Her parents tried many remedies to no avail. After only one month of Ayurveda the condition disappeared.

Ayurveda Is Appropriate For Ages

- It is appropriate from birth to adulthood. How well the treatment works on which age varies according to the nature and degree of the imbalance.
- Some treatments work on all ages, including infants, while others require greater active participation, so the child must be older.

Children & Youth's Reactions To Ayurveda

- Children usually enjoy the wide variety of therapies employed in their treatment.

Extra Care Is Needed

- Beyond taking herbal medicines, Ayurveda requires a lot of work on the part of both child and parent.

Contraindications: When Ayurveda Should Be Avoided

- There are none that apply all of the time.
- Severe, sudden onset of symptoms and/or severe conditions should be evaluated by a medical doctor.
- A lack of involvement by the patient or parents makes treatment very difficult.
- Herbs alone may help, but the whole treatment brings about the best results.

History

- Ayurveda evolved in India approximately 5,000 years ago.
- Complete Ayurvedic hospitals and universities exist in India.
- Although Ayurveda is new to America it has been growing in popularity for about 20 years.
- Key figures in Ayurveda include Dr. David Frawley, Dr. Vasant Lad, Dr. John Doulliard, and Dr. Deepak Chopra.

Basic Concepts And Components Of Ayurveda
- Disease is caused by living out of harmony with our environment.
- Health is the natural result of living in harmony.
- Healing is the process of returning to harmony.
- We are all unique (as defined by our constitution) and our path toward healing is also unique.
- Ultimately, the cause of all disease is forgetting our true nature as spirit. This separation causes us to act only as a body and sense organ. This leads to indulgences, which cause disease.

Description Of A Typical Session
- On the initial visit, a full and complete history is taken on the physical, emotional, and spiritual states of the individual.
- Tongue and pulse examinations are performed along with observation of body structure.
- Time is spent in consultation, examination, and on patient education.
- In the follow-up, time is spent checking how the patient is implementing the treatment plan.

Major Differences Of Opinion Between Practitioners
- Some practitioners may rely entirely on pulse diagnosis while others may rely more on the complete history and examination.
- Some practitioners may focus only on diet, herbs, and lifestyle while others may include the additional modalities of yoga, meditation, aroma, color, sound, and massage.

Fees/Costs In 2007
- Initial visits vary from $75 to $225.
- Follow-ups are from $75 to $175.
- Fees vary according to location in the country and experience of practitioner.

Average Time Per Session
- Session time varies according to training and experience, but the initial visit is generally two hours and follow-ups are 45 minutes.

Recommended Length Of Time Between Sessions
- Recommended time between sessions is one week to four weeks.

Estimated Length Of Time Before Improvements Can Be Expected
- This varies between four to eight sessions.

Suggestions To Make Ayurveda More Effective
- The practitioner should have experience working with children.
- Herbs can be mixed with juice to improve the taste.
- Parents need to support the plan made by the practitioner.
- Parents may need to be in an Ayurvedic program as well.

Other Methods That Are Similar To Ayurveda
- None

Other Methods That Complement Ayurveda
- Acupuncture
- Chiropractic

Nature And Length Of Training To Be A Practitioner
- In the U.S., education varies and includes on-site and home study.
- Hours of education vary up to 1,700 hours.
- Independent and home study increase the number of hours significantly.
- Certification may take up to three years. Training at the California College of Ayurveda includes more than 1,700 hours of total education, including internship. Training covers all aspects of Ayurvedic science.

Special Training Needed To Work With Children & Youth
- None

Certifications/Licenses Held By Practitioners
- Clinical Ayurvedic Specialists receive state-approved certification.
- There is currently no licensing required for Ayurvedic practice.

Professional Associations To Contact For Names Of Local Practitioners
- National Ayurvedic Medical Association. Website: www.ayurveda-nama.org
- California Association of Ayurvedic Medicine. Website: www.ayurveda-caam.org
- Please see the website of the California College of Ayurveda for a listing of practitioners. Go to: www.ayurvedacollege.com.

Number Of Certified Practitioners In U.S, Canada, And Mexico
- Approximately 500 in the United States

What To Look For When Choosing The Best Practitioner
- Check the amount of training.
- Check the amount of experience.
- Check references.
- Check reputation.
- Evaluate their curiosity about your child or youth.
- Ask the practitioner about the extent of their training: where and for how long, and how were they tested for competency.
- Has the practitioner been certified, and by whom?
- Contact the certifying organization and verify.

Leading Clinics, Centers, Practitioners
- California College of Ayurveda; 1117A East Main Street; Grass Valley, CA 95495; 530-274-9100; Fax 530-274-7350; Website: www.ayurvedacollege.com; Email: info@ayurvedacollege.com; Founder: Dr. Marc Halpern
- The Ayurvedic Institute; P.O. Box 23445; Albuquerque, NM 87192-1445; 505-291-9698; Fax: (505) 294-7572; Website: www.ayurveda.com/index.html. Founder: Dr. Vasant Lad

Resources, Research Papers, Books, DVD's, Websites
- There are hundreds in the U.S. and thousands in India, mostly on the pharmacological aspects of the herbs and on the benefits of meditation.
- Dozens of articles/research papers are available on the website of the California College of Ayurveda: www.ayurvedacollege.com.

Bibliography
- Atreya, David Frawley. *Practical Ayurveda: Secrets for Physical, Sexual & Spiritual Health*. ME: Weiser Books, 1998.
- Frawley, David, M.D. *Ayurveda and the Mind: The Healing of Consciousness*. WI: Lotus Press, 1997.
- Frawley, David, M.D. *Yoga & Ayurveda: Self-Healing and Self-Realization*. WI: Lotus Press, 1999.

Helpful Tips For Parents
- To improve digestion, make sure the child eats in a quiet, peaceful environment without the distractions of television, reading, or excessive talking.
- To improve digestion and many other conditions, avoid feeding children all junk foods including white sugar, canned foods, old foods, and fast foods.
- To calm children's minds, spend more time with them in nature.
- To help heal children of many conditions, parents need to cultivate greater faith, compassion, and unconditional love, and then bring this into their relationship with the child.

Biography Of Dr. Marc Halpern, DC, CAS, Author
- Years Experience: Fifteen
- Approximate number of children & youth patients: 200 in Ayurveda, 500 in Chiropractic
- Degrees: Doctor of Chiropractic through Palmer West Chiropractic College
- Post Graduate Certification in Holistic Health Care through New York Chiropractic College
- Ayurveda Certification through the American Institute of Vedic Studies

Statement By Dr. Marc Halpern, DC, CAS
I became interested in Ayurveda and meditation in an effort to heal myself of a life-threatening and debilitating disease. In 1987, I was crippled with severe arthritis, anemia, and liver dysfunction. Utilizing Ayurveda, meditation, and other methods of alternative medicine, I was able to heal myself. My work today is the result of that journey.

Today, I teach Ayurvedic seminars around the world, and am the President of the California College of Ayurveda. I am on the founding board of the National Ayurvedic Medical Association and California Association of Ayurvedic Medicine.

To Contact Dr. Marc Halpern, Who Contributed This Chapter

Dr. Marc Halpern; California College of Ayurveda; 1117A East Main St.; Grass Valley, CA 95495; Ph: 530 274-9100; Fax: 530 274-7350; Web: www.ayurvedacollege.com; Email: info@ayurvedacollege.com

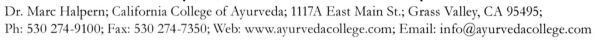

Marie Mulligan's Comment About Ayurveda: My family has benefited from Ayurveda. I have referred patients to Ayurveda providers and most have done well. Unlike Chinese Medicine there is no licensing for Ayurveda practitioners at the state or national levels at this point. Make sure you carefully choose practitioners.

Rick Geggie's Comment About Ayurveda: Any healing system that is as old as Ayurveda must work well. How both the complexity and the simplicity of it work so well to help children fascinate me. Children find Ayurvedic practices calming so they tend to like going to Ayurveda practitioners. Over the years I noticed that children from families following an Ayurvedic lifestyle did very well in living and learning. Picking an experienced practitioner is important.

CHAPTER 8

BIOFEEDBACK FOR CHILDREN & YOUTH

by Bill Barton, PhD,   © Copyright 2008.

Biofeedback Has Helped Kids With

• Anorexia/Bulimia	• Digestion problems
• Anxiety	• Epilepsy
• Asthma	• Hyperactivity
• Attention Deficit Disorder (ADD)	• Learning difficulties
• Attention Deficit/Hyperactivity Disorder (ADHD)	• Migraine headaches
• Cancer	• Rage
• Chronic fatigue syndrome	• Seizures
• Dental problems (TMJ)	• Sleeping difficulties
• Depression	• Stress
• Diabetes	• Raynaud's syndrome

Biofeedback Can Help In The Following Areas

Spirit: Yes
Body: Yes
Mind: Yes
Emotions: Yes
Social: Somewhat, as a person gains confidence in abilities to relax with others

Brief Description Of Biofeedback

• Biofeedback is a painless, non-invasive technique for learning control of the processes of the mind and body.

- Instruments are used that give precise, immediate and meaningful auditory and/or visual feedback of the child's physiology.
- Biofeedback is used to increase relaxation, relieve pain and the effects of stress.
- Biofeedback is also used to train awareness and mindfulness for the promotion of healthier and more comfortable life patterns.
- Each session can be fun, challenging and helpful.

Success With Biofeedback
- Using biofeedback, imagery, and breathing techniques, a 9 year-old boy was able to reduce his frequency of asthma attacks and lessen his reliance on his inhaler. He accomplished this in eight sessions.
- A 10 year-old girl suffering from anxiety, depression, and Raynaud's syndrome after the sudden death of her father was helped considerably by six sessions of biofeedback. She wrote me of her success for several years.
- Combining both brainwave (neurofeedback) and body measures, a young boy of 12 learned to effectively focus and concentrate better. The biofeedback techniques also helped him to fall asleep more easily at night. The quality of his school work improved dramatically. Many gains were noticed after six sessions but further gains continued through twenty sessions.
- A 12 year-old boy receiving chemotherapy found that biofeedback gave him success at managing discomfort and nausea more effectively. In only four sessions he learned a sense of control.
- A 17 year-old girl was able to reduce the amount of insulin she used after some twelve sessions of biofeedback training. This is attributed to a reduction in anxiety, as anxiety often exacerbates diabetic conditions.
- A 9 year-old girl dramatically reduced the frequency and severity of her migraine headaches after eight sessions. She conscientiously practiced her biofeedback exercises at home.

Biofeedback Is Appropriate For Ages
- Seven and older

Children & Youth's Reactions to Biofeedback
- Children report really enjoying the sessions and feeling comfortable with the therapist.
- Children can quickly relate to challenges of self-regulation and self-quieting.
- Children particularly like computer generated puzzles and games that are linked to their learning and mastery of these skills.
- The child takes pride in the opportunity to train and gain control over symptoms and may be excited to tell others what they are doing.
- The child is eager to return, as sessions are fun and meaningful.

Extra Care Is Needed
- Anytime a practitioner is having unexpected results with a client

Contraindications: When Biofeedback Should Be Avoided
- It should be avoided if the child is unmotivated or would be better served with medication or another intervention.
- If a child is working on reducing seizure activity, certain biofeedback frequencies (theta and delta) should be suppressed and not reinforced.

History

- In the late 1960's several researchers were active in biofeedback research: Dr. Neal Miller at Rockefeller University; Dr. Elmer Green (all modalities) at the Menninger Clinic; Dr. Joe Kamiya (EEG) at the University of Chicago; Dr. Barbara Brown (EEG) at UCLA; Dr. Thomas Basmajian in muscle feedback (electromyography or EMG), and others.
- Early successes in biofeedback were in addressing physical problems such as Raynaud's, high blood pressure and other circulatory problems, insomnia, migraine and tension headaches, and other areas of pain management.
- Since the mid 1970's, electro-encephalogram (EEG) or "neurofeedback" has become popular for treating such conditions as ADD and ADHD, seizures, anxiety and panic disorders, phobias, acute and post traumatic stress, habit control and chemical dependency.
- EEG feedback training is also being applied to enhance mental states such as increased awareness, focusing and improved learning states.
- Currently, Biofeedback is being widely used to treat incontinence with electromyographic feedback and cardiac problems via heart rate variability training.

Basic Concepts And Components Of Biofeedback

- Biofeedback uses instruments that send immediate clues to the child about how they can control their physical, mental and emotional states.
- It is founded on two basic mind/body laws:
    1. Any change in our physical state results in a change in our mental/emotional state;
    2. Any change in our mental/emotional state results in changes in our physical state.

Description Of A Typical Session

- Depending on the presenting problem, the most appropriate feedback tools or modalities will be selected and introduced in the first session.
- Sensor pads are taped to the child's skin to monitor brain or bodily activities.
- The child and therapist use the instruments to learn how the child's own movement, tension or relaxation, breath changes, and mental states affect the instruments and how the child can learn to control them.
- Results are reviewed in a positive way and training goals are discussed.
- The child or youth will have a meaningful experience in learning self-regulation. It is painless and fun.
- Subsequent sessions focus on practice to increase skills in order to achieve the goals.

Major Differences Of Opinion Between Biofeedback Practitioners

- Only a small percentage of biofeedback practitioners are experienced in EEG (brainwave or neurofeedback). Those who are EEG qualified often are limited in working with the whole person.

Fees /Costs In 2007

- $75 - $150 per session (in Northern California)

Average Time Per Session

- 45 to 50 minutes

Estimated Length Of Time Before Improvements Can Be Expected

- 4 to 8 sessions

- After 4 or 5 sessions, symptoms usually show some diminishing or improvement.

Suggestions To Make Biofeedback More Effective

- Parents can make sure the relationship between child and practitioner is good and should not hesitate to sit in on the first session.
- Parents can make sure the child gets regular appointments or uses instruments at home.
- Parents can get to know the process themselves by having sessions on their own.

Other Methods That Are Similar To Biofeedback

- Counseling
- Hypnosis
- Mindfulness
- Autogenic Training
- Meditation
- Yoga

Other Methods That Complement Biofeedback

- Physical therapy
- Counseling
- Massage
- Interactive Metronome™
- The learning is accelerated and enhanced by the use of auxiliary techniques such as Autogenic Training, Progressive Relaxation, Systematic Desensitization, diaphragmatic breathing, by practice with and without instruments, and by the expert guidance, coaching and teaching of a trained and skilled therapist.

Nature And Length Of Training To Be A Practitioner

- A license in a counseling profession is recommended: Clinical psychology, marriage and family therapy, clinical social work, or nursing.
- Several years of biofeedback experience is preferable.

Special Training Needed To Work With Children & Youth

- On the job experience working with children & youth is needed.

Certification/Licenses Held By Practitioners

- Biofeedback practitioners are not licensed but are certified. Look for a B.C.I.A. (Biofeedback Certification Institute of America) certificate.
- Additionally, some states have their own certification (e.g., BSC: Biofeedback Society of California). Certification indicates a level of competence even in licensed professionals.

Professional Associations To Contact For Names Of Local Practitioners

- Association for Applied Psychophysiology and Biofeedback; 10200 W. 44th Ave., #304; Wheat Ridge, CO 80033; 303-422-8436; Fax: 303-422-8894; Website: www.aapb.org
  E-mail: AAPB@resourcenter.com

- Biofeedback Certification Institute of America (BCIA); 10200 W. 44th Ave., Suite 310; Wheat Ridge, CO 80033-2840; 866-908-8713; Fax: 303-422-8894; Website: www.bcia.org Email: info@bcia.org
- Biofeedback Society of California; 1925 Francisco Blvd. E. #12; San Rafael, CA 94901; 415-485-1345; Fax: 415-485-1348; Website: www.biofeedbackcalifornia.org Email: bsc@biofeedbackcalifornia.org
- International Society for Neurofeedback and Research; PO Box 832925; Richardson, TX 75083-2925; 800-847-4986; Fax: 972-437-1212; Website: www.isnr.org: Email: annmarie@isnr.org

Number Of Certified Practitioners In U.S., Canada, And Mexico
- Approximately 1,600.

What To Look For When Choosing The Best Practitioner
- Competence: practitioner should be licensed in some helping profession and certified by the Biofeedback Certification Institute of America.
- Experience with children: practitioner needs to really enjoy working with children. Being a parent themselves often ensures greater sensitivity to being effective with children.
- Meet and interview several practitioners to find the one with whom your child will be most comfortable.

Leading Clinics, Centers, Practitioners
- Menninger Clinic; 2801 Gessner Drive; P.O. Box 809045; Houston, TX 77280; 800-351-9058; Fax: 713-275-5107; Website: www.menningerclinic.com
- Scripps Health; 4275 Campus Point Court; San Diego, CA 92121; 800-326-3776; Website: www.scripps.org

Resources
- Barton, William G. *Relax To Sleep* CD. Website: www.biobill.org
- Barton, William G. *Clinical Biofeedback & How It Works* DVD. Website: www.biobill.org

Research Papers Pertaining To Biofeedback
- "Clinical Applications of Biofeedback and Applied Psychophysiology"; a series of White Papers prepared in the public interest by the Association for Applied Psychophysiology and Biofeedback (each paper includes references to articles, and research): available from AAPB phone: 303-422-8436 (in 2001) Website: www.aapb.org

Bibliography
- *Biofeedback: A Practitioner's Guide, 3rd edition*, by Mark S. Schwartz and Associates, 2003 The Guilford Press; New York. "This is a gold mine of clinical chapters with tons of references." Dr. Barton.
- Criswell, Eleanor. *Biofeedback and Somatics: Toward Personal Evolution*. Novato, CA: Freeperson Press, 1995.
- Green, Alyce and Elmer. *Beyond Biofeedback*. Knoll Publishing, 1989.
- Tursky, Bernard and Leonard White (Editors). *Clinical Biofeedback: Efficacy and Mechanisms*. New York: Guilford Press, 1982.

Helpful Tips For Parents
- Use home training cassettes or cd's for guided relaxation.
- Use simple home training monitors: temperature, muscle tension, electrodermal (arousal), heart rate monitors, EEG or neurofeedback home training devices.

- Practice relaxed, diaphragmatic breathing.

Biography of Bill Barton, Author

William G. Barton, PhD, MA, MBA., is a clinical psychologist that has been using biofeedback in his clinical practice in San Francisco for over 35 years. He is certified by the B.C.I.A. in both general biofeedback and neurofeedback. He is a two-time past president of the Biofeedback Society of California.

To Contact Bill Barton, Who Contributed This Chapter

Bill Barton, MBA, MA, PhD; 2166 Hayes St., Suite 203A; San Francisco, CA 94117-1033; Ph: 415-775-9222; Fax: 415-775-9222; Website: www.biobill.org; E-mail: BioBill@pacbell.net

. . . .

Marie Mulligan's Comment About Biofeedback: There can be additional benefits when people get involved with biofeedback practiced by people licensed in other healing modalities. I have referred many children and adults to biofeedback practitioners.

Rick Geggie's Comment About Biofeedback: Biofeedback has helped me on many occasions. Biofeedback has helped so many children or youth with a wide variety of problems. They enjoy learning how to control their bodies and emotions using Biofeedback. They especially like the changes they experience. I am continually impressed with the process and the potential of the many new developments in the field.

CHAPTER 9

CHILD PSYCHIATRY

By Kristi Panik, MD,   © Copyright 2008.

Child Psychiatry Has Helped Kids With

- Sadness
- Irritability
- Anxiety
- Fears
- Nightmares
- Defiance
- Aggression
- Difficulty making and keeping friends
- Problems in school/refusing to go to school
- Divorce of parents
- Family problems
- Any other issue that's holding a child or teen back from progressing and growing emotionally or socially

Child Psychiatry Can Help In The Following Areas

Spirit: Because Child Psychiatry can positively affect physical, emotional and social aspects of a child or teen's life, it can greatly enhance a person's overall essence or spirit. It can also help kids work through spiritual or religious questions or issues.

Body: Because emotions and the body work together in concert, help with emotional disorders affects the body in positive ways; such as improved immune function or decreased pain, to name just two. The Child Psychiatrist can help children and teens deal with chronic medical disorders like diabetes or cerebral palsy.

Mind: Child Psychiatry can help young people with problems in thinking that may be related to emotional or learning disorders. Some kids have scary experiences of seeing or hearing things not perceived by other people. Child Psychiatry can help to get those kids back on track. Help from a Child Psychiatrist can also restore motivation or will. Creativity and/or imagination can come alive!

Emotions: Child Psychiatry can help young people with sadness, anxiety, mood swings, out-of-control anger or any emotion that is troubling. The goal of Child Psychiatry is essentially to enhance positive emotional states like good self-esteem, tolerance, empathy, fortitude and joy!

Social: Child Psychiatry can help kids feel better so they feel more like being with friends. It can help some kids learn how to make or keep friends. It can help families get along better.

Brief Description of Child Psychiatry

- Child Psychiatry in the United States is a way of helping children with a variety of disorders and difficulties. It begins with a thorough assessment of the difficulties the child or adolescent is having.
- A Child Psychiatrist carefully investigates the current and past circumstances of the young person's and family's lives and how the young person and family members interact with one another and within their environment. The Child Psychiatrist explores the strategies that have already been put in place (or attempted) by the young person and family to deal with difficulties.
- Drawing upon years of training and experience, the Child Psychiatrist attempts to determine factors that may be contributing to the young person's difficulties. The Child Psychiatrist then suggests things that can be helpful. These may include ideas about how to approach the issues in a different way: talk or play therapy; extra help at school; further evaluations or tests; close attention to diet, exercise and sleep; and sometimes, prescription medication or over-the-counter treatments.
- In American Child Psychiatry the child or teen may be involved with psychologists, social workers and family therapists who do the talk or play therapy sessions. Psychologists may also administer psychological tests for further information when needed.
- Child Psychiatrists consult with schools or any organizations such as a medical clinic or child protective agency that are also working for the young person's welfare.

Success With Child Psychiatry

- Steven is an 8 year old boy who lives with his mom and sisters, except for every other weekend when he and his sisters live with his dad and dad's girlfriend.
- His mom brought him in because he was having anxiety so badly he was having trouble sleeping at night, his grades were dropping in school and he had lost his appetite.
- A careful interview revealed that Steven was most nervous just before going to his dad's house. Initially, Steven stated that his reluctance to go to his dad's was because he thought his mom would be lonely with all the kids gone. Mom tried to reassure him and wondered if medication may help.
- Over several more sessions trust was gained and Steven revealed that, as the male, his father saw Steven in a dominant role. Steven was pulled aside regularly, given details about his father's relationship difficulties and told he needed to be responsible for the welfare of his sisters. Scared of his father's disapproval, Steven just sat and listened. He felt an enormous responsibility that he did not want.
- Through talk therapy Steven became empowered to eventually tell his father that he was expecting too much of an eight year old boy. Steven chose this solution instead of having adults talk to his father for him. And he did all of this without the help of medication! Sleep and appetite improved right away and grades improved over time.
- Rachel is a 14 year old girl who wanted help for feeling sad or angry most of the time. For the past few months she has been having trouble getting up in the morning and has been taking long naps during the day. She's been hanging out with her friends less and less. Most interactions with her parents or sister turn into arguments. Usually a B student, she is now getting Cs, Ds and Fs.
- She began seeing the counselor at school on a weekly basis and after two months Rachel's mother found a letter in Rachel's trash can detailing her continuing despair and wish to "end it all."
- They were referred to a Child Psychiatrist. After finding out that Rachel had no specific plans to kill herself, her family agreed to monitor Rachel's safety at home. It was confirmed that illicit drugs and alcohol were not involved. Medical conditions like anemia or thyroid disease, which can play a role in depression, were also ruled

out by laboratory testing. Close attention to a healthy diet and good sleep habits were discussed, again employing help from Rachel's family.

- Anti-depressant medication was discussed and agreed upon by Rachel and the family after the third meeting, as things seemed to be getting worse. Rachel continued her counseling at school. After about 2 weeks it was noted that Rachel was less irritable and was talking to her friends a bit more often. The school counselor felt Rachel was able to identify issues more readily in sessions. Rachel "felt like herself again" after about three months!

Child Psychiatry Is Appropriate For Ages
- It is appropriate for ages birth to 18, or older if someone has a developmental delay or disorder such as autism.

Children & Youth's Reactions To Child Psychiatry
- On average most people are a bit nervous coming to a Psychiatrist for the first time. However, children and teens can begin to feel comfortable as early as the first session - just in taking that step in dealing with the difficulties.
- Many children and teens have ambivalence about coming, noticing positive changes but wanting to avoid reminders of their difficulties.
- It is important that parents encourage the young person to come if she or he is reluctant. It's like getting a child or teen to do their chores or homework: kids often resist, but it is good to insist in order to promote learning and overall growth.

Extra Care Is Needed
- When the young person's parents live apart, the Child Psychiatrist should consider talking to everybody - parents and step-parents alike. Legal custody issues must be talked about and decisions made based on these factors.
- Opposing custody lawyers may subpoena the child's psychiatric records in court. Whenever the courts request anything from a Psychiatrist, a lawyer should be consulted.
- Care must always be taken in considering issues of privacy and confidentiality.

Contraindications: When Child Psychiatry Should Be Avoided
- Parents need to feel comfortable with the Child Psychiatrist and should ensure that a thorough evaluation has been conducted before any treatment is begun, especially medication.

Basic Concepts And Components Of Child Psychiatry
- The young person needs to be viewed in the context of his whole being and surroundings. The environment plays a big role in a child's difficulties. The word environment here refers to the family, school, and any other aspect of the child's or teen's life outside of them: friends, the neighborhood, grandma's house, and so on. Consideration is paid to after-school activities, weekend activities, weekend residence (if different), spiritual beliefs or practices, abuses of any kind and parenting styles, to name a few important environmental factors.
- Possible biologic causes of difficulties must be explored as well. Some disorders are passed on within families. Biologic causes of difficulties could also be from medical illnesses, reactions to medications, or nutritional problems. Substance abuse in the mother can contribute to or cause difficulties that appear later in the child's life and substance abuse by the young person can lead to a variety of symptoms.

Description Of A Typical Session
- Each session is as different as is each child.

- During the first session, it is helpful if the assessment process is explained: what to expect in terms of length and structure. The concept of confidentiality is discussed: this concerns what is kept private and what is not. It's important for parents to know that the young person may talk about things with the Child Psychiatrist that are kept private. This is to promote trust so that the child or teen will feel comfortable talking about difficult issues. If the young person tells the Child Psychiatrist something that indicates that the child or teen may endanger themself or another person, the Child Psychiatrist will then make sure the parents are informed.
- Often two or three sessions are needed for a full assessment. The first session typically involves the parents with the child or sometimes the parents alone. The child is generally seen alone for a session. If another session is needed, it can be structured as seems best.
- During the assessment, questions are asked detailing the difficulty the child or teen is having: What is happening now? What has led up to the difficulties? There may be discussion about what has already been utilized to deal with the difficulties. Information about any kind of treatment by medical doctors or mental health professionals is obtained. Details about life at home and school are very important. The Child Psychiatrist asks about the young person's early life - from the time of pregnancy forward. The Child Psychiatrist will probably ask permission to talk with teachers or other doctors.
- During the assessment session with a child on their own, the Child Psychiatrist and child may "play." During this "play" the Child Psychiatrist is getting a view into what the parents may experience at home. It can help the child to act more spontaneously than sitting talking face to face. The Child Psychiatrist is looking for certain themes or issues to be expressed through play. An older child or teen may prefer to talk rather than play. A teen may feel more comfortable going for a walk.
- When the assessment is complete the Child Psychiatrist will meet with parents and the young person to discuss their thoughts and impressions and to work out a treatment plan together.

Major Differences Of Opinion Between Practitioners
- Length of evaluation – one brief visit or an extended period for evaluation
- How much to include the family in the evaluation and within the treatment
- Prescribing medication alone as treatment, or using Play or Talk Therapy in conjunction
- Some disagree on which medications to use and which dosage. It is not an exact science but more of an art.

Fees/Costs In 2007 (Averages In Northern California)
- First session – intake: $200 to $400 or sometimes more; ongoing sessions may be $150 to $300 for an hour, or less for half an hour.
- Most health insurance covers part of the visit.

Average Time Per Session
- Sessions are usually 45 to 60 minutes long.
- The first session is often longer.
- Sometimes sessions discussing primarily medication can be completed in 30 minutes.

Recommended Length Of Time Between Sessions
- If the Child Psychiatrist, child and family are working together in therapy, meetings are often weekly.
- If the Child Psychiatrist is only prescribing medications while the therapy is being done elsewhere, visits to the Child Psychiatrist can be monthly or even every couple of months.

Estimated Length Of Time Before Improvements Can Be Expected
- Sometimes the decision to get help facilitates some change, or change can happen after the first meeting.

- With medication, while relief can sometimes begin in a few days or weeks, play or talk therapy is important in helping to ensure that changes stick.
- In some cases, it may take months or even years of therapy before significant change is achieved.

Suggestions To Make Child Psychiatry More Effective

- Children and teens like seeing a Child Psychiatrist when parents feel hopeful that the Psychiatrist is going to help and that improvement in the child's life is going to happen. Young people seem to be able to know when their parents don't feel good about Psychiatry.
- Consistency and commitment from the young person and the family are good predictors of a positive outcome.

Other Methods/Practices That Are Similar To Child Psychiatry

- Child Psychiatry combines aspects of psychology and medicine – linking mind and emotions with body and physical health.

Other Methods/Practices That Complement Child Psychiatry

- Psychological testing
- Occupational therapy
- Speech and language therapy
- Sensory integration therapy

Nature And Length Of Training To Be A Practitioner

- After high school, one completes four years of college.
- This is followed by four years of general medical school and three to four years of Psychiatry Residency Training working with adults.
- Finally, two years of additional Psychiatry Residency Training working with children and adolescents is completed.

Certification/Licenses Held By Practitioners

- First, a Bachelor's degree is acquired.
- Then a Medical Doctor (MD) or Doctor of Osteopathy (DO) degree is acquired.
- Then each state grants licenses to individuals to practice medicine after many tests have been passed.
- An optional certification is Board Certification by the American Board of Psychiatry and Neurology in Adult and/or Child and Adolescent Psychiatry through the taking of further examinations.

Professional Associations To Contact For Names Of Local Practitioners

- American Academy of Child and Adolescent Psychiatry (AACAP); 3615 Wisconsin Ave., NW; Washington, DC 20016-3007; 202-966-7300; Fax: 202-966-2891; Website: www.aacap.org
- American Psychiatric Association (APA); 1000 Wilson Blvd., Suite 1825; Arlington, VA 22209-3901; 703-907-7300; Fax: 703-907-1088; Website: www.psych.org; Email: apa@psych.org
- National Alliance on Mental Illness (NAMI); Colonial Place Three; 2107 Wilson Blvd., Suite 300; Arlington, VA 22201-3042; 888-999-6264; Fax: 703-524-9094; Website: www.nami.org; Email: available on website

Other Methods Of Locating A Good Practitioner

- Look in the phone book or on the world wide web.
- Consult with your family doctor or pediatrician.
- Consult with psychotherapists.
- Ask school psychologists and teachers.

Number Of Certified Practitioners In U.S., Canada, And Mexico

- The AACAP represents over 7,500 Child Psychiatrists, mostly in the U.S. but also internationally.
- Many Child Psychiatrists are not members of this organization.

What To Look For When Choosing The Best Practitioner

- Look for someone who is going to gather a significant amount of information before recommending any plan of treatment.
- Find someone with whom you are comfortable. This is extremely important for success!
- Look for someone who appears knowledgeable and is confident speaking about the child's or teen's difficulties.

Bibliography

- *Your Child: What Every Parent Needs To Know.* American Academy of Child and Adolescent Psychiatry (AACAP) and David B. Pruitt. New York: Collins, 1998.
- *Your Adolescent: Emotional, Behavioral and Cognitive Development from Early Adolescence Through the Teen Years.* AACAP and David B. Pruitt. New York: Collins, 2000.

Helpful Tips For Parents

- Consistency in parenting is key.
- Modeling effective conflict resolution at home is very important.
- Frequent reminders of love and affection are important. Children need to know that no matter how angry their parents may get, they will love their kids no matter what.
- Attention to nutrition, sleep patterns and exercise can make a world of difference.

Biography Of Kristi Panik, Author

- I grew up in Florida and went to college and medical school at the University of South Florida in Tampa. I then completed my General and Child and Adolescent Psychiatry training at the University of California in Irvine.
- Since I've completed my training in 1998, I have worked in public clinics in Southern California, New Zealand, and at Sonoma County Mental Health Services in Santa Rosa, California. Until 2007 I worked for public systems in both outpatient and inpatient child, adolescent, and adult psychiatry.
- I began a private practice serving children, adolescents and adults in January 2007 in Berkeley, California.
- In addition, I work a limited number of hours at the student health center at the University of California, Berkeley and at La Cheim School for seriously emotionally disturbed teens.

Kristi Panik's Personal Statement

Young people are our future teachers, police officers, doctors, CEOs and entrepreneurs. I love working with this energetic population and their families to help effect positive change and the motivation to always grow emotionally.

My hope is that in the future, my work and that of other Psychiatrists will be more about the preventative work of strengthening positive emotions and traits, and less about trying to solve problems.

To Contact Kristi Panik, Who Contributed This Chapter

Kristi Panik, MD; 2428 Dwight Way, Suite 5; Berkeley, CA 94704; Ph: 510-845-5155; Email: drpanik@gmail.com

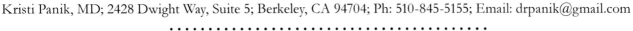

Dr. Marie Mulligan's Comment About Child Psychiatry: Many children & youth benefit from psychiatric medications. There is concern that psychiatric medications are being used in the place of human contact and more time intensive therapies.

Rick Geggie's Comment About Child Psychiatry: I am sad that Child Psychiatry is so misunderstood by the public. I believe that it is one of the most challenging of all medical specialties. I have referred hundreds of children/teens to Child Psychiatrists. Results were most often excellent when the children's parents really wanted the child's life to change and were willing to change their own behavior and beliefs. Child Psychiatrists most often gave excellent advice to me and to my fellow educators on how we could help the children grow easier.

One of their biggest contributions to me was teaching me that the child's behavior is just another language that the child/teen uses when they cannot use words directly.

The other great contribution was in helping me see how body chemistry greatly affects behavior/growth/living – especially in children and adolescents.

CHAPTER 10

CHIROPRACTIC FOR CHILDREN & YOUTH

By Lana Surgenor, DC,   © Copyright 2008.

Chiropractic Has Helped Kids With

• Misalignment of a spinal vertebra that puts pressure on the nerve system (called Subluxation(s))

• Acute and chronic illness	• Colic	• Mood swings
• ADD	• Constipation	• Nausea
• ADHD	• Developmental challenges	• Neck pain
• Allergies	• Digestive issues	• Neurological disorders
• Asthma	• Ear infections	• Overall health and wellness optimization
• Athletic performance	• Epilepsy	
• Autism	• Fatigue	• Postural issues
• Bed-wetting	• Headaches	• Seizures
• Birth trauma	• Injury recovery	• Sleep disorders
• Breastfeeding/latching issues	• Joint aches	• Vertigo
• Chronic colds/flu	• Mid-back pain/low back pain	• Vision trouble

Chiropractic Can Help In The Following Areas

Spirit: Chiropractic care empowers children and youth to reconnect and embrace the power that made their bodies, and deepens the inner connection to their own spirit.

Body: It promotes proactive wellness care and healthy lifestyle choices that translate into better health with greater ability to grow, develop, adapt and evolve as a human being throughout one's lifespan.

Mind: The nerve system sends mental impulses from the brain cells to the tissue cells. Chiropractic promotes optimal transfer of life force information from the brain to the rest of the body, ensuring harmonious body function and balance.

Emotions: With greater ease in the nerve system, Chiropractic care is involved in supporting the resolution of many emotional/behavioral and mental challenges.

Social: Everyone in the family unit - and the greater community, benefits from proactive wellness care. Developing strong, balanced, healthy children and youth is critical for creating peaceful and harmonious communities.

Brief Description of Chiropractic

- Chiropractic includes numerous techniques or sets of practices that use the spinal vertebrae as access points to reduce nerve system pressure or interference, to optimize health, healing and wellbeing throughout the body.
- Techniques employed range from adjusting upper cervical-specific (upper neck only), to full spinal adjustments. Extremity adjustments and instrument use are also incorporated into some approaches. The Chiropractic spinal adjustment (chiro="hand", practic="done by") is a way to access the nerve system which is being protected by the spine. An adjustment releases life force, improves physiological function, frees stuck neural patterns, releases stress and returns our bodies to a state of dynamic healing.
- Chiropractic is based upon the principles of life, health, healing, wellness and wellbeing. It embraces the inarguable truth that every living being is born with an innate intelligence that knows how to organize, adapt, heal and experience life fully.
- A growing body of scientific research and careful observation is supporting Chiropractic care for all ages.
- Although Chiropractors are trained in Chiropractic school to address all ages and aspects of health, some Chiropractors take further training in order to concentrate in different specialties which include but are not limited to; pediatrics, prenatal care, family wellness care, geriatric care, radiology, athletics, neurology, nutrition and physical therapy.
- Chiropractic care is delivered in private offices, multi-disciplinary clinics and some hospitals.
- Millions of people in all age groups - including babies & kids, have enjoyed positive symptomatic results through Chiropractic care.

Success With Chiropractic

- Becky, age 3, had chronic ear infections with multiple antibiotic treatments and recommendation to surgically implant tubes into ears. After one month of care, Becky no longer had any fluid or infection in her ears and was not a candidate for the surgical procedure. Becky is now 5 years old and has had no further incidence of ear infections and consequent need for antibiotics. She continues to receive wellness adjustments to this day.
- Noah, age 2 months, had colic symptoms with difficulty opening mouth to breastfeed. After one month of care, symptoms of colic significantly decreased with greater ability to open jaw and latch successfully. Both mother and son experienced greater ease, intimacy, bonding and health benefits following this improvement.
- Justin, age 1, had constipation for 6 days with intestinal cramping and stomach upset. Immediately following the adjustment the child was able to have a successful bowel movement (in the Chiropractic office) and has had no further episodes of constipation to date. He is now 3 years old and gets checked by his Chiropractor regularly for wellness.

Chiropractic Is Appropriate For Ages

- It is appropriate for all ages!

Children & Youth's Reactions to Chiropractic

- This depends on the nature of the Chiropractor, the environment the practice is in and the techniques used. Some techniques, instruments or machines used can be scary for kids and youths.
- Gentle Chiropractic care delivered with masterful skills is an enjoyable experience for kids that they love to receive again and again!

- Most children & youth appreciate the fact that Chiropractic is non-invasive and doesn't involve any 'yucky' pills, medicines or scary shots.
- Most children & youth understand and embrace the philosophy that their bodies contain inborn and infinite healing wisdom that needs to be expressed fully for their optimum health and wellbeing.

Extra Care is Needed
- When children & youth have been frightened by past medical procedures or other Chiropractic experiences
- When the child or youth and/or family are uncertain, inexperienced or frightened about Chiropractic care in general
- When the child or youth has experienced extensive injury, poor habits or detrimental lifestyle choices, which complicate their Chiropractic care plan
- Pregnancy, newborns and infants

Contraindications: When Chiropractic Should Be Avoided
- Contraindications need to be addressed on an individual basis.
- Generalized contraindications include fractures, spinal tumors, generalized osteoporosis, acute/severe injury and any life-threatening emergency.

History
- The roots of Chiropractic were shown to go back as far as prehistoric times, when pictures depicting spinal manipulation were discovered in cave paintings in southwestern France. Ancient Chinese, Japanese, Egyptians, Hindus, Tibetans and Babylonians all practiced spinal manipulation dating back to 1500 B.C. Even ancient American Indian hieroglyphics illustrated walking on the back of a person as a method of curing ailments.
- The famous Greek physician, Hippocrates wrote over seventy books on health and healing and he was an advocate of spinal manipulation. He believed we had a "vital spirit" and that only nature could heal the body, so it was the physician's responsibility to remove any interference that would prevent the body from optimal healing. He is quoted as saying "Get knowledge of the spine, for this is the requisite for many diseases," Hippocrates, 460-377 B.C.
- Modern Chiropractic was born on September 18, 1895 when D.D. Palmer performed the first specific spinal adjustment to correct vertebral subluxation (nerve interference). The specific adjustment was performed on Harvey Lillard, a janitor who had been deaf for seventeen years. The man's hearing returned following Palmer's spinal adjustment and modern Chiropractic began.
- In the late 1800's, D.D. Palmer opened the Palmer School & Infirmary of Chiropractic in Davenport, Iowa to teach and develop the Chiropractic profession. His son, B.J. Palmer graduated from his school in 1902 and is credited as the developer of Chiropractic. His relentless work over his lifetime to develop, promote, expand and communicate Chiropractic was critical for the profession as we now flourish in the 21st century.
- Chiropractors are now recognized as Primary Healthcare Providers. They have extensive education and training of the human body, life principles, scientific method and Chiropractic philosophy.
- More and more evidence-based scientific research is being done to prove the efficacy, safety and benefits of Chiropractic care.

Basic Concepts And Components Of Chiropractic
- True health, wellness and healing only come from the inside out, not from the outside in.
- Every being is born with an innate intelligence and ability to develop, heal, organize and adapt to changes in its internal and external environments to maintain itself in a state of health. This innate intelligence is carried over the nerve system and any interference to this system results in a lack of function, communication and dis-ease in the body. Vertebral subluxation is the term used for interference or pressure on the nerve system.

- Chiropractic does not treat any symptoms, illnesses or injuries specifically. Rather, it improves and increases the overall function of the nerve system which affects ALL areas of the body and allows the innate healing intelligence, with which we are all born, to work unimpeded. Although Chiropractors do not claim to treat any specific ailment or disease, Chiropractic has seen powerful results from the inside out with a vast number of symptoms and health concerns.
- Conducting and paying attention to scientific research is important.
- There is a responsibility to protect client confidentiality..
- There is a responsibility to give clear information to our clients in regards to known risks, benefits, alternatives and proper referrals to other healthcare providers when necessary (specialists, allied healthcare professionals, medical Doctors).
- There is a responsibility to get consent from clients and/or family before providing Chiropractic care.
- Chiropractic unifies mind, body and spirit so that you and your children can live life to its fullest expression.
- Up until recently, a child was said to be healthy if she or he had no symptoms. However, this has now been found to be misleading and inappropriate. Health is better defined as the ability of the child's body and nerve system to interpret and then respond appropriately to lifestyle and environmental stresses, regardless of the presence or absence of symptoms.
- Regular Chiropractic care will ensure that the child's nerve system is better able to handle all that life has to offer.

Description Of A Typical Session
Initial Chiropractic Visit
- Chiropractor will take special time and attention getting to know the child or youth and parent(s) by providing a warm, friendly environment.
- The practitioner will take a full life and health history, including; current situation, past concerns, family history, lifestyle habits, stress level, spiritual growth and emotional/social circumstances.
- A thorough and complete neuro-spinal assessment will be made by the Chiropractor on the child or youth's initial visit.
- Some Chiropractors take x-rays or order other tests/medical imaging of the body.
- The necessity for such tests may be determined on an individual basis and can usually be avoided through a thorough neuro-spinal biodynamic assessment.
- A Chiropractic wellness plan will be designed that is individualized, comprehensive and specific to each child or youth assessed.
- In addition to adjustments, the Chiropractor will make healthy lifestyle recommendations that will educate the child or youth on wellness practices that promote greater physical, mental, emotional and spiritual wellbeing throughout their lives.

Regular Chiropractic Visit
- Chiropractor will inquire with the child or youth and the parent(s) as to any physical, emotional, mental or spiritual changes noticed since the last Chiropractic visit. These can include questions about activities, bumps/tumbles/falls, emotional concerns, behavioral tendencies, symptoms, nutrition, chemical exposure, etc.
- Chiropractor performs a hands-on neuro-spinal assessment to determine if there is any interference to the child's nerve system (subluxations).
- Chiropractor delivers a gentle spinal adjustment to alleviate any pressure on the nerve system, if necessary.
- Recommendations or strategies to promote improved health and wellbeing in various areas may be made at the end of the visit by the Chiropractor. These include such things as; stretching/strengthening exercises, nutritional suggestions, emotional and chemical stress reduction ideas and other recommendations that promote healthy personal evolution.

Major Differences of Opinion Between Practitioners
- There are various techniques or approaches used by Chiropractors.
- Chiropractic is an Art; like all Arts there are various artistic expressions. Some of these include; upper cervical care (only the upper neck adjusted), full-spine techniques, instruments, traction devices, physical therapy, low-force energy work, high velocity specific adjustments or a combination of approaches.
- Differences in approaches are helpful because there are so many different people with different needs.
- The most important factor is that the child or youth feels very comfortable with the choice of Chiropractor the family made. Getting to know the Chiropractor, seeing the environment they practice in and getting a "feel" for the Chiropractor's energy is critical for getting the most out of their care.
- The other major difference between practitioners is the focus on symptom-based care versus wellness Chiropractic care.
- Many chiropractors focus on pain, symptoms and injury recovery.
- Other Chiropractors embrace a holistic wellness approach that looks deeper into health and healing, not merely the presence or absence of symptoms.

Fees/Costs In 2007
- Cost of Chiropractic care varies from area to area, office to office and health plan to health plan, if insurance is utilized. A typical adjustment may range from $25-75 depending on the office. A typical initial assessment visit may range from $50-150.
- Many insurance health plans cover Chiropractic care on a fee for service basis. Insurance plans vary considerably and can be assessed by the Chiropractic office staff, if insurance is accepted within the office. For more information on HMO and PPO insurance plans, please reference the *Western Medicine* chapter of this book.
- Some counties and states have assistance programs set up for families who cannot afford Chiropractic care. Ask your Chiropractor or Primary Healthcare Provider to direct you to these programs to gain more information.

Average Time Per Session
- Session time varies from office to office, Chiropractor to Chiropractor and technique to technique.
- New visits are typically 30 to 60 minutes - longer under special circumstances.
- Daily adjustment sessions typically average 5 to 20 minutes.
- Wait times vary, depending on the Chiropractic office.

Recommend Length Of Time Between Sessions
- This depends on the program of care that the Chiropractor recommends and is based on the child or youth's individual and unique experience.

Estimated Length Of Time Before Improvements Can Be Expected
- Results can be experienced almost instantaneously, or can take many months or even years, depending on the symptom/problem. Healing is a process and it takes time!
- Reducing interference to the nerve system, unleashing the body's healing potential and experiencing greater life/light expression occurs immediately upon receiving an adjustment, regardless if a change in the symptom/problem is noticed.
- You do not need to be sick to get well! We don't feel our hair and nails growing, but they are and we notice it in retrospect. Greater health and wellness is happening whether you see it or not.

Suggestions to Make Chiropractic More Effective

- Choose a Chiropractor who will provide the exceptional Chiropractic experience: one full of love, service, masterful skills and grounded in the principles of life, health, healing, wellness and wellbeing. One who embraces Chiropractic as a vocation and their life's true calling.
- Choose a Chiropractor who you feel good about; who will take time to answer your questions; who cares for you/your child as a unique and special person; who truly listens to you & respects you; who can help you make decisions and employ strategies to experience a greater quality of life.
- Parents/caretakers and Chiropractic staff remaining calm, relaxed and fun loving helps the child or youth to be at ease during their adjustments—especially on their very first experience.
- Follow the care plan and recommendations as outlined by your Chiropractor to minimize nerve system interference. Do not confuse lack of symptoms with optimal wellness.
- Eat a well-balanced, nutrient dense diet. Decrease intake of inflammatory foods such as dairy, refined sugar, red meat, soy products, gluten and especially processed foods.
- Avoid unnecessary exposure to chemical toxins such as preservatives, sugar, caffeine, excessive prescription or over-the-counter drugs and vaccines.
- Drink plenty of water every day to cleanse and detoxify the body.
- Receive proper rest each night (7-8 hours).
- Maintain a positive and flexible mental attitude.
- Make regular exercise and play a consistent part of your life and your child's life.
- Stretching the body and/or practicing YOGA is a wonderful way to keep the body flexible, pliable and resilient.
- Remember to truly BREATHE.
- Reduce and eliminate unnecessary stress.
- Take quality time with family and friends to laugh, play, support and enjoy one another.
- Spend time in nature marveling at the beauty and intelligence all around. The same beauty and intelligence found in nature resides within our bodies.

Other Methods That Are Similar To Chiropractic

- It is difficult to compare it to any other method because Chiropractic is the only method that adjusts the spinal vertebrae to reduce nerve system interference in order to experience better physical, mental, social and spiritual wellbeing.
- Osteopaths and some Traditional Chinese Medicine body workers use spinal manipulations of spinal segments to improve the body's overall form and function, similar to Chiropractors.
- Other approaches that embrace the body's ability to heal from the inside out include; Acupuncture, Reiki, Massage therapy, Yoga, Chinese Medicine, Craniosacral therapy, Feldenkrais, Homeopathic Medicine, Naturopathic Medicine and Ayurvedic Medicine.

Other Methods That Complement Chiropractic

- Most methods work well with Chiropractic and it is always great to have a team of healthcare professionals working with you and your family for greater health.
- Allied medical fields: Western/allopathic medicine, Acupuncture, Massage Therapy, Midwifery, Lactation consulting, Physical Therapy, Osteopathy, Reiki, Chinese Medicine, Homeopathy, Naturopathic Medicine, Yoga, Nutrition, Fitness, Health Education, Personal/Professional Life Coaching.

Special Training Needed To Work With Children & Youth
- All Chiropractors receive some generalized pediatric training while in Chiropractic school.
- If a Chiropractor adjusts many babies, kids and pregnant women in their offices and focuses on family wellness care, they most likely have had specialized training and experience in pediatrics and prenatal Chiropractic care. Many Chiropractors take continuing education and training from such organizations as the International Chiropractic Pediatric Association (www.icpa4kids.org) in order to have greater skills, knowledge and experience with these specialized populations.
- Chiropractors can choose to take intensive training and education to become fully certified as a Chiropractic Pediatric Diplomate by the International Chiropractic Pediatric Association (ICPA). To have this status, a Chiropractor must successfully complete 180 hours of pediatric class work and 48 hours of Advanced Elective classes, participate in two Practice Based Research Network studies, author an article for the Chiropractic magazine for family wellness called "Pathways", have proof of CPR certification and complete a written, oral and practical final exam administered by the ICPA. Other requirements by the ICPA may apply to be fully certified as a Pediatric Diplomate.

Certification/Licenses Held By Practitioners
- Chiropractors have to be licensed by state and federal governments, as well as certified by professional associations.
- Board certified Chiropractors have basic training of a minimum 3 years of undergraduate study, followed by 3-4 more years of Chiropractic graduate school study (3 years on the accelerated program, 4 years on regular program). Chiropractors must also successfully complete an internship with various requirements depending on the school, country and state/provincial obligations.
- Continuing education is a requirement for licensing annually.
- Specialists have much more training (Chiropractic Neurologists, Pediatric Chiropractors).

Professional Associations To Contact For Names of Local Practitioners
- There are different Chiropractic associations for each state/province.

Number Of Certified Practitioners In U.S. And Canada
- According to The National Directory of Chiropractic, there are currently over 65,000 licensed Chiropractors in the United States.
- According to The Canadian Chiropractic Association, there are currently around 6,600 licensed Chiropractors in Canada.

What To Look For When Choosing The Best Practitioner
- Recommendations from family members, friends and other people in your life are a great way to choose a Chiropractor.
- Interview the Chiropractor to see if they are a good fit for you and your family.
- For Chiropractors in your area that have taken specific pediatric and prenatal training, check out www.icpa4kids.org, or other pediatric Chiropractic specific organizations.
- Check your state or province's Chiropractic board Internet site to see if the practitioner is being investigated for negligence, unprofessional or unethical conduct or if they have any on-going liability law suits pending.
- Check out your state or province's board Internet sites to find out if the practitioner has passed all competency examinations and has completed all annual continuing education requirements.
- Although often time consuming, you can access a list of providers in your area who accept your insurance plan in their office if you have Chiropractic insurance benefits.

- Make sure the Chiropractor communicates clearly, listens intently and answers all your questions so everyone is on the same page. This is a team effort between you and your Chiropractor.
- Find a Chiropractor who educates regularly on healthy lifestyle choices, life principles and the astonishing power of the body and its healing potential.
- Ensure your Chiropractor provides gentle, honoring Chiropractic for the whole family with special interest toward pediatric and prenatal populations.

Leading Clinics, Centers, Practitioners

- Dr. Jeanne Ohm, DC is the Executive Coordinator of the International Chiropractic Pediatric Association and the editor of *Pathways* magazine: www.ohmchiropractic.com, or www.icpa4kids.org
- Dr. Arno Burnier, DC is a renowned national and international speaker on life, health, healing, wellness and Chiropractic. Dr. Burnier has had a lifelong dedication to promoting Chiropractic wellness care for the WHOLE family including babies and kids: www.cafeoflife.com.
- Dr. Sue Brown, DC is the Founder of Bio-Geometric Integration (BGI) and renowned international speaker on the principles of Chiropractic: www.bgiseminars.com.
- Dr. Lou Corleto, DC is the President of AdJustWorld, Inc., a non-profit company which organizes worldwide humanitarian Chiropractic missions of light, providing Chiropractic care to people in countries such as Brasil, Panama, El Salvador and India: www.lifeexpressionschiropractic.com, or www.AdJustWorld.com.
- Oklahaven Children's Chiropractic Center is celebrating over 45 years of helping sick and disabled children back to health through Chiropractic care, specializing in treating children whom traditional medicine was unable to help: www.chiropractic4kids.com.

Resources, Research Papers, Books, DVD's, Websites

- Many reputable Chiropractic schools have reliable sources of information and guidance. To name a few: www.lifewest.edu; www.life.edu; www.sherman.edu; www.parkercc.edu; www.palmer.edu.
- For more specific information on Chiropractic for kids and family wellness care, check out these websites: www.icpa4kids.org; www.cafeoflife.com; www.soulshinechiro.com; www.hpakids.org; www.mothering.com; www.holisticanarchy.com.
- General books on Chiropractic care to start with: *Chiropractic First*, by Terry A. Rondberg, DC; *Discover Wellness: How staying healthy can make you rich*, by Dr. Bob Hoffman, DC and Dr. Jason A.Deitch; and *Enhance Your Life Experience*, by Dr. Joseph B. Strauss, DC.
- Resources to help you make an informed decision on vaccinations for your child or youth are the following: www.generationrescue.org; www.gval.com; www.nvic.org; www.vaers.hhs.gov; and www.thedoctorwithin.com.

Bibliography

- Blanks RH, Schuster TL, Dobson M. "A retrospective assessment of network survey of self rated health wellness and quality of life." *Journal Vertebral Subluxation Research* 1997; 1:4-9.
- "Café of Life," *Café of Life International, Inc.*, 2008. Website: www.cafeoflife.com.
- Langley C. "Epileptic Seizures, Nocturnal Enuresis, ADD." *Chiropractic Pediatrics* 1(1): 22, April 1994.
- Lipton, PhD, B. *The Biology of Belief.* California: Mountain of Love/Elite Books, 2005.
- Mariano MJ, Langrell PM. "A longitudinal assessment of chiropractic care using a survey of self rated health, wellness and quality of life: A pilot study." *Journal of Vertebral Subluxation Research* 1999; 3:78-82.
- Phillips N. "Vertebral Subluxation And Otitis Media: a case study." *Journal of Chiropractic Research and Clinical Investigation* 8(2): 38, July 1992.
- Rubinstein H. "Case Study: Autism." *Chiropractic Pediatrics* 1(1): 23, April 1994.

Helpful Tips For Parents

- Proper nutrition is critical for healthy childhood development and growth.
- Incorporate daily physical exercise for you and your child. Help your children develop healthy lifestyle habits at a very young age so that they will continue with these wellness choices throughout their lives.
- It has been proven that our cells respond to patterns of thought, both negatively and positively. Teach your children the importance and power of happy, positive thoughts and loving affirmations.
- Reduce the chemical stress your child's nerve system is exposed to as much as possible. Eat organic, non-processed foods, use natural skin & body care products, reduce or eliminate when possible the use of prescription, over-the counter drugs and vaccinations, use natural or non-toxic cleaning products in your home and make your home as chemical-free as possible (furniture, toys, paint, gases, etc.).

Biography of Dr. Lana Surgenor, DC, Author

- I did my undergraduate studies in Alberta, Canada and then graduated Summa Cum Laude from Life Chiropractic College West as an Honors Intern.
- I have served on 6 Chiropractic humanitarian mission trips to Nicaragua, El Salvador and Brasil and have served as a staff member of Master Piece Training Camp numerous times.
- I have been practicing Chiropractic for 4 years in my private practice, Soul Shine Family Chiropractic in downtown Santa Rosa, California.
- I have special training in pediatric and prenatal care through the International Chiropractic Pediatric Association and I currently see between 30-40 babies, children and youths per week.

Dr. Lana Surgenor's Personal Statement

Why wait until your health is impaired to take good care of ourselves? Proactive wellness care is for the entire family.

To Contact Lana Surgenor, Who Contributed This Chapter

Lana Surgenor; Soul Shine Family Chiropractic; 858 Second Street; Santa Rosa, CA 95404; 707-525-9950; Website: www.soulshinechiro.com; E-mail: drlana@soulshinechiro.com

· ·

Marie Mulligan's Comment About Chiropractic: Chiropractic is a readily available healing practice. I refer patients to Chiropractors, and my children and I have benefited from Chiropractic care. There are wide varieties of Chiropractic schools and skill levels. Take time and care in choosing the best Chiropractor for your child.

Rick Geggie's Comment About Chiropractic: I know many children and adults who have been helped a great deal by Chiropractors. One Chiropractor helped her local high school football team become winners, against all odds.

CHAPTER 11

CRANIOSACRAL FOR CHILDREN & YOUTH

By Hugh Milne, DO,   © Copyright 2008.

Craniosacral Has Helped Kids With
- Asthma
- ADHD
- Dyslexia
- Headache: all types
- Traumatic birth
- Mood swings

Craniosacral Can Help In The Following Areas
Spirit: Yes
Body: Yes
Mind: Yes
Emotions: Yes

Brief Description Of Craniosacral
- Craniosacral is a form of bodywork that utilizes extremely delicate finger and hand contacts to cranium, spine, and pelvis.
- It works with cranial bones, central nervous system, energy fields, membranes and cerebrospinal fluid.
- It can have a dramatic effect on dyslexia, headache, TMJ, and ADHD, and is effective in correcting cranial molding after birth.

Success With Craniosacral
- **Headache:** Girl aged 8 had a stroke. Her mother called me because while the after-effect of the stroke had stabilized, she still had headaches. I was curious: How does an 8 year-old have a stroke? It turned out that she

223

had been lifting a heavy breadboard down from a counter at home and lost her grip and it had slammed into her forehead. It hurt for a day or two and then she thought no more of it. About three weeks later one of her classmates kicked a soccer ball straight into her face, and it impacted her forehead in exactly the same place as the breadboard. Later that night a blood vessel in her brain hemorrhaged.

My work with her consisted of relieving the pressure and impactation (something wedged) on her forehead, unwinding the tension, compressions and contraction in her upper neck, and helping the more delicate central bones of her head to regain their normal fluid vacancy.

After two 45-minute sessions a week apart, she had no more headaches.

- **Dyslexia and coordination problems:**

A teacher of a ten year old approached the girl's mother. The daughter was doing so poorly in class with her reading and writing skills that something would have to be done, perhaps special tutelage, or to repeat the grade. She kept hurting herself in gym because her motor skills seemed uncoordinated. I sat with both the mother and daughter at the beginning of the session, tuning in to the deeper reasons for this dyslexia. It seemed to me that the parents were fighting, and at the same time attempting to hide this from their daughter.

Since it seemed to me appropriate to discuss the subject, I asked the mother's permission to do so. When this was granted, I explained to the daughter that what she was sensing, and what was disturbing her so much was in fact happening, and that the tensions and anxiety she was experiencing had slowly caused her cranial bones to become displaced.

I encouraged the mother to take her daughter for a long walk by the river and be frank and open with her, and treat her as an equal, not as a child from whom things should attempt to be hidden. I pointed out that you couldn't hide emotional realities from a child.

I then worked on the daughter's head to correct and normalize the position and movement patterns of her sphenoid - the most central bone of the head and the one most often associated with learning difficulties. This took about 20 minutes.

A week later the teacher asked the mother, "What have you done with Anne - this is a different child!" Her dyslexia had disappeared, and her learning abilities fully normalized. (When Craniosacral is successful in children with dyslexia, it is often successful immediately and permanently, as it was with Anne.)

Two years later Anne's coordination had improved to the point that she was the top gymnast in her grade school, excelling on the single bar.

Craniosacral Is Appropriate For Ages

- All ages, including in utero (pre-birth) and even during birth

Children & Youth's Reactions To Craniosacral

- May be immediate, gradual or long term
- The younger the child, the more rapid the response

Extra Care Is Needed Treating

- Brain tumor
- Epilepsy
- Hydrocephalus
- Cerebral Palsy
- If child is unable to stay still

Contraindications: When Craniosacral Should Be Avoided

- Should be avoided in the first four to six weeks after surgery

History
- It originated prehistorically in Shamanism and bone setting.
- American Osteopath, William G. Sutherland, formulated it in the 1900's.
- It is practiced today by Osteopaths, Chiropractors, and Massage Therapists.
- Craniosacral is also known as: Cranial Osteopathy, Visionary Craniosacral, Craniosacral Therapy, Sacro-Occipital Technique, and Craniology.

Basic Concepts And Components Of Craniosacral
- It regards the body's energy field as a source of information and intelligence that can be "listened to" through the fluctuations of cranial bones, spine, and sacrum.
- It helps the body to heal and correct itself; restores natural health and well-being.
- Children inherently understand what the work is because they appreciate being touched carefully, compassionately, intelligently, in a meaningful way.

Description Of A Typical Session
- It is done fully clothed.
- Begins by establishing contact with the child—eye contact, movement contact, and verbal contact.
- It moves to contact with specific cranial bones in a quiet, meditative way.
- Great care is taken with the child's sensibilities, regarding pressure and length of contact.

Major Differences Of Opinion Between Practitioners
- Some give very short five to ten-minute sessions.
- Training and skill levels vary enormously.
- Some practitioners work in a purely technical way, others in a technical and intuitive way.

Fees/Costs In 2007
- The cost is $30 to $110 per 30 minute cranial session, depending on practitioner skill level and location.

Average Time Per Session
- At birth, ten to fifteen minutes
- After age five, fifteen to twenty minutes
- After age twelve, thirty to forty minutes

Recommended Length Of Time Between Sessions
- Five days

Estimated Length Of Time Before Improvements Can Be Expected
- Improvements can be expected in one to four sessions.
- Four to six sessions are typically needed.

Suggestions To Make Craniosacral More Effective
- Make sure that postural, diet and/or home situation suggestions are followed.

- Specific homework tasks are fulfilled.

Other Methods That Complement Craniosacral
- Acupuncture
- Massage
- Homeopathy
- Tai chi
- Yoga
- Osteopathy
- Chiropractic
- Ayurveda
- Meditation
- Leadership development courses

Nature And Length Of Training To Be A Practitioner
- Training may be a four-day seminar.
- Training may be a part time two-year training of approximately 750 hours.
- Training may be an integral part of Osteopathy or Chiropractic training.
- It may be a part of a DO (Doctor of Osteopathy), M.D., or D.D.S. (Doctor of Dental Surgery) training.

Certification/Licenses Held By Craniosacral Practitioners
- There are no state or federal licensing requirements.

Professional Associations To Contact For Names Of Local Practitioners
- Milne Institute Inc.; P.O. Box 220; Big Sur, CA 93920; 831-667-2323; Fax: 831-667-2525; Website: www.milneinstitute.com; Email: infomilne@aol.com
- Upledger Institute Inc.; 11211 Prosperity Farms Road, Suite D-325; Palm Beach Gardens, FL 33410; 561-622-4334; Fax: 561-622-4771; Website: www.upledger.com; Email: edsrv@upledger.com
- The Cranial Academy; 8202 Clearvista Parkway #9-D; Indianapolis, IN 46256; 317-594-0411; Fax: 317-594-9299; Website: www.cranialacademy.org; Email: info@cranialacademy.org

Number Of Craniosacral Practitioners In U.S., Canada, And Mexico
- Several hundred

What To Look For When Choosing The Best Practitioners
- Sensitivity, presence, responsiveness
- Referrals or testimonials from people you trust

Leading Clinics, Centers, Practitioners
- Milne Institute Inc.; P.O. Box 220; Big Sur, CA 93920; 831-667-2323; Fax: 831-667-2525; Website: www.milneinstitute.com; Email: infomilne@aol.com
- Upledger Institute Inc.; 11211 Prosperity Farms Road, Suite D-325; Palm Beach Gardens, FL 33410; 561-622-4334; Fax: 561-622-4771; Website: www.upledger.com; Email: edsrv@upledger.com

Resources, Research Papers, Books, DVD's, Websites
- Feeley, Richard; "Clinical Cranial Osteopathy"
- Blood, S.D. "The Craniosacral Mechanism and the Temporomandibular Joint." *Journal of the American Osteopathic Association* 86, no. 8 (1986): 512-9

Bibliography
- Milne, Hugh. *The Heart of Listening: A Visionary Approach To Craniosacral Work.* Berkeley, CA: North Atlantic Books, 1995.
- Upledger, John and Jon Vredevoogd. *Craniosacral Therapy.* Seattle: Eastland Press, 1983.

Helpful Tips For Parents
- Entirely dependent on practitioner's evaluation

Biography of Hugh Milne, Author
- Third Generation Scottish Osteopathy
- 40 years of experience
- Degrees: N.D. (Doctor of Naturopathy), DO (U.K.)

To Contact Hugh Milne, Who Contributed This Chapter
Hugh Milne; P.O. Box 220; Big Sur, CA 93920-0220; Ph: 831-667-2323; Fax: 831-667-2525; Website: www.milneinstitute.com; Email: infomilne@aol.com

. . . .

Marie Mulligan's Comment About Craniosacral: There can be additional benefits when people get involved with Craniosacral practiced by people licensed in other healing modalities. Parents are advised to have one or two sessions themselves so they can feel the practitioners' competency and can understand the process. My children have benefited from this work.

Rick Geggie's Comment About Craniosacral: I have seen many quite remarkable benefits from good CS work with children & youth. The process is very gentle. Children often fall asleep. CS also tends to enhance the good effect of many other practices. Results are often quite rapid.

CHAPTER 12

DEVELOPMENTAL OPTOMETRY FOR CHILDREN & YOUTH

By Dr. Tanya Mahaphon, OD, FCOVD, FAAO,   © *Copyright 2008.*

Developmental Optometry Has Helped Kids With

• Amblyopia (lazy eye) • Accommodative disorders (inability to keep eyes focused at distance or near) • Anxiety • Arithmetic difficulties • Attention Deficit Disorder (ADD) • Attention Deficit Hyperactive Disorder (ADHD) • Autism • Balance problems • Behavior problems • Brain damage • Cerebral palsy	• Chronic fatigue syndrome • Conduct disorder problems • Convergence insufficiency (inability to cross eyes for near-work) • Convergence excess (over crossing of the eyes) • Coordination • Depression • Developmental retardation • Developmental delays • Difficulty with rhythm and sequencing • Digestion problems • Down's Syndrome	• Dyslexia/letter reversals/left-right confusion • Fetal alcohol syndrome • Handwriting • Hyperactivity • Headaches • Learning differences • Learning disabilities • Rage • Reading difficulties • Spatial disorganization • Speech problems • Short term memory deficiency • Strabismus (eye turns in or out) • Stress

Developmental Optometry Can Help In The Following Areas

- Spirit: A child's spirit is healed when vision is improved. The child learns that he/she is not stupid or lazy, but that their vision was holding them back from achieving success in school, with reading and math, and in sports.

- Body: Body awareness and being able to overcome gravity to stand upright is the foundation for visual and spatial awareness. Developmental optometry enhances a child's coordination by using visually-guided motor activities, reinforces a child's midline and bilateral integration of the body and eyes, then develops the ability to cross midline efficiently and effectively. The child develops a more grounded self and can start to explore visually rather than through tactile senses.
- Mind: A picture is worth a thousand words. A child's mind that learned to utilize vision can learn non-phonetic spelling of words through visual memory, rather than using spelling rules and verbal/auditory memory. Higher levels of visual processing include the ability to create visual pictures in the mind's eye; such as seeing a movie play in your mind while reading words in a book, which is important for reading comprehension.
- Emotions: A child's emotions become more stable through vision therapy. Vision therapy teaches a child to become more flexible and how to adapt to new and different situations. For example: Prism therapy with bean bag toss. The prism alters the child's perception of objects by physically bending light. The child learns how to adapt to this new visual situation and compensate in order to throw the bean bag into the bucket.

Brief Description Of Developmental Optometry

- Developmental optometry is the practice of using lenses, prisms, and/or visually-guided motor activities to enhance visual performance.
- The main goals of developmental optometry are to achieve "single, clear, comfortable binocular (two-eyed) vision" and to develop visual-spatial, visual analysis, and visual-integration skills.
- Vision therapy is a medically supervised program that can treat conditions such as amblyopia (lazy eye), strabismus (turned or crossed eyes), poor eye movements needed in tracking or reading a book, visual spatial skills (such as left/right confusion and letter reversals), visual analysis skills (such as visual memory, visual figure/ground, visual form constancy), visual integration skills (such as visual-motor integration/eye-hand coordination, visual-verbal integration/rapid naming, and visual-auditory integration/seeing and hearing match.

Success With Developmental Optometry

- An 8 year old developmentally delayed young girl had tested mildly mentally retarded at a full scale IQ 70, and learning disabled with performance two grades below. After receiving 30 sessions of vision therapy she still tested borderline full scale IQ of 80, but her academic achievement was on grade level and above her potential IQ!
- A 7 year old boy in second grade with possible attention deficit was struggling with school. He had 20 sessions of vision therapy and has become more focused in school with improved grades, and he has more hits in little league baseball.
- A 13 year old girl with headaches and double vision in school was diagnosed with convergence insufficiency (inability to cross the eyes for reading). After 20 sessions of vision therapy, her headaches and double vision were eliminated and her reading and school grades improved as well.

Developmental Optometry Is Appropriate For Ages

- Birth to death

Children & Youth Reactions To Developmental Optometry

- Most children respond positively to developmental optometry since many of the therapy sessions involve visual-motor activities; such as throwing and catching balls, building blocks, and/or three dimensional pictures. An experienced developmental optometrist with trained vision therapists will know how to create situations that are challenging and achievable by the child, which will then foster self-esteem and increased motivation to succeed.
- Depending on the therapist or doctor, most children enjoy vision therapy and react to vision therapy as if they were playing games at school.

- Many of the vision therapy activities are similar to visual processing games; such as Hidden Pictures, Mazes, Concentration, Bean Bag Toss, Trampoline, and Balance Beam.
- Other vision therapy activities involve crossing and uncrossing the eyes, three dimensional pictures, and eye focusing exercises and patching. These activities may cause some discomfort to children in the beginning as the visual-motor-neurological strength of the eyes improve, which is similar to weight training for the eyes.

Extra Care Is Needed

- Children & youth with short attention spans and poor behavior may require shorter and more frequent vision therapy sessions; such as twice weekly-30 minute sessions, versus a once a week-50 minute session.

Contraindications: When Developmental Optometry Should Be Avoided

- The only contraindication with developmental optometry is when a serious medical condition exists that needs to be treated prior to vision therapy. There are some serious neurological conditions that have symptoms of double vision, blurred vision, headaches, poor memory, and reduced/poor eye movements. These neurological conditions need to be ruled out with a comprehensive vision examination with a dilated fundus exam before vision therapy is started.

History

- The father of developmental optometry was an optometrist named A. M. Skeffington. He was one of the founders of the Optometric Extension Program in the 1920's.
- Optometrist G. N. Getman and an educator, Glenna Bullis, combined Skeffington's theories with their training in the Gesell Institute for Child Development, and their written works have emerged to be the foundation of developmental optometry.

Basic Concepts And Components Of Developmental Optometry

- Vision is a learned process, which begins at birth and continues into adulthood. Vision is being able to receive visual information through the eyes, process the information in the brain, and then output or integrate the information using another motor response such as verbal communication, handwriting or catching/kicking a ball.
- The Developmental Model of Vision is Skeffington's Four Circles:
  * Antigravity - the ability of the body to develop into an upright/vertical position and gain balance
  * Centering - the ability for a person to locate where he/she is located in space, through the use of the eyes and body; i.e., Where am I?
  * Identification – the ability to analyze information through the eyes and senses; i.e., What is it?
  * Speech-Language aspect - the ability to communicate what a person sees
- Most developmental optometrists will integrate visually guided gross motor/body exercises to develop a foundation for the higher level visual processing skills.
- Many vision therapy activities include sensory-integration techniques such as auditory stimuli of a metronome, balance with a trampoline or balance board.

Description Of A Typical Session

- A child or youth will perform 3 to 5 different visual tasks in each session. An example would be a child will perform Angels in the Snow while lying on her/his back for body awareness, bilateral integration, and midline development.
- The child or youth will then follow a Marsden/swinging ball with letters for smooth eye tracking and crossing midline.
- The child or youth will then clear letters using lenses of different powers, similar to eyeglass lenses.

- The child or youth will look at three-dimensional pictures and learn how to cross and uncross their eyes.

Major Differences Of Opinion Between Practitioners

- Some optometrists that practice vision therapy are not Developmental Optometrists. These optometrists have an eye muscle approach and will train the eyes to focus (accommodate) and to cross/uncross (vergence) without the visually-guided gross motor activities. This sort of vision therapy is also effective; however, may not have as lasting effect as a developmental approach, which works on a strong eyes-mind-body approach.

Fees/Costs In 2007 – Northern California

- Average of $85 to $175 per session

Average Time Per Session

- Bi-weekly 30 minute sessions, to weekly 45-50 minute sessions

Recommended Length Of Time Between Sessions

- At least once a week for maximum effect – with daily home activities for reinforcement

Estimated Length Of Time Before Improvements Can Be Expected

- About one month (or 4-8 sessions)

Suggestions To Make Developmental Optometry More Effective

- Parents need to be consistent with having the child attend the vision therapy sessions regularly.
- Ensure the home vision exercises are performed as directed by your doctor.

Other Methods That Are Similar To Developmental Optometry

- Occupational therapy would be the most similar practice to developmental optometry; however, occupational therapists are not authorized to use lenses and prisms to train the eyes.

Other Methods That Complement Developmental Optometry

- Physical therapy for low or high muscle tones and to improve gross motor or core foundation of the body
- Occupational therapy for fine muscle control of the fingers for eye-hand coordination
- Speech/language therapy to help integrate visual-verbal integration
- Auditory therapy to help with rhythm, timing, and sequencing
- Any physical activity that works on bilateral coordination such as karate, tae kwon do, yoga, and swimming
- I highly recommend that parents who have had children in multiple therapies focus on vision therapy first and then add any additional therapies when vision is improved. A significant improvement in all aspects of life will be seen after vision therapy, such as improvement with speech-language, body coordination for sports, dance, and karate, improved eye movements so that reading remediation/tutoring will be more effective.

Nature And Length Of Training To Be A Practitioner

- All optometrists must complete a Bachelor's degree from an accredited undergraduate college and then complete a four year graduate program in the field of optometry and obtain an OD (Optometry Degree).

- Afterwards, some optometrists complete an optional one year residency in vision therapy, binocular vision, and pediatric optometry.
- Developmental optometrists can obtain a Board Certified Fellowship in Developmental Optometry (F.C.O.V.D.) which is granted by the College of Optometrists in Vision Development. This fellowship consists of written essays, three written case reports, 100 hours of vision therapy experience, a written examination and an oral interview.

Certification/Licenses Held By Practitioners
- All optometrists must be licensed and certified by state and national board license exams and requirements.
- There are no specific certification and licenses required for optometrists to practice developmental optometry; however, board certification for Developmental Optometry (F.C.O.V.D.) is highly regarded by the optometric community.
- Affiliations and memberships to the College of Optometrists in Vision Development (COVD) and Optometric Extension Program (OEP) are also considered Developmental or Behavioral optometrists.

Professional Associations To Contact For Names Of Local Practitioners
- College of Optometrists in Vision Development; 215 West Garfield Rd., Suite 210; Aurora, OH 44202; Ph: 330-995-0718; Fax 330-995-0719; Website: www.covd.org; Email: info@covd.org
- Optometric Extension Program; 1921 E. Carnegie Ave., Suite 3-L; Santa Ana, CA 92705-5510; Ph: 949-250-8070; Fax: 949-250-8157; Website: www.oep.org

Number Of Certified Practitioners In U.S., Canada, And Mexico
- Several hundred

What To Look For When Choosing The Best Practitioner
- How well does the developmental optometrist interact with your child? Communication and trust between the child and the doctor/vision therapist is critical for the success of vision therapy.
- Does the developmental optometrist have experience with similar problems that your child has? For example, not all developmental optometrists specialize in special needs, head trauma or strabismus (cross-eyed).
- Look for consistency of relating and disciplining the children.
- Look for a loving person with clear boundaries and solid communication skills.
- Look for a convenient location. Vision therapy is only successful if you, the parent, can bring the child or youth in for consistent and regular sessions. If there is a will, there is a way.
- Look for clear movement/instruction from the practitioner.
- Look for emphasis on safety and injury prevention.

Research Papers
- Pediatric Eye Disease Investigator Group. "A Randomized Pilot Study of Near Activities versus Non-near Activities During Patching Therapy for Amblyopia." (ATS6) JAAPOS 9, no 2 (2005): 129-36.
- Granet DB, Gomi CF, Ventura R, Miller-Scholte A. "The Relationship between Convergence Insufficiency and ADHD." Strabismus 13, no 4 (2005): 163-8.
- Scheiman M, Mitchell GL, Cotter S, et al. "A randomized clinical trial of treatments for convergence insufficiency in children." Arch Ophthalmol 123 (2005): 14-24.
- Maples WC. "Visual factors that significantly impact academic performance." Optometry 74, no 1 (2003): 35-49.

Bibliography

The following books may be obtained directly from the Optometric Extension Program (OEP). (See: www.oep.org.)

- Getman, G.N. How to Develop Your Child's Intelligence. Santa Ana, CA: OEP/VisionExtension, Inc.
- Getman, G.N. Smart in Everything… Except School. Santa Ana, CA: OEP/VisionExtension, Inc.
- Bing, Lois, and George D. Spache and Lillian Hinds. *Vision and School Success*. Santa Ana, CA: OEP/Vision-Extension, Inc.
- Cook, David. *When Your Child Struggles The Myths of 20/20 Vision: What Every Parent Needs To Know*. Marietta, GA: Cook Vision Therapy Centers, 1992.
- Richmond, Hazel and Dawkins. *Suddenly Successful: How Behavioral Optometry Helps You Overcome Learning, Health and Behavior Problems*. Santa Ana, CA: OEP/VisionExtension, Inc., 1990.

Helpful Tips For Parents

- Allow your child to explore his/her world with all the senses: touch, smell, taste, hearing, and vision. This provides the child with sensory memory matches to objects seen visually. For example, an orange fruit: let the child explore the fruit and if the child is old enough, write a flash card that spells orange. Soon a child will be able to visualize the look, smell, taste, and feel of an orange just from the symbolic word "orange".
- Make sure your child has developed the ability to creep and crawl in a coordinated fashion using the right arm/left leg, left arm/right leg pattern. This helps develop a midline and ability to use both the right and left brain. If your child has difficulty creeping and crawling, get their eyes thoroughly examined. Depth perception and blurry vision can make the activity of creeping and crawling a frightful experience.
- Have your child perform activities such as building blocks, wooden puzzles, coloring, tracing pictures with tracing paper, dot-to-dot pictures, mazes, hidden pictures, concentration game/flash cards. All of these activities develop visual processing skills of eye-hand coordination, visual closure (seeing completed pictures from fragments), visual figure-ground (seeing hidden images within a distracting background), visual memory.
- Practice left to right/top to bottom eye tracking patterns. When you read with a child or youth have them use their finger to point from left to right/top to bottom with the sentence you are reading.
- At the end of the day before bed, have your child or youth tell you about his/her day and see if they can get a mental image in detail of what they experienced for the day. For example, what the child ate for lunch or the clothes worn. This builds visual memory and visualization.

Biography Of Dr. Tanya Mahaphon, Author

- Years Experience: 9
- Approximate number of children and youth treated: over 200+
- Degrees: B.S. in Animal Physiology and Neuroscience; Optometry Degree from Pacific University, College of Optometry
- B.S. in Animal Physiology and Neuroscience from UC San Diego
- Residency
- Residency certification in Vision Therapy from SUNY, State College of Optometry

Dr. Tanya Mahaphon's Personal Statement

I have seen numerous children's and parent's lives changed by vision therapy and it has been a blessing to be part of the process. Children who were non-readers become avid readers, failing students become honor students, poor self-esteem children become social butterflies, and frustrated parents become happy and proud parents again. Please see: www.visiontherapysuccessstories.com; and: www.pavevision.org.

To Contact Dr. Tanya Mahaphon, Who Contributed This Chapter

2291 Soscol Avenue; Napa, CA 94558; Ph: 707-253-7111; Website: www.eyespyvision.com; Email: eyespyvision@sbcglobal.net

. . . .

Marie Mulligan's Comment About Developmental Optometry: I have had many friends and children of friends who have been helped a great deal by Developmental Optometry.

Rick Geggie's Comment About Developmental Optometry: Developmental Optometry is one of the most powerful tools in helping children be ready to learn. The time and expense are worth the investment. It works!

One adult client, who started the program totally unable to read, spell or write, thanked her Toronto-based Developmental Optometry practitioner for "giving me back my life; I want to name my soon-to-be born child after you".

CHAPTER 13

DRUMMING FOR CHILDREN & YOUTH

by Christine Stevens, MT-BC, MSW, MA; Heather MacTavish, © *Copyright 2008.*

Drumming Has Helped Kids With
- ADD
- Attachment Disorder
- Autism
- Cerebral Palsy
- RETT (female autism)
- Group drumming can be used as a preventative to increase multicultural awareness in school children and decrease prejudice and violence in school.

Drumming Can Help In The Following Areas
Spirit: Yes
Body: Yes
Mind: Yes
Emotions: Yes
Social: Yes

Brief Description Of Drumming
- Trained therapists or facilitators use drums and rhythm, in groups or individually, to help children and youth overcome the challenges they face.
- Drumming gives all children & youth a voice.
- Drumming is accessible and allows non-verbal communication.

Success With Drumming

- An autistic child, age 6, who was non-verbal, used the drum while the therapist played piano and saxophone. They played "call and response" to increase attention and communications and decrease emotional outbursts.
- Two sisters, ages 15 and 17, were suffering from attachment disorder as a result of being removed from the home. The therapist worked with both the biological and foster families to increase bonding, listening, boundary/rule setting, and emotional expression.
- A 13 year-old child, who was severely impaired, suffered from RETT (female autism) syndrome, was wheelchair bound and appeared to look only about 5 years old. She was constantly wringing her hands, which impaired her ability to communicate and perform other tasks. After placing her hands on a remo ocean drum, there was a decrease in the occurrence of hand wringing.

Drumming Is Appropriate For Ages

- All ages, but the earlier the better

Children & Youth's Reactions To Drumming

- Children love it because drumming is fun and involves them physically through their senses.
- Children are immediate and natural drummers. They find it to be fun and immediately rewarding.
- They enjoy being in control of themselves and feeling powerful. They remind us that there is an innate need to express our human biology in rhythm and sound. They experience an increase in self-esteem, confidence and ability to focus.
- Some children can be shy at first, however this does not usually last long.

Extra Care Is Needed

- Some children require adaptive mallets or drums due to movement impairment.
- With severely traumatized children, group drumming can re-traumatize. Use one-on-one.

Contraindications: When Drumming Should Be Avoided

- Some practitioners feel that children and teens with autism should work one-on-one but not in groups.
- Drumming is not recommended for those with sound sensitivity.

History

- Drumming began in ancient times. For as old as drumming is, it is still pretty new as a youth empowerment and therapeutic modality.
- In 1991 the senate had a hearing on the effects of music therapy on older Americans. It is included in the Older Americans Act.
- The Association On Aging (AOA) funded research on the effects of drumming all over America. The Rhythm for Life organization was born (now defunct), to train people to use drumming with older populations. That project produced more research and acknowledgment of the need for drumming with kids with special needs.
- Today there are several organizations training people in how to use rhythm therapeutically.

Basic Concepts And Components Of Drumming

- Rhythm is innate.
- Drumming gives all children a voice.
- It's an intelligence that exists without any impairment, regardless of the disability.

- Drumming provides successful experience, enhancing self-esteem of even the most "disabled children."
- Drumming increases attention span and creates a non-verbal modality to feel human connection.

Description Of A Typical Session
- Work one-to-one or in groups to accomplish non-musical goals through non-verbal interaction:
  * One-to-one: rhythm games and activities are created which are improvisational and goal directed, such as copying sound if the goal is to create auditory attention.
  * Groups: children are empowered towards creative expression, listening skills, motor skills, thinking skills, social connection and psychologically boosting self-esteem.

Major Differences Of Opinion Between Practitioners
- There is disagreement about the use of drumming with groups of autistic children.

Fees/Costs In 2007 (Averages in California)
- Costs are similar to mental health workers fees: ranging from music therapists, psychologists, etc.
- Cost depends upon geography and experience.
- Free drum circles often exist in your community.

Average Time Per Session
- Sessions are 30 to 60 minutes - depending upon attention span of child.

Recommended Length Of Time Between Drumming Sessions
- Sessions are typically once to twice a week.
- Frequency is determined by need. Some children benefit by drumming daily.

Estimated Length Of Time Before Improvements Can Be Expected
- Immediate

Suggestions To Make Drumming More Effective
- Directly participate in the sessions.
- Encourage continued music work.
- Work with your therapist on how to continue the work at home.

Other Methods That Are Similar To Drumming
- None

Other Methods That Complement Drumming
- Movement/dance therapy
- Art
- Poetry
- Drama
- Singing

Nature And Length Of Training To Be A Drumming Practitioner

- Music therapist earn a 4-year bachelor's degree and 6 months clinical internship.
- Drum circles are not a currently established system - training is offered by some individuals like:
  * Barry Bernstein of Healthy Sounds: P.O. Box 40304; Overland Park, KS 66204; 913-888-5517; Website: www.healthysounds.com; Email: barry@healthysounds.com
  * Arthur Hull of Village Music Circles; 719 Swift St., Suite 65; Santa Cruz, CA 95060; 831-458-1946; Fax: 831-459-7215; Website: www.drumcircle.com; Email: teambuilding@drumcircle.com
  * Heather MacTavish of New Rhythms; P.O. Box 1070; Tiburon, CA 94920; 415-435-4870; Website: www.NewRhythms.org; email: rhythms@rcn.com
  * Christine Stevens and Dr. Barry Bittman, MD of Remo Inc. HealthRHYTHMS; 28101 Industry Drive; Valencia, CA 91355; 661-294-5600; Website: www.remo.com; Email: healthrhythms@remo.com
  * UpBeat Drum Circles One Day Intensive Training; PO Box 55245 Valencia, CA. 91385-0245; 661-799-1636 Website: www.ubdrumcircles.com; Email: info@ubdrumcircles.com

Special Training Needed To Work With Children & Youth

- Clinical internship or specialized training
- There are two ways:
  * A music therapist who uses drumming
  * A drummer or drum circle facilitator who is trained in clinical application

Certification/Licenses Held By Practitioners

Board Certification by American Music Therapy Association (AMTA): 8455 Colesville Road; Suite 1000; Silver Spring, MD 20910; 301-589-3300; Fax: 301-589-5175; Website: www.musictherapy.org; Email: info@musictherapy.org

Professional Associations To Contact For Names Of Local Practitioners

- American Music Therapy Association (AMTA): See above.
- HealthRHYTHMS: See above.
- NAMM Recreational Music Making database; rmm.namm.org, Facilitator Corner

What To Look For When Choosing The Best Practitioner

- Make sure the person is qualified - has had proper training.
- Make sure the person is experienced.
- Check references.
- Make sure that a therapy protocol is set: assessment, make plan, set goals, and evaluate the progress.

Leading Clinics, Centers, Practitioners

- Barry Bernstein/Healthy Sounds: See above.
- Robert Lawrence Freedman and Drumming Away Stress; New York, NY; 212-229-7779; Fax: 718-554-7686; Website: www.stress-solutions.com; Email: info@stress-solutions.com
- Deforia Lane of University Hospitals Health System; Ireland Cancer Center; 11100 Euclid Avenue; Cleveland, OH 44106-5065; 216-844-5298; Fax: 216-844-7832; Website: www.musicasmedicine.com; Email: deforia.lane@uhhospitals.org
- Heather MacTavish: See above.
- Christine Stevens: See above.

- Connie Tomaino of the Beth Abrhmam Institute for Music and Neurologic Function; 612 Allerton Avenue; Bronx, NY 10467; 718-519-5880; Website: www.bethabe.org/Music_Therapy213.html; Email: info@bethabe.org

Research Papers And Articles Pertaining To Drumming

Note: Most of the research has been done on adults so papers pertaining to children specifically are not available.

- Lang (1990).Supplementary Motor Area Activation While Tapping Bimanually Different Rhythms in Musicians. *Experimental Brain Research*, 79, 504-514.
- "Central timing system" found in bimanual motor sequences. Central mesial cortex prevails, including parietal cortex, cerebellum and basal ganglia.
- Mark Anshel and D.Q. Marsi (1978). "Effect of Music and Rhythm on Physical Performance". *Research Quarterly*, 49, 109-113.
- Bittman et al, Composite Effects of Group Drumming Music Therapy on Modulation of Neuroendocrine-Immune Parameters in Normal Subjects (2001) *Journal of Alternative Therapy*. Jan, 2001. p. 38-47.
- Stevens, Christine. "Rainbows of Rhythm: Rebuilding After the Storm of Columbine." Accessed through the UpBeat Drum Circles website: www.ubdrumcircles.com/article_rainbow.html.

Bibliography

- Stevens, Christine. *The Art and Heart of Drum Circles*. Milwaukee: Hal Leonard Co., 2003.
- Stevens, Christine. *The Healing Drum Kit*. Louisville, CO: Sounds True, 2005.
- Tomaino, Concetta. (1998). "Clinical Applications of Music in Neurologic Rehabilitation." St. Louis. MMB Music, Inc.
- Friedman, Robert. *The Healing Power of the Drum*. Gilsum, NH: Whitecliffs Media, 2000.
- Bradway, Deborah. Website: www.remo.com; "Music Therapy as a treatment with at-risk children and adolescents"; 661-294-5600.

Helpful Tips For Parents

- Sit down, across from your child with a frame drum and two mallets. Start a beat and have them join you. Let improvisation happen.
- Follow the ame instructions as above. This time play a "call and response" game.
- Drum your name or your child's name. Take turns and have a drum conversation. Drum along with your favorite CD.

Biography of Christine Stevens, Co-Author

- Founder, UpBeat Drum Circles
- Consultant, Remo Inc, HealthRHYTHMS™
- 20 Years Experience
- Approximate total number of clients who are infants, children, or teens: 2,000
- Degrees: BA and MA in Music Therapy, MSW, Board Certified in Music Therapy

To Contact Christine Stevens, Who Co-Contributed This Chapter

Christine Stevens; P.O. Box 55245; Valencia, CA 91385-0245; Ph: 661-799-1636; Website: www.ubdrumcircles.com and www.remo.com/health; E-mail: info@ubdrumcircles.com

Biography of Heather MacTavish, Co-Author

- Executive Director, New Rhythms Foundation

• Has worked with thousands of infants, children and youth

To Contact Heather MacTavish, Who Co-Contributed This Chapter

Heather MacTavish of New Rhythms Foundation; P.O. Box 1070; Tiburon, CA 94920; Ph: 415-435-4870; Website: www.NewRhythms.org; email: rhythms@rcn.com

. . . .

Marie Mulligan's Comment About Drumming: Drumming is now also used by licensed psychotherapists. Benefits can come from the joy of taking drumming lessons and just drumming.

Rick Geggie's Comment About Drumming: Throughout time, many native people around the world have considered drumming and music in general to be healing. I think children respond to drumming with enthusiasm because they feel good when they drum. Drumming is easy and helps children communicate. It energizes and relaxes children, taking them out of their thoughts of the past and of the future. I use drumming whenever I get tired or tense.

CHAPTER 14

EMDR FOR CHILDREN & YOUTH
Eye Movement Desensitization & Reprocessing

By Sandra Wilson, PhD and Robert Tinker, PhD, © *Copyright 2008.*

EMDR Has Helped Kids With
- Fears, anxieties, compulsive behavior, depression, sleep, and eating disorders
- The effects of big traumas such as ongoing abuse of any kind, war, many surgeries, or a death in the family.
- The effects of little traumas, such as single scary accidents, failures, social problems, animal nips, and nightmares
- Instances where the child feels stuck and wants to change her or his feelings or behavior but can't do it alone
- Phantom limb pain (when pain is felt to be coming from an amputated body part)
- Emotional effects of all degrees of abuse -- emotional, physical, sexual, and social (abandonment and betrayal)
- Fixes "broken feelings"
- Children who act up or are depressed because they don't know who loves them and don't know how to love because they have not bonded to their parents, show huge improvement and participation in life after EMDR sessions
- Children of all ages, who have been traumatized by war, earthquakes, volcanoes, floods, etc., can recover the urge to live after EMDR sessions

EMDR Can Help In The Following Areas
Spirit: EMDR helps children recover their damaged souls.
Body: It helps children recovering from challenges such as bedwetting, facial tics, and phantom limb pain.
Mind: EMDR is especially useful for depression, anxiety, obsessive-compulsive disorder, withdrawal, and poor school performances caused by traumas.
Emotions: EMDR is great for children with low self-esteem caused by physical and/or sexual abuse.
Social: EMDR helps children who are violent, anti-social, or difficult to get along with in general due to trauma and abuse.

Brief Description Of EMDR

- EMDR is used to help children recover from strong emotional reactions to difficult things (traumas) that have happened in their lives.
- Only licensed mental health professionals, such as psychiatrists, social workers, and psychotherapists, can be trained in EMDR.
- EMDR uses eye, or hand movement, or tapping with talking, to achieve emotional release and to gain new ways of reacting to what has occurred.

Success With EMDR

- Juan, a three year old, was able to relax and sleep through the night after fears brought on by many surgeries on his mouth and face to correct a severe birth defect.
- Amy, a child who had been raped repeatedly and was in shock, recovered after EMDR sessions.

EMDR Is Appropriate For Ages

- Two and up

Children & Youth's Reactions To EMDR

- They like it when they can be free of troublesome feelings.
- They can experience intense emotion during sessions, and highly-trained therapists can help them as these feelings change.

Extra Care Is Needed

- Very complex traumas can be present when many different and difficult things have happened to the child.
- Extra care is needed when the child has many overlapping problems.

Contraindications: When EMDR Should Be Avoided

- A consulting physician must check out existing medical conditions, such as diabetes, vision problems, etc.
- Use with caution during pregnancy.
- When the causes of the traumatic reactions have not yet stopped.

History

- In 1987, Dr. Francine Shapiro, in dealing with her own cancer, discovered that her negative thoughts disappeared when she moved her eyes back and forth in a certain way.
- She researched her discovery with rape victims and with shock victims of the Vietnam War, and learned that it worked with them as well.
- Methods were developed to train therapists to use EMDR as part of the efforts to help children and adults heal from the effects of the Oklahoma bombing by Sandra Wilson, PhD.
- As part of the Humanitarian Assistance Programs (HAP) of the Spencer Curtis Foundation, Eye Movement Desensitization and Reprocessing-HAP has now been used throughout the world, wherever there are natural or manmade disasters--such as Rwanda, Kosovo, Albania, Scotland, Turkey, and Japan.

Basic Concepts And Components Of EMDR
- Whenever humans get emotionally overwhelmed, it is like a logjam in the river of life. EMDR helps to release the logjam.
- In the child's brain and nervous system, EMDR produces something similar to intensified brain waves usually associated with sleep and dreaming - yet the child is fully awake.
- When used by trained mental health workers, EMDR speeds up the healing of "broken feelings."

Description Of A Typical Session
- At the first session the therapist takes a history of the child's traumas from the parents (and from the child if 12 or older). The practitioner explains to the parent what EMDR is and how it works. Together, the practitioner, the parent - and the child when appropriate, set goals for the work.
- In the next and following sessions if needed, EMDR is practiced. The work is done with the child fully clothed. Parents are generally not in the room with the child, unless the child is very young or is too fearful.
- The practitioner has the child establish a safe place in his/her mind and "sets" the place with eye movements or other methods.
- The practitioner has the child picture in his/her mind whatever the problem is and asks them questions about the thoughts and feelings it brings up, and again has them do eye movements or other techniques.
- Both the safe exercise and the exercise about the problem may be repeated several times, until the safe place has replaced the problem space in the child's mind.
- Goals and targets are reset during and after each session.

Major Differences Of Opinion Between Practitioners
- Highly directive structured framework is needed to allow EMDR to work. There are two basic rules; if moving, stay out of the way; if stuck, certain techniques are used to help get it unstuck. Differences may occur over when to think of a child as being stuck.
- Some practitioners add their own methods to their use of Eye Movement Desensitization and Reprocessing; others may omit some EMDR steps.

Fees/Costs In 2007
- Costs vary according to geographic location and the practitioner's training.
- EMDR is used by qualified mental health professionals, psychiatrists, psychologists, social workers, and psychotherapists, so expect to pay their usual fees - which may be covered by many insurance plans.

Average Time Per Session
- Time per session depends upon the age of the child.
- There might be ten minutes of actual EMDR work for a five year old; up to an hour for older children.
- Most sessions are 50 to 60 minutes long and often include other things such as talk, play, drawing, etc.

Recommended Length Of Time Between Sessions
- Generally one week

Estimated Length Of Time Before Improvements Can Be Expected
- Two or three sessions

Suggestions To Make EMDR More Effective

- Parents need to pay attention to any changes that occur after sessions and reward improved behavior.
- Parents need to tell the EMDR therapist about these changes.
- Parents can be taught some of the exercises to perform at home.

Other Practices That Are Similar To EMDR

- There are none like it.

Other Methods That Complement EMDR

- Practically all therapeutic methods; especially expressive art therapies, such as art, dance, music and theater

Nature And Length Of Training To Be A Practitioner

- Only licensed, certified mental health professionals, such as psychotherapists, social workers, psychologists, doctors, and psychiatrists, can take the training. Make sure your practitioner is one of these.
- The training is highly structured and lasts for two weekends.
- Level one trains practitioners for use of EMDR with simple traumas. Level two focuses on working with more complex challenges.
- There is also specialty training for particular traumas and age groups.

Special Training Needed To Work With Children & Youth

- Part One EMDR training

Certification/Licenses Held By Practitioners

- The EMDR Institute (see below) grants EMDR certificates.

Professional Associations To Contact For Names Of Local Practitioners

- Eye Movement Desensitization and Reprocessing International Association; 5806 Mesa Drive, Suite 360; Austin, TX 78731; Ph: 866-451-5200; Fax: 512-451-5256; Website: www.emdria.org; Email: info@emdria.org
- EMDR Institute; P.O. Box 750; Watsonville, CA 95077; Ph: 831-761-1040; Fax 831-761-1204; Web: www.emdr.com; Email: inst@emdr.com

Number Of Certified EMDR Practitioners In U.S., Canada, And Mexico

- There were 5,000 in the USA as of 2001.

What To Look For When Choosing The Best Practitioner

- Look for someone who is kind and compassionate.
- Check for EMDR Institute Level Two certification.
- Check for two years of experience.

Leading Clinics, Centers, Practitioners

- EMDRIA Eye Movement Desensitization and Reprocessing International Association Institute (See above.)

- Spencer Curtis Foundation; Colorado Springs CO; 719-630-8212
- Carol York MSW; Austin TX; 512-451-0381
- Joan Lovett MD; Berkeley CA; 510-524-0488
- Ricky Greenwald PsyD; c/o Child Trauma Institute; P.O. Box 544; Greenfield, MA 01302-0544; 413-774-2340; Fax 413-772-2090; Website: http://www.childtrauma.com; Email: cti@childtrauma.com
- Frankie Klaff; Wilmington, DE; 410-392-6086; Email: fklaff@crosslink.net
- Margaret Moore MSW, Albuquerque, NM 505-247-8915

Resources, Research Papers, Books, DVDs, Websites
- Refer to the EMDR Institute – See above.
- Carlson, JG, Chemtob, CM, Rusnak, K, Hedlund, NL, and Muraoka, MY. "EMDR (Eye Movement Desensitization and Reprocessing) Treatment for Combat-Related Posttraumatic Stress Disorder." *Journal of Traumatic Stress* 11, no. 1 (1998): 3-24.
- Chemtob, CM, Nakashima, JP, and Carlson, JG. "Brief treatment for elementary school children with disaster-related PTSD: A field study." *Journal of Clinical Psychology* 58, no. 1 (2002): 99-112.
- De Jongh, A, Ten Broeke, E. and Renssen, MR. "Treatment of specific phobias with EMDR (Eye Movement Desensitization and Reprocessing): Protocol, empirical status, and conceptual issues." *Journal of Anxiety Disorders* 13, no. 1-2 (1999): 69-85.
- Greenwald, R. "Applying EMDR in the treatment of traumatized children: Five case studies." *Anxiety Disorders Practice Journal* 1, (1994): 83-97.
- Puffer, MK, Greenwald, R, and Elrod, DE. "A single session EMDR study with twenty traumatized children and adolescents." *Traumatology* 3, no. 2 (1998).
- Wilson, SA, Logan, C, Becker, LA, and Tinker, RH. (1999, June). "EMDR as a stress management tool for police officers." Paper presented to the annual conference of the EMDR International Association, Las Vegas, Nevada.

Bibliography
- Refer to the EMDR Institute: www.emdr.com.
- Tinker, Robert and Sandra Wilson. *Through the Eyes of a Child*. New York: W.W. Norton & Company, 1999.
- Shapiro, Francine and Margot Silk Forrest. *EMDR: The Breakthrough "Eye Movement" Therapy for Overcoming Anxiety, Stress, and Trauma*. New York: Basic Books, 1997.
- Parnell, Laura. *Eye Movement Desensitization and Reprocessing: Transforming Trauma*. New York: W.W. Norton & Company, 1997.
- Lovett, Joan. *Small Wonders: Healing Childhood Trauma with EMDR*. New York: The Free Press, 1999.

Helpful Tips For Parents
- Children can be taught by the EMDR therapist to do some of the processes at home, to soothe themselves.
- Parents can remind their children by learning self-soothing techniques from the EMDR therapist.

Biography of Sandra Wilson, PhD, Co-Author
- Sandra has 10 years experience.
- She has worked with hundreds of infants, children and teens.

Sandra Wilson's Personal Statement

EMDR brings a gift of health and normal development to children individually and in groups, worldwide.

To Contact Sandra Wilson, Who Co-Contributed This Chapter

Sandra A. Wilson; c/o Spencer Curtis Foundation; 18 East Monument St.; Colorado Springs, CO 80903; Ph: 719-630 8212; Fax: 719-630-2213; Email: drswilson@msn.com

Biography of Robert Tinker, PhD, Co-Author

- Robert has16 years experience with EMDR: 35 years as a psychologist.
- Has worked with thousands of infants, children and teens.

To Contact Robert Tinker, Who Co-Contributed This Chapter

Robert H. Tinker; c/o Spencer Curtis Foundation; 18 East Monument St.; Colorado Springs, CO 80903; Ph: 719-630 8212; Fax 719-630-2213

. . . .

Marie Mulligan's Comment About EMDR: I have many patients, young and old, who have benefited from EMDR. I recommend it to parents whose own childhood traumas prevent them from supporting their children effectively. I strongly recommend that children & youth receive EMDR from licensed mental health or medical practitioners.

Rick Geggie's Comment About EMDR: EMDR is surprising and strangely effective. Most children appear to enjoy it. They can recover their quality of life quickly and the changes seem to be long lasting. I have used it and am still amazed. Choosing a practitioner who resonates with the child appears to be very important. (Look for a practitioner who has experience and training in other healing modalities.)

CHAPTER 15

ENVIRONMENTALLY HEALTHY HOME CONSULTANTS

By Susan Bahl,   © Copyright 2008.

Environmentally Healthy Home Consultants Have Helped Kids With

• Allergic reactions of all kinds	• Digestive disorders	• Loss of, or reduction in smelling and tasting
• Asthma	• Eating disorders	• Mood swings
• Autism	• Epilepsy	• Nausea
• Multiple Chemical Sensitivities	• Fatigue	• Sleep disorders
• Multiple Sclerosis	• General malaise	• Rashes and skin disorders
• Seizures/Tremors	• Hair loss	• Violent behavior
• Hyperthyroid	• Headaches	• Vision
• Cancer	• Joint ache	
• Depression	• Learning disabilities	

Environmentally Healthy Home Consultants Can Help In The Following Areas

Spirit: Children and youth's natures are often distorted by the body/mind challenges caused by environmental pollution in their homes and schools.

Body: Pain, many diseases, burning eyes, sore muscles and joints, skin rashes, cramping, and diarrhea.

Mind: Thinking is difficult in environmentally polluted environments. Children & youth often appear "foggy brained", irritable, disconnected, speech impaired, or not able to communicate needs clearly.

Emotions: Emotional overreaction can often be caused by environmental chemical pollution.

Social: Having friends is difficult when emotions, mind, and body are not harmonious.

Brief Description Of How Environmentally Healthy Home Consultants Work

- Environmentally Healthy Home Consultants are concerned with having healthy environments for children and youth.
- Environmentally Healthy Home Consultants help parents locate contaminants and hazards in children or youth's home environment.
- Environmentally Healthy Home Consultants help parents make realistic plans about what to do about toxins that are present.

Success With Environmentally Healthy Home Consultants

- A school age child had violent outbursts due to glued down synthetic carpeting and polyurethane being applied to a gymnasium floor. The outbursts stopped when the contaminants were removed.
- A little boy had seizures when a synthetic carpet was introduced into his home. His seizures stopped when he was out of the house. The family lawyer and parents tracked down the chemicals that were causing the problem. They discovered the carpet manufacturers were giving misleading information. The boy stopped having seizures when the carpet was removed.
- A little girl started sleep-walking after her mother put a new comforter and new drapes into her bedroom. The mother washed all the materials to remove the stain, mold and fungal repellant, and fire retardant which had been sprayed on the material. This was not enough. The child only stopped sleep-walking when all the new materials were removed and replaced with organic, natural fibers.

Environmentally Healthy Home Consultants Are Appropriate For Ages

- All ages

Children & Youth's Reactions To Environmentally Healthy Homes

- Children & youth can get frightened if they learn how contaminated their homes and schools are.
- Children & youth's fears are reduced when they know their parents are taking action.
- Children can occasionally notice when contaminants are removed if they are very chemically damaged and are very sensitive.
- Children feel more protected and relaxed.
- They are alert, happy, compassionate, and healthier.
- Bothersome symptoms often disappear.

Extra Care Is Needed

- When people are in panic and fear about their household environment and the high financial costs of environmentally safe homes and schools.
- Where the investigation is not comprehensive enough or not focused on health issues.
- Many unethical companies are trying to make profits without concern for health issues.
- Many companies are offering a service without having the proper training.

Contraindications: When Environmentally Healthy Home Consultants Should Be Avoided

- None

History

- Many ancient Romans went insane due to poisoning from lead plumbing.
- Environmental Medicine was started in the 1930's by Dr. William Randolf in the United States. He noticed that people were getting sick from home and workplace contamination.
- Dr. Randolf noticed that different people often had different reactions to the same chemicals.
- There is now a new form of medical practice called Environmental Medicine and there are currently thousands of such doctors.
- Rachel Carson wrote a book called *Silent Spring* outlining the extent and effects of pesticide pollution.
- People living in a community called Love Canal, which was built beside a chemical dump, became so ill that the government condemned all their homes.
- In another community, Times Beach, the dumping of waste chemicals on the roads to reduce dust poisoned the community.
- The movie, *Erin Brockovich*, starring Julia Roberts, recounted the true story of a power company that poisoned a community to save money.
- Bill Moyer's television program, *Trade Secrets*, documented the chemical industry's suppression of evidence that they knowingly poisoned workers and surrounding communities.
- Movies and television programs like these are awakening people to environmental pollution issues.
- In many cities, families are finding high levels of lead and asbestos pollution in and around their homes. Both are very dangerous to children.
- The combined effects of chemicals and molds are not known. What is known is that children and adults develop problems when exposed to chemical and mold contaminated environments.
- Despite ample evidence to the contrary, government and industry (chemical, agricultural, building, and household products, etc.) have consistently denied the cause-and-effect relationship between health effects and environmental products. They have worked together to try to pass laws limiting the amount of money people can be awarded in law suits over pollution-caused health damages.
- Industry has been effective in legally stopping government agencies from warning people about the scientific data proving a connection between health effects and chemicals.
- As of 2007 there are still few companies offering environmentally healthy home consultant services. Most often families must hunt up specialists in each area: water, air, mold, chemicals, and electromagnetic fields, etc.
- Consumers are asking questions about products. Manufacturers are spending billions on marketing campaigns that mislead consumers. Consumers are told that products are safe when there are no government standards or credible research. For example: Consumers are told that synthetic carpets only off-gas (releasing toxic gasses and compounds into the home/school) for 72 hours, when off-gassing could take one to two years. (An organic wool carpet does not off-gas any volatile chemicals.)
- The Internet is giving people a chance to gather information so they can more often make better purchases.

Basic Concepts And Components Of Environmentally Healthy Homes

- The chemical industry has created over 200,000 chemicals. New chemicals are being invented and put into household products all the time.
- Thousands of petrochemicals are in construction materials, interior finishings, cabinets, furniture, carpeting, glues, paints, solvents, cleaners, insecticides, fire retardants, and mildew and mold removers.
- Many of these chemicals move freely in the environment and interact with each other to create new, unnamed chemicals about which no one has information.
- Many of the chemicals and the new combinations of chemicals can be hazardous to humans, especially to children - because they are growing.
- The building and furnishing materials that are available for use in homes and schools are often not health supportive. Since the 1950's Asthma has increased in children by 75%. This is thought to be due to the chemical soup environments in which children live. Other diseases have also been connected to the chemicals in our home environments.

- Weatherization and energy-reducing heating and air conditioning processes can cause air to become polluted with chemicals, dust, and molds due to lack of fresh air.
- Air, water, soil, and building materials can all have contaminants that cause strong reactions in sensitive children, resulting in damage to their nervous, immune and reproductive systems.
- Air and water can also be contaminated with molds, pollens, dust, radiation, and chemical residues.
- Molds and mildews, which can cause illness, collect in homes and on furnishings.
- The label "Sick Building" is being given to buildings, which have many contaminants that can chemically compromise children. A child or youth's symptoms can vary to this accumulation of chemicals.
- Everyday our children are surrounded by toxic VOC (volatile organic compounds – natural and synthetic) which are released into air, water and dust by all materials. Many of these compounds are unhealthy for children/youth/adults/pets. For example: Recycled rubber tires are used in schools as floor covering. However, rubber tires are not rubber but are made of a chemical called Styrene Butadiene. This chemical causes cancer.
- Contaminated gases can seep into homes and schools from the earth.
- Water in wells and in municipalities is often contaminated and is affected by minerals and chemicals in water pipes, such as polychlorinated biphenyl (pcb's), lead and copper.
- Illnesses can be caused by electromagnetic fields found in cathode ray tubes, electric blankets, laptop computers, video games, and high voltage wires – especially near sleeping areas.
- Natural and full-spectrum lighting (like sunlight) is healthier than fluorescent lighting.
- The "Green Movement" does not always approach the solution and may often involve products that are not interior air quality friendly.
- It is important for parents to realize that, at this point, there are no government regulations about which materials can and cannot be used for homes and schools. Even though people think they are protected by the government agencies like the Food and Drug Administration (FDA) and the Environmental Protection Agency (EPA), these organizations have no standards for construction of buildings or the sale of home products, some of which create poor interior air quality. In fact some materials, like fire retardants, are required by law to be used, even though they cause diseases.
- Trained, knowledgeable consultants, using monitoring equipment can identify which toxins are in the home.
- The consultants teach parents ways to make the home as safe as possible, attempting to work within the family budget.
- Because of this complicated situation, parents need experts to help them find out what can be done.
- Parents and school officials are advised to take action regardless of the cost or inconvenience.
- Parents must take responsibility and assume that any products near children could pose a risk until proven to be safe.
- Parents must also be aware that hygiene issues are extremely important. It is essential to wash food, cooking and eating utensils; floors, bedding, sinks and toilets with non-toxic substances.
- Hazards in the home environment can cause reproductive system problems in both parents - before children are conceived. The fundamental health of the child can be affected if these hazards are not removed before conception.
- Conception, birth, infancy, childhood, and adolescence can all be improved when hazards in the home, community, and school environment are eliminated.
- Environmentally safe homes should be built with organic materials and furnished with safe household products.

Major Areas Needing Environmentally Healthy Home Consultants
- Portable classrooms
- Emergency homes/mobile homes
- Low cost housing
- New homes/new schools

- Home decorating products: bedding, mattresses, carpet, carpet under-padding, particle board furniture, cabinetry, laminated flooring, lawn and garden products, insecticides, paints, wood finishes, flooring sealants and fungicides (for mildews and molds).

Description Of A Typical Session
- The consultant visits the home or school and interviews the occupants or owners.
- An assessment is made about health conditions, building materials, home products, insect spraying, agricultural spray drift, heating and air conditioning systems, and water supply. The presence of electromagnetic fields may be checked. Samples of air, water, and dust may be taken back to a laboratory.
- The consultant later returns with a written report, and a plan to remedy the problems.
- Corrective action is taken.
- The consultant may return to recheck after the plan is carried out.

Brief Description Of How Environmentally Healthy Home Consultants Do Their Work
- Environmentally Healthy Home Consultants go to homes and schools to identify toxins in the environment coming from building materials, furniture, supplies and equipment. There are some investigators who specialize in one or two areas such as Electromagnetic Fields (EMF's), air quality, Radon gas, and heating.
- Inspections and plans are made to correct the presence of hazards and toxins.
- Attention is paid to allergies which may be symptoms of reactions to chemicals in school and homes.
- Parents receive information and support on how to identify and correct the possible sources of toxins. This can support the cure of the physical, mental and emotional impairments.

Major Differences Of Opinion Between Consultants
- Consultants may give different possible solutions.
- Consultants working for the industry and those working for householders often disagree about what substances are toxic. Consultants can often find research to back up their contradictory claims.
- The effect of electromagnetic fields from appliances and house wiring is a hotly debated topic.

Fees/Costs In 2007 - Averages
- Fees vary among consultants depending upon qualification and location.
- $150 an hour is typical.

Average Time Per Session
- Initial consultation is normally two hours.
- There may be a need for several follow-up calls to make sure remedies could be implemented.

Recommended Length Of Time Between Sessions
- A month apart, plus any needed follow-up to check the progress.

Estimated Length Of Time Before Improvements Can Be Expected
- After at least two sessions (if recommendations are followed) - if the problems are not large and long term
- In cases where toxins have long term effects, changes may not be noticed immediately.
- Often no immediate response occurs because the effects are long term.
- Unfortunately, some damage is slow to heal.

Suggestions To Make Environmentally Healthy Home Consultants More Effective
- Follow the plan you work out with the Healthy Homes & Schools/Holistic Health Interiors Consultant.
- Try not to panic the children.
- Take action carefully.
- Keep noticing your child's reactions as an indicator of success.
- Be prepared to make life changes for your child or youth even if the changes involve big sacrifices of time and money.

Other Practices That Complement Environmentally Healthy Home Consultants
- Use health supportive construction materials: building supplies, heating, air filtration, paints, carpeting, furniture, household goods and household cleaners.
- Use environmental medicine.
- Use environmental specialists and companies that specialize in testing magnetic fields, and/or water, air; and for the presence of gases or radiation or molds; and/or any other common household materials. Many consultants bring equipment to measure gases, radiation, etc.
- Eliminate fabric softeners, perfumed detergents, and flame retardants on mattresses.

Nature And Length Of Training To Be An Environmentally Healthy Home Consultant
- Many practitioners train themselves.
- A two-year certificate program is given by the International Institute for Bau – Biologie and Ecology; 1401 A Cleveland Street; Clearwater, Florida 33755; 727-461-4371; Fax: 727-441-4373. Website: http://building-biology.stores.yahoo.net.

Special Training Needed To Work With Children & Youth
- None

Certification/Licenses Held By Consultants
- As of 2007 there are no state standards.
- There a few states that have standards or certification/licensing requirements for some of the possible tests made by Environmentally Healthy Home Consultants.

Professional Associations To Contact For Names Of Local Consultants
- As of 2007 there are none.
- Most practitioners are independent, unregulated and unsupervised.
- To compensate for this, a large selection of websites, books and magazines are given to you below so you can become your own expert.

Number Of Certified Environmentally Healthy Home Consultants In U.S., Canada, And Mexico
- The number of consultants is unknown as of 2007.
- There are far fewer than needed.

What To Look For When Choosing The Best Consultant
- Ask questions about their understanding of environmental illness and Multiple Chemical Sensitivity (MCS).
- Determine their understanding of symptoms that develop as a result of contaminants in the home and schools.
- Ask for certificates of training they have had in identifying molds, harmful chemicals, electromagnetic fields, gases, and water and air quality.
- Trust your own judgment.

Famous Practitioners/Famous Centers
- Chemical Injury Information Network; P.O. Box 301; White Sulphur Springs, MT 59645; 406-547-2255; Fax: 416-547-2455; www.ciin.org
- Dr. Doris J. Rapp; 1421 Colvin Blvd.; Buffalo, NY 14223; 716-875-0398; Fax: 716-875-5399; www.drrapp.com.
- Environmental Research Foundation; P.O. Box 160; New Brunswick, NJ 08903-0160; 732-828-9995; Fax: 732-791-4603; www.rachel.org
- Healthy House Institute; 13998 West Hartford Dr.; Boise, ID 83713; 208-938-3137; Fax: 208-938-3138; www.healthyhouseinstitute.com
- International Institute for Bau-Biologie and Ecology; 1401 A Cleveland Street; Clearwater, FL 33755; 727-461-4371; Fax: 727-441-4373; www.buildingbiology.net
- Natural Home Design Center; 461 Sebastopol Ave.; Santa Rosa, CA 95401; 707-571-1229; Fax: 707-571-1711; www.naturalhomesource.com

Resources, Research Papers, DVD's, Websites
Please look up papers outlined on these websites: (If you don't have a computer, ask your local librarian to help you.)
- Centers for Disease Control and Prevention Environmental Health; 1600 Clifton Rd.; Atlanta, GA 30333; 800-311-3435, or 404-498-1515. Website: http://www.cdc.gov/Environmental/. http://www.cdc.gov/health/environm.htm.
- Children's Environmental Health Network http://www.cehn.org/cehn/resourceguide/rghome.html.
- American Lung Association, Indoor Air Quality Education for Schools, Parents, etc.: http://www.lungusa.org/air/air00_iaq.html.
- Home water testing/treatment: http://epa.gov/safewater/faq/faq.html#test.
- Water quality standards are also available at the website of the Environmental Protection Agency: http://epa.gov/safewater/faq/faq.html#test.
- Advice from EPA on mold: http://www.epa.gov/iaq/molds/moldguide.html.
- Healthy House Institute provides extensive information about creating a healthy home environment. Their website is: http://www.healthyhouseinstitute.com.
- There are videos covering a variety of topics available from the website of Dr. Doris J. Rapp: http://www.drrapp.com/publications.htm.
- American Chemical Society. Available at: www.acs.org.
- Natural Home Magazine. Available at: www.naturalhomemagazine.com.
- Newsletter: Our Toxic Times by Chemical Injury Information Network. Available online at: http://www.ciin.org.

Bibliography
- Hidden Exposures: Many people, including pregnant women, come into contact with things in their day-to-day environment that may affect their health and their ability to have a healthy child. Website: http://www.womenshealthmatters.ca/centres/environmental/Healthy-Environments/hidden_exposures.html.
- Baker-Laporte, Paula, Erica Elliott and John Banta. *Prescriptions for a Healthy House: A Practical Guide for Architects, Builders and Homeowners*. Pennsylvania: New Society Publishers, 2001.

- Bower, Lynn Marie. *Creating A Healthy Household: The Ultimate Guide For Healthier, Safer, Less-Toxic Living.* Indiana: Healthy House Institute, 2000.
- Colborn, Theo, Dianne Dumanoski and John Peter Myers. *Our Stolen Future: Are We Threatening Our Fertility, Intelligence and Survival? A Scientific Detective Story.* New York: Penguin, 1996.
- Dadd, Debra Lynn. *Home Safe Home: Protecting Yourself and Your Family from Everyday Toxics and Harmful Household Products.* New York: Tarcher/Penguin, 1997.
- Pinsky, Mark. *EMF Book: What You Should Know About Electromagnetic Fields, Electromagnetic Radiation & Your Health.* New York: Grand Central Publishing, 1995.
- Rapp, Doris J. *Is This Your Child?: Discovering and Treating Unrecognized Allergies.* New York: William Morrow & Co (Harper), 1991.
- Rapp, Doris J. *Is This Your Child's World? How You Can Fix the Schools and Homes That Are Making Your Children Sick.* New York: Bantam, 1997.
- Lewis, Grace Ross. *1001 Chemicals in Everyday Products.* New York: Wiley-Interscience, 1998.
- Schettler, Ted, Jill Stein, Fay Reich, Maria Valenti and David Wallinga. *In Harms Way: Toxic Threats to Child Development.* Massachusetts: Greater Boston Physicians for Social Responsibility, 2000. No longer in print. May be downloaded here: http://psr.igc.org/ihw-download-report.htm.
- Steinman, David and Samuel S. Epstein. *The Safe Shopper's Bible: A Consumer's Guide to Nontoxic Household Products, Cosmetics, and Food.* New York: John Wiley & Sons, 1995.

Helpful Tips For Parents Made By Environmentally Healthy Home Consultants
- Eliminate products that have high volatile compounds. The "new house", "new car", "new carpet" smell means there are dangerous chemicals being released into the home.
- Create non-toxic bedrooms as soon as possible because children spend most time there.
- Eliminate synthetic carpets and toys.
- Use non-perfumed detergents and fabric softeners.
- Stop dry cleaning your clothing.
- Have mattresses with no flame retardants.
- Use organic mattresses and bedding.
- Find and remove molds and mildews using various techniques, including renovation.
- Avoid using mildew and mold removers as a solution. They are also toxic. Find the sources.
- Replace furniture paint and wall paints with organic paint.
- Replace particle board furniture with solid wood furniture.
- Avoid plastics, vinyl furniture, decorations and toys.
- Create non-toxic bathrooms.
- Avoid scented soaps.
- Avoid air fresheners and toilet deodorants.
- Avoid chlorine cleaners (chlorine is only given by prescription in parts of Europe).
- Find and remove molds and mildews in the bathroom and kitchen.
- Replace new furniture that has been treated with stain, mold and mildew repellants.
- Check for radon gas and take corrective measures.
- Check municipal and well water supplies for contamination.
- Check for Electrical Magnetic Fields (EMF's), cell phone towers, microwave towers, electrical transformers and transmission lines, as well as home electrical fuse boxes, and then take corrective action, including moving.
- Find a new place to live if necessary.

Helpful Tips For Parents
- Make sure no child's bedroom is near garages where cars and chemicals are stored.
- Give new homes, new carpets, new furniture, and new paint jobs lots of time to release off gases. Some people "cook" them off by turning up the heat for many weeks, while living somewhere else.

- Be tactile; use your senses. Look at your body for inflammations of the eyes, headaches, ongoing flu-like symptoms. Look for molds and stale air.
- Make a list of possible dangerous new products brought into the home in the last six months to one year.
- Try to get material safety data sheets (MSDS) when you purchase new products.
- Purchase a carbon monoxide detector.
- Get natural rather than chemical-based products whenever possible.
- Air out your home as much as possible (as long as there is good quality air outside).
- Assume any manufactured food or product is dangerous until proven otherwise.
- Serve organic food to strengthen the body and further reduce the child's chemical load.
- Get involved politically, contact politicians, and boycott hazardous goods.

Biography of Susan Bahl, Author

- Degrees: BA, 25 years of Interior Design
- Years Experience: 17 locating safe products
- Approximate total number of clients who are infants, children, or teens: 8,000
- Owns and operates Natural Home Products retail outlet

Susan Bahl's Personal Statement

The government building and manufacturing standards were set in the 1950's. This has created a silent epidemic of children and adults with compromised immune systems.

Reactions to chemical pollutants vary for each individual. Some get multiple sensitivities; others may become depressed, or exhibit other conditions, while others may appear healthy for years and years.

Unexplained illnesses due to pollutants can appear much later in life as the body accumulates toxins over years of exposure. Soon buildings and products will be created that support humans and their health.

Some professionals might tell you that your child's conditions are hysterical reactions.

Pay attention to how you and your child feel.

Strange, and often unexplained, symptoms that do not respond to standard medical and psychological testing often have environmental causes.

It is good that you care and are concerned about your family's environment, despite what "experts" may say.

~ Susan

To Contact Susan Bahl, Who Contributed This Chapter

Susan Bahl; 2661 Gravenstein Hwy South, Suite G, Sebastopol, CA 95472; Phone: 707-824-0914; Fax: 707-824-4366; Web page: www.NaturalHomeSource.com; E-mail: info@NaturalHomeProducts.com

. . . .

Marie Mulligan's Comment About Environmentally Healthy Homes: This chapter is a great overview of these complicated issues. There is a lot you can do on your own. Check out www.medlineplus.gov. If problems still persist, investigate further by hiring the most qualified consultant you can afford.

There are a few simple approaches to take that make the issue more manageable and comprehensible:

1. Think carefully and critically about the environments you live in and the materials and products you use.
2. Make changes you can manage at a pace you can manage. Many lifestyle and environment changes are easy to make, others less so. Making smaller, manageable changes over an extended period of time ends up being more realistic and effective over the long term.
3. Practice the precautionary principle. Assume that something could pose a hazard to health and well-being until it is proven otherwise. Don't wait for science or government to officially "decide" that something poses a risk. Lead was considered "safe" for many decades; pesticides were considered generally "safe" for decades and are only now being seriously questioned. My guess is that within the next decade using pesticides in the home will be as taboo as using lead paint!

Rick Geggie's Comment About Environmentally Healthy Homes: The complexity and scope of this issue is staggering - it can seem that everything around you is toxic! This may make it seem impossible to ever feel like you've done "enough" to create a safe and healthy environment for yourself, the people you care about and the broader community.

We humans are not distinct from the environment; we are part of it. What we do, what we use, what we eat, what we buy, how we travel, all have an impact. Do what you can. Follow the advice in this chapter as much as you can. You will make a difference.

I look forward to the day when people who make lots of money from selling chemicals and other products that harm people and the environment realize this and deal with products that contribute to health or at least do no harm. I am sure things will change when they wake up to the terrible suffering caused by their hazardous chemicals. I also look forward to companies and governments paying for long-term impartial research and publicity on the effects of products and manufacturing processes. I want my grandchildren's grandchildren to have environmentally safe homes and schools.

CHAPTER 16

EXPRESSIVE ARTS THERAPY FOR CHILDREN & YOUTH

By Lore Caldwell LCXMHC, ATR-BC,   © Copyright 2008.

Expressive Arts Therapy Has Helped Kids With
- Anxiety
- Attention Deficit Disorder (ADD)
- Attention Deficit Hyperactive Disorder (ADHD)
- Behavior disorder
- Depression
- Migraine headaches
- Rage

Expressive Arts Therapy Can Help In The Following Areas
Spirit: It fosters the child's natural spirit and expressiveness.
Body: It is used in the medical field to facilitate healing, recovery and to explore pain.
Mind: It helps the child to better focus on the present.
Emotions: It helps the child express their feelings and emotions without words.
Social: The child is able to practice social skills through role-play in a non-threatening environment.

Brief Description Of Expressive Arts Therapy
- Expressive Arts Therapy uses art and creativity to help children connect to their problems, give voice to their emotions, and learn techniques to heal.
- It uses a variety of techniques including art, drama, movement, music, poetry, puppetry, and sand play.
- Through the experience of Expressive Arts Therapy, the child's individuality and self-esteem are supported and enhanced.

Success With Expressive Arts Therapy

- Sam was a 7 year old boy with control issues. He felt that he always had to have things his way, and if he didn't, he would "tantrum" for hours. Using sand play, the games Sam created frequently involved power struggles. He agreed that from now on the opposing players could ask questions before beginning play, or if power struggles developed. Practicing this skill helped Sam learn to compromise. His behavior at home improved, and he explained to his parents that, "Sometimes we can all get our way, but just a little different".
- Roger was an 8 year old boy who experienced angry outbursts in school. Through role-play, using puppets for demonstration, Roger was able to master the technique of breathing deeply for a count of ten to stay calm. Roger's school and his mother began to encourage the use of the technique at school and home. His outbursts decreased significantly.
- A 15 year old girl named Jane came in one day after several weeks of Expressive Arts Therapy. She began to draw with great intensity because other students had sexually harassed her after school that day. By the end of the session Jane had gotten all her emotions out through drawing and felt quite calm. She integrated this process into her life at home, and now uses the techniques whenever she needs them. Using art helped give her a voice and confidence in sharing her feelings.

Expressive Arts Therapy Is Appropriate For Ages

- Three years through adolescence

Children & Youth's Reactions To Expressive Arts Therapy

- They show enjoyment.
- They show enthusiasm.
- It feels natural.
- Some children fear Expressive Arts Therapy because they believe they are not "good enough" at drawing, singing, dancing, etc. These fears are put to rest through the non-judgmental stance of the therapist.
- They begin to take techniques they have learned into their home life.
- The child is demonstrating enjoyment or excitement in going to therapy.
- The child may begin to verbalize more about their feelings and problems.
- The child may begin using the expressive techniques at home to help themselves.

Extra Care Is Needed

- Care is needed when a child remembers a traumatic event for the first time.
- Therapists should always allow adequate time to process the meaning of a "piece" the child creates.

Contraindications: When Expressive Arts Therapy Should Be Avoided

- A child is threatening to hurt herself/himself or others.

History

- From the early 1970's, therapists, social workers, and medical professionals began to document improvements in clients and patients who used Expressive Arts.

Basic Concepts And Components Of Expressive Arts Therapy

- When people are in pain or under stress, words are often unavailable to express their depth of emotion. They often turn to some form of art or drama to express these emotions.

- Often children don't have the language skills to verbalize their problems. Expressive Arts Therapy taps into the right brain where the language of images, ideas, and creative expression exist.
- There is a natural yearning in all of us to create without judgment.
- The therapist will explore with the child his or her interests.

Description Of A Typical Session
- The first session is for information-gathering about the child and family, including such things as: the child's strengths, family strengths, goals for treatment, family history, developmental history, social and school experiences, mental status, and harm to self or others.
- The following sessions are conducted using modalities in which the child has demonstrated interest. For example: The child may be asked to draw the family doing something together and to discuss it with the therapist.
- The techniques used will be designed around each individual child.

Major Differences Of Opinion Between Practitioners
- None

Fees/Costs In 2007 (Average)
- $75.00-$150.00 per session, depending on practitioner's experience and geographical location

Average Time Per Session
- 50 minutes to 1 ½ hours

Recommended Length Of Time Between Sessions
- One to two weeks

Estimated Length Of Time Before Improvements Can Be Expected
- Depending on the child, in as little as three to four weeks after the first information-gathering session

Suggestions To Make Expressive Arts Therapy More Effective
- Parent and/or family can be involved in the therapy sessions if appropriate, and may be asked to do a project during sessions, or for homework.
- The therapist is exploring all the different modalities to find the one that works best for each child.
- Collaborate with other people familiar with the child (school, friends, family outside the home).

Other Methods That Are Similar To Expressive Arts Therapy
- Drama therapy
- Music therapy
- Both of these modalities can be included in Expressive Arts Therapy.
- Art Therapy

Other Methods That Complement Expressive Arts Therapy
- Discussion or talk therapy
- Drama therapy
- Narrative therapy
- Art Therapy

Nature And Length Of Training To Be A Practitioner
- Both Master's and Doctoral programs are available in Expressive Arts Therapy.
- In most states, licensed therapists have completed at least 60 credits in graduate school and have received a Master of Arts degree in psychology and counseling or a Master of Social Work degree.
- Other routes to become an Expressive Arts Therapist are: psychologists, social workers, and counselors.
- Therapists interested in Expressive Arts Therapy can take courses in that field.

Special Training Needed To Work With Children & Youth
- Course work in child/human development
- Child and adolescent psychology is very beneficial.
- Expressive Therapy Course
- Internships or practicums with children
- Workshops and conferences in Expressive Arts Therapy on an ongoing basis

Certification/Licenses Held By Practitioners
- Therapists are licensed on state and national levels.
- Some receive certifications from Expressive Arts Therapy associations.

Professional Associations To Contact For Names Of Local Practitioners
- American Art Therapy Association, Inc.; 5999 Stevenson Ave.; Alexandria, VA 22304; 888-290-0878; Website: www.arttherapy.org; E-mail: info@arttherapy.org
- National Coalition of Creative Arts Therapies Associations (NCCATA); c/o AMTA; 8455 Colesville Rd., Ste. 1000; Silver Spring, MD 20910; Website: www.nccata.org
- The National Expressive Therapy Association (NET); Website: www.expressivetherapy.com
- International Expressive Art Therapy Association; P.O. Box 320399; San Francisco, CA 94132; 415-522-8959; Website: www.ieata.org; For names of registered therapists, Email: reat@ieata.org

What To Look For When Choosing The Best Practitioner
- Ask your Pediatrician or school guidance counselor for names of Expressive Arts Therapists in your area.
- Contact Expressive Therapy Associations listed in this section.
- Ask for references from the therapist you consider and check them out.
- Ask therapist for the names of parents who have found Expressive Arts Therapy beneficial in their families.

Leading Clinics, Centers, Practitioners
- Expressive Therapy Institute, founded by Natalie Rogers; Website: www.nrogers.com
- Society for the Arts in Healthcare; 2437 15th St., NW; Washington, DC 20009; 202-299-9770; Fax: 202-299-9887; Website: www.thesah.org; Email: mail@thesah.org

Research Papers

- Brooke, Stephanie. "Art Therapy: An approach to working with sexual abuse survivors." *The Arts in Psychotherapy* 22, no. 5, (1995): pp. 447-466.
- Group Art Therapy with mothers of sexually abused children. Hagood, Marilyn M. MFCC ATR, *Arts in Psychotherapy*. 1991, vol.8: #1.

Bibliography

- Allen, Pat. *Art Is a Way of Knowing*. Boston: Shambala Publications, 1995.
- Lewis, Penny and David Read Johnson, (Editors). *Current Approaches in Drama Therapy*. Springfield, IL: Charles C. Thomas Publisher, 2000.
- Dossick, Jane and Eugene Shea. *Creative Therapy: 52 Exercises for Groups*. Sarasota: Professional Resource Exchange, 1988.

Helpful Tips For Parents

- Once a technique has demonstrated its usefulness in a therapeutic setting, it can be repeated at home.
- If a child is having a difficult time expressing their feelings, they can draw how they are feeling, and that can help facilitate the communication.
- Oftentimes, an Expressive Art Therapist will give homework assignments for the child, and occasionally the parents.

Biography Of Lore Caldwell, LCMHC, AT, RDT, Author

- Degrees: Bachelor of Science from Springfield College, School of Human Services; Master of Arts in Counseling Psychology from Antioch New England Graduate School; CAS in Art Therapy from Springfield College
- Currently in private practice in Littleton, New Hampshire as a Licensed Clinical Mental Health Counselor, Registered Art Therapist and Registered Drama Therapist
- Recently employed as an adjunct professor at Springfield College and Lyndon State College
- Experience: 18 years working with children using art and drama as a pathway to healing
- Approximate number of children & youth: 8-15 per week

Lore Caldwell LCXMHC, ATR-BC's Personal Statement

I am an artist and therapist specializing in combining art and drama therapy to facilitate healing and personal growth with my clients.

The effectiveness of art therapy, sand tray therapy, play therapy, puppetry, and mask-making is evident as I observe both adults and children begin the process of healing in their own personal way, each one using her or his own medium which feels most comfortable and safe.

To Contact Lore Caldwell, Who Contributed This Chapter

Lore Caldwell; 15 Main Street; P.O. Box 661; Littleton, NH 03561; Ph: 603-444-8830

. . . .

Marie Mulligan's Comment About Expressive Arts Therapy: There can be additional benefits when people get involved with Expressive Arts practitioners who are licensed in other healing modalities. I wish I had access to Expressive Arts therapy when I was a child & youth.

Rick Geggie's Comment About Expressive Arts Therapy: Expressive Arts of any kind can be healing. Joining good therapeutic practice with the Expressive Arts is a powerful combination. Children learn through creating and expressing, which is why play is so vitally important. They also heal the same way. Creating and expressing themselves helps them rid themselves of painful and non-productive patterns. It helps them create new ways of being who they are.

CHAPTER 17

THE FELDENKRAIS METHOD® FOR CHILDREN & YOUTH

By Russell Delman and Linda Evans Delman, © *Copyright 2008.*

The Feldenkrais Method® Has Helped Kids With

• Autism	• Breathing difficulties	• Posture
• Accidents (recovery from)	• Cerebral Palsy	• Sitting
• ADD	• Coordination (large muscle and	• Standing
• Athletics	hand-eye)	• Walking
• Balance	• Compulsive disorders	• Running
• Behavior problems	• Disorganized thinking	• Scoliosis
• Lordosis	• Learning disabilities	• Tourette's Syndrome

The Feldenkrais Method® Can Help In The Following Areas
Spirit: Yes
Body: Yes
Mind: Yes
Emotions: Yes
Social: Yes

Brief Description Of The Feldenkrais Method®
- Through the gentle touch and respectful interaction of the Feldenkrais practitioner, children are able to learn to move themselves more effectively, easily and enjoyably.
- The Feldenkrais movements organize the whole brain and therefore affect the thinking, feeling, and behavioral functions of the child.

- The Feldenkrais Method® helps children sense themselves more clearly and develop a more accurate self-image and a more accurate image of the world around them.

Success With The Feldenkrais Method®

- Mother Teresa's Mission in Calcutta, India took in a street child whose name was "Child of Light." At age 4, he was crib bound, could not walk or stand and was blind. In the course of 6 weeks of applying the Feldenkrais Method®, Child of Light learned to crawl, took his first steps, and spoke his first words.
- A girl, about 9, brought in from living on the streets, was spiritually and emotionally absent, unresponsive and depressed. She was completely in her own world and un-communicable. In the course of being touched with the Feldenkrais Method® work, she discovered herself, started to smile, giggle, and come alive.
- A 6-year-old boy with severe cerebral palsy couldn't crawl, feed himself or hold up his head. After consistent sessions for a year all of these functions became possible.
- A girl of 12 with severe scoliosis, postural difficulty, movement problems, and distressing body image learned to sit, stand and walk in ways that gave her enjoyment and pride.

The Feldenkrais Method® Is Appropriate For Ages

- All ages: one day old children and up

Children & Youth's Reactions To The Feldenkrais Method®

- They like how it feels.
- They notice that they can do things differently and with more ease.
- Most children enjoy the sessions.
- The touch is gentle and the atmosphere playful.
- As they discover that they can do things more easily it becomes self-rewarding.

Extra Care Is Needed

- When parents need specific scientific reasons for everything, they can have difficulty with the lack of research.
- When parents need guarantees that the Feldenkrais Method® will work for their child.
- When parents confuse the Feldenkrais Method® with a primary care system. It is an educational process.
- Parents need to take children with serious injury for standard medical examination before they engage a Feldenkrais Method® practitioner.
- Practitioners have to work hard exploring movement with children who do not want to be touched or who are frightened or defensive.

Contraindications: When The Feldenkrais Method® Should Be Avoided

- If trauma has been recent
- If the child feels he gets attention by having or being a problem
- If one of the parents is invested in their child having a problem or if child seems to be forming an identity as a 'problem' from seeing too many health care providers
- If the parents are skeptical of the Feldenkrais Method®
- If parents can't accept the learning, as opposed to 'fixing', model

History

- Moshe Feldenkrais PhD was an engineer and physicist who discovered the basic principals while healing his own crippling knee injury.

- Dr. Feldenkrais combined his studies of children, the development of movement, and human behavior with his deep understanding of the bio-mechanics, biology, and the neurology of movement.
- Since his death in 1984 practitioner training programs are conducted all over the world.
- Contact the Feldenkrais Guild® for further training information.

Basic Concepts And Components Of The Feldenkrais Method®
- Learning through movement
- Intelligent play
- Concentrated listening
- Entering a state of meeting themselves
- Stimulating brain potential

Description Of A Typical Session
- With clothes on, we work on the floor or on a low table in a friendly environment.
- There is a strong effort to keep the child comfortable and at ease.
- We focus on keeping the experience playful and interactive.
- The Feldenkrais Method® practitioner gives movement directions by voice or gentle touch.
- Parents are often encouraged to stay during the learning sessions.

Major Differences Of Opinion Between Practitioners
- There are some Feldenkrais Method® practitioners who mix other technologies into their practices.
- Some Feldenkrais Method® practitioners see a child two or three times a week for a set period, while others prefer to see children once a week.

Fees/Costs In 2007
- Our fees are $150 per session.
- Fees vary around the country and with practitioner.
- Higher fees do not necessarily indicate higher quality Feldenkrais Method® work.

Average Time Per Session
- 20 to 60 minutes

Recommended Length Of Time Between Sessions
- 1 to 6 days depending upon the child

Estimated Length Of Time Before Improvements Can Be Expected
- On average you should notice a change after 5 sessions.

Suggestions To Make The Feldenkrais Method® More Effective
- Follow the practitioner's recommendations.
- Stay for sessions; don't just drop the child off.
- Consider the practitioner the family's teacher.

- Learn about the quality of touch and the quality of interaction that the Feldenkrais Method® practitioner is modeling for them.
- Don't be afraid to develop a home program based upon the Feldenkrais Method® practitioner's recommendations.
- The practices closest to the Feldenkrais Method® are: sensory integration work, pro-perceptive neurological work and body-mind centering.

Other Methods That Are Similar To The Feldenkrais Method®
- Nothing is like the Feldenkrais Method®.

Other Methods That Complement The Feldenkrais Method®
- Depends upon the child
- Homeopathy
- Acupuncture
- Therapies using special devices such as large screen computers that assist with perception

Nature And Length Of Training To Be A Practitioner
- The Feldenkrais Guild® of North America accredited certification programs involve 800 hours of training over a 4-year period.
- 10 years of experience is needed to be a trainer of practitioners.

Special Training Needed To Work With Children & Youth
- The skills to work with children are a part of the general training.
- The Feldenkrais Guild® of North America requires practitioners to engage in continuing education.
- Many post-graduate, continuing education programs focus upon children.

Certification/Licenses Held By Feldenkrais Method® Practitioners
- Certification by the Feldenkrais Guild® of North America (FGNA)
- Certification by the International Feldenkrais Federation (IFF)
- Please be aware there are unauthorized practitioners. Look for practitioners certified by the FGNA and IFF.

Professional Associations To Contact For Names Of Local Practitioners
- Feldenkrais Guild® of North America (FGNA); 5436 N. Albina Ave.; Portland, OR, 97217; 800-775-2118; 503-221-6612; Fax: 503-221-6616; Website: www.feldenkrais.com

Number Of Certified Practitioners In U.S., Canada, And Mexico
- Hundreds

What To Look For When Choosing The Best Practitioner
- Rapport: are you and your child comfortable with the Feldenkrais Method® practitioner?
- Do you feel they see your child as a person?
- Do they listen well?
- The more years of experience the better.

- Ask for references and recommendations.

Leading Clinics, Centers, Practitioners

- Contact the North American Feldenkrais Guild, 3611 SW Hood Ave. Suite 100; Portland, Oregon 97239, 800-775-2118, 503-221-6612; Website: www.feldenkrais.com; Email: guild@feldenkrais.com

Resources, Research Papers, Books, DVD's, Websites

- You will find many research papers available on the International Feldenkrais Federation website. Go to: http://feldenkrais-method.org/en/flexinode/list/5.
- Shelhav-Silberbush, Chava. "The Feldenkrais Method for Children with Cerebral Palsy." MS Thesis. Boston University School of Education, *Feldenkrais Resources*, 1988.

Bibliography

- Rosenfeld, Albert. "Teaching the Body How to Program the Brain is Moshe's Miracle." *Smithsonian*, (January 1981): pp52-58.
- RosenHoltz PhD, Stephen. "*Monkey Moves*" Video. Available through Amazon.com.
- Shafarman, Steven. *Awareness Heals*. Reading, MA: Perseus Books, 1997.

Helpful Tips For Parents

- Get on the floor and play with balls.
- Pretend to be different animals and move like the animals move.
- Touch each other, be kind, and use humor.
- Do puzzles that teach thinking in new ways.
- Take 5 deep breaths.

Biography of Linda Evans Delman, Co-Author

- Years Experience: 25 as of 2008
- Approximate total number of clients who are infants, children, or teens: Several hundred
- Degrees: BA
- FGNA Trainer Certification, teaching practitioners and general public all over the world

Biography of Russell Delman, Co-Author

- Years Experience: 34 as of 2008
- Approximate total number of clients who are infants, children, or teens: Several hundred
- Degrees: BA
- FGNA Trainer Certification, teaching practitioners and general public all over the world

Statement By Linda And Russell Delman

The Feldenkrais Method® is a gentle, respectful approach to learning. Most families feel great gratitude for both the learning and the way the learning takes place. It is much less stressful and more enjoyable than traditional physical therapy. Our intention is to interact with the intelligence that is alive within all human beings.

To Contact The Feldenkrais Guild® Of North America

5436 N. Albina Ave.; Portland, OR, 97217, 1.800-775-2118; 503-221-6612
Website: www.feldenkrais.com; E-Mail: www.feldenkrais.com/about/contact_us

. . . .

Marie Mulligan's Comment About The Feldenkrais Method®: There can be additional benefits when people get involved with The Feldenkrais Method® practiced by people licensed in other healing modalities. There can also be benefits from working with practitioners who learned from having their own conditions healed through Feldenkrais work. Members of my family have benefited from Feldenkrais work.

Rick Geggie's Comment About The Feldenkrais Method®: I became so convinced about the effectiveness of the Feldenkrais Method® that I became a practitioner. I was motivated to go through the lengthy training after seeing the looks of awe, amazement and glee that children exhibit when they can do something that they could not do before. The Feldenkrais Method® has helped children do what was impossible for them such as raising their arms over their head, running without pain, or paying attention easily.

CHAPTER 18

FLOWER ESSENCES FOR CHILDREN & YOUTH

By Katharina Johnson, MD (Austria),   © Copyright 2008.

Flower Essences Has Helped Kids With

• Acne & rosacea • Allergic skin reactions • Deodorant (replaces harmful chemical deodorants) • Dental problems (toothache, teething pain, gum infections, abscesses, etc.) • Eczema	• Hair problems (lice, itchy scalp, dandruff, etc.) • Immune system • Insomnia • Itching • Menstrual disorders (PMS, hormonal imbalances, painful or irregular menses, etc.)	• Mental alertness, clarity & focus • Nausea • Psoriasis • Relaxation • Scars • Spasms

Flower Essences Can Help In The Following Areas

Spirit: Lack of clarity about higher purpose, loss of connection with the higher self and spirit guide, confusion about psychic abilities

Body: Trauma and shock, bedwetting, lack of energy, burns, tension, sexual abuse, fainting, low blood pressure, insomnia, dental problems, cramps, menstrual problems

Mind: Lack of mental clarity and focus, unwillingness to learn from past mistakes, non-accepting of authorities, lack of motivation, lack of self-reliance, indecisiveness, lack of patience, guilt, lack of creativity, courage and self-discipline, perfectionism, stubbornness, resignation, lack of prospects, school problems, suicidal thoughts

Emotions: Fear and anxiety, depression, phobias, panic attacks, addictions and co-dependency, worry, self-doubt, aggressive behavior, homesickness, jealousy, hypersensitivity, lack of self-confidence, mood swings, mourning, desperation, shyness

Brief Description Of Flower Essences

- Flower Essences are gentle but powerful vibrational healing remedies, which act to balance harmonies in the emotional and spiritual bodies.
- They have the ability to help us heal, to stabilize and support us, to stimulate self-responsibility and self-awareness, to clear energy blockages, to transform old beliefs and open us to new possibilities.
- They do not operate at a biochemical level – as prescription drugs do, but work on a vibrational level, and by doing so, they affect the subtle energy body which is present in the human field.
- Upsetting emotions are the result of an interruption in the natural flow of energy.
- By ingesting Flower Essences, or when used topically as an ointment, Flower Essences interact with our own energy field and can help us rebalance our energy and our emotions.
- Flower Essences are one of the safest self-help remedies available, as they do not have any known side effects.
- They can be used safely with children, adults, animals and plants.

Success With Flower Essences

- Julia, a nine year old girl suddenly started to become anxious and nervous and had troubles falling asleep without her mother, after having witnessed a terrible street accident. Flower Essences ("Mimulus", "Aspen", "Star of Bethlehem" and "Honeysuckle"), quickly helped Julia to get over this incident. To this day, her anxiety has not returned.
- Tom (13), became self-conscious after being ridiculed in school by one of his friends. Essence of "Larch" helped him regain his self-esteem.
- Anne's (10) exam nerves went away after taking "Chestnut Bud", "Elm", "Hornbeam" and "Rock Water". During the exam, "Gentian", "Mimulus" and "White Chestnut" helped Anne stay calm and focused. Also, the black-outs, normally experienced by Anne in stressful situations, were gone.

Flower Essences Are Appropriate For Ages

- Flower remedies have been shown to be effective for children of all ages.
- Some practitioners and midwifes even use Flower Essences to help the newborn baby to recover from birth and to adjust to life outside the womb more quickly. In this case, Flower remedies (Star of Bethlehem, Rock Rose) are used topically, gently massaged into the soles of the feet. This will give the newborn inner peace and the feeling of belonging to the universe.
- During pregnancy is also a sensitive time to take essences. Because the unborn is connected so intensely with the mother, every emotion which is experienced by the mother will affect the unborn in some way or another. Therefore it is very beneficial for the mother-to-be to use Flower Essences to help balance the intense emotions, which can occur during pregnancy and while giving birth.
- It is also safe to use Flower Essences through the time of nursing, as the baby will receive the essences through the mother's milk.

Children & Youth's Reactions To Flower Essences

- In general, children react to Flower Essences very quickly and some notice dramatic changes immediately.
- For others, the changes are more gradual and they feel that "something" has changed in a week or two.
- Some report a change in emotional states and a feeling of peace, harmony and wellbeing; others will experience changes of attitudes and a greater connection to nature.

Extra Care Is Needed

- Some practitioners recommend not applying undiluted essences directly onto the skin. Very sensitive children & youth can develop a strong emotional reaction. In that case, it is best to continue using the essences, but in a diluted form until the emotions subside.

Contraindications: When Flower Essences Should Be Avoided

- There are not many contraindications.
- Flower Essences are among the safest self-help remedies available on the market.
- They do not have common side effects.
- Homeopathic remedies and Flower Essences should not be taken together, as they can interfere with each other and their healing properties will be diminished.

History

- It is believed that Flower Essences have been in existence throughout the ages.
- Some people even think they were already popular forms of healing in the forgotten civilizations of humankind: i.e., Atlantis and Lemuria.
- Today, some of the most popular Flower Essences are the "Bach Flower Essences", which were rediscovered in the 1930's by Dr. Edward Bach, a British physician. Dr. Bach was a very sensitive soul and he relied on his intuition for guidance. He had the ability to directly communicate with plants and by doing so he was able to develop 36 different flower remedies which address 36 different emotional states. Dr. Bach found that dis-eases of the body came about as a result of imbalances or negativity at the level of the soul and by correcting the problems at that level, healing would result on all levels.
- Flower Essences are among the most popular forms of self-help remedies on the market and they are especially popular in Europe.
- Today, more and more therapists, complementary health care practitioners and health care professionals are discovering their various healing properties and are using and incorporating them into their practice.
- Other popular Flower Essences are: Alaskan flowers, Australian Bush flowers, North American flowers, Californian flowers, and many, many more.

Basic Concepts And Components Of Flower Essences

- Flower Essences are diluted extracts of various types of flowers and plants.
- The wildflowers are picked at the peak of their blooming cycle.
- For optimal results and potential, attention is also paid to the time of the day when the flower is picked, the ideal season and the moon phase.
- The blooms are then put into a bowl of water and infused with the sun. The power and energy of the sun transfers the healing energies into the water. This is called the "mother essence".
- To preserve the mother essence, brandy is added and the infusion is further diluted into what is called the "stock level". This is the level which is commonly available in health care shops.
- The flower essence practitioner then prepares the "dosage level". Only four drops of the stock level are needed. After that, brandy and water are added again.
- For alcohol sensitive adults or children, cider vinegar can be used as a preservative instead of brandy, even though the percentage of alcohol found at this level of dilution is insignificant.
- Some health care shops also offer Flower Essences in the form of globuli, which have a sweet taste, contain no alcohol and are widely accepted by children.
- Most commonly, Flower Essences are used orally, placed with a dropper directly under the tongue, or put into a glass of water or juice (not milk).
- Another common procedure is to mix the essences with ointments and creams to use them topically.

- Essences can also be used in the form of mist sprays or as an additive for bathwater.

Description Of A Typical Session

- First, a skilled and experienced practitioner will begin to establish a good relationship with the child or youth.
- Depending upon the age of the child, the parents may be present during the session.
- After the practitioner has clarified which challenges the child is facing and where help is needed the most, the Flower Essence consultant will choose up to 6 different essences and then prepare a dosage bottle.
- Occasionally, it can also be useful to simply let the child pick one flower essence. Children are very sensitive and in tune with their needs and emotions and often they will intuitively pick the most important flower essence for themselves.
- At the end of the consultation, the practitioner will explain how and when the Flower Essences should be taken.
- A good practitioner will also schedule a follow-up session, either over the phone or in person after about six days. This will assure reactions and changes in behavior are being discussed and if necessary, the practitioner will change the dosage.

Major Differences Of Opinion Between Practitioners

- The major differences of opinion lie in the number of Flower Essences to be taken at a time. Some practitioners prefer to work with just one single flower; others combine up to 8 different ones.
- Another difference of opinion is the dosage. The recommendations here vary greatly.

Fees/Costs In 2007

- Fees vary widely depending on the practitioner's level of training and location, and the number of Flower Essences to be used.
- Overall rates are between $30 and $120. This typically includes the consultation, a customized blend of essences, and sometimes a follow-up session.
- Single Flower Essences at the stock level can be found in good health care shops for about $10 each.

Estimated Length Of Time Before Improvements Can Be Expected

- Children react to Flower Essences very quickly and some notice dramatic changes immediately. For others, the changes are more gradual and they feel that "something" has changed in a week or two.
- If many different Flower Essences are combined, changes will be noticed within about a month.
- In general, it can be said that the fewer essences selected, the sooner positive effects will appear.

Suggestions To Make Flower Essences More Effective

- Flower Essences will only be effective if a skilled practitioner is choosing the right essences. If essences are chosen which are inappropriate, the desired effect will simply fail to appear.
- It is also important to notice that the fewer flower remedies selected, the more effective they will be. A good number is up to six different Flower Essences. Too many different Flower Essences can result in a state of confusion and a sense of uneasiness, as the body will be overstrained with too many different frequencies.
- It is also extremely important to take flower remedies on a regular, consistent basis. The rhythmic, frequent use ensures the flower remedies can develop their full healing forces. Therefore, a greater effect will not be achieved by increasing the number of drops, but by using them more frequently, since they do not work on a biochemical basis but on a vibrational level.
- Before taking Flower Essences make sure you shake the bottle a few times. This will re-activate the life force of the plants and their full healing properties can unfold again.

- Another thing to be aware of is not to contaminate the plastic dropper of the bottle. Try to avoid direct contact with the dropper and the tongue.
- Do not store flower remedies next to electromagnetic devices, such as cell phones, TV's or computers.
- Be aware that due to cosmic radiation, the healing frequencies of the essences will be affected after about four hours of air travel.

Dosage Directions For Children & Youth

- The standard dosage for preschool and gradeschool children is two to three drops of stock concentrate a day. The best times are upon rising and before going to bed.
- If necessary, the dosage can be slightly increased up to five times a day.
- Best times to take them are 15 minutes before a meal or on hour after.
- For older children or adults, four drops three times a day is a good place to start with.
- As an additive to bathwater, 15 drops are a good amount.
- When prepared as an oinment, take 15 to 20 drops and add it to one ounce of body cream.
- Spraying the crib or bed with the essences in a misting bottle is helpful as well, therefore 5 drops are used for one ounce of water.
- Any combination of the above is possible. For safety reasons, start with the lowest dose and slightly increase it until the desired effects appear.

Other Methods That Are Similar To Flower Essences

- Homeopathy

Other Methods That Complement Flower Essences

- Energy work: such as Reiki, Shiatsu and Breath work
- Psychotherapy
- Aromatherapy
- Physical therapy
- Acupuncture
- Cranialsacral work
- Massage
- Many other forms of healing work

Nature And Length Of Training To Be A Practitioner

- Length and nature of training involved to become a certified flower essence practitioner vary widely. Some certification classes only take 2 days, while others take up to one year, including field research.
- As there are no strict regulations, it is important to ask the practitioner with whom you are working, where he/she received training and about their experience.
- Make sure your child feels comfortable with the practitioner.

Special Training Needed To Work With Children & Youth

- There is no special training needed to work with children. The working principles are the same as for adults. The major difference is the dosage.

Professional Associations To Contact For Names Of Local Practitioners
- Flower Essence Society; P.O. Box 459; Nevada City, CA 95959; 800-736-9222; Fax: 530-265-0584; Website: www.flowersociety.org; Email: mail@flowersociety.org.
- British Flower and Vibrational Essences Association; BM BFVEA; London; WC1N 3XX; 01372-744426; Website: www.bfvea.com; Email: webmaster@bfvea.com.
- World Wide Essence Society: Website: www.essences.com; Email: wwes@essences.com.
- Dr. Edward Bach Foundation: Website: www.bachcentre.com; For general advice on dosage etc. and for help finding a practitioner near to you, email: Kathy@bachcentre.com.

Number Of Certified Practitioners In U.S., Canada, And Mexico
- Difficult to know at this point.

Leading Clinics, Centers, Practitioners
- Patricia Kaminski, Richard Katz, FES – Flower Essence Society. (See listing above).
- The International Association of Flower Essence Producers: Website: www.floweressenceproducers.org.
  For North/Central/South America:
  Steve Johnson; Ph: 907-235-2188; Fax: 907-235-2777; Email: steve@FlowerEssenceProducers.org.
  For Europe and the rest of the world:
  Bram Zaalberg; 31-77-398-7826; Fax: 31-77-398-7827; Email: bloesem@Worldonline.nl.

Research Papers Pertaining To Flower Essences
- Recent research into the links between emotions and the immune system supports and reinforces the view that emotional balance and well-being directly affect and influence our physical health. More and more medical experts now agree that a healthy mind really does ensure a healthy body.
- The Flower Essence Society does research on Flower Essences on an ongoing basis. Studies are published on their website. (See listing above.)

Bibliography
- Kaminski, Patricia and Richard Katz. *Flower Essence Repertory.* Nevada City, CA: Flower Essence Society, Rev Ed 1994.
- Mazzarella, Barbara. *Bach Flower Remedies for Children: A Parents' Guide.* Rochester, VT: Healing Arts Press, 1994.
- Arnos, Kathy. *The Complete Teething Guide: From Birth to Adolescence.* Van Nuys, CA: Spirit Dance Publishing, 2003.
- Soo Hwa, Yeo. *Healing the Family with Bach Flower Essences.* Sunnyvale, CA: 2005.
- Wesson, Nicky. *Natural Mothering: A Guide to Holistic Therapies for Pregnancy, Birth, and Early Childhood.* Rochester, VT: Healing Arts Press, 1997.

Helpful Tips For Parents
- In a crisis of any kind, one of the best things you can do to help your child is to have a bottle of Rescue Remedy at home. Rescue Remedy is a combination of five of the original Bach flower remedies: Cherry Plum, Impatiens, Clematis, Star of Bethlehem and Rock Rose.
- Rescue Remedy can reduce stress and help to restore a sense of calm and control.
- Rescue Remedy is very useful for all types of crisis, shocks and stressful situations: such as trauma, injury, going to the dentist and relationship breakdowns.

- Rescue Remedy is also available in a soothing cream for minor scrapes and dry skin conditions.
- If you want to choose Flower Essences for your child or youth by yourself, but are not sure which one to choose, observe how your child reacts to situations around him. You will notice very quickly that each child or youth reacts very differently to the same circumstances. For instance, one child will react with fear to a given situation, another will become angry and upset, while another will become quiet and will retreat. Once you have observed this, you can then use a good Flower Essence repertory book (found in health food stores) to find which flower fits the child or youth the best. If you are unsure, it is best to contact an experienced flower essence consultant.

Biography of Katharina Johnson, Author

- Dr. Katharina Johnson is a medical doctor, licensed and trained in Austria. She holds a degree in Orthomolecular therapy (Nutritional Medicine), is trained in Acupuncture and Bach Flower Essences as well.
- Due to her interest in Energy psychology, Katharina studied to become a certified Seemorg Matrix Work and EFT (Emotional Freedom Technique) practitioner. By applying those healing modalities, Katharina is able to provide clients with lasting relief from a range of psychological disorders, physical diseases and spiritual impasses.
- Katharina recommends Bach Flower remedies to all her clients, to improve their emotional, physical and mental states of wellbeing.
- Katharina lives and works in San Francisco, CA.

Katharina Johnson's Personal statement

Growing up in Austria in a very progressive family, I was very lucky to have parents who introduced me to Flower Essences and homeopathy at an early age. I have been taking Flower Essences throughout my whole life and I have seen dramatic shifts in emotional states happening in a very short time, not only within myself, but also within my clients. Flower Essences are safe and effective, and one of their most beautiful gifts is their ability to reconnect us with our innermost nature, being one of love, joy and compassion.

To Contact Dr. Katharina Johnson, Who Contributed This Chapter

Dr. Katharina Johnson; 79 Brosnan; San Francisco, CA 94103; Ph: 415-637-3196; Website: www.DrKatharina.com; Email: Katharina@DrKatharina.com

. . . .

Marie Mulligan's Comment About Flower Essences: Flower Essences, when used as directed, can be a safe, wonderful and cost effective home remedy to address a wide range of common difficutlies. For addressing serious and/or complex and/or chronic conditions, get care from a Flower Essence practitioner. There can be additional benefits when people get involved with Flower Essences practiced by people licensed in other healing modalities. My family and patients and I have benefited.

Rick Geggie's Comment About Flower Essences: I have used Flower Essences for years with my family and friends. They work. They are inexpensive. How they work is a mystery to me; however the relief that they bring is undeniable.

CHAPTER 19

HERBOLOGY FOR CHILDREN & YOUTH

By Karyn Sanders,   © Copyright 2008.

Herbology Has Helped Kids With

- Asthma
- Broken Bones
- Cancer
- Colds & Flu's
- Emotional issues
- Eczema

Herbology Can Help In The Following Areas

Spirit: Children live much closer to their spiritual selves. Even very low doses of the correct herb can be very effective.

Body: It's good for all kinds of illnesses; chronic asthma, allergies, acute-colds, and ear infections. Works well with measles, mumps and other childhood illnesses against which some parents may choose not to immunize.

Mind: Herbs work very well for children with brain dysfunction and similar problems.

Emotions: Herbs work well for depression, anxiety, etc.

Social: It's best to treat the whole family if challenges are on a social/emotional level. Usually, the herbalist gives herbs to the child and counsels the parents, but sometimes the whole family receives herbs.

Brief Description Of Herbology

- Uses herbs to bring the child's body back into balance.
- Good health depends on the mind, body and spirit of the child being in harmony with each other. If one is off, they're all off. Herbology restores that balance.
- An herb is anything that is plant matter.
- Healing comes about through the alignment of the sick child's energy, the illness, and the herb.

- The challenge is to get to the root of the illness. Why is it there, and what is causing the symptoms? Herbology meets that challenge.

Success With Herbology

- Bill, six years old, had severe asthma attacks. His herbalist gave him herbs in an herbal syrup, which she made just for him. She also discussed with Bill's parents the amount of time he spent playing video games and using the computer, and explained she felt these kept him too wired to breathe deeply. Bill's parents report he hasn't had an asthma attack in months.
- Janie, a two year old, cut off the tip of her little finger in a fan. Her parents didn't believe in Western medicine or surgery as a first option. The herbalist bound the injured tip onto the child's finger with herbs and made up an herbal salve for the parents to apply. The finger tip and even the nail bed grew back in time.
- Jeff, a nine year old, was a very violent child and had been since he was three. He was isolated and taunted by other kids, which made him depressed, miserable, and even more violent, especially toward his younger sister. The herbalist gave him several spirit plants to help him control his impulses. As he began to calm down, he was then given other remedies to lift his depression and help him make friends. Over the course of a year, Jeff became much more cooperative with his parents and teachers and developed a good relationship with his sister.
- Jimmy was seven when he developed bone cancer. Along with surgery and chemotherapy, he took herbal remedies. His recovery went much smoother than expected by the surgeons and the cancer specialists. He also had less side effects from the chemotherapy.

Herbology Is Appropriate For Ages

- Newborn through adolescence
- There are herbs to help heal circumcision, treat colds, earaches, acne, PMS, etc.

Children & Youth's Reactions To Herbology

- Most children are drawn to the herbs. They love the colors and smells of the herbs. They can feel the magic. They understand when they feel better.
- Some children love the taste, others aren't fond of it. Of course, a lot depends on both the child's age and which herb they're given.
- They like it--not necessarily taste. Practitioners often tell children the taste of it is the plant's "voice." "Don't say "Yuck!" when you take an herb or it will hurt the plant's feelings."
- Children desire harmony. If they believe the remedy will bring harmony to them, they will cooperate in taking it.
- Herbalists often make the remedy fun, with games and songs and stickers for small children. This increases their cooperation and it aids in healing.
- Children usually notice some positive change right away. They usually like to take their remedies.

Extra Care Is Needed

- The herbalist needs to be completely objective and not approach working with the child with any assumptions.

Contraindications: When Herbology Should Be Avoided

- Pregnancy - with some herbs
- With multiple health issues, one has to be careful. A remedy could be good for asthma for example, but bad for an ulcer. An experienced practitioner is needed for this.

History

- The use of herbs for healing dates back to the first appearance of people on the planet. In ancient times, the connections between people and plants were obvious and apparent everywhere.
- In intact indigenous cultures, herbalism is still practiced today, as it has been for thousands of years. This has never been lost.
- In the Western European cultures, most modern medicines have been developed from plants.
- Today, in Western European cultures, the value of learning about and from the plants in their original forms is once again becoming obvious and the number of herbal practitioners is growing profusely.

Basic Concepts And Components Of Herbology

- Energetic Herbalists work with energy--the energy of the child, the illness, and the plant--to achieve balance.
- It takes several hours with the parent and the child to determine, through a series of questions and observations, what the basic nature of the child is when they are well.
- During that same time period, the practitioner also determines the exact nature of the illness.
- Using knowledge, experience, and wisdom, the practitioner determines what remedy works best with that illness, then creates the remedy and administers it.
- Often, once the immediate symptoms of an illness--such as asthma attacks--have been relieved, the herbalist then uncovers the deeper cause of the illness; such as depression, anxiety, poor nutrition, over-stimulation, etc., and then treats the deeper cause.
- Most herbalists use herbs from the continental biosphere in which the child lives.
- Herbs may be administered in many different ways: orally through syrups, teas, tinctures, or drops; and externally through poultices, baths, smudges, or creams, depending on the nature of the illness and the age of the child.

Description Of A Typical Session

- When the child comes in for a session, the herbalist gives the parent a long intake form that goes over every organ system. It also asks for a detailed history of the child.
- If the child is old enough, the herbalist asks them many questions about themselves. If not, the herbalist questions the parent and observes the child at play.
- It's very important that the herbalist listens to and observes the child/patient in a non-judgmental way. It's also important the herbalist is respectful of the child or youth.
- The herbalist examines the child and usually gives them a remedy before they leave. In some cases, however, the herbalist needs to "sit" with the problem for awhile before deciding on the best course to follow.
- The herbalist trusts that between the interaction of the plant and the child, balance can be restored.
- Sometimes the parents or the whole family also receive a remedy.

Major Differences Of Opinion Between Practitioners

- Dosage levels: Some herbalists believe a dose of 6 drops is enough of a remedy, while others may prescribe up to 60 drops.
- Some Western herbalists don't have an energetic system and are just working on a physical level.
- There are several schools of thought amongst herbalists and sometimes they complement one another; sometimes they conflict.

Fees/Costs In 2007

- A sliding scale fee from $0-$135 with an openness to trade for everything from eggs to carpentry.
- This covers the initial session and a six week supply of herbs.

Average Time Per Session
- The initial visit takes two to three hours.
- Follow-up sessions, if needed, may take up to an hour.

Recommended Length Of Time Between Sessions
- In acute cases, the herbalist may need to be present with the child to administer herbs every fifteen minutes.
- Sometimes the child and their family move in with the practitioner and stay for a few weeks.
- Ordinarily, the time between sessions is five to six weeks.

Estimated Length Of Time Before Improvements Can Be Expected
- In acute cases such as measles, colds and earaches, results will often be noticed in moments to hours.
- In long-term chronic illnesses, most clients notice some immediate change. However, it can take up to a year for complete recovery and different remedies will be needed over time as conditions change.

Suggestions To Make Herbology More Effective
- Make sure your child or youth takes the prescribed remedies as directed.
- Remind the children the herbs are medicine and may not taste good but will help them.
- Believe in the healing power of the herbs.

Other Methods That Are Similar To Herbology
- Since Herbology works with the child's energy systems - their vital forces, other energetic bodywork such as massage, Bowen, or Feldenkrais can be a great addition to working with herbs.
- Homeopathy is similar.
- Use of Flower Essences and essential oils is similar.

Other Methods That Complement Herbology
- Almost all healing modalities blend well with herbology, including homeopathy, acupuncture, body work, and traditional Western medicine. Since we carry things on a cellular level, shifts in energy that restore balance can be achieved by many paths toward wellness.

Nature And Length Of Training To Be A Practitioner
- There are a number of herbal schools in the United States and Canada. Each has its own standards and length of training.
- Ideally, an herbalist should do a lengthy, in-depth apprenticeship of seven to ten years with an experienced practitioner.

Special Training Needed To Work With Children & Youth
The practitioner must:
- Make sure they have done work on themselves, on their power dynamics.
- Train themselves to be perceptive in many different ways - not simply verbally.
- Learn to be quiet and patient, so they can wait for the child's revelations.

Certification/Licenses Held By Practitioners
- There are no licenses for Western herbalists.

Professional Associations To Contact For Names Of Local Practitioners
- Herbs are the people's medicine. Herbs are about people, for people, and belong to people to use and grow themselves.
- There are herbalists trained in many different approaches all over the world.
- Use the word-of-mouth approach.
- It's best to ask people for referrals to practitioners they know and trust.

Number Of Certified Herbology Practitioners In U.S., Canada, And Mexico
- Herbalists are not certified.
- However there are thousands of practitioners in all three countries.

What To Look For When Choosing The Best Practitioner
- Do they pay close attention to the child and the parent?
- Do they respond without judgment or blame?
- Are they able to set aside ego, and let the child and the plants guide them to the healing remedy?
- Are they willing to take plenty of time and are not motivated by greed?

Leading Clinics, Centers, Practitioners
- Rosemary Gladstar at www.rosemarygladstar.com
- Contact Michael Moore at the Southwest School of Botanical Medicine; P.O. Box 4565, Bisbee, AZ 85603; Website: www.all-natural.com/herbindx.html. "After 28 years, we have retired and closed down our 500 hour residency program. We now offer two distance learning programs with residency segments…"

Resources, Research Papers, Books, DVDs, Websites
- Numerous articles by Michael Moore, including Herbal Energetics in Clinical Practice: www.all-natural.com/herbindx.html
- Karyn Sanders at www.blueotterschool.com

Bibliography
- Gladstar, Rosemary. *Herbal Remedies for Children's Health*. Pound, Vermont: Storey Books. 1999.
- Hutchins, Alma R. *Indian Herbs of North America*. Boston: Shambala Press, 1991.
- Moore, Michael. *Herbal Formulas for Clinic and Home*. Keats Publishing Inc, 27 Pine St., New Canaan, CT 06840. 1995.

Helpful Tips For Parents
- Get a book about using herbs with children.
- Grow simple herbs like comfrey, aloe vera, peppermint, etc. with your child, and share the uses with them.
- Don't treat complicated issues by yourself. Find a good practitioner.

Biography of Karyn Sanders, Author

- Karyn Sanders has been practicing herbal medicine for 33 years. She sees about 40 children each month. She has a full-time practice and is founder and head instructor of the Blue Otter School of Herbal Medicine. She produces and hosts a weekly live radio show about herbal medicine on KPFA 94.1 FM in the San Francisco Bay area.

Karyn Sanders' Personal Statement

Herbal medicine has a profound healing effect in a gentle way with very little side effect. Energetic herbalism gets to the core of the issue and heals the whole illness and not just the symptoms.

To Contact Karyn Sanders, Who Contributed This Chapter

Karyn Sanders; 13310 Patterson Creek Rd.; Fort Jones, CA 96032; Ph: 530-468-4342; Fax: 530-468-4342; Website: www.blueotterschool.com; Email: cohosh.karyn@gmail

. . . .

Marie Mulligan's Comment About Herbology: Energetic Herbalism can be wonderfully healing for children, youth, and parents. It is the spirit of the plant that can be helpful. There are safety concerns regarding the use of herbal medicines with children & youth, especially long term use. What safety data we have involves adults. Proceed with caution by getting the help of a practitioner experienced in working with children & youth.

Rick Geggie's Comment About Herbology: One of my grandmothers was an herbalist. She and her herbs helped me grow up easier. My family could not afford prescription or over the counter remedies and drugs. A practice that is thousands of years old must work or else people would not make use of it.

CHAPTER 20

HOMEOPATHY FOR CHILDREN & YOUTH

By Dian Wagner; Randy Jane Reitzes, LVN, CMT, CCHH; Lisette Narragon CCH, BRCP,   © Copyright 2008.

Homeopathy Has Helped Kids With

Short term (acute) illnesses	Long term (chronic) illnesses:	Terminal illness/End of life:
• Ear infections • Respiratory infections • Diarrhea and vomiting • Injuries • Sore throats • Teething • Constipation • Fevers • Neonatal jaundice • Parasites • Colic	• Recurrent infections of all kinds: ear, throat, respiratory • Frequent colds • Asthma • Skin conditions: eczema, impetigo, acne • Constipation • Diarrhea • Teething discomfort • Behavioral problems: ADD, hyperactivity, aggression, depression and anxiety	• Ease physical pain and terminal restlessness without sedation

Homeopathy Can Help In The Following Areas

Spirit: It brings about change on the deepest level so the child can reach his/her highest potential.

Body: It treats many common childhood illnesses, both acute and chronic.

Mind: It increases concentration and focus, and stimulates the child's ability to understand and learn.

Emotions: It restores balance to the child who is nervous, restless, angry or unhappy.

Social: It balances the child's nature, allowing the child to interact with others in a positive way.

Brief Description Of Homeopathy

- Homeopathy treats the whole child on all levels: mental, physical and emotional for both short and long term conditions.
- Homeopathic remedies prevent or treat illness by stimulating the body's defense mechanisms.

Success With Homeopathy

- Eight year old Jeff refused to eat almost anything if it didn't have sugar in it--and he'd been a difficult and picky eater since age three. His mother felt guilty and anxious about his lack of appetite and was worn out by the everyday struggle at mealtime. Jeff was also clingy and disruptive, demanding constant attention. After three weeks on the remedy prescribed for him, Jeff started eating regular meals and exhibiting independence and self-confidence. His mom said, "At last I can enjoy being a mother again."
- Julie, a bright seven year old, was having a very hard time at school. She was restless, uncooperative and getting into fights. She didn't want to talk to the practitioner and refused to even look at her. The practitioner gave her a remedy and when she returned a month later for her follow-up visit, she was a changed child. Smiling, she handed the homeopath a bouquet of flowers she'd picked herself. She said she was getting along great at school and making friends with her classmates.
- Eliza had constant ear infections and runny noses. Her parents were afraid her hearing would be affected if the infections didn't stop. The homeopath gave her a remedy that cleared up her immediate symptoms and, a few weeks later, gave a different remedy to boost her vital force and help her resist future infections.

Third-Party Testimonials

- "My son is not in the principal's office anymore!"
- "I have not used my inhaler all winter. Usually I have a cold and cough all winter long and this year, only one!"
- "I feel happy...(spoken by a 14 year old who had been depressed)."
- "My daughter is more resilient, less upset by small things, and more cooperative."

Homeopathy Is Appropriate For Ages

- Homeopathy is for all ages, from conception on, can be treated successfully with homeopathic remedies.
- Homeopaths gather information from observation as well as the report from the parent and child.

Children & Youth's Reactions To Homeopathy

- Homeopathic remedies are easily dissolved under the tongue or in water. Children love the taste and often ask for more!
- Many children like visiting a homeopath because it is a time when the child is able to speak freely, without judgment or interruption.

Extra Care Is Needed

- Life threatening illnesses such as Asthma
- Severe skin conditions
- Acute illnesses where the condition changes quickly

Contraindications: When Homeopathy Should Be Avoided

- Homeopathy should not be used in conjunction with other energetic treatments as this confuses the practitioner's ability to determine which treatment is working and what to do next.

- The action of the homeopathic remedy can be interrupted by the following: camphor, menthol, eucalyptus and/ or tea tree oil.
- Don't use such things as deep heating rubs, liniments, Tiger Balm, Vicks, Ben Gay, Noxzema products and some calamine lotions. Carefully read the labels of lip balms, mouthwashes and throat lozenges. Avoid teas that contain menthol. Avoid prolonged breathing of mothball vapors.

History

- Homeopathy was founded by Samuel Hahnemann, a German physician, in the late 1700's. The concept actually dates back to the time of Hippocrates, the first official physician.
- Homeopathy comes from the Greek words homoios (similar) and pathos (suffering).
- Hahnemann believed the doctor's role should be to help the patient's own body heal itself. He developed the Law of Similars, (which means remedies have healing properties which match the symptoms of the patient).
- Hahnemann also developed a method of energizing the remedies which eliminates or greatly reduces side effects. The smaller the dose of medicine, the greater its potency and its effect on the body's healing ability.
- It came to the United States in the 1800's and was very popular until the mid 1920's. Homeopathy is regaining popularity in the U.S. today with many schools across the nation, thousands of practitioners, several national homeopathic organizations and pharmacies. The remedies are widely available by mail and in natural foods stores.
- Homeopathy has spread all over the world; including India, Europe, Russia, Brazil, Israel, Canada and Mexico.

Basic Concepts And Components Of Homeopathy

- A very small amount of the proper medicine stimulates the body to heal itself.
- It cures the person by treating the root of the illness, not just the symptoms.
- When given correctly it is safe and without side effects.
- Homeopathy uses natural, non-toxic substances.
- Homeopathy heals physical, mental and emotional symptoms.
- It is effective for both acute (short term) and chronic (long term) conditions.
- Homeopathy is simple, cost-effective and quick for conditions such as teething, earache and injuries.
- It does not dampen or depress a child's spirit—in fact the child's overall health benefits from the treatment.

Description Of A Typical Session

- The first session begins with the patient's own description of his/her symptoms. Then the practitioner may ask questions if more information is needed. The practitioner is interested in what is unique about the child – sleep patterns, food desire and aversions, details about the pregnancy and birth, the child's response to discipline, etc.–and listens without judgment or comment to the answers.
- The practitioner studies the case and then prescribes a remedy.
- A week after taking the remedy, a brief check-in phone call is done by some practitioners.
- After four to five weeks, a one-hour follow-up session is done to review all the symptoms reported at the first session.

Major Differences Of Opinion Between Practitioners

- Single remedy vs. combination remedies
- Single dose vs. repeated doses
- Single remedy vs. alternating remedies
- Treatment of the whole person vs. focus on one complaint
- High doses vs. low doses

Fees/Costs In 2007 – (Northern California Averages)
- Initial consultation (for under age 18): $150-200
- Follow-up visits: $50-100
- Acute Treatment: $50-100

Average Time Per Session
- Young children: The first visit lasts 1 ½ - 2 hours. Depending on the age and the willingness of the child, the practitioner may see the child separately from the parent as well as together.
- Adolescents: The first visit lasts 2 - 3 hours and should be done directly with the practitioner if possible. The parent would then meet with the practitioner individually.

Recommended Length Of Time Between Sessions
- For at least the first six months there should be no more than 4-5 weeks between sessions. This allows time for the remedies to act and keeps the treatment on track. Too much time between sessions can interrupt or stall the healing process.

Estimated Length Of Time Before Improvements Can Be Expected
- Changes can often be seen within the first month of treatment. However, it is best to allow several months for significant improvement to occur.

Suggestions To Make Homeopathy More Effective
- Report accurate information.
- Give the remedy as instructed.
- Observe closely.
- Report changes to the practitioner.
- Keep follow-up appointments.

Other Methods That Are Similar To Homeopathy
- Other energetic treatments may try to improve the body's ability to heal itself, such as Acupuncture, Network Chiropractic and other forms of energy work. However, only Homeopathy uses energetic medicines to cure the person.

Other Methods That Complement Homeopathy
- Chiropractic
- Osteopathy
- Physical Therapy
- Naturopathy
- Tai chi
- Yoga
- Ayurveda
- Massage
- Counseling
- Meditation
- Leadership development courses

Nature And Length Of Training To Be A Practitioner
- Homeopathic training can range from self-paced online courses to four-year, full time programs.
- Training should include in-depth study of the Homeopathic Philosophy, Homeopathic remedies in the Materia Medica books and use of Repertories (books of symptoms) along with appropriate medical science classes for non-medical students. Some clinical experience is very valuable and should be included in the program.

Special Training Needed To Work With Children & Youth
- Lectures in taking the case of a child
- Observation of children in the training clinic
- In-depth study of remedies often prescribed in early life

Certification/Licenses Held By Practitioners
- Licensing varies from state to state. However, many states have passed a bill allowing non-licensed practitioners to practice legally. Graduates from Homeopathic programs receive a certificate of completion and may go on to obtain a certification from one of several organizations.

Professional Associations To Contact For Names Of Local Practitioners
- National Center for Homeopathy (NCH); 801 North Fairfax St., Suite 306; Alexandria, VA 22314; 703-548-7790; Fax: 703- 548-7792; Website: www.nationalcenterforhomeopathy.org; Email: available through the website
- Council for Homeopathic Certification; 16915 SE 272nd St., Suite 100; Covington, WA 98042; 866-242-3399; Fax: 815-366-7622; Website: www.homeopathicdirectory.com; Email: chcinfo@homeopathicdirectory.com
- North American Society of Homeopaths (NASH); P.O. Box 450039; Sunrise, FL 33345-0039; 206-720-7000; Fax: 208-248-1942; Website: www.homeopathy.org; Email: NashInfo@homeopathy.org
- American Institute of Homeopathy; 801 N. Fairfax St., Suite 306; Alexandria, VA 22314; 888-445-9988; Website: www.homeopathyusa.org; Email: aih@homeopathyusa.org
- Homeopathic Academy of Naturopathic Physicians (HANP); P.O. Box 126; Redmond, WA; 98073-0126; 253-630-3338; Fax: 815-301-6595; Website: www.hanp.net; Email: info@hanp.org

Number Of Certified Practitioners In U.S., Canada And Mexico
- There are several thousand practitioners in these countries.

What To Look For When Choosing The Best Practitioner
- School they attended
- Length of time practicing Homeopathy
- Method of practicing Homeopathy
- Experience with children
- Certification level

Leading Clinics, Centers, Practitioners
- Dr. Judyth Reichenberg-Ullman and Robert Ullman of The Northwest Center for Homeopathic Medicine; 131 Third Avenue, N.; Edmonds, WA 98020; 425-774-5599; Fax: 425-670-0319; Website: www.healthyhomeopathy.com; Email: nchmclinic@gmail.com
- Miranda Castro; 3051 N. Federal Highway, # 201 Fort Lauderdale, Florida 33306, USA 352-505-8545; Email: email@mirandacastro.com

- Andre Saine of The Canadian Academy of Homeopathy; 1173 boul. du Mont-Royal; Outremont (Québec), Canada H2V 2H6; 514-279-6629; Fax: 514-279-0111; Website: www.homeopathy.ca; Email: cah@videotron.ca
- Paul Herscu of The New England School of Homeopathy (NESH); 356 Middle Street; Amherst, MA 01002; 413-256-5949; Fax: 413-256-6223; Website: www.nesh.com; Email: available through the website

Research Papers Pertaining To Homeopathy

- J.Kleijnan, P.Knipschild, and G ter Riet. "Clinical Trials of Homeopathy." British Medical Journal, 302 (1991): 316-23.
- Jacobs, L., M. Jimenez, S.Gloyd, and D. Crothers, "Treatment of Acute Childhood Diarrhea with Homeopathic Medicine: A Randomized Clinical Trial in Nicaragua." Pediatrics 93, 5 (1994): 719-25.
- National Center for Complementary and Alternative Medicine and the National Institutes of Health website on homeopathic research: http://nccam.nih.gov.
- The Samueli Institute's website provides numerous articles on Homeopathy. Website: www.siib.org.

Bibliography

- The best sources for books on Homeopathy are the two largest Homeopathic booksellers in the U.S.:
    1. Minimum Price Books; P.O. Box 2187; Blaine, WA 98231; (UPS only: 250 H Street, Blaine, WA 98230); Orders: 800-663-8272; Fax: 604-597-8304; Website: www.minimum.com: Email: orders@minimum.com;
    2. Homeopathic Educational Services; 2124B Kittredge St.; Berkeley, CA 94704; 510-649-0294; Fax: 510-649-1955; Website: www.homeopathic.com; Email: available through the website.
- Homeopathy Today: The magazine of the National Center for Homeopathy. (See above.)
- Reichenberg-Ullman, Judyth, and Robert Ullman. *Rage Free Kids*. Roseville, CA: Prima Lifestyles, 1999.
- Shalts, Edward. *The American Institute of Homeopathy Handbook for Parents: A Guide to Healthy Treatment for Everything from Colds and Allergies to ADHD, Obesity, and Depression*. San Francisco: Jossey-Bass, 2005.
- Lansky, Amy. *The Impossible Cure: The Promise of Homeopathy*. Portola Valley, CA: R. L. Ranch Press, 2003.
- Kruzel, Thomas. *The Homeopathic Emergency Guide: A Quick Reference Guide to Accurate Homeopathic Care*. Berkeley, CA: North Atlantic Books, 1992.

Helpful Tips For Parents

- It is recommended that you openly discuss the use of Homeopathy with your own physician.
- Never give repeated doses of a remedy without the advice of a Homeopathic practitioner.
- Only repeat a remedy if improvement has been seen.

Biography of Randy Jane Reitzes, LVN, CMT, CCHH, Co-Author

- Randy has 6 years of experience.
- 25% of her practice is with children & youth under 18.
- Randy is affiliated with the National Center for Homeopathy.
- Degrees: Randy is a Licensed Vocational Nurse, Certified Massage Technician, and Certified Classical Hahnemannian Homeopath.

Randy Jane Reitzes, LVN, CMT, CCHH' Personal Statement

As a nurse for almost 30 years and specializing in hospice care for the past 8 years, I am concerned with the increase in chronic disease and the low rate of cure in conventional medicine. The philosophy of Homeopathy, particularly the way in which health, disease and cure are viewed, resonates with me in a very profound way. After experiencing the positive curative response both personally and professionally with my clients, I am convinced that cure is possible...

which means not only the elimination of symptoms, but also the restoration of health at the deepest core of one's being.

To Contact Randy Jane Reitzes, LVN, CMT, CCHH, Who Co-Contributed This Chapter

Randy Jane Reitzes; 690 5th Street, Suite 101; San Francisco, CA 94107; or, 907 Key Route Blvd.; Albany, CA 94706; Ph: 510-528-4146; Fax: 510-528-4146; Website: www.bayareahomeopathy.com; Email: randy@bayareahomeopathy.com

Biography of Lisette Narragon CCH, BRCP, Co-Author

- Lisette has 8 years of experience.
- 50% of her practice is with children & youth under 18.
- Degrees: Bachelor of Science; Certification of Classical Hahnemannian Homeopathy.
- Affiliations: National Center for Homeopathy; and British Registry of Complementary Practitioners.

Lisette Narragon CCH, BRCP's Personal Statement

I came to Homeopathy through my own personal experience in curing my son's recurrent throat infections, and my younger son's ear infections. Being treated Homeopathically as a child is a true blessing, as it sets a great foundation of good health for one's whole life. My wish is to be able to grow the numbers of children using Homeopathy in the years ahead by educating more parents about the benefits of Homeopathic treatment.

To Contact Lisette Narragon CCH, BRCP, Who Co-Contributed This Chapter

Lisette Narragon; 2672 Bayshore Parkway, Suite 810; Mountain View, CA 94043; Ph: 650-494-3199; Fax: 650-494-3199; Website: www.bayareahomeopathy.com; Email: lisette@bayareahomeopathy.com

Biography of Dian Wagner, Deceased.

- Dian will be remembered in the Sebastopol, California area for a long time. She was an excellent Homeopath who worked with thousands of children over many decades. She was an early supporter of the Growing Up Easier/Help For Children Project. Lisette and Randy have included some of her contributions in this chapter.

. . . .

Marie Mulligan's Comment About Homeopathy: My children have benefited from over-the-counter Homeopathic remedies and Homeopathic consultation with Dian Wagner. I have also had patients benefit from Homeopathic care. Be careful in choosing practitioners because Homeopaths are not licensed. Generally, with rare exceptions, Homeopathic remedies are safe.

Rick Geggie's Comment About Homeopathy: I use Homeopathy often. I have told many parents about it and they have reported very good results. Homeopathy is very effective with children's emotional issues. Picking a good Homeopath is important. Pick one who asks a great number of questions. Homeopathy is much disputed by many people in the mainstream medical field. According to modern scientific theory, it should not work; however it does work and it is very effective. I think that every home with children benefits from having a Homeopathic remedy called Rescue Remedy. It is very handy for calming children when they are upset from accidents, traumas and fear.

CHAPTER 21

HYPNOTHERAPY FOR CHILDREN & YOUTH

By Randi Farkas, MA, MFT, © Copyright 2008.

Hypnotherapy Has Helped Kids With

- The most common challenge is some kind of anxiety or fear. These situations include performance anxiety (test-taking, public speaking, sports); medical or dental visits, and also ongoing medical interventions for chronic illness; school phobia; and such common but often terrifying fears as fear of the dark.
- Hypnotherapy helps with anything that involves letting go of problematic memories.
- Hypnotherapy helps with pediatric asthma and a wide range of medical problems.
- Hypnotherapy helps with nightmares.

Hypnotherapy Can Help In The Following Areas

Spirit: It can help with post-traumatic stress; creativity; boundary issues; adoption issues.

Body: I can help stuttering; sports; bleeding and pain including menstrual cramps; asthma; skin problems; enuresis; headaches; pre and post-surgery; comfort during terminal illness.

Mind: It can help issues like, "I hate arithmetic" and other beliefs about oneself which block learning, growth and healthy self-esteem.

Emotions: It can help with difficulty accepting a new sibling, or a divorce ; death of a pet, friend or family member; trauma of a car accident, fire or assault; fears and phobias, which are numerous in some children.

Social: It can help with friendship skills; setting healthy boundaries with bullies and with friends.

Brief Description Of Hypnotherapy

- Hypnotherapy is a method for accessing and changing buried memories, fears or habits that interfere with the full expression of the child's true nature. The bonus of using Hypnotherapy, as compared to other equally effective modalities like play therapy, art or drama therapy, is that with Hypnotherapy, many issues can be resolved in a handful of sessions. Often one meeting is all it takes to resolve a child's problem.
- Hypnotherapy is a naturally-occurring state, easily observed in children when they stop playing and stare off into space. Teens and adults experience Hypnotherapy while watching a movie, listening to music, daydreaming, or

driving "on automatic pilot" while thinking about something else. The feeling is generally of relaxation coupled with intent focus and receptiveness.

> * "We might compare it to a teeter-totter. In the waking state the conscious mind is at the high end of the teeter-totter and the subconscious mind at the low end. Under Hypnotherapy they reverse and the subconscious is at the high end, and the conscious mind at the low end, but it is still present. Thoughts rise from the inner mind into consciousness." Leslie M. LeCron

- Hypnotherapy uses this natural state to bring about positive change by engaging the child with a game, story or some other focus of interest.
- Next comes the healing work: suggestions are given that help the child believe and act in new ways. These suggestions may be quite concrete and matter-of-fact ("Would it be alright for the pain to move to the tip of your little finger?"). Or, they may be presented in images and metaphors. For example, a story about a sad little dog being adopted by a loving family might help a child connect to her adoptive family. Or the image of a rain cloud letting go of its drops of water at exactly the right time for the farmers' fields could help with persistent bed-wetting. A professional hypnotist always asks the child's subconscious mind for permission to deal with a topic.
- How the hypnotist decides to work depends on both her/his style and what they've observed about the child. Often, children like the idea of creating a "control room" in their minds where they can view their problem on a screen, making it smaller or different to bring about the desired results. Or the healing work may consist of a story constructed to echo the child's situation but with a twist that brings about positive change. The idea here is to allow the child to tap into their imagination in order to free themselves from the problem.

Success With Hypnotherapy

- Tracy, a thirteen year old girl, had refused dental work for years. She developed gum disease and was at risk of losing teeth. In one session she figured out a way to control the situation with her subconscious mind. She decided she'd like to distract herself with a favorite TV show. She laughed as she imagined it. I asked if there were some words to describe how she was feeling, and she giggled, "This is outrageously funny!". We practiced letting those words take her into a delightful state, free of fear or pain.

  I talked with her dental assistant, who agreed to say the phrase "This is outrageously funny!" when Tracy was ready for her procedure. With the cue, Tracy was able to enter and maintain her private fantasy of watching an absorbing, comical show in her imagination while she was sitting in the dental chair.

  In more traditional therapy, we would have looked for and talked about the origins of Tracy's dental phobia. These different approaches don't need to be seen as opposite; rather, they are along a continuum and sometimes blend together.

- A boy I'll call Kenny was the one who convinced me years ago that I was on the right track offering Hypnotherapy to children suffering from post-traumatic stress.

  With a few figures and blocks as props, he acted out a horrible car accident that had taken place near his house. Showing all the signs of being in a light trance, he re-enacted the scene several times. Each time the damage was milder. By the end, the figure representing Kenny was able to say, "Whew, I'm glad that's over. It's not as bad as I was afraid it was."

- The following is a story from Sister Xavier McPhee, a wonderful local Hypnotherapy practitioner and teacher who died recently: "James, a 6-year old boy, had dreadful asthma, used a nebulizer, and was on medication. He was often rushed to the hospital.

  I asked him what he did with things he didn't want anymore. He said he threw them in the trash. In trance, I asked him to put the asthma and the memory of it in the garbage. He had no further asthma attacks after that."

- We work on the memories that created the ongoing anxiety or fear. For instance, "an 8-year old girl was petrified of loud noises and would start crying uncontrollably whenever she heard them. From her mother I learned the girl had been born in a very noisy hospital environment. In three hypnosis sessions the child was able to recall and release the effects of the birth memories freeing her from her fear of loud noises."

Hypnotherapy Is Appropriate For Ages

- All ages beyond two

Children & Youth's Reactions to Hypnotherapy

- They love it because it uses their own power.
- It's mysterious and magical.
- Learning how to go into a trance is, for most children, a skill like bike riding which they enjoy mastering and which, once learned, they never forget.
- Children respond to Hypnotherapy with enjoyment, pride and sometimes a shrug of "no big deal".
- One boy gleefully commented, "This is weird, weirder than weird."
- Sometimes a child will not want to talk about the experience, which should be respected.
- Teens report enjoying Hypnotherapy for the opportunity to take a break from stress: they like the relaxation, the vivid imagery, and the sense of control.

Contraindications: When Hypnotherapy Should Be Avoided

- If the child or youth is very seriously emotionally disturbed or dissociated, cannot follow directions, or is too frightened to relax.
- A child or youth with epilepsy may need special strategies for entering trance.

History

- Strongly-accented singing, clapping, repetitive dancing, rhythmic language (including poetry), marching, and certain visual patterns are entries to this state which have been used throughout humanity's history.
- Hypnotherapy was enthusiastically researched from the 1700's on.
- It fell out of popularity during the early 20th century. However it regained favor after World War II with successful treatment of battlefield injuries and "shellshock".
- The last twenty years have seen Hypnotherapy reach its peak of acceptance by the medical community and the general public.
- Most medical benefits include coverage for hypnotherapy as a form of psychotherapy.

Basic Concepts And Components Of Hypnotherapy

- Hypnotherapy is an altered state of consciousness, which people may go into when they concentrate on something, meditate, relax and let their minds drift, or when they are faced with a mind-altering stressor.
- Working with a hypnotist is a way of using this state intentionally for positive benefits.
- Hypnotherapy works with the part of the mind that dreams and imagines. Sometimes we refer to it as the subconscious mind, or inner mind.
- The child has the control. The hypnosis therapist follows the nonverbal and spoken cues of the child to bring about healing.
- Because the subconscious mind can access new ways of looking at things and solving problems as it bypasses a child's everyday way of thinking, Hypnotherapy can help children with many challenges both mild and severe. For example, a rash can be seen as a burning desire to express oneself, and appropriate ways to do that will just "pop" into one's mind.

- While in trance, hand signals may be used by the patient to indicate "yes" or "no".
- We work on the memories that created the ongoing anxiety or fear.
- Hypnosis is almost always successful, if the person is able to relax.
- What happens in the first session is a good indicator of whether or not Hypnotherapy is going to be successful with a particular child and topic.
- Hypnotherapy is not long-term therapy.
- No one ever "stays in trance" or does things they don't want to do.

Description Of A Typical Session

- A history is taken from parents before the child or youth comes in. It's important to find out what the family has already tried in order to resolve the issue for which they are seeking help.
- Children are made comfortable by choosing their own chair or sitting on the rug. If a child wants her/his parent present, that's fine.
- To an onlooker, the therapy may resemble storytelling or an art activity.
- There may be silences. The child may have their eyes open, or closed.
- Some children move about while in trance; this doesn't interfere with the work.
- If the child is wary I sometimes ask him/her to help me hypnotize his parent, or me.
- I respect the child's subconscious mind. They must be told very directly what is going to be done.
- Imagery, repetition and humor are common features of hypnotherapy.
- Suggestions are always positive and in the present tense. For example, "It feels so good to sleep all through the night" rather than "I'm not going to lie awake at night anymore."
- I often give children a special object like a rock or a shell to take with them. The object can help the child re-enter the trance or simply become "peaceful" on their own.

Fees/Costs In 2007 - Northern California

- In the Bay Area, fees range from $70 to $125 per session.
- Some practitioners offer sliding scale fees, and health insurance may apply, depending on your provider.
- Often, follow-ups are briefer and thus have a lower fee.

Average Time Per Session

- Sessions are usually an hour.
- The length of sessions depends on the age and distractibility of the child.
- With a young child, it's common to do shorter sessions.

Recommended Length Of Time Between Sessions

- One week
- If in crisis, 2 or 3 days (a rare occurrence)

Estimated Length Of Time Before Improvements Can Be Expected

- Improvement is often achieved in one trance session.
- There is rarely a child who does not resolve challenges within a few sessions.

Suggestions To Make Hypnotherapy More Effective

- Parents can sit in on sessions - out of the child's view. In this way, parents can provide safety for the child and can see the changes.

- Parents can show approval for Hypnotherapy and for any changes in attitude and behavior. But again, sometimes it's better not to talk about the changes. Ask your practitioner for their opinion.
- A parent can also be hypnotized so the child can see that it is safe.

Other Methods That Are Similar To Hypnotherapy
- Meditation
- Contemplation
- Dream Reentry (Therapeutic Imaging)

Other Methods That Complement Hypnotherapy
- Games, stories, play, and mystery activate the imaginative mind.

Special Training Needed To Work With Children & Youth
- Nationwide, professional associations and individual practitioners such as child psychologists and medical doctors offer trainings focused on child and adolescent issues for hypnotherapists.
- Sadly, not many hypnotherapists are trained in working with children. People who like children and have experience such as teaching or child-care are usually the ones who specialize in working with them.

Certification/Licenses Held By Practitioners
- While some people hold that Hypnotherapy practitioners should also be licensed to practice medicine or psychotherapy, I don't agree with this. I have received training from highly professional, expert hypnotherapists who do not hold clinical licenses.
- The reason that hypnotherapy is not regulated by the state of California is that it is not held to be a dangerous or high-risk practice.
- As with any health-care provider, a parent should ask for and check out references and use their own common sense when interviewing a potential hypnotist.
- Most practitioners in Sonoma County have at minimum 100-150 hours of basic training. This is the minimum coursework for "certification" which, again, is not required in California. Anyone who is a serious, ethical professional follows up with continuing education and consults with his peers on a regular basis.
- The American Society of Clinical Hypnotherapy requires that a trainee must be licensed as a practitioner of another healing art (psychology, medicine, counseling, nursing, dentistry).

Professional Associations To Contact For Names Of Local Practitioners
- The American Society of Clinical Hypnosis; 140 N. Bloomingdale Rd. Bloomingdale, IL 60108; Ph: 630-980-4740; Fax 630-351-8490; Website: www.asch.net; Email: info@asch.net
- The Milton H. Erickson Foundation; 3606 North 24th Street; Phoenix, AZ 85016; Ph: 602-956-6196; Fax 602-956-0519; Website: www.erickson-foundation.org; Email: office@erickson-foundation.org
- RECAMFT (Redwood Empire Chapter of the California Association of Marriage and Family Therapists), has a referral service and can provide names of licensed MFTs (Marriage and Family Therapists) who specialize in hypnotherapy in Sonoma County. RECAMFT; P. O. Box 2443; Sebastopol, CA 95473; Telephone/Fax: 707-575-0596; Website: www.recamft.org; Email: therapy@RECAMFT.org
- The California Association of Marriage and Family Therapists (CAMFT) maintains a database of licensed California professional therapists. Website: www.camft.org; then click on therapistfinder.com

What To Look For When Choosing The Best Practitioner
- Ask for references from people you know such as pediatricians, principals and school counselors. I receive many referrals from school counselors.
- Look for experience and maturity, and someone who has a good attitude toward children: trusting, loving and caring with the ability to build rapport.
- Follow the guidelines for choosing any healthcare provider: look for clear communication; upfront discussion of fees; respect for you and your child; and a willingness to collaborate with other professionals who may be involved with your child.
- If the presenting problem is a physiological one, be sure the child has had a recent medical evaluation and be willing to provide a release for the hypnotist to speak with your child's doctor.
- Caveat: If a practitioner is taught by someone who is not licensed as a healthcare provider, they may not learn reliable information regarding psychological issues, particularly those concerning children.

Famous Practitioners/Famous Centers
- The Milton H. Erickson Foundation; 3606 North 24th St.; Phoenix AZ 85016; Ph: 602-956-6196; Fax: 602-956-0519; Website: www.erickson-foundation.org; Email: office@erickson-foundation.org

Bibliography
- Olness et al: (1998) Wart Regression in Children, in *The American Journal of Clinical Hypnotherapy*.
- Ames, R., Madrid, A., Skolek, S., and Brown, G. "Does Maternal-Infant Bonding Therapy Improve Breathing in Asthmatic Children?" *The Journal of the Association of Prenatal and Perinatal Psychology and Health* 15, no. 2 (2000): 99-117.
- The journal that has great articles about Hypnotherapy in general is the *American Journal of Clinical Hypnotherapy*. When you access ASCH's website (see above), you can find short versions of articles.
- Haley, Jay. *Uncommon Therapy: The Psychiatric Techniques of Milton H. Erickson*, M.D. New York: W.W. Norton, 1993.
- Olness, Karen and Daniel Kohen. *Hypnosis and Hypnotherapy with Children: Third Edition*. New York: The Guilford Press, 1996.
- Temes, Roberta: *The Complete Idiot's Guide to Hypnosis, 2nd Edition*. New York: Alpha Books, 2004.
- Mills, Joyce and Richard Crowley. *Therapeutic Metaphors for Children and the Child Within*. Philadelphia: Brunner/Mazel, 1986.
- Duke, Robert. *Hypnotherapy for Troubled Children. East Rutherford*, NJ: New Horizon Press, 1985.

Biography of Randi Farkas, MA, MFT, Author
- Randi has twenty-three years of experience working with children & youth.
- Randi has a private practice as a Marriage and Family Therapist. Hypnotherapy is not the only modality she uses, but it her my favorite. Adolescents make up half of her practice. She sees younger children only for hypnotherapy or as part of a family.
- Degrees: She earned an MS in Education; MA in Counseling; Special Education Certification; CA Marriage and Family Therapist license; EMDR Level II training; holds certificates in specialized areas of Hypnotherapy.

Randi Farkas' Personal Statement
One of my special interests is working with the mother and/or father of a child who's dealing with physical or emotional issues.

I have been strongly influenced by Tony Madrid's work with the parent-child bond. This powerful connection, which has a strong impact on a child's (and family's) well-being, is quite amenable to positive change using Hypnotherapy with the parent(s). Also, teaching self-Hypnotherapy to both adults and children is one of my loves, and I incorporate that into much of my work.

To Contact Randi Farkas, Who Contributed This Chapter

Randi Farkas; 555 W. College Ave.; Santa Rosa, CA 95401; Ph: 707-578-5321; Fax: 707-578-5321

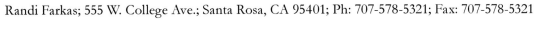

Marie Mulligan's Comment About Hypnotherapy: In my experience, Hypnotherapy has been useful in helping children & youth with headaches and reducing anxiety. I recommend seeking care from a hypnotherapist who is licensed in another healing modality, such as psychotherapist, psychologist, nurse, etc.

Rick Geggie's Comment About Hypnotherapy: Hypnotherapy works very well with most children suffering from most emotionally based problems. I have seen children and adults experience quite amazing changes of negative belief, attitude and performance after they have had hypnotherapy sessions. Experienced, trained, licensed psychotherapists who use hypnotherapy and who like working with children can help in profound and positive ways in a short period of time. I look forward to the day when it is used routinely to increase learning and performance levels.

CHAPTER 22

INDEPENDENT STUDY FOR CHILDREN & YOUTH

By June Nason, MsEd,   © Copyright 2008.

Independent Study Has Helped Kids With

- It has helped gifted students who are not challenged in regular classrooms and want to accelerate their studies.
- It has helped students who want an individualized approach that allows them to delve more deeply into areas of special interest.
- It has helped students who need to make up credits, or who have fallen behind in their studies and need targeted instruction and materials to fill in gaps in their learning.
- It has helped students who feel frustrated, bored, disconnected or frightened in a regular school environment.
- It has helped students who face particular challenges such as health issues, or the necessity of employment, thus making classroom attendance difficult.
- It has helped students who feel frustrated because teaching strategies in the traditional classroom are directed toward the needs of students who are learning at a slower rate, thus slowing the pace of learning for the whole.
- It has helped students and parents who are overwhelmed by the amount of homework associated with regular classroom instruction.
- It has helped students who have had negative interactions with classroom teachers or with other students.
- It has helped students who feel the need for more connection with parents and family.
- It has helped students who are suffering from shock, trauma, or a significant loss.

Independent Study Can Help In The Following Areas

Spirit: Independent Study honors the individuality of the student, without excluding the benefits of the school system.

Body: The structure of Independent Study can be physically less stressful than conforming to routines that make up a traditional school day, such as sitting for several hours at a desk.

Mind: Independent Study students learn at their own pace and are not distracted by classroom problems and peer pressures.

* Independent Study develops the child's or youth's curiosity.

* It avoids the common feeling of some children & youth that they are wasting their time in regular classrooms where learning is slowed by misbehavior, social problems, and other students who learn more slowly.
* Independent Study is good for children & youth who are very bright, self-motivated and yet easily distracted.
* Being in regular programs can be very difficult for gifted students who are eager to learn.
* Independent Study benefits gifted and talented children, as well as students who are behind in their academic learning, due to a variety of regular classroom conditions.
* Independent Study helps students to learn the discipline of time management, self-monitoring and assessment, and promotes the development of independent learning abilities.

Emotions: Independent Study can reduce frustrations, stresses, and feelings of being unmet, unseen and unheard. Independent Study can also reduce the feeling of "overwhelm" and fear that can come from the expectations, work load, peer pressures, and disruptions associated with regular classrooms.

Social: Independent Study avoids problems of peer pressure and distraction; allows for choosing social activities that are most interesting and satisfying to the student.

Brief Description Of Independent Study

* Independent Study is an alternative instructional strategy whereby students work independently and generally at home, according to a written agreement, and under the supervision of a credentialed teacher(s). Parents and family members provide additional support for their student as needed.
* Public school districts can operate Independent Study as a program within a regular school, or as a charter school or an alternative school. There are some private schools that use an Independent Study strategy as well as online Independent Study programs.
* Always check out the accreditation policies of an Independent Study program.
* Not all school districts offer Independent Study as an alternative option. In some cases, parents can request a school district transfer, enabling their student to enroll in a neighboring school district that offers Independent Study.
* The curriculum and instructional materials are provided by the public, state supported school system.
* Independent Study students follow a school district's course outlines – or state standards, and meet the district graduation requirements.
* Independent Study offers flexibility to meet a student's interests and styles of learning, within the context of required course content standards.
* Independent Study students can achieve a state government education department approved High School Diploma and pursue a college education.
* With Independent Study, parents can take back responsibility for their child's or youth's education by becoming more involved in their student's education.
* Independent Study is offered as an alternative to regular classroom attendance for children and youth by some, but not all, public school systems.
* Outside California, Independent Study may have another legal name such as "Home Study."
* Independent Study education provides support and resources to parents and families.
* The Independent Study teacher files reports on pupil progress with state education authorities.
* There are now websites about Independent Study, Home Study, Alternative Education, and Home Schooling.
* Independent Study is different from Home Schooling because Home Schooling parents most often receive no assistance, no materials, and no guidance from local school districts.
* Students enrolled in Independent Study can receive all the benefits and services the school district has to offer: psychological services, counselors, sports programs, music programs, foreign language classes, school libraries, and special education service.

Success With Independent Study

- "My Husband and I chose to educate our children through Independent Study to individually give each of them what they needed on an academic level. Happily, they are both experiencing great success. The added bonus however, is that our lives have become more family-centered and balanced. In the past, the public school, with its homework and many demands, set the tone and speed at which our family moved. Too often, it was a crazy whirlwind of rush-rush-rush, and quite frankly, unmanageable chaos. Now, we have time to linger over meals, really talk with each other, read good books, take weekly hikes and outings, and visit with family and friends. Each of our children pursues sports and activities fully and passionately. There is a renewed sense of purpose and energy in each of us now that we, as parents, lead the way for our children." Theresa Schroth, parent.
- "I like Independent Study because I never hear any of that noise that I get with public school. It enables me to do a lot of work. I am able to study what I want to study…"Wesley Schroth, 6th grade student.
- A young gymnast was able to maintain a rigorous training and competition schedule because she was able to complete her assignments at home in the mornings, on weekends and on training breaks at the gym.
- A family enrolled their 5 year old daughter in an Independent Study program because their religious values were in conflict with all the holiday themes at regular school.
- Two successful High School girls were harshly teased by their peers about their appearance. The pressure was so bad, they did not want to go to school anymore. Independent Study enabled them to continue succeeding with their course work in the safety and protection of their homes. They could choose their friends and make time to socialize with people they enjoyed.
- A 16 year old young woman is on a fast track to graduate high school and begin her career education. She is very bright and can complete a lot of work in a short period of time. She is having a great time.
- Two high school Independent Study students are collaborating on a special project and are creating an organic garden on the Independent Studies school site while earning elective credits.

Independent Study Is Appropriate For Ages

- All ages - Kindergarten through 12th grade

Children & Youth's Reactions To Independent Study

- Students are calm, happier and less stressed about education.
- Students enjoy learning and feel they have some control over their education.
- Students enjoy the responsibility to be well organized.
- Since most Independent Study students rate very well on standardized tests, they appreciate their program.

Extra Care Is Needed

- When students who are new to Independent Study are far behind their grade level achievement levels.

Contraindications: When Independent Study Should Be Avoided

- Children & youth that are in the habit of power struggling and resisting parents will not do well.
- Independent Study is not very helpful to children with emotional and disruptive behavior problems/habits.
- Independent Study does not work when the home environment is chaotic, with no suitable place to study, concentrate and complete assignments.
- For Elementary age children, Independent Study should be avoided if parents are working during the day. Having Daycare staff or babysitters supervising the student usually does not work.
- Independent Study does not work when children & youth have very complicated intellectual, physical or developmental challenges.

- Local school districts have special teachers who visit homes when a child or youth is medically ill or recovering from surgery.
- Independent Study is less effective when parents have difficulty learning how to be supportive of their children or youth's learning by engaging them with curiosity and enjoyment.

History

- At one point in history all pioneers home schooled their children. When children were forced to go to school by the government, reading levels were lowered.
- Independent Study started in response to parents and educators being concerned that very bright students were dropping out of school because they felt schooling was irrelevant. Bright students felt slowed down by the usual rate of progress in schools and by the distractions of some student behavior. Alternative educational programs started to become a popular way of helping such students get a usable education.
- Parents, educators and politicians were concerned that some home-schooled children & youth were not learning enough skills to allow them to choose their own careers. Programs like Independent Study were started, allowing parents to be very involved in their children or youth's education with the help of qualified teachers, modern curriculum and good educational materials.
- Many parents have become very dissatisfied with, and even frightened of, what happens to their children or youth when they attend modern traditional schools that do not reflect home values.
- Many parents of Independent Study students are concerned that modern traditional schools have a hidden curriculum of compliance and obedience.
- Many parents are concerned that modern traditional schools take away time from family relationships. They find family life enhanced by Independent Study programs.

Basic Concepts And Components Of Independent Study

- Students are self-disciplined, self-motivated, and want to learn.
- Parents are willing to get involved with their child's or youth's education.
- The Independent Study teachers are inspired and qualified.
- The Independent Study teachers are curriculum experts, have good one-on-one communication skills, and can teach students and parents how to learn.
- Resources, materials, teaching/learning aides, and books are available through the program.
- Independent Study is completed through legitimate, accredited public school programs – with all the resources of the local school district, state education departments, etc. (availability of art, music, gymnastics, science labs, advanced foreign language classes, psychological services, and counseling).

Description Of A Typical Session

- The teacher completes legal enrollment procedures, gets records from past schools, and notifies the state of student's enrollment.
- The teacher completes an inventory of student's strengths, interests and needs.
- The Child and parent attend a weekly one-hour meeting with the teacher. Youth attend a weekly one-hour meeting with the teacher(s) - without the parent.
- The teacher evaluates, responds to, corrects, and discusses the past week's completed learning assignments.
- The teacher records information about the completed learning assignments with state education authorities to ensure compliance to state standards.
- The teacher and student (and parent, if in attendance) develop the coming week's learning assignments.
- The teacher loans appropriate materials to child or youth and parent.
- The teacher checks to make sure that the new learning assignments are understood by the child or youth.
- The teacher instructs the parent on how to best support the student in getting the learning assignments completed.

- The teacher is occasionally available by telephone for brief consultation.

Major Differences Between Independent Study and Home Study/Home Schooling

- In Home Schooling, parents take total responsibility for providing their child's or youth's curriculum and education.
- Unlike Independent Study, parents who are using Home Schooling provide their own materials, teachers, guidance, training, curriculum, and educational opportunities. Happily, there are many Home Schooling resources available today and some are free of charge.
- Parents using Home Schooling must prove to state authorities that their child's or youth's at-home educational program and accomplishments are meeting state education requirements. Some states have educational departments that are becoming very involved in this process.
- Since state education requirements for Home Schooling differ so much, parents are advised to contact education authorities before beginning Home Schooling. There are many resources available on the Internet.
- Be very careful to determine which companies are more interested in profits than in children & youth.

Fees/Costs In 2007 - Averages

- It is free. Supplies and teacher salary are paid for by taxes to school district.
- Families pay transportation costs to and from supervision sessions with Independent Study teacher.
- Parents pay for private lessons in art, music, gymnastics, or their child or youth can drop in for those classes at local schools free of charge.

Average Time Per Study Session With Teacher

- For Elementary and Junior High/Middle School: One hour per week supervision time with the program teacher/guide.
- For High School: one half-hour per week supervision with a teacher per course.

Average Length Of Independent Study Time At Home

- Check with your local Independent Study School for specific time requirements.
- In California, students in Kindergarten need an at-home program of 15 hours a week; Elementary/Middle School age = 20 hours a week minimum; Secondary = between 20 and 30 hours a week.

Estimated Length Of Time Before Improvements Can Be Expected

- Almost immediately, to a few months

Suggestions To Make Independent Study More Effective

- Children & youth have to want Independent Study. They have to want to do their learning and school work at home.
- Home School must be voluntary.
- Elementary and middle school students need a lot of parental support. One parent needs to be at home supervising all the time. Babysitters are less effective.
- Parents and the students need to have a good working relationship where the student is open to their direction, instruction and suggestions.
- Parents need to be patient with their kids.
- Children & youth who are resisting their parents, and who power-struggle, will not do well with an Independent Study educational approach and would do better in school.

Other Methods That Complement Independent Study

- Community service
- Activities offered by local Home Schooling Associations
- Community Sports and Activities
- Music Lessons

Nature And Length Of Training To Be An Independent Study Teacher

- Independent Study teachers must have 3 to 4 years of university education in Education.
- Independent Study teachers are encouraged to have Postgraduate degrees in Education or related fields.
- Independent Study teachers are encouraged to have experience in regular classrooms.

Professional Associations To Contact For Names Of Local Independent Study programs

- The are currently none.
- Contact your county or state department of education.
- Home Schooling associations occasionally will list Independent Study programs.

Number Of Certified Education/Home Schooling/Apprenticing Practitioners In U.S., Canada, And Mexico

- The number is unknown at this time.

What To Look For When Choosing The Best Independent Study Program/Teacher

- Talk with parents of other children & youth in the program.
- Make an appointment and visit the program.
- Choose teachers who are curious about your child or youth.
- Choose teachers with whom you are comfortable.
- Choose teachers with whom your child or youth is comfortable.

Resources And Websites

- A-Z Home's Cool: This is a list of California home school organizations with state charters. See their website: http://homeschooling.gomilpitas.com.
- California Department of Education's Independent Study Program: See their website: http://www.cde.ca.gov. This site is designed for schools wanting to run an independent study program as well.
- California Department of Education Manual for Independent Study outlines curriculum and instruction for independent study teachers from the California Department of Education…useful information for community resources to enhance curriculum. See: http://www.cde.ca.gov.
- California Consortium for Independent Study: Website for Independent Study Teachers and a state wide organization interested in the advancement of independent study programs. See: http://www.ccis.org.
- Currie, Carol. "History of Homeschooling." *EzineArticles*: This website has various links and information to read more about Homeschooling. See: http://ezinearticles.com.
- Emery, Kathy. "Alternative Schools: Diverted but not Defeated." (July 2000): Paper submitted to Qualification Committee At UC Davis, California.
- Hill, Elizabeth G. "Alternative Education California." (2007). *The Legislative Analyst's Office*. Website: http://www.lao.ca.gov. The history of alternative education in California. Independent Study is one of four alternative options for education mentioned. Page 6 has information on Independent Study.

- Home School Association of California provides information regarding the legalities of Homeschooling: website: http://www.hsc.org.
- Stephanie Hood's article on Public Independent Study Programs and Charter Schools can be found on the Gifted HomeSchoolers Forum website. See: http://giftedhomeschoolers.org.
- Gordon, Edward E. and Elaine H. "Centuries of Tutoring: A History of Alternative Education in America and Western Europe." *History of Education Quarterly* 32, no. 3 (Autumn, 1992): pp. 379-381.
- Miller, Ron. "A Brief History Of Alternative Education." (1996). *The Alternative Education Resource Organization* (AERO). See: http://www.educationrevolution.org/history.html.
- National Home Education Research Institute has a wealth of information available. See: http://www.nheri.org.

Bibliography

- For books related to Home Study, see the website of the Alternative Education Resource Organization (AERO): http://www.educationrevolution.org.
- Education Resource Organization (AERO): http://www.educationrevolution.org/homeschooling.html.
- Gordon, Edward E. and Elaine H. Gordon. *Centuries of Tutoring: A History of Alternative Education in America and Western Europe.* Lanham, MD: University Press of America, 1990.

Helpful Tips For Parents

- Acknowledge effort and success. Avoid taking responsibility for getting the child or youth's assignments completed.
- Have a calm uncluttered study space if possible.
- Have regular learning times if possible.
- Complete the assignments as soon as possible: Avoid last minute rushing.
- Provide time to practice.
- Chart and acknowledge effort and accomplishment.
- Keep emotional contact with your child or youth while they are doing their learning assignments: Avoid isolation while learning.
- Avoid doing the assignment for the child or youth. Express faith that they will figure out how to do it.
- Become a life-long learner yourself. Take a correspondence course and work on it while your child or youth works on their assignments.
- Avoid telling your child or youth about the academic areas in which you had difficulty. Rather, become a learner and take a course and get more comfortable with those trouble areas. Your comfort will help your child or youth.
- Do not feel guilt or shame if you or your child or youth has had difficulty learning in one or all academic areas. These emotions might reflect your own lack of support in the past. These emotions are not helpful to your child.
- Work to get your child or youth's school programs based on your child or youth's interests and not solely on memorizing textbook/computer program information.
- Be aware that textbook publishing companies pay large amounts of lobbying money to politicians who are in charge of educational programs.

Biography Of June Nason, Author

- June holds a Master's Degree in Education; plus many other certificates.
- She has 30 years of experience, teaching over a thousand children.
- She started learning how to be a teacher while enrolled in alternative education as a youth.

June Nason's Personal Statement

Independent Study can be one the best learning strategies for children & youth who have unique traits in their personalities and intellects: they are extremely motivated and self-directed; they thrive on the independence; they can learn better in the quiet of their own homes.

As an Independent Study supervising teacher I've had the opportunity to be of service providing quality education to children & youth and their families. The program allows them freedom and independence while meeting the educational criteria mandated by the state and local governments. I have been able to serve students who have a lot of ambition and intelligence and whose needs were not being met in regular schools. However, Independent Study is by no means the best educational strategy for all students.

To Contact June Nason, Who Contributed This Chapter

June Nason; c/o Valley Oaks School; 540 Vallejo St.; Petaluma CA, 94952; Email:
JuneNason@GrowingUpEasier.com

. . . .

Marie Mulligan's Comment About Independent Study: I used an Independent Study program with my sons while living in Mexico for a few years. While making family life richer, the boys learned well.

Rick Geggie's Comment About Independent Study: I am sad that this option was not available for my family. Independent Study is not suitable for all families and all students.

For me, Independent Study offers something that can help children & youth grow up much easier. Having paid attention to the home schooling, Independent Study, Alternative Education movements for over 45 years, I am convinced that Independent Study offers the best of all worlds.

For many of the reasons listed in this chapter and for many other very complex reasons, Independent Study will become increasingly popular as time goes on.

CHAPTER 23

LIGHT THERAPY FOR CHILDREN & YOUTH

By John Downing, OD, PhD, © Copyright 2008.

Light Therapy Has Helped Kids With

• Allergies	• Chronic fatigue syndrome	• Headaches
• Anxiety	• Conduct disorder problems	• Hyperactivity
• Arithmetic difficulties	• Coordination	• Learning differences
• Arthritis	• Depression	• Learning disabilities
• Attention Deficit Disorder	• Developmental delays	• Rage
• Attention Deficit Hyperactive Disorder	• Developmental retardation	• Reading difficulties
• Autism	• Digestion problems	• Seizures
• Balance problems	• Disorganization	• Short term memory deficiency
• Behavior problems	• Down's Syndrome	• Speech problems
• Borderline personality structure	• Dyslexia	• Stress
• Brain damage	• Epilepsy	• Wandering eye problems

Light Therapy Can Help In The Following Areas

Body: Light Therapy eliminates physical problems such as fatigue, insomnia, hyperactivity, poor coordination, balance difficulties, autonomic and endocrine imbalances.

Spirit: Light Therapy gives the soul back its light and helps the spirit soar. It takes the innate energy of the child or youth, which the mind sends out into the world, and grounds it more deeply into the soul. It allows the child or youth to control their energy instead of the energy controlling the child.

Mind: Intellectual difficulties are lessened; including poor reading comprehension, pronunciation, concentration, memory, organizational ability, and mathematical ability.

Emotions: Emotional problems are reduced or eliminated; including low self-esteem, depression, fears and anxieties, SAD (Seasonal Affective Disorder).

Social: When the body, mind and emotions of a child are functioning optimally and the spirit is soaring, social interactions will be appropriately smooth and rewarding.

Brief Description of Light Therapy

- Colored Light Therapy utilizes specific colors of light shined into the eyes to stimulate and enhance brain function.
- This therapeutic light stimulates almost every cell in the brain, which in turn improves brain and body chemistry and function.
- Colored Light Therapy is a medically supervised program that guides the patient through a series of therapies that result in better vision, improved mental functioning, emotional processing and improved coordination.

Success With Light Therapy

- A nine year old girl with hyperactivity, poor concentration and reading difficulties, received one month of Light Therapy. Afterward her behavior improved and she began passing all her school subjects.
- A sixteen year old girl suffered form headaches and allergies. After 40 Light Therapy sessions, her physical symptoms improved, as well as her reading and learning abilities.
- A seven year old boy, who had suffered a series of minor head injuries and the separation of his parents, had poor self-esteem, learning disabilities, and a severe withdrawal from life. His emotional distress would cause him to vomit. After 14 sessions of colored Light Therapy he made a complete reversal in personality. He began verbalizing emotional problems, and was comfortable making eye contact for the first time in his life! His self-esteem skyrocketed and his learning ability improved. He is now interacting normally with other children and making friends.
- My six year old son has come out of his withdrawn, non-communicative state and is now for the first time in his life talking to me like a regular, normal human being. He has also moved from the slow reading group to the fast reading group and from failing math to getting A's. His mother says that he now goes to sleep without being told several times and that he sleeps much better. All of these positive changes are the result of his experiencing the Colored Light Therapy.

  ~Father, Oakland, California

- All eight learning-disabled students who used the Downing technique of colored Light Therapy showed a significant expansion of their visual fields. Four students demonstrated reading rate gains of 2.1 to 3.4 grade levels and one student tested 8.8 grade levels higher after therapy. All reported gains in visual clarity, mental clarity and emotional well-being.

  ~Learning Disability Specialist, California State University

Light Therapy Is Appropriate For Ages

- Three to adult

Children & Youth's Reactions To Light Therapy

- Children usually find the experience of looking at the gently flashing light to be fun and captivating.
- Approximately 85% of children receiving Light Therapy experience significant improvements.
- When a child's abilities have been suppressed for so long and when these abilities are given back to them over such a short period of time, they can open up and blossom.

Extra Care Is Needed

- The child or youth should be closely observed during Light Therapy by an experienced practitioner, in order to ensure that each color stimulus given is appropriate.

Contraindications: When Light Therapy Should Be Avoided

- Children suffering from photo-convulsive seizures should not be stimulated with a flashing light. In these instances, the practitioner will use a non-flashing light source for therapy.

History

- In 1903, Niels Finsen was awarded the Nobel Prize for the use of Light Therapy in the treatment of tuberculosis.
- In the 1920's, Medical Doctor and Optometrist, Riley Spitler, began successfully using Light Therapy for the correction of vision problems.
- In 1958, Robert Gerard PhD's research supported a therapeutic use of light for psycho-physiological functions.
- In the 1970's, Dr. Downing developed a therapeutic application of light that focuses on the development of overall brain function which enhances mental, emotional, physical well-being and performance. This protocol has been taught to thousands of health care practitioners who are practicing world-wide.

Basic Concepts And Components Of Light Therapy

- When the brain-vision connection is not working properly, a myriad of dysfunction can occur in the individual.
- Deficiencies in the brain-vision connection can be eliminated or reduced by stimulating the optic nerves and neural pathways going to the brain, with specific exposure to colored lights.
- Once stimulated, the improved brain-vision connection will continue even after the therapy has ended.

Description Of A Typical Session

- A child sits comfortably in front of a Light Therapy device that shines the appropriate color and flash rate of light into the child's eyes.

Major Differences Of Opinion Between Practitioners

- Most practitioners use Light Therapy to directly and immediately start rebalancing the system.
- Some practitioners, primarily psychologists, will use Light Therapy to initially provoke a negative response in order to bring unresolved trauma to the surface. This negative response is then dealt with through continued color stimulation and psychotherapy until balance is achieved.

Fees/Costs In 2007 – Averages

- $45.00 per Light Therapy session

Average Time Per Session

- Initial Evaluation: 1 hour
- Daily light therapy sessions: 20 minutes
- A "series" of therapy is one month of daily sessions (30 total sessions)

Recommended Length Of Time Between Sessions
- 3 to 4 sessions per week are the minimum.
- 5 to 7 sessions of Light Therapy per week gives the best results.

Estimated Length Of Time Before Improvements Can Be Expected
- Beneficial results should be noted after one to seven sessions of therapy.

Suggestions To Make Light Therapy More Effective
- Make sure the child does the therapy regularly.

Other Methods That Are Similar To Light Therapy
- There is probably no other health care technique that safely goes directly into the brain in a similar way to enhance brain and body function in such a profound way.

Other Methods That Complement Light Therapy
- All other methods of health care complement Light Therapy.

Nature And Length Of Training To Be A Practitioner
- This varies widely, but light therapists are often licensed as some type of health care professional; such as, medical doctors, psychiatrists, psychologists, optometrists, acupuncturists, chiropractors or naturopaths.

Special Training Needed To Work With Children & Youth
- The same protocol is used with both children and adults.

Certification/Licenses Held By Practitioners
- There are no state or federal license requirements.

Professional Associations To Contact For Names Of Local Practitioners
- College of Syntonic Optometry; Website: www.syntonicphototherapy.com

Number Of Certified Practitioners In U.S., Canada, And Mexico
- Several hundred

What To Look For When Choosing The Best Practitioner
- How long has the practitioner been doing Light Therapy?
- Do they have experience with the problems your child is experiencing?
- Ask them to explain their technique.
- Does what they say make sense physiologically.

Research Papers

- Rustigan, CJ. "Effects of Colored Light and Relaxation Exercise Therapy on Adults with Learning Disabilities." *Education Resources Information Center* 1996.
- Liberman, J. "The Effects of Syntonic Stimulation on Certain Visual and Cognitive Functions." *Journal of Optometric Vision Development* 1986; 17 (June).
- Kaplan, R. "Changes in Form Visual Fields in Reading Disabled Children Produced by Syntonic Stimulation." *The International Journal of Biosocial Research* 1983: 5 (1):20-33.
- Gerard, R. Differential Effects of Colored Lights on Psychophysiological Functions. Unpublished Doctorial Dissertation, University of California, Los Angeles, California. (1976).

Bibliography

- Breiling, Brian (Ed). *Light Years Ahead: The Illustrated Guide to Full Spectrum and Colored Light in Mindbody Healing.* Berkeley, CA: Celestial Arts, 1996.
- Wurtman, Richard, Michael Baum and John Potts. "The Medical and Biological Effects of Light" (*Annals of the New York Academy of Sciences*) Volume 453, September 20, 1985.
- Hollwich, Fritz. *The Influence of Ocular Light Perception on Metabolism in Man and in Animal.* New York: Springer-Verlag, c1979.

Helpful Tips For Parents

- Colored Light Therapy should be supervised by an experienced practitioner.
- Some practitioners will provide colored Light Therapy instruments for use in the home while they guide the parent and child through therapy by telephone.

Biography Of John Downing, Author

- John has over 30 years of experience.
- He has worked with hundreds of children and youth.
- He holds an OD, PhD in Vision Science.

To Contact John Downing, Who Contributed This Chapter

John Downing; c/o Light Therapy Institute; 708 Gravenstein Hwy. North #286; Sebastopol, CA 95472; Ph: 707-829-1478; Fax: 707-829-3444; Email: johndowning88@comcast.net

. . . .

Marie Mulligan's Comment About Light Therapy: I have not had much experience with Light Therapy. I have had children/patients benefit from it.

Rick Geggie's Comment About Light Therapy : Light Therapy is one of the most amazing practices I have encountered and experienced. I have used it myself for years. I have been very impressed with the results with all the Light Therapy referrals I have made. I look forward to the day when Light Therapy is used in every school. I have found that it compliments almost every other helpful practice for children, including Western Medicine.

CHAPTER 24

MASSAGE FOR CHILDREN & YOUTH

By Alan Jordan, BA, LMT, NCTMB & Peggy Jones Farlow, LMT, MsEd, CIMI, © Copyright 2008.

Massage/Touch Has Helped Kids With

• Cerebral palsy • Down syndrome • Cancer (with medical permission) • Autism	• Anxiety • Body image • ADD and ADHA • Asthma/Respiratory problems • Premature infant weight gain	• Developmental delayed • Speech/language delayed • Many other special needs • Tactile defensive/autistic

Massage/Touch Can Help In The Following Areas

Spirit: Massaging with compassion and love strengthens the ties that bond between parent and child.

Body: It improves circulation and skin nutrition, stimulates growth, offers passive exercise reducing atrophy of muscles and easing aches and pains, increases flexibility and function of muscles and joints.

Mind: It supports and increases thinking and verbal skills.

Emotions: It helps children relax and learn to calm themselves and be better able to manage stress. Helps relieve depression and anxiety.

Social: It can increase speech and language skills and help to build trust, friendship and respect.

Brief Description Of Massage/Touch

Massage/Touch provides an opportunity for increased bonding and attachment between parent and child. It balances the child's muscle tone by increasing floppy muscle tone and decreasing tight muscle tone. Massage/Touch supports respiration and deeper breathing patterns. It enhances the immune system by increasing circu-

315

lation and lymph flow. When done in specific ways, Massage/Touch can increase the child's verbalization and socialization.

Success With Massage/Touch
- Children with symptoms of Autism have shown increased relaxation when they received massage during activities, more than those who received other forms of relaxation methods.
- Premature infants provided with 10 minutes of massage three times a day increased their weight gain, allowing release from the hospital 3 weeks earlier than those infants who did not receive massage.
- A mother felt an increase in her love and emotional attachment with her son after learning massage. Her son, with severe cerebral palsy, seemed to "cuddle" more.
- Massage helped children with dermatitis and other chronic skin conditions.

Massage/Touch Is Appropriate For Ages
- Infants, toddlers, preschoolers, growing children and adolescents all benefit from massage and positive touch.
- Newborns and premature infants respond positively to monitored massage.
- Some teenagers often go through a few years where they are no longer comfortable with massage.

Children & Youth's Reactions To Massage/Touch
- Children really enjoy it, relaxing and smiling after just a few moments.
- Children with cerebral palsy extend previously flexed muscles.
- Children given massages at bedtime fall asleep easier.

Extra Care Is Needed
- Feeding tubes
- Shunts
- Under-control diabetes
- Immediately after surgery
- Skin diseases
- Seizures, undiagnosed conditions
- Unusual skin condition

Contraindications: When Massage/Touch Should Be Avoided
- Medical consultation is needed before massage is given to children with critical and chronic medical conditions.
- Massage should be avoided with children who have any swelling, fever, open sores, active diabetes, acute infection, and/or staph infections.

History
- Touch is a human experience. Many cultures have utilized infant/child massage for centuries. For example, references to Massage/Touch are found in Chinese literature as early as 3000 B.C. Massage was used in various forms by the ancient Greeks and Romans.
- Hippocrates, the first physician, understood the value of massage and thought every physician should be experienced in the art.

- Massage was formally introduced to the United States in 1856 by George and Charles Taylor and it was used extensively during World Wars I and II. It moved out of favor after World War II as people turned to technology, machines and pharmaceuticals for quick cures.
- Ashley Montagu provided extensive information on the importance of human touch and the therapeutic value of massage.
- Vilima McClure brought infant massage to the United States from India in the early 1970's. She established the International Association of Infant Massage in the 1980's.
- Today, people are becoming more aware of alternative health care methods and are learning to take responsibility for their own bodies. As a result, massage therapy is experiencing phenomenal growth in the U.S. and throughout the modern world.

Basic Concepts And Components Of Massage/Touch

- Massage/Touch includes stroking, rubbing, pressure, gliding, gentle stretching, or rocking.
- Touch supports trust, emotional security, communication and health.
- Pediatric massage is compassionate, honors the child's boundaries and desires, and helps form stronger family relationships.

Description Of A Typical Session

- Before massage, the professional therapist conducts a thorough interview to determine the needs of the child and to confirm that there are no reasons the child should not be massaged.
- Appropriate dress is always discussed and modesty is always respected. Some children prefer to have their clothes on, others prefer just their underwear, while some enjoy being covered with only a sheet.
- Parents can remain in the treatment room but should be prepared to sit quietly during the session.
- The typical treatment room is softly lit, often with gentle music or environmental sounds being played. The room is warm and comfortable.
- Massage/Touch is applied for varying lengths of time: 10 minutes to an hour, depending on age and needs of the infant/child.
- Sessions end with a short, quiet time to allow the treatment to sink in.

Major Differences Of Opinion Between Practitioners

- Some therapists work on a therapeutic/medical/condition-based model.
- Other therapists work on the whole child, paying attention to the connection between mind, body and spirit, and focusing upon respect, self-worth and communication.

Fees/Costs In 2007

- Costs are $23-$40 for 30 minutes; $50-$75 for one hour.
- Prices vary in different parts of the country.
- Parents who want to massage their own children can ask the therapist to teach them massage techniques.

Average Time Per Session

- Thirty minutes to one hour, depending on the age of the child and the child's willingness
- Ten minutes of massage daily - if provided by a trained parent
- Twenty to thirty minute weekly sessions for children with special needs

Recommended Length Of Time Between Sessions
- The frequency of massage depends upon the child's ability to tolerate the stimulation.
- For pain management, injury rehabilitation or surgery, children may see a massage therapist once or twice a week for two to six weeks.

Estimated Length Of Time Before Improvements Can Be Expected
- Improvement can sometimes be noticed immediately; but it usually takes one to three sessions.

Suggestions To Make Massage/Touch More Effective
- Quietly stay in the room with the child and therapist, out of the child's vision range.
- Make sure the therapist always asks permission of the infant/child no matter what age.
- Create a warm, quiet and safe space (may be indoors or out).
- Communicate with the child and respect his or her needs for touch/no touch.

Other Methods That Are Similar To Massage/Touch
- Acupressure
- Touch Therapy
- Reiki
- Yoga
- Movement/awareness therapies
- Craniosacral therapy
- Myofascial release

Other Methods That Complement Massage/Touch
Most massage/bodywork approaches that offer gentle, nurturing touch, including:
- Compassionate Touch
- Craniosacral work
- Feldenkrais Method
- Yoga for the Special Child
- Chiropractic
- Acupressure

Nature And Length Of Training To Be A Practitioner
- Massage schools differ. Most requirements are from 500 hours to 1000 hours of massage training.
- Few massage schools offer specific training in pediatric massage.

Special Training Needed To Work With Children & Youth
- Massage therapists seek further training to work with children through continuing education programs such as: Touch to T.E.A.C.H.; various workshops; Pediatric Myofascial Release, and Crainosacral Therapy.
- Check credentials and ask with whom the therapist has trained.
- Pick therapists who have experience working with children and children with special needs.

Certification/Licenses Held By Practitioners
- The International Association of Infant Massage certifies instructors of massage for children and for teaching parents how to massage their own children.
- AMTA (American Massage Therapy Association) provides list of reputable member therapists.
- If you live in a state that requires a license to practice massage therapy, make sure that your therapist has one.
- Nationally Certification of Therapeutic Massage and Bodywork (NCTMB) indicates that the therapist has met certain basic standards of training and experience, and compliance to a code of ethics.

Professional Associations To Contact For Names Of Local Practitioners
- American Massage Therapy Association (AMTA), 500 Davis Street, Evanston, IL 60201-4695, Ph: 877-905-2700; Fax: 847-864-1178; Website: www.amtamassage.org; Email: info@amtamassage.org
- National Certification Board for Therapeutic Massage and Bodywork (NCBTMB); 1901 South Meyers Road, Suite 240; Oakbrook Terrace, IL 60181; Ph: 800-296-0664; Website: www.ncbtmb.com; Email: info@ncbtmb.com.
- International Association of Infant Massage, P.O. Box 6370; Ventura, CA 93006; Ph: 805-644-8524, Fax: 805-830-1729; Website: www.iaim.ws; Email: IAIM4US@aol.com

Number Of Certified Practitioners In U.S., Canada, And Mexico
- There are currently 37,000+ massage therapists who are Nationally Certified in Therapeutic Massage and bodywork.

What To Look For When Choosing The Best Practitioner
- Look for compassion and the ability to relate to children.
- Confirm the amount of experience they have working with children.
- Watch the practitioner's interest in your child. Make sure your child is more important than their attachment to their method.
- Notice your child's interest in the therapist.
- Have a massage yourself and feel the quality of their touch.
- Check to make sure the therapist has training in pediatric/infant massage for normal and at-risk children.

Leading Clinics, Centers, Practitioners
- International Association of Infant Massage; P.O. Box 6370; Ventura, CA 93006; 805-644-8524; Fax: 805-830-1729; Website: www.iaim.ws; Email: IAIM4US@aol.com
- International Institute of Infant Massage, Maria and Wayne Mathias; 605 Bledsoe Rd., NW; Albuquerque, NM 87107; 505-341-9381; Fax: 505-341-9386; Website: www.infantmassageinstitute.com; Email: info@infantmassageinstitute.com
- Touch to T.E.A.C.H (Trust, Emotional security, Attachment & attending, Communication & cognition, and Healthier children, families & world). Private instruction for primary and professional caregivers in pediatric massage for children with special needs. 18092 Blue Springs Rd; Athens, AL 35611; 256-729-0070; Website: www.touchtoteach.org; Email: pegfarlow@aol.com
- Touch Research Institute (TRI); Dr. Tiffany Field; University of Miami School of Medicine; Mailman Center for Child Development; 1601 NW 12th Ave.; 7th Floor, Room 7037; Miami, FL; 305-243-6781; Fax: 305-243-6488; Website: www6.miami.edu/touch-research; Email: tfield@med.miami.edu

Resources, Research Papers, Books, DVD's, Websites
- Contact the Touch Research Institute in Miami (see above). Dr. Tiffany Field has multiple research papers on the positive benefits of massage for children.

Bibliography
- Jordan, Alan, "Massage Through the Ages" July/August 2000 edition of Massage Magazine.
- Farlow, Peggy. "Touch to T.E.A.C.H. - Guidebook for Professional and Primary Caregivers for Children With Special Needs." Available through: www.touchtoteach.org.
- Field, Tiffany. *Touch Therapy*. London: Churchill Livingstone, 2000.
- Heller, Sharon. *The Vital Touch*. New York: Henry Holt, 1997.
- Martin, Chia. *The Art of Touch: A Massage Manual for Young People*. Prescott, AZ: Hohm Press, 1996.
- Sinclair, Marybetts. *Massage for Healthier Children*. Oakland, CA: Wingbow Press, 1992.

Helpful Tips For Parents
- The best time to massage is when your child is alert and ready for interaction.
- Relax and have fun with massage and your child.
- Do massage before your child goes to bed or after bath when you are both more relaxed.
- Involve both fathers and mothers in the massage for the child with special needs.

Biography Of Peggy Jones Farlow, Co-Author
- Peggy Jones Farlow has 30 years experience providing speech therapy to special children.
- She has 15 years LMT (Licensed Massage Therapist).
- She holds the following degrees: MEd., Special Education Speech/Language Pathology; Licensed Massage Therapist (LMT); Certified Infant Massage Instructor (CIMI).

To Contact Peggy Jones Farlow, Who Co-Contributed This Chapter
Peggy Jones Farlow; Creator of Touch to T.E.A.C.H (a program for special needs children); 18092 Blue Springs Rd.; Athens, AL 35611; Ph: 256 -729 0070; Website: www.touchtoteach.org; Email: pegfarlow@aol.com

Biography Of Alan Jordan, Co-Author
- Alan Jordan has 20 years experience as massage therapist and massage therapy educator.
- He holds a B.A.
- He published "Touch Listen and Be: Creating Nonviolent People".
- He is presently director of the Helma Institute of Massage in Saddle Brook, New Jersey (website: http://www.helma.com).

Peggy Jones Farlow's Personal Statement
By teaching a caregiver or family how to successfully offer nurturing touch and massage to their child with special needs, I believe we begin to heal the world. - Peggy

Alan Jordan's Personal Statement
Healthy touch is essential to producing a healthy child. Children who receive abundant touch cry less, are happier, more energetic and more alert. Children deprived of touch develop severe developmental disorders. Dr. James Prescott, a

former member of the National Institute of Child Health and Human Development, has concluded that the presence or absence of touch, as well as cultural practices regarding touch, are the two most important factors that differentiate violent or non-violent cultures. He states, "The principal cause of human violence is a lack of bodily pleasure derived from touching and stroking during the formative years."

To Contact Alan Jordan, Who Co-Contributed This Chapter
Alan Jordan; 10 Frances Street; Clifton NJ 07014; Ph: 201-280-8654; Email: alankjordan@aol.com

Marie Mulligan's Comment About Massage/Touch: Massage really helps children & youth.

Rick Geggie's Comment About Massage/Touch: Touch is a language that teaches us who we are and what our world is about. Massage is a form of touch that teaches us that we can be gentle, loveable, peaceful and well. It relaxes children and puts them in touch with their bodies. When children are touched they feel real to themselves. I look forward to the day when all of us, including children, are massaged at least once a week.

CHAPTER 25

MEDITATION – INSIGHT MEDITATION FOR CHILDREN & YOUTH

By Heather Sundberg, Meditation Teacher, © *Copyright 2008.*
Heather is the Spirit Rock Meditation Center Family Program Teacher and Manager.

Insight Meditation Has Helped Kids With

• ADHD and other attention challenges • Experiencing chronic illness • Concentration problems • Emotional intelligence	• Emotional reactivity • Emotional pain • Family dynamics • Loneliness	• Physical pain • Self-esteem issues • School performance • Social relations stress

Insight Meditation Can Help In The Following Areas

Spirit: Meditation is a spiritual practice. It is helpful because it allows children & youth to access what is true in their own experience. From that experience they can develop confidence in themselves and have a wider range of choice for themselves.

Body: Meditation cultivates relaxation and a deep sense of rest. The body can then rejuvenate. Statements such as, "this feels like the first time I've rested all week," are often heard.

Mind: Fundamentally, meditation is a mind training. It teaches kids and youth that they are not enslaved to their thoughts and that they have choices.

Emotions: Meditation creates a container for kids and youth to safely feel their emotions in their bodies. Meditation helps them to regulate their emotions. Mindfulness Meditation teaches children that they have a choice about how to respond to their emotions.

Social: Even though a person practices meditation individually, what is learned is that everything is connected. A deeper, more authentic social connection develops when meditation is practiced in a family or group. Meditation tends to foster a sense of trust in one's own experience and that translates into trust socially.

Brief Description Of Insight Meditation
- Mindfulness Meditation is a training, wherein the child or youth develops moment to moment, non-judgmental, curious attention to the direct experience of mind and body.

Insight Meditation Is Appropriate For Ages
- Some people would disagree with me, but I have found that children can begin to meditate in groups at age four and up.
- Under age four, meditating with an adult can work.

Children & Youth's Reactions To Insight Meditation
- Most children & youth like meditation, if they are not being forced to do it.
- Feeling calmer, more peaceful and relaxed are common responses.
- Sometimes children & youth will feel a sense of wellbeing, while other times meditation will reveal emotions that can be difficult for them. This is why debriefing meditations are important. After children have accepted the difficult feelings they most often feel better.
- Often youth will get a much clearer sense of who they are (a sense of authenticity).

Extra Care Is Needed
- Meditation sessions have to be modified to accommodate certain psychological issues.
- Extra care has to be taken by the teacher when a child is experiencing intense emotions.
- Insight Meditation can be very helpful; however, care always has to be taken. Care may mean altering the meditation instruction slightly to accommodate the child or youth. For example: when a child is experiencing intense grief over a death, or a divorce.
- Lessons have to be modified when a child/teen is in early recovery from addiction or eating disorders. Meditation sessions should be shorter.

Contraindications: When Insight Meditation Should Be Avoided
- Sitting meditation should be avoided during acute trauma. It is not helpful to meditate because the trauma is too intense and painful. Mindful meditation during such times could be eating meditation and/or movement meditation.

History
- Meditation has been practiced in one way or another in every major world religion.
- Meditation is practiced in some way in most indigenous traditions.

Basic Concepts And Components Of Insight Meditation
- Mindfulness involves paying attention, being non-judgmental, curious, being kind with one's self, as well as sensations, thoughts, emotions and with reactions to other people.
- Mindfulness of sound
- Mindfulness of body
- Mindfulness of breath
- Mindfulness of emotions
- Mindfulness of thoughts
- Insight Meditation can be done sitting cross-legged, sitting in a chair, standing, walking, or lying down.

- Insight Meditation can also be done with eyes closed or eyes opened.

Fees/Costs In 2007
- In many traditions, payment is done by donation.
- At Spirit Rock, group classes cost about $10 a class. However, no one is turned away.
- Costs vary from teacher to teacher, and place to place.

Average Time Per Session
- At Spirit Rock with beginning students: 5 minutes for Elementary School age children; 10 minutes for Middle School age youth; 15 minutes for High School aged youth.
- As students gain more experience, the length of time can be increased up to 30 minutes for children in High School.
- A good rule of thumb is one minute for each year of life. For example: an eight year old would meditate for eight minutes.

Recommended Length Of Time Between Sessions
- Sessions are practiced in many schools three times a week.
- Classes for children and for teens are held weekly at Spirit Rock.
- Children & youth are encouraged to meditate once each day.

Estimated Length Of Time Before Improvements Can Be Expected
- Improvements totally depend upon the child or youth, family and meditation teacher.
- It is rare that a child or youth comes out of a retreat unchanged. (A retreat is an intensive residential training experience in meditation, ranging from three days to many months.)
- For many students, families will notice change after the child or youth has attended a six week class.

Suggestions To Make Insight Mediation More Effective
- Create a quiet safe space.
- Have a qualified teacher.
- Avoid forcing children & youth to meditate.

Other Methods That Are Similar To Insight Meditation
- Mindfulness Practice can be integrated into any activity.
- Movement meditations including Aikido and Yoga are similar.
- Expressive Arts and Contact Improvisation can be similar.
- Dancing/moving arts is similar.
- Other martial arts (in certain ways) are similar.
- Yoga is similar.

Nature And Length Of Training To Be An Insight Meditation Teacher
- It varies.
- At Spirit Rock, training takes at least 4 years.
- Other centers have different qualifications and time requirements.

Special Training Needed To Work With Children & Youth
- Apprenticing with an experienced teacher working with children & youth for at least a year
- Having an ongoing personal practice, which includes retreats (A retreat is an intensive residential training experience in meditation, ranging from three days to many months.)
- Having other experience working with children & youth, such as teaching, childcare, and/or summer programs

Certification/Licenses Held By Practitioners/Teachers
- Check out who trained the practitioner and whether or not that person is a recognized meditation teacher.

Professional Associations To Contact For Names Of Local Practitioners/Teachers
- Contact the centers and people listed below. It is a small community.

Number Of Certified Teachers In U.S., Canada, And Mexico
- There are hundreds.

What To Look For When Choosing The Best Teachers/Practitioners
- For private lessons or for group lessons: check out their prior experience as a meditator and as a teacher.
- Check to make sure the person has been meditating for at least 5 years and has attended several retreats (a retreat is an intensive residential training experience in meditation, ranging from three days to months).

Leading Centers, Practitioners
- Spirit Rock Meditation Center's Family Program; PO Box 169; Woodacre, CA 94973; 415-488-0164; Fax: 415-488-1025; Website: www.meditation-center.com; Email: SRMC@spiritrock.org
- Spirit Rock Meditation Center Teen Program. (See above for contact information.)
- Insight Meditation Society (the first Vipassana Center), The Retreat Center; 1230 Pleasant Street; Barre, MA 01005; 978-355-4378; Website: www.dharma.org/ims; Email: rc@dharma.org
- San Francisco Zen Center/Green Gulch Zen Center; 300 Page Street; San Francisco, CA 94102; 415-863-3136; Website: www.sfzc.org; Email: ccoffice@sfzc.org
- Tsultrum Allioni of Tara Mandala; P.O. Box 3040; Pagosa Springs, CO 81147; 970-731-3711; Website: www.taramandala.org; Email: info@taramandala.org
- Youth Programs of the Shambala Centre; 1084 Tower Rd.; Halifax, NS, B3H 2Y5 Canada; 902-420-1118; Fax: 902-423-2750; Website: www.halifax.shambhala.org; Email: halifax@shambhala.org
- Susan Kaiser Greenland, founder of Inner Kids; 1739 Berkeley Street, Suite 105; Santa Monica, CA 90404; 310-440-4869; Fax: 310-828-4733; Website: www.innerkids.org
- Diana Winston, Director of Mindfulness Education at the Mindful Awareness Research Center (MARC); University of California at Los Angeles; Box 951759; Los Angeles, CA 90095-1759; 310 206 7503; Fax: 310 206 4446; Website: www.marc.ucla.edu; Email: marcinfo@ucla.edu. (This e-mail address is being protected from spam bots, you need JavaScript enabled to view it.)
- Oakland, California school board mindfulness meditation program, taught by Richard Shankman. He may be contacted through his email address: Richard@sati.org.
- The Association for Mindfulness in Education; 650-575-5780; Website: www.mindfuleducation.org; Email: info@mindfuleducation.org
- Impact Foundation; 264 Quari Street; Aurora, CO 80011; 303-317-5767; http://www.theimpactfoundation.org; Email: info@theimpactfoundation.org

Leading Meditation Programs
- Meditation is practiced in some form or another by every religion.
- Meditation classes in every tradition - Muslim, Christian, Judaism, Hindi, (and other Buddhist traditions) can be found searching the Internet, community resources, churches, temples, mosques, meditation halls and ashrams.

Bibliography
- Alexander, Shoshana. *In Praise of Single Parents: Mothers and Fathers Embracing the Challenge.* New York: Houghton Mifflin Company, 1994.
- Conover, Sarah. *Kindness: A Treasury of Buddhist Wisdom for Children and Parents.* Spokane: Eastern Washington University Press, 2001.
- Eastoak, Sandy. *Dharma Family Treasures: Sharing Mindfulness With Children.* Berkeley, CA: North Atlantic Books, 1994.
- Hanson, Rick, Jan Hanson and Ricki Pollycove. *Mother Nurture.* New York: Penguin Books, 2002.
- Kabat-Zinn, Jon and Myla. *Everyday Blessings: The Inner Work of Mindful Parenting.* New York: Hyperion, 1998.
- Kornfield, Jack. *A Path with Heart: A Guide Through the Perils and Promises of Spiritual Life.* New York: Bantam Books, 1993.
- Nhat Hanh, Thich. *A Pebble For Your Pocket.* Plum Blossom Books, 2002.
- Miller, Karen Maezen. *Mama Zen: Walking the Crooked Path of Motherhood.* Boston: Trumpeter Books, 2006.

For Teens:
- Gordhamer, Soren. *Just Say Om!: Your Life's Journey.* Cincinnati: Adams Media Corp, 2001.
- Loundon, Sumi. *Blue Jean Buddha: Voices of Young Buddhists.* Somerville, MA: Wisdom Publications, 2001.
- MacLean, Kerry Lee. *Peaceful Piggy Meditation.* Morton Grove, IL: Albert Whitman & Co., 2004.

For Children:
- Hendricks, Gay and Russel Wills. *The Centering Book: Awareness Activities for Children and Adults to Relax the Body and Mind.* Upper Saddle River, NJ: Prentice Hall Trade, 1992.

Helpful Tips For Parents
- Have a quiet place to meditate – one that is free of distractions.
- Meditate together as a family.
- A lot of families have a simple mindfulness bell. If the bell is rung, everyone stops and takes three breaths –this is especially useful during times of conflict, over-busy times, or during moments of transition (stopping one activity and moving to another activity). Families don't have to know how to meditate to do this. They just have to take in and let out three breaths.

Biography of Heather Sundberg, Author
- Experience: Heather has worked with youth since 1991 and has taught meditation to youth since 1999. She is in Spirit Rock Teacher Training under the guidance of Jack Kornfield.
- Degrees: She holds a BA; California Teaching Credential (expired).
- She has approximately 250 children students and 150 Teens – personally and as Program Director.

To Contact Heather Sundberg, Who Contributed This Chapter
Heather Sundberg; c/o Spirit Rock Meditation Center; P.O. Box 169; Woodacre, CA 94973; 415-488-0164 ext. 227; Fax: 415-488-1025; Website: www.SpiritRock.org; Email: SRMC@spiritrock.org

Marie Mulligan's Comment About Meditation: I meditate every day. My children meditate on an as-needed basis. For children experiencing major depression and other serious mental illness, I recommend getting clearance from a mental health professional before beginning any meditation practice.

Rick Geggie's Comment About Meditation: I meditate and have done so for years. When I was a school principal I helped oversee a research project investigating the effects of meditation on high school children & youth.

The chief of the board of education research department was a meditator and felt that it was important to know if meditation helped children & youth. The study was very carefully designed. The results were quite amazing. Academic achievement went up. Truancy and violence went down. Self-concept went up. Teacher morale improved. Unfortunately, the program was curtailed after over 3000 students had learned to meditate. This was done by some misguided elected trustees who were afraid of meditation, confusing it with something else. This group of caring trustees also wanted to ban kindergarten children from sitting in a circle while they talked.

Meditation can take children & youth some time to settle into, however it works. I advise parents to learn it too. Meditating as a family as often as possible can lead to amazing results.

CHAPTER 26

MUSIC LESSONS FOR CHILDREN & YOUTH

By Nick Simmons, BA, © Copyright 2008.

Music Lessons Can Help Kids With

• Addictions to video games • ADHD • Anger/aggression management • Anxiety • Autism • Communication difficulty • Conflict resolution	• Cooperation • Coordination issues • Depression • Family problems • Lack of success • Learning disabilities • Listening	• Loneliness • Prolonged stress • Relationships • Self-confidence issues • Shyness • Traumas of all kinds

Music Lessons Help In The Following Areas

Spirit: Music gives children freedom and space to explore their own creativity and uniqueness. Making music empowers their spirit.

Mind: Music lessons focus the mind through patterns of rhythm, melody, harmony, body movements and techniques. Music also develops the memory and recognition of patterns, necessary for logic, language, and mathematics.

Body: It relaxes, organizes coordination through repetition, and brings awareness. Music has the ability to give energy to the body by releasing tensions.

Emotions: It gives a tool for safe, creative, individual emotional release and expression. It helps children & youth explore their emotions, know their feelings, and express themselves.

Brief Description Of Music Lessons

- I set the scene by greeting the student as they enter. I often mirror their behavior and try to adapt to them. One way to do this is to be playing music they like as they enter - from loud rock to a lullaby. Sometimes they have lots of energy so I mirror their excitement. Other students are quiet and mellow and I try follow in the same way.
- The 'initial check-in' is very important. Sometimes a student will want to talk about something not related to music. This usually feels okay as it gives an output for releasing things that could be distracting them when we do begin to focus on music. It is important to see if there are any questions or challenges that arose during the week. I often give a review of the last week's lesson.
- I then ask questions to get a sense of what the student wants to work on. This helps create a flow to the time we have together. I make it clear that I work for them and that the lesson is their time. I also try to emphasize the value of not wasting our time together. Structure is important. Depending on age and maturity, redirection and focusing is sometimes needed.
- Lessons revolve around the student's musical preferences. They are empowered by making decisions about what they want to learn. This leads to the child or youth learning more because they are more relaxed. Students are more motivated to practice at home because they enjoy what they are playing.
- Many pupils bring the songs they want to learn as recorded music (cd's, iPods) or printed music they find on the Internet. I also have an extensive library of recorded music which I share. Often I learn the song on the spot and teach them until we play it together. Learning is made easier and more enjoyable when students choose songs to play that they like and are familiar with.
- A major part of the lesson involves using what the student chooses to focus on as a launching point for basic music theory and techniques (rhythm, scales, chords, pattern recognition…). For example: the child or youth wants to learn a punk rock song; I point out that the song uses a particular scale. I then expand on that scale and show them how to connect that scale to the song we're learning. This often leads the student to improvising and composing their own music. Many times I make CD's for them to practice along with at home.
- Another tool involves making music without an agenda. We create music together spontaneously, sometimes with only a few notes. We play together and I back them up so that they sound great to themselves. In these moments I point out their successes and courage at taking risks and expressing themselves. I often record and make CD's of these songs for them to enjoy at home with family and friends. This can give them encouragement.
- Many parents confuse leaning standard musical notation with learning music. For most children it is useful to learn a musical language which organizes their understanding of rhythm, melody, harmony, and ways of communicating these ideas. I frequently encourage students to learn to read music and write what they hear in many ways suited to their skill level. There are many different ways. Depending on the instrument and style being played, learning standard notation methods is often not the most efficient way to begin to read music. By teaching these effective tools for reading and writing music, the students learn to organize their ideas, express themselves and share their music with others.
- Some children are very self-conscious and frightened by learning new things and by expressing themselves. The pleasure and relaxation that comes from music often creates an ideal atmosphere to work with these challenges. Many students go on to start their own groups and to create original music.
- Lessons often end with clearing up any misunderstandings, and making sure that the home practice ideas are understood.
- I always thank them for their time and effort. I honor their efforts and accomplishments.

Basic Concepts And Components Of Music Lessons

- Training and practice listening, remembering, coordination, self control, and awareness – all with enjoyment and satisfaction are all very important.

History Of Music Lessons

- Music, playing instruments and singing have been taught since the beginning of civilization, and perhaps before.
- One hundred years ago most people could sing or play an instrument, as sharing live music was a major foundation of entertainment.
- Today most people do not play instruments or sing. The advent of recorded music and the development of a market-driven popular culture has been a possible reason for this decline of lots of people playing music.
- Many people today have a fear of musical expression, and worry because they don't sound "professional."
- Many modes of musical instruction in the past have put an emphasis on striving for perfection, instead of simply enjoying the process. I think this is a reason why many people have not had a positive experience with taking music lessons.
- I am amazed at the amount of information available in this day and age. With the advancements in communication, a music lover can now experience sounds from almost any part of the world with the push of a button.
- I am very curious about how the evolution of music on the planet will unfold.
- It is truly an exciting time to be exploring music.

Is Appropriate For Ages:

- Music is appropriate for all ages, young children to adults.

Estimated Length of Time Before Improvements Can Be Expected

- It depends on each child.
- Some children struggle due to their challenges.
- Most children enjoy the lessons from the start.

Children & Youth's Reactions To Music Lessons

- After the first lesson, most children want to continue because the lessons are fun.

Fees/Costs In 2007 (In California)

- $25 to $100.
- Depends on the instrument, level, and teaching style

Average Time Per Session

- Usually 30 minutes to an hour - sometimes longer

Suggestions To Make Music Lessons More Effective

- Make sure the child is well rested.
- Keep the teacher up-to-date on what is happening with the child.
- Don't over-schedule the child.
- Give enough time to practice.
- Be encouraging, however encourage but don't force practice sessions.
- Ask to listen to the music.
- Be with the child while they practice if they enjoy the company and attention.
- Let the child be alone to practice if they ask.
- Help them get the instrument and supplies they need.

Other Methods That Are Similar To Music Lessons
- Learning anything: Sports, martial arts, expressive arts, dance, drama, school, and other disciplines

Other Methods That Complement Music Lessons
- Sports, martial arts, artistic expression, dance, learning foreign languages, communication training, mathematics and science

Major Differences Of Opinion Between Music Teachers
- To teach a set curriculum vs. adapt what is learned to the student's preferences
- Forced practice vs. enjoyable practice
- Learning patterns of music towards perfection vs. a student being perfectly connected to what they are feeling, intending and playing

What To Look For When Choosing The Best Teacher
- The child or youth should get along with the teacher.
- The teacher should get along with the child.
- The teacher should be happy, relaxed, patient, and have a good sense of humor.
- The teacher should be very curious and non-judgmental.
- Sit in on a few lessons and watch the process.

Training And Education To Be A Music Teacher Working With Children & Youth
- The teacher should be experienced in working with children— summer camps, classrooms, or sports.
- The teacher should be skilled in music.
- The teacher should have studied with many good teachers who teach individuality.
- The teacher should have the ability to play many different types of music.

Professional Associations To Contact For Names Of Local Teachers
- I advise asking friends, neighbors, other parents.
- Contact local music stores, local schools, colleges, or university music departments.
- There are many national and state organizations of music teachers and musical education.
- These certifications and/or degrees in music may be useful, but don't necessarily guarantee effective teaching skills.

Bibliography
- Mathieu, W.A. *The Listening Book: Discovering Your Own Music.* Boston and London: Shambhala, 1991.
- Nachmanovitch, Stephen. *Free Play: The Power of Improvisation in Life and the Arts.* Los Angeles: Jeremy P. Tarcher, Inc, 1990.

Biography Of Nick Simmons, Author
- Began studying music (flute) in school at age nine
- Had private lessons in guitar at age 12
- Worked at summer camps from age 13 to 21
- Toured with his high school choir

- Built music program for summer camp
- Studied music at Santa Rosa Junior College
- Holds a BA in music from Sonoma State 2003
- Worked with emotionally disturbed children
- Worked in a home for men with autism
- Taught music to students with autism
- Plays guitar, (electric, acoustic, bass) drums, piano, flutes, and more
- Has performed with various bands – rock, jazz, pop, etc
- Presently has more than 40 students
- Has taught many students who have gone on to be successful musicians

Nick Simmons' Personal Statement

Bringing awareness through music is an amazing adventure with limitless possibilities. How wonderful it is to be able to share something that I care for so deeply and see it create the same joy in the students that it gives me. I give thanks to my many teachers, mentors and students.

To Contact Nick Simmons, Who Contributed This Chapter

Nick Simmons: P.O. Box 4474, Santa Rosa, CA 95402; Ph: 707-303-6482; Website: www.nicksimmons.org; Email: nrs200@hotmail.com

. . . .

Marie Mulligan's Comment About Music Lessons: My sons are thriving on Nick Simmons' music lessons. So am I!

Rick Geggie's Comment About Music Lessons: Where was Nick Simmons when I was told to move my lips and not let any sound come out as well as told "that's not music"– it has taken over 60 years to recover my music.

CHAPTER 27

NONVIOLENT COMMUNICATION FOR CHILDREN & YOUTH

By Inbal Kashtan, © Copyright 2008.

Nonviolent Communication (NVC) Can Help In The Following Areas

Spirit: NVC is inspired in part by the work of the Indian leader, Gandhi, who encouraged people to have such open hearts that they could see every person's humanity. When we can see people's humanity, we have no enemies. By the term "Nonviolent" we mean, as Gandhi did, living with such open hearts that we can see the humanity of all people. Long-term practice of NVC supports the capacity to live in peace within oneself and with others, even when our needs are not met.

Body: NVC can sometimes support children with stress, which has an impact on our bodies.

Mind: NVC provides clarity and understanding about why people behave in the ways they do. It moves people from judging others or judging themselves toward acceptance and understanding.

Emotions: NVC helps everyone understand their own emotions, instead of reacting from habits that don't work for them or others.

Social: NVC helps people get along with each other (children and adults). With practice, it can help people resolve conflicts effectively.

Brief Description Of Nonviolent Communication

- Nonviolent Communication is a process that supports people to understand themselves and each other, and to develop skills to resolve conflicts peacefully.
- It is used around the world by people in many situations - including places of work, schools, prisons and in personal relationships, among others.
- NVC can help parents understand their children's behavior and treat the children with compassion and care.
- Using NVC, children can be helped to understand themselves, their friends, and the adults in their lives, and to come up with solutions to problems that are more likely to work for everyone.
- NVC principally helps parents connect with their children. It supports parents who are struggling with anger or ongoing frustration in relation to their children.

- NVC supports parents who don't have a sense of mutual care and understanding with their children. It also supports parents who are generally satisfied with their parenting, but who want to have more connection with their children.

Success With Nonviolent Communication

This is a story shared with me by a mother of three sons who had been studying and implementing NVC with her family for a few years:

"When David was about 13 ½ years old, he was really angry one day and about to hurt one of his 10-year-old twin brothers as they sat near each other on the couch. So, I did what I now do whenever physical violence is about to happen between them and got in the middle of the two.

David was breathing heavily and had his fists clenched as he sat in a chair next to me. His brother was on the other side of me on the couch. I went with habit and started to tell David about anger management and how he needed to go for a walk or go to his room until he cooled off.

He continued to breathe heavily and clench his fists.

Then his brother actually started using NVC! He said: "David, did you just want to be included?"

I realized then that what David needed was empathy and repeated his brother's guess. I saw David's fist relax just slightly. I guessed again, "are you needing to feel that you belong?" His fist relaxed even more and his breathing began to slow down some.

Then I guessed that his need for belonging had been unmet for a really long time with his twin brothers. David's fist relaxed more along with his body.

Then I guessed that maybe if his need for belonging were met his need for love would be met, and tears began to roll down his cheeks.

I will be forever grateful for the tools of NVC for allowing me to get to this place of awareness and healing with my son."

Nonviolent Communication Is Appropriate For Ages

- Any age
- However, for most parents it is easier to apply with school-age children. For younger children it is primarily a non-verbal practice.

Children & Youth's Reactions To Nonviolent Communication

- Most children are happy with the integration of Nonviolent Communication into their family's life because they experience more understanding, compassion and support for meeting their needs.
- Some children are very interested in NVC and want to learn to use it themselves.
- Some children do not like the verbal component of NVC.

Extra Care Is Needed

- Some NVC trainers are also trained in the Waldorf educational approach. From their perspective as Waldorf teachers, they tend to recommend not using the verbal form of NVC with children younger than 7 or 8.

Contraindications: When Nonviolent Communication Should Be Avoided
- There are none.
- However, the *verbal* element of NVC does not always contribute to connection.
- As long as the focus is on the underlying assumptions and intentions of NVC, and not on the verbal communication, there are no situations in which is it contraindicated.

History
- NVC was developed by Dr. Marshall Rosenberg starting in the 1960's. It has since spread around the world into many different settings. Parenting is just one application of NVC.
- In 1994 UNICEF selected NVC for introduction into schools in Yugoslavia and by 1998 over 1,500 teachers from 40 towns had received 6 full days of training.
- Subsequently, the European Union funded NVC trainers to introduce it into four Israeli and four Palestinian schools and to schools in Northern Ireland.
- Since then, the Israeli government has appointed an NVC trainer to a national education post with the mandate to introduce NVC into Israeli schools.
- The European Union funding for NVC has now been extended to other countries.
- NVC is taught by trainers around the United States, Canada and the rest of the world.

Basic Concepts And Components Of Nonviolent Communication
- Adults learn to distinguish between the following sets of concepts:
    * Observations vs. judgments/interpretations
    * Feelings vs. thoughts/interpretations
    * Needs vs. strategies
    * Requests vs. demands or vague wishes
    * Empathy vs. advice or sympathy
- Study of NVC is needed for effective practice.

Assumptions Underlying the Practice of Nonviolent Communication
- Following are key assumptions upon which NVC practice is based. Many traditions share these assumptions. NVC gives us concrete, powerful tools for putting them into practice. (Note: There are a lot of details to each of these headings.)
    1. All human beings share the same needs.
    2. Our world offers sufficient resources for meeting everyone's basic needs.
    3. All actions are attempts to meet needs.
    4. Feelings point to needs being met or unmet.
    5. All human beings have the capacity for compassion.
    6. Human beings enjoy giving.
    7. Human beings meet many needs through interdependent relationships.
    8. Choice is internal.
    9. The most direct path to peace is through self-connection.
- When we live based on these assumptions, self-connection and connection with others become increasingly possible and easy.

Key Intentions when Using Nonviolent Communication

We hold the following intentions when using NVC because we believe that they help us contribute to a world where everyone's needs are attended to peacefully. (Note: There are a lot of details to each of these headings.)

Open-Hearted Living
- Self-compassion
- Expressing from the heart
- Receiving with compassion
- Prioritizing connection
- Beyond "right" and "wrong"

Choice, Responsibility, Peace
- Taking responsibility for our feelings
- Taking responsibility for our actions
- Living in peace with unmet needs
- Increasing capacity for meeting needs

Sharing Power (Partnership)
- Caring equally for everyone's needs
- Protective use of force

Description Of A Typical Session
- Each learning environment is different.
- There are different groups for parents, children, and organizations.
- Individual sessions focus on coaching and empathy.
- All types of workshops include both teaching and practice opportunities.

Fees/Costs In 2007
- About $200 for a 12-week course for parents
- Courses are always offered on a sliding scale basis: no one is turned away for lack of funds.

Average Time Per Session
- Individual or family sessions typically last 1-2 hours.
- Foundation Course is a beginning.
- There are also daylong workshops, short introduction workshops, and continuing learning opportunities for people who want to integrate NVC into their lives.

Estimated Length Of Time Before Improvements Can Be Expected
- Some people experience a change after just 1 or 2 sessions.
- However, this practice is intended as a life-long process, changing the dynamic between parents and children toward mutual understanding and connection.

Suggestions To Make Nonviolent Communication More Effective
- The intention of NVC is to foster a quality of connection between people that supports them to meet everyone's needs as well as possible.
- To work effectively, NVC cannot be focused on changing behavior, but on deep mutual understanding and connection. When this happens, both parents' and children's behavior often changes.

MARIE MULLIGAN • RICK GEGGIE

Other Methods That Are Similar To Nonviolent Communication
- *Parent Effectiveness Training*, by Tom Gordon shares some key elements with NVC

Other Methods That Complement Nonviolent Communication
- Attachment parenting for infants

Nature And Length Of Training To Be A Trainer
- See The Center for Nonviolent Communication's website: http://cnvc.org/trnrtobe_en.htm, for guidelines for becoming a certified trainer.
- Anyone is welcome to share NVC as a lay leader, provided they follow the guidelines listed here: http://cnvc.org/guidelines_en.htm.

Special Training Needed To Work With Children & Youth
- None is needed.
- There are special trainings for parents and for educators. See: www.cnvc.org and www.baynvc.org . Particularly, see the page for the Peaceful Families, Peaceful World Project: http://www.baynvc.org/peaceful_families.php.
- For information about trainings for schoolteachers see the Train for Life Communication website: http://www.trainforlifecommunication.com.

Certification/Licenses Held By Trainers
- Certification from the Center for Nonviolent Communication

Professional Associations To Contact For Names Of Local Trainers
- Center For Nonviolent Communication; 5600 San Francisco Rd. NE, Suite A; Albuquerque, NM 87109; Ph: 800-255-7696; Fax 505-247-0414; Website: http://cnvc.org/index.htm

Number Of Certified Trainers In U.S., Canada, And Mexico
- There are more than 200 worldwide.

What To Look For When Choosing The Best Trainers
- Ask the person what training they have had, especially if they are not a certified trainer.
- Ideally they have been actively studying NVC for more than 2 years, as it takes a while to integrate the principles of NVC into daily life.
- Your own level of comfort with the person is most important.
- If the trainer is working with your child, your child's comfort with that person is most important.

Resources, Research Papers, Books, DVD's, Websites
- There are many other books and materials about NVC that are not specific to parents. They are available for purchase at: www.cnvc.org.

Bibliography
- Kashtan, Inbal. *Parenting From Your Heart: Sharing the Gifts of Compassion, Connection, and Choice (Nonviolent Communication Guides)*. Encinitas, CA: PuddleDancer Press, 2004.
- Rosenberg, Marshall B., PhD *Raising Children Compassionately: Parenting the Nonviolent Communication Way*. Encinitas, CA: PuddleDancer Press, 2005.
- Sura Hart and Victoria Kindle Hodson. *Respectful Parents, Respectful Kids: 7 Keys to Turn Family Conflict Into Co-operation*. Encinitas, CA: PuddleDancer Press, 2006.
- Inbal Kashtan. "Connected Parenting: NVC in Family Life." CD. Available through: www.baynvc.org.
- Rosenberg, Marshall B., PhD *Nonviolent Communication: A Language of Life*. Encinitas, CA: PuddleDancer Press, 2005. (This is a foundation book on Nonviolent Communication; not specific to parenting.)

Helpful Tips For Parents
- Remember that every time your child acts in a way you don't like, it means they have some need they are trying to communicate to you.
- Get curious and try to understand their need. This will help them experience care and trust that they matter, and help both of you find ways to attend to both your needs.
- Tell your child what you want, instead of what you don't want.
- Be as specific as possible.
- If they say "No", try to find out what they are needing instead of using consequences or rewards.
- There is always a need that is in the way when a human being says "no".
- Look for a way to meet both your needs, instead of focusing on getting your child to do what you want.

Biography Of Inbal Kashtan, Author
- Inbal is a certified Nonviolent Communication trainer. She directs Peaceful Families, Peaceful World, a joint project of the international Center for Nonviolent Communication and BayNVC, and is a co-founder of BayNVC.
- Inbal facilitates public workshops and retreats, as well as trainings in organizations, co-leads an NVC leadership development program, and creates curricula for learning NVC.
- She is the author of *Parenting from the Heart: Sharing the Gifts of Compassion, Connection, and Choice*, a booklet about parenting with NVC. Inbal's greatest teacher has been her son, who is mentoring her on what it means to live nonviolently.

To Contact Inbal Kashtan, Who Contributed This Chapter
Bay Area Nonviolent Communication; 55 Santa Clara Ave, Ste 203; Oakland, CA 94610; Ph: 510-433-0700; Toll Free (outside Bay Area): 866-4-BayNVC; Fax 510-452-3900; Website: www.baynvc.org; Email: nvc@baynvc.org

Marie Mulligan's Comment About Nonviolent Communication: I find Nonviolent Communication to be extremely effective. I am no expert and I use it daily. My children are beginning to use it. Make sure you learn from someone who has experience with children & youth.

Rick Geggie's Comment About Nonviolent Communication: I am so very impressed with this process. I am sad that I was not aware of Nonviolent Communication when I was a parent, teacher and principal. I make use of it in my relationships.

CHAPTER 28

NUTRITION CONSULTING FOR CHILDREN & YOUTH

By Paula Bartholomy, MS, CNC,   © Copyright 2008.

Nutrition Consultation Has Helped Kids With

• Addictions	• Fatigue	• Infections
• Allergies	• Food cravings	• Mood swings
• Asthma	• Hormonal imbalances	• Nervous conditions
• Autism	• Hyperactivity	• Personality disorders
• Depression	• Immune concerns and deficiencies	• Respiratory concerns
• Digestive disturbances	• Impulsiveness	• Seizures
• Emotional imbalances and disturbances		• Weight problems

Nutrition Consultation Can Help In The Following Areas

Spirit: Nutrition affects balance, allowing the spirit to soar.

* **Body:** Nutrition is beneficial for all childhood illnesses--ear, nose, throat, asthma, stomach ailments, skin problems, hyperactivity, mood disturbances, and fatigue.

Mind: Nutrition stabilizes biochemical reactions resulting in a calm, clear, and focused mind.

Emotions: Nurturing the body soothes the nervous system and calms the body while providing steady, reliable energy. This is stabilizing to a child who is nervous, anxious, has trouble sleeping or has wide emotional mood swings.

Social: Nutrition supports a child's natural rhythms, allowing them adequate and appropriate physical and mental energy to engage with others of all ages at home, at school, and while playing.

Brief Description Of Nutrition Consultation

A Nutrition Educator or Consultant can assist individuals with self-healing by:

- Educating the client regarding appropriate diet, herbs, supplement and lifestyle needs.
- Offering support on a broad range of health conditions.
- Considering each person to be biochemically unique.
- Individualizing diet plans to help individuals overcome their health challenges.
- Suggesting appropriate diet and lifestyle changes to help restore health and balance.
- Emphasizing that many illnesses are diet related and diet-modifiable.
- Noting that illness is related to problems of the digestion and/or liver detoxification processes and their influence on immune, nervous and endocrine function.
- Stressing that nutrition has a positive impact on the whole person--physical, mental, and emotional.

Success With Nutrition Consultation

- Justin, an 18-month-old boy of vegetarian parents, was having great difficulty digesting his food. While he was still nursing he was introduced to the foods his parents ate. This resulted in diarrhea, gas, bloating and pain. Justin's father had allergies. Lab tests concluded that Justin was allergic to several of the foods in his diet. When these foods were removed from the diet and others introduced, Justin's symptoms began to improve immediately. Supplements addressed the healing of the intestinal lining and resulted in additional improvement. His digestive distress was resolved within a month.
- As a 14-month-old, Gloria was very small for her age. Her mother had stopped nursing at eight months and began a formula on her pediatrician's advice. A high bulk diet of dairy and meat was advised with no water or fruit. The child became severely constipated, and the iron in the formula contributed to the binding of her bowels. The child was extremely stressed by painful, weekly bowel movements. I discovered that many of her ancestors were very small people. She was encouraged to drink fluids freely--especially water; eat fruit, stop the formula; and add good oils to her diet of fresh, whole foods. Her bowels started moving with ease the next day.
- Robin, an 8-year-old boy, was having great difficulty in school and at home. He was extremely hyperactive - never still unless he was asleep. He couldn't sit still in class or pay attention to his lessons, and he fought frequently with others. His teacher and mother were exhausted. Labeled with Attention Deficit Disorder by two other professionals, Ritalin was suggested as the solution. Changing from mostly refined and fast foods with only apple juice and sodas to drink, to a whole-foods, non-allergenic diet brought steady improvement. A special protein drink loaded with essential nutrients stabilized his energy and moods, as well as his behavior.
- Julie, a 13-year-old-girl, came in with PMS and bumpy skin on her arms. She picked at these bumps so badly that her arms were covered with scabs and she would not wear anything but long-sleeve blouses, even in the summer. Her PMS was so bad she could not go to school two days a month because of cramps. A review of her diet showed a severe deficiency of vitamin A and essential fatty acids. Adding the foods rich in these nutrients, and temporarily supplementing these nutrients, resolved her distress.

Nutrition Consultation Is Appropriate For Ages

- Prenatal through young adult

Children & Youth's Reactions To Nutrition Consultation

- Initially children may miss some of their old favorite foods. Over time, this changes as they experience an increased sense of well-being.
- Children are excited to learn how their bodies work and what they require to feel well.
- They show willingness to participate in their healing by learning and trying new things.
- Improved health is demonstrated in strengthened immunity, digestion, and nervous systems.
- Children enjoy the one-on-one attention, as well as learning about their bodies and how to care for them.

- Children & youth's response to nutrition is quite rapid, usually demonstrating improvement in a few days and seeing resolution within weeks to a month, in more chronic conditions.

Extra Care Is Needed
- If the child is chronically ill, working in partnership with other health care providers may be beneficial.

Contraindications: When Nutrition Consultation Should Be Avoided
- Nutrition Consultation and principles are always relevant and will support any other therapy, treatment or modality.

History
- For the last 5000+ years, our major health systems around the world have focused on nourishing the body, mind and spirit.
- "Food is our best medicine," is ancient wisdom. Nutrition Consultation uses diet, herbs, healing waters and exercise or movement as remedies.

Basic Concepts And Components Of Nutrition Consultation
- The basic premise is to support the client, to encourage them to fully participate and take responsibility for their ongoing health by educating them as to the basic and essential needs of their unique constitution and condition.
- There is belief that the body has the ability to heal itself and remain in balance, and needs ongoing support in the form of self-awareness, essential nutrients found in our foods and lifestyles that support rejuvenation.
- It works to discover factors that contribute to illness and replace them with ones that support health.
- It supports the whole person; does not just treat symptoms.
- It helps the person become fully independent with the necessary tools and knowledge to live a healthful life.

Description Of A Typical Session
- An initial session of 60-90 minutes with a nutrition educator or consultant includes; compiling a complete health and family history, including diet and activity records, and review of medical tests. The child and the caregiver both participate.
- The questions are focused on accessing all the contributing factors: genetics, current and past diet, medications used, metabolism, and ancestry.
- The practitioner may offer some initial recommendations, but usually will review the information and present an individually tailored plan for the child within a few days.
- Follow-ups (to check in) can be done by phone.
- If needed, follow-up appointments are usually 20-40 minutes to review the child's progress and current status, so as to advance the protocol.

Major Differences Of Opinion Between Nutrition Consultation Practitioners
- Some practitioners will determine the pace that a child and the family can maintain while transitioning into a healthier diet and lifestyle, working slowly over a period of one to three months.
- Others will evaluate the child's health condition and present the desired health plan all at once, expecting the family to implement the changes on their own over time.

Fees/Costs In 2007
- Fees are $40-$100 per hour, depending on the practitioner's training and experience, as well as their geographical location.

Average Time Per Session
- Initial visits average from 60-90 minutes. Follow-up visits are generally 30 minutes.

Recommended Length Of Time Between Sessions
- After the first session, a follow-up appointment is scheduled for one to two weeks.
- Sessions occur monthly thereafter to check on the progress of the child's or youth's recommended protocol.

Estimated Length Of Time Before Improvements Can Be Expected
- Depending on the severity and duration of the health condition, expect symptoms to begin improving within a few days to a week.
- For chronic and debilitating conditions, symptoms will improve gradually and continue to improve with time, as the depleted status of the child's health rebuilds.

Suggestions To Make Nutrition Consultation More Effective
- Parents need to communicate extensively with the nutrition educator or consultant regarding the child's health history and any changes they see after the start of the new dietary program.
- Families who participate with the child in the process of learning and implementing the changes in diet and lifestyle demonstrate confidence in the program, which helps the child to feel he or she is on the path to healing. This avoids making the child feel too different, as well as having other family members benefit from the improvement in diet.

Other Methods That Are Similar To Nutrition Consultation
- Nutrition is specific unto itself.
- Many modalities include nutrition, or value its importance.

Other Methods That Complement Nutrition Consultation
- All natural, traditional and conventional therapies are compatible with nutrition.

Nature And Length Of Training To Be A Practitioner
- The field of nutrition is currently a non-licensed profession.
- Several schools offer certification with their one to two year training.
- Some universities offer degrees for Bachelor's, Master's, and PhD programs.
- The field of nutrition is constantly evolving. Nutrition educators are lifelong students. It is essential for practitioners to keep current by attending ongoing seminars, conferences, and training.
- The practitioners should practice what they teach.

Special Training Needed To Work With Children & Youth
- Nutrition educators and consultants are educated in human anatomy and physiology. They understand the basic requirements of the human body to maintain optimal health, as well as understanding of the patterns of disease that are typical in the various life cycles; including babies, children and young adults.
- Many practitioners will specialize in children's concerns.

Certification/Licenses Held By Practitioners
- Nutrition Educator Certification
- Nutrition Consultant Certification (NCC)
- Bachelors, Masters, Doctorate, and PhD in Nutrition

Professional Associations To Contact For Names Of Local Practitioners
- American Holistic Health Association; P.O. Box 17400; Anaheim, CA 92817; 714-779-6152; Website: www.ahha.org
- National Association of Nutrition Professionals; P.O. Box 1172; Danville, CA 94526; 800-342-8037; Fax: 510-580-9429; Website: www.nanp.org

Number Of Certified Practitioners In U.S., Canada, And Mexico
- This is difficult to know since it is a non-licensed profession.
- Some health professionals also specialize in nutrition such as: DO (Doctor of Osteopathic Medicine); DC (Doctor of Chiropractic); L.Ac. (Licensed Acupuncturist), and N.D. (Doctor of Naturopathy).
- Some people practice without certification or degree. Always check their educational and training references.

What To Look For When Choosing The Best Practitioner
- Check their training and certification.
- Ask for references from someone you trust.
- Trust your instincts.
- Do you connect and communicate well with this person?
- You want to work with someone who respects you, is compassionate and caring, is a good listener, and is thorough.
- Seek out people who have worked with the nutrition professional whom you are considering to work with your child:
    * Have they been treated well?
    * Did they achieve positive results?
    * Were they pleased with the outcome, as well as the experience?

Leading Clinics, Centers, Practitioners
- Janet Zand: UPDATE: November 2007 Dr. Zand suggests using this email if anyone has questions for her: drjanetzand@gmail.com
- Dr. Doris Rapp; 1421 Colvin Blvd.; Buffalo, NY 14223; Ph: 716-875-0398; Fax: 716-875-5399; www.drrapp.com
- Nori Hudson; 1952 Yosemite Road; Berkeley, CA 94707-1651; Ph: 510-847-3197(messages); Website: www.radiant-vitality.com; Email: Nori@Radiant-Vitality.com
- Emily Bender; Ph: 415-259-4471; Website: www.gourmethelping.com; Email: emily@nutritionforthewholefamily.com

- Julie Matthews; Ph: 415-437-6807; Email: Julie@HealthfulLiving.org
- Liz Lipski; 4 Sunny Ridge Drive; Asheville, NC 28804; Ph: 828-645-7224; Website: http://www.innovativehealing.com; Email: liz@innovativehealing.com
- Jane Sheppard; c/o Future Generations; 1275 Fourth Street, #118; Santa Rosa, CA 95404; Ph: 707-570-0408; Website: www.healthychild.com/index.html

Research Papers
- Anything by Dr. Stephen Schoenthaler, which can be found by doing a search on the Internet using Google.
- Weston A. Price Foundation for Wise Traditions in Food, Farming and the Healing Arts. The Weston A. Price Foundation; PMB 106-380, 4200 Wisconsin Ave., NW.; Washington DC 20016; Ph: 202-363-4394; Fax: 202-363-4396; Website: www.westonaprice.org; Email: info@westonaprice.org .

Bibliography
- Zand, Janet, Robert Roundtree, and Rachel Walton. *Smart Medicine for a Healthier Child*. New York: Avery, 2nd Ed. 2003.
- Zimmerman, Marcia. *The A.D.D. Nutrition Solution: A Drug-Free 30 Day Plan*. New York: Henry Holt and Co., 1999.
- Rapp, Doris J. *Is This Your Child?: Discovering and Treating Unrecognized Allergies*. New York: William Morrow, 1991.
- Lipski, Elizabeth. *Digestive Wellness for Children: How to Strengthen the Immune System & Prevent Disease Through Healthy Digestion*. Laguna Beach, CA: Basic Health Publications, Inc., 2006.
- Kelly Burgess. "Snacks for Tiny Tummies: Healthy Foods for Toddlers." Available from iParenting Media: www.toddlerstoday.com/articles/3627/1.
- Kelly Burgess. "The Clean Plate Club: Why Your Family *Shouldn't* Join." Available from iParenting Media: http://recipestoday.com/resources/articles/cleanplate.htm.
- Shaw, William. *Biological Treatments for Autism and PDD*. Lenexa, KS: Great Plains Laboratory, 2002.
- McCandless, Jaquelyn. *Children with Starving Brains: A Medical Treatment Guide for Autism Spectrum Disorder*. Putney, VT: Bramble Books, 2003.
- Seroussi, Karyn. *Unraveling the Mystery of Autism and Pervasive Developmental Disorder: A Mother's Story of Research and Recovery*. New York: Simon & Schuster, 2000.
- Nourishing Hope: Nutrition and Diet Intervention for Autism Spectrum Disorders. A website of Julie Matthews, a Certified Nutrition Consultant: www.nourishinghope.com.
- Nourish the Future: Holistic Nutrition for Preconception, Pregnancy, and Postpartum. A website of Julie Matthews, a Certified Nutrition Consultant: www.healthfullivingsf.com/seminars/pregnancy.php
- Sears, William. *The Family Nutrition Book: Everything You Need to Know About Feeding Your Children - From Birth through Adolescence*. New York: Little, Brown and Company, 1999.
- Burney, Lucy. *Optimum Nutrition for Babies and Young Children: Over 150 Quick and Tempting Recipes for the Best Start in Life (Optimum Nutrition Handbook)*. London: Judy Piatkus Ltd., 1999.
- Ward, Elizabeth. *Healthy Foods, Healthy Kids: A Complete Guide to Nutrition for Children from Birth to Six-Year-Olds*. Cincinnati: Adams Media, 2002.
- Arsenault, Anne. *Real Solutions to Children's Health*. Bloomington, IN: AuthorHouse, 2006.
- Internet link for Autism information: www.healthfullivingsf.com/resources/bookswebsites/#autism#autism.
- Internet link for healthful diet information: www.healthfullivingsf.com/resources/bookswebsites/#diets#diets.
- Vaccinations/Heavy Metal Toxicity; www.healthfullivingsf.com/resources/bookswebsites/#vacc#vacc.
- Family Resources; www.healthfullivingsf.com/resources/bookswebsites/#family#family.
- Mind, Energy, Spirit; www.healthfullivingsf.com/resources/bookswebsites/#mes#mes.
- Environmentally-Friendly Products and Product Safety: www.healthfullivingsf.com/resources/bookswebsites/#product#product.

- Food Safety, Organics vs. GMO, Food Additives: www.healthfullivingsf.com/resources/bookswebsites/#food#food.
- Classes:
  * Foundations of Traditional Foods: Recipe for a Healthy Family: www.healthfullivingsf.com/seminars.
  * Cooking for Baby: www.healthfullivingsf.com/seminars.
  * Nutrition for Pregnancy, Pre-Conception & Postpartum: www.healthfullivingsf.com/seminars.
  * Traditional Healing Foods for Children on the Autistic Spectrum including ADHD: www.healthfullivingsf.com/seminars.
- Workshops:
  * Nourishing Our Children: www.healthfullivingsf.com/seminars.
  * Natural Resources - Pregnancy and Postpartum Nutrition: www.healthfullivingsf.com/seminars.
  * Natural Resources - Introducing Solids: www.healthfullivingsf.com/seminars.
- Newsletters
  * Holistic Pediatric Association's "Family Wellness First" newsletter: www.hpakids.org/e-news.html. Amy Yasko: www.autismanswer.com.
  * Autism Research Institute: www.autism.com.
  * Autism Solution Center: www.autismsolutioncenter.com.
  * Cure Autism Now, recently merged with Autism Speaks. You can sign up for their newsletter by going to: www.autismspeaks.org/be_informed.php.
  * Dana's View - a parent's perspective: www.danasview.net.
  * Developmental Delay Resources. You can receive a complimentary issue of their newsletter by writing to, or calling: The Developmental Delay Resources; 5801 Beacon St.; Pittsburgh, PA 15217; Ph: 800-497-0944; Fax: 412-422-1374; Website: www.devdelay.org; Email: devdelay@mindspring.com.
  * "Enzymes for Autism and other Neurological Conditions", by Karen DeFelice: www.Enzymestuff.com.
  * Families for Early Autism Treatment: www.feat.org.
  * Thoughtful House: www.thoughtfulhouse.org.
  * Unlocking Autism: www.unlockingautism.org.

Helpful Tips For Parents
- I suggest all parents take a basic nutrition class.
- Develop an appreciation for, routinely purchase, prepare and serve fresh, whole foods and liquids.
- Exercise and be active with your children.
- Learn, teach, and practice stress reduction techniques with your children.
- Instill healthful attitudes and appreciation for life.

Biography Of Paula Bartholomy, Author
- Paula has 30 years of experience.
- Approximate total number of clients who are infants, children, or teens: She has worked with several hundred families and their children.
- Degrees: She holds a Bachelor of Science and Masters in Holistic Nutrition. She is a Certified Clinical Nutrition Consultant, Certified Transformational Hypnotherapist and Certified Creative Healer.
- She is Board Certified in Holistic Nutrition
- Paula is the School Director of Hawthorn University. Hawthorn University offers online degree and certificate programs in holistic health and nutrition. Visit www.hawthornuniversity.org for more information.

Paula Bartholomy's Personal Statement

I appreciate the ability of children to heal when they receive the essential nutrients and support. Nutrition is essential to life and is the foundation upon which we all depend. I have witnessed minor miracles occur when a child was supported with diet and lifestyle.

To Contact Paula Bartholomy, Who Contributed This Chapter

Paula L. Bartholomy; P.O. Box 275; Whitethorn, CA 95589; Ph: 707-986-9745; Fax: 707-238-1468; Email: paulab@sonic.net

. . . .

Marie Mulligan's Comment About Nutrition Consulting: I recommend nutrition consultation if your child or youth is overweight or underweight, or if they eat an unbalanced diet.

- It is a good idea to give children & youth an appropriate multivitamin/multimineral supplement when their diets are low in vegetables, fruit, whole grains and/or high iron foods (meats, beans, lentils, broccoli). The supplement should give 100% of the DIR (daily reference intakes) of vitamins and minerals recommended by the USDA (United States Department of Agriculture).
- Ask your medical provider/nutritionist for their recommendations for your child or youth.
- Many foods and dietary supplements are vitamin and mineral fortified, so consult your medical provider/nutritionist to avoid giving too much Vitamin A and/or Vitamin D.
- Avoid giving children or youth adult strength supplements.

Rick Geggie's Comment About Nutrition Consulting: I used to marvel at the connection between the food children ate, how they grew, learned and behaved. I found that many well-intended parents had little idea about good nutrition, let alone nutrition that helped children be their best.

Over the years, I discovered that government recommendations about daily requirements of food were simply not enough—especially when children were under stress. Children today need optimal nutrition because they face stress from the environment, the fast pace of family life, and from the complex social problems of society. Given excellent nutrition, children have a better chance of thriving mentally, emotionally and physically.

CHAPTER 29

OSTEOPATHY FOR CHILDREN & YOUTH

By Carlisle Holland, DO,   © Copyright 2008.

Osteopathy Has Helped Kids With

• Anxiety	• Digestive problems	• Repetitive stress injuries
• Arthritis	• Ear infections	• Rheumatological problems
• Asthma	• Emotional distress	• Scoliosis
• Allergies	• Eye coordination problems	• Seizure Disorders
• Balance or coordination problems	• Headaches	• Sinus problems
• Birth trauma	• Head injuries	• Sleep problems
• Cancer	• Jaw problems (TMJ)	• Spinal disc problems
• Cerebral palsy	• Learning problems	• Stomachaches
• Chronic Fatigue Syndrome	• Menstrual pain	• Strains & injuries
• Chronic pain	• Migraines	• Traumatic injuries (motor vehicle and others)
• Depression	• Neurological disorders (including ADD, ADHD, PDD)	• Vertigo/dizziness

Osteopathy Can Help In The Following Areas

Spirit: Since the spirit suffers when the body suffers, treating the physical relieves the spiritual.

Body: Osteopathy is excellent for many physical conditions including asthma, cerebral palsy, sports injuries, sleep apnea and ear infections.

Mind: Decreasing pain and suffering increases the child's ability to concentrate and relieves the depression that often accompanies physical illness.

Emotions: Emotions are stored in the body. Release them and many physical and emotional problems are also released.

Social: Children are able to enjoy more social activities when they feel better physically.

Brief Description Of Osteopathy

- Osteopathy, a practice that includes a combination of Osteopathic Manipulative Treatment and standard Western Medicine, helps children with a wide range of challenges. Osteopaths understand that humans function as a complete working system. The body structure, organ systems, mind and emotions are all interrelated and mutually interdependent.
- Manipulation balances muscular and autonomic reflexes. There is much focus on easing muscular tension, which not only alleviates pain and stiffness; it also allows for the unimpeded flow of blood and lymph fluids.

Success With Osteopathy

- Billy, age 4, had chronic ear infections, to the point where another doctor had recommended putting in tubes. With one osteopathic treatment, however, normal physical movement was restored and the infections disappeared.
- Jenny, age 5, developed asthma. Her parents tried conventional treatments, including an inhaler. With three osteopathic treatments to her chest wall, normal breathing patterns were restored. She receives follow-up treatments each spring during allergy season.
- Janie, age 8, had spina bifida, and one of her hip bones kept popping out of her pelvis. Surgery was recommended. The osteopath manipulated her pelvis, moving the bone back into place. He also measured her legs and, finding that one was shorter than the other, he recommended a lift in her shoes. The need for surgery was eliminated.

Osteopathy Is Appropriate For Ages

- Newborn through adolescence

Children & Youth's Reactions to Osteopathy

- They often respond very quickly to treatment.
- They usually enjoy sessions with their doctors.
- They are relieved to be treated with respect and careful attention.
- Most children love their treatments since it doesn't hurt them and often makes them feel better very quickly.
- Children need to feel they are perfect. The osteopath shows them they are perfect - they just have a problem that needs to be fixed.

Extra Care Is Needed

- During pregnancy

Contraindications: When Osteopathy Should Be Avoided

- There are no absolute contraindications for involving Osteopathy.

History
- Begun in 1873 in Missouri by Dr. Andrew Taylor Still. He conceived of what is now known as holistic medicine in an effort to reform what he felt were some of the more extreme excesses of traditional Western medicine as it was then practiced.
- Dr. Still and his sons founded the first college of Osteopathy in Kirksville, Missouri in 1892.
- Despite opposition from the American Medical Association, the number of osteopathic colleges and the number of osteopaths grew. Today there are 23 osteopathic colleges throughout the United States and over 60,000 osteopathic physicians.

Basic Concepts And Components Of Osteopathy
- The body is a unit.
- Structure and function are reciprocally related. (Form follows function and the properly functioning body displays balance and harmonious motions in all its processes.)
- The body tends to heal and DOs are taught to trust the inherent healing powers of the body's physiology.

Description Of A Typical Session
- During the first visit, the practitioner listens to the chief complaint, then takes a complete history and conducts a complete traditional and structural exam.
- The practitioner chats with the child and tries to develop an understanding of her/him as a person.
- The practitioner checks the child's posture and does a biomechanical test on all the joints - from the toes to the top of the head.
- During the course of the exam the practitioner treats the child all over, then manipulates the restricted joints - starting from the biggest one. An osteopath often uses a vibrator as part of the treatment.
- Lastly, the practitioner performs a cranial treatment, which is very subtle movement of the head.
- The practitioner not only treats the child for the chief complaint, but also finds hidden symptoms and treats them as well.
- Drugs may also be prescribed as necessary.

Major Differences Of Opinion Between Practitioners
- Some osteopaths are more inclined to prescribe drugs than others.

Fees/Costs In 2007
- Fees are $100 - $200 per visit.
- Insurance Companies usually cover some or all of the cost.

Average Time Per Session
- One hour for the first visit
- 20-30 minutes on subsequent visits

Recommended Length Of Time Between Sessions
- Usually treatments start out weekly, then move to biweekly, monthly, etc. for up to six months.

Estimated Length Of Time Before Improvements Can Be Expected
- Three to five sessions

Suggestions To Make Osteopathy More Effective
- Have confidence that treatment will be effective and express that belief to the child.
- Parents need to be united in their treatment of the child. If parents are at war, the child senses this and has a harder time getting well.
- Parents can learn some simple manipulations, drainage techniques, etc.
- Be aware of child's sensitivities to foods, animals, down, plants, etc.

Other Methods That Are Similar To Osteopathy
- Some forms of chiropractic manipulation are similar.
- Many traditional Western medical doctors have studied Osteopathy.
- Naturopathy, nutrition, and holistic healers are similar.

Other Methods That Complement Osteopathy
- Acupuncture, homeopathy, nutrition, and phytotherapy (medicinal herbology)

Nature And Length Of Training To Be A Practitioner
- A minimum of three years of undergraduate education (98% have four years or more) is needed.
- Four years, or the equivalent, of osteopathic medical school, and a one year rotating internship is needed.
- All graduate programs in physical therapy teach Osteopathic Manipulation techniques.
- DO specialists have spent an additional two to five years of residency, training in hospital situations.
- DOs are now all required to do three-year postdoctoral residencies to practice.

Special Training Needed To Work With Children & Youth
- There are residency programs in pediatrics, but 90% of children's problems can be handled by a general practitioner.

Certification/Licenses Held By Practitioners
- A degree from a certified Osteopathic College of Medicine
- A license from the state certifying that the physician has passed the state medical examination

Professional Associations To Contact For Names Of Local Practitioners
- The American Osteopathic Association; 142 E. Ontario Street; Chicago, IL 60611; Ph: 800-621-1773; Fax: 312-202-8200; Website: www.osteopathic.org; Email: available through website
- The American Academy of Osteopathy; 3500 DePauw Boulevard, Suite 1080; Indianapolis, IN 46268; Ph: 317-879-1881; Fax: 317-879-0563; Website: www.academyofosteopathy.org
- Each state has its own osteopathic association to contact for referrals.

Number Of Certified Practitioners In U.S., Canada, And Mexico
- There are thousands in all three countries.

What To Look For When Choosing The Best Practitioner
- Check their licenses.
- The practitioner has compassion and patience with both the child and the parent.
- The practitioner has the willingness to take the time to take a thorough history and do a complete exam before making a diagnosis.
- The practitioner has a good sense of humor.

Leading Clinics, Centers, Practitioners
- Viola Frymann and the Osteopathic Center for Children and Families; 4135 54th Place; San Diego, CA 92105; Ph: 619-583-7611; Fax: 619-583-0296; www.osteopathiccenter.org; Email: info@osteopathiccenter.org
- Pat Crampton, Executive Director of the Cranial Academy; 8202 Clearvista Parkway, Ste. 9D; Indianapolis, IN 46256-1457; Ph: 317-594-0411

Research Papers
- Viola Frymann's articles on academic difficulties, vision problems, scoliosis, asthma, etc. can be found at the Osteopathic Center for Children and Families' website: www.osteopathiccenter.org/articles.html.

Bibliography
- Collinge, William. *The American Holistic Health Association Complete Guide to Alternative Medicine*. New York: Warner Books, 1996.
- Jones, Bob E. *The Difference A DO Makes*. Oklahoma City: 1978. Now available through the Oklahoma Educational Foundation for Osteopathic Medicine; 4848 North Lincoln Boulevard; Oklahoma City, OK 73105-3335; Ph: 800-522-8379; Website: http://www.okosteo.org.
- Frymann, Viola. Articles available online at: www.osteopathiccenter.org/articles.html.

Helpful Tips For Parents
- Provide the child with a calm, peaceful environment.
- Be sure your child is eating lots of fresh fruits and vegetables.
- Use any treatment techniques the practitioner has provided at the time of the child's office visit.

Biography of Carlisle Holland, Author
- Years experience: 30
- Approximate number of children and youth patients: 10 – 15 per week
- Degrees: B.A. in Biology – University of Texas at Austin; DO (1977) from Texas College of Osteopathic Medicine, Fort Worth, TX.

To Contact Dr. Carlisle Holland, Who Contributed This Chapter
Dr. Carlisle Holland; c/o Holonomic Institute; 130 S. Main St. #104; Sebastopol, CA 95472; Ph: 707-824-8764; Fax: 707-824-8766; Website: www.holonomicinstitute.com; Email: info@holonomicinstitute.com

. . . .

Marie Mulligan's Comment About Osteopathy: I have seen Osteopathy help many children & youth, especially after accidents.

Rick Geggie's Comment About Osteopathy: Classic Osteopaths who still practice Osteopathic manipulation really impress me. I have seen many children helped dramatically. While Osteopaths in the United States are licensed as medical doctors, they also have a superior knowledge of how the body works mechanically. As a result, I have noticed they can help children who have not been helped by traditional medicine.

CHAPTER 30

PRECISION TEACHING FOR CHILDREN & YOUTH

By Elizabeth Haughton, MA, © Copyright 2008.

Precision Teaching Has Helped Kids With
- Reading
- Spoken and written language
- Spelling
- Handwriting
- Arithmetic
- Mathematics
- Physical coordination

Precision Teaching Can Help In The Following Areas
Spirit: Confidence is built through the child's awareness of his/her progress.

Body: Physical skills can improve if they are a goal for Precision Teaching.

Mind: The primary focus of Precision Teaching is the increase in the intellectual and expressive aspects of an individual.

Emotion: Children feel secure knowing that their progress is built on solid success. Many become more at ease.

Social: Social skills appear to improve with the confidence that results from Precision Teaching work.

Brief Description Of Precision Teaching
- Precision Teaching is a learning system that helps children & youth who have a difficult time focusing, learning, and achieving their goals.
- Precision Teaching does this by providing continuous, minute-by-minute monitoring and feedback of progress to students and teachers.
- This is accomplished by pinpointing skills, charting progress, and analyzing learning pictures.
- Fluency aims are used to guarantee retention, endurance, and application of skills.

- Students set fluency aims, chart their progress, achieve "personal bests," and celebrate their learning.

Success With Precision Teaching
- Albert was nine years old and could not read. We worked on his ability to process sounds in words, to understand and retain what he heard. He was carefully taught phonemic awareness and a systemic multi-sensory phonics program. Within two years he was up to grade level. He is now an above-average reader.
- Terry was a six year old boy with Cerebral Palsy symptoms, who was unable to write. Doctors felt his lack of muscle control would never allow him to do so. He needed over 1,000 repetitions to do this. Years later, Terry has now finished college. He easily writes about 80 clear letters a minute.
- Stephanie, an eight year old girl, was diagnosed as having Dyslexia. She could not learn to read. She was also having behavior problems in school. Precision Teaching work revealed that her real problem was remembering the order of visual symbols and tracking from left to right. Using Precision Teaching tutoring on her rapid automatic naming (RAN), phonics and reading-in-context skills, Stephanie was eventually able to work easily at grade level. As her school performance improved, so did her behavior. She is now in college and doing well.

Precision Teaching Is Appropriate For Ages
- Four through adult

Children & Youth's Reactions To Precision Teaching
- Students want to practice because they enjoy reaching their personal best.
- Children & youth get excited about the learning experiences because of the immediate feedback.
- Most have an immediate boost of confidence.
- Children & youth are enthusiastic and excited about reaching their personal aims.
- Children & youth learn to be good decision-makers.
- Older children & youth often say things like, "This is the first program that really helps me. I can see the charts that show I'm improving."

Extra Care Is Needed
- If the child has severe emotional problems

Contraindications: When Precision Teaching Should Be Avoided
- Problems can occur when teachers have not been properly trained to do the whole method. In such cases, children & youth can feel pressured, and the method will not work.
- Children & youth who feel extremely pressured need to have control of the time period.

History
- Precision Teaching has been in use for 30 years.
- Developed by Dr. Ogden Lindsley and Dr. Eric Haughton, professors of Psychology at Kansas University, it uses principles from psychology in humane ways.
- Lindsley and Haughton trained many graduate students on how to use Precision Teaching.
- Many applications have been developed.

Basic Concepts And Components Of Precision Teaching
- Precision Teaching holds that very strong basic skills are needed as a foundation for any future learning.

- Precision Teaching holds that learning is a step-by-step, task-by-task process.
- Precision Teaching builds skill levels purposefully, moving carefully from one expertly planned learning task to the next task - only as mastery is achieved.
- Children's performance of their "personal best" is timed and/or counted as they work toward specific learning aims.
- Each student's performance is thoroughly analyzed to understand and pinpoint exactly where the problems are occurring.
- The measuring and charting of the child's progress builds the child's confidence and, as a result, their future performance is made easier.
- Precision Teaching is not like standardized tests, as standardized tests do not measure daily performance.
- Research has shown that auditory processing delays (hearing, understanding, and remembering what has been heard) are a primary cause of problems in reading, language, and spelling. These problems kill confidence, which in turn causes more problems (many children are misdiagnosed with Attention Deficit Disorder). Precision Teaching is extremely effective in dealing with these problems.
- After foundation skills are fluent, time and effort must be spent catching up any missed skills and knowledge so students can use their full potential.

Description Of A Typical Session
- The student and the teacher work one-on-one.
- The student does tasks in the area under study while the tutor times, charts, and evaluates to see if more practice is needed before moving to the next set of tasks.
- Acknowledgement and celebration of success is very important.

Major Differences Of Opinion Between Precision Teaching Practitioners
- Goals for fluency performance (Automaticity levels) may differ considerably between practitioners.
- Use of the Standard Celeration Chart differs between practitioners. (The Standard Celeration Chart is a six-cycle chart which lasts 20 weeks.)

Fees/Costs In 2007
- The cost is $60 for one hour one-to-one sessions.
- The cost is $500 for consultation/assessment.
- Usually 120 to 240 hours are needed.

Average Time Per Session
- Sessions last one hour to four hours.

Recommended Length Of Time Between Sessions
- Sessions are recommended at least twice a week.
- If a student is a year or so behind in school, the intensive summer school is suggested, with four one-hour sessions daily.

Estimated Length Of Time Before Improvements Can Be Expected
- Attitude change is often noticed immediately.
- Significant academic change is noticed within twenty hours of Precision Teaching.

Suggestions To Make Precision Teaching More Effective

- Pay attention to the charts of learning each week. Celebrate learning success and personal best.
- Become educated on the latest research concerning child development.
- Make sure the child feels good about the program.
- Occasionally, observe the tutoring sessions.

Other Methods That Are Similar To Precision Teaching

- Precision Learning
- Direct Instruction
- Precision Measurement
- Fluency Based Instruction
- Curriculum Based Measurement

Other Methods That Complement Precision Teaching

- Vision therapy
- Physical therapy
- Speech and language therapies
- Direct instruction

Nature And Length Of Training To Be A Practitioner

- 80 hours of training, followed by two years of advising by an experienced Precision Teaching teacher is needed.

Special Training Needed To Work With Children & Youth

- Participate in conferences; chat room on website for Precision Teaching.
- Practitioners need to keep investigating and use their data to make decisions.
- Having a background in education is not necessary.

Certification/Licenses Held By Practitioners

- There is no standard license given, although some centers may certify their trainees.

Professional Associations To Contact For Names Of Local Practitioners

- Contact Standard Celeration Society (SCS) (also holds conferences); PO Box 3351; Kansas City, Kansas 66103; Website: www.celeration.org; Email is available through website.

Number Of Certified Practitioners In U.S., Canada, And Mexico

- There are hundreds - scattered around the continent.

What To Look For When Choosing The Best Practitioner

- Look for well-trained and caring Precision Teaching practitioners who are able to communicate clearly.
- Carefully investigate references and claims.

Leading Clinics, Centers, Practitioners

- Achieve Fluency (Autism and related disabilities); c/o Danusia Pawska, Christine Cukar-Capizzi; Breakthru Family Fit 4 Life; 48 Union St.; Stamford, CT; Ph: 203-698-0247; Website: www.achievefluency.com; Email: achievefluency@gmail.com
- This is a site where there is an effort to collect many Precision Teaching links of interest and FAQ's in one place; Website: http://precisionteaching.pbwiki.com
- The Learning Incentive, Inc., home of the Ben Bronz Academy; 139 North Main Street; West Hartford, Connecticut 06107; Ph: 860-236-5807; Fax: 860-233-9945; Website: www.learningincentive.com; Email: Inquire@learningincentive.com
- Cache Valley Learning Center (private school and learning center); 75 South 400 West; Logan, UT 84321; Ph: 435-753-8811; Website: www.cvlc-logan.org; Email: penny@cvlc-logan.org
- Charter Day School/Roger Bacon Academy (public charter school); 7055 Bacons Way; Leland, NC 28451; Ph: 910-655-1214; Fax: 910-655-1549; Website: www.charterdayschool.com
- Binder Riha Associates (Strategic Performance Consulting); 281 Shepard Way NW; Bainbridge Island WA 95404; Ph: 206-780-8578; Fax: 206-780-3279; Website: www.binder-riha.com; Email: Info@Binder-Riha.com
- Organization for Research and Learning; Website: www.o4rl.com
- Haughton Learning Center; 10315 Amador St.; Jackson CA 95642; Ph: 209.257.1613; Fax: 209-257-1613; Website: www.HaughtonLearningCenter.com; Email: elizabeth@haughtonlearningcenter.com
- Morningside Academy; 201 Westlake Ave. N.; Seattle, WA 98109; Ph: 206-709-9500; Fax: 206-709-4611; Website: www.morningsideacademy.org; Email: info@morningsideacademy.org

Resources, Research Papers, Books, DVD's, Websites

- Go to Fluency.org for hundreds of articles and research papers on Precision Teaching.
- Binder, Carl. "Behavioral Fluency: Evolution of a New Paradigm." *The Behavior Analyst* 19, no. 2 (1996): 163-197.
- Kubina, RM, Morrison, R. "Fluency in Education." *Behavior and Social Issues* 10 (2000): 83-99.
- Lindsley, Ogden R. "Ten Products of Fluency." *Journal of Precision Teaching and Celebration* 13, no. 1 (1995): 2-11.

Bibliography

- Precision Teaching Fluency Based Curriculum Packets, (2001); Haughton Learning Center, Jackson, CA; order through www.HaughtonLearningCenter.com. (Source for teachers' manuals, phonics, math, word patterns, etc.)
- Contact Behavior Research Co., the source of Standard Celeration Charts, books, charts and other materials: www.behaviorresearchcompany.com.
- Morningside Press; Fluency supplements for core curriculum: www.morningsidepress.org.

Helpful Tips For Parents

- Work on your child's strengths and then begin to look at their needs.
- Make sure that your child develops a strong skill foundation.
- Make sure they know their phonics, math facts, how to correctly hold their pencil, and how to think independently.
- Continue to read to your child until they go to college.
- Help them use more language. Have them describe events, objects, and pictures.
- Feed them a good diet.
- Give them a massage once a week. A relaxed child or youth learns better.

Biography Of Elizabeth Haughton, Author

- Elizabeth Haughton has, for over thirty years, devoted her professional life to providing children and adults with programs that guarantee learning success. Elizabeth is a specialist in teaching academic and language foundation skills to children with special needs.
- Combining teacher with science, Elizabeth works with students who need development of their visual, auditory, language and motor processing systems. She has put into operation and honed the ground breaking work of Eric Haughton, which demonstrated that learning rates accelerate once a student obtains a certain optimum level of fluency in the basic component skills of reading, math and other academic activities.
- Elizabeth has trained numerous educators and parents on how to identify a child's strengths and needs; determine how best a child's performance can be brought into line with his/her potential; and then implement and measure highly efficient learning programs. She has repeatedly demonstrated that with consistent, dedicated instruction, ongoing measurement, well designed practice materials and the student's involvement in decision making, learning success is possible for anyone.
- Elizabeth was a public school teacher in Canada and the USA; director of the Haughton Learning Center in Napa; educational consultant to schools and agencies; teacher trainer; and author. Currently, Elizabeth consults with the Morningside Academy, as well as schools in California, Wisconsin, and New Hampshire.

Elizabeth Haughton's Personal Statement

Each child has special strengths and needs. It is essential that a child's potential and school performance match.

If you have concerns about your child's learning development, it is important to immediately seek help before the family experiences emotional stress. This will prepare everyone for a lifetime of learning success.

To Contact Elizabeth Haughton, Who Contributed This Chapter

Elizabeth Haughton, Director, Haughton Learning Center; 10315 Amador St.; Jackson CA 95642; Ph: 209.257.1613; Fax: 209-257-1613; Website: www.HaughtonLearningCenter.com; Email: elizabeth@haughtonlearningcenter.com

. . . .

Marie Mulligan's Comment About Precision Teaching: Precision Teaching helps children & youth master the foundation steps they need for future learning. I hope someday Precision Teaching and programs like it are available to all children & youth.

Rick Geggie's Comment About Precision Teaching: I first learned of Precision Teaching decades ago. I have remained very impressed with its ability to help challenged children as well as children already doing well who want to increase their performance levels. The expense of the practice is offset by the overall amount of learning time and self-esteem that it saves. Childhood does not last long. The effects of low esteem and poor academic performance can last a lifetime.

CHAPTER 31

PSYCHOTHERAPY FOR CHILDREN & YOUTH
Psychodynamic Psychotherapy

By Peter Carnochan, PhD,   © Copyright 2008.

Psychotherapy Has Helped Kids With
- Depression and anxiety
- Problems in school, attention and learning difficulties
- Adjustment to loss, divorce, or death
- Impulse control, defiant behavior, and aggression
- Social skills, peer and sibling relationships, loneliness
- History of trauma, abuse, or neglect
- Coping with troubled family members or parents with addictions

Psychotherapy Can Help In The Following Areas
Spirit: Yes
Body: Yes
Mind: Yes
Emotions: Yes
Social: Yes

Brief Description Of Psychotherapy
- Psychotherapy is a method for helping children, teenagers and families with emotional and behavioral problems.
- Psychotherapy can help with behavior problems at home and at school.
- Psychotherapy can support children during separations, divorces, and/or grief.
- Psychotherapy can help children heal from the damages of abuses of all kinds.
- There are various methods of psychotherapy (a list of methods can be found later in this chapter). One of these methods is Psychodynamic Psychotherapy.

Brief Description of Psychodynamic Psychotherapy

- Psychodynamic Psychotherapy is based on the idea that many surface behavior and relationship problems are rooted in conscious or unconscious emotional difficulties.
- Using Psychodynamic Psychotherapy, children and parents can begin to understand and become comfortable with underlying feelings that can be confusing.
- During sessions, the therapist will talk to both parents and children to gain greater understanding about the underlying issues.
- With younger children, the primary language of the therapy session is play.
- Through play, children can begin to show the therapist how they have experienced the important situations in their life. A girl who has difficulties making friends, for instance, may learn about making friends by playing a game with the therapist about a group of imaginary animals.
- Psychodynamic psychotherapy (PP) is a practice that requires a significant commitment in terms of time and resources.
- PP has the potential to help change the long term course of a child's life.
- Because it focuses on underlying emotions and relationships, this type of therapy offers the promise of change that is more than superficial.

Success With Psychotherapy

Mark (not his real name) first came to see me at age six. He had been removed from his home before he turned one, after suffering abuse from his father that had left him with broken ribs and a collapsed lung. Since then, he had been in and out of fifteen foster care placements.

At the beginning of our time together, Mark didn't have many ideas about how to use his time during the sessions.

I usually give each child I work with their own box, where they can keep whatever they make during a session.

Mark realized that once he had changed some of the art supplies by cutting or drawing, they became his and were moved into his box.

He began to test the limits about how much he could have. In one session he cut a whole ball of string into ten inch pieces. Mark just felt like he needed something, a lot of something, and he couldn't count on adults to give it to him. At the end of that session his box was full of scraps, useless in themselves, but there were lots of them, and they belonged to him.

As we worked together to make some sense of his feelings of hopelessness and lack, and as he settled into his very good new adoptive home placement, Mark's ability to imagine and tolerate knowing about his history grew.

After several months of therapy together, he returned to the scraps of string and asked me to tie them together for him. We spent the next several sessions tying the string together with a growing sense of excitement.

As we talked about our project I said: "This string is kind of like your life. It was all cut apart. You feel now like maybe you can tie it together again." At this point the string began to have meaning and use. He would tie it around the doorknob to keep out potential intruders. He thought he might be able to use it as an escape ladder to crawl out the window. He started to talk about the string as his life ball.

Mark was in therapy for three years. By the end of his therapy, he had developed understanding about his past and a greater sense of trust and safety with me-his therapist, and with his parents. He used these strengthened relationships as a basis for relationships with friends and school.

Several years after the end of his therapy his parents reported that he was doing well in school and was happy.

Psychotherapy Is Appropriate For Ages
- Three to eighteen years.
- When working with children birth to 3, the child needs to be seen with the parent. This therapy focuses on strengthening the attachment between parent and child.

Children & Youth's Reactions To Psychotherapy
- Some children really love therapy. They feel they have a trusted ally and like the creative activity.
- Other children can feel threatened by therapy and make strong complaints about going, even though the therapy may be helpful.
- If the child complains, parents and the therapist have to determine whether the complaints are part of recovery.

Extra Care Is Needed
- Kids who have gone through significant trauma may need more help in developing the ability to keep out invading, troublesome thoughts and worries. With these children, the therapist needs to be careful not to move too quickly to speak about the painful events because the child can experience this as a repetition of the trauma.
- Before remembering the painful experience, the child must get permission to forget and take part in living. When the child has emotional skills and strengths they can start to remember the trauma – which can be helpful. Being forced to remember too soon can be another painful demand.
- The child has to feel safe enough and ready to remember the painful experience.
- Another area that requires caution is parental commitment.
- It is important that the parents have a commitment to the therapy and understand how emotions can be stirred up in the process.
- Parents need to be committed to a lengthy process. A bit of therapy is usually not helpful when the child has been very hurt.

History
- Psychodynamic Psychotherapy has its roots in the work of Sigmund Freud. Freud was a Viennese medical doctor who began trying to understand the roots of emotional disorders during the 1880's. He continued to develop his thought through the early 1930's.
- Freud developed a type of therapy that he called psychoanalysis where he encouraged his adult patients to free-associate, to say whatever they wanted to. He realized that eventually, using this method, most patients would begin to talk about the thoughts and feelings that were most important to them.
- Freud's daughter, Anna Freud, and a therapist named Melanie Klein (both students of Freud) began working with children in the 1920's.
- Children, however, are not ready to talk abstractly about their thoughts and feelings.
- To reach children, Anna Freud and Melanie Klein realized that another approach was required.
- They recognized that for children, play is the language of the unconscious. Playing is how children free-associate.

Basic Concepts And Components Of Psychotherapy
- For children to flourish, they need to learn certain skills that allow them to relate with other people.
- They need to be able to adjust their feelings, and know how to use their feelings effectively when interacting with others.
- In health, children should be able to experience a wide range of feelings without becoming overwhelmed.
- In their relationships, children should be able to play cooperatively and competitively with peers.
- With adults, children should be able to put up with the reasonable demands of authority, and make their wishes and concerns known.
- These skills are usually learned in the family setting, and early school environment.
- When children have difficult temperaments or they have a challenging situation at home, it can be hard for them to develop these skills.
- Beginning psychotherapy early can make a big difference in bringing development back on track.
- For children, play is the language of the imagination and feeling.
- Play offers children an avenue to express their strongest feelings and conflicts. In this way, play provides an avenue into the child's inner world.
- In the context of play, difficult thoughts and feelings can be expressed in a non-threatening way. For example, a child who has a hard time expressing his troubles in words, might be able to draw a detailed picture, using images that reveal his inner feelings. By talking about the drawing instead of the underlying problem, the child can address his issues in a way that feels safe.
- Play offers a controlled setting where a child can try out new behaviors, in the same way that an athlete might work on a new skill during practice.
- Problematic behavior is often an attempt to manage anxiety and feelings of danger.
- In psychotherapy, safety is created by the relationship between the child and the therapist.
- The regular meetings, the therapist's consistent and careful focus on the child's worries and the therapist's acceptance of the child, all add to an increased sense of security.
- When the family understands the nature of the child's behavior, it can help them find more effective and less frightening responses to the child's behavior.
- As things begin to feel more safe in their environment, children can take the risk of leaving their old methods of managing anxiety behind, and can begin to develop new, more positive behavior.
- It is important for parents to understand that throughout a course of helpful psychotherapy, children may have intense positive and negative feelings toward their therapist.
- This is part of what allows the therapy to reach the child at the deepest level.

Description Of A Typical Session
- When I work with a child, I begin by meeting with the parents.
- I gather information about the nature of the child's difficulties and the family's background.
- After getting a history of the child's development, I meet with the child.
- Often children will want their parents to stay with them during the first session.
- I tell children that I'm a doctor who helps people with their troubles and worries.
- During a session, children are invited to play with the toys and art supplies in the office.
- With teenagers, I explain to them what I have been told about their situation and ask them to give me their perspective on themselves and their family.
- Some teenagers are quite ready to speak about their thoughts and feelings. Other teenagers may feel unsure about opening up with a stranger.
- With these teens, I work hard to create a more comfortable context for discussion.
- We may begin by speaking about music, movies, or other ordinary topics and allow this to become a springboard for more personal conversation.
- After meeting with the child for several sessions, I will then schedule another meeting with the parents. At this time I will talk to the parents about my impressions of the case and talk about a possible course of treatment.

- It is important for parents to understand the reason for treatment, and to have a good sense of the commitment involved.
- As the therapy continues, the child's worries and concerns are expressed increasingly in play and drawings.
- As the child starts to trust the therapist, there is room for the therapist to begin to talk with the child about how the themes in the child's play may be connected to issues and feelings in the child's own life.

Major Differences Of Opinion Between Practitioners
- There are a lot of differences. Most of the differences are too complicated for a short discussion.
- One important area of difference is about whether it is better to teach new skills, or to deal with underlying fears and anxiety before change can be long lasting.

Fees/Costs In 2007
- In San Francisco, the cost is $100 to $175 per session.
- Parents who need a significantly reduced fee or a fee based upon income, can often find interns who are in training and who are under the supervision of more experienced therapists.

Average Time Per Session
- Sessions last 45 to 50 minutes, one to four times a week.
- Therapy seems to work best when children have at least two sessions a week.

Estimated Length Of Time Before Improvements Can Be Expected
- Some children are able to be helped quite quickly.
- With most children, therapy requires time for enough safety and depth to be established. This process usually takes at least a year.
- When problems are severe, many years of work can be required.

Suggestions To Make Psychotherapy More Effective
- Parents should meet with the therapist regularly: once a week to once a month.
- They can keep the therapist informed about the events in the child's life.
- The therapist can coach the parents on ways of being more effective at home.
- Parents sometimes have the idea that children should talk about their troubles with the therapists.
- Parents must realize that, for the therapy to go well, there has to be room for playing.
- Parents should understand that conflict and strong emotions are an important part of the therapeutic process.
- During difficult periods in the treatment, parents should collaborate closely with the therapist.

Different Methods of Psychotherapy For Children & Youth
- There are many forms of Psychotherapy for kids: Psychodynamic, Cognitive, Behavioral, Expressive Art.

Other Methods That Complement Psychotherapy
- Occupational therapy
- Family therapy
- Social skills training

Special Training Needed To Work With Children & Youth
- Regardless of their specific degree, clinicians need to have training and supervision in working with children. Inquire about the amount of child experience the clinician has.
- A skilled child therapist will know about child development, and be familiar with the physical, emotional and intellectual issues that effect children.

Education/Certification/Licenses Needed By Practitioners
- In the United States, licenses and training to be a psychotherapist vary by state.
- In the United States, there are a variety of degrees that qualify people to work as therapists: most are Masters Degree programs – that is, education that follows graduation from a university with a Bachelor's degree.
    * Look for degrees like: MSW (Master of Social Work), MFT (Master of Family Therapy). These usually take two years of schooling with additional years of supervised practice.
- After completing a Master's degree, a therapist can pursue a Doctorate, or PhD.
  This qualifies the therapist to be called a Psychologist or Ph.D Social Worker. These degrees usually take a minimum of 4 years in addition to years of supervised practice.
- At the medical level, doctors who have had four years of medical education then complete residencies in psychiatry. Psychiatrists have an MD and this allows them to prescribe medication when indicated.

Professional Associations To Contact For Names Of Local Psychotherapists
- To locate a practitioner, start by asking friends. Word of mouth referral is often a good way to find therapists. Pediatricians, school counselors and officials, and some ministers will also know local therapists.
- The American Psychological Association's website provides a link to locate a local psychologist: www.apa.org.
- Contact the American Medical Association; 515 N. State St.; Chicago, IL 60610; 800-621-8335; Website: www.ama-assn.org.
- Contact the American Family Therapy Academy (AFTA, Inc.); 1608 20th St., NW; 4th Floor; Washington, DC 20009; Ph: 202-483-8001; Fax: 202-483-8002; Website: www.afta.org.

What To Look For When Choosing The Best Practitioners
- Skill in psychotherapy is a combination of who the therapist is as a person, combined with their training and experience.
- Look for personal qualities you respect: a therapist who is thoughtful, empathic, warm, and is able to think clearly about the child and family.
- Look for someone who can form a positive bond with the child.
- Inquire about their training.

Bibliography
- Greenspan, Stanly and Jacqueline Salmon. *The Challenging Child: Understanding, Raising, and Enjoying the Five "Difficult" Types of Children*. Jackson, TN: Perseus Books, 1995.
- Miller, Alice. *The Drama of the Gifted Child: The Search for the True Self*. Jackson, TN: Basic Books, 1997.
- Altman, Neil (Editor), Richard Briggs (Editor), Jay Frankel (Editor), and Daniel Gensler (Editor). *Relational Child Psychotherapy*. New York: Other Press, 2002.
- Axline, Virginia. *Play Therapy*. New York: Ballantine Books, 1947.

Peter Carnochan's Personal Statement

When children are having difficulties at home or at school, I believe psychotherapy can play a key role in helping develop new possibilities and insights. Parents often report that children gain confidence and greater empathy over the course of the therapy. This can result in better relationships and increased focus and enjoyment in school.

To Contact Peter Carnochan, Who Contributed This Chapter

Peter Carnochan; 3609 Sacramento Street; San Francisco, CA 94118; Ph: 415-922-5570; Email: pcarnochan@mindspring.com

. . . .

Marie Mulligan's Comment About Psychotherapy: The right therapist and the right therapy can transform a child's or youth's life. I have seen it over and over again. Choose carefully.

Rick Geggie's Comment About Psychotherapy: I wish every child could be in therapy for as long as they need to be, in order to know themselves, to like themselves and to know how to find trustworthy people from whom to learn. As a principal, I was very sad that therapy was not available to more children. I have seen therapists perform miracles, bringing children and teens back from lives of anger, confusion, and creating havoc. I believe society should spend more money on getting therapy for children. Jails, which are more costly than therapy, would be far less necessary.

CHAPTER 32

SAFE SCHOOL AMBASSADORS® FOR CHILDREN & YOUTH

By Rick Phillips, MsEd,   © Copyright 2008.

Safe School Ambassadors® Has Helped Kids With
- Schools with active Safe School Ambassadors® (SSA) find reductions in drug abuse, gang involvement, interpersonal violence and bullying occur after having implemented the SSA program. These reductions, in turn, help alleviate stress and anxiety in the whole student body.
- Improvement can be seen in statistics on self-esteem, dropout rates, academic performance, and attendance.
- The program also increases positive communication among students and between Ambassadors and the adults trained in the SSA program.

Safe School Ambassadors® Can Help In The Following Areas
Spirit: Embody the spirit of inclusion. Students like to feel that "We are all in this community together."
Body: Help prevent children and teens from getting assaulted. Help students to experience less fear and stress as interpersonal violence and bullying are reduced. Lessen the physical abuse caused by use of alcohol/drugs, since these are used less frequently.
Mind: Teach young people high level, nonviolent communication skills. Ambassadors help their friends to reason more carefully before acting.
Emotions: Reduce stress and fear. Promote self esteem and more positive affiliations with the school and within peer social networks.
Social: Encourage problem solving and nonviolent communication to manage conflicts. Increase confidence and competence for Ambassadors and those they influence directly.

Brief Description Of Safe School Ambassadors® Program
- Community Matters staff assist students and school staff to identify appropriate students to be trained as Safe School Ambassadors®.
- These students must fulfill several criteria, including being natural student leaders from within the various social groups in a school.

- The SSA program training then teaches intervention techniques to these youth leaders to use informally, in the moment, when they see their friends doing things that might lead to trouble. The training also encourages and offers methods for Ambassadors to support targeted students and to befriend or include students who have been mistreated and excluded from social networks.
- The SSA program training includes a small number of school staff and they then meet regularly with the trained student leaders to help them keep practicing these intervention skills and problem solve about common interpersonal difficulties. These trained adults from the campus community meet with Ambassadors in small groups, consistently and frequently, for ongoing skill building and to provide personal support, as well as to gather data about safety and students' interactions on their campus.

Success With Safe School Ambassadors®

- An unpopular high school girl was being harassed by other students in the hall between classes. The students were kicking her books and belongings that had fallen from her school bag. She had lost her glasses. The most popular cheerleader in the school had been trained as a Safe School Ambassador. When she saw what was happening, she dropped to her knees and began helping the girl gather her stuff – without saying a word. Almost immediately, other students stopped harassing the girl, and began helping gather her belongings.
- A gang leader who was trained as a Safe School Ambassador was on his way home from school when he saw groups of boys gathering in a park in preparation for a gang fight. Using his skills and social status, he prevented a battle. By doing this he stopped much violence, physical injury, and another cycle of retribution.
- Another Safe School Ambassador reported that he used his skills to defuse fights at home between his mother and father.

The Safe School Ambassadors® Program Is Appropriate For Ages

- SSA works well with students in Elementary and Secondary schools.
- Ambassadors can be drawn from grades 4 and higher, with students who are aged ten years and older.

Children & Youth's Reactions To The Safe School Ambassadors® Program

- The effects on schools can be felt after several months.
- The Safe School Ambassadors® feel pride in being able to use their status to make a difference. They like being able to help their friends and to help make their school a better place. They take direct ownership of the school and community because they are making decisions about the quality of life in the school.
- Initially, some Ambassadors feel uneasy about confronting their peers, and some of their peers are unsure of the reasons that these leaders' behaviors and attitudes are changing so much. There can be friction between these leaders who are trained and intervening as Ambassadors and some of their friends, but usually the Ambassadors' higher social status encourages the other students to be receptive and to follow their lead.
- Some students do not like having their behaviors or attitudes challenged by their peers. However, most of the students have already learned how to deal with being questioned by or corrected by the leaders of their group, and there is not much resistance. Students who have not been trained start imitating these leaders, using the SSA skills with each other.

History

- The SSA program was developed by Rick Phillips and Chris Pack in 2000, after the tragedies at Columbine occurred. The format and methods are based upon their own experiences and expertise in youth development and on the bullying in schools research of experts Dr. Ron Slaby, Dr. Dan Olweus and Dr. Wendy Craig. The first Safe School Ambassadors® program was launched in December, 2000, in Palm Beach County, Florida.

- Between 2000 and 2006, the SSA program became implemented in over 500 schools and 18,000 students have been trained as Ambassadors. In the fall of 2006, there were 10 trainers who conducted program trainings in 44 schools in one month.

Basic Concepts And Components Of The Safe School Ambassadors® Program

- Students are more likely than adults to know when trouble is about to happen or has already been occurring.
- Students listen and respond to other students more than they will listen and respond to adults.
- Student leaders are the most likely to know when trouble is about to happen, and to be able to, and willing to challenge their friends to change their negative behaviors. Because of their social status, these leaders are not as afraid to speak up to their friends.
- Both school staff and students identify who the leader students are in the school's social groups.
- Student leaders appreciate learning usable skills to intervene on behalf of their friends' and everyone's safety.
- With effective intervention skills, student leaders are in the best position to reduce school violence and other behaviors that will cause harm and trouble.
- Safe School Ambassadors® need regular, ongoing, consistent support from adults to strengthen their intervention skills and to maintain their courage and commitment for being Ambassadors.

How Safe School Ambassadors® Operate In Their Schools

- Safe School Ambassadors® start taking action almost immediately after being trained.
- As they gain confidence and competence, the number of interventions steadily rises over the first several months, and often levels off after that.
- At first their interventions are sometimes "after the fact," or just as mistreatment is occurring.
- Once Ambassadors have been operating on a campus for several years, the social norms change significantly and mistreatment occurs less often.
- The need for their interventions steadily declines and the timing of their interventions moves to earlier in the mistreatment continuum.

Variations For Implementation Of The Safe School Ambassadors® Program

- Visibility of the Safe School Ambassadors® varies from school to school, in that some Ambassadors operate "undercover" and some are known to their peers.
- Trainers leave these decisions to each group, and inform them of the benefits and risks of both approaches.
- Timing, duration, activities and frequency of the ongoing small group meetings of Ambassadors with their adult leader vary from school to school.
- It is important for the meetings to be regular and consistent, and to include time for Ambassadors' intervention skills to be supported and data collected; the rest of the choices are up to each school.

Some Examples Of Safe School Ambassadors' Interventions

- Safe School Ambassadors® are taught six or seven verbal and nonverbal/nonviolent interventions.
- Interventions are used when trouble is about to happen or has already begun.
- The interventions are simple and can be done quickly.
- Example: Two boys are calling a smaller boy names. The Safe School Ambassador, who knows the two boys, might say, "Hey, the kid's ok. Leave him alone." An invitation to the kid who has been excluded might be made as well. The Ambassador's higher social status is enough to get the bullies to change their behaviors.
- Informal interventions tend to happen where there are no adults available. Children and teens often know what is happening or is about to happen long before any adults.
- Another example: An Ambassador sees that a student has a gun and hears him talking about planning to use it to hurt another student. The Ambassador goes to notify his group leader, who was trained along with him in

the program. The adult notifies authorities, who find the armed student, disarm and escort him off campus, and no one gets hurt.
- Getting adult help is newly conceived as valuable in protecting their friends. Safe School Ambassadors® are empowered to be responsible for their social group, have formed positive, trusting adult relationships with at least one other adult, and are trained to get adult help if they hear of a threat their own interventions cannot manage.

Description Of A Typical Training Session
- For two consecutive school days, one Safe School Ambassador trainer assembles 26 - 40 carefully chosen student leaders and some appropriate adults from the campus community (school staff, parents, and faculty) for a ratio of one adult to six or seven students, and conducts the training.
- The students come together, perhaps for the first time without danger, in this consciously established, controlled setting.
- In this training, Ambassadors build trust, bridges between social groups, respect among these student leaders, and between the students and adults present.
- During the training, Ambassadors learn the benefits and purposes of being able to identify and prevent mistreatment.
- Ambassadors practice non violent communication and intervention skills to help their friends and to improve school safety by preventing, mitigating and stopping these negative effects and occurrences.
- Guided role playing is used extensively.
- Confidence and competence are gained with practicing these skills.

Fees/Costs Per Two-Day School Training Session In 2007
- Elementary schools - $3,550, plus trainers' travel expenses
- Middle schools - $3,950, plus trainers' travel expenses
- Secondary schools - $3,950, plus trainers' travel expenses
- This works out to about $100 to $150 per Ambassador/per training.

Estimated Length Of Time Before Improvements Can Be Expected
- The effects on schools can usually be felt after several months.

Conditions That Ensure Success When Implementing
The Safe School Ambassadors® Program
- Key school staff (administration, counselors, and teachers) must support the program, and encourage and allow for the two days of training plus the regular small group meetings to occur during school time for the trained Ambassadors and adults.
- The "right" students (those who fulfill all the criteria for being effective Safe School Ambassadors®) and appropriate adults (those who will actively support and encourage the Ambassadors' efforts) must be selected to become trained.
- The small group meetings must occur regularly and frequently, and the time must be used well to support and encourage the Ambassadors.

Suggestions To Make Safe School Ambassadors® More Effective
- Ask children specific questions about school life. Listen without over reacting.
- Have discussions about school life. Be hopeful.
- Set examples of speaking up and standing up for other people.

- Encourage children who are selected to be Safe School Ambassadors® to take it seriously and be committed.
- Encourage children to speak up and stand up for other people.
- Encourage and promote students to be peacemakers.
- Model peacemaking and negotiating in the home.

Other Programs That Are Similar To Safe School Ambassadors® Program

- There appear to be few other intervention programs that train students to intervene in the moment, informally, when incidents are about happen.
- Some conflict resolution programs offer prevention/intervention skills, but often lack ongoing support for students to practice or utilize these skills.
- Peer mediation and peer helping/counseling programs train students to assist other students to manage already existing conflicts and require more formal meetings and appointments.
- A Challenge Day (CD) assembly is not a program, but it does start the process of identifying mistreatment, raising awareness of bullying and begins the bridge-building process across social groups on a campus. A Challenge Day is a good launching pad for the SSA program. CDs are only used in secondary schools.

Other Programs That Complement Safe School Ambassadors® Programs

- Peacemaking/Peace builders
- Youth Empowerment and Development programs
- Character education curricula
- Service learning
- School-wide anti-bullying curricula
- Positive Behavioral Intervention and Support (PBIS)
- Building Effective Schools Together (BEST)
- Olweus Bullying Prevention programs
- Classroom based respect programs/curricula
- TRIBES

Process For Becoming A Safe School Ambassadors® Program Trainer

- The training process begins with observing an SSA program training.
- Being open to supervision and coaching is important.
- Attending a few more trainings while taking increasing responsibility for 20, 50, 80, and then 100% of training occurs, all under supervision.
- Attendance at a yearly retreat is also part of ongoing training.
- Trainers consider themselves to be members of a learning community.
- Training local trainers using a similar process is also offered.
- SSA program trainers need to be certified by Safe School Ambassadors® parent organization's senior staff after completing the graduated competence steps listed above.

Characteristics Of Effective Safe School Ambassadors® Program Trainers

- Trainers ought to have a charismatic presence and experience working with groups of youth.
- They must also be well organized and able to manage activities and time, as well as be adept at handling several activities simultaneously.
- Trainers must be comfortable with diversity and respectful of differences.

Professional Associations To Contact For Names Of Local Trainers
- There are currently none.

Resources, Research Papers, Books, DVDs, Websites
- Safe School Ambassadors® book and web site: www.safeschoolambassadors.org.
- Fein, Robert A., Bryan Vossekuil, William Pollack, Randy Borum, William Modzelski, and Marisa Reddy. *Threat Assessment in Schools: A guide to Managing Threatening Situations And To Creating Safe School Climates.* U.S. Department of Education, Office of Elementary and Secondary Education, Safe and Drug-Free Schools Program and U.S. Secret Service, National Threat Assessment Center, Washington, DC, 2004.
- University of Colorado - Center for the Study & Prevention of Violence. They have a "Safe Communities - Safe Schools" initiative launched in 1999 and it includes some models and fact sheets that would help a reader of the book understand more about the issue from a school perspective, including steps a school can take. "CSPV developed the Safe Communities~Safe Schools Model to assist each school in designing an individualized safe school plan. The goal of this model is to create and maintain a positive and welcoming school climate, free of drugs, violence, intimidation and fear — an environment strongly supported by the community in which teachers can teach and students can learn." For more on this topic, see: http://www.colorado.edu/cspv/safe-schools/index.html.
- The Center for Evaluation and Education Policy at Indiana University, Bloomington, has a Safe and Responsive Schools Project; Russell Skiba is the Director. For a news release from the University, and a helpful overview of the Center's findings about Zero Tolerance, see: http://newsinfo.iu.edu/news/page/normal/1333.html.

Biography Of Rick Phillips, PhD, Author
- Father, Teacher, Principal, Superintendent
- Co-Founder of Safe School Ambassadors®

Rick Phillips' Personal Statement
Every child deserves to attend a school where they feel welcome, safe, and connected. As adults, we must recognize that we alone cannot protect our children from emotional and physical violence. We must support young people in bringing voice to their values, and courage to their actions, if we are to truly create safe schools. We must engage, equip, and empower the students who are in the best position to speak up and intervene when they witness peer on peer mistreatment. The Safe School Ambassadors® program provides a proven and effective approach for creating safer school climates where it's cool to be compassionate, not cool to be cruel.

To Contact Rick Phillips, Who Contributed This Chapter
Rick Phillips; Community Matters; P.O. Box 14816; Santa Rosa, CA 95402; Ph: 707-823-6159; Fax: 707-823-3373; Website: www.safeschoolambassadors.org; Email: info@safeschoolambassadors.org

. . . .

Marie Mulligan's Comment About Safe School Ambassadors®: I am still learning about this. It sounds promising.

Rick Geggie's Comment About Safe School Ambassadors®: Violence and bullying have been long time concerns for me as a parent, teacher, principal, and now grandfather. Safe School Ambassadors® is the best program I have ever seen. It empowers and equips students to get involved with each other in helpful ways. I have been very moved by listening to very tough gang members talk about the changes in their lives and in the lives of their friends. School staff speak very highly of this program as well. I want this program in my granddaughter's schools.

CHAPTER 33

SUPPORT FOR PARENTS

By Theresa Beldon, MA, MFTI, Bodynamic Analyst,   © Copyright 2008.

Support Has Helped Parents Whose Children & Youth Have Experienced

• Abuses of all kinds (Emotional, Educational, Intellectual, Physical, Psychological, Spiritual) • Accidents • Being assertive • Bonding • Boundary Problems/Violations (Emotional, Educational, Intellectual, Physical, Psychological, Spiritual) • Bullying	• Developmental arrests and delays • Death in the family • Confidence problems/feeling powerless • Eating disorders • Illnesses • Impulse control • Learning containment and boundaries • Parental burnout around their child's problems	• Parent/child relationship/attachment problems • Separation/divorce/death of family members/illness/military service/imprisoned • Severe medical problems • Violence • Self-esteem problems • Shy, withdrawn • Speaking/talking effectively

Brief Descripton Of Support For Parents
- All parents need support.
- Everyone needs support, especially parents.
- Getting and giving support is part of being healthy humans.
- Raising children & youth is a very difficult job, for which most parents have no training.
- Many parents were not understood, nurtured, protected or encouraged as children and teens.
- All parents do the best job they can, depending upon their own childhoods, and levels of knowledge and experience.

- At the present time, a great deal more is known about how children can thrive and develop more effectively.
- More information is being discovered each year.
- Dealing with children & youth who are having challenges can be difficult.
- Extra effort, time, money, concern have to be given if the child is to deal with his/her challenges.
- Parents of children/teens with challenges often burn out and make the situation worse.
- Far too often, parents feel as unsupported and misunderstood as their children.
- Parents can begin to argue and fight in ways that don't result in anything but more pain. In the worst case scenario, they might even separate or divorce. This hurts the child even further.
- It is of the utmost importance that parents heal their own childhood injuries, so they can better assist their children or youth.

Parents' Reactions To Getting Support

- Most parents are often very excited and relieved because they get energy and comfort from getting the support they need.
- Parents getting support often don't feel so alone with their feelings and frustrations.
- Being able to express emotions in a safe place with a safe person can be healing.
- Parents can get more understanding of, and connection with their children. They appreciate the information and the support.
- Some parents can temporarily become defensive, ashamed or anxious about their children and how they have been as parents. They are helped to understand and move through these feelings.
- Some parents feel bothered when they start remembering what happened to themselves as children. It is important to keep getting support when this happens, since these forgotten memories can make parenting very difficult – especially when their child is having problems.

Extra Care Is Needed

- Extra care is needed if there are any developmental or medical issues. Additional support is needed for these difficulties.
- Additional support may also be needed if the parents are deeply embarrassed, ashamed, shy and/or withdrawn.

Children & Youth's Rights And Needs

The Bodynamic Institute USA describes a child's developmental needs as follows:
- The right to exist and be part of a family (prenatal through birth)
  "I am glad you exist." "I am glad you are part of our family."
- The right to get their needs met—emotionally and physically (0 to 18 months)
  "I want to meet your needs." "I will work to understand and honor them."
- The right to be loved for who they are and to be independent, and to expect and get support when needed (8 months to 2 .5 years)
  "I am proud of what you are able to do but I am available if you need help or support."
- The right to have their own power, want what they want, and have their feelings acknowledged (2 to 4 years)
  "I like to see you in your own power and feelings and I will hold family rules when necessary."
- The right to feel proud of themselves and their gender identity (4 to 6 years)
  "I am happy I have a little girl/little boy." "I want you to feel comfortable being who you are."
- The right to stand for their own opinion and to be with others (6 to 8 years)
  "I'm glad you have your own opinion and I respect you even if it is different from my own."
- The right to do their personal best and still be part of the group (8 to 12 years)
  "I'm happy seeing you do your best and I also want you to feel comfortable in your peer group."

Basic Concepts And Components Of Support For Parents
- Change and healing are possible.
- Healing happens when positive mutual connection occurs between people: adults and adults; parents and children; children and children.
- Injuries can happen because of the lack of positive and mutual connection between parent and child.
- Parents of children with challenges need support.
- To be able to help their suffering children, it is necessary for parents to be clear of the affects of their own unresolved childhood injuries in regards to the rights and needs of children.
- The development of healthy boundaries is essential for children. A boundary is the capacity to sense one's self as separate from another and yet still feel a connection to the other.
- Support for parents is needed because the problems the parents experienced in their own childhood affect how they react to their own children's problems.
- Support for parents can take many forms including talk, appropriate touch, learning new information about children and what they need, and how they need to be treated.
- Referrals to other professionals for specific support are often necessary.
- Understanding children's rights and needs is essential for parents, teachers, therapists, and society.

Fees/Costs In 2007
- The cost depends on the type of support/therapy.
- Fees can range from a few dollars to hundreds.
- Fees can often be negotiated. Sliding scales are usually available.

Average Time Per Session
- Session length depends upon the type of support.
- Quite often, sessions are an hour and a half.
- Ten sessions are recommended.
- Workshops can be weekly, monthly, or on weekends.

Estimated Length Of Time Before Improvements Can Be Expected
- When parents get support around their own issues, the children respond almost immediately.
- What has been missing for the parent is being addressed, so the parent can be more effective with the challenged child.
- Children like getting what they really need from parents. If the child has very complicated problems, progress can be slower.

Suggestions To Make Support For Parents More Effective
- Taking courses and workshops in child development.
- Learning about the rights and needs of children.
- It is sad that parents are not exposed to learning this before they are parents.
- Most people learn more about buying a new car or a new dishwasher than they do about the needs of children.

Special Training Needed For Supporting Parents
- Experience with, and education in, Developmental Child Psychology is very helpful.
- Adults who have work experience with young children; such as teachers, day care providers, therapists, and psychologists, are helpful.

Support For Parents Providers And How To Find Them

- Since there are many levels of challenges that children face, the type of Support For Parents needed may be different.
- Parents may need help for themselves from some of the following: Psychiatrists; Family Medical Doctors; Psychologists; Psychotherapists; Child and Marriage Family Counselors (different states and countries have different names for these supporters); religious leaders – rabbis, priests, ministers, pastors; school counselors.
- Ask friends for referrals, look in the yellow pages, look on the Internet. Interview your choices. They need to work for you and be of support in a way that helps both you and your child.
- Bodynamic Institute USA is a nonprofit organization dedicated to promoting healthy human connections by removing mental and physical blocks to the formation of relationships. For more information, please see their website: www.Bodynamicusa.com.
- Another source of support for parents can be found in organizations of parents whose children have similar problems. You can find these on the w and local mental and physical health agencies.
- Be careful to pick support groups where people are positive and appreciative of who you are and what is possible for you.
- Some of these groups can be unhelpful and tyrannical. Don't be afraid to start your own.
- Watch out for websites which are selling products.
- Attending classes on Parenting and parent skills can be a good source of support and can lead to finding supportive people who have training. These often can be found through local Junior College evening programs.
- Also check out local courses in Nonviolent Communication to learn helpful ways of communicating during challenging times. See the Center for Nonviolent Communication's website: http://www.cnvc.org.
- One of my favorite sources for low cost support is something called co-counseling or re-evaluation counseling. This is a self-help group. Information can be found at The Re-evaluation Counseling Communities' website: http://www.rc.org.
- If there are parental addiction problems involved, 12 step meetings can be very helpful as a starting place. Local yellow pages usually have listings. There are also support groups which teach Tough Love concepts to parents with addicted children/teens. People with training in Bodynamics Analysis can be of great help as well.

What To Look For When Choosing The Best Practitioner

- Look for people who have had the most training and who have had their own children, or have done a lot of work with children in other areas – preschool, elementary school, or in clinical therapeutic settings.
- If you can, choose someone who has education up to a Masters degree in Psychology/Counseling/Marriage and Family Counseling/Education.
- Choosing people who have had Developmental Psychology training can be particularly useful.

Resources, Research Papers, Books, DVDs, Websites

- Bodynamic Institute USA; P.O. Box 1708; Novato, CA 94948; 415-258-4805; Website: www.Bodynamicusa.com; Email: info@bodynamicusa.com
- The Re-evaluation Counseling Communities; 719 Second Avenue North; Seattle, WA 98109; Ph: 206-284-0311; Fax: 206-284-8429 http://www.rc.org; Email: ircc@rc.org

Theresa Beldon's Personal Statement

When you understand the rights of your child or youth at his or her various stages of development, it is so much easier to have empathy for her/his behavior. Education which is grounded in your own experience is the best way to learn to understand and nurture your child. This information helped me raise my own children as well as supporting many of my clients.

To Contact Theresa Beldon, Who Contributed This Chapter

Theresa Beldon; 11725 Bodega Hwy; Sebastopol, CA 95472; Ph: 707-823-5216; Email: tbodynamicusa@yahoo.com

. . . .

Marie Mulligan's Comment About Support For Parents: Every caregiver and parent needs support. There are many types of support for parents: financial, emotional, practical support (babysitting, food preparation, respite care, family-friendly employment), parenting classes.

Rick Geggie's Comment About Support For Parents: I wish my pride and fear had not been in my way when my son was little. Parenting was hard and confusing. Even his smallest challenges were very difficult on his mom and me. We did not know what to do. We did not get Parental Support. His mother and I burned out and broke up. He suffered more.

CHAPTER 34

TRADITIONAL CHINESE MEDICINE FOR CHILDREN & YOUTH

By Bob Flaws, L.Ac., FNAAOM (USA), FRCHM (UK), © Copyright 2008.
Bob is a Practitioner, Teacher and Publisher.

Traditional Chinese Medicine Has Helped Kids With

• Allergies	• Fever	• Premature menstruation
• Asthma	• Restlessness	• Rubella
• ADD	• Teething	• Skin diseases, rashes
• Bronchitis	• Kidney disorders	• Sleep disorders
• Chicken pox	• Learning disabilities	• Sore throats
• Colic	• Measles	• Traumatic injuries
• Colds	• Mumps	• Slow growth
• Constipation	• Nausea	• Retarded development
• Diabetes	• Neonatal jaundice	• Hyperactivity
• Diarrhea	• Physical pain	• Vomiting
• Earaches	• Poor appetite	• Worms
• Emotional disorders		

Traditional Chinese Medicine Can Help In The Following Areas
Spirit: Yes
Body: Yes
Mind: Yes
Emotions: Yes
Social: Yes

Brief Description Of Traditional Chinese Medicine

- Traditional Chinese Medicine is the oldest continually practiced professional medicine in the world today. It is a complete system of medicine that treats old and young, men and women, boys and girls - for acute and chronic complaints.
- Traditional Chinese Medicine is based on the concept of identifying various kinds of imbalances within the body and correcting them.
- Traditional Chinese Medicine treats the whole person.
- The main method of treatment is to use herbs in water-based mixtures. Other methods include acupuncture, herbal heat treatment, massage, osteopathy, dietary therapy, and meditation.

Success With Traditional Chinese Medicine

- Jennie was three weeks old and had colic. Every afternoon, she would begin to cry restlessly and to pump her legs to her abdomen. If she passed gas, she quieted for a bit. When she cried, her face became red and her hands and feet were warm to the touch. The vein at the base of Jennie's index finger was slightly more purple and visible than normal. Therefore, her Traditional Chinese Medicine practitioner knew she was suffering from food stagnation.

  She was given a Chinese herbal formula to be administered several times per day with an eyedropper. In addition, her mother was advised to switch to feeding based upon a schedule, rather than on demand. She was also taught how to massage her daughter's abdomen to remove stagnation.

  After two days, Jennie's colic quieted noticeably, and disappeared entirely within four days.
- Benjamin, age two, had a history of recurrent earaches for which he had been prescribed numerous rounds of antibiotics. His face was pale; his appetite was poor; and his stools tended to be loose.

  Benjamin's hands and feet were cool to the touch, and he had a blue vein at the top of his nose between his eyes. The vein at the base of his index finger was purple and prominent. Thus, Benjamin's Chinese pattern discrimination was spleen vacuity with food stagnation, causing heat in his stomach and intestines, which traveled up to his inner ear via certain network vessels.

  Benjamin was prescribed a Chinese herbal formula, his diet was adjusted and he was given Chinese herbal eardrops. Following this diet and taking this formula for eight months, Benjamin's current earache quickly cleared up without antibiotics and he was free from further earaches the rest of that year.

Traditional Chinese Medicine Is Appropriate For Ages

- Birth through adolescence

Children & Youth's Reactions To Traditional Chinese Medicine

- Children usually tolerate it.
- Babies usually have no problem drinking Chinese herbal decoctions (mixed medicines).
- Older children may not like the taste. In that case, the medicine can be administered via pills or capsules.
- Different children react to acupuncture and Chinese infant massage differently. Some enjoy it, some do not. For those who are needle shy, other methods of stimulating the points and channels of life energy can be used. These include the use of magnets, Chinese herbal plasters and poultices (patches attached to the skin).

Extra Care Is Needed

- Traditional Chinese Medicine produces no side effects or adverse reactions when prescribed properly.
- A fully trained and licensed Traditional Chinese Medicine practitioner should prescribe Chinese herbs (often grown in the US) because prescriptions are based on Chinese medical patterns, and not a disease diagnosis.
- Chinese medicinals are only free from side effects when correctly prescribed.

- Chinese medicinals are suspended when the condition is half eliminated, and then the Chinese dietary therapy will complete the treatment.

Contraindications: When Traditional Chinese Medicine Should Be Avoided
- When Traditional Chinese Medicine should be avoided depends on the training and experience of your local Traditional Chinese Medicine practitioner. It is impossible to make a blanket statement.

History
- The first surviving Chinese medical books - still in use today, were written 2,500 years ago.
- The first government-sponsored Chinese medical schools, hospitals, and administrative agencies were created 1,500 years ago.
- The literature on Traditional Chinese Medicine is comprised of 30,000 volumes written before 1900. Hundreds of new books and thousands of journal articles are being published each year in the People's Republic of China.
- National standards for the teaching and professional practice of Chinese medicine were created in China in the 1960's and are annually updated.
- The current popularity of acupuncture/Traditional Chinese Medicine in the United States of America dates from the late 1970's.

Basic Concepts And Components Of Traditional Chinese Medicine
- Traditional Chinese Medicine is based on the concept of balance and harmony between ying-yang (positive and negative, dynamic and magnetic) polarities.
- Traditional Chinese Medicine treats the whole person, not just the major complaint. It treats the root of the problem, not just the symptoms.
- When practiced properly, Traditional Chinese Medicine treats without adverse reactions or side effects.

Description Of A Typical Session
- The usual first session with either a child or adult lasts one hour. Information is gathered about the patient by:
    * Looking, listening, smelling
    * Questioning
    * Palpation (tapping and listening)
    * Taking the pulse (different than taking the pulse of the heart)
- These are the so-called four examinations. In particular, there are specific pulse examinations in infants and young children.
- The child's pattern of disharmony is determined based on information gathered from the above examinations, and the necessary treatment principles are written down.
- Based on these principles, a Chinese herbal, acupuncture-moxibustion (herbal heat treatment), or Chinese infant massage treatment plan is created. With this information, the first treatment is given. In addition, the prescribed Chinese dietary therapy is usually explained, as well as any other "home remedies."
- Follow-up sessions are usually brief and, in the case of Chinese herbal medicine, may be conducted by phone.

Major Differences Of Opinion Between Practitioners
- Traditional Chinese Medicine is the proper name of a specific style of Chinese medicine, which has professional standards of care.

- Some Traditional Chinese Medicine practitioners practice either acupuncture-moxibustion, Chinese infant massage, or Chinese herbal medicine as their sole or main modality, especially when it comes to pediatrics. However, any of these three may be equally effective for most common pediatric conditions.
- There are a number of differences in theory and practice between Traditional Chinese Medicine and Korean, Vietnamese, and Japanese medicines, and Western schools of so-called Chinese medicine. All of these may be effective. However, they are not necessarily the same as Traditional Chinese Medicine.

Fees/Costs In 2007

- The fee is $75 – $100 for the initial visit.
- The fee is $30 – 50 for follow-up visits.
- Fees vary widely, depending on the practitioner's education and experience.

Average Time Per Session

- Initial visit lasts one hour.
- Follow-up visits last 20–30 minutes, without acupuncture and/or Chinese infant massage.
- 45 minutes with either acupuncture or Chinese infant massage.

Recommended Length Of Time Between Sessions

- As needed

Estimated Length Of Time Before Improvements Can Be Expected

- Typically speedy relief of most acute symptoms happens within a few hours or one or two days.
- In chronic conditions, allow for a week.
- Progress thereafter is gradual with marked, readily apparent improvement occurring in most chronic conditions.

Suggestions To Make Traditional Chinese Medicine More Effective

- Make sure the practitioner takes a complete medical history of the child and be sure to answer all of the practitioner's questions as factually and completely as possible.
- After medicine or treatment, the parents should report any changes in the child's condition to the practitioner so that the child's prescription or treatment plan can be appropriately adjusted. (If the child's symptoms change, so usually should their Chinese medicinal prescription.)
- Study the book, *Keeping Your Child Healthy with Chinese Medicine*, by Bob Flaws.
- Follow the Traditional Chinese Medicine practitioner's dietary recommendations that are coordinated with acupuncture and/or Chinese herbal treatments.

Other Methods That Are Similar To Traditional Chinese Medicine

- Ayurvedic medicine.
- Tibetan medicine.
- Unani medicine.
- Greco-Roman scholastic medicine.

Other Methods That Complement Traditional Chinese Medicine

- Modern Western medicine.

- Treatments can often complement and alleviate the side effects of modern Western medicines.

Special Training Needed To Work With Children & Youth
- Look for a professional practitioner of Chinese Medicine specifically trained and experienced in the specialty of pediatrics, with at least one semester in Traditional Chinese Medicine pediatrics combined with a one-semester rotation in a Traditional Chinese Medicine pediatric clinic.

Certification/Licenses Held By Practitioners
- Practitioners need three to four years minimum entry level education.
- It takes two to three years to become a Traditional Chinese Medicine acupuncturist.
- Three to six years of training are needed to become a Traditional Chinese Medicine internal medicine practitioner.
- Most Traditional Chinese Medicine practitioners in the U.S. practice under the title and license of acupuncturists. Acupuncture/Traditional Chinese Medicine is a legal profession in approximately 45 out of 50 states. Licensed acupuncturists typically append Lic.Ac. or Reg.Ac. after their names.
- The National Commission for the Certification of Acupuncture and Oriental Medicine (NCCAOM) certifies practitioners as diplomats of acupuncture, Chinese herbal medicine, and/or oriental massage via national board examinations.
- Blue Poppy Seminars, a division of Blue Poppy Enterprises, Inc., is currently the only organization in the U.S. that offers a certification program specifically in Traditional Chinese Medicine pediatrics.

Professional Associations To Contact For Names Of Local Practitioners
- To locate a Traditional Chinese Medicine center, clinic, or practitioner near you, look in your local yellow pages under "acupuncturists." Or contact the NCAAOM or other organizations located below.
- NCCAOM (National Certification Commission for Acupuncture and Oriental Medicine); 76 South Laura Street, Suite 1290; Jacksonville, FL 32202; Ph: 904-598-1005; Fax: 904-598-5001; Website: www.nccaom.org; Email: info@nccaom.org
- AAAOM (American Association of Acupuncture and Oriental Medicine); P.O. Box 162340; Sacramento, CA 95816; Ph: 866-455-7999; Fax: 916-443-4766; Website: www.aaaomonline.org
- Other on-line resources:
  * www.acupuncture.com
  * www.craneherb.com
  * www.redwingbooks.com

Number Of Certified Practitioners In U.S., Canada, And Mexico
- There are approximately 15,000 practitioners in the United States.
- The number in Canada and Mexico is unknown.

What To Look For When Choosing The Best Practitioner
- Check their education and certification.
- Ask if they have been specifically trained, both theoretically and clinically in Traditional Chinese Medicine pediatrics.
- Ask for references from patients previously treated for the same condition.
- Be sure you can communicate freely and easily with the practitioner.

Bibliography, Research Papers, Resources

- Allen, John J.B. "Depression and Acupuncture: A Controlled Clinical Trial." *Psychiatric Times*, March 2000, Vol. XVII, Issue 3.
- Flaws, Bob. *Keeping Your Child Healthy with Chinese Medicine*. Boulder: Blue Poppy Press, 1996.
- Barlow, Teresa and Julian Scott. *Acupuncture in the Treatment of Children*. Seattle: Eastland Press, 3rd Ed., 1991.

Biography of Bob Flaws, Author

- Bob Flaws is a teacher of Traditional Chinese Medicine. He is also a Traditional Chinese Medicine gynecologist and is director of Blue Poppy Press which publishes materials on Chinese medicine in its many forms.

Bob Flaws' Personal Statement

Because I am a Traditional Chinese Medicine gynecologist, and because women have children, I have seen many infants and children (between 300 and 600) over the past 25 years. I am convinced that Traditional Chinese Medicine provides exceptionally effective treatment for all of the most common pediatric complaints. Not only is Traditional Chinese Medicine without side effects and adverse reaction when practiced correctly, but also it treats imbalances at their root; thus promoting long-term health and well-being. In addition, Traditional Chinese Medicine can be used as a complement to modern Western medicine, reducing or eliminating that medicine's side effects, and making it even more effective.

To Contact Bob Flaws, Who Contributed This Chapter

Bob Flaws; C/O Blue Poppy Enterprises, Inc.; 5441 Western Ave., #2; Boulder, CO 80301;
Ph: 800-487-9296; Fax: 303-245-8362; Website: www.bluepoppy.com; E-mail: bobflaws@earthlink.net

. . . .

Marie Mulligan's Comment About Traditional Chinese Medicine : TCM can support healing and transform the lives of children & youth. I recommend getting evaluation and treatment from both Western Medicine and TCM practitioners for serious medical conditions, such as Asthma. Please be aware that there are concerns about the safety of some Chinese herbal medicines. Please discuss safety concerns with your TCM practitioner before giving your child or youth a Chinese herbal product. I have seen benefits particularly with Asthma, recurrent ear infections, and improving vitality. On your own you can try implementing TCM dietary recommendations, which are widely available and effective. In particular, eating seasonal food seems to improve health.

Rick Geggie's Comment About Traditional Chinese Medicine: Traditional Chinese Medicine works. It has been practiced for thousands of years. It has thousands of remedies and techniques that produce excellent, cost-effective results with practically every type of childhood problem. New applications are being discovered all the time.

I have been going to elderly Traditional Chinese Medicine practitioners from mainland China for years. Traditional Chinese Medicine complements Western medicine more than western doctors/therapists may usually know. With proper practitioner experience and proper training, TCM produces excellent results, especially for children & youth. Select the practitioners who have the most training and experience.

CHAPTER 35

WESTERN MEDICINE FOR CHILDREN & YOUTH

(Also known as Bio Medicine or Allopathic Medicine)

By Marie Mulligan MD,   © Copyright 2008.

Western Medicine Has Helped Kids With
- Health emergencies
- Acute and chronic illnesses
- Mental health issues
- Birth and developmental challenges
- Comfort care at the end of life

Western Medicine Can Help In The Following Areas
Spirit: Caring for the mind/body in skillful and respectful ways heals the child's or youth's spirit.
Body: Western Medicine is designed to cure illness, manage chronic disease and prevent illness.
Mind: Western medicine is rapidly expanding its understanding of the brain and the mind.
Emotions: Western Medicine is involved in treating many mental/emotional/behavioral challenges and illnesses.
Social: The skillful use of Western Medicine supports healthy development and socialization of children and youth.

Brief Description of Western Medicine
- It includes a vast set of practices to treat diseases, injuries and to maintain health.
- It includes specialties of practice addressing every physical and emotional aspect of human beings.
- It is based upon careful observation, scientific methods, a growing body of evidence research, as well as trial and error.
- Practitioners are licensed by state governments and may be certified by professional associations. The federal government grants the ability to prescribe controlled drugs.

- Service is divided into specialties.
- Primary medical care is delivered in offices, clinics, local community hospitals, by: Pediatricians; Pediatric Nurse Practitioners; Pediatric Physician Assistants; Family Physicians; Family Nurse Practitioners; and Family Physician Assistants. These practitioners refer people with complicated challenges to specialists, such as Speciality Pediatric Physicians.
- Specialty Pediatric Physicians deliver their services in offices, clinics, local community hospitals, specialist hospitals, and regional centers. Specialists are usually available in larger cities and are less available in smaller cities and towns.
- Non-Surgical Specialties:
  * Allergy (for allergies); Cardiology (for heart); Dermatology (for skin); Developmental (neurological and behavioral development); Emergency; Endocrinology (for glands and hormones); Gastroenterology (for stomach and intestines); Genetics; Hematology (for blood); Infectious Disease; Neurology (for brains and nerves); Nephrology (for kidneys); Oncology (for cancer); Physical Medicine (rehabilitation); Psychiatry (for mental health, learning and behavior); Pulmonology (for lungs); Radiology (for diagnostic imaging and interventional radiology; for options to surgery procedures); Rehabilitation; Rheumatology (for arthritis and autoimmune conditions); Sports Medicine
- Surgical Specialties:
  * Cardiothoracic (for heart and chest); Dental; General (non-specialist surgeons); Neurosurgery (for brain and nerves); Obstetrics and Gynecology (for female reproductive organs); Ophthalmology (for eyes); Oral and Maxillofacial (for teeth, mouth and face); Orthopedics (for bones); Plastic or Reconstructive surgery; Otolaryngology (for head and neck); Transplant; Trauma; Urology (for kidney and bladders); Vascular (for veins and arteries)
- Allied Medical Fields:
  * Audiology (for hearing); Chiropractic; Dentistry; Dietetics (about nutrition); Epidemiology (health and illness research about large groups of people); Health Education; Medical Social Work; Nursing; Optometry; Pharmacy; Physical Therapy; Psychiatry; Psychology; Podiatry (for feet); Public Health and Preventive Medicine; Respiratory Therapy (for breathing); Speech and Language Therapy

Success With Western Medicine
- Ask your primary care provider. Each one has countless stories.

Western Medicine Is Appropriate For Ages
- All ages

Children & Youth's Reactions To Western Medicine
- This depends upon emotions and expectations of the parents/caretakers/children when they come for help.
- This depends on the nature of the practitioner, diagnosis and treatment methods. Some of the machines and procedures can be scary.
- Parent/caretaker/and medical staff staying calm, relaxed and friendly and patient with the child or youth can help.
- Most children & youth appreciate being helped, especially when frightening parts are over.

Extra Care Is Needed
- Care is needed when children & youth have been terribly frightened by past medical procedures.
- Care is needed when the child or youth and family are very frightened in general.
- When the child or youth do not have medical insurance, families need help in finding foundations, state and federal programs to cover the cost of medical care and procedures.

- Some medical practitioners make medical decisions based upon influences.
- Studies showing that something does not work or might be dangerous may not get published. As a result, health providers are forced to make decisions based upon incomplete information. There is some movement to correct this problem.

History

- The roots of Western Medicine go back to ancient Greece when they moved away from believing that gods do the healing, to physicians relying upon observation and logic.
- Modern Western Medicine is about 500 years old.
- In the late 1800's Canadian Sir William Osler founded the first modern medical residency program, emphasizing bedside history taking and physical examination skills, combined with studying medical records and texts.
- Western Medicine replaced native and traditional healing practices. There is now much interest in researching these ancient practices and making use of what is effective.
- In the last century there has been an explosion in medical knowledge and technology: e.g., the research and development of drugs by the pharmaceutical industry; and the development of new surgical techniques.
- Evidence-based or scientific medicine is a new trend. Doctors make decisions about diagnosis and treatment based on the best research possible. Good research is costly. Research often does not address the real life choices a provider must make when a patient has several problems and requires multiple treatments. A person's conditions and their medications can become very complicated. For these reasons there are limits to its usefulness in taking care of individual, unique persons.
- The cost of modern medicine in the U.S. has become extremely expensive, pricing it beyond many families—even those with health plans.

Basic Concepts And Components Of Western Medicine

- Continue rapid improvement of practices through research.
- Extensive training gives detailed knowledge of the human body, how it works and about what can go wrong.
- Conduct and apply scientific research.
- Be dedicated to not causing harm.
- Keep accurate records.
- License who gets to practice medicine and medical procedures.
- Continuing medical education is a requirement for licensing.
- There is a responsibility to protect patient confidentiality.
- There is a responsibility to give clear information about procedures – known risks, benefits and alternatives for medical interventions.
- There is a responsibility to get consent from patients or family before doing any medical procedure.

Description Of A Typical Session

- Method of payment for service will be reviewed by office staff, determining the level of care to be given. (See Cost Of Service below.)
- Licensed medical personnel get to know the child or youth by being friendly and taking a history of the current situation, past illnesses and conditions, family history and social circumstances. They will talk with parents and the child or youth.
- Ideally, a review is made of all past medical records.
- A physical examination will be made by medical provider–possibly by a doctor, nurse practitioner or physician's assistant.
- Tests and further examinations will be ordered and given and possibly medical imaging of the body will be made.
- Repeat appointments may be necessary.

- Many other tests and diagnostic procedures could be required: medical imaging: x rays, CT scan, MRI, ultrasound, etc.
- A treatment plan will be made based on the existing information and availability of service and medications.
- May recommend self-care, the use of over-the-counter medications or prescriptions for medications.
- Further observation, changes in lifestyle, referrals to allied health professionals, and referrals to specialists, surgeries or other procedures may also be recommended.

Major Differences Of Opinion Between Practitioners
- Pharmacological studies are producing many new medications. There is criticism that negative studies are not published. This hampers provider's ability to make fully informed decisions.
- It is important to get second and third opinions from different doctors about major conditions and treatment plans – if financially possible.
- Computers and the Internet have made home research possible. It is now possible to check out a variety of sources of information.
- Check out information from governments (USA and others); university medical information sites; patient advocacy groups; and independent reviews.
- Caution is needed when checking medically related websites. Many websites have information that is biased toward selling products. Seek sources that are as independent from financial gain as possible.
- Much research is now funded by large medical/pharmaceutical manufacturing companies.
- There is a growing debate about the influence of pharmaceutical companies on what physicians prescribe.

Fees/Costs In 2007
- Costs of all medical procedures vary from area to area, health plan to health plan.
- United States has amazing health care if you are very wealthy or if you have very good health insurance.
- The present system in the US is a minefield for ordinary families and it is constantly changing.
- Often insurance plans appear worthwhile until the fine print of the contract is studied carefully.
- You have some complicated things to deal with if you are not very wealthy or do not have very good insurance.
- State and Federal health care rules change every month…or quicker.
- The medical system in the United States is set up as follows:
    * Fee For Service paid by medical insurance companies
    * HMO (Health Maintenance Organization)
    * PPO (Preferred Provider Organization)
- The federal government in cooperation with state governments provides health insurance for low income women and children. Families have to apply. Programs differ by state.
- Many people are not poor enough to qualify for the programs for people in poverty, but are not rich enough to pay adequate insurance or high co-pays and high deductibles, which lower the cost of insurance.
- Check your municipal and state government for any assistance programs.
- Often programs are funded, but are not well advertised.
- Some nonprofit corporations and some states help provide service for some families in this group.
- County Public Health departments and community and free clinics may have this information.
- *Fee For Service*
    * People can pay directly or can pay an insurance company to pay most of your medical costs.
    * You pay more of your medical costs when you have a less expensive policy.
    * You get to choose your health care provider.
    * The insurance company may have limits on how much they will cover and for what conditions they will pay.
    * You have to keep your own records of your medical expenses. This is complicated if your child or youth needs a lot of medical attention.

* If your doctor charges more than the fees paid by the insurance companies, you will be expected to pay the difference. Check this out before you have anything done. If you can, shop around for a better price.
* Check out the size of the deductible - the amount that you have to pay before the insurance company starts to pay. The size of the deductible often relates to the cost of insurance.
* Check the upper limits (or cap) of your coverage for procedures, hospitalization, medicines, etc. These caps can be by month, year, lifetime, or condition.
* Check the size of the co-pays and for what services they are needed.
* Check to see if certain conditions are excluded from coverage.
* Check if your plan pays for chronic conditions your child or youth had before getting the policy.
* If a referral for a medical procedure, medication, hospitalization is made by a practitioner, make sure that the insurance company will pay before you get the procedure done. The health practitioner's office can often check with the insurance company for you.

• *HMO (Health Maintenance Organization)*
  * For a monthly fee, you get to use only the health practitioners and facilities designated by the HMO.
  * You may get to choose the doctor of your choice within that organization.
  * Check out fees called co-pays which may be charged for office visits, medicines, tests etc.
  * Some medicines and some procedures may not be available or covered.
  * Check out the size of the deductible - the amount you have to pay before the HMO starts to cover.
  * Check out the upper limits (or cap) of your coverage for medicines, procedures, hospital stays, etc. Caps can be made by month, year, lifetime or condition.

• *PPO (Preferred Provider Organization) - a combination of Fee for Service and HMO*
  * Check to make sure your health care provider is listed in your health insurance company's list of network providers. If they are not, the co-pay will be higher. You will likely have to pay much more than you would if you used a provider listed by your health insurance company.
  * Check how much the insurer will pay if your provider is not associated with the PPO.
  * Check out the size of the deductible - the amount that you have to pay before the insurance company starts to pay. The size of the deductible often relates to the cost of insurance.
  * Check the upper limits (or cap) of your coverage for procedures, hospitalization, medicines, etc. These caps can be by month, by year, by lifetime, by condition.
  * Check the size of the co-pays and for what services they are needed.
  * Check to see if certain conditions are excluded from coverage.
  * Check out if your plan pays for chronic conditions your child or youth had before getting the policy.
  * If a referral for a medical procedure, medication, hospitalization is made, make sure that the insurance company will pay before you get the procedure done. The health practitioner's office can often check with the insurance company.

• *Information to check out for all types of coverage*
  * Check to see if your insurance plan adequately covers what you want for your child or youth. For example, different plans pay different amounts for: psychotherapy, occupational therapy, nutritional consultation, preventative health care, or chemical addiction programs. Some plans do not cover these services at all.
  * The network of help for uninsured people or underinsured people varies from community to community.
  * Some services are offered for children/teens but not for older teens.
  * In order to have better health care and to reduce medical bills, families need to find a primary health care provider. Avoid using the Emergency Room as a substitute for having a primary care/health care provider.
  * Your health care provider, free clinic or county clinic staff may have suggestions for you on your search for resources for your child or youth.
  * Some religious organizations can help you through the medical payment minefields.

    * County public health departments and local churches may be useful in connecting you and your child or youth with health care.

    * Expect frustrating waits, and questions you may find intrusive. Keep your focus on your child or youth's needs.

    * Do not give up. Keep looking for resources.

    * If you do not have funds remember to locate city, county, and federally funded health centers.

- To help navigation through the health care system, find a primary health care provider for your child or youth.
- Check out the website: www.nlm.nih.gov/medlineplus. It has many links, including JAMA Patient Page, Health Care Insurance; The Basics.

Average Time Per Session

- This depends upon the problem being addressed.
- New visits are usually 30 to 60 minutes – longer under special circumstances.
- A basic medical visit typically averages 10 to 15 minutes.
- Wait times vary depending upon the provider.

Estimated Length Of Time Before Improvements Can Be Expected

- Results can be almost instantaneous or can take many months or even years, depending upon the problem.

Suggestions To Make Western Medicine More Effective

- If possible, get second or third opinions for major surgeries and procedures in order to build confidence.
- Choose medical providers: who you feel good about; who treat you with respect; who answer your questions; who work with you to make decisions; and who can help you stay calm.
- Communicate clearly with medical professionals.
- Write down questions and observations before consultations.
- During important appointments - which could be frightening or confusing, make sure to take a friend or family member with you.
- Make sure you and the practitioner agree on a treatment plan for your child or youth.
- Follow recommendations carefully and thoroughly. If the plan is not working for you or your child or youth, notify the practitioner immediately. Make another plan.
- Pay attention and report unexpected changes quickly.
- Learn how to use the Internet and get information from government and university medical information websites. Be cautious with websites sponsored by private companies wanting your medical business.

Other Methods That Are Similar To Western Medicine

- Western Medicine is comprehensive and has a unique perspective on the body, illness, and healing. Traditional Chinese Medicine and Ayurveda are comprehensive also and have unique perspectives on the body, illness and healing.

Other Methods That Complement Western Medicine

- Most methods work well with Western Medicine.

Special Training Needed To Work With Children & Youth

- This is different for each medical specialty. (See above.)

Certification/Licenses Held By Practitioners

- This varies depending upon nature of training. For example, doctors have more training than Nurse Practitioners who have more training than nurses.
- Specialists have much more training.
- Board Certified Physicians have basic training of four years of college, four more years of medical school, three to seven years of post-graduate residency and/or fellowship training.

Professional Associations To Contact For Names Of Local Practitioners

- There are different associations for each medical specialty and subspecialty. (See above.)
- Check out recommendations from family members, friends, and other people you trust.
- Interview the medical practitioner. They work for you.
- Check out your state's medical board Internet site to see if the practitioner is being investigated for unprofessional conduct, negligence or if they have outstanding ongoing medical liability law suits.
- Check out state medical board Internet sites to see that the practitioner has passed competency examinations that are required every six or seven years.
- Although it may take a lot of time, check out the financial terms of both your health insurance company and medical provider.

What To Look For When Choosing The Best Practitioner

- Make sure the practitioner communicates clearly. Look for someone who answers your questions so you can understand and who checks with you to see that you understand.
- Look for a practitioner who has good listening skills.
- Choose a practitioner who is willing to consider your values and lifestyle.
- Find a practitioner who uses what is called a 'Shared Decision Making Process' with you, so that what you know and feel is taken seriously.
- Check for availability, including after-hours care.
- Check for approachability.

Resources, Research Papers, Books, DVD's, Websites

- Many reputable medical schools and health care institutions have reliable sources of information. To name a few: www.aap.org; www.familydoctor.org; www.mayoclinic.com; www.health.harvard.edu; www.healthletter.tufts.edu; and many others.
- Check out the website: www.nlm.nih.gov/medlineplus.
- Check out "medicine" in the Wikipedia website: www.wikipedia.org.
- Wolinski, Howard and Judi. *Healthcare Online For Dummies.* New York: Hungry Minds, Inc., 2001.
- An excellent source for evidence-based Complementary and Alternative Medicine: http://denison.uchsc.edu/education/cam2/database.html
- More General western medicine info sources:
  - * Harvard Health Publications: http://www.health.harvard.edu
  - * www.familydoc.org
- Dr. Mulligan's Published Works:
  - * Contributor, Natural Medicines Comprehensive Database, Publishers of Pharmacist's Letter, Stockton, CA, 2007. See: http://www.naturaldatabase.com.
- Farley M, JM Golding, G Young, M Mulligan, JR Minkoff. "Trauma history and relapse probability among patients seeking substance abuse treatment." *Journal of Substance Abuse Treatment* 27, no. 2 (2004): 161-167.

Biography of Marie Mulligan, Author

- Marie has been practicing for over 23 years. Currently she sees between 20 to 30 infants, children and youth per week.

To Contact Marie Mulligan, Who Contributed This Chapter

E-mail: mariemulligan@GrowingUpEasier.org

. . . .

Marie Mulligan's Comment About Western Medicine: It is a privilege being a family physician, being able to provide health care to people at all stages of their lives. I find patient centered care particularly rewarding where what is happening in each patient encounter has more to do with the needs of the patient and their family than with my own agenda.

Rick Geggie's Comment About Western Medicine: Western Medicine has saved my life many times. It has saved my son's life as well. I have found Western Medicine to be very dependable in emergencies. My experience with Western Medicine's solutions to long term chronic problems has been mixed. The high cost of Western Medicine is understandable because so much technical development and research is involved. The cost factor has lead to cost-cutting practices which have shortened the amount of time doctors and medical staff can give to patients.

As a Canadian American I am a proponent of universal health coverage. I see grave danger in having so many families, children and youth without access to health care. Solutions to these problems are on the way.

As with any other practice I am concerned when practitioners are not curious about the value of other practices – which may be less costly and more efficient in making a child or youth's growing, living and learning much easier.

CHAPTER 36

WILDERNESS THERAPY FOR CHILDREN & YOUTH

By Robert Cooley, PhD,   © Copyright 2008.

Wilderness Therapy Has Helped Kids With

• Impulsive/uncontrollable behavior • Alcohol/drug problems • Violent behavior • Anorexia/Bulimia • Anxiety • Attention Deficit Disorder (ADD) • Behavior disorder	• Bipolar disorder • Borderline personality structure • Brilliant but underachieving, disorganized • Conduct disorder • Depression • Developmental delay • Fetal Alcohol Syndrome (mild)	• Learning differences • Learning difficulties • Multiple personality disorder • Personality disorder • Schizophrenia (when previously identified and stabilized) • Stress • Unorganized

Wilderness Therapy Can Help In The Following Areas

Spirit: Wilderness Therapy allows the soul to emerge and participants experience powerful spiritual feelings of meaning, support, guidance and beauty. It fosters understanding the inner self and learning how to manage one's life in harmony with the self. Wilderness Therapy helps youth appreciate the goodness of life.

Body: Wilderness Therapy gives regular physical exercise and healthy diet to support inner well-being. From taking care of themselves in the outdoors, many adolescents develop a strong sense of personal competence along with self confidence.

Mind: Wilderness Therapy programs that provide the therapy component lead participants to understand problems and solutions and foster a determination to live more effectively.

Emotions: Through Wilderness Therapy, emotions calm and clarify. Participants learn to control their impulses and recognize and accept their true feelings.

Social: After Wilderness Therapy, most participants get along much better with their families and are able to stop seeing negative friends.

Brief Description Of Wilderness Therapy

- Wilderness Therapy is an extended period of time, usually 3-8 weeks, spent in remote outdoor locations with a knowledgeable staff. It usually involves backpacking in remote areas. In modern programs this is not rigorous or challenging, but is rather designed to provide healthy physical activity and a sense of mastery.
- The primary antidotes to what is ailing the participant are natural beauty and the need to provide for one's own basic needs (shelter, food, sleep, etc.), along with a sense of emotional and physical safety. These provide a peaceful "time out" from the high risk lives most participants have been living.
- The outdoor component is supplemented in some programs by a therapy component in which experienced therapists enrich reflection, help deepen the experience, and clarify participants' needs and goals in life.

Successes With Wilderness Therapy

Excerpted from parent letters:

- "We have never met, however, I feel that I know you through the fine people that you have chosen to be a part of your organization. It is important that you are aware of the impact your programs and therapists have made in our life.
- "…before going through treatment, I was afraid of [Jessie]. …he was becoming very aggressive. Since the trek, Jessie has taken and passed a Lifeguard course and a Water Safety Instruction course. He is now working part-time at a theater. He is graduating from high school. He is preparing to go to a community college and apply for the Fire Sciences Program. I am so proud of him, but more importantly, he is very proud of himself."
- "I was extremely impressed with the changes I saw in my child and the other children in just 21 days. I never expected to see the progress we did in such a short amount of time."
- "My son is like a different person. Thanks."
- "I wanted to let you know that your wilderness program that my daughter experienced while she was an angry and surly 16 year old has stayed in her heart and soul. She is now 20 and is in her third year of college…Although she had many more wild and crazy adventures following her expedition, something changed within her about two years later. I believe that the wilderness experience continues to have a profound effect on every decision that she makes…She is a loving and passionate young adult, and is grateful that we tried so hard to help her. Thank you."
- "Thank you once again for saving our son's life. Kevin is happy, successful …and drug and alcohol free for four years…Your program works."

Wilderness Therapy Is Appropriate For Ages

- 14 to 22
- Sometimes 12 or 13

Children & Youth's Reactions To Wilderness Therapy

- Most experience a "turn around" in attitude.
- Desire to change negative behaviors is sincere.
- They return home happy to be with their families.
- Most describe their experience as difficult and challenging but appreciate the learning, parents' gift of such treatment and the beauty and power of nature.
- Many find it challenging and arduous.
- Most prefer not to do it again but recognize that it helped, even saved their life.
- Most are grateful to parents for sending them - despite frequent initial resistance.

- Most feel healthier, more confident, and happier with themselves.
- Most feel healed.

Extra Care Is Needed
- Milder versions of the contraindications below
- Personality disorders

Contraindications: When Wilderness Therapy Should Be Avoided
- Physical problems that rule out 5-8 mile hikes with a 30-35 pound backpack
- Uncontrolled schizophrenia or severe bipolar
- Severe depression with sincere desire to die (as opposed to suicide gestures)
- Violent behavior with no remorse/conscience/feelings
- Emotionally very dependent on parents
- Not able to manage activities of daily life
- Children & youth are also usually excluded from the program when they have severe eating disorders, diabetes, and/or epilepsy.

History
- It began in 1980's with survival training schools in Utah and Idaho.
- 1990's changed focus to teaching effective life habits, clarifying values, and providing psychotherapy.

Basic Concepts And Components Of Wilderness Therapy
- Removing a child from the noise and distractions of urban/suburban life allows for personal clarity and healing.
- Natural setting supplemented with quality therapy is beneficial.
- Self-reliance for daily essentials bring deep revelation.

Description Of A Typical Session
- Wake early and prepare breakfast.
- Individual therapy session and journaling
- Morning hike
- Lunch and educational group
- Afternoon hike
- Set up evening camp.
- More journal work or short hike
- Dinner
- Campfire group therapy session
- Sleep.

Major Differences Of Opinion Between Practitioners
- Some programs emphasize therapy component while others have few or no therapists on staff.
- Program focuses vary between delinquent youngsters, those with non-criminal behavior problems, and adolescents with serious emotional or substance abuse problems.
- 8-week programs tend to wait for the child to come around, while shorter programs may push to achieve the same "turn around" in less time.

Fees/Costs In 2007

- $9, 845 for 3 week programs (includes $500 equipment purchase)
- $23, 195 for 7 week programs

Average Time Per Session

- 3 weeks, or 7-8 weeks

Estimated Length of Time Before Improvement Can Be Expected

- At the end of the first session/trek

Suggestions To Make Wilderness Therapy More Effective

- Engage in Family Therapy for at least two months before wilderness program (even if your child refuses to attend), during the program and for 6-18 months afterwards.
- Pick a program length and approach that is appropriate for your child.
- Take part in Parent Training /Coaching programs.
- Undertake Alcohol & Drug Education while the child is in the program.
- Changes in home life, schooling, friends, and activities must take place as soon as the child returns, to prevent slipping back into negative behavior patterns.

Other Methods That Are Similar To Wilderness Therapy

- Outward Bound programs
- NOLS (National Outdoor Leadership School)
- 8-24 month "base camp" programs in the Eastern U.S.: Three Springs, 888-758-4356, www.threesprings.com/index.html; Eckerd Academy, 800-554-HELP (4357), www.eckerdyouthalternatives.org/index.html
- Weekend Adventure Therapy

Other Methods That Complement Wilderness Therapy

- Family Therapy
- Parent Training/Coaching

Nature And Length Of Training To Be A Practitioner

Guides should:
- Be at least 22 years old
- Have 100+ days of outdoor expedition experience
- Have Wilderness First Responder certification
- Have 6 weeks of training with the program before becoming a lead guide

Therapists should:
- Have at least an MA in counseling or psychology, or be certified Alcohol and Drug Counselors (CADC)
- Be well trained in alcohol and drug treatment
- Have one year of post-degree experience

Special Training Needed To Work With Children & Youth
- See above qualifications.

Certification/Licenses Held By Practitioners
- WFR (Wilderness First Responder) or EMT
- CADC (Certified Alcohol and Drug Counselor)

Professional Associations To Contact For Names Of Local Programs
- Outdoor Behavioral Healthcare Industry Council; Box 1064; Albany OR 97321; Ph: 541-926-7252 ext. 202; Email: trish@cfreer.com

Number Of Certified Practitioners In U.S., Canada, And Mexico
- It is difficult to count number of practitioners.
- There are several qualified programs being run in the United States.

What To Look For When Choosing The Best Program
- Check program safety for a nurturing approach with quality therapy work.
- Check age/maturity of field staff, their credentials and average tenure with the program.
- Check program licensure and accreditation, management credentials, and experience.
- Pick program length and approach appropriate for your child.
- Check state licenses.
- Check national accreditation (CAHO, COA, CARFF).
- Make sure that it operates under permits/regulations issued by national organizations (i.e. U.S. Forest Service, Bureau of Land Management, U.S. Fish and Wildlife Service).
- Check program and staff association memberships.
- Check staff degrees and licenses.
- Check average age and tenure of Field Staff.

Leading Clinics, Centers, Practitioners
Some leading programs working separately and together to upgrade standards of care and treatment:
- Anasazi Foundation; 1424 South Stapley Dr.; Mesa, Arizona 85204; 800-678-3445; Fax 480-892-6701; Website: www.anasazi.org; email: info@anasazi.org
- Ascent; Ruby Creek Road @ County Road 12; P.O. Box 230; Naples, ID 83847; 800-974-1999; Fax 208-267-2295; Website: http://www.ascent4teens.com/index.html; Email: janice.pannell@uhsinc.com
- Aspen Achievement Academy; 98 South Main Street; P.O. Box 509; Loa, UT 84747; 800-283-8334; Website: www.aspenacademy.com/index.html
- Catherine Freer Wilderness Therapy Expeditions; Albany, OR; 800-390-3983; Contact through Website: http://www.cfreer.com
- RedCliff Ascent Wilderness Treatment Program; 757 South Main; Springville, UT 84663; 800-898-1244; Contact through Website: http://www.redcliffascent.com
- School of Urban and Wilderness Survival – SUWS of the Carolinas; 363 Graphite Road; Old Fort, NC 28762; 888-828-9770; Fax 828-668-7959; Contact through Website: www.suwscarolinas.com/index.htm
- Summit Achievement Academy; 69 Deer Hill Road; Stow, ME 04037; Ph: 207-697-2020; Fax: 207-697-2021; Website: www.summitachievement.com; Email: admissions@summitachievement.com

- Wilderness Quest; P.O. Box 12; 580 N. Main; Monticello, UT 84535; 888-929-2225; Fax 435-587-3164; Website: http://www.wildernessquest.com/home.html; Email: admissions@wildernessquest.com
- Sunhawk Academy; 948 North 1300 West; St. George, UT 84770; 800-214-3878; Contact through Website: www.sunhawkacademy.com/index.html

Resources, Research Papers, Books, DVD's, Websites
- Dr. Keith Russell's dissertation and program of Wilderness Treatment outcomes research. This comes with a comprehensive bibliography. It is available from Dr. Russell. Contact through Email: krussell@umn.edu.

Bibliography
- "Wilderness Therapy Can Help Troubled Adolescents," by Rob Cooley.
- "How Big Is The Risk of Wilderness Treatment of Adolescents," by Rob Cooley.
- The above are available by request from Freer Wilderness Therapy.

Biography Of Dr. Robert Cooley, Author
- Since 1979 Rob Cooley has specialized in family and adolescent therapy at Oregon's child protective services agency and in private practice. He also ran a whitewater rafting outfit in the summers. In 1988, he combined his outdoor and therapy interests in founding Catherine Freer Wilderness Expeditions, a 3 week adolescent program with a strong therapy emphasis, which is licensed in Oregon for both chemical dependency and mental health treatment.
- He holds a PhD and is a licensed psychologist.
- Catherine Freer Wilderness is licensed by Oregon for Mental Health and Alcohol and Drug treatment for adolescents; and as an Oregon Outdoor Youth Program; and is nationally accredited by JCAHO (Joint Commission on Accreditation of Healthcare Organizations).
- He has 34 years of experience as Therapist and 19 years as Director of Catherine Freer Wilderness.
- He works with approximately 325 children and youth per year.

Robert Cooley's Personal Statement
Wilderness stands to benefit as much from this new use as do the young clients who voyage into it. Wilderness treatment makes perfectly clear the underlying value to our culture of wild areas, which is less obvious in adult recreational and youth camp use. Wilderness has the potential to provide a kind of essential healing through a partial return to our natural human eco-niche, which cannot be provided in any other way. While wild areas have other important uses — such as to preserve habitats, species, and healthy aquatic systems, it is crucial for their long range preservation that our culture fully grasp how meaningful they are for humans too—not just for casual recreation, but for basic healing and renewal that are vital to our success as a human community.

To Contact Robert Cooley, Who Contributed This Chapter
Robert Cooley, PhD; Director, Catherine Freer Wilderness Therapy Expeditions; P.O. Box 1064, Albany, OR 97321; Ph: 800-390-3983; Fax: 541-812-0116; Website: www.cfreer.com

· ·

Marie Mulligan's Comment About Wilderness Therapy: Wilderness Therapy programs that actively involve families before, during and after the wilderness interventions are more likely to be helpful than programs that focus primarily on the youth.

Rick Geggie's Comment About Wilderness Therapy: Over the years I have seen many youth saved by Wilderness Therapy programs from lives of self-destruction, incarceration, and wasted opportunity. My hope is that politicians can see the cost benefits of funding Wilderness Therapy programs rather than jails. Nature heals, especially with the help of highly trained and skillful Wilderness Therapy guides and therapists.

CHAPTER 37

YOGA FOR CHILDREN & YOUTH

By Brenda Bakke, MEd, PT, CYT, © *Copyright 2008.*

Yoga Has Helped Kids With
- It is worth trying with practically every childhood & youth challenge.
- Always consult your physician before beginning a Yoga program.

Yoga Helps In The Following Areas
Spirit: Yoga allows children to connect to their inner spirit, be in tune to their energy and develop mindfulness and self-awareness.

Body: Yoga helps develop controlled movement, exercises every muscle and joint throughout the body, improves posture and balance, develops speech and respiration, tones internal organs promoting better digestion, circulation, respiration, and joint formation.

Mind: Yoga helps children to calm the mind, while teaching them to concentrate, become clear-headed and alert. Yoga provides tools for self-regulation (alerting and calming) in order to live in harmony with ourselves and with others.

Emotions: Yoga helps children develop self-awareness, release tension, work through their fears and be more in control of their emotions in order to effectively express them. Yoga fosters creativity and imagination.

Social: Yoga is non-competitive, develops self-esteem and confidence, and can be done with partners or in groups. It promotes cooperation, teamwork and family unity.

Brief Description Of Yoga
- Yoga means union, a joining of the body, mind, and spirit. Yoga for children is an actively engaging way for children to develop their physical, mental, and emotional health. Through Yoga, children learn how to relax, focus their energy and develop poise, strength, balance, and flexibility.
- Yoga helps the child create connections in body, mind, and spirit by developing mindfulness and self-awareness.

- The therapeutics of Yoga provides a methodology to improve mental and motor skills in children with learning and developmental disabilities.

Success With Yoga
- Linda, a 5 year old with a right-sided weakness, had difficulty with bilateral hand skills. With the practice of Yoga she has made big improvements with balance and the use of her right side and is now able to use both hands more effectively.
- Ralph is a 2 year old who is developmentally delayed and has extreme sensitivities to touch and loud noises. Yoga has helped him calm down and to learn to fall asleep easily.
- Julia, a 17 year old, had William's Syndrome - a genetic developmental delay with some learning and motor disabilities. She was very stressed and experienced headaches and backaches. She had steel rods in her spine to correct Scoliosis. After a few months of practicing Yoga, she was able to learn to relax, feel comfortable in her body and she had fewer headaches.
- Billy, a 10 month old baby with Downs' Syndrome, has been doing Yoga since he was 2 months old. His mother feels that he is making great progress in muscle tone, attention span, awareness, and motor skills and is close to meeting his developmental milestones. He's a very happy baby.

Yoga Is Appropriate For Ages
- Birth through adulthood

Children & Youth's Reactions To Yoga
- It's play and it's fun.
- It helps them relax when they do it at school.
- They notice their bodies getting stronger and they have better balance.
- They can take responsibility for doing their exercises.

Extra Care Is Needed
- Extra care is needed with children who have Down's Syndrome. Evaluation for the presence of a condition called Atlanto Axial Instability must be made.

Contraindications: When Yoga Should Be Avoided
- Medical consultation is necessary when using Yoga with children challenged with seizures, shunts, cardiac, or spinal problems.
- Any chronic medical condition or orthopedic condition should have medical consultations.

History
- Yoga is thousands of years old. It is an ancient science from India.
- Yoga is a system of physical and mental exercises meant to synchronize the mind and body, promote health and well being, and increase awareness of self.
- There are many different schools of Yoga.
- Children's Yoga should focus on Hatha Yoga - which addresses the physical/structural level.

Basic Concepts And Components Of Therapeutic Yoga
- A therapeutic Yoga program for children will integrate mind, body, and spirit.

- Yoga is an actively engaging way for children to develop their physical, mental and emotional health.
- Therapeutic Yoga is appropriate for all ages and all developmental abilities.
- Yoga improves balance, strength, and flexibility through postures, breathing, visualization, imitation, and play.
- Yoga stimulates and strengthens the nervous system, which benefits the spinal column by keeping it healthy and flexible.
- Yoga is gentle and noncompetitive.
- Yoga techniques and methods vary for children, depending on their unique and individual needs.

Description Of A Typical Session

- A session begins with Pranayama (breathing exercises) to increase the flow of vital energy throughout the body. Yoga teaches us how to move with the breath and how to use the breath to connect the mind and body and develop a sense of calmness.
- Mantra – the vibration and vocalizations from music and sound activities help to warm up the body, focus energy, develop concentration, and increase breath support. Motor skills are improved by adding imitation in the form of clapping, hand, and body movements.
- Asanas (physical postures) are steady, relaxed, and done without discomfort. Asanas may be static or dynamic. Using the breath is a key component during Asana to help the body stay relaxed and focused while performing the movements. Physical postures improve body awareness, balance, strength, and coordination as well as increase confidence and self-esteem.
- Relaxation allows the body to receive complete benefits of the Yoga session. May include foot and/or body massage, creative visualization, and guided meditation. Relaxation ends with bringing awareness back into the mind and body.

Fees/Costs In 2007

- Depends on the geographic area and experience of the teacher. Generally, $75 to $100 an hour for individual, therapeutic instruction and $10 to $15 for a group class.

Average Time Per Session

- For infants, 30 to 45 minutes
- For two and older, 60 minute sessions

Recommended Length Of Time Between Sessions

- One to two times per week is recommended. However, it's great to do it more often when parents understand the program and are able to develop a home practice with their child.

Suggestions To Make Yoga More Effective

- Be supportive and patient; give Yoga a chance to work.
- Be creative and explore ways to engage children.
- Parents are encouraged to do Yoga with their children.
- Teach children to appreciate and respect their body.
- Be simple with directions and use visualization.
- Provide a suitable, quiet space to do Yoga at home.
- Be joyful! The goal is to teach children that exercise is fun.

Other Methods That Complement Yoga
- Massage therapy
- Expressive arts therapies
- The Feldenkrais Method®
- Tai Chi and Martial Arts for older children
- Aromatherapy
- Physical therapy, occupational therapy, and other similar therapies

Nature And Length Of Training To Be A Practitioner
- Adapted and therapeutic Yoga training
- Completed adult Hatha Yoga training in order to demonstrate a strong foundation in Yoga
- Ongoing advanced training is strongly advised.

Special Training Needed To Work With Children & Youth
- The more advanced training the teacher has completed, the better.
- Additional training in related fields such as physical, occupational, or Massage Therapy is helpful.

Certification/Licenses Held By Practitioners
- This will vary between practitioners.
- Should have a minimum 200 hour Hatha Yoga certificate.
- Advanced training in Yoga for Children

Professional Associations To Contact For Names Of Local Practitioners
- For a directory of certified teachers, contact: Yoga Alliance®; 7801 Old Branch Ave., Ste. 400; Clinton, MD 20735; Ph: 877-964-2255 (toll free); Fax: 301-868-7909; Website: http://yogaalliance.org/teacher_search.cfm)
- International Association of Yoga Therapists. Website: www.iayt.org

What To Look For When Choosing The Best Practitioner
- Make sure your practitioner is patient and compassionate.
- Practitioners should have a good knowledge of child development, including anatomy and physiology.
- The best practitioners must have many years of Yoga practice.
- Make sure your practitioner is involved in ongoing training.

Leading Clinics, Centers, Practitioners
- Bakke Yoga and Physical Therapy Services; 23606 5th Ave.; W. Bothell, WA 98021; Ph: 425-485-1554; Fax: 425-485-1554; Email: bbyogakids@verizon.net
- Relaxing Resources; Ph: 206-612-6201; Website: www.relaxingresources.com; Email: mary@relaxingresources.com
- The Samarya Center; 1806 ½ E. Yesler Way; Seattle, WA 98122; Ph: 206-568-8335; Website: www.samaryacenter.org
- Radiant Children's Yoga Program; Website: www.childrensyoga.com; Email: info@childrensyoga.com
- Yoga for the Special Child®; 2100 Constitution Blvd, Suite 125; Sarasota, FL 34231; Ph: 888-900-YOGA (toll free); Fax: 941-925-9433; Website: www.specialyoga.com; Email: info@specialyoga.com

Resources, Research Papers, Books, DVDs, Websites
- International Association of Yoga Therapists (IAYT) displays research papers, articles, and current studies on a variety of medical conditions and diseases. Website: www.iayt.org.

Bibliography
- Sumar, Sonia; Leonaro Dinis; Jeffrey Volk; and Adriana Marusso. *Yoga for the Special Child*. Special Yoga Publications, 1998.
- Khalsa, Shakta Kaur. *Fly Like a Butterfly*. Sterling Publishing, 1998.
- Wenig, Marsha. "Yogakids", DVD. Livings Arts, 2004. Available through Amazon.com.
- Komitor, Jodi; and Eve Adamson. *The Complete Idiot's Guide to Yoga with Kids*. Alpha, 2000.

Helpful Tips For Parents
- Parents can learn and teach their children various Yoga breathing exercises to use throughout the day to increase awareness and relieve tension.
- Children can use breathing techniques before tests to help relax and focus.
- Children can use the postures from Yoga sessions while playing outside, walking, relaxing at home, etc.
- In order to help improve sleep patterns, parents can read meditative, calming stories-that include visualization, before their children go to bed.

Biography Of Brenda Bakke, Author
- Brenda has 25 years of experience as a Physical therapist with children and 10 years of experience with therapeutic Yoga with children.
- She has hundreds of Yoga clients who are infants, children, or teens.
- Her degrees include Bachelor of Science in Physical Therapy; Masters in Education; Certified Adult and Children's Yoga teacher (200 hour level).

To Contact Brenda Bakke, Who Contributed This Chapter
Brenda Bakke; 23606 5th Ave.; W. Bothell, WA, 98021; Ph: 425-485-1554; Fax: 425-485-1554; Email: bbyogakids@verizon.net

. . . .

Marie Mulligan's Comment About Yoga: Yoga can help with the healing of both physical and emotional challenges and it can be fun.

Rick Geggie's Comment About Yoga: Yoga has been practiced and developed for thousands of years. It works. I do it each day. Brenda and others have done a great service in adapting it to working with children. I have seen many adults and children helped by Yoga.

CHAPTER 38

ON OUR OWN WE WOULD TRY

Back Rubs and Foot Massages

Studies have shown that all human beings need touch from other human beings to feel loved, safe, appreciated and relaxed. Infants who are not regularly touched with love, die or become very troubled adults.

Back rubs and foot massages are a wonderful way to bond with your child or youth. They are a way for him/her to relax and reduce stress. These tension relievers show the child or youth that she/he is loved, cared for, and important. They build self-confidence and teach the child or youth how to give and receive love, caring and attention as well as connecting the child or youth to his/her body in calm ways.

Most children & youth like some form of foot rubs, back massages, back scratches, or hair stroking, especially before sleep. These help children & youth calm down and release tension.

Human feet are remarkable. Rubbing them and massaging them will cause almost instantaneous relaxation. Much healing can happen through skillful massaging of the feet. Check out Reflexology if you want more information.

Massaging the human back also has a great benefit in releasing tension and evoking what is called the relaxation response.

Massage your children or youth's back, shoulder, spine above the belt line, and arms, hands, legs beneath the knee, ankles, feet. Avoid touching children or youth in the groin area, upper thighs, chest and breast area (male or female). Children get very confused and can get into trouble later in life when they are touched there because a number of nerve endings in these areas gives strong pleasurable sensations that affect emotions and thinking. Always use "safe touch."

Expressing love to children may be difficult for some parents. Some parents don't touch their children because they are so afraid of sexually or physically abusing their children. Touching your child or youth may evoke strong emotions which can be frightening and confusing for some parents. Memories of how they were touched in a harmful way as children may make it difficult to feel comfortable touching their children or youth.

Teach your children about good touch and bad touch. Make sure to teach your children as soon as they are old enough to understand that they should tell you when someone touches them with "bad touch". Teach children where it feels okay with them to be touched and where it is not okay to be touched without permission.

Pay attention to times when children or youth don't like to be touched. It can be a signal of a loss of trust in you, adults in general, fear or anger towards parents and/or adults, as a sign of isolation and alienation, a time of deep hurt, a time of embarrassment about their bodies. Not liking touch may be a sign of communication breakdown, and/or a sign of some kind of abuse.

You can also ask your child to help you reduce your tension by giving you a rub or a massage. Stick to feet, lower legs, upper backs, shoulders, arms and hands. Children often enjoy helping their parents/caregivers. The important thing is that human touch is happening for the child or youth. This helps her/him calm down, relax, and refresh.

Bedtime Stories and Chats (And Lullabies)

Bedtime stories and chats help relax and refresh children & youth. They teach caring, connection, communication, focus and use of the mind and imagination. Bedtime stories and chats teach children & youth that they deserve attention and caring. They involve emotional education. The nearness of another human, along with the sound of the voice of a person who is caring, is relaxing and creates a sense of safety that builds over time. The routine of stories and chats is very calming for children and youth as well.

Children learn language by hearing it. Words and phrases have to be heard many times before the child will try them.

Children's ability to read and write is directly connected to how they talk, how much they talk and how much talking they have heard. Being relaxed while talking and listening is the best way for children to learn language. Lying in their cozy warm beds while their parents/caregivers read or talk with them in a soft voice is certainly relaxing.

Studies have suggested that children who are read to and sung to by their parents and caregivers grow up to be better learners. TV shows, radio, and audiotapes do not carry the same effect. The child cannot ask the TV questions about what something means.

Another benefit of reading bedtime stories and having chats is that children & youth fall asleep with less fear and tension. They are more relaxed when they are listening to a live human voice.

Children & youth wake up more refreshed if they sleep calmly and have sweet dreams of things they have heard/talked about. Pay attention to the last things that go into your children or youth's minds and hearts before they fall asleep. Make sure they are not being filled with frightening or disturbing stories.

The rich language found in stories helps children & youth develop their own speaking skills. Vocabularies increase. Ability to understand the spoken and written word increases as well. Children learn how to understand and use complicated sentences. Children who do not know how to put two ideas in one sentence by the time they start school will have a very hard time being successful.

If you have trouble reading don't worry about it. Keep doing it. Deep down, your child will appreciate it even if they can't tell you. You will get better.

The same goes for singing lullabies to your children. Even if you aren't a really good singer, it's good for your children to have you sing to them at bedtime. And, experts also say that music helps develop mathematical ability in children by stimulating the part of the brain that is used for math.

Children & youth pick up that you are giving them the gift of your time, your love, your wanting to be with them. They can use the memory for strength throughout their lives and when they get to be parents.

Bedtime stories, chats and lullabies may well be the most nourishing thing you can do for yourself and for your child. You will never forget the feelings of intimacy you experience and neither will your children or youth.

Experiencing this closeness helps children or youth grow into people who know what love and real intimacy feel like. As adults, they can draw on this experience to choose the right partners for themselves. And if they have children of their own, they will be more likely to read to, talk to, and sing to them, too.

Help make your child or youth a successful adult. Read stories and talk with them at bedtime. Let the child or youth pick the stories or topics of conversation. If they can't or won't, you pick the topic.

Less or No TV, Movies, Video/Computer Games

Staying away from television, movies video/computer games for a few days, or a few weeks—or completely if need be—eventually can help many children & youth calm down, relax, get focused, find other interests, and be more physically active.

Television, movies, video/computer games can soak up a child's learning time like nothing else except illnesses. Children can waste enormous amounts of time lulled by exciting action. This is time they should be doing things, trying things, learning things, using language, learning what is interesting, mastering skills, learning to entertain themselves, talking with adults and each other.

Truly being entertained is relaxing and refreshing. TV and movies can make people happy and pleasantly sad. But they can also shock and frighten. Children & youth can get addicted to shock and fear sensations –like putting your tongue into a sore tooth. Shock and fear are irritants.

The Dali Lama once observed that many people in North American were very careful to eat only clean healthy food, but were not so careful about what they put in their minds and hearts.

TV, movies, video/computer games are great pacifiers. Children and youth enjoy them. They are designed so that children & youth will watch, see advertisements, and bug parents to buy things. One famous movie producer admitted that he would not let his own children see one of his own movies that was marketed to children.

There are some TV shows that are designed to be educational. Children and youth rarely get to practice whatever they are learning because they cannot interact with the characters and images on the screen.

Of course, TV, movies, video/computer games may have some social value. Children and youth can talk about experiences they have all seen. However, since the content of most TV, movies, video/computer games is not very rich, the level of conversation about them is usually not very rich either.

If your children or youth have particularly strong reactions to restrictions in these areas try to get directly involved with their experiences. Watch television and movies with them. Play the video and computer games with them. This gives you a chance to have conversations to counteract the aggressive ideas that they are being given. Racism, sexism, materialism, thrillism, are all part of the television/movie/video and computer game experience. Almost all involve conflict, winners and losers. Talk about these ideas as you watch. Notice your own attachment to excitement and stimulation.

If your child or youth have impossibly strong reactions to restrictions in these areas, try to look for television programs, movies and video/computer games that have some positive value to your child/teen. Some televisions shows, movies and video/computer games do convey messages of calm, harmony, beauty, loving kindness, and compassion. Others are good sources of quickly absorbed useful information. They are hard to find, but they are there.

Get to know the programs and movies your children like to watch. Become aware of the values that are being taught to your child. Expect great resistance when you throw away your TV or restrict viewing time or censor which programs can be watched or games that can be played. Watch for the activities we suggest that fill in the time in a more positive way.

Long Walks/Hikes

Long walks and hikes reduce stress. They relax the body and mind, improve mood and enhance health. When done together, walks and hikes create opportunity to deepen relationships and enjoy comfortable companionship with your child or youth. They also build self-confidence.

Walk for walking's sake. Go for a walk. Go for long walks.

Walking is a great healer. Our bodies are designed to move. Walking helps the body stay strong, gets rid of chemical toxins, gets rid of mental tensions, clears the mind, clears emotions, relaxes us and aids digestion.

Walking helps us breathe more deeply. Walking and breathing help control weight, regulate energy and help with overall health. Children & youth who walk regularly have more controlled, sustained energy and less jumpy, jittery energy. Walking appears to help children & youth pay attention and focus better.

Walking helps get us out of ruts. Walking exposes us to new and interesting things that can distract us from our troubles. When possible, have fun. Laugh. Point out interesting things to one another. Play games of "Do you see the _____?"

Children & youth need attention from us and they also need time by themselves. Walking with children & youth gives them company. When they walk behind or ahead, it gives them safe time to be alone because you are still in view. Try to tune in to when they need to be alone and when they desire your company.

Walking without talking is often a good way for children & youth to start talking about things that are difficult or important to them. Sometimes children & youth need to discharge anger, fear, frustration, or sadness. Learn how to listen and acknowledge. Avoid bringing up your own fears, complaints, etc. as much as possible.

Make walking a habit--even if you only do it once a week. Try for once a day. Walk for more than hour if you can. Waking up early to walk can help. This usually means earlier bedtimes, which usually means less TV, which is good.

If possible, walk in nature where there are no cars or trucks. The body and mind can relax a bit more. Seeing live trees, flowers, bugs, and animals appears to help children & youth relax--especially if they already have the habit of being in nature.

Traveling to interesting places to walk helps children & youth learn to notice novelty. However, walking the same route often can be interesting too--observing the subtle changes that nature provides can be great topics of conversation.

Walking works when it is enjoyable. If walking with your children or youth becomes an ugly chore you need to re-evaluate and ask yourself what needs to change for it to become an enjoyable experience. Remember that children & youth's behavior and attitudes are languages that can help you know what is going on with them. Learn Nonviolent Communication skills to help you break through communication blockages that may be making walking less than enjoyable.

Above all, avoid making walking/hiking a competitive activity between yourself and your child or youth. Keep their physical limitations in mind and set a pace and find a place that is comfortable for everyone involved.

Walking can become a lifelong habit that can reduce stress and bring pleasure. Do it!

Nature/Beauty/Harmony

Nature/beauty/harmony heals, relaxes, reduces stress, reduces worry and anxiety. It also aids in thinking and calming the mind so clear thinking and concentrating are possible. It engages all the body, not just the mind.

Being around life in nature can help children and youth both calm down and get energized. Children & youth who are around nature/beauty/harmony appear to have an easier time growing up. Children & youth can slow down and relax when they have beauty and when life is harmonious without drama and excitement. They are happier and more focused.

Sometimes children and youth need encouragement to expose themselves to nature, beauty, and harmony. Children and youth might feel awkward being around nature, beauty and harmony. Many children and youth love fast-paced television, movies and loud, pulsing music because it temporarily distracts them from their tensions, frustrations, sadness, and depression. Persist. They will usually get hooked on the relaxed and alive feelings that result from turning off the distractions and tuning in to a calmer environment.

Being in nature, around beauty, and in harmony may take some practice and learning for parents as well, especially parents who spend their own lives in a fast-paced, urban environment.

Exposure to nature, beauty and harmony can be easy: a bunch of flowers in a vase; walking on a beach, in a park or forest; gardening; habitat restoration. Traveling to beaches and parks as a family can be part of the fun, but even if money or time doesn't allow for a long vacation, a short time in a neighborhood park just lying in the grass with your child or youth and watching the clouds or the stars overhead can be relaxing and bonding.

Pets

Pets can be great fun. They do the unexpected, they react, and they interact. Pets can do amusing things that cheer up children & youth and adults, as well.

Pets are very good for children & youth who have suffered from abandonment, betrayal, loneliness, depression, hopelessness and abuses of all kinds.

Pets can help families reduce stress, loneliness, and boredom. If the pet is a dog, take the child with you when you walk the dog. For a traumatized child or youth, pets also can be very soothing. By acting as an emotional anchor, they can become one of the constants in a child or youth's life. Since they need to be looked after in a regular fashion, they can create routines to help structure day-to-day life.

Horses, ponies, cats, dogs, ferrets, rats, budgies, snakes, chickens – and other animals which can develop a relationship with humans can also give children & youth attention when they need it.

Animals seem to have a way of receiving emotional energy from humans and of giving affection, love, or at least reaction. Children & youth need the unconditional love, affection, and comfort that pets can give.

When choosing a pet for your child or youth, be sure and consult them about what pet they want. But also remember to be realistic and that a pet is also an additional responsibility for you as well. Choose carefully.

Regular Physical Activity and Fun

Regular physical activity and fun reduces stress, promotes relaxation, improves mood, increases vitality, promotes health, stimulates the brain, increases capacity to learn, and contributes to love of life.

Children and youth do much better when they exercise their bodies and when they enjoy themselves. Finding what is fun for them can be difficult for some children & youth who have had too many worries and troubles. Fun is sometimes mistakenly connected with feeling good after discharging tension in a negative way. For example, bullies enjoy being bullies because being a bully passes their pain to someone else.

Parents/caretakers have to help children and youth find what is truly fun for them. The child or youth needs to be encouraged lightly, not pushed into activities. Trying lots of things may be necessary before the child finds interests that are fun.

Thinking up things that are fun for children has become a very big business. Advertising on television creates the illusion that fun comes from buying expensive and complicated toys and games or going to expensive theme parks. Try to help your child or youth find simple things that are fun, rather than costly things that are faddish, demand little from the child or youth in terms of imagination or creativity, and are only popular for a short time.

Daily physical exercise is best learned when the whole family is active physically, for fun. Going for walks and hikes with your children & youth, playing simple outdoor games--like tag--with them, swimming in pools or natural bodies of water, or throwing snowballs are all fun, inexpensive and easy things to do.

Replace Sodas, Juices, Sugars, Fats, Fast Foods With Water, Veggies, Whole Grains, Nuts, Protein, Fruit, Slow Food

Fast food slows children and youth down.

Sugars, refined processed foods, caffeine, excess salt and not enough water make children anxious, grumpy, overactive, and tired. These things also slow learning and concentration a great deal.

Try an experiment:

- For one week, feed your child or youth lots of chocolate, sodas, cookies, and pre-cooked food, sugar-coated cereals, fruit juice.

- Keep a record of the number of times you have to deal with her/him having temper tantrums, being grumpy and uncooperative, having too much energy, not being able to stay focused and concentrated, having to be reminded to do simple chores.

- The next week, feed your child or youth lots of water, vegetables, whole grains, protein from meat, fish, beans, or nuts. Cook the food yourself from scratch and eat meals together slowly. If he/she really wants fruit juice, limit it to one half cup per day.

- Take as much time as you can cooking and encourage your children & youth to join you in the kitchen. Even very young children can help with some food preparation if you have the patience to teach them.

- Avoid sodas, fast food meals, pre-cooked and prepared foods and meals. Avoid chocolate, sugars, sugar-coated cereals, breads, and dairy products. (Expect rebellion. Try to get cooperation by saying it is all an experiment.)

- Keep the same record listed above.

- Notice how much more relaxed, focused, energetic, and cooperative your child or youth has become after just a week of this wholesome diet.

Many studies similar to this one have been done and the results are always the same. Children & youth and adults function much better in every way when they have a wholesome diet. Schools are beginning to respond to these studies by feeding their students more wholesome meals and taking out vending machines full of candy and soda. Many schools now have gardens on their grounds where students and parent volunteers work together to grow organic vegetables. Parents and caregivers can encourage the schools their kids attend to take these actions if they haven't yet done so.

It is not easy to change eating habits of children & youth or adults, but it can be done. And once you and your family have witnessed the benefits of doing so, you are more likely to do your best to make sure everyone eats the freshest, most wholesome food you can afford. And you'll be pleasantly surprised to find that some wholesome foods—a pound of oatmeal say, versus those little pre-packaged servings full of sugar and additives—are actually less expensive.

You can also save money—and resources—by buying an inexpensive water filter and using refillable bottles to supply your family with pure water rather than buying bottled water, soda, or juice.

If at all possible, grow some organic fruits and vegetables of your own with your children & youth. Even if you only have a small porch, you can usually grow a few containers of herbs or tomatoes. Children also love to care for a few hens if you have space for them. If available, take your children & youth to farmers' markets to buy fresh produce. Establishing a link in children & youth's lives between where their food comes from and how it gets to their tables will increase their enjoyment of wholesome meals.

Wholesome Pleasures

Wholesome pleasures include regular, predictable shared family meals, predictable routines, playing board, card, or outdoor games, doing art and craft projects, rituals, celebrations, and religious observances--all with extended family if possible.

Wholesome pleasures reduce stress. They provide the opportunity for family interactions, relaxed conversations, for doing things together, and for emotional and social nourishment.

Doing simple activities that the child or youth enjoys together as a family really helps the whole family. Activities don't have to cost money. Wholesome pleasures just have to be as free from stress as possible. Even routine chores such as washing the dishes, preparing food, doing the laundry can be enjoyable times in which relaxed conversations can happen.

Wholesome pleasures are simple, everyday activities that bring the child or youth joy and pleasure. They can be done alone, together, with family, friends, or organizations. The experience of joy, pleasure and happiness is deeply healing. Everyone needs this experience every day or as often as possible.

- **Regular, Predictable Shared Family Meals**
  Sitting down together to a nourishing, home cooked meal that everyone has participated in preparing to whatever extent possible—even a very young child can snap beans—and talking over the day's events at work and school is a time for sharing, caring, and pleasure. Try to make sure that everyone has a chance to talk if they'd

like to, but don't force anyone to talk if they're not feeling like it. When it comes to table manners, try to set a good example and avoid criticizing a child's or youth's manners or eating habits. Also, when you are introducing a new food that the child or youth may be timid about tasting, present it in a way that makes the child or youth eager to try it.

- **Regular, Predictable Family Routines**
  Unpredictable family life creates stress. Predictable routines like regular meals, homework, fun and bedtimes help children & youth relax and refresh themselves. Predictable family routines reduce stress.

- **Rituals, Celebrations, Religious Observances**
  These reduce stress and can give confidence, build self-esteem and give children & youth good ideas of who they are and a sense of belonging to a particular family, religious or ethnic group.

  The routine of rituals, celebrations and religious observances are good anchors for children and youth. They teach the children & youth spiritual values while being a break in the routines of everyday life. Special times like these can be a great time to learn more about a family's original or adopted culture. Learning how to make special times enjoyable – and not a tedious chore, is a skill worth knowing and passing on to your children & youth. And again, giving every member in the family some part—no matter how small, in creating the celebrations is another way of building family unity.

- **Extended Family And Friends**
  Children and youth can benefit from connection with extended family and friends because they can get support, other perspectives and ideas about solving problems and feel part of a multi-age social group.

  Keep in mind, however, that some family members or friends may not know how to behave appropriately with children & youth. Parents do need to respond immediately to any indications from the child or youth of emotional, physical, or sexual abuse from extended family members or friends.

  Knowing that you are part of a family and a network of friends helps children and youth learn to socialize, to give affection and to receive it.

- **Other Ideas Of Wholesome Pleasures**
  Other examples of wholesome pleasures include playing games together, having arts and crafts nights, working picture puzzles, baking bread, making cookies, creating family photo albums and scrapbooks together. Drawing your child or youth a nice hot bubble bath is a simple but special and calming treat that demonstrates your care. Volunteering to perform community service of some sort in a project that interests both you and your child or youth is both fun and rewarding.

  Use your imagination and knowledge of your child's or youth's special needs and interests to come up with your own wholesome pleasures.

CHAPTER 39

RAISING MONEY FOR HEALING PRACTICES

The ideas listed below have proven helpful to other parents/caregivers faced with this situation. If you truly believe that your child or youth would benefit from a particular practice that is beyond your financial means, the following information on ways to raise money may prove useful.

Parents and caregivers are often disturbed by the high out-of-pocket cost of some practices, and the high costs of getting help for children & youth with problems should deeply concern us all. Every child & youth's unique gifts and talents are needed in the world. As more and more people begin to realize this, getting the best help for each child & youth will become a priority.

So far, insurance companies and most government programs rarely pay for many of the healing practices we have suggested. It is the rare parent today who finds the money they need for treatments easily available. What is often overlooked are the extremely high costs, both in money and anguish, of children & youth continuing to have unsolved problems. Methods of raising money are discussed below. Meanwhile, keep in mind that the money, time and heart that you invest today could save even more money, time and heartache in the future.

Some practitioners charge what seems like a lot of money for their services. Parents and caregivers should "shop around" for practitioners to find the best quality that can be had for the money you can pay. But remember, sometimes the best help your child or youth needs is only available from the more expensive practitioner. And some of these practices take quite a lot of time and energy with your child or youth on the practitioner's part before results are visible. Directness and commitment to a practitioner's services may produce some creativity about getting that help. A passionate appeal from you can sometimes lower a practitioner's fee to one that works for both of you and for your child or youth. If your practitioner gives you and your youth/child homework, you can often speed recovery and save money by doing it diligently.

If insurance coverage is not an option, and if parents really can't afford practitioners, you should speak with practitioners about other modes of payment. Although practitioners may not volunteer information about occasionally offering reduced fees, some will provide special rates to a limited number of clients each month. A child or youth may have to be on a waiting list for these less expensive vacancies to become available. Parents and practitioners have to determine whether waiting is advisable and what can be done in the meantime. Phone consultations are a good possibility. Even though some practitioners charge for telephone calls, it is usually less than a visit in person.

Parents may also seek the practitioner's help in finding donors. Practitioners often know of helpful foundations, individual donors, and other sources that may assist people who are seeking alternative therapies. Parents must be direct. Every child is worth the effort it takes to get help! You must have faith that the money will come.

When Asking For Financial Assistance

Ask for a specific dollar amount. Have a specific plan. Your planning and research demonstrates your commitment to helping your child. Be as specific as you can. Include when you would like the Healing Practice to begin. Include the name and address of the practitioner you have chosen.

Prayer and Visualization

Prayer and visualization, have helped many people a great deal. If these words don't resonate with you, it is helpful to find words that do: manifestation, focus, positivity, attentiveness, gratitude, and hope are all good substitutes. These have sometimes miraculously produced the money needed for alternative treatments. Worry, feeling poor and harboring a sense of lack, tend to bring even more of the same. Feeling grateful for what you have and expecting even better things to happen tends to bring good results.

Consider seeking out groups of people who pray. Prayer circles often produce amazing results. Expect miracles: they do happen.

Brainstorming Sessions with Family and Friends

Desire to raise money to help your child or youth can fuel creativity. Hold brainstorming sessions with family and friends. Making lists of ideas, without judgement or criticism, can often unleash interesting results. Groups of people can generate more good plans because one person's idea will spark another's creativity. Solutions to money raising problems may not immediately appear, so more than one brainstorming session may be necessary.

It is important for everyone involved with the child or youth to spend some time thinking about how to raise money for helpful practices. Avoid isolating yourself or being shy about asking relatives and friends to help. Carefully explain your child's or youth's problem and why the money is needed. Family and friends may want to help because it feels good to help. If practitioners are able, they can be valuable in getting family support by sharing information about their practice personally. Practitioners have been known to lower their fees because they were so moved by the parents', family's and friends' commitment and everyone's willingness to help.

If you can't see yourself leading the fund raising, perhaps a friend or relative will be willing to take the job. It is often easier to raise money for someone else.

Loans From Family and Friends

Remember that loans have to be paid back—even/especially—to family members. Not paying back money owed to family and friends can damage relationships. It is very important to make a plan of payment and to keep to the plan as much as possible. It is equally important for both lender and borrower to be in good communication about the child or youth's progress and about the loan repayment.

A Fund for the Child & Youth

An excellent money-raising idea is to have a group of family and friends set up a fund to pay for alternative practice for your child or youth. They can send a letter or make personal contact with anyone who knows the child or youth, inviting participation in raising money for the fund.

The letter or contact should include a picture of the parent and child or youth, as well as a simple explanation of the problem and information about the practice chosen, including any pamphlets the practitioner can provide. A photocopy of the appropriate section of this book may also help. The total expected cost of the treatments should also be noted. It is a good idea to list the names of the people who will be making sure the fund is used properly. Funds can be informal or can be legally set up by lawyers and bankers.

The letter should ask people to donate a lump sum gift, or they can send postdated checks to cover a monthly amount of ten or twenty dollars for a period of six or twelve months. Checks can be made payable to the practitioner.

Some people have had fundraising parties and other social events where people can read the literature about the practice, learn about the costs, and if possible, meet the practitioner.

Insurance Companies

Occasionally, a medical insurance company will pay some or all of the costs of going to a practitioner of some of the healing practices in this book. This can often be accomplished by getting the family doctor and other medical specialists to prescribe the practice desired. Taking this book, along with research documents and books about the chosen healing practice, might help you in getting a prescription. Sometimes medical insurance companies agree to pay for some of the healing practices in this book simply because they can be less expensive than traditional methods.

Shopping around for doctors who are open to prescribing some of the healing practices is sometimes necessary. Practitioners of the healing practices in this book often know doctors who support their work and will make needed prescriptions.

Service Organizations

Service organizations such as the Rotary Club, American Legion, Kiwanis, Lions, Shriners, Chamber of Commerce, etc. can often be a big help in paying for practices that help children. They often need convincing.

If you are not comfortable making approaches, family and friends can make presentations for you. Locating a person who is already a member of the organization is a good idea because they can help with information about the best ways to approach the organization.

With some extra effort, you might find individual members of these groups who can write grant proposals to them. Taking practitioners and this book to meetings with these organizations can be useful as well.

Religious Organizations, Churches, Temples, Mosques, Meeting Halls

Churches, temples, synagogues, mosques, and other religious congregations have been known to raise money for healing practices —especially when the persons applying are members in good standing. Occasionally they will even help non-members.

Ask for help from these organizations in getting grants. Religious groups often have members who are skilled at writing grant proposals. Grant-giving foundations often do not give money to individuals. They do give to organizations that can then pass the money on to the practitioners. Local librarians can help locate foundations to approach.

Including this book, research papers, pictures of your child or youth, along with practitioners, can often help in getting action from both religious organizations and grant-giving foundations.

Grants

Grants of money are given by foundations. Usually each foundation has its own special interest and geographic area. You and your friends can go to a public library and look at the lists of foundations that provide various types of grants.

Foundations usually require detailed proposals, applications, and reporting at specific times of the year. Usually each foundation has its own preferred format. Keep in mind that it is wise to meet these criteria or you can become quite frustrated.

Some foundations do not give out all the money that is available because people did not ask them correctly. Contacting a professional grant writer, or taking a course in grant writing have helped other parents to receive grants in the past. Books are available about grants, grant proposals, and grant writing.

Local religious organizations can be approached for help in grant writing. Most spiritual organizations have volunteers who write grant proposals. They have the skills that are needed. Persistence is necessary.

The *Free Money* book series by Laurie Blum is a very good resource. *Free Money* is a treasure of information about where and how to apply for grants. WWW.ProgresivePubs.com is a website that lists foundations by subject.

Money may have to funneled through a nonprofit, tax-exempt organization such as a religious group, a service organization, other nonprofit social organization or club. Having their support can be a big help in acquiring a grant.

It does take time and energy to research and write grant proposals as well as finding an organization to administer the money. Getting relatives and friends to help with this is a good idea if you do not have time or comfort working with grants.

Loans From Banks

Parents have successfully gone to banks to get loans, even when they did not have good credit or collateral. Contacting banks is a good idea only when very dramatic improvements have already been seen. Taking this book, research papers, pictures of your child or youth, progress reports and even, when possible, the practitioner to the bank can also help. Bankers aren't always as hardhearted as their reputations make them out to be. After all, most of them are also parents.

Schools

Schools in general are not on the list of good sources of money for alternatives. Most public schools are so financially limited they avoid any commitment that could lead to more parents wanting money, even for a worthwhile cause.

School boards are wary of lawsuits that may result from recommending or endorsing anything outside of accepted mainstream practices.

Happily for some children, a few progressive private schools will recommend some of the healing practices in this book. Since children & youth with problems tend to disrupt classroom programs, an increasing number of private schools actually share the cost of treatments. This makes excellent sense economically because the children & youth become better learners, thus requiring less teacher effort.

Making Presentations

When you are making presentations for financial support to family, friends, religious organizations, banks, service organizations, and grant-awarding foundations, pay attention to your appearance and manner. When money is being given or handled, it is important to project credibility, responsibility, reliability and sincerity. It is also important to show respect and maintain a serious attitude.

Giving help is easier when it is more personal. Unless it is too difficult or embarrassing for all concerned, whenever you talk to anyone about raising money, you should take your child or youth along, or at least bring good photos or videos. The people being approached for support will see your love and desire as well as the child or youth's need. The child or youth or the pictures will help people better realize the value of their help.

Practicing presenting your request with a friend is a good idea. Be sure you have all the papers and documents you'll need carefully prepared and in order. Practicing presenting these papers and documents can help you feel relaxed and at ease when you're doing the real thing.

Remember that your appearance will help you make a good impression, so be as well groomed and dress as neatly as you can for your presentation. It also helps to have calm eyes, slow movements, quiet speech, and good eye contact. Remembering to exhale helps you stay calm. Visualizing a good outcome to your presentation helps as well. And remember, too, that you're not asking for pity for your child's or youth's condition. You're asking for help to make things better. Project your own and your child's or youth's great and beautiful spirits.

Records and Updates

Like all people receiving donations, you are well advised to keep careful, clear records of who sent money, how much was collected, where it was spent, and what progress is being made. It is very important to also keep track of dates, appointments, and all receipts, and send a report containing this information to the people who sent money.

It makes a good impression on donors when they receive a record of how their money is being spent and what effect it is having. These records often prove useful in future fundraising efforts. The records show that the recipients are responsible and are worthy of additional contributions.

Taxes

To avoid paying taxes on donations, have them paid directly to the practitioners or to a nonprofit group that has agreed to work with you on this project.

Thank You Letters

It is very important to build and maintain a sense of community. Keeping in touch and giving updates helps maintain community. If you receive any financial support, write thank you letters and send records and progress reports, along with pictures to whoever gives you money–regardless of the amount.

Letters are usually better than phone calls because they show more intent and caring. However phone calls are better than nothing, especially from very busy parents.

The acknowledgment of assistance helps donors become a part of the process and a part of the miracle of the child's or youth's healing. Letters, pictures, and reports help people and organizations feel a sense of accomplishment which can help them want to continue their support of your child or youth in the future.

Ethics

If you receive any financial support for your children or youth, you are advised to ensure that the money was used for the intended practice. If you change your plans and want to spend the money on something else, you should contact the donors to get approval of the new plan. This builds trust and can encourage additional support.

Closing

Invite people and organizations to become part of your child or youth's life. Invite people to join in and enjoy growing up easier.

CLOSING

We hope the information in *Healing Practices To Help Children Grow Up Easier* has been valuable to you and your family. We hope that it has directed you towards addressing the problems your child or youth is facing at this time.

We hope you are successful in assisting your children & youth to grow up easier so they can develop their gifts and talents, lead a full life, and help the world heal as well.

We hope you have been successful in making this useful information available to other people who are caring for children and youth.

We are grateful for the exciting honor of amassing and organizing all this information in easy-to-understand ways.

We are continuously gathering information on more healing practices and will include additional practices in future editions of *Healing Practices To Help Children Grow Up Easier*. Visit our website, *www.GrowingUpEasier.org*, often as new information will be posted there.

Please write to us with your reactions, comments, corrections, and suggestions at: Growing Up Easier, P.O. Box 94, Sebastopol, California, USA. or through our website at *www.GrowingUpEasier.org*.

BIBLIOGRAPHY

CHAPTER 3 - PROBLEMS AND HEALING PRACTICES
by Marie Mulligan, MD and Rick Geggie, MEd

Books:
* *Attunement: Reading the Rhythms of the Child*, by Dr. Bruce Perry
* *Real Boys: Rescuing Our Sons from the Myths of Boyhood* and *Real Boys' Voices*, by William Pollack
* *Reviving Ophelia: Saving the Selves of Adolescent Girls*, by Mary Pipher
* *The Mood Cure*, by Julie Ross

Websites:
* www.acestudy.org; The Adverse Childhood Experiences Study website.
* www.actionforhealthykids.org; childhood overweight and obesity information.
* www.autismtreatmentcenter.org; now the Center for the Son-Rise Program® - offering a unique treatment for autism.
* www.bbc.co.uk/relationships/coping_with_grief/bereavement_effectschildren.shtml; discusses the ways in which kids of varying ages can be affected by grief.
* www.becomingtheparent.com/subsections1/question28.html; an article on "Rude Behavior."
* http://california.startingouthealthy.com/index.html; California Pacific Medical Center's kids' health information.
* www.Childtrauma.org; a Houston, Texas-based nonprofit working toward improving the lives of high-risk children.
* www.chionline.org; for children's hospice and end of life care information.
* www.critpath.org/pflag-talk/gid.htm; gender identity concerns.
* www.drsimonelli.com; the website of Dr. Shannon Simonelli, supporting kids and families with emotional, intellectual and educational healing.
* www.edap.org; the largest nonprofit dedicated to providing assistance for the prevention and treatment of eating disorders.
* www.KidsHealth.org; the largest website for doctor-approved, kids' health information.
* www.kidshealth.org/teen/your_mind/relation¬ships/peer_pressure.html; information regarding peer pressure and kids.
* www.marypipher.net; books and videos discussing the challenges facing today's teenagers-especially girls.
* http://medlineplus.gov; MedLine Plus – a combined website of the National Institutes of Health and the U.S. National Library of Medicine.
* www.mentalhelp.net; an enormous resource for wellness and mental health education.
* www.mentalhealth.samhsa.gov/15plus/aboutbullying.asp; The National Mental Health Information Center's website article about bullying.
* www.nctsn.org; National Child Traumatic Stress Network – an enormous site with information on assisting traumatized children.
* www.nlm.nih.gov/medlineplus/bereavement.html; bereavement information.
* www.nlm.nih.gov/medlineplus/childnutrition.html; information on nutrition for kids.
* www.nlm.nih.gov/medlineplus/exerciseforchildren.html; information regarding exercise for kids.
* www.partnershipforlearning.org; an award-winning nonprofit, which brings schools and communities together to boost learning.
* www.pbs.org/wgbh/misunderstoodminds; a companion site for the PBS special regarding learning disabilities.
* www.raisingkids.co.uk/abt/abt.asp; online discussions and professional opinions for help in raising kids.

- wwwSchwabLearning.org (Now known as "Great Schools"); provides support for parents of kids struggling with learning.
- www.shakeyourshyness.com/parentingshychildren.htm; help for dealing with shyness in children.
- www.stopitnow.com; to stop the sexual abuse of children.
- www.traumasoma.com (very technical); the website of Dr. Robert Scaer for assistance in the recognition and healing of trauma.
- Web search: Relaxation Techniques
- http://wso.williams.edu/orgs/peerh/stress/relax.html; two relaxation techniques, in written form.

CHAPTER 4 - AIKIDO FOR CHILDREN & YOUTH
by Isaiah Wisdom

Resources, Research Papers, Books, DVDs, Websites
- AikiWeb - The Source for Aikido Information: Its principal purpose is to serve the Internet community as a repository and dissemination point for aikido information. Website: www.aikiweb.com.
- Downloadable video (mpeg) clips of aikido in action: www.stenudd.com/aikido/video.htm.

Bibliography
- Stevens, John. *Abundant Peace*. Boston: Shambhala Publications, 1987.
- Deguchi, Kyotaro. *The Great Onisaburo Deguchi*. Japan: Oomoto Foundation, 1973.
- Dobson, Terry and Jan Watson. *It's a Lot Like Dancing: An Aikido Journey*. Berkeley, CA; Frog, Ltd., 1993.

CHAPTER 5 - AROMATHERAPY FOR CHILDREN & YOUTH
by Julia Fischer

Resources, Research Papers, Books, DVD's, Websites
Books:
- Schnaubelt, Kurt. *Medical Aromatherapy*. Berkeley: North Atlantic Books, 1999.
- Schnaubelt, Kurt. *Advanced Aromatherapy: The Science of Essential Oil Therapy*. Rochester, VT: Healing Arts Press, 1995.
- Sheppard-Hangar, Sylla. "Aromatherapy Practitioner Reference Manual." Available from the Atlantic Institute of Aromatherapy; Website: http://atlanticinstitute.com/index.html.
- Balazs, Tony and Robert Tisserand. *Essential Oil Safety: A Guide for Health Care Professionals*. London: Churchill Livingstone, 1995.
- Gattefosse, Rene-Maurice and Robert Tisserand. *Gattefosse's Aromatherapy: The First Book on Aromatherapy*. United Kingdom: Random House, 2004 (2nd Rev. Ed.).
- L'Aromatherapie Exactement/Pierre Franchomme & Dr. Daniel Penoel (in French).

Periodicals:
- *Aromatherapy Journal*. Available from the National Association for Holistic Aromatherapy; Website: http://www.naha.org/journal.htm.

Bibliography
- Rose, Jeanne. *Aromatherapy Book: Inhalations and Applications*. Berkeley: North Atlantic Books, 1992.
- Rose, Jeanne. *375 Essential Oils and Hydrosols*. Berkeley: Frog, Ltd/North Atlantic Books, 1999.
- Lavery, Sheila. *Aromatherapy: A Step-By-Step Guide*. London: Element Books, 1997.
- England, Allison and Lola Borg. *Aromatherapy for Mother and Baby: Natural Healing With Essential Oils During Pregnancy and Early Motherhood*. Rochester, VT: Healing Arts Press, 1994.
- Tisserand, Maggie. *Aromatherapy for Women: A Practical Guide to Essential Oils for Health and Beauty*. Rochester, VT: Healing Arts Press, 1985.
- Tisserand, Robert. *The Art of Aromatherapy*. C.W.Daniel, 2004 (Rev. 2nd Ed.).
- Tisserand, Robert. *Aromatherapy: To Heal and Tend the Body*. Wilmot, WI: Lotus Press, 1988.

- Fischer-Rizzi, Susanne. *Complete Aromatherapy Handbook: Essential Oils for Radiant Health*. Sterling Publishers, 1991.
- Worwood, Valerie Ann. *The Complete Book of Essential Oils & Aromatherapy: Over 600 Natural, Non-Toxic and Fragrant Recipes to Create Health - Beauty - a Safe Home Environment*. Novato, CA: New World Library, 1991.
- Catty, Suzanne. *Hydrosols: The Next Aromatherapy*. Rochester, VT: Healing Arts Press, 1991.
- Lawless, Julia. *The Illustrated Encyclopedia of Essential Oils: The Complete Guide to the Use of Oils in Aromatherapy and Herbalism*. London: Element Books, 1995.
- Penoel, M.D. Daniel. *Natural Home Health Care Using Essential Oils*. Essential Science Publishing, 1998.
- Valnet, Jean and Robert Tisserand. *The Practice of Aromatherapy: A Classic Compendium of Plant Medicines and Their Healing Properties*. Rochester, VT: Healing Arts Press, 1982.

CHAPTER 6 - ATTITUDINAL HEALING FOR CHILDREN & YOUTH
by Kathy Harris, Carolyn Smith, Marilyn Robinson

Resources, Research Papers, Books, DVD's, Websites
- Center for Attitudinal Healing; 33 Buchanan Drive; Sausalito, CA 94965; 415-331-6161; Fax 415-331-4545; Website: www.attitudinalhealing.org; Email: info@attitudinalhealing.org.

Bibliography
- Bearison, David. *They Never Want to Tell You, Children Talking About Cancer*. Boston: Harvard University Press, 1991.
- Huber, Cheri and June Shiver. *How You Do Anything Is How You Do Everything: A Workbook*. Keep It Simple Books, 1988.
- Jampolsky, Gerald, G. *There is a Rainbow Behind Every Dark Cloud*. Berkeley: Celestial Arts, 1979.
- Jampolsky, Gerald G. *Love Is Letting Go of Fear*. Berkeley: Celestial Arts, 1979.
- Foundation for Inner Peace. *A Course In Miracles*. Mill Valley: Foundation for Inner Peace, 1975.

CHAPTER 7 - AYURVEDA FOR CHILDREN & YOUTH
by Dr. Marc Halpern, DC, CAS

Resources, Research Papers, Books, DVD's, Websites
- There are hundreds in the U.S. and thousands in India, mostly on the pharmacological aspects of the herbs and on the benefits of meditation.
- Dozens of articles/research papers are available on the website of the California College of Ayurveda at www.ayurvedacollege.com.

Bibliography
- Atreya, David Frawley. *Practical Ayurveda: Secrets for Physical, Sexual & Spiritual Health*. ME: Weiser Books, 1998.
- Frawley, David, M.D. *Ayurveda and the Mind: The Healing of Consciousness*. WI: Lotus Press, 1997.
- Frawley, David, M.D. *Yoga & Ayurveda: Self-Healing and Self-Realization*. WI: Lotus Press, 1999.

CHAPTER 8 - BIOFEEDBACK FOR CHILDREN & YOUTH
by Bill Barton, Ph.D

Resources, Research Papers
- Barton, William G. *Relax To Sleep CD* and *Clinical Biofeedback & How It Works DVD*. Website: www.biobill.org.
- Clinical Applications of Biofeedback and Applied Psychophysiology; a series of White Papers prepared in the public interest by the Association for Applied Psychophysiology and Biofeedback (each paper includes references to articles, and research): available from AAPB phone: 303-422-8436 (in 2001); Website: www.aapb.org.

Bibliography
- *Biofeedback: A Practitioner's Guide 2nd edition* by Mark S. Schwartz and Associates, 1995 The Guilford Press; New York. "This is a gold mine of clinical chapters with tons of references." Dr. Barton
- Criswell, Eleanor. *Biofeedback and Somatics: Toward Personal Evolution*. Novato, CA: Freeperson Press, 1995.
- Green, Alyce and Elmer. *Beyond Biofeedback*. Knoll Publishing, 1989.
- Schwartz, Mark and Associates. *Biofeedback: A Practitioner's Guide*. New York: Guilford Press, 2 Ed., 1998.
- Tursky, Bernard and Leonard White (Editors). *Clinical Biofeedback: Efficacy and Mechanisms*. New York: Guilford Press, 1982.

CHAPTER 9 - CHILD PSYCHIATRY
by Kristi Panik, MD

Bibliography
- American Academy of Child and Adolescent Psychiatry (AACAP) and David B. Pruitt. *Your Child: What Every Parent Needs To Know*. New York: Harper Collins, 1998.
- *Your Adolescent: What Every Parent Needs To Know: What's Normal, What's Not, and When to Seek Help*, as above.
- American Academy of Child and Adolescent Psychiatry (AACAP) and David B. Pruitt. *Your Adolescent: Emotional, Behavioral, and Cognitive Development from Early Adolescence Through the Teen Years*. New York: Collins, 2000.

CHAPTER 10 - CHIROPRACTIC CARE FOR CHILDREN AND YOUTH
By Lana Surgenor, DC

Resources, Research Papers, Books, DVD's, Websites
- Many reputable Chiropractic schools have reliable sources of information and guidance. To name a few: www.lifewest.edu; www.life.edu; www.sherman.edu; www.parkercc.edu; www.palmer.edu.
- For more specific information on Chiropractic for kids and family wellness care, check out these websites: www.icpa4kids.org; www.cafeoflife.com; www.soulshinechiro.com; www.hpakids.org; www.mothering.com; www.holisticanarchy.com.
- General books on Chiropractic care to start with: *Chiropractic First*, by Terry A. Rondberg, DC; *Discover Wellness: How staying healthy can make you rich*, by Dr. Bob Hoffman, DC and Dr. Jason A.Deitch; and *Enhance Your Life Experience*, by Dr. Joseph B. Strauss, DC
- Resources to help you make an informed decision on vaccinations for your child or youth, check out: www.generationrescue.org; www.gval.com; www.nvic.org; www.vaers.hhs.gov; and www.thedoctorwithin.com.

Bibliography
- Blanks RH, Schuster TL, Dobson M. "A retrospective assessment of network survey of self rated health wellness and quality of life." *Journal Vertebral Subluxation Research* 1997; 1:4-9.
- "Café of Life," *Café of Life International, Inc.*, 2008. Website: www.cafeoflife.com.
- Langley C. "Epileptic Seizures, Nocturnal Enuresis, ADD." *Chiropractic Pediatrics* 1(1): 22, April 1994.
- Lipton, PhD, B. *The Biology of Belief*. California: Mountain of Love/Elite Books, 2005.
- Mariano MJ, Langrell PM. "A longitudinal assessment of chiropractic care using a survey of self rated health, wellness and quality of life: A pilot study." Journal of Vertebral Subluxation Research 1999; 3:78-82.
- Phillips N. "Vertebral Subluxation And Otitis Media: a case study." *Journal of Chiropractic Research and Clinical Investigation* 8(2): 38, July 1992.
- Rubinstein H. "Case Study: Autism." *Chiropractic Pediatrics* 1(1): 23, April 1994.

CHAPTER 11 - CRANIOSACRAL FOR CHILDREN & YOUTH
by Hugh Milne, DO

Resources, Research Papers, Books, DVD's, Websites
- Feeley, Richard; "Clinical Cranial Osteopathy".
- Blood, S.D. "The Craniosacral Mechanism and the Temporomandibular Joint." *Journal of the American Osteopathic Association* 86, no. 8 (1986): 512-9.

Bibliography
- Milne, Hugh. *The Heart of Listening: A Visionary Approach To Craniosacral Work.* Berkeley, CA: North Atlantic Books, 1995.
- Upledger, John and Jon Vredevoogd. *Craniosacral Therapy.* Seattle: Eastland Press, 1983.

CHAPTER 12 - DEVELOPMENTAL OPTOMETRY FOR CHILDREN & YOUTH
by Dr. Tanya Mahaphon, OD, FCOVD, FAAO

Research Papers
- Pediatric Eye Disease Investigator Group. "A Randomized Pilot Study of Near Activities versus Non-near Activities During Patching Therapy for Amblyopia." (ATS6) *JAAPOS* 9, no 2 (2005): 129-36.
- Granet DB, Gomi CF, Ventura R, Miller-Scholte A. "The Relationship between Convergence Insufficiency and ADHD." *Strabismus* 13, no 4 (2005): 163-8.
- Scheiman M, Mitchell GL, Cotter S, et al. "A randomized clinical trial of treatments for convergence insufficiency in children." *Arch Ophthalmol* 123 (2005): 14-24.
- Maples WC. "Visual factors that significantly impact academic performance." *Optometry* 74, no 1 (2003): 35-49.

Bibliography
The following books may be obtained directly from the Optometric Extension Program (OEP). (See: www.oep.org.)
- Getman, G.N. *How to Develop Your Child's Intelligence.* Santa Ana, CA: OEP/VisionExtension, Inc.
- Getman, G.N. *Smart in Everything…Except School.* Santa Ana, CA: OEP/VisionExtension, Inc.
- Bing, Lois, and George D. Spache and Lillian Hinds. *Vision and School Success.* Santa Ana, CA: OEP/VisionExtension, Inc.
- Cook, David. *When Your Child Struggles The Myths of 20/20 Vision: What Every Parent Needs To Know.* Marietta, GA: Cook Vision Therapy Centers, 1992.
- Richmond, Hazel and Dawkins. *Suddenly Successful: How Behavioral Optometry Helps You Overcome Learning, Health and Behavior Problems.* Santa Ana, CA: OEP/VisionExtension, Inc., 1990.

CHAPTER 13 - DRUMMING FOR CHILDREN & YOUTH
by Christine Stevens and Heather MacTavish

Research Papers
Note: Most of the research has been done on adults, so papers pertaining to children specifically are not available.
- Lang (1990). "Supplementary Motor Area Activation While Tapping Bimanually Different Rhythms in Musicians." *Experimental Brain Research*, 79, 504-514.
- "Central timing system" found in bimanual motor sequences. Central mesial cortex prevails, including parietal cortex, cerebellum and basal ganglia.
- Mark Anshel and D.Q. Marsi (1978). "Effect of Music and Rhythm on Physical Performance." *Research Quarterly*, 49, 109-113
- Bittman et al, Composite Effects of Group Drumming Music Therapy on Modulation of Neuroendocrine-Immune Parameters in Normal Subjects (2001) *Journal of Alternative Therapy.* Jan, 2001. p. 38-47.

- Stevens, Christine. "Rainbows of Rhythm: Rebuilding After the Storm of Columbine." Accessed through the UpBeat Drum Circles website: www.ubdrumcircles.com/article_rainbow.html.

Bibliography
- Stevens, Christine. *The Art and Heart of Drum Circles*. Milwaukee: Hal Leonard Co., 2003.
- Stevens, Christine. *The Healing Drum Kit*. Louisville, CO: Sounds True, 2005.
- Tomaino, Concetta. (1998). "Clinical Applications of Music in Neurologic Rehabilitation." St. Louis. MMB Music, Inc.
- Friedman, Robert. *The Healing Power of the Drum*. Gilsum,NH: Whitecliffs Media, 2000.
- Bradway, Deborah. *Music Therapy as a treatment with at-risk children and adolescents*. Available at the Remo website: www.remo.com.

CHAPTER 14 - EMDR: EYE MOVEMENT DESENSITIZATION & REPROCESSING FOR CHILDREN & YOUTH

by Sandra Wilson, PhD and Robert Tinker, PhD,

Resources, Research Papers, Books, DVDs, Websites
- Refer to the EMDR Institute – See above.
- Carlson, JG, Chemtob, CM, Rusnak, K, Hedlund, NL, and Muraoka, MY. "EMDR (Eye Movement Desensitization and Reprocessing) Treatment for Combat-Related Posttraumatic Stress Disorder." *Journal of Traumatic Stress* 11, no. 1 (1998): 3-24.
- Chemtob, CM, Nakashima, JP, and Carlson, JG. "Brief treatment for elementary school children with disaster-related PTSD: A field study." *Journal of Clinical Psychology* 58, no. 1 (2002): 99-112.
- De Jongh, A, Ten Broeke, E. and Renssen, MR. "Treatment of specific phobias with EMDR (Eye Movement Desensitization and Reprocessing): Protocol, empirical status, and conceptual issues." *Journal of Anxiety Disorders* 13, no. 1-2 (1999): 69-85.
- Greenwald, R. "Applying EMDR in the treatment of traumatized children: Five case studies." *Anxiety Disorders Practice Journal* 1, (1994): 83-97.
- Puffer, MK, Greenwald, R, and Elrod, DE. "A single session EMDR study with twenty traumatized children and adolescents." *Traumatology* 3, no. 2 (1998).
- Wilson, SA, Logan, C, Becker, LA, and Tinker, RH. (1999, June). "EMDR as a stress management tool for police officers." Paper presented to the annual conference of the EMDR International Association, Las Vegas, Nevada.

Bibliography
- Refer to the EMDR Institute: www.emdr.com.
- Tinker, Robert and Sandra Wilson. *Through the Eyes of a Child*. New York: W.W. Norton & Company, 1999.
- Shapiro, Francine and Margot Silk Forrest. *EMDR: The Breakthrough "Eye Movement" Therapy for Overcoming Anxiety, Stress, and Trauma*. New York: Basic Books, 1997.
- Parnell, Laura. *Eye Movement Desensitization and Reprocessing: Transforming Trauma*. New York: W.W. Norton & Company, 1997.
- Lovett, Joan. *Small Wonders: Healing Childhood Trauma with EMDR*. New York: The Free Press, 1999.

CHAPTER 15 - ENVIRONMENTALLY HEALTHY HOME CONSULTANTS

by Susan Bahl

Resources, Research Papers, Books, DVD's, Websites
- Please look up papers outlined on these websites: (If you don't have a computer, ask your local librarian to help you.).
    * Centers for Disease Control and Prevention Environmental Health; 1600 Clifton Rd.; Atlanta, GA 30333; 800-311-3435, or 404)-498-1515; Website: http://www.cdc.gov/Environmental/.

- * Children's Environmental Health Network: http://www.cehn.org/cehn/resourceguide/rghome.html.
- * American Lung Association, Indoor Air Quality Education for Schools, Parents, etc.: http://www.lungusa.org/air/air00_iaq.html.
- * Home water testing/treatment: http://epa.gov/safewater/faq/faq.html#test.
- * Water quality standards are also available at the website of the Environmental Protection Agency: http://epa.gov/safewater/faq/faq.html#test.
- * Advice from EPA on mold: http://www.epa.gov/iaq/molds/moldguide.html.
- * Healthy House Institute provides extensive information about creating a healthy home environment. Their website is: http://www.healthyhouseinstitute.com/.

- There are videos covering a variety of topics available from the website of Dr. Doris J. Rapp: http://www.drrapp.com/publications.htm.
- American Chemical Society. Available at: www.acs.org.
- Natural Home Magazine. Available at: www.naturalhomemagazine.com.
- Newsletter: *Our Toxic Times* by Chemical Injury Information Network. Available online at: http://www.ciin.org/.

Bibliography
- Hidden Exposures: Many people, including pregnant women, come into contact with things in their day-to-day environment that may affect their health and their ability to have a healthy child. Website: http://www.womenshealthmatters.ca/centres/environmental/Healthy-Environments/hidden_exposures.html.
- Baker-Laporte, Paula, Erica Elliott and John Banta. *Prescriptions for a Healthy House: A Practical Guide for Architects, Builders and Homeowners.* Pennsylvania: New Society Publishers, 2001.
- Bower, Lynn Marie. *Creating A Healthy Household: The Ultimate Guide For Healthier, Safer, Less-Toxic Living.* Indiana: Healthy House Institute, 2000.
- Colborn, Theo, Dianne Dumanoski and John Peter Myers. *Our Stolen Future: Are We Threatening Our Fertility, Intelligence and Survival? A Scientific Detective Story.* New York: Penguin, 1996.
- Dadd, Debra Lynn. *Home Safe Home: Protecting Yourself and Your Family from Everyday Toxics and Harmful Household Products.* New York: Tarcher/Penguin, 1997.
- Pinsky, Mark. *EMF Book: What You Should Know About Electromagnetic Fields, Electromagnetic Radiation & Your Health.* New York: Grand Central Publishing, 1995.
- Rapp, Doris J. *Is This Your Child?: Discovering and Treating Unrecognized Allergies.* New York: William Morrow & Co (Harper), 1991.
- Rapp, Doris J. *Is This Your Child's World? How You Can Fix the Schools and Homes That Are Making Your Children Sick.* New York: Bantam, 1997.
- Lewis, Grace Ross. *1001 Chemicals in Everyday Products.* New York: Wiley-Interscience, 1998.
- Schettler, Ted, Jill Stein, Fay Reich, Maria Valenti and David Wallinga. *In Harms Way: Toxic Threats to Child Development.* Massachusetts: Greater Boston Physicians for Social Responsibility, 2000. No longer in print. May be downloaded here: http://psr.igc.org/ihw-download-report.htm.
- Steinman, David and Samuel S. Epstein. *The Safe Shopper's Bible: A Consumer's Guide to Nontoxic Household Products, Cosmetics, and Food.* New York: John Wiley & Sons, 1995.

CHAPTER 16 - EXPRESSIVE ARTS THERAPY FOR CHILDREN & YOUTH

by Lore Caldwell, LCMHC, AT, RDT

Research Papers
- Brooke, Stephanie. "Art Therapy: An approach to working with sexual abuse survivors." *The Arts in Psychotherapy* 22, no. 5, (1995): pp. 447-466.
- Group Art Therapy with mothers of sexually abused children. Hagood, Marilyn M. MFCC ATR, *Arts in Psychotherapy.* 1991, vol.8: #1.
Bibliography
- Allen, Pat. *Art Is a Way of Knowing.* Boston: Shambala Publications, 1995.

- Lewis, Penny and David Read Johnson, (Editors). *Current Approaches in Drama Therapy.* Springfield, IL: Charles C. Thomas Publisher, 2000.
- Dossick, Jane and Eugene Shea. *Creative Therapy: 52 Exercises for Groups.* Sarasota: Professional Resource Exchange, 1988.

CHAPTER 17 - THE FELDENKRAIS METHOD® FOR CHILDREN & YOUTH
by Russell Delman and Linda Evans Delman

Resources, Research Papers, Books, DVD's, Websites
- You will find many research papers available on the International Feldenkrais Federation website. Go to: http://feldenkrais-method.org/en/flexinode/list/5.
- Shelhav-Silberbush, Chava. "The Feldenkrais Method for Children with Cerebral Palsy." MS Thesis. Boston University School of Education, *Feldenkrais Resources,* 1988.

Bibliography
- Rosenfeld, Albert. "Teaching the Body How to Program the Brain is Moshe's Miracle." *Smithsonian,* (January 1981): pp52-58.
- RosenHoltz PhD, Stephen. "Monkey Moves" Video. Available through Amazon.com.
- Shafarman, Steven. *Awareness Heals.* Reading, MA: Perseus Books, 1997.

CHAPTER 18 - FLOWER ESSENCES FOR CHILDREN & YOUTH
by Katharina Johnson, MD (Austria)

Research Papers
- Recent research into the links between emotions and the immune system supports and reinforces the view that emotional balance and well-being directly affect and influence our physical health. More and more medical experts now agree that a healthy mind really does ensure a healthy body.
- The Flower Essence Society does research on Flower Essences on an ongoing basis. Studies are published on their website.

Bibliography
- Kaminski, Patricia and Richard Katz. *Flower Essence Repertory.* Nevada City, CA: Flower Essence Society, Rev Ed 1994.
- Mazzarella, Barbara. *Bach Flower Remedies for Children: A Parents' Guide.* Rochester, VT: Healing Arts Press, 1994.
- Arnos, Kathy. *The Complete Teething Guide: From Birth to Adolescence.* Van Nuys, CA: Spirit Dance Publishing, 2003.
- Soo Hwa, Yeo. *Healing the Family with Bach Flower Essences.* Sunnyvale, CA: 2005.
- Wesson, Nicky. *Natural Mothering: A Guide to Holistic Therapies for Pregnancy, Birth, and Early Childhood.* Rochester, VT: Healing Arts Press, 1997.

CHAPTER 19 - HERBOLOGY FOR CHILDREN & YOUTH
by Karyn Sanders

Resources, Research Papers, Books, DVDs, Websites
- Numerous articles by Michael Moore, including Herbal Energetics in Clinical Practice: www.all-natural.com/herbindx.html.
- Karyn Sanders at www.blueotterschool.com.

Bibliography
- Gladstar, Rosemary. *Herbal Remedies for Children's Health.* Pound, Vermont: Storey Books. 1999.

- Hutchins, Alma R. *Indian Herbs of North America*. Boston: Shambala Press, 1991.
- Moore, Michael. *Herbal Formulas for Clinic and Home*. New Canaan, CT: Keats, 1995.

CHAPTER 20 - HOMEOPATHY FOR CHILDREN & YOUTH
by Dian Wagner, Randy Jane Reitzes, LVN, CMT, CCHH and Lisette Narragon CCH, BRCP

Research Papers

- J.Kleijnan, P.Knipschild, and G ter Riet. "Clinical Trials of Homeopathy." *British Medical Journal,* 302 (1991): 316-23.
- Jacobs, L., M. Jimenez, S.Gloyd, and D. Crothers, "Treatment of Acute Childhood Diarrhea with Homeopathic Medicine: A Randomized Clinical Trial in Nicaragua." *Pediatrics* 93, 5 (1994): 719-25.
- National Center for Complementary and Alternative Medicine and the National Institutes of Health website on homeopathic research: http://nccam.nih.gov.
- The Samueli Institute's website provides numerous articles on Homeopathy. Website: www.siib.org.

Bibliography

- The best sources for books on Homeopathy are the two largest Homeopathic booksellers in the U.S.:
  1. Minimum Price Books; P.O. Box 2187; Blaine, WA 98231; (UPS only: 250 H Street, Blaine, WA 98230); Orders: 800-663-8272; Fax: 604-597-8304; Website: www.minimum.com: Email: orders@minimum.com.
  2. Homeopathic Educational Services; 2124B Kittredge St.; Berkeley, CA 94704; 510-649-0294; Fax: 510-649-1955; Website: www.homeopathic.com; Email: available through the website.
- Homeopathy Today: The magazine of the National Center for Homeopathy. (See above.)
- Reichenberg-Ullman, Judyth, and Robert Ullman. *Rage Free Kids*. Roseville, CA: Prima Lifestyles, 1999.
- Shalts, Edward. *The American Institute of Homeopathy Handbook for Parents: A Guide to Healthy Treatment for Everything from Colds and Allergies to ADHD, Obesity, and Depression*. San Francisco: Jossey-Bass, 2005.
- Lansky, Amy. *The Impossible Cure: The Promise of Homeopathy*. Portola Valley, CA: R. L. Ranch Press, 2003.
- Kruzel, Thomas. *The Homeopathic Emergency Guide: A Quick Reference Guide to Accurate Homeopathic Care*. Berkeley, CA: North Atlantic Books, 1992.

CHAPTER 21 - HYPNOTHERAPY FOR CHILDREN & YOUTH
by Randi Farkas, MA, MFT

Bibliography

- Olness et al: (1998) Wart Regression in Children, in *The American Journal of Clinical Hypnotherapy*.
- Ames, R., Madrid, A., Skolek, S., and Brown, G. "Does Maternal-Infant Bonding Therapy Improve Breathing in Asthmatic Children?" *The Journal of the Association of Prenatal and Perinatal Psychology and Health* 15, no. 2 (2000): 99-117.
- The journal that has great articles about Hypnotherapy in general is the *American Journal of Clinical Hypnotherapy*. When you access ASCH's website (see above), you can find short versions of articles.
- Haley, Jay. *Uncommon Therapy: The Psychiatric Techniques of Milton H. Erickson, M.D.* New York: W.W. Norton, 1993.
- Olness, Karen and Daniel Kohen. *Hypnosis and Hypnotherapy with Children: Third Edition*. New York: The Guilford Press, 1996.
- Temes, Roberta: *The Complete Idiot's Guide to Hypnosis, 2nd Edition*. New York: Alpha Books, 2004.
- Mills, Joyce and Richard Crowley. *Therapeutic Metaphors for Children and the Child Within*. Philadelphia: Brunner/Mazel, 1986.
- Duke, Robert. *Hypnotherapy for Troubled Children*. East Rutherford, NJ: New Horizon Press, 1985.

CHAPTER 22 - INDEPENDENT STUDY FOR CHILDREN & YOUTH

by June Nason, MsEd

Resources And Websites

- A-Z Home's Cool. This is a list of California home school organizations with state charters. See their website: http://homeschooling.gomilpitas.com.
- California Department of Education's Independent Study Program. See their website: http://www.cde.ca.gov. This site is designed for schools wanting to run an independent study program as well.
- California Department of Education Manual for Independent Study outlines curriculum and instruction for independent study teachers from the California Department of Education…useful information for community resources to enhance curriculum. See: http://www.cde.ca.gov.
- California Consortium for Independent Study. Website for Independent Study Teachers and a state wide organization interested in the advancement of independent study programs. See: http://www.ccis.org.
- Currie, Carol. "History of Homeschooling." *EzineArticles*. This website has various links and information to read more about Homeschooling. See: http://ezinearticles.com.
- Emery, Kathy. "Alternative Schools: Diverted but not Defeated." (July 2000). Paper submitted to Qualification Committee At UC Davis, California.
- Hill, Elizabeth G. "Alternative Education California." (2007). *The Legislative Analyst's Office*. Website: http://www.lao.ca.gov. The history of alternative education in California. Independent Study is one of four alternative options for education mentioned. Page 6 has information on Independent Study.
- Home School Association of California provides information regarding the legalities of Homeschooling. See: http://www.hsc.org.
- Stephanie Hood's article on Public Independent Study Programs and Charter Schools can be found on the Gifted HomeSchoolers Forum website. See: http://giftedhomeschoolers.org.
- Gordon, Edward E. and Elaine H. "Centuries of Tutoring: A History of Alternative Education in America and Western Europe." *History of Education Quarterly* 32, no. 3 (Autumn, 1992): pp. 379-381.
- Miller, Ron. "A Brief History Of Alternative Education." (1996). *The Alternative Education Resource Organization (AERO)*. See: http://www.educationrevolution.org/history.html.
- National Home Education Research Institute has a wealth of information available. See: http://www.nheri.org.

Bibliography

- For books related to Home Study, see the website of the Alternative Education Resource Organization (AERO): http://www.educationrevolution.org.
- Gordon, Edward E. and Elaine H. Gordon. *Centuries of Tutoring: A History of Alternative Education in America and Western Europe*. Lanham, MD: University Press of America, 1990.

CHAPTER 23 - LIGHT THERAPY FOR CHILDREN & YOUTH

by John Downing, OD, Ph.D

Research Papers

- Rustigan, CJ. "Effects of Colored Light and Relaxation Exercise Therapy on Adults with Learning Disabilities." *Education Resources Information Center* 1996.
- Liberman, J. "The Effects of Syntonic Stimulation on Certain Visual and Cognitive Functions." *Journal of Optometric Vision Development* 1986; 17 (June).
- Kaplan, R. "Changes in Form Visual Fields in Reading Disabled Children Produced by Syntonic Stimulation." *The International Journal of Biosocial Research* 1983: 5 (1):20-33.
- Gerard, R. "Differential Effects of Colored Lights on Psychophysiological Functions." Unpublished Doctorial Dissertation, University of California, Los Angeles, California (1976).

Bibliography
- Breiling, Brian (Ed). *Light Years Ahead: The Illustrated Guide to Full Spectrum and Colored Light in Mindbody Healing.* Berkeley, CA: Celestial Arts, 1996.
- Wurtman, Richard, Michael Baum and John Potts. "The Medical and Biological Effects of Light" *(Annals of the New York Academy of Sciences).* Volume 453, September 20, 1985.
- Hollwich, Fritz. "The Influence of Ocular Light Perception on Metabolism in Man and in Animal." New York: Springer-Verlag, c1979.

CHAPTER 24 - MASSAGE/TOUCH FOR CHILDREN & YOUTH

by Peggy Jones Farlow & Alan Jordan

Resources, Research Papers, Books, DVD's, Websites
- Contact the Touch Research Institute in Miami (see above). Dr. Tiffany Field has multiple research papers on the positive benefits of massage for children.

Bibliography
- Jordan, Alan, "Massage Through the Ages" July/August 2000 edition of *Massage Magazine.*
- Farlow, Peggy. "Touch to T.E.A.C.H. - Guidebook for Professional and Primary Caregivers for Children With Special Needs." Available through: www.touchtoteach.com.
- Field, Tiffany. *Touch Therapy.* London: Churchill Livingstone, 2000.
- Heller, Sharon. *The Vital Touch.* New York: Henry Holt, 1997.
- Martin, Chia. *The Art of Touch: A Massage Manual for Young People.* Prescott, AZ: Hohm Press, 1996.
- Sinclair, Marybetts. *Massage for Healthier Children.* Oakland, CA: Wingbow Press, 1992.

CHAPTER 25 - MEDITATION (INSIGHT MEDITATION) FOR CHILDREN & YOUTH

By Heather Sundberg, Spirit Rock Meditation Center Family Program Teacher and Manager

Bibliography
- Alexander, Shoshana. *In Praise of Single Parents: Mothers and Fathers Embracing the Challenge.* New York: Houghton Mifflin Company, 1994.
- Conover, Sarah. *Kindness: A Treasury of Buddhist Wisdom for Children and Parents.* Spokane: Eastern Washington University Press, 2001.
- Eastoak, Sandy. *Dharma Family Treasures: Sharing Mindfulness With Children.* Berkeley, CA: North Atlantic Books, 1994.
- Hanson, Rick, Jan Hanson and Ricki Pollycove. *Mother Nurture.* New York: Penguin Books, 2002.
- Kabat-Zinn, Jon and Myla. *Everyday Blessings: The Inner Work of Mindful Parenting.* New York: Hyperion, 1998.
- Kornfield, Jack. *A Path with Heart: A Guide Through the Perils and Promises of Spiritual Life.* New York: Bantam Books, 1993.
- Nhat Hanh, Thich. *A Pebble For Your Pocket.* Plum Blossom Books, 2002.
- Miller, Karen Maezen. *Mama Zen: Walking the Crooked Path of Motherhood.* Boston: Trumpeter Books, 2006.
For Teens:
- Gordhamer, Soren. *Just Say Om!: Your Life's Journey.* Cincinnati: Adams Media Corp, 2001.
- Loundon, Sumi. *Blue Jean Buddha: Voices of Young Buddhists.* Somerville, MA: Wisdom Publications, 2001.
- MacLean, Kerry Lee. *Peaceful Piggy Meditation.* Morton Grove, IL: Albert Whitman & Co., 2004.
- Hendricks, Gay and Russel Wills. *The Centering Book: Awareness Activities for Children and Adults to Relax the Body and Mind.* Upper Saddle River, NJ: Prentice Hall Trade, 1992.

CHAPTER 26 - MUSIC LESSONS FOR CHILDREN & YOUTH
by Nick Simmons, BA

Bibliography
- Mathieu, W.A. *The Listening Book: Discovering Your Own Music.* Boston and London: Shambhala, 1991.
- Nachmanovitch, Stephen. *Free Play: The Power of Improvisation in Life and the Arts.* Los Angeles: Jeremy P. Tarcher, Inc, 1990.

CHAPTER 27 - NONVIOLENT COMMUNICATION FOR CHILDREN & YOUTH
by Inbal Kashtan

Resources, Research Papers, Books, DVD's, Websites
- There are many other books and materials about NVC that are not specific to parents. They are available for purchase at www.cnvc.org.

Bibliography
- Kashtan, Inbal. *Parenting From Your Heart: Sharing the Gifts of Compassion, Connection, and Choice (Nonviolent Communication Guides).* Encinitas, CA: PuddleDancer Press, 2004.
- Rosenberg, Marshall B., PhD *Raising Children Compassionately: Parenting the Nonviolent Communication Way.* Encinitas, CA: PuddleDancer Press, 2005.
- Sura Hart and Victoria Kindle Hodson. *Respectful Parents, Respectful Kids: 7 Keys to Turn Family Conflict Into Co-operation.* Encinitas, CA: PuddleDancer Press, 2006.
- Inbal Kashtan. "Connected Parenting: NVC in Family Life." CD-ROM. Available through: www.baynvc.org.
- Rosenberg, Marshall B., PhD *Nonviolent Communication: A Language of Life.* Encinitas, CA: PuddleDancer Press, 2005. (This is a foundation book on Nonviolent Communication; not specific to parenting.)

CHAPTER 28 - NUTRITION CONSULTING FOR CHILDREN & YOUTH
by Paula Bartholomy, MS, CNC

Research Papers
- Anything by Dr. Stephen Schoenthaler, which can be found by doing a search on the Internet using Google.
- Weston A. Price Foundation for Wise Traditions in Food, Farming and the Healing Arts. The Weston A. Price Foundation; PMB 106-380, 4200 Wisconsin Ave., NW.; Washington DC 20016; 202-363-4394; Fax: 202-363-4396; Website: www.westonaprice.org; Email: info@westonaprice.org .

Bibliography
- Zand, Janet, Robert Roundtree, and Rachel Walton. *Smart Medicine for a Healthier Child.* New York: Avery, 2nd Ed. 2003.
- Zimmerman, Marcia. *The A.D.D. Nutrition Solution: A Drug-Free 30 Day Plan.* New York: Henry Holt and Co., 1999.
- Rapp, Doris J. *Is This Your Child?: Discovering and Treating Unrecognized Allergies.* New York: William Morrow, 1991.
- Lipski, Elizabeth. *Digestive Wellness for Children: How to Strengthen the Immune System & Prevent Disease Through Healthy Digestion.* Laguna Beach, CA: Basic Health Publications, Inc., 2006.
- Kelly Burgess. "Snacks for Tiny Tummies: Healthy Foods for Toddlers." Available from iParenting Media: www.toddlerstoday.com/articles/3627/1.
- Kelly Burgess. "The Clean Plate Club: Why Your Family *Shouldn't* Join." Available from iParenting Media: http://recipestoday.com/resources/articles/cleanplate.htm.
- Shaw, William. *Biological Treatments for Autism and PDD.* Lenexa, KS: Great Plains Laboratory, 2002.

- McCandless , Jaquelyn. *Children with Starving Brains: A Medical Treatment Guide for Autism Spectrum Disorder.* Putney, VT: Bramble Books, 2003.
- Seroussi, Karyn. *Unraveling the Mystery of Autism and Pervasive Developmental Disorder: A Mother's Story of Research and Recovery.* New York: Simon & Schuster, 2000.
- Nourishing Hope: Nutrition and Diet Intervention for Autism Spectrum Disorders. A website of Julie Matthews, a Certified Nutrition Consultant: www.nourishinghope.com.
- Nourish the Future: Holistic Nutrition for Preconception, Pregnancy, and Postpartum. A website of Julie Matthews, a Certified Nutrition Consultant: www.healthfullivingsf.com/seminars/pregnancy.php
- Sears, William. *The Family Nutrition Book: Everything You Need to Know About Feeding Your Children - From Birth through Adolescence.* New York: Little, Brown and Company, 1999.
- Burney, Lucy. *Optimum Nutrition for Babies and Young Children: Over 150 Quick and Tempting Recipes for the Best Start in Life (Optimum Nutrition Handbook).* London: Judy Piatkus Ltd., 1999.
- Ward, Elizabeth. *Healthy Foods, Healthy Kids: A Complete Guide to Nutrition for Children from Birth to Six-Year-Olds.* Cincinnati: Adams Media, 2002.
- Arsenault, Anne. *Real Solutions to Children's Health.* Bloomington, IN: AuthorHouse, 2006.
- Internet link for Autism information: www.healthfullivingsf.com/resources/bookswebsites/#autism#autism.
- Internet link for healthful diet information: www.healthfullivingsf.com/resources/bookswebsites/#diets#diets.
- Vaccinations/Heavy Metal Toxicity: www.healthfullivingsf.com/resources/bookswebsites/#vacc#vacc.
- Family Resources: www.healthfullivingsf.com/resources/bookswebsites/#family#family.
- Mind, Energy, Spirit: www.healthfullivingsf.com/resources/bookswebsites/#mes#mes.
- Environmentally-Friendly Products and Product Safety: www.healthfullivingsf.com/resources/bookswebsites/#product#product.
- Food Safety, Organics vs. GMO, Food Additives: www.healthfullivingsf.com/resources/bookswebsites/#food#food.

Classes:
- Foundations of Traditional Foods: Recipe for a Healthy Family: www.healthfullivingsf.com/seminars.
- Cooking for Baby: www.healthfullivingsf.com/seminars.
- Nutrition for Pregnancy, Pre-Conception & Postpartum: www.healthfullivingsf.com/seminars.
- Traditional Healing Foods for Children on the Autistic Spectrum including ADHD: www.healthfullivingsf.com/seminars.

Workshops:
- Nourishing Our Children: www.healthfullivingsf.com/seminars.
- Natural Resources - Pregnancy and Postpartum Nutrition: www.healthfullivingsf.com/seminars.
- Natural Resources - Introducing Solids: www.healthfullivingsf.com/seminars.

Newsletters
- Holistic Pediatric Association's "Family Wellness First" newsletter: www.hpakids.org/e-news.html.
- Amy Yasko: www.autismanswer.com.
- Autism Research Institute: www.autism.com.
- Autism Solution Center: www.autismsolutioncenter.com.
- *Cure Autism Now recently merged with Autism Speaks.* You can sign up for their newsletter by going to: www.autismspeaks.org/be_informed.php.
- Dana's View - a parent's perspective: www.danasview.net.
- Developmental Delay Resources. You can receive a complimentary issue of their newsletter by writing to, or calling: The Developmental Delay Resources; 5801 Beacon St.; Pittsburgh, PA 15217; 800-497-0944; Fax: 412-422-1374; Website: www.devdelay.org; Email: devdelay@mindspring.com.
- Enzymes for Autism and other Neurological Conditions by Karen DeFelice: www.Enzymestuff.com.
- Families for Early Autism Treatment: www.feat.org.
- Thoughtful House: www.thoughtfulhouse.org.
- Unlocking Autism: www.unlockingautism.org.

CHAPTER 29 - OSTEOPATHY FOR CHILDREN & YOUTH
by Carlisle Holland, DO

Research Papers
- Viola Fryman's articles on academic difficulties, vision problems, scoliosis, asthma, etc. can be found at the Osteopathic Center for Children and Families' website: www.osteopathiccenter.org/articles.html.

Bibliography
- Collinge, William. *The American Holistic Health Association Complete Guide to Alternative Medicine*. New York: Warner Books, 1996.
- Jones, Bob E. *The Difference A DO Makes*. Oklahoma City: 1978. Now available through the Oklahoma Educational Foundation for Osteopathic Medicine; 4848 North Lincoln Boulevard; Oklahoma City, OK 73105-3335; 800-522-8379; Website: http://www.okosteo.org.
- Frymann, Viola. Articles available online at: www.osteopathiccenter.org/articles.html.

CHAPTER 30 - PRECISION TEACHING FOR CHILDREN & YOUTH
by Elizabeth Haughton, MA

Resources, Research Papers, Books, DVD's, Websites
- Go to www.Fluency.org for hundreds of articles and research papers on Precision Teaching.
- Binder, Carl. "Behavioral Fluency: Evolution of a New Paradigm." *The Behavior Analyst* 19, no. 2 (1996): 163-197.
- Kubina, RM, Morrison, R. "Fluency in Education." *Behavior and Social Issues* 10 (2000): 83-99.
- Lindsley, Ogden R. "Ten Products of Fluency." *Journal of Precision Teaching and Celebration* 13, no. 1 (1995): 2-11.

CHAPTER 31 - PSYCHOTHERAPY FOR CHILDREN & YOUTH (PSYCHODYNAMIC PSYCHOTHERAPY)
by Peter Carnochan, Ph.D

Bibliography
- Greenspan, Stanly and Jacqueline Salmon. *The Challenging Child: Understanding, Raising, and Enjoying the Five "Difficult" Types of Children*. Jackson, TN: Perseus Books, 1995.
- Miller, Alice. *The Drama of the Gifted Child: The Search for the True Self*. Jackson, TN: Basic Books, 1997.
- Altman, Neil (Editor), Richard Briggs (Editor), Jay Frankel (Editor), and Daniel Gensler (Editor). *Relational Child Psychotherapy*. New York: Other Press, 2002.
- Axline, Virginia. *Play Therapy*. New York: Ballantine Books, 1947.

CHAPTER 32 - SAFE SCHOOL AMBASSADORS® FOR CHILDREN & YOUTH
by Rick Phillips, MsEd

Resources, Research Papers, Books, DVDs, Websites
- Safe School Ambassadors website: www.safeschoolambassadors.org.
- Fein, Robert A., Bryan Vossekuil, William Pollack, Randy Borum, William Modzelski, and Marisa Reddy. *Threat Assessment in Schools: A guide to Managing Threatening Situations And To Creating Safe School Climates*. U.S. Department of Education, Office of Elementary and Secondary Education, Safe and Drug-Free Schools Program and U.S. Secret Service, National Threat Assessment Center, Washington, DC, 2004.

- University of Colorado - Center for the Study & Prevention of Violence. They have a "Safe Communities - Safe Schools" initiative launched in 1999 and it includes some models and fact sheets that would help a reader of the book understand more about the issue from a school perspective, including steps a school can take. "CSPV developed the Safe Communities~Safe Schools Model to assist each school in designing an individualized safe school plan. The goal of this model is to create and maintain a positive and welcoming school climate, free of drugs, violence, intimidation and fear—an environment strongly supported by the community in which teachers can teach and students can learn." For more on this topic, see: http://www.colorado.edu/cspv/safeschools/index.html.
- The Center for Evaluation and Education Policy at Indiana University, Bloomington, has a Safe and Responsive Schools Project; Russell Skiba is the Director. For a news release from the University, and a helpful overview of the Center's findings about Zero Tolerance, see: http://newsinfo.iu.edu/news/page/normal/1333.html.

CHAPTER 33 - SUPPORT FOR PARENTS
by Theresa Beldon, MA, MFTI, Bodynamic Analyst

Resources, Research Papers, Books, DVDs, Websites
- Bodynamic Institute USA; P.O. Box 1708; Novato, CA 94948; 415-258-4805; Website: www.Bodynamicusa.com; Email: info@bodynamicusa.com.
- The Re-evaluation Counseling Communities; 719 Second Avenue North; Seattle, WA 98109; 206-284-0311; Fax: 206-284-8429; website: http://www.rc.org; Email: ircc@rc.org.

CHAPTER 34 - TRADITIONAL CHINESE MEDICINE FOR CHILDREN & YOUTH
by Bob Flaws, Practitioner, Teacher, Publisher

Bibliography/Research Papers/Resources
- Allen, John J.B. "Depression and Acupuncture: A Controlled Clinical Trial." *Psychiatric Times*, March 2000, Vol. XVII, Issue 3.
- Flaws, Bob. *Keeping Your Child Healthy with Chinese Medicine*. Boulder: Blue Poppy Press, 1996.
- Barlow, Teresa and Julian Scott. *Acupuncture in the Treatment of Children*. Seattle: Eastland Press, 3rd Ed., 1991

CHAPTER 35 - WESTERN MEDICINE FOR CHILDREN & YOUTH (ALSO KNOWN AS BIO MEDICINE OR ALLOPATHIC MEDICINE)
by Marie Mulligan, MD

Resources, Research Papers, Books, DVD's, Websites
- Many reputable medical schools and health care institutions have reliable sources of information. To name a few: www.aap.org; www.familydoctor.org; www.mayoclinic.com; www.health.harvard.edu; www.healthletter.tufts.edu; and many others.
- Check out the website: www.nlm.nih.gov/medlineplus.
- Check out "medicine" in the Wikipedia website: www.wikipedia.org.
- Wolinski, Howard and Judi. *Healthcare Online For Dummies*. New York: Hungry Minds, Inc., 2001.
- An excellent source for evidence based Complementary and Alternative Medicine: http://denison.uchsc.edu/education/cam2/database.html.
- More General western medicine info sources:
    * Harvard Health Publications: http://www.health.harvard.edu.
    * www.familydoc.org.
- Dr. Mulligan's Published Works:

* Contributor, Natural Medicines Comprehensive Database, Publishers of Pharmacist's Letter, Stockton, CA, 2007. See: http://www.naturaldatabase.com.
* Farley M, JM Golding, G Young, M Mulligan, JR Minkoff. "Trauma history and relapse probability among patients seeking substance abuse treatment." *Journal of Substance Abuse Treatment* 27, no. 2 (2004): 161-167.

CHAPTER 36 - WILDERNESS THERAPY FOR CHILDREN & YOUTH
by Robert Cooley, Ph.D

Resources, Research Papers, Books, DVD's, Websites
• Dr. Keith Russell's dissertation and program of Wilderness Treatment outcomes research. This comes with a comprehensive bibliography. It is available from Dr. Russell. Contact through Email: krussell@umn.edu.

Bibliography
• "Wilderness Therapy Can Help Troubled Adolescents," by Rob Cooley.
• "How Big Is The Risk of Wilderness Treatment of Adolescents," by Rob Cooley.
• The above are available by request from Freer Wilderness Therapy.

CHAPTER 37 - YOGA/THERAPEUTIC YOGA FOR CHILDREN & YOUTH
by Brenda Bakke, Med, PT, CYT

Resources, Research Papers, Books, DVD's, Websites
• International Association of Yoga Therapists (IAYT) displays research papers, articles, and current studies on a variety of medical conditions and diseases. Website: www.iayt.org.

Bibliography Of Books And Articles
• Sumar, Sonia; Leonaro Dinis; Jeffrey Volk; and Adriana Marusso. *Yoga for the Special Child*. Special Yoga Publications, 1998.
• Khalsa, Shakta Kaur. *Fly Like a Butterfly*. New York: Sterling Publishing, 1998.
• Wenig, Marsha. "Yogakids", DVD. Livings Arts, 2004. Available through Amazon.com.
• Komitor, Jodi; and Eve Adamson. *The Complete Idiot's Guide to Yoga with Kids*. New York: Alpha Books, 2000.

GRATITUDES & ACKNOWLEDGEMENTS

We wish to thank Rick's wife, June Nason for all the love, patience and support she has given for so many years.

Next we wish to thank our parents, Denis and Kathleen Mulligan and Thomas and Bernice Geggie whose love and hard work helped us be who we are and who gave us our lives.

We give special thanks to the late Anapurna Broffman and to Michael Broffman who were so instrumental in our connection with each other.

Producers And Sponsors

Very special thanks to the many people who have contributed to this book by being much appreciated producers and sponsors. Thank you for sharing our dream and taking part in helping the most kids possible. Your contributions have made this book possible.

Bill Alexander, Joel Alter, Deborah Boyer, Bread For The Journey-Sebastopol, Meri Collier, Paul Copeland, Teresa Devine, Fran Dincin, Rob Evens, Jan Fischer, Chris Geggie, Wayne Heldt, Bill Herr, Ross Jones, Tito La Rosa, Jeff Leifer, Tiage Liner, Heather MacTavish, Allan Mayfield, June Nason, Nan Palmer, Dan Perlitz, Jess Perlitz, Alison Pinto, Rony Rengifo, Ailish Schutz, Mary Smith, Joanne Sulman, Alan Sumpter and Pattie Walker.

Contributors

We remain gratefully inspired by all the contributors for their dedication to making life better for kids. They have all worked very hard in making their chapter as easy to read and thorough as possible. A few have passed away. Others had to leave the project. Each left their positive mark on the whole process. Beyond words, we appreciate everyone's contribution, hard work, good-will and patience as they have waited for publication.

Many thanks to: Lore Anderson, Susan Bahl, Brenda Bakke, Denise Barry, Paula Bartholomy, Dr. Bill Barton, Teresa Beldom, Susanne Burkhard, Dr. Rob Coolie, Rick Corrigan, Russell Delman, Dr. John Downing, Linda Evans Delman, Randi Farkas, Julia Fischer, Dr. Bob Flaws, Dr. Mel Fox, Peggy Furlow, Dr. Marc Halpern, Kathy Harris, Elizabeth Haughton, Dr. Carlisle Holland, Randy Jane Reitzes, Dr. Katharina Johnson, Dr. Alan Jordan, Cynthia Kupper, Donna Lampke, Dr. Penny Lewis, Tiaga Liner, Dr. Tanya Mahophon, M. Xavier McPhee, Heather McTavish, Dr. Hugh Milne, Dr. Marie Mulligan, Lisette Narragon, June Nason, Dorisse Neale, Dr. Kristi Panik, Marilyn Robinson, Karen Sanders, Dr. Stephen Schoenthaler, Nick Simmons, Carolyn Smith, Christine Stevens, Sonia Sumar, Heather Sundberg, Dr. Robert Tinker, Dr. Dian Wagner, Dr. Sandra Wilson and Asaiah Wisdom.

Inspiration

Much inspiration and encouragement has been given over the years of preparation. Without this great inspiration this book would not exist.

Many thanks to: All the families, children, youth, and co-workers who shared of their lives, Stephen Aldridge, Dr. Bill Alexander, Julie Alexander, Dr. Joel Alter, Briege Aranaga, Goyo Aranaga, Anglese Arrien, Sai Baba, Gail Badel, Kristina Baker, Margaret Barkely, Mike Bell, Dawn Berney, Allan Bernstein MD, Billy, Quest Books, Bill Boygen, Joanne Brem, Anapurna Broffman, Michael Broffman, Michael Broffman LAc, John Brown, Kay Brownfield, Buddha, Jose

Campos, Brown Camps, Art Cecchine, Dawson Church, Ricci and Jack Coddington, Paul Copeland, Zen DeBrucke, Ron Deson, Lauren and Teresa Devine, Fran Dincin, Laura Dincin, Maya and Olivia Dincin, Dr. John Downing, Jackie Dugay, Al Dunikowsky, Will Dwyer, Bob Eisenberg, Ellen Eisenberg, Katherine Elber-Wenner, Dave Ellis, Trisha Ellis, Vince Filetti MD, Andrew Fischer, Maeve Freeman, Pete Freeman, Zorah Freeman, Peter Friedberg, Nan Fuchs, Christopher Geggie, Cleo Geggie, Irma Geggie, Simone Geggie, Tanya Geggie, Mary Cay Glendening, Burton Goldberg, Zorah Goldberg, Harley Goldberg DO, Betsy Gordon, Diane Greenberg, Kristina Grof, Dr. Stanislov Grof, Nini Guerard LAc, Walter Gunn, Meg Hamill, Sandra Hansen–Velloo, Robert Harris, Sara Harris, Mary Harris DC, Katherine Hemmens, Bob Henry, Pheobe Henry, Terry Hess MSW, Adam Holland, Martha Howden, Dr. Mary Ann Huckabay, Jeromy Johnson, Mark Jones, Neal Katz, Pat and Eileen Keogh, Meredith Kieschnick MD, Patricia Kirby, Susan Kirk RN, Ben Klip, Patricia Kulawiak MD, Getty Lee, Alex Lifeson, Lew Lightstone, Joan Lovett, Nancy Lunney, Kate and David Mack, Naomi Magdeleno, Lynn Martin, Leah Martino LAc, Jim Matthews, George and Christine McCaffery, Dr. Eileen McIntyre, Dr. Maura McIntyre, Dr. Robert McIntyre, Nina McKinney, Alix McLaughlin, Peter McLaughlin, Hector McNeil, Michael, Walter Mills MD Jerry Minkoff MD, Andra Mitchel, Phillip Mo, John and Karen Mulligan, Denis and Susan Mulligan, Miyoko Munakata PT, Michael Murphy, Denise Muscorella, Nancy Olin, Laura Onofre, Itamar Pacaya, Kirk Pappas MD, Neville Pather, Tony Penegos, Jake Perlitz, Jess Perlitz, Fletch Pheonix, Dr. Cheri Quincy, Rony Renifo Yon, Dr. June Robinson, Neil Rogen, Jakusho Kwong Roshi, Santen, Joe Scherger MD, Kathy Schneider, Bob Schultz MD, Florence Silver, David Slabotsky, Gregory Slater, Hugh Smith, Lorin Smith, Voge Smith, Kate Spelman, Esalen-LimeKiln staff, Marg Starbuck, Paul Sullivan, Dr. Joanne Sulman, Alan Sumpter, Dr. Thynn Thynn, David Tucker, Sabine Tucker, Lynn Twist, Dr. John Upledger, Robert Van, Palani Velloo, Dr. Neva Walden, Pattie Walker, Jennifer Ware, Jennifer Ware, Warrendale, Laurie Weaver, Martha Webster, Ann Weiser, Eric Welham, Ronnie Wells, Annette Whan, Eric Whan, Kevin Whan, Neil Whan, Rob and Eileen White, Bill Wiener, Barbara Wilt LAc, Dr. David Wise, Dr. John Wiser, Beverly Yates, Anne Yoeman, Tom Yoeman, Jason Zheng, Jan Zieglan, Sandy Ziggle, Dr. Jon Kabbat Zinn, North York Board of Education administration, and the members of the East York Drop In Center. There are so many others. You know who you are. Thank you!

Writers, Editors And Researchers

The book would not be as thorough or easy to read without the skills of these writers, editors and researchers. Thank you all for your skill and care.

Ken Collier, Rick Corrigan, Soren Gordhammer, Cheryl Halde, Meg Hamill, Ruth Harris, Leslie Ann Hartman, Dr. Ross Jones, Greg King, Heather Lennox, Tiaga Liner, Kristy McCollough, Lilth Rogers, Ginger Rose, Dr. Shannon Sammonelli, Diana Schauffer, Nick Simmons, Sabine Tucker, Gina Van Dicken, Gayle Van Dyke and "Whitefire".

Completion Team

Thanks to our amazing completion team. Your skill, care, focus and dedication has been invaluable. Goyo Aranaga, Peter Carnochan, Ken Collier, Meg Hamill, Jody Heckenlively, Wayne Heldt, Lori Ingerman, Jim Matthews, Allan Mayfield, Kristy McCollough, Elizabeth Palmer, Lilith Rogers, Mary Smith, Sabine Tucker, Gina Van Dicken and Mark Wiley. We especially thank Mary Smith for her formatting and design skills. Thank you Mark Wiley, for always being there for us with your computer savvy.

Marie Mulligan & Rick Geggie

BIOGRAPHIES

Marie Mulligan, M.D. *American Medical Doctor*

- Mother of two boys, 10 and 13 (in 2008).
- The oldest daughter of hard working parents who immigrated to USA from Ireland.
- Has six brothers and sisters.
- Continues to be a successful life long learner with ADHD and other learning challenges.
- Brings wisdom gained healing anorexia nervosa as a youth to her entire practice.
- Presently associate medical director of a community health center in Santa Rosa, CA.
- Practicing medicine for over 20 years.
- Has worked with thousands of adults, infants, children and teens.
- For her entire medical career has sought effective healing practices to help suffering families.
- Encourages self-care and sound decisions within the family budget.
- Contributed to Natural Medicines Comprehensive Database published by Therapeutic Research Faculty.
- Spearheaded an aromatherapy program at CASA Midwifery Hospital in San Miguel de Allende, Guarnajuato, Mexico.
- Served as chairperson of botanical medicine committee in a major medical system.
- Directed an outpatient chronic pain clinic, integrating alternative practices with conventional medicine.
- Received M.D. from University of California Davis School of Medicine.
- Completed Family Medicine Residency at University of California Davis Sacramento Medical Center.
- Received B.A. in Biophysics from University of California Berkeley – Regents' Scholar.
- Completed University of California Los Angeles Extension Medical Acupuncture course.
- Lives in Sebastopol, California.

Rick R. Geggie, M.Ed. *Canadian American teacher*

- Father, Stepfather, Grandfather, and Godfather.
- Continues to learn from successes and failures as a parent.
- Was the only child of loving, hard working, blue collared parents, who lived in relative poverty caused by paying many high medical bills (before Canadian Universal Health Care).
- Has become happy and successful, despite severe childhood learning and behavior difficulties.
- Harvested useful wisdom recovering from childhood abandonment, abuses and addictions.
- Became a successful lifelong learner dedicated to seeking and learning effective healing practices.
- Credits his successes in life to most of the practices in this book.
- Was a grade school teacher then vice principal for ten years with the North York Board of Education (NYBE).
- Retired after being an NYBE elementary school principal for 24 years.
- Was very involved in introducing daily physical education as a way of students increasing physical, emotional and academic well-being, as well as building self-confidence.
- Took part in a major study that revealed the academic and emotional benefits of meditation.
- Established a school for emotionally disturbed children and teens.
- Directed a community support and diversion center for youth and gangs.
- Focused on schools being safe, non-violent, non-abusive havens, free of sexism and racism, encouraging all students to achieve their personal best, with individual curriculum and appropriate learning styles.
- Helped parents explore effective healing practices wherever possible.
- Taught discipline and conflict management workshops for parents and professionals.
- Developed a public housing project community reliance mental health program.
- Advocated for curriculum suited to traumatized children and youth.
- With others, attempted to birth a program in Big Sur, California combining challenged children, their families, teachers of healing practices and their students.
- Earned a BA from Queen's University in Kingston, Ontario.
- Received MEd from University of Toronto.
- Teaches the Feldenkrais Method of neurologic education to adults and children—focusing on how to learn.
- Coaches individuals and families toward achieving their goals.
- Lives in Sebastopol California.
- As a father, stepfather, teacher, principal, wanted a book like this one on a daily basis.

INDEX

HOW TO ORDER THIS BOOK

By Phone:
707-874-1789

By Fax:
707-874-1788

By Mail, send a check payable to Growing Up Easier Publishing:
P.O. Box 94, Sebastopol, CA 95473

By internet:
www.GrowingUpEasier.org

For Bulk Rates and Discounts for Gifts or Resale, Contact:
sales@GrowingUpEasier.org.

For School and Library Discount Rates, Contact
sales@GrowingUpEasier.org

Healing Practices To Help Kids Grow Up Easier Addresses Over 100 Problems

- Abandonment
- Abuse
- Accident, Accident Prone
- Acne
- Addictions
- Adoption
- Anti-Social Behavior
- Anxiety
- Arithmetic/Mathematics Challenges
- Ashamed, Blamed, Suffering Debilitating Guilt
- Asthma
- Attachment Disorders
- Attends Schools With:
  - Drug/Alcohol Use Challenges
  - Gangs/Violence
  - Low Performance
- Attention Deficit Disorder (ADD)
- Attention Deficit Hyperactive Disorder (ADHD)
- Attitude Challenges
- Autism
- Attracted To Strangers
- Bereavement/Death Of Family Member
- Birth Trauma
- Bored A Lot Of The Time
- Brain Damage
- Bullying – Aggressive
- Can't Accept Love, Kindness,
- Cancer: Tumors: Leukemia
- Colds And Flus: Frequent And Long
- Communication Challenges: Interpersonal, Emotional, Social
- Communication Challenges: Physical: Neurological
- Concentration Problems
- Concussion: Head Trauma: Head
- Injuries
- Coordination Challenges
- Daydreams
- Depressed Parent(s)/Caregiver(s)
- Depressed
- Disorganized: Scattered
- Dying: Child Has Terminal Illness
- Dyslexia
- Ear Challenges
- Eating Disorders
- Educational Abuse/Wounding
- Emotional/Psychological Abuse
- Emotional Challenges
- Eye Challenges
- Exposure To Drug/Alcohol Intoxicated Family Members
- Exposure To Violence
- Exposure To Suffering Depression, Economic Despair, Addictions, Illness, Homelessness
- Failure
- Falling
- Fidgets And Squirms
- Fights
- Focusing Challenges
- Food And Beverage Dangers
- Frustration
- Gender Identity Concerns
- Grief
- Handwriting/Printing Is Ineffective
- Head Injuries
- Has Repeated A Grade At School
- Inactivity: Habitual Physical Inactivity
- Injury
- Intellectual/Educational Abuse
- Isolation
- Language/Speaking Difficulties
- Language/Written Problems
- Learning Difficulties/Disabilities
- Life Threatening Illness
- Listening Challenges
- Low Grades
- "Low Intelligence"
- Low Self-Esteem/Lacks Confidence
- Lying
- Memory Challenges
- Mood Swings
- Moving Often
- Music Difficulties
- Nervous
- Not Loving To Family, Friends
- Obesity - Overweight Parent Hospitalized
- Parent/Family Member Dying/ Dead
- Parental Addiction
- Parental Fighting, Arguing, Family Unhappiness
- Parental Worry About The Child Or Youth
- Parents Not Having Enough Money To Pay For Healing Practices And Treatments For Their Children Or Youth
- Peer Pressure
- Physical Abuse
- Post Traumatic Stress Disorder
- Reading Problems
- Rude Behavior
- Sarcastic/Critical
- Self-Abuse
- Seeing Stranger Killed
- Self-Critical
- Separation/Divorce
- Sexual Abuse
- Shock
- Shy/Timid
- Socializing Challenges
- Spelling Challenges
- Stealing
- Study Skill Challenges
- Substance Abuse/Substance Experimentation
- Temper Tantrums
- Trauma
- Uncooperative
- Underachieving
- Unsocial
- Victim
- Violence In The Home, School And Community

40 Practitioners Write About Their Healing Practice

- Aikido
- Aromatherapy
- Attitudinal Healing
- Ayurveda
- Biofeedback
- Child Psychiatry
- Chiropractic
- Craniosacral
- Developmental Optometry
- Drumming
- EMDR
- Environmentally Healthy Homes
- Expressive Arts Therapy
- Feldenkrias Method
- Flower Essences
- Herbology
- Home Study
- Homeopathy
- Hypnotherapy
- Light Therapy
- Massage
- Meditation
- Music Lessons
- Nonviolent Communication
- Nutrition Education
- Osteopathy
- Parental Support
- Precision Teaching
- Psychotherapy
- Safe School Ambassadors
- Traditional Chinese Medicine
- Western Medicine
- Wilderness Therapy
- Yoga

Printed in the United States
151316LV00001B/8/P

9 780981 670218